Learning Computer Literacy
Generic—for PC and Mac

Paul Wray

275 Madison Avenue, New York, NY 10016

Acknowledgments

*To Leona Veach, whose forgiving love surrounds us all, and
to Floyd Veach, who's hauled a lot of timber and plays Scrabble like a champ.
To Ginny for 20 years and more.
To Julie and D for choosing me as their Dad.*

Thanks to Jennifer for her patient disagreement and sensible suggestions, to Kathy Berkemeyer for capturing the peer-to-peer network illustrations, to all DDC Chicago for laughing, and to the DDC NY desktop crew, alphabetically: Elsa, Elviro, Maria, and Shu, for making the office a place to enjoy. Special thanks to Elsa for her help with the Web simulation.

Managing Editor	**English Editor**	**Technical Editors**	**Design and Layout**
Jennifer Frew	Ginny Wray	Cheryl Brumbaugh-Duncan	Maria Kardesheva
		Joyce Nielsen	Elviro Padro
			Paul Wray

Contents

Contents

Introduction

About this Book

This book is designed to help you become computer literate as you learn to use features of both the Windows and Mac operating systems and applications.

Lesson 1 **introduces computers** and summarizes their components, types, and the workers who make their livings directly in the computer industry.

Lesson 2A shows you how to use some of the features of **Mac OS** (the operating system for Apple computers). If you are working on Apple machines, complete the exercises in Lesson 2A. It introduces the desktop and describes how to become familiar with the way Mac OS works. It also has exercises to help you learn to find files and programs.

Lesson 2B shows you how to use some of the features of **Windows** with information about both Windows 95 and Windows 98. It introduces the desktop, My Computer, and Windows Explorer. It also has exercises to help you learn to find files and programs.

Lessons 3 through 7 cover important features of the following four applications:

- **Word processing**, a program used for creating and editing documents and for **desktop publishing**. Direct reference is made to the following word processors:
  - AppleWorks word processing (Mac OS)
  - Microsoft Word 98 (Mac OS)
  - Microsoft Works 4.5 word processor (Windows)
  - Microsoft Word 97 (Windows)
  - Microsoft Word 2000 (Windows)
  - Corel WordPerfect 8 & 9 (Windows)
- **Spreadsheet**, a program used for analyses and graphing of numerical data. Direct reference is made to the following spreadsheet applications:
  - AppleWorks spreadsheet (Mac OS)
  - Microsoft Excel 98 (Mac OS)
  - Microsoft Works 4.5 spreadsheet (Windows)
  - Microsoft Excel 97 (Windows)
  - Microsoft Excel 2000 (Windows)
  - Corel Quattro Pro 8 & 9 (Windows)

- **Database**, a program used for organizing and sorting information. Direct reference is made to the following presentations applications:
  - AppleWorks database (Mac OS)
  - Microsoft Works 4.5 database (Windows)
  - Microsoft Access 97 (Windows)
  - Microsoft Access 2000 (Windows)
  - Corel Paradox 8 & 9 (Windows)
- **Presentations**, a program used for creating sales and other presentations that can be shown via computer or given using overhead transparencies. Direct reference is made to the following presentations applications:
  - AppleWorks drawing (Mac OS)
  - Microsoft PowerPoint 98 (Mac OS)
  - Microsoft PowerPoint 97 (Windows)
  - Microsoft PowerPoint 2000 (Windows)
  - Corel Presentations 8 & 9 (Windows)

Lesson 8 introduces **computer communications**, including local area networks and the Internet.

Lesson 9 deals with **personal computer care**, giving simple instructions for keeping your machine running efficiently. This lesson includes information about backup, hard disk management, and general care and use instructions.

Appendix A presents a brief **history of computers**.

Appendix B contains step-by-step directions for using **Windows 98 help**.

Appendix C contains step-by-step directions for using **Mac OS help**.

Appendix D contains information about using **Access 97 and Access 2000 data files**.

Appendix E contains information about using **Paradox data files and databases**.

How to Use this Book

Each exercise contains two main parts:

NOTES explain the application and its features. These notes contain **Try It!** activities that lead you step-by-step through the feature being presented. You should perform the steps described in each Try It! activity.

- The Notes contain often contain gray boxes in the right-hand column. These gray boxes present definitions of terms, hints, cautions, or additional information about the topic or feature discussed in the notes.

- Where appropriate, in the right column of the page next to a Try It!, is a reference that looks like the following:

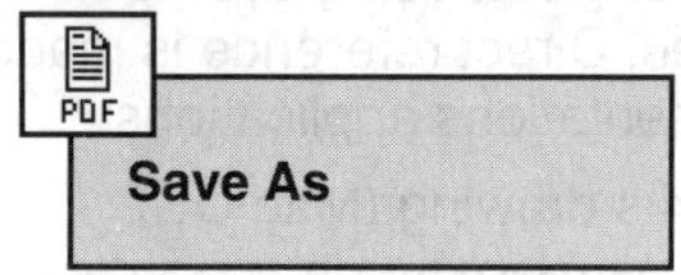

- These gray boxes refer to files on the CD-ROM that accompany this book. They give the title of **procedures** that give step-by-step directions for using an application feature. These procedures are specific to the applications and are in the following files on the CD:

  - AppleWorks.pdf
  - Microsoft Office 98.pdf
  - Microsoft Works.pdf
  - Microsoft Office 97.pdf
  - Microsoft Office 2000.pdf
  - Corel Suite.pdf

- The files are in PDF (Portable Display Format), which can be read and printed using Adobe Acrobat or Adobe Acrobat Reader. Acrobat Reader can be installed for either Mac OS or Windows from the CD-ROM. Many machines already have an Acrobat version installed because Web sites often provide information in downloadable PDF files.

- You may print out the procedures specific to the suite of applications installed on your machine. Each file includes a detailed table of contents and an index to help you locate the procedure you need.

EXERCISE DIRECTIONS give step-by-step instructions for using the software to perform a function or create a particular document. These instructions reinforce the learning presented in the Notes and Try It! activities.

Menu Items and Keyboard Shortcuts

Throughout this book you will see directions like the following:

Click **Alt** + **F**.

The words refer to menu options. The black key symbols (**Alt** + **F**) indicate a keyboard shortcut. It means to hold down the Alt key and press the F.

For example, **⌘** + **Tab** in a procedure for a Mac OS application means, "Hold down the command (Apple) key, and press the Tab key."

If the keys are separated by a comma, for example, **F10**, **F** you press and release one key, then press the next in the sequence.

The Mac OS keyboard has a key labeled *delete* and the Windows keyboard have one labeled *Delete*. In this book, the **Del** symbol is used to represent these keys. The Windows keyboard contains a key labeled *Insert*, which is represented by the **Ins** symbol.

Data and Solution Files

The **data files** on the accompanying CD-ROM are provided so that you can concentrate on the tasks essential to the exercise's objective rather than on typing or data entry. Data files are preceded in the text by a CD-ROM symbol ⊙ to indicate that a data file can be used.

Some exercises are based on files created in earlier exercises. Directions use a keyboard symbol ⌨ to indicate files created in previous exercises.

When a keyboard and diskette appear within the same direction, you may use either the file you created or the data file.

For example, a typical direction might read:

Open ⌨**Firstdoc**, or open ⊙**02Firstdoc** from the data disk.

Solutions disks may be purchased separately from DDC Publishing. You can compare your work with the final version or solution on disk. Each solution filename includes the letter "S" and is followed by the exercise number and descriptive file name.

For example, **S02Firstdoc** contains the solution to directions that changed the Word document *Firstdoc* in Exercise 2.

A directory of data disk and solutions disk file names are provided in the Log of Exercises section of this book.

✓ *If you save files to a network, longer file names may automatically be truncated to a maximum of eight characters.*

The Teacher's Manual

While this book can be used as a self-paced learning book, a comprehensive Teacher's Manual is also available. The Teacher's Manual contains the following:

- Lesson objectives
- Exercise objectives
- Related vocabulary
- Points to emphasize
- A Log of Exercises, which lists file names in exercise number order
- A Directory of Documents, which lists file names alphabetically along with the corresponding exercise numbers
- Solution illustrations

The CD-ROM that accompanies this book contains:

- **Data files**, as described on page vi.
- **Procedure (PDF) files**, as described on page vi.
- **Adobe Acrobat Reader installation files**, needed to view and print the procedures.
- **Typing tests** with automatic scoring can be used to test typing speed and accuracy.

Copy Data Files

You can copy data files to a hard drive.

Mac OS

1. Open the CD-ROM drive window on your desktop, and locate the folder that contains data files for your suite of applications—AppleWorks or Microsoft Office 98.

2. Open the hard drive to which you want to copy the files, and open the folder (if any) to which you want to place the data files.

3. Drag the folder from the CD-ROM drive window to the folder on the hard drive.

Windows

1. Open Windows Explorer (Right-click on the **Start** button **Start** and click **Explore**).

2. Be sure that the CD is in your CD-ROM drive. Select the CD-ROM drive letter in the left pane of the Explorer window.

3. In the right pane, locate the folder that contains the data files for your suite of applications (Microsoft Works, Microsoft Office 97, Microsoft Office 2000, or Corel WordPerfect Suite).

4. Press **Ctrl**+**C** to copy the files.

5. In the left pane of Windows Explorer, select the drive and folder (if any) to which you want to copy the data files.

6. Press **Ctrl**+**V** to copy the files.

   Be aware that if you copy the files to a network drive to make them available to a larger group of students, the file names may be truncated to eight characters. Some networks do not allow the long file names permitted by Windows 95 and 98.

HTML Files

The data files include several HTML files that can be used to practice use of the World Wide Web if you do not have Internet access. You can open the files using your browser and click on active links to practice using the Web without needing a modem or other connection to the Internet. Lesson 8, Exercise 3 gives directions for using these files.

You may copy the HTML files to a hard drive or network volume. Follow the procedure outlined for the data files. Be sure to **copy the entire HTML folder from the CD**; otherwise, the directions in Lesson 8 will not work correctly.

Acrobat Reader

Mac OS

If you have already installed Adobe Acrobat or Reader, you do not need to go through these steps.

1. Shut down all programs and turn off extensions.

2. Insert the CD in your CD-ROM drive.

   The CD-ROM icon 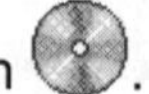 *will appear on your desktop.*

3. Double-click the CD-ROM icon.

4. Click the Adobe Acrobat installer in the **MacFiles** folder.

5. Follow on-screen prompts.

Windows

If you have already installed Adobe Acrobat or Reader, you do not need to go through these steps.

1. Shut down all programs.

2. Locate the Acrobat Reader folder on the CD.

3. Locate the installation files for your operating system.

4. Double-click the Setup icon.

5. Respond to the prompts to install Acrobat Reader.

After installing Acrobat Reader, you may either:

- Leave the procedures on the CD and open, view, and print them from the CD. These files are in a folder called **Procedures**. Be sure to open and print out the procedures for your operating system.
- Copy the appropriate procedure files to your hard drive. Once on your hard drive you can open, view, and print the files. These files are in a folder called **Procedures**.

Automated Typing Program (Windows only)

System Requirements

Software	Windows 95, Windows 3.1 (or higher), or Windows NT 3.51 (or higher)
Hardware	386/33MHZ or higher (486 or higher recommended), 8 MB RAM, 256 color monitor, and CD-ROM Drive
Disk Space	10 MB available hard disk space for a "Typical" installation.

1. Click **START** on the desktop, Click RUN and then type: **(CD-ROM drive letter):\TIMINGS\SETUP**.
2. Click **NEXT** twice to proceed to the Choose Directory Location screen.
3. Click **NEXT** to accept the default directory (or click **BROWSE** to select another directory) for installing program files.

   TYPICAL *is recommended for most users.*
4. At the Setup Type screen, click a setup option based on your system needs and click **NEXT**.
5. At the Select Program Folder screen, click **NEXT** to accept the default folder (or select another folder) for storing the program icons.
6. At the Setup Complete screen, click **FINISH**.
7. Start Automated Typing Program

   Steps 3, 6, and 7 are only necessary the first time you log into the program or if you wish to make any program adjustments.

8. If program and program icons were installed to the default locations, click **START** on the desktop, click **PROGRAMS**, then click **All the Right Type DDC Edition.**
9. When the introductory screen appears, click anywhere to continue.
10. At the Sign On screen, click **EDIT USERS**, then click **ADD**, type your name, click **OK**, and then click **DONE** to add it to the program.
11. Click your name in the User list and click **SELECT**.
12. Click **CONTINUE** at the welcome screen.
13. Click **Options** on the menu bar and select **Set Options**.

TO SET A SPEED GOAL:

1. Click Speed Goal.
2. Select a speed goal from the drop-down list and click **OK.**
3. The User Prompt option allows you to manually adjust the speed goal for each exercise with out returning to the Options screen.
4. Double-click the exercise for which you wish to be timed.
5. Follow the online instructions.

TO SET A TIME GOAL:

1. Click Timed Writing.
2. Select a time goal from the drop-down list.

   The User Prompt option allows you to manually adjust the timing goal for each exercise without returning to the Options screen. However, the User Prompt option does not enable you to select 30-second timings, whereas the Timed Writing drop-down option does. THE TIMED WRITING, USER PROMPT OPTION IS THE RECOMMENDED SETTING FOR THIS PROGRAM.
3. At the FACULTY OF A.R.T. main campus screen, click the **TESTING CENTER** to access the timed writing exercises that accompany this book.
4. Double-click the exercise for which you wish to be timed.
5. Follow the online instructions.

Log of Exercises

LESSON	EXERCISE	FILE NAME	DATA FILE	SOLUTION FILE	PAGE
2A Mac OS	3	—	—	SMacOS.txt	34
2B Windows	2	—	—	Swindows.txt	82
3 Word Processing	1	MyDoc	—	S01MyDoc	133
		Firstdoc		S01Firstdoc	133
	2	Firstdoc	02Firstdoc	S02Firstdoc	134
		Advice	—	S02Advice	139
	3	Firstdoc2	03Firstdoc2	S03Firstdoc3	142
		Marianne	03Marianne	S03Marianne	143
		Goode	03Goode	S03Goode	144
	4	Goode	04Goode	S04Goode4	149
		Coyote	04Coyote	S04Coyote	152
	5	Spelling	05Spelling	S05Spelling	156
		Spelling2*	05Spelling2	S05Spelling5	157
		Words	05Words	S05Words	158
		Godzilla	05Godzilla	S05Godzilla	158
		Vegetables	05Vegetables	S05Vegetables	160
		Synonym	05Synonym	S05Synonym	161
		Horace	05Synonym	S05Horace	161
	6	Bullets	—	S06Bullets	162
		Diamonds	—	S06Diamonds	163
		Numbers	—	S06Numbers	163
		Letters	—	S06Letters	163
		Rules	06Rules	S06Rules1	165
			06Rules	S06Rules2	165
	7	AnimalFarm	07AnimalFarm	S07AnimalFarm	168
		Thayer	07Thayer	S07Thayer	170
		Carol	07Carol	S07Carol	171
		Memo	07Memo	S07Memo	172
	8	WebPage	08WebPage	S08WebPage	177
		Report	08Report	S08Report	186
	9	Fairmaiden	09Fairmaiden	S09Fairmaiden	192
		Gourmet	09Gourmet	S09Gourmet	194
		Latin Club	—	S09Latin Club	196

*Not used with AppleWorks and MS Works

LESSON	EXERCISE	FILE NAME	DATA FILE	SOLUTION FILE	PAGE
4 Desktop Publishing	1	My Letterhead	—	S01My Letterhead	201
		Guppy	01Guppy	S01Guppy	203
		Flyer	01Flyer	S01Flyer	204
	2	My Letterhead	02My Letterhead	S02My Letterhead	209
		Guppy	02Guppy	S02Guppy	211
		Flyer	02Flyer	S02Flyer2	212
	3	Extreme	03Extreme	S03Extreme	214
		Wakeboard	03Wakeboard	—	215
		Newsletter	—	S03Newsletter	217
		Announce	03Announce	—	219
		Retire	03Retire	—	219
		Website	03Website	—	220
		Summer	03Summer	—	220
5 Spreadsheets	1	Book1	—	S01Book1	227
		Shopping	—	S01Shopping	230
	2	Lunch	02Lunch	S02Lunch	232
		Shopping	02Shopping	S02Shopping2	237
	3	Students	03Students	S03Students	238
		Scrabble	03Scrabble	S03Scrabble	241
	4	Perfect	—	S04Perfect	244
		Scrabble	04Scrabble	S04Scrabble2	248
	5	Stocks	05Stocks	S05Stocks	250
		Basketball	05Basketball	S05Basketball	253
	6	Online	06Online	S06Online	254
		Basketball	06Basketball	06Basketball2	257
	7	IF		S01IF	260
		Scores	07Scores	S07Scores	262
		Pass Fail	07Pass_Fail	S07Pass_Fail	263
	8	Enrollment	08Enrollment	S08Enrollment	266
		Flueghel	08Flueghel	S08Flueghel1	266
		Acme	08Acme	S08AcmeSales	267
		Enrollment	08Enrollment	—	269
		Flueghel1	08Flueghel1	S08Flueghel2	269
	9	Checkbook	—	S09Checkbook	274

LESSON	EXERCISE	FILE NAME	DATA FILE	SOLUTION FILE	PAGE
6 Databases	1	Classical Music	01Classic	—	281
	2	Library	02Library	S02Library	286
		Glasser	02Glasser	S02Glasser	290
	3	Library	03Library	S03Library	292
		Glasser	03Glasser	S03Glasser	294
	4	GoodStuff	—	S04GoodStuff	296
		My Address Book	—	S04My Address Book	298
	5	Glasser	05Glasser	S05Glasser	300
		My Address Book*	05My Address Book	S05My Address Book	301
		Library	05Library	S05Library5	303
		School*	05School	S05School	303
	6	Library	06Library	S06Library	304
		Glasser	06Glasser	S06Glasser	305
7 Presentations	1	Wright	—	S01Wright1	308
		Treacher	—	S01Treacher1	316
	2	Wright	02Wright1	S02Wright2	318
		Treacher	02Treacher1	S02Treacher2	321
	3	Wright	03Wright2	S03Wright3	325
		Treacher	03Treacher2	S03Treacher3	332
	4	Wright	04Wright3	S04Wright4	334
		Treacher	04Treacher3	S04Treacher4	338
8 Communications	3	si-edu	www-si-edu.htm	—	369

*Access 97, Access 2000, and Corel Paradox only.

Directory of Documents

Lesson 3: Word Processing

File Name	Exercise
Advice	2
AnimalFarm	7
Bullets	6
Carol	7
Coyote	4
Diamonds	6
Fairmaiden	9
Firstdoc	1, 2
Firstdoc2	3
Godzilla	5
Goode	3, 4
Gourmet	9
Horace	5
Latin Club	9
Letters	6
Marianne	3
Memo	7
MyDoc	1
Numbers	6
Report	8
Rules	6
Spelling	5
Spelling2	5
Synonym	5
Thayer	7
Vegetables	5
WebPage	8
Words	5

Lesson 4: Desktop Publishing

File Name	Exercise
Announce	3
Extreme	3
Flyer	1, 2
Guppy	1, 2
My Letterhead	1, 2
Newsletter	3
Retire	3
Summer	3
Wakeboard	3
Website	3

Lesson 5: Spreadsheets

File Name	Exercise
Acme	8
AcmeSales	8
Basketball	5, 6
Book1	1
Checkbook	9
Enrollment	8
Flueghel	8
Flueghel1	8
IF	7
Lunch	2
Online	6
Pass Fail	7
Perfect	4
Scores	7
Scrabble	3, 4
Shopping	1, 2
Stocks	5
Students	3

Lesson 6: Databases

File Name	Exercise
Classical Music	1
Glasser	2, 3, 5, 6
GoodStuff	4
Library	2, 3, 5, 6
My Address Book	4, 5
School	5

Lesson 7: Presentations

File Name	Exercise
Wright	1, 2, 3, 4
Treacher	1, 2, 3, 4

Lesson 8: Communications

File Name	Exercise
www-si-edu.htm	3

Lesson 1: Introduction to Computers

Learn about Computers and Computer Careers

- **What is a Computer?**
- **Personal Computer Hardware**
- **Peripherals**
- **Bits and Bytes**
- **Computer Speed and MHz**
- **Software**
- **Computer Types**
- **Computer Workers**

Introduction to Computers

Learn about Computers and Computer Careers

■ What is a Computer? ■ Personal Computer Hardware ■ Peripherals ■ Bits and Bytes
■ Computer Speed and MHz ■ Software ■ Computer Types ■ Computer Workers

NOTES

What is a Computer?

■ A computer is a machine that receives **input** (data), performs **processing**, and produces **output** (information).

■ Uses of the computer can be viewed as variations of input-processing-output. This is as true of complex tasks, like computer simulations of weather events, as it is of common ones, like typing a letter. Some examples of input-processing-output are given in the following table.

INPUT	PROCESSING	OUTPUT
Text typed on the keyboard	Formatting and preparation for printing by word processing program	Letter, book report, memo, story
Text typed on the keyboard and pictures inserted from disk drive or diskette	Text formatting, picture placement, sizing, and scaling in desktop publishing program	Newsletter, advertisement, flyer
Text and numbers typed on the keyboard	Calculations performed in spreadsheet program	Banking record, budget, grade book
Text and numbers typed on the keyboard	Formatting into tables, sorting, searching, selection of data in database program	Address book, membership list, product sales report, employee information
Temperatures, wind velocities and direction, air pressure readings, frontal boundaries, humidity readings, jetstream location and speed	Calculations based on meteorological research and assumptions and comparisons with a database of weather patterns	Weather forecast

■ If the input contains errors, the output will contain errors. Sometimes computers break down. But most "computer errors" result from human errors—bad data or bad programming.

Personal Computer Hardware

■ **Hardware** refers to all the pieces of equipment that make up a computer system. The computer hardware you are most familiar with is probably the **personal computer** or **PC**.

Input
Data entered into a computer.

Processing
Actions that computer programs perform on the input.

Output
Results of processing.

Personal Computer
A distinction is often made between a PC and a personal computer made by Apple or some other manufacturer. In this book, however, the term *personal computer* or PC is used as a generic term that applies to any computer intended for the use of one person.

Personal Computer Hardware

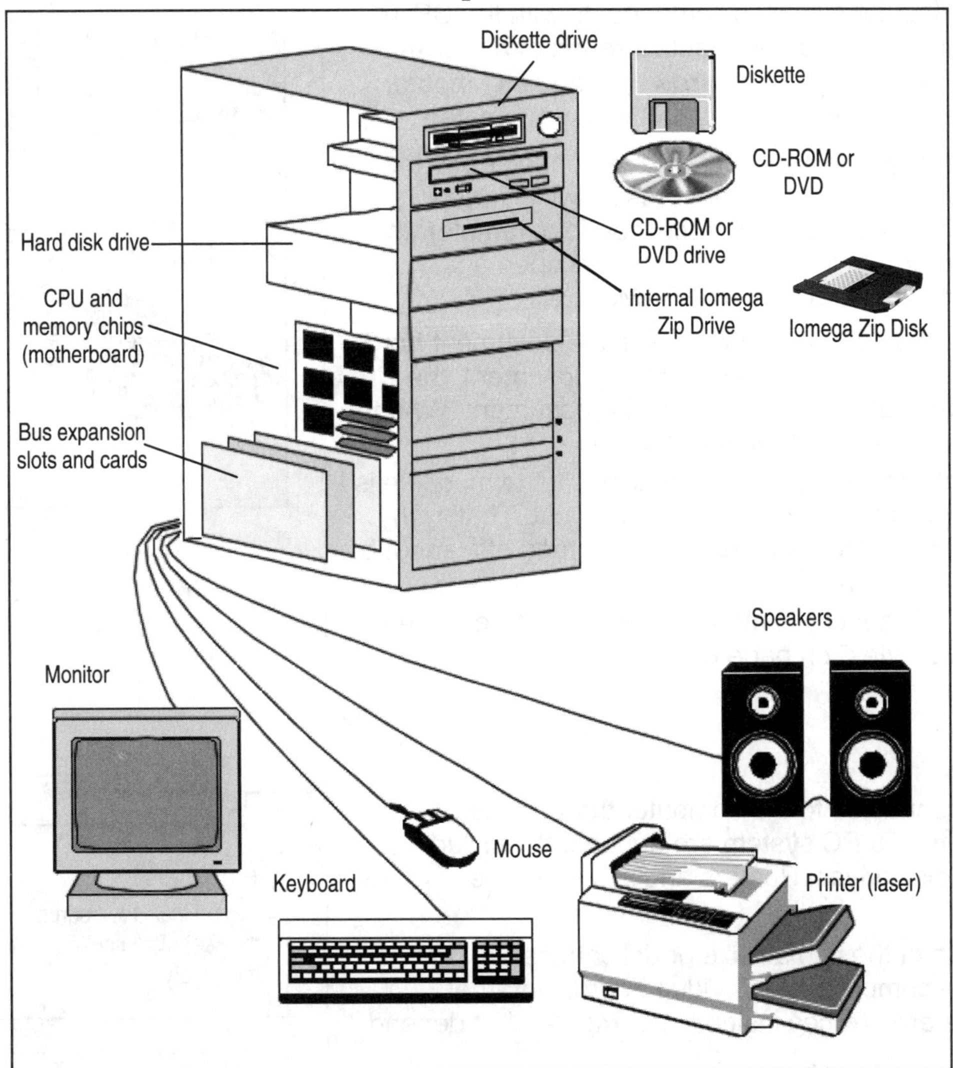

- A PC includes several pieces of hardware:
  - The **power supply** is a device (not shown in the illustration) that distributes electricity to the various components of the system. The electrical cord runs from the power supply to an electrical outlet. The power supply also includes a fan that cools the internal components.

  - The **motherboard** is the largest circuit board inside your personal computer. It contains millions of electronic circuit elements on chips of silicon. These chips store programmed instructions in active memory (see RAM on the next page). They also execute the instructions stored in other chips. The motherboard has expansion sockets or slots (known as the bus, see the next page). These slots permit installation of additional circuit boards.

  - The **CPU (Central Processing Unit)** is a chip, located on the motherboard, that performs mathematical calculations and logic functions (determining if one value is greater than another, and so on). The CPU is often referred to as the brain of the computer because it administers the functions of the other components. When users say their machine has a Pentium III processor, they are talking about the CPU chip.

- The **bus** is the main communication path, or series of paths, on the motherboard, connecting the system's components with the CPU. The bus also connects external components through **expansion slots**. These slots can contain plug-in **cards** that let the computer communicate with other devices, such as monitors and printers.

- **RAM (<u>R</u>andom <u>A</u>ccess <u>M</u>emory)**, special chips connected to the CPU, is the area where programs and data reside while in use. When you start an application (a word processor, for example), the computer places the program into RAM. If you then open a document, it also loads the document into RAM.

  - When you save a document, the CPU copies the document from RAM to permanent storage. When you close a document, the CPU frees up the memory that was occupied by the document. When you close a program, memory is also freed up.

  - RAM holds data only so long as it has electricity. If the machine is turned off or loses power, information in RAM is lost. That's why any changes not saved before the machine is turned off cannot be retrieved.

  - In modern PCs, RAM capacity is measured in megabytes. (See the section "Bits and Bytes" on page 6 for a definition of bits and bytes.)

Peripherals

- A **peripheral** is a device connected to the computer through the bus. Many essential components of a PC system are peripherals, including monitors, keyboards, and disk drives. Printers and scanners are also peripherals.

- Some peripherals, because of their small size or delicate nature, are mounted directly inside the computer case. Video boards, internal modems, and sound cards are devices inside the computer that depend on the bus.

- Peripherals are often divided into two categories—input devices and output devices. Some peripherals serve as both input and output devices, so the categories are not exclusive. Some common peripherals and their functions are described below.

  - The **monitor** is an output device that displays input and the results of processing. Most monitors on PCs use a <u>c</u>athode <u>r</u>ay <u>t</u>ube (CRT) similar to that used in television sets. (In fact, some computers can use TV sets as monitors.) Laptop computers more often use <u>l</u>iquid <u>c</u>rystal <u>d</u>isplay (LCD) technology in their monitors.

  - The **mouse** is an input device that you lets you control a pointer that displays on the monitor. When the pointer is located at the spot where you want the software to respond, you press a button on the mouse; this action is called **clicking**.

    On the **Mac**, the mouse generally has only one button, although you can buy two-button mice that are programmable.

    On a **Windows** machine, the mouse generally has two buttons. In Windows you press and release the left button once (**click**), the right button (**right-click**), or the left button twice rapidly (**double-click**). The IntelliMouse, supported by Microsoft Office applications, includes

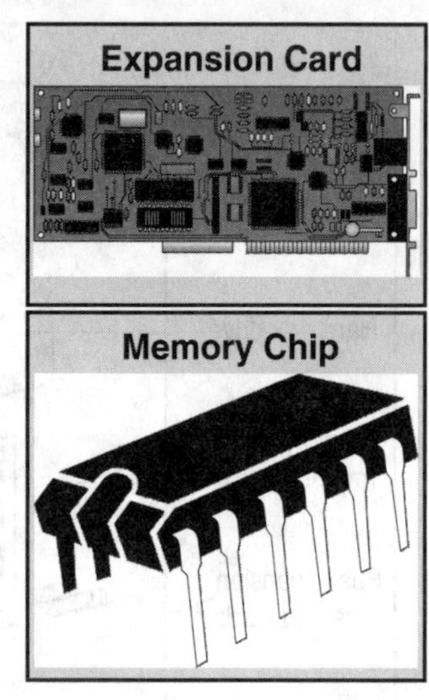

Expansion Card

Memory Chip

Peripheral
Device that is not part of the central computing machinery.

LCD Monitor

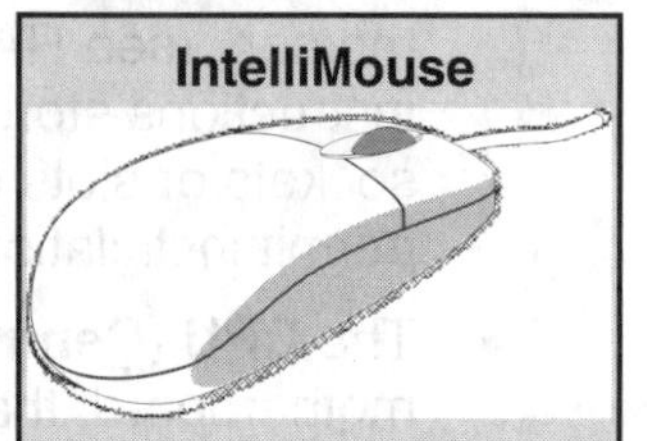

IntelliMouse

a wheel between the two buttons. The wheel can be used for scrolling and zooming.

- The **keyboard** is an input device with alphabetic, numeric, punctuation, and auxiliary keys in a standardized layout. (Some keyboards change the location of certain keys and include keys that other keyboards do not have.) The auxiliary keys are used alone or in combinations to send commands to the central processing unit. They include

  - Function or F keys (F1 - F12)
  - Control (Ctrl) key.
  - Option (Option) key Mac OS
  - Alt (Alt) key in Windows
  - Mac OS command or Apple key (⌘)

- Most computers contain a **hard disk** (also called a hard drive) and a **diskette drive**. You may have another kind of removable storage drive, such as an Iomega® Zip® or Jazz® drive, with disks that store 100 or more megabytes. Diskettes and Zip disks can be removed and carried from one computer to another; hard disks are installed inside the computer and are not considered portable.

  On Windows machines, disk drives are identified by letter. The typical Windows personal computer has a diskette drive identified as **A:**. It probably also has a hard drive known as **C:**.

  On the Mac, all drives appear on the desktop (if they have disks inserted) and are identified by name, such as Macintosh HD or ZIP-100.

  Hard disks and diskettes and their drives serve as both input and output devices.

  - When output, such as a letter, is stored (saved) on a hard disk or diskette, the disk is an output device.
  - When you retrieve data from a disk, it serves as an input device.

- **CD-ROM** (<u>C</u>ompact <u>D</u>isk-<u>R</u>ead-<u>O</u>nly <u>M</u>emory) and **DVD** (<u>D</u>igital <u>V</u>ideo <u>D</u>isc or <u>D</u>igital <u>V</u>ersatile <u>D</u>isc) disks are input devices. Without special equipment, you cannot save data to a CD-ROM or DVD, but you can retrieve information from one if you have a CD-ROM/DVD drive on your computer.

- **Modems** and other telecommunication hardware (when used with the appropriate software) serve as sources of both input and output. Telecommunication gives you access to the world outside your personal computer—to such services as America Online (AOL) and that vast network of computers known as the **Internet** or **World Wide Web**. A modem may be installed inside the computer case (an internal modem) or the modem may be connected through a communications port (external modem).

- **Printers**, next to monitors and disk drives, are the most common output devices. A wide variety of printer types is available:

  - **Impact** printers push images of letters and symbols (cast in metal or plastic) through a ribbon onto the paper. These are usually the slowest and oldest of the printer types and generally cannot print

**Examples of
Storage Devices**

Hard Disk

Iomega Zip Disk

**External Iomega
Zip Drive**

graphic images. Some of these printers are called "daisy wheel" printers because the printing element looked like a flower with its petals containing the characters to be printed.

- ♦ **Dot-matrix** printers use a pattern of steel pins in a moving print head to imprint dots through a ribbon onto paper. Like all the other following printer types, they generally can print graphic images.
- ♦ **Ink Jet** and **Bubble Jet** printers spray ink onto paper to produce the output.
- ♦ **Laser** printers use copier-like technology to spread patterns of toner and affix it to paper using heat.
- ♦ **Plotters** use a needle to draw on paper; they are frequently used by engineers to produce schematic drawings.

- **Scanners**, which let you create files from pictures, drawings, or text, are input devices.

- **Voice input** devices are becoming more common as hardware and software makers improve their efficiency.

Bits and Bytes

■ Your personal computer operates through a vast number of on/off switches called **binary digits** or **bits** (bit is short for **B**inary dig**IT**). All the reception of input, processing, and output are accomplished by bits that are either turned on or turned off.

■ Bits are grouped together into **bytes**, a string of 8 bits that can be translated by the computer into a letter or an action. For example, when you press the capital letter A on the keyboard, a signal from the keyboard passes to the computer and gets translated into a string of 8 bits that are represented like this: 01000001. Each 0 represents a switch that is turned off and a 1 represents a switch that is turned on.

■ A byte is the most common measurement of storage in the digital computer.

Size	Number of Bytes
Kilobyte	1,024 (8,192 bits) 1 thousand bytes
Megabyte	1,024,000 1 million bytes
Gigabyte	1,024,000,000 1 billion bytes
Terabyte	1,024,000,000,000 1 trillion bytes

Computer Speed and MHz

■ The speed of your personal computer is measured in megahertz (MHz). A hertz is a single oscillation (up-and-down movement) of an electromagnetic wave. When coupled with the prefix *mega*, it refers to millions of wave oscillations per second.

■ In the computer, the activity of the CPU microchip is coordinated by a clock that is part of the chip. Thus, a 400 MHz chip has a clock that receives electricity and switches on and off 400 million times per second. It is twice as fast as a chip that has a 200 MHz clock.

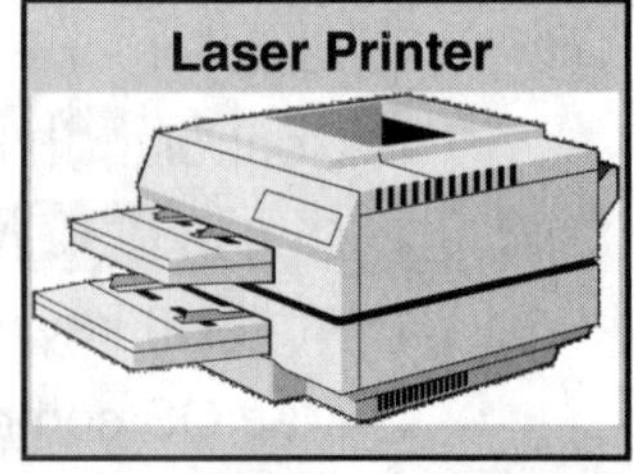

More on Printers

The following Web site contains a brief description of the operation of "daisy wheel," dot matrix, ink jet, and laser printers.

http://www.repairfaq.org/REPAIR/F_printfaq.html

Heinrich Hertz

German physicist Heinrich Hertz (1857-1894), showed that electricity can be transmitted in electromagnetic waves. The *hertz* (Hz), which is named after him, combines with Greek prefixes to describe the number of cycles (wave oscillations) per second of electromagnetic radiation.

http://www.ideafinder.com/history/inventors/hertz.htm

- A personal computer's overall speed, however, depends not only on the speed of the CPU but also on its interaction with the bus system. If the CPU operates at 400 MHz and the bus at 50 MHz, the bus slows the computer down when the CPU is communicating with cards in the bus slots. More recent bus speeds, however, reach 100 MHz and faster.

Software

- **Software** refers to the instructions that allow a computer to run and act on the data that is entered. Software is usually divided into two types: operating system software and application software. Software and **computer programs** mean the same thing.

- **Operating system software** includes instructions that allow a computer to **boot up** (start). Startup involves checking for equipment attached to the computer, such as the keyboard, to ensure that it is working and can communicate with the computer's operating system. Windows 98 and Mac OS are examples of operating systems.

- **Application software** includes programs that allow you to make the computer do what you want—write a letter, browse the Internet, draw a picture, create a computer program.

- Application software depends on the operating system. It uses operating-system-specific instructions to tell the operating system to do something. Because application software interacts with the operating system in this way, applications designed for one operating system (Windows, for example) cannot run on a different operating system (Unix or Mac OS, for example).

  - **Data files**, however, can be shared between operating systems. For example, a Macintosh Word 98 file can be opened in Word 2000 and vice-versa. If the data file to be shared is on a network, either application can access and open the document. (Not all features of the two applications are necessarily compatible, so some formatting may change when the file is opened.)

  - If the file is on a 3.5" floppy or Zip disk, sharing works best when the disk is formatted for Windows. Mac OS can read disks formatted for Windows, but Windows usually cannot read disks formatted for the Mac. Thus, to transfer files between the two systems, use a Windows disk.

Computer Types

- The computer with which you are most familiar, and the one with which you will probably have the most direct contact throughout your life, is the personal computer. But you will have indirect contact with other, larger computers. For example, every time you use the Internet, you are using larger computers; most Web site run on large computers.

- If you make a career in science, higher mathematics, advanced computing, or military or industrial research, you may use a **supercomputer**. Supercomputers are the fastest problem solvers available. They work at extremely high speeds. Often, they process data in "parallel," breaking a complicated problem into smaller units, each of which is handled by a part of the computer, then combined to produce the final result.

Application

The term *application* comes from the idea that a group of programs work together to *apply* the abilities of the computer to a specific task, such as word processing or weather forecasting.

Source for Definitions

For more definitions of mainframes and minicomputers, see the following Web sites:

http://foldoc.doc.ic.ac.uk/foldoc

http://www.currents.net/resources/dictionary/dictionary.phtml

- **Mainframes** are machines that many large companies use to manage the huge amounts of data required to keep their operations running. For example, your local telephone company gathers usage data from a large number of telephone users, calculates the charges, and produces telephone bills. For this huge undertaking, the company requires a machine that can handle a large database, process rapidly, and print quickly. While many personal computers manage several gigabytes (billions of bytes) of storage, mainframe computers control and process terabytes (trillions of bytes) of storage.

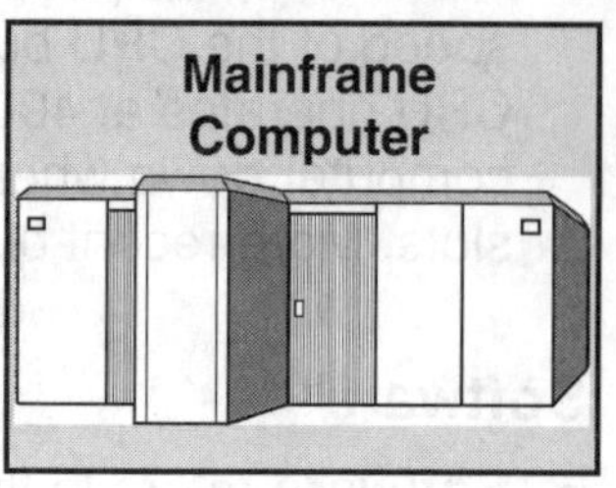

- Mainframes may still control as much as 90% of the data major businesses rely on for their critical applications, such as inventory, manufacturing, billing, and other accounting activities. For such applications they offer superior performance, reliability, and security compared to microprocessors, and they are usually easy to expand as the business grows.

- If you work at a telephone company, you may use a PC to gain access to the large amounts of information stored under the control of a mainframe. You may also use a "dumb" terminal (keyboard and monitor) directly connected by network wires to the mainframe. The terminals are called "dumb" because, unlike PCs, they have no processing capabilities of their own but simply give users direct access to mainframe computing capacities.

- **Minicomputers**, first developed in the late 1960s and early 1970s, used to be distinguished from mainframe computers because they had smaller processing and storage management capabilities. The distinction has broken down in recent years for two reasons (which have also contributed to the growth of the personal computer):

  - Computer chips and storage capacities have increased rapidly and small machines can now manage much more storage and process much more rapidly than earlier ones.

  - Minicomputers are often linked in networks so companies (and universities, in particular) can use several networked minicomputers to perform the same tasks as one mainframe. Access to minicomputers, like access to mainframes, may be through dumb terminals or PCs.

Minicomputers

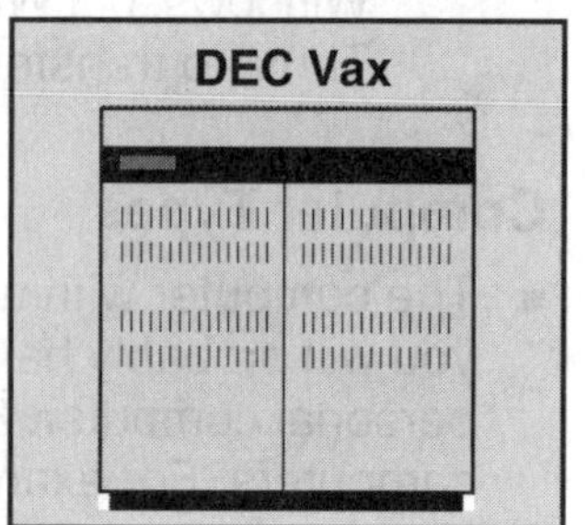

- **Personal computers** come in a wide variety of styles and sizes. Some are designed for the **desktop**, with a cathode ray tube monitor separate from the rest of the computer. Some newer desktop computers, like the iMac, have reintegrated the CPU case and the monitor.

- **Laptop** and **hand-held** computers grow lighter and sturdier with each new version. Laptops are compact with built-in liquid crystal display monitors that provide crisp displays. Most hand-held computers are used for a specific purpose, such as taking notes and sending/receiving messages. Their portability makes them ideal for salespeople and other business professionals who travel a great deal.

Computer Workers

- Computer chips, hard disks, diskette drives, CD-ROM and DVD drives, and all other computer components are designed by **electronics engineers**. These professionals specialize in micro-circuitry or imaging technology or hundreds of other areas involved with the design and manufacture of computing equipment.

- Supercomputers, mainframes, and minicomputers require specially trained personnel to keep them running efficiently. Most mainframe installations have a **systems programmer** who has studied the inner workings of the mainframe operating system and knows how to keep it working correctly.

- In addition, such installations may have a person in charge of managing disk storage, called a **DASD** (Direct Access Storage Device) manager. Just as you may accumulate a great deal of data that you no longer need on your personal computer, a mainframe installation may pile up data it should archive (file permanently elsewhere) and information needed only temporarily. The DASD manager sees to it that the installation gets the most efficient use of its storage capacity.

- Mainframe installations usually also have a staff of **application programmers** who ensure that the programs the organizations need are created, maintained, and improved. Such programmers work on fixing problems in programs, adding new features, and creating special programs to perform specific tasks. Application programmers are necessary because many of the programs that run on mainframes are not purchased from a software supplier.

- **Database administrators and developers** are people who specialize in designing and overseeing the maintenance of databases.

- **Network administrators** are people who specialize in making sure that a company's local area network (see Lesson 9) operates efficiently. They need to be well-acquainted with the operation and maintenance of personal computers.

- **Help desk professionals** are people who are trained to provide help to users of applications. They work in the information processing department of large organizations and are called upon to install programs on PCs, answer questions about how to use programs, and help users recover from problems.

- Those who manage, support, and maintain computer installations are often known as **information systems** personnel. Their specialties may be housed in a department called **MIS** (Management Information Systems) or **IT** (Information Technology), and the department head may be a corporate officer called the **CIO** (Chief Information Officer).

- **Web site designers and programmers or developers** are those who decide what Web pages should look like and those who prepare the code that make Web pages perform properly. Sometimes Web page design and programming are done by the same person. In many cases, however, a graphics professional designs the look of a Web site, and a programmer makes sure that the Web site looks and works as designed.

  Web site programmers know how to use Web building tools like **HTML** (**h**ypertext **m**arkup **l**anguage) and Java, and special-purpose programs like Microsoft FrontPage or Dream Weaver.

Personal Computers

Laptop Computer

Palm V Personal Organizer

Computer Workers

WINDOWS EXERCISE DIRECTIONS

Windows Users

To illustrate input-processing-output, the following exercise asks you to start Windows' Calculator and perform some addition.

In this book, "Click" means to press and release the left mouse button. "Double-click" means to press and release the left mouse button twice quickly. "Right-click" means to press and release the right mouse button.

Start the Calculator

1. Move your mouse pointer to the Start button on the Windows desktop.

2. Click the Start button Start.

3. Move your mouse pointer up to Programs

    Programs

4. Move the mouse pointer to the right and find Accessories.

5. Move the mouse pointer to the right and find Calculator, as shown below.

Illustration A. Start Calculator

6. Click Calculator.

    The Calculator starts and displays as shown in Illustration B.

Illustration B. Calculator

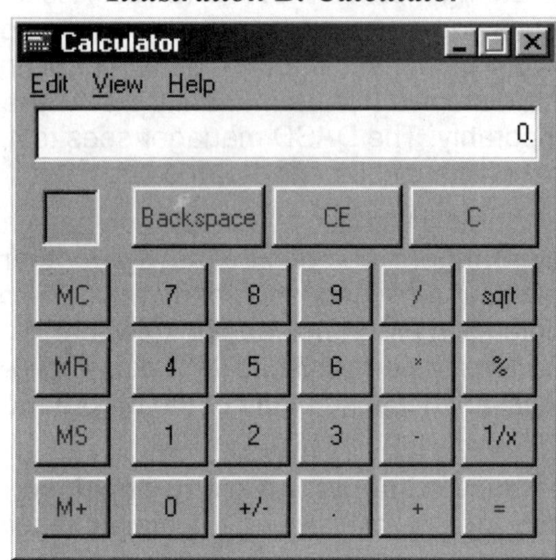

INPUT—Enter Data

In the remaining directions, you can use any of the following to enter data:

- **Point** to the appropriate buttons on the Calculator window and **click** the mouse button.

- **Press** the appropriate key on the number pad at the right of the keyboard if the Num Lock indicator is lit. (To turn Num Lock on and off, press the Num Lock key on the number pad.)

- **Press** the appropriate key on the top row of the keyboard.

    1. Enter the number *50*.

        The number 50 appears in the Calculator's display.

    2. Enter the + (plus sign).

    3. Enter the number *49*.

        The number 49 appears in the Calculator's display.

PROCESSING—Get Result

1. Press Enter, enter the = (equal sign), or enter the + (plus sign).

    The number 99 appears in the Calculator display.

2. Leave the number displayed; don't clear the display.

Additional Input-Processing-Output

1. Click the MS (memory save) button 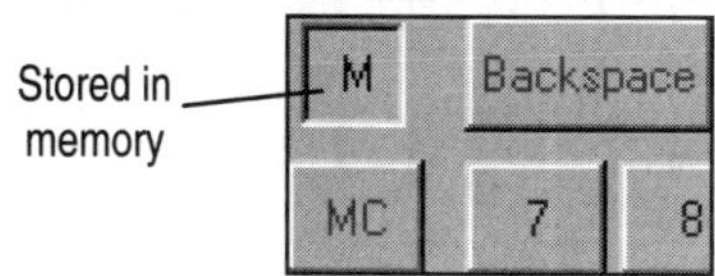 on the calculator, or press **Ctrl**+**M** (hold down the **Ctrl** key and press **M**).

   The result is stored in the Calculator's memory, as indicated by the M in the upper left just below the display, as shown in Illustration C.

   ### *Illustration C. Stored Memory Indicator*

   Stored in memory → [M] [Backspace] [MC] [7] [8]

2. Click the Clear button [C], or press the **Esc** key to clear the 99 from the display.

3. Enter the number *37*.

   The number 37 appears in the Calculator's display.

4. Enter the + (plus sign).

5. Enter the number *48*.

   The number 48 appears in the Calculator's display.

6. Enter the + (plus sign).

   The number 85 appears in the Calculator's display.

7. Enter the number *59*.

   The number 59 appears in the Calculator's display.

8. Enter the + (plus sign).

   The number 144 appears in the Calculator's display.

9. Enter the + (plus sign).

10. Click the MR (memory recall) button [MR].

    The data stored in the calculator's memory by Memory Save is recalled for processing.

11. Enter the = sign.

    The number 243 appears in the Calculator display, as shown in Illustration D.

OUTPUT—View Results

By following the directions, you have:

- Entered numbers (input).
- Requested the program to add those numbers (perform processing).
- Reviewed the output.

Illustration D. Final Result

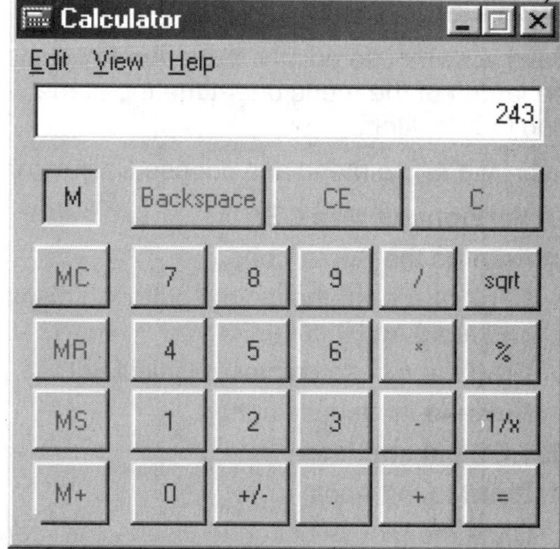

Clear and Close the Calculator

1. Click the MC (memory clear) button [MC] or press **Ctrl**+**L** to clear the Calculator's memory.

2. Click the Clear button [C], or press the **Esc** key to clear the display.

3. Click the Close button [X] in the upper right of the Calculator, or press **Alt**+**F4** to exit the calculator.

MAC OS EXERCISE DIRECTIONS

To illustrate input-processing-output, the following exercise asks you to start the Mac OS Calculator and perform some addition.

In this book, "Click" means to press and release the mouse button. "Double-click" means to press and release the mouse button twice quickly.

Start the Calculator

1. Move your mouse pointer to the Apple symbol at the far left of the menu bar at the top of the Mac OS desktop.

2. Open the Apple menu and choose Calculator.

   All Versions of Mac OS:
   a. **Point** to the Apple icon.
   b. **Click and hold** the mouse button to display the menu and it open.
   c. **Drag** the mouse pointer to Calculator.
   d. **Release** the mouse button.

   Mac OS 8.0 and later:
   a. **Point** to the Apple icon.
   b. **Click** the mouse button to display the menu.
   c. **Slide** the mouse pointer to Calculator.
   d. **Click** the mouse button.

Illustration E. Start Calculator

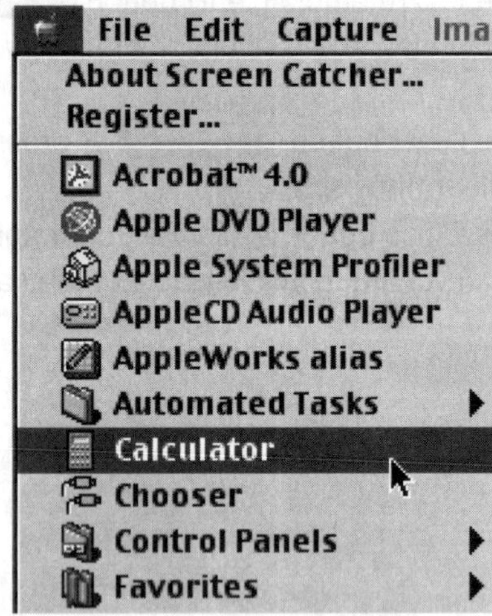

The Calculator starts and displays as shown in Illustration F.

Illustration F. Calculator

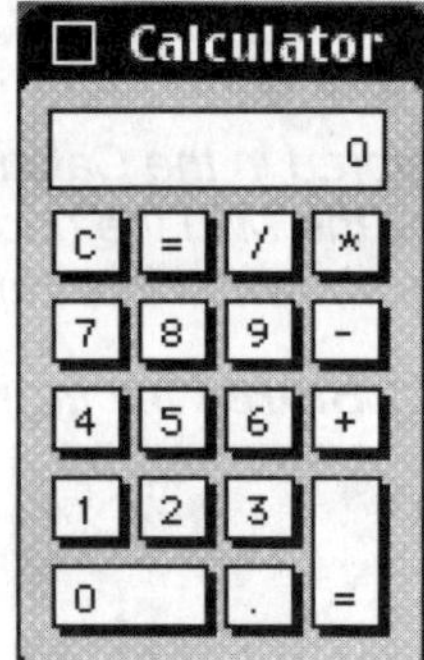

Note that the Calculator displays buttons in the same positions as the keys on the number pad at the right side of the keyboard. When the Calculator is active, you may use the number pad keys to enter data and request processing.

INPUT—Enter Data

In the remaining directions, you can use any of the following to enter data:

- **Point** to the appropriate buttons on the Calculator window and **click** the mouse button.

- **Press** the appropriate key on the number pad at the right of the keyboard. Note that the buttons on the Calculator window are laid out in the same pattern as the keys on the number pad.

- **Press** the appropriate key on the top row of the keyboard.
  1. Enter the number *50*.
     The number 50 appears in the Calculator's display.
  2. Enter the + (plus sign).
  3. Enter the number *49*.
     The number 49 appears in the Calculator's display.

PROCESSING—Get Result

1. Complete the Calculator entry by doing one of the following:
   - Press the **Enter** key.
   - Click or press the **=** (equal sign).
   - Click or press the **+** (plus sign).

   The number 99 appears in the Calculator display.

2. Click the C button **C** on the Calculator, or press the **num lock** **Num Lock** key on the number pad.

   The Calculator's memory is cleared and the number 0 appears in the Calculator's display.

Additional Input-Processing-Output

1. Enter the number *37*.

   The number 37 appears in the Calculator's display.

2. Enter the + (plus sign).
3. Enter the number *48*.

   The number 48 appears in the Calculator's display.

4. Enter the + (plus sign).

   The number 85 appears in the Calculator's display.

5. Enter the number 99.

6. Press the Enter key or click the ▣ button.

   The number 184 appears in the Calculator's display, as shown in Illustration G.

OUTPUT—View Results

By following the directions, you have:

- Entered numbers from the keyboard for input.
- Requested the program to add those numbers (perform processing).
- Reviewed the output.

Illustration G. Final Result

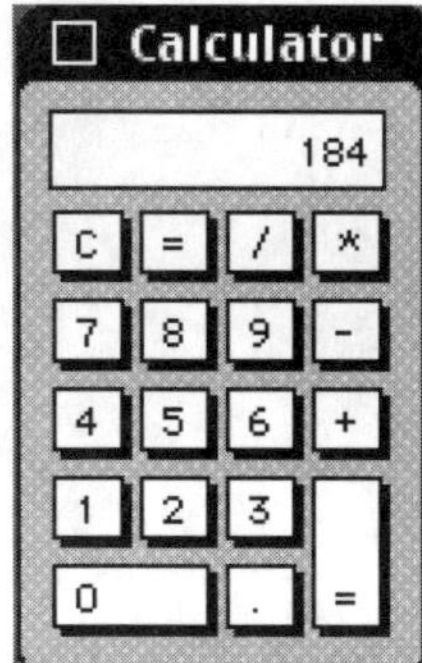

Clear and Close the Calculator

1. Click the C button ⬚ or press the Num Lock key to clear the Calculator.

2. Click the Close box ▣ in the upper left of the Calculator, or press ⌘+Q to quit the calculator.

GENERAL EXERCISE DIRECTIONS

Your Computer

How many of the following peripherals are accessible to your computer? Note that they may be directly attached or accessible through a network connection.

Keyboard

Monitor

CD-ROM or DVD player

Diskette or other drive with removable disks to which you may save data

Scanner

Printer

Mouse

Sound system

Printer

Voice input system

Computers and Careers

To learn more about careers in computing, use the library, Internet, or interviews with computer professionals and write a brief report about any of the following as a career:

Applications programmer

Systems programmer

Computer operator

Network administrator

Web site developer

Database administrator

Database developer

Help systems developer

Technical writer

Look in the Help Wanted ads of the newspaper from a fairly large city. Look at classifications other than Computers, Computing, and so on. List the number of different software applications mentioned in requirements for the jobs.

Do any of the positions mention specific hardware?

Lesson 2A: Introduction to Mac OS

Exercise 1: Learn Mac OS Basics

- **About Mac OS**
- **The Desktop**
- **Use the Mouse**
- **Mouse for Mac OS**
- **Mouse Pointer Shapes**
- **Use the Keyboard**
- **Insertion Point Movement**
- **Other Mac OS Keys**
- **Use Menus**
- **Use Dialog Boxes**

Exercise 2: Getting Started with Mac OS

- **Finder Menu**
- **Apple Menu**
- **Help Menu**
- **Application Menu**
- **Shut Down Mac OS**

Exercise 3: Mac OS Windows

- **Use the Hard Disk Window**
- **Explore the Hard Disk Window List**
- **Use Alternate Views**
- **Use Collapse, Zoom, and Size Boxes**

Exercise 4: Use the Control Panels

- **The Control Panels Folder**
- **Work with Sections (Appearance Control Panel)**
- **The Active Window**

Exercise 5: Find Files Using Sherlock

- **The Sherlock Dialog Box**
- **Other Sherlock (Find) Options**

Exercise 6: Managing Your System

- **Create a Folder**
- **Create an Alias**
- **Save an Item to the Desktop**
- **The Desktop Folder**
- **Add an Item to the Apple Menu**
- **Remove an Item from the Apple Menu**
- **Use Trash**
- **Select Multiple Items**
- **Create a Folder**
- **Rename an Item**
- **Copy or Move Items by Dragging**
- **Arrange Items on the Desktop**

Exercise 7: Use Applications

- **Launch or Start Applications**
- **Use Launcher**
- **Locate a Folder Using a Dialog Box**

Learn Mac OS Basics

■ **About Mac OS** ■ **The Desktop** ■ **Use the Mouse** ■ **Mouse for Mac OS**
■ **Mouse Pointer Shapes** ■ **Use the Keyboard** ■ **Insertion Point Movement**
■ **Other Mac OS Keys** ■ **Use Menus** ■ **Use Dialog Boxes**

NOTES

About Mac OS

- Apple computers generally run on **Mac® OS** (**M**acintosh **O**perating **S**ystem). Mac OS provides a **GUI** (**G**raphical **U**ser **I**nterface).

- The GUI was first developed at a Xerox® think tank in California's famed Silicon Valley in the early 1970s. It was then adapted by Steve Jobs and Steve Wozniak when they created the first Apple computers. With a GUI, you most often use a mouse pointing device to interact with the computer through a variety of menus, icons, options, and buttons. Many of these actions can also be performed from the keyboard, but the primary interaction is visual—point and click, click and drag.

- Applications that run on Apple machines use the Mac OS GUI, which provides a similar appearance and consistent usage from one application to another. When you work in Mac OS, you can take some things for granted regardless of the software program, as you'll see as you work through the exercises in this lesson.

The Desktop

- When you start your machine, Mac OS displays the desktop. A sample desktop from Mac OS 8.5 is shown on the next page. Your desktop may include **icons** not shown in the illustration. (In computer terms, an *icon* is a symbol that represents a program, application, or other computer feature.) The elements in this illustration are described in the following table.

GUI

Acronym for **Graphical User Interface** (an acronym is a shortened form of a phrase).

Prior to GUI, users had to type commands at the keyboard to work with the computer. The GUI is convenient for many users because they point with the mouse to an icon or menu item and click. (This visual method of interaction is not so convenient for the blind and visually impaired.)

Interface

The method by which a computer system presents information to another computer or to a user.

Icon	Description
	**Apple menu.** Click to see a list of all items in the Apple Menu Items folder within the System folder on the hard disk. Some items are placed in the Apple Menu Items folder automatically during installation. You can add items, such as an alias for a file or application, to this folder.
Menu bar	The menu options change as the active application and window change. For example, when you start AppleWorks, the menu bar offers options for AppleWorks. When you start an MS Office 98 application, the menu for that application appears.
11:36 AM	Shows the current time of day or the date. Click it to switch between the time and the date.
Finder	Application menu lets you switch quickly from one open application to another. Finder is the application that runs the desktop; its use is described in the next exercise.

Icon	Description
Macintosh HD	Double-click to list all folders on the hard disk. The name of your hard disk may be different. The disk from which the Mac starts is always in the upper-right-hand corner of the desktop. The one illustrated here is the default name as it appears on the Mac OS machine used to capture illustrations for this book. **Note:** When you insert a disk in a peripheral drive, such as the CD-ROM or floppy disk drive, an icon for that drive also appears on the desktop. In the Desktop illustration the icon ZIP-100 indicates that there is a disk in the Iomega® Zip™ drive in the computer.
Browse the Internet	Double-click an **alias** (indicated by a curving arrow and an italicized name) to start the application or open the folder it represents. The Browse the Internet alias starts the application that connects you to the Internet. The *Mac PPT 98 data* alias in the illustration opens a folder as indicated by the folder symbol in the icon.
Trash	Double-click this icon to see the list of files and folders you have deleted. Each disk from which you can erase files has its own Trash. You can retrieve files and folders deleted by mistake from this list or you can empty the Trash to free up space on a disk. (Deleted files are not actually removed from a disk until you empty the Trash.)
Control Strip	Provides access to many control panels options. Click the right end of the strip to collapse it. When the strip is collapsed, click the right end to expand it.

Sample Mac OS 8.5 Desktop

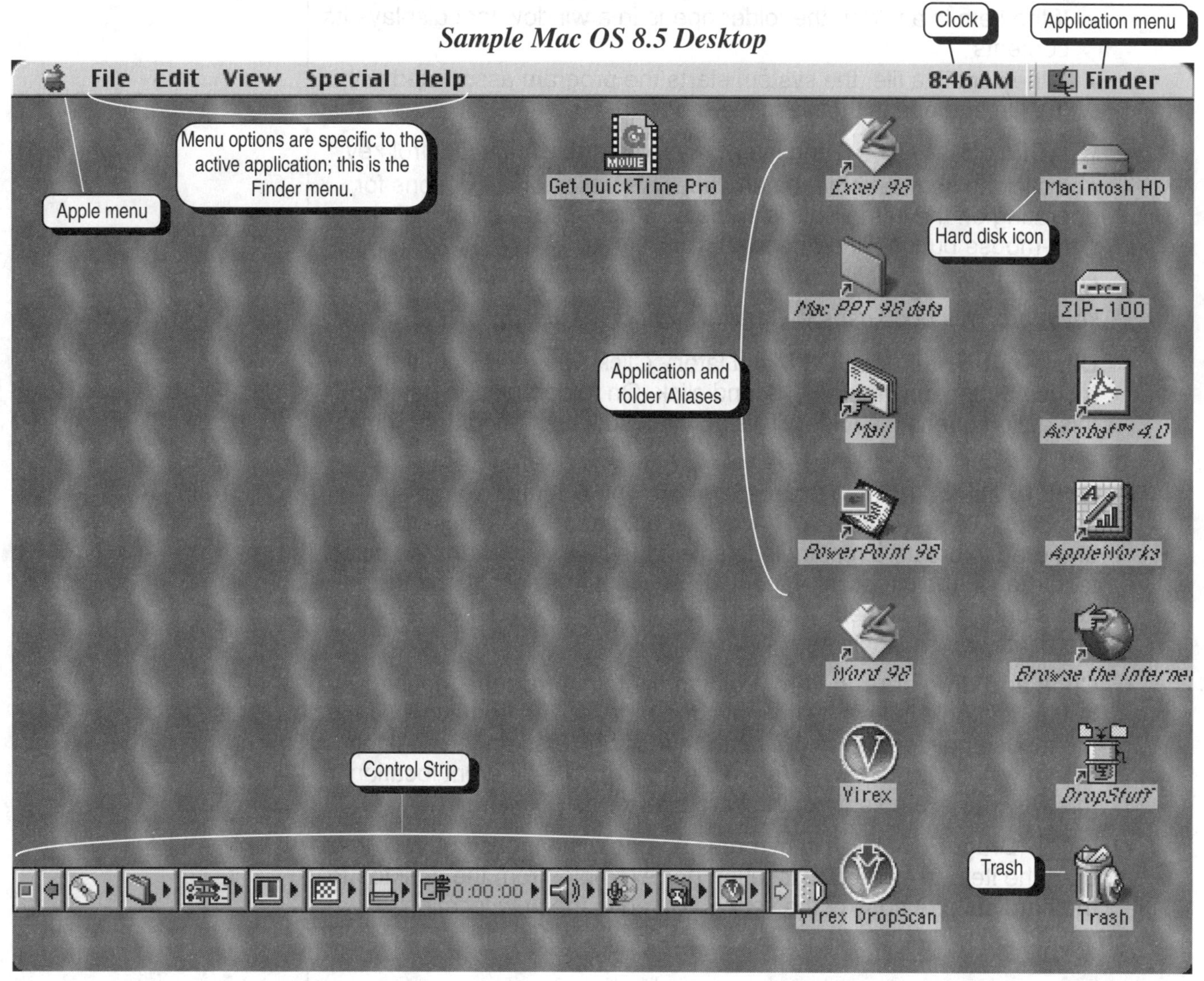

Use the Mouse

■ The mouse is a device that controls a pointer on the computer monitor. When you slide the mouse across a surface, the pointer moves across the screen. The pointer initially is an arrow ▲. When the arrow points to an **item**, you can click a mouse button to request the operating system to act upon that object.

Mouse for Mac OS

■ The mouse for the Mac usually has one button. With it, you can perform the following actions:

Item
Any element on the screen that can be selected, opened, or executed.

- **Click**. Point at an item on the screen, press the mouse button once, and release it. If the item is an icon, folder, or file, the item is selected. If the item is a menu or a button, the item opens.

- **Double-click**. Press and release the mouse button rapidly two times. Double-clicking opens the item.
    - If the item is an icon for a program, the program starts.
    - If the item is a folder, the folder opens in a window that displays its contents
    - If the item is a file, the system starts the program associated with the file and opens the file in the program.

- **Ctrl+Click** (Mac OS 8.0 and later). If you hold down the Control key and click an item, a context menu appears which offers options for operating on the item. (This is same as a right-click—clicking the right-mouse button—in Windows.)

    *Note that although the word **control** is spelled out on the Mac OS keyboard, this book uses* **Ctrl** *as the symbol for the key.*

- **Click-and-a-half** (Mac OS 8 and later). Click twice and hold the mouse button down on the second click. On folders on the desktop, this action opens the folder. This action also works on folders within a window to open the folders.

- **Drag to select**. Point to the place where you want to begin the selection. To select items in a window, hold down the mouse button and drag to create a rectangle to select the items you want. To select text, drag in the direction of the text you want to select. Once the items or text is selected, you can drag the selection as if all selected elements were a single item.

- **Click and drag** or **drag item**. Point to an item, press the mouse button and hold it down, then move the mouse. The item moves as the mouse pointer moves. You can reposition items on the desktop or in a window in this way. You move an item to a different location in this way (for example, from the hard disk to the desktop).

- **Option+ Drag**. Point to an item, press and hold the mouse button, then drag the item to a different location (for example, from the desktop to the hard disk). A copy of the item is placed in the new location.

Mouse Pointer Shapes

- The following table describes some of the mouse pointer shapes that appear as you use Mac OS. Other pointer shapes are described as necessary throughout this book.

Pointer	Description	Where Effective
	Normal select. Left-slanted arrow points to items, such as icons, menu options, or toolbar buttons.	Everywhere in Mac OS
	Wait. The system is busy processing. The hands on the watch go around and the beach ball spins to indicate that the system is working.	Everywhere in Mac OS
	Column adjust. Arrow on a vertical bar lets you change the width of a column. You drag the boundary between two columns or the left or right boundary.	Mac OS AppleWorks Office 98
	Text select. I-beam shows where the insertion point will be positioned when you click the mouse button. If you drag it, you select text. The insertion point (a blinking vertical bar) shows where the next key you press will take effect. For example, if you press the Del key, the insertion point moves left and deletes the character.	Mac OS text fields All AppleWorks applications All Office 98 applications
	Contextual Menu pointer. When you hold down the Ctrl key and click an item on the desktop or in a window, displays a menu appropriate to the selected item.	Mac OS Finder application (the desktop)
	Cell select. The fat cross appears as the standard pointer in the spreadsheet application. You point to a spreadsheet cell and click to select the cell.	AppleWorks spreadsheet Excel 98

Use the Keyboard

- The Macintosh keyboard shown in the following illustration has the alphanumeric keys in the traditional QWERTY arrangement, with the Shift, Caps Lock, Tab, Return, and Delete keys.

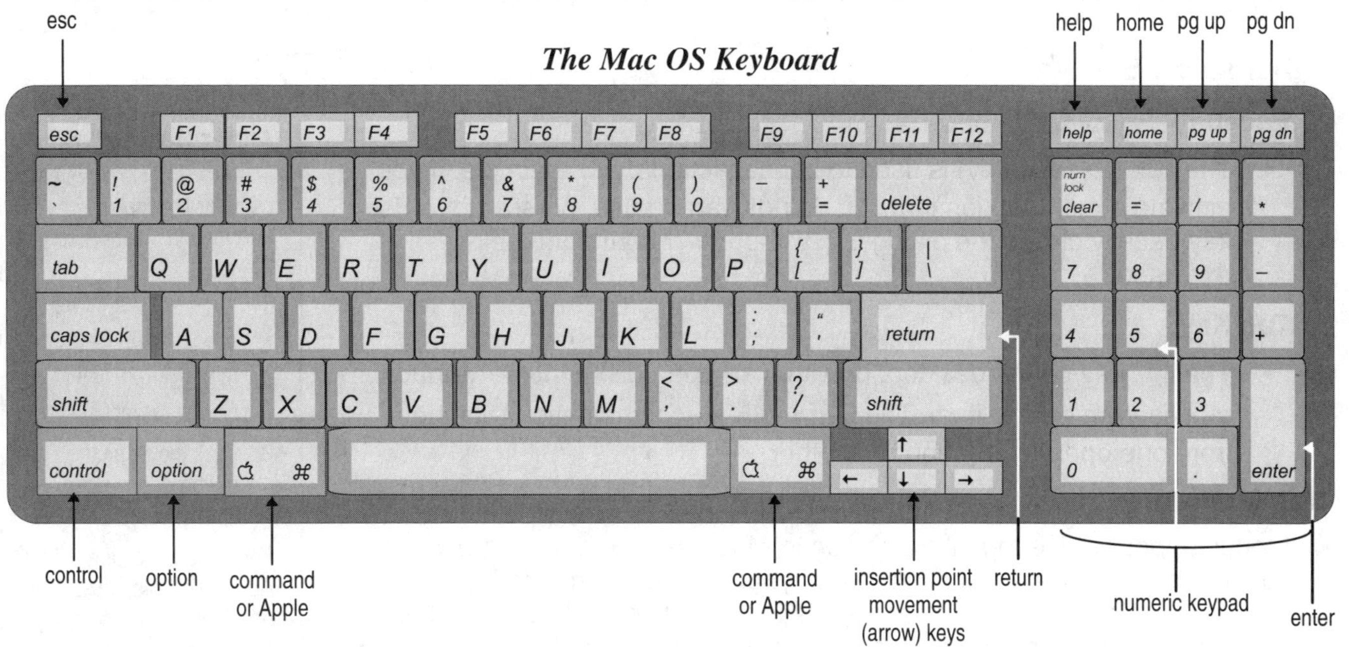

The Mac OS Keyboard

- Along the bottom row, to the left of the spacebar are the Control, Option, and Command keys. To the right of the spacebar are another copy of the Command key and the insertion point movement or arrow keys. Along the top row are the Escape (Esc) key and twelve function keys (F1 - F12).

- To the right is the numeric keypad. The top row of keys above the numeric keypad includes the Help, Home, Page Up (pg up), and Page Down (pg dn) keys.

- The uses of special modifier keyboard keys, such as Command ([Command]) Option ([Option]), and Control ([Ctrl]), are described as necessary throughout this book. (The symbols are used throughout the book to indicate these keys.)

Insertion Point Movement

- You can move the insertion point (a blinking vertical line |) by pointing with the mouse and clicking to position the insertion point at the mouse pointer, usually the pointer is the I-beam when you are working with text.

- You can also move the insertion point by using the arrow keys on the keyboard. The arrow keys are located at the lower right of the standard keyboard next to the command (Apple) key.

Insertion Point Movement Keys (Mac OS Keyboard)

- Each key may be pressed by itself or combined with other keys to move the insertion point. For example, [Command]+[↑] moves the insertion point to the top of the document. The Mac OS PDF document on the CD-ROM contains a reference table of keystrokes for moving the Insertion point.

Other Mac OS Keys

Escape Key

- The [Esc] (Escape key) is used to cancel actions. For example, if you activate a menu option that you do not want to use, pressing the Esc key usually closes the dialog box without any command being executed.

Tab Key

- The [Tab] key on the desktop, or within an open disk or folder window, moves from item to item. The [Command]+[Tab] key combination switches from one open application to another.

Use Menus

- Menus appear at the top of the screen in Mac OS. The menus are specific to the active application. When your computer first starts, the desktop appears and the Finder application, which lets you work with the desktop, is active. The Finder menu appears at the top of the screen.

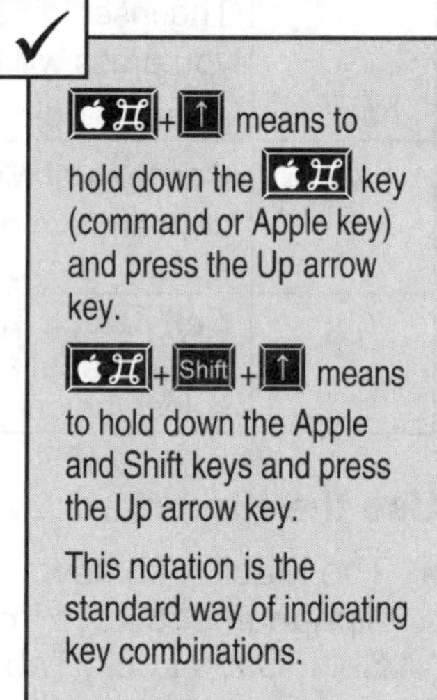

Other Resources

The Mac OS Help system contains extensive information on shortcut keys.

1. From the **Help** menu, choose **Help Center**.

2. In the search text box type *shortcut keys*.

3. Click the Search button or press the Return key.

The support section of the Apple Web site (URL http://www.apple.com/support) offers advice about getting started with Mac OS 8.5 and later.

- Menus offer a list of commands from which you choose the one you want to execute. Sometimes the command is executed immediately. Sometimes the option displays a submenu, as indicated by a right-pointing arrowhead. Sometimes the option displays a dialog box. The Finder menu bar and the Finder File menu are shown in the following illustrations.

Finder Menu

File   Edit   View   Special   Help

File Menu (Finder Application) with Submenu

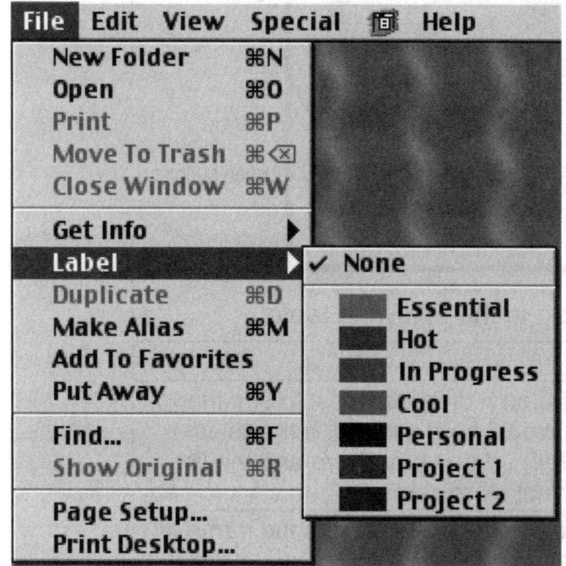

- Note that some commands appear in black letters while others are gray or dim. Options in black are available for selection; options in gray or dim letters are not available. Available options depend on the item (icon, folder, text, and so on) selected for processing.

- To activate a menu and command:
  1. Click the name of the menu you want to display and hold down the mouse button.
  2. Drag until you reach the item you want to activate. If the menu item offers a submenu, drag to the submenu item you want to activate.
  3. Release the mouse button.
     The system executes a command or opens a dialog box.

  OR
  1. Click the name of the menu.
  2. Point to the item you want to select. If the menu item offers a submenu, point to the submenu item you want to select.
  3. Click the mouse button.
     The system executes a command or opens a dialog box.

Use Dialog Boxes

- Dialog boxes are formatted windows that let you tell the system what work you want to perform. Dialog boxes are used for such things as opening files, printing documents, specifying margins for documents, and setting preferences. The dialog box in the following illustration is the Save As dialog box from AppleWorks for a word processing document.

AppleWorks Save As Dialog Box

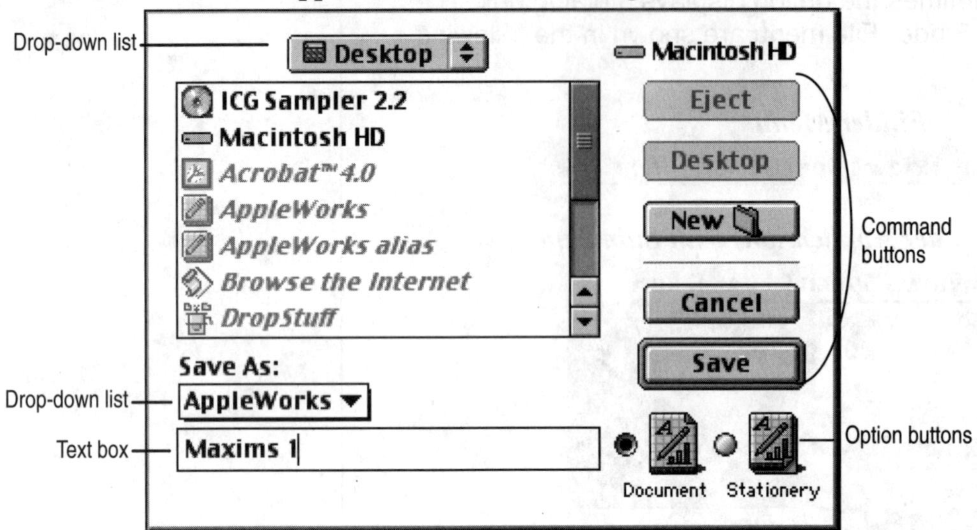

- The elements of a dialog box are described in the following table.

Element	Description
Drop-down list	Click the name or the arrow(s) on a drop-down list to see the choices. Choose just as you would from a menu. If the list is longer than can fit on the screen, drag up or down and the list will scroll automatically to reveal more items.
Text box	Type the desired text in the box. Usually the text is the name of a document or a search criterion.
Command buttons	Click a command button to activate the command. The dialog box illustrated above, has two inactive buttons (the ones in gray) and three active commands.
Option buttons	Round option buttons—sometimes called radio buttons—indicate options that are mutually exclusive (only one of the options can be chosen). Check box option ☑ buttons indicate options that are not mutually exclusive.

- When a dialog box appears, you complete the options as necessary and click the command button you wish to process the entries.

- For example, in the Save As dialog box shown above, you can:

  1. Choose a location to save the file from the drop-down list at the top of the dialog box.

  2. Choose a type of file in the Save As drop-down list.

  3. Type a name in the text box.

  4. Choose a document type by clicking an option button.

  5. Click the Save button **Save** to save the document

     OR

     Click the Cancel button **Cancel**, the Close box ☐, or the Esc key to close the dialog box without processing the options selected.

- Some dialog boxes offer other command buttons, such as **OK**. These buttons will be described as necessary throughout the lessons in this book.

> **In this exercise, you will work with the hard disk window.**

EXERCISE DIRECTIONS

1. Start on the desktop.

2. Double-click the icon for your hard disk.
   The hard disk window opens and displays a list of folders and files or icons for the items on the drive.

3. Click the Collapse box ▤.
   The hard drive window collapses into the title bar. It looks similar to the following:

4. Click the Collapse box ▤ again to restore the window to its previous size and position.

5. Click the Zoom box ▤.
   If the window was small, it enlarges; if it was enlarged, it becomes smaller. The Zoom box alternates between window sizes.

6. Click the Close box ▫ in the upper left of the window.
   The hard disk window closes.

7. Reopen the hard disk window.

8. Make sure the hard drive window is at its smaller size. Click the Zoom box if necessary to shrink it.

9. Move your mouse pointer to the hard drive title bar.

10. Hold down the mouse button and drag the window around on the desktop. (Careful not to double-click.)
    The window changes its position on the desktop.

11. When the window is in a position that you like, release the mouse button.
    Any window that is not collapsed can be moved in this way. You may find it useful to move a window around to be able to see elements on the desktop that the window hides.

12. Click the Close box ▫ in the upper left of the window to close the hard disk window.

Exercise 2

Getting Started with Mac OS
■ Finder Menu ■ Apple Menu ■ Help Menu
■ Application Menu ■ Shut Down Mac OS

NOTES

Finder Menu

- When you start your machine, Mac OS displays the desktop and the Finder application's menu. The Finder application gives you access to the desktop, your hard disk, and any removable media, such as a diskette or Iomega® Zip™ drive, and the CD-ROM or DVD drive.

- The Finder menu, shown in the following illustration, has at least five options or menus. In the illustration, these are the options with names. (The icon in the illustration is the Aladdin Systems MagicMenu™ associated for StuffIt® application, which compresses files so they take less time to transmit. Your menu may have no icon or a different one.) You can review the commands offered by these menus.

The Finder Menu

File   Edit   View   Special   📧   Help

- You will learn more about the options on the Finder menu as you work through the exercises in this lesson.

💻 Try It!

1. Click on a blank area of the desktop
   Finder *appears in the upper right of the screen. The symbol indicates that Finder is active.*

2. Point to the **File** menu and click and hold the mouse.
   The File menu opens, as shown in the illustration on the next page. (Different options may be available on your menu.)

3. Slide the mouse pointer across the other menu names.

4. As the mouse pointer touches each name, the menu commands appear.

5. Click the **View** menu.

6. Click the **as Buttons** option.
   The icons on the desktop turn into buttons. Buttons can be activated by a single click rather than a double-click.

7. Click the **View** menu.

8. Click the **as Icons** option.
   The buttons turn into icons again.

File Menu for Finder (Desktop) Application

Apple Menu

- The Apple menu is a list of the items in the Apple Menu Items folder in the System folder. It lists up to 52 items, some of which, such as Control Panels, are installed as part of the operating system. Other options may be placed in the folder when applications are installed, and you can place any item you wish in the Apple Menu Items folder to make it appear on the Apple menu. (You can have as many items in the folder as you like, but only the first 52 alphabetically appear on the menu.) A portion of a sample Apple menu is shown in the following illustration.

Portion of Sample Apple Menu

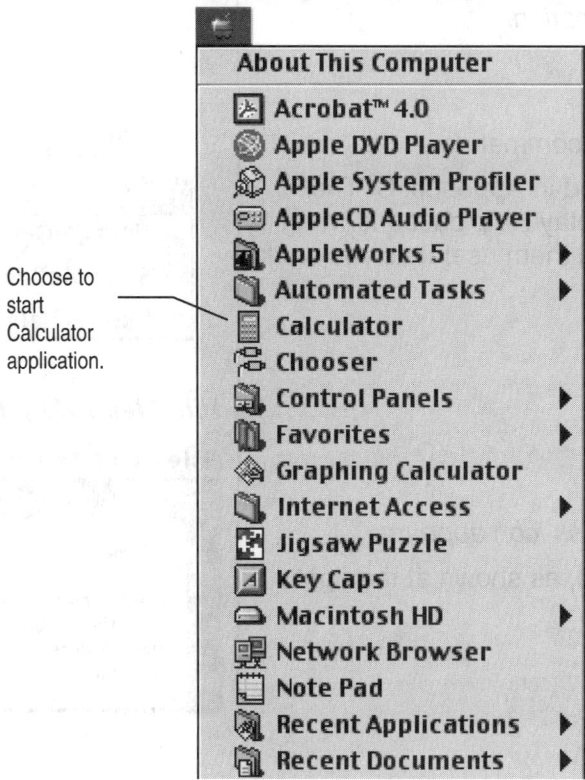

Choose an Item from a Menu

- To choose an item from a menu:
    1. Click the menu name and hold down the mouse button.
    2. Drag down until you reach the item you wish to activate.
    3. Release the mouse button.

    OR

    1. Click the menu name.
    2. Slide the mouse pointer until you reach the item you want.
    3. Click the item.

Try It!

1. Click the Apple menu icon to display the Apple menu for your computer.

2. Choose the **Calculator** option.
   The Calculator appears on your desktop.

3. Click the **C** button to clear the display area of any numbers.

4. Click the 8 key, then the 9 key to enter the number *89*.

5. Click the asterisk (*) key. (* is the symbol for multiplication.)

6. Click the 2 key.

7. Click the = key.
   The number 178 should display in the calculator display area.

8. Click **C** button to clear the display window.

9. Click the Close box to close the calculator window.

   OR

   Click **File**, **Quit** or press ⌘+Q.

   Either action always closes the active application.

Help Menu

- The Help menu, shown at the right, offers three commands.

- The Help Center and Mac OS Help are described in Appendix C. The Show Balloons option causes the system to display Help balloons when you point to objects on the screen. You may find them useful as you work with your Apple computer.

Try It!

1. Click the **Help** menu.

2. Click **Show Balloons**.

3. Point at the hard disk icon.
   A balloon with information about the hard disk icon appears.

4. Point to the **File** menu, and read the balloon, as shown at the right.

5. Click the **Help** menu.

6. Click **Hide Balloons**.

Help Menu

File Menu Help Balloon

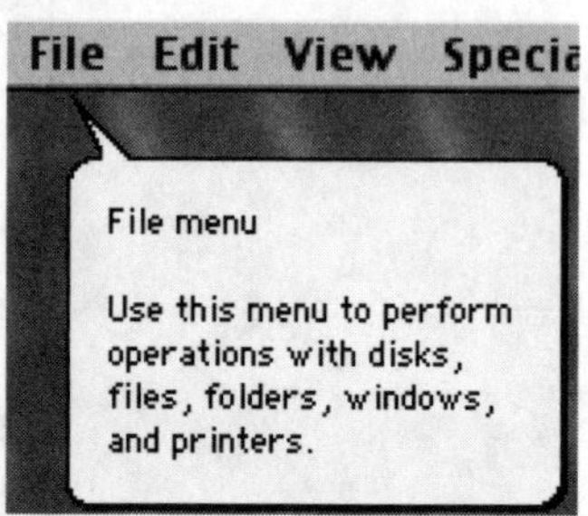

Application Menu

- The Application menu in the upper-right corner of the desktop screen lists the **open** applications. In the following illustration, Finder, AppleWorks, and Screen Catcher (the program used to capture the Mac OS screen images in this book) are the applications.

Application Menu

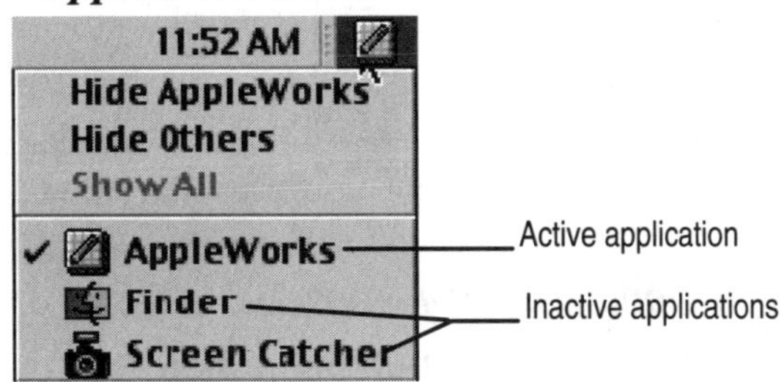

- The other menu choices let you:
  - Hide the windows of the **active** application
  - Hide the windows of all other applications so only the windows of the active application are showing.
  - Show all hidden windows.
  - Make another application the active one by clicking its name. The lower portion of the menu is called the Application Switcher.

- If you are running Mac OS 8.5, you can "tear off" the Application menu and display it as a small window called the Application Switcher.

Try It! (Mac OS 8.5 and later)

1. Click on the **Application** menu.
2. Hold down the mouse button
3. Drag down until you pass the bottom of the menu.
   An outline of a box appears, and items on the desktop show through the box outline, as shown in the following illustration.

Create Application Switcher (Mac OS 8.5 and later)

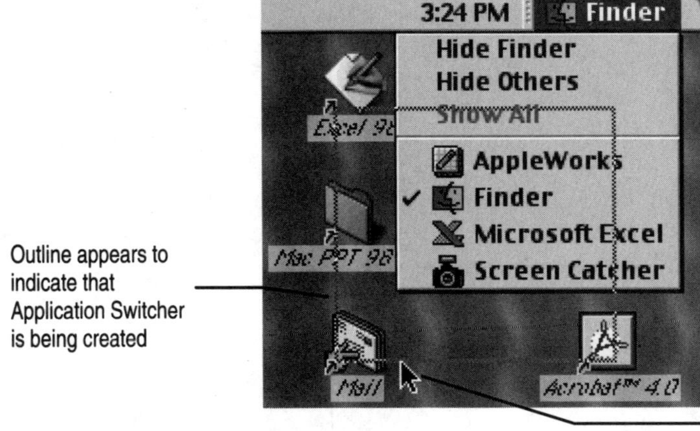

4. Release the mouse button.
   The Application Switcher appears, as shown on the left in the following illustration.
5. Click the Zoom box.

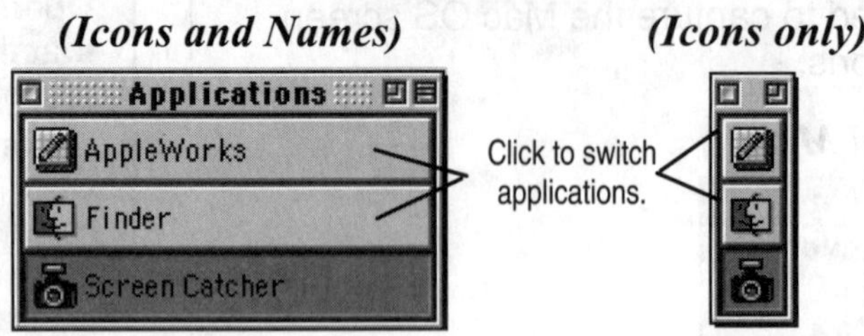

6. Click the Zoom box  again.
    The applications' names appear along with their icons.

- To switch from one application to another, click the button for the
  application you want to activate.

- To remove the Application Switcher from the desktop, click the
  Close box ☐. Then, to switch from one application to another, use the
  Application menu.

Shut Down Mac OS

- To shut down Mac OS, click **Special** on the Finder menu. If the Special
  menu is not on the menu bar, switch to the Finder application using the
  Application menu (or click anywhere on the desktop without selecting an
  icon or window). The Special menu is shown at the right.

- Select one of the three options:

  - **Sleep** puts the computer into system sleep. The computer's memory
    maintains its contents and conserves power. To wake the computer,
    press any key on the keyboard except the Caps Lock key.

  - **Restart** quits all open applications and programs, giving you the
    opportunity to save any unsaved documents. It ejects any removable
    disks and restarts the computer.

  - **Shut Down** quits all open applications and programs, giving you the
    opportunity to save any unsaved documents. It ejects any removable
    disks and shuts down the computer. To restart the computer, you
    must turn it back on using the on/off switch.

In this exercise, you will use the Help balloons to learn more about the desktop and the control strip. You will also start an application, use it, and quit it.

EXERCISE DIRECTIONS

Use Help Balloons

1. Click the Help menu.
2. Click Show Balloons.
3. Open (expand) the control strip at the bottom of the desktop if it is collapsed.
4. Point to each button on the control strip.
5. Click the Monitor Resolution button.
   The current resolution of your monitor is marked by a round bullet.
6. Click the Printer Selector button.
   The current printer selected for your computer is marked by a round bullet.
7. Click the right end of the control strip to collapse it.
8. Point to the Trash and read the Help balloon.
   What directions for using the trash appear?

Use the Apple Menu

1. Click the Apple menu icon to open the Apple menu.
2. Drag until you reach the Recent Applications entry.
3. Release the mouse button.
   The Recent Applications window opens and lists all recently-used applications in icon form.
4. Click the View menu.
5. Choose as List.
   The items are shown in list format.
6. Click the View menu.
7. Choose as Buttons.
   The items appear as buttons.
8. Click the View menu.
9. Choose as Icons.
   The items appear as icons.
10. Click the Close box on the window, or press +.

Use an Application

1. From the Apple menu, choose Jigsaw Puzzle.
   The Jigsaw Puzzle application opens, with its window displaying a map of the word in a modified Mercator projection.
2. Click the Options menu and choose Start New Puzzle.
   A dialog box opens asking you to choose the size of pieces.
3. Choose Large and click OK.
4. Click Help and choose Hide Balloons.
5. Solve the puzzle by clicking on a piece and dragging it to its correct position.
   If your computer is equipped for sound, a sound (called the wild eep) indicates when a piece is in the right place.
6. When the puzzle is complete, click the Close box on the Jigsaw Puzzle window.

Mac OS Windows
**■ Use the Hard Disk Window ■ Explore the Hard Disk Window List
■ Use Alternate Views ■ Use Collapse, Zoom, and Size Boxes**

NOTES

Use the Hard Disk Window

- The hard disk window displays the contents of the hard disk. The hard disk contains files stored in folders, which, like folders in a filing cabinet, are containers for information. On your computer, the folders contain the files that start and run applications and the files that you create and save.

- The hard disk from which your Macintosh starts always appears in the uppermost right-hand corner of the desktop. It can have any name that is fewer than 32 characters long. On the Macintosh machine used for the illustrations in this book, the default name *Macintosh HD* was used.

🖳 Try It!

1. Double-click the hard disk icon **Macintosh HD** on the desktop.
   The hard disk window opens.

2. Click the View menu and choose **as List**.
   The contents are displayed as a list of items, as shown in the following illustration.

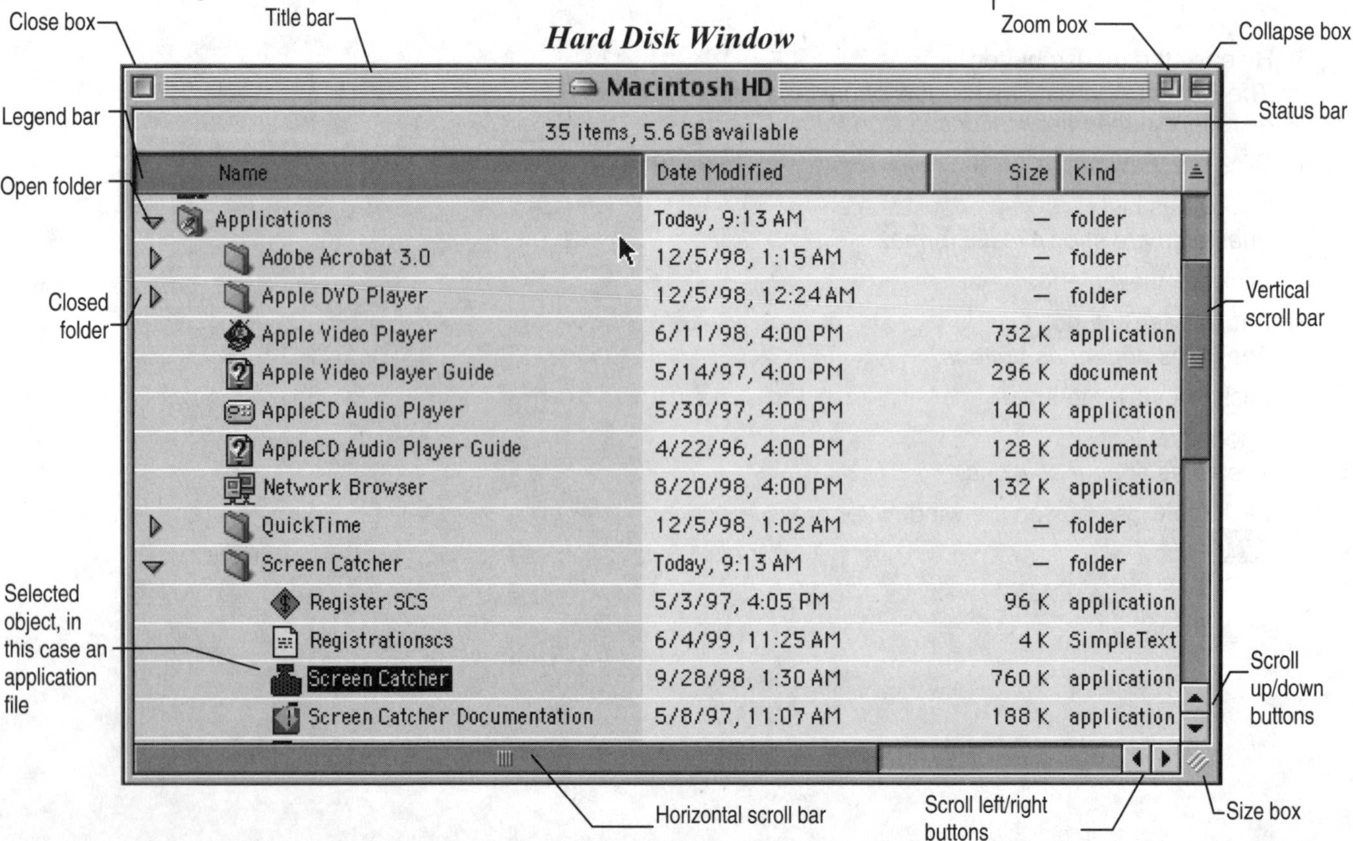

Hard Disk Window

■ The hard disk window has several important elements that are common to all Mac OS windows, as described in the table that follows.

Window Element	Description
Title bar	Identifies the window. When the window contains a document, the name of the document appears in the title bar.
Collapse box	Rolls up the window into the title bar so that only the title bar remains displayed. When a window is collapsed, you can return it to its previous position by clicking the Collapse box again.
Zoom box	Causes the window to expand or shrink.
Close box	Closes the window. If the window is an unsaved document, you are asked if you want to save it before the window closes.
Status bar	On disk drive windows, indicates the number of items and the remaining disk space. On application windows, such as AppleWorks for example, the status bar appears at the bottom of the window
Legend bar	On disk drive windows in List view, shows the Name, Date Modified, Size, and Kind of file listed. You can click any of these column headings to sort the contents by these headings.
Scroll bars and buttons	You can scroll (move the window across the contents) up, down, left, and right when the scroll bars and scroll buttons appear on a window. (If they are grayed out, the entire contents of the window is displayed.) Drag a scroll bar in the direction you want to move; click a button to move the window in the direction you desire.
Size box	Click and drag this box to change the size of the window.

Explore the Hard Disk Window List

■ In List view, you can see icons for folders and icons for applications. If a folder is closed, you can open it in List view by clicking the right-pointing triangle at the left of the folder name. The triangle then points down. To close the folder, click the down-pointing triangle.

■ If you double-click a folder name, you open a window that displays the folder's contents. You can open an application by double-clicking its icon.

Try It!

1. With the hard disk window open, locate the System Folder
   ▶ 🗑 System Folder.

2. Click the right-pointing triangle at the left of the folder to open the folder.

   When you click the triangle, the folder displays its contents as a list in the current window.

3. Double-click the Apple Menu Items entry in the folder
   ▶ 🗂 Apple Menu Items.

   The Apple Menu Items folder opens in a new window. Its contents display in the view that was in effect when the window was last closed.

Double-clicking a folder name in a list opens the folder in a new window.

4. Click the Close box  on the Apple Menu Items window to close it.
5. Locate the System Folder name ▽ 📁 System Folder.
6. Click the down-pointing triangle to close the folder.
   The list collapses and the triangle points to the right again.
7. Leave the hard disk window open.

Use Alternate Views

- You can view the items in the hard disk window as a list as illustrated in the previous Try It! activity. You may instead choose to view the items as icons or as buttons. You control the view of the hard drive window (and many others) through the View menu on the Finder menu bar.

- The difference between List view and the other two views is that in List view, you can remain within the hard drive window to work with the contents of the hard disk. With Icon and Button view, each time you double-click an icon or click a button, another window opens. You may prefer to remain within a single window, or your working style may be more compatible with multiple windows. You can choose the format you prefer.

 **Try It!**

Use *as Buttons* View

1. Click the View menu and choose **as Buttons**.
   The contents are displayed as buttons.

2. Locate and click the System Folder button System Folder.

   The System Folder window opens. The view in this window depends on the view in effect when it was last closed.

3. If it does not display buttons, click the View menu and choose **as Buttons**.

4. Click the Apple Menu Items button Apple Menu Items to open the Apple Menu Items window.

5. Click the Close box on the Apple Menu Items window to close it.

6. Click the Close box on the System Folder window.

7. Leave the hard disk window open.

Use *as Icons* View

1. Click anywhere in the hard disk window to activate it.
   The hard disk window is activated.

2. Click the View menu and choose **as Icons**.
   The contents are displayed as icons.

Double-click in List View

If you double-click a folder name in List view, a folder window opens just as in icon view.

3. Locate the System Folder icon ▽ 🗺 System Folder and double-click it.
   The System Folder window opens.
   The view in this window depends on the view in effect when it was last closed.
4. Click the View menu and choose **as Icons**.
5. Double-click the Apple Menu Items icon to open the window.
6. Click the Close box ▢ on the Apple Menu Items folder window.
7. Click the Close box ▢ on the System Folder window.

Use Collapse, Zoom, and Size Boxes

- You have used the Close box ▢ to close windows. On the other end of the title bar are the Collapse box ▤ and the Zoom box ▥.
- When you click the Collapse box ▤, the window appears to roll up into the title bar, revealing any windows hidden behind it. When you click it again, the window expands to its former state. The Collapse box ▤ is an example of a **toggle**.
- When you click the Zoom box ▥, the window expands or shrinks.
- In the lower-right corner of the window is the Size box ▧. When you click and drag this box, the window expands or shrinks in the direction you drag.

💻Try It!

1. Click the Collapse box ▤ on the right end of the title bar of the hard disk window.
   The window collapses into the title bar.
2. Click the Collapse box ▤ again.
   The window returns to its previous state.
3. Click the Zoom box ▥ on the title bar.
   The hard disk window expands or shrinks depending on whether it was previously zoomed.
4. Click the Zoom box ▥ again.
   The window returns to its previous size.
5. Click the Size box ▧ in the lower right of the window and drag it to the left until the window shows only a couple of columns of icons.
6. Click the Zoom box ▥.
   The hard disk window expands to full size.
7. Click the Zoom box ▥ again.
   The hard disk window shrinks to the size you created by dragging the size box.

Collapse by Double-clicking Title Bar

- You can set an option so that you can double-click the title bar to collapse a window. Once the option is set, all windows can be collapsed and restored by double-clicking their title bars.

Try It!

1. From the **Apple** menu, choose **Control Panels**, **Appearance**.
2. On the Appearance window, click the **Options** tab.
3. Click the option **Double-click title bar to collapse windows** if it is not already checked.
4. Double-click the Appearance window's title bar.
   The Appearance window collapses.
5. Double-click the Appearance window's title bar again.
   The Appearance window is restored.
6. Close the Appearance window (click its Close box █).
7. Double-click the hard disk window's title bar.
   The hard disk window collapses.
8. Double-click the title bar again to restore the window.
   The hard disk window is restored.

In this exercise, you will identify the parts of a disk window. Refer to the hard disk window illustration on page 30 for help.

You will also use the Collapse, Zoom, Size, and Close boxes to vary the size and look of a window on the desktop.

EXERCISE DIRECTIONS

Identify Parts of a CD-ROM Disc Window

- Illustration A on the following page shows a CD-ROM window in list format.
- The parts of the window are marked by letters. Write the correct letters from the illustration beside the elements listed in the table.

Letter	Button
	Title bar
	Open folder
	Closed folder
	Vertical scroll bar
	Horizontal scroll bar
	Close box
	Zoom box
	Collapse box
	Status bar
	Vertical scroll buttons
	Horizontal scroll buttons

Illustration A. CD-ROM Disc Window

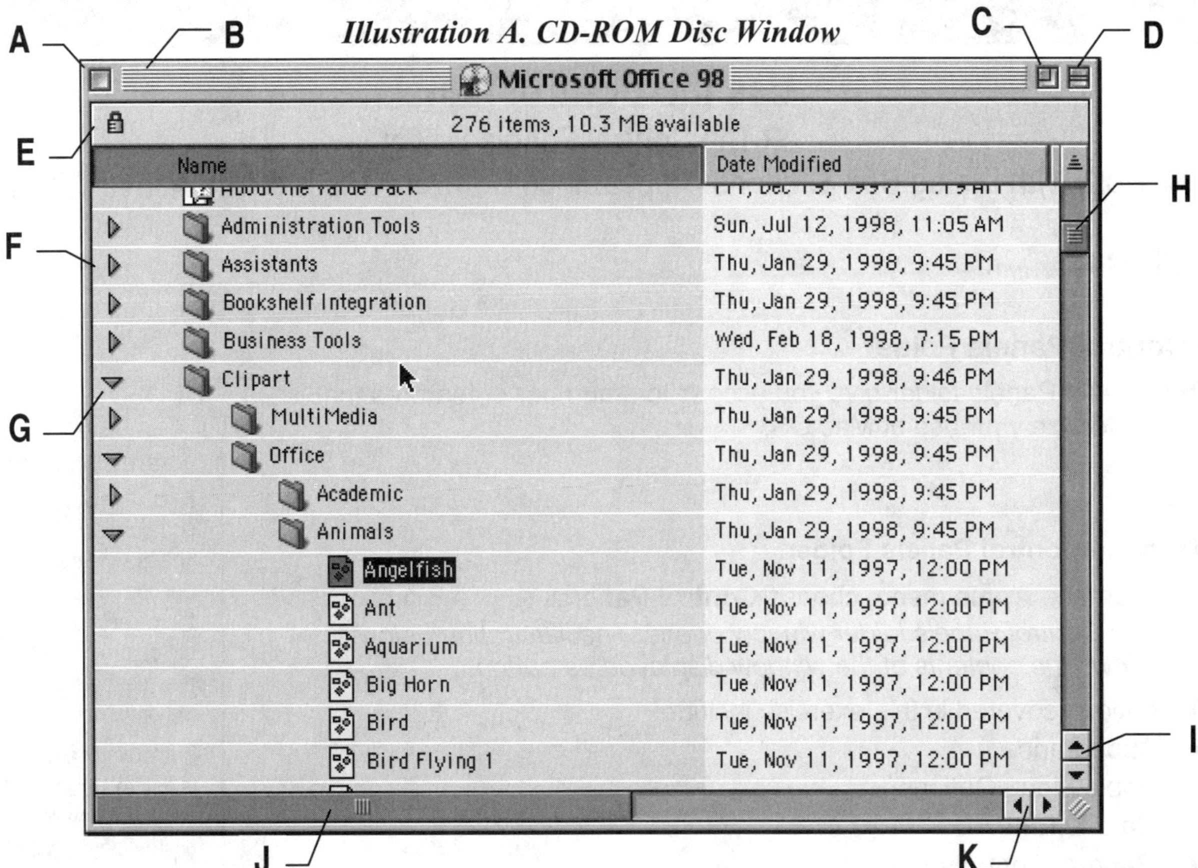

Manage Window Views

1. Open the hard disk window.
2. From the View menu, choose *as Buttons*.
3. Collapse the window.
4. Restore the window.
5. Use the Size button [Size] to shrink the window.
6. Use the Zoom box to expand the window.
7. From the View menu, choose *as List*.
8. Open the System folder without opening a new window.
9. Open the Control Panels folder without opening a new window.
10. Close the Control Panels folder.
11. Double-click the Control Panels folder to open it as a window.
12. View the Control Panels window as icons.
13. View the Control Panels window as buttons.
14. Close the Control Panels window.
15. Leave the System folder open.

Sort Objects Using Legend Bar

1. Enlarge the hard disk window until you can see the Name, Date Modified, Size, and Kind buttons.
2. Click the Size button [Size] on the legend bar.
   The items are sorted in ascending order by their size. Objects within folders are sorted by size within folder.
3. Click on the Name button [Name].
   The items are sorted alphabetically by name.
4. Click the Date Modified button [Date Modified].
   The items are sorted in ascending order by the date they were last modified. Items within folders are sorted by date within folder.
5. Click the Close box to close the hard disk window.

Exercise 4

Use the Control Panels
■ The Control Panels Folder
■ **Work with Dialog Box Sections (Appearance Control Panel)** ■ **The Active Window**

NOTES

The Control Panels Folder

■ The Control Panels folder give you access to a number of features that let you customize your use of Mac OS.

Try It!

Open the Control Panels Folder

• From the **Apple** menu, choose **Control Panels**.
The Control Panels folder window opens. The illustration below shows the contents of the window displayed as buttons.

■ The options covered in this exercise include:
• Appearance
• Apple Menu Options
• Date & Time
• General Controls
• Monitors & Sound
• Mouse

Control Panels Folder Window

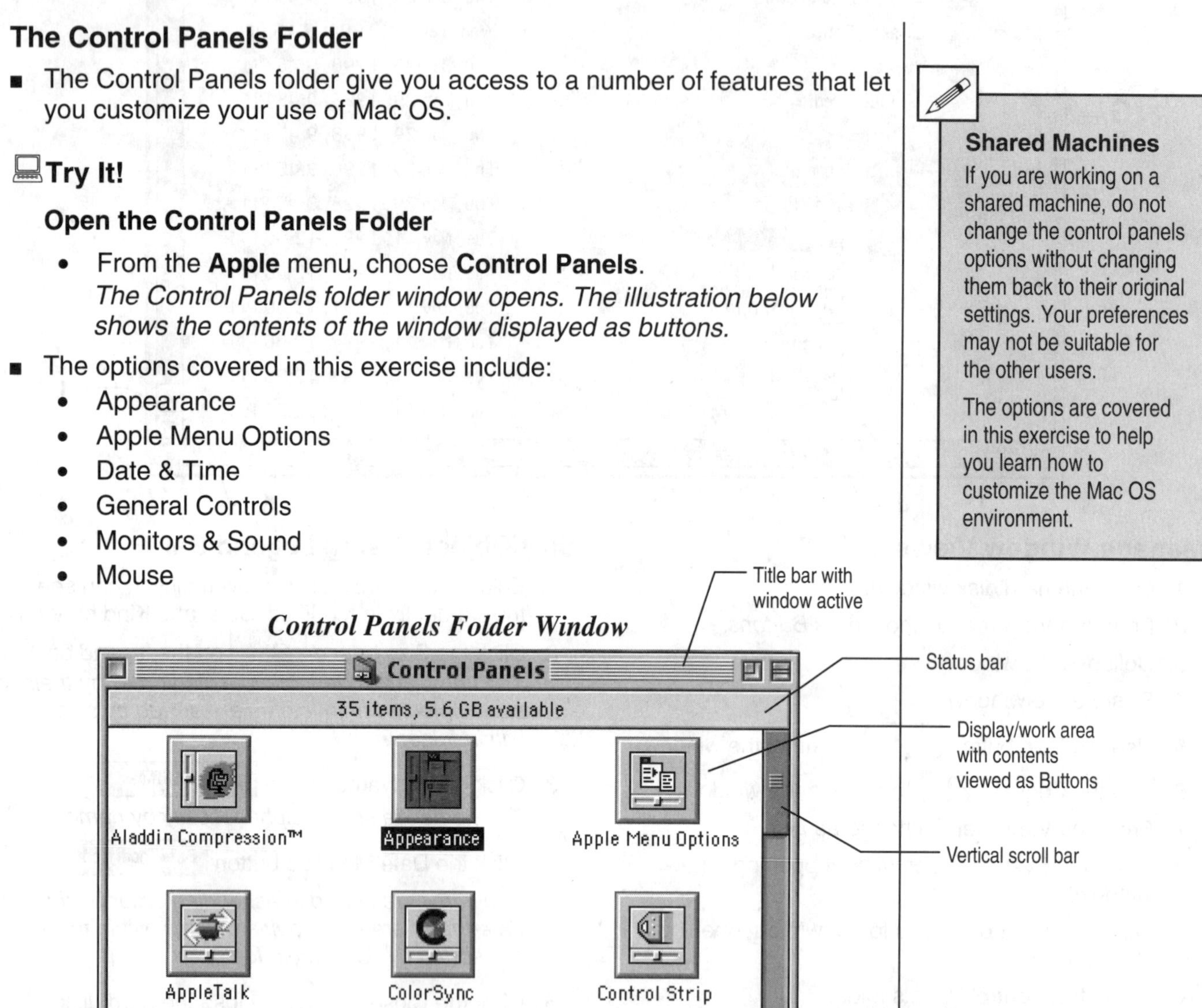

Work with Dialog Box Sections (Appearance Control Panel)

- When you select an item in the Control Panels window, a new window opens to let you customize the Mac OS system. The illustration below shows the Appearance control panel window with the Themes section displayed. (To activate a section, click the appropriate tab within the work/display area of the window.)

Appearance

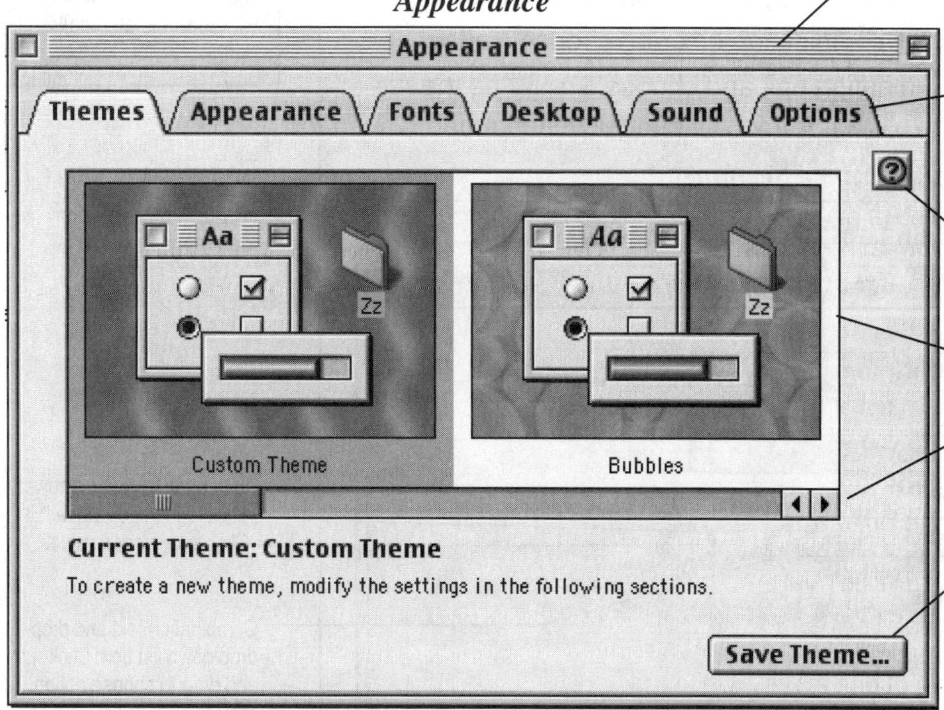

Title bar with window active

Sections indicated by tabs; Themes section active

Help command button

Display work/area with sections

Horizontal scroll bar and buttons for current section

Command button

- The **Themes** section lets you select one of several system-defined themes. You alter a theme by changing options in the other sections.

- The **Appearance** section lets you choose an appearance option and a highlight and variation color for the selected theme.

- The **Fonts** section lets you choose fonts for the selected theme.

- The **Desktop** section lets you choose a pattern for the desktop. It also lets you place a picture of your choice on the desktop. Mac OS provides several pictures for the desktop. You can place a picture of your own on the desktop.

- The **Sound** section lets you specify whether sound effects play for different operations.

- The **Options** section lets you specify where the scroll buttons will appear and whether you can double-click the title bar to collapse a window.

- If you select a different theme from the one currently in use, check the settings, particularly in the Options section, to be sure that the scroll buttons and double-click to collapse options are set as you prefer.

- By selecting a theme, changing it, and saving it, you can create your own customized theme.

Set Appearance Options

1. Open the **Appearance** control panel.
2. Note the name of the current theme.
3. Select the **Bubbles** theme.
4. Click the **Appearance** tab to display the Appearance section.
5. Click the **Highlight Color** combination box and choose **Yellow**.
6. Click the **Variation** combination box and choose **Sunny** as the variation color, as shown in the work/display area below.

> **Field**
> An area of a window where data is entered or displayed. The place that data is saved in a file or database is also called a field.

Appearance Section

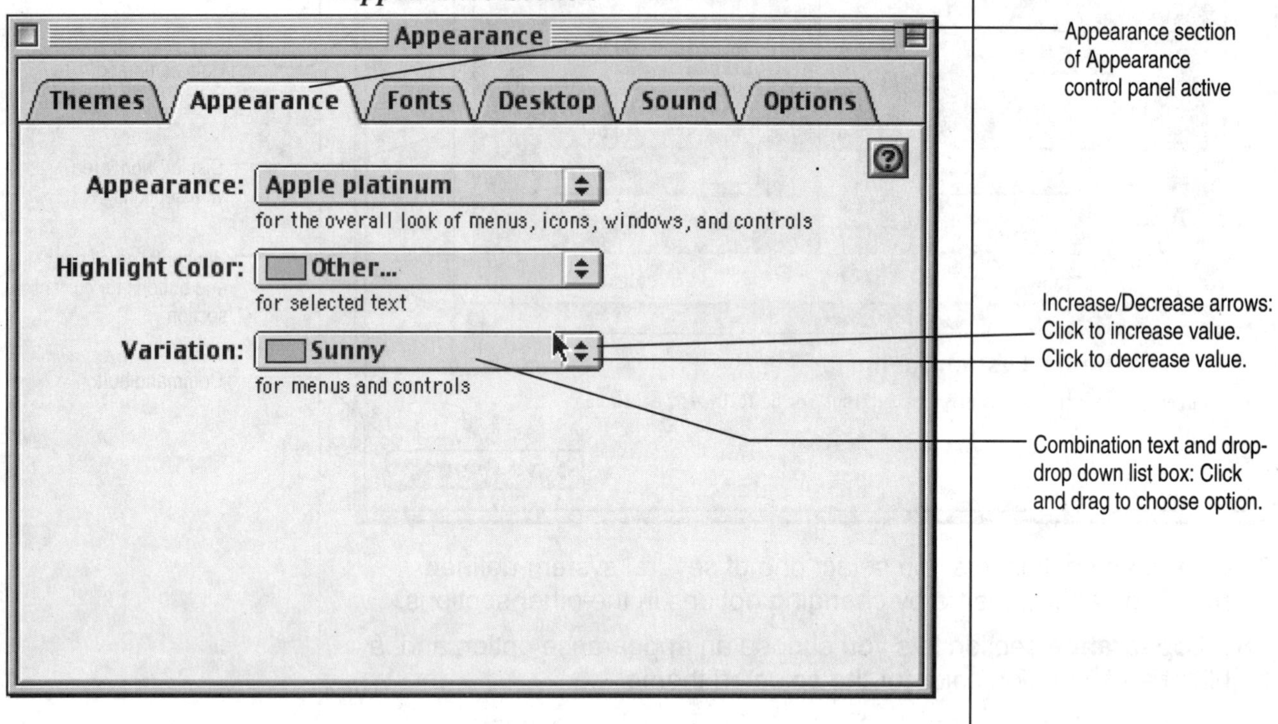

Appearance section of Appearance control panel active

Increase/Decrease arrows: Click to increase value. Click to decrease value.

Combination text and drop-drop down list box: Click and drag to choose option.

Set Other Options

1. Click the **Fonts** tab to display the Fonts section.
2. Select **Gadget** as the large system font.
3. Display the **Desktop** section.
4. For the pattern, choose **Waves Sunny**.
5. Click the Set Desktop button [**Set Desktop**].
6. Display the **Sound** section.
7. For sound track, choose **Platinum Sounds**, if available.
8. Select all the sound effects options.
9. Display the **Options** section.
10. Select both the **Smart Scrolling** and **Double-click title bar to collapse windows** options.

Save Customized Theme

1. Display the **Themes** section.
2. Click the Save Theme button **Save Theme...**.
3. Save the theme as *yo Custom 1,* replacing *yo* with your initials.
4. Scroll to find the original theme with which you started.
5. Select that theme to return your desktop to its original appearance.

The Active Window

- You should now have three windows open—Appearance Control Panel, Control Panels window, and the hard disk window. You may be able to view all three or only one. The one in which you are working is called the **active window**. You can tell which window is active because:

  - Its Close, Zoom, and Collapse boxes are visible.

  - The name on its title bar is dark.

  - The gray horizontal lines on the title bar are visible.

- In the illustration on the following page, Control Panels, Appearance is the active window and the Macintosh HD window is inactive and partially hidden by Control Panels. Note the help balloon pointing to the **inactive window**. A portion of the desktop forms the background.

- If you cannot see a window that you want to activate, collapse windows until a portion of the window you want is visible.

- To activate a window, click anywhere within the window or on its title bar.

- If an application, such as AppleWorks, is active, and you wish to switch to the desktop, you can use the Application menu and choose Finder, or press ⌘+Tab or ⌘+Shift+Tab to cycle through the open applications until Finder is activated. (Finder is the application that gives you access to the desktop, as described in Exercise 1 of this lesson.)

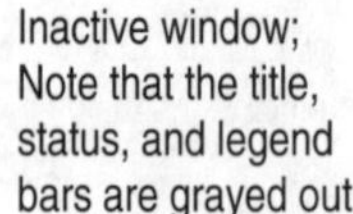

Inactive window;
Note that the title,
status, and legend
bars are grayed out.

Mac OS Desktop with Active and Inactive Windows

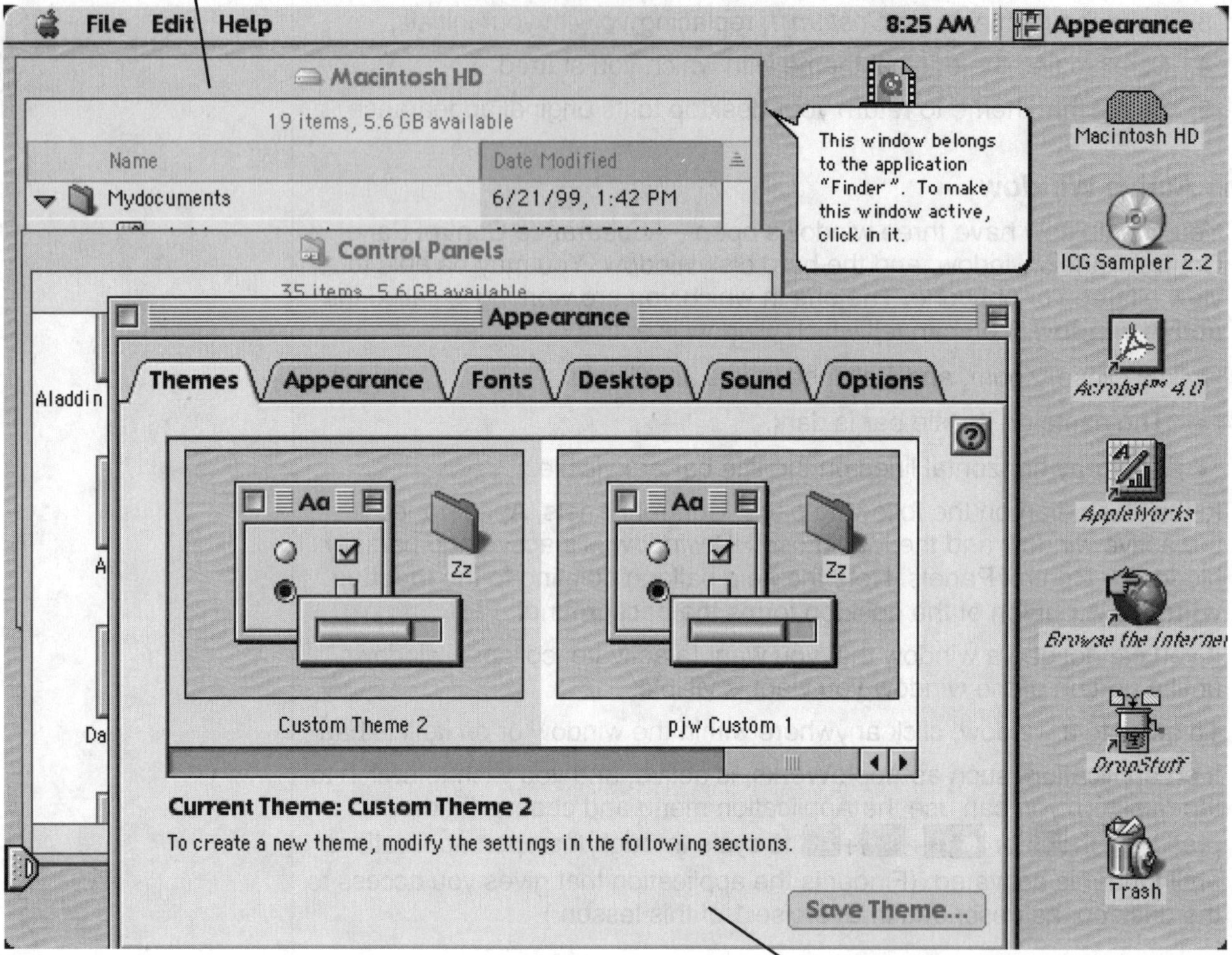

🖥️ Try It!

1. Click the hard disk window to activate it.

2. Click the Control Panels window to activate it.

3. Double-click the Trash icon [Trash] on the desktop.
   The Trash window opens.

4. Click the hard disk window to activate it.

5. Collapse the hard disk window.

6. Collapse the Control Panels window.

7. Click the collapsed hard disk window.

8. Activate and close the Appearance control panel window.

9. Activate and close the Trash window.

10. Restore the hard disk and Control Panels windows.

11. Close all open windows to display the desktop with the Finder
    application active.

> **In this exercise, you will work with Control Panels windows.**

EXERCISE DIRECTIONS

Change General Controls

1. Open the Control Panels window if it is not already open.
2. Display its contents as Buttons.
3. Click the General Controls button to open the General Controls control panel.
4. Deselect Show Desktop when in background.
5. Select Off for Menu Blinking.
6. Close the General Controls window.

Test the Results

1. Open the Apple menu and choose the Jigsaw Puzzle.

   Note that the Jigsaw Puzzle menu item does not blink when it is activated.

   Note that the icons and windows on the desktop are hidden.
2. Open the Application menu (upper right of the screen) and choose Finder.

   The desktop items reappear and the Jigsaw Puzzle window is inactive.
3. Press ⌘+Tab or ⌘+Shift+Tab to reactivate the Jigsaw Puzzle.

   The desktop items disappear again.

Reset the Options

1. Switch to Finder.
2. Activate the Control Panels window.
3. Click the General Controls button.
4. Select Show Desktop when in background.
5. Select 3 for Menu Blinking.
6. Close the General Controls window.
7. Close the Jigsaw Puzzle.

Change the Mouse Tracking Option

1. In the Control Panels window, click the Mouse button.

   The Mouse control panel opens.
2. For Mouse Tracking, select Very Slow.
3. Slide your mouse pointer across the screen.

   Note how far you must move the mouse to move the pointer.
4. Click the right-most Mouse Tracking option.
5. Move the mouse pointer across the screen.

   Note the difference from the previous setting.

Change the Double-Click Speed

1. For Double-Click Speed, click the left-most option.
2. Close the Mouse control panel.
3. Activate the Control Panels window.
4. From the View menu, choose as Icons.
5. Slowly double-click the Mouse icon.

   The Mouse control panel opens.
6. Close the Mouse control panel.
7. Experiment to see how long you can wait between clicks and still open the Mouse control panel.
8. With the Mouse control panel open, choose the right-most double-click speed.
9. Close the Mouse control panel.
10. Try to double-click slowly to open the Mouse control panel.
11. Double-click quickly to open the Mouse control panel.
12. Set the double-click speed to its original setting.
13. Close the Mouse control panel.
14. Close the Control Panels window.

Exercise 5

Find Files Using Sherlock
■ The Sherlock Dialog Box ■ Other Sherlock (Find) Options

NOTES

The Sherlock Dialog Box

- **Important Note:** The Sherlock method of finding files was introduced in Mac OS 8.5. If you are running on an earlier version of the operating system, you will use the Find File feature, which offers fewer options than Sherlock.

- A **dialog box** lets you specify criteria (input) to set **parameters** for processing. You complete the elements in the dialog box, then click a button to request processing of the options selected. In this section, you'll learn the parts of a dialog box by learning about the Sherlock dialog box.

🖥 Try It!

1. Activate the Finder application (the desktop manager). (Use the **Application** menu in the upper right of the screen and choose **Finder** if Finder is not already active.)

2. From the **File** menu, choose **Find**.

   OR

   Press ⌘+F.

   The Sherlock dialog box, shown below, opens. The Find File dialog box is similar but it does not have the Find By Content section or the Search Internet section.

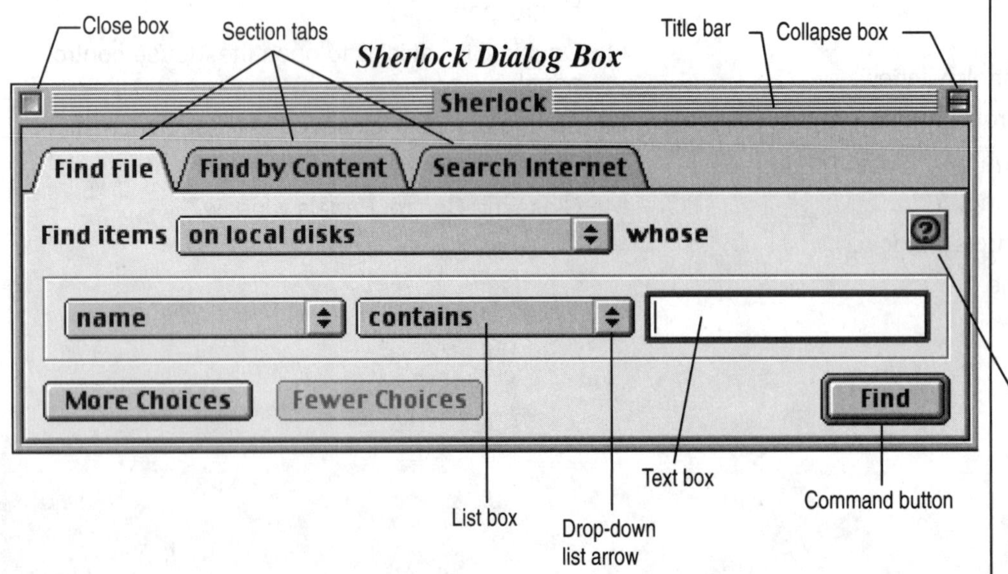

Parameter

An entry that sets a condition or a limit for processing. For example, when you specify a word that you want a program to search for, you are setting a parameter for the search.

✓ Open Sherlock Dialog Box

You can also open the Sherlock dialog box by completing the following steps:

1. Open the **Apple** menu.

2. Drag the mouse pointer to **Sherlock** (or **Find**) and release the button.

- The Sherlock dialog box lets you specify criteria (input parameters) for folders and files that you want to locate on your computer. The parts of the dialog box are described in the following table.

Element	Description
Title bar	Identifies the dialog box. Has the same purpose as the title bar on other windows.
Close box **Collapse box** **Help button**	The Sherlock dialog box offers the Close ▢ and Collapse ▤ boxes that you have seen on other windows; it also has a Help button ❓, which appears on other dialog boxes, such as the control panels.
Section tabs	The Sherlock dialog box is divided into sections, each serving a specific purpose. The Sherlock dialog box offers several ways to specify what you want to find. The Find File section lets you set parameters (conditions) to look for files in your local environment by a variety of criteria.
Combination text box and drop-down list	When a field in a dialog box allows you to type text, it is called a text box. If the field displays a list of choices, it is called a drop-down list. The list is displayed when you click box or the arrows ⬍. When you can type text or display a list, the field is called a combination box because it lets you type text or use a drop-down list.
Command buttons	Dialog boxes offer command buttons. A command button initiates processing.

- When you use a dialog box, complete your input then click one of the command buttons to request processing.

- If you open a dialog box by accident or decide at any time that you do not want to complete the action, close it before processing by:

  - Clicking the Close box ▢ on the dialog box.

  - Clicking the Cancel button if the box has one.

- You will learn about other elements of dialog boxes as you encounter them in this lesson and in other lessons in this book.

Other Sherlock (Find) Options

- The Sherlock dialog box gives you a wide variety of options for locating files and information. You click drop-down lists and choose different options, click the **More Choices** button More Choices to increase the number of available options, and complete the options that appear.

- The **Find by Content** section of Sherlock lets you look for words that appear within files on indexed volumes. (If the volume, such as your hard disk, is not indexed, you can index it through this dialog box.)

- The **Search Internet** section lets you specify words to search for on a variety of search engines and Web sites. This section works only if you can connect to the Internet.

Reference

For complete documentation of the Find options and other features of Mac OS, use the Help system or a reference work such as Sharon Zardetto Aker's *The Macintosh Bible*.

EXERCISE DIRECTIONS

Find Files

1. Activate the Finder application.

2. Press **⌘**+**F** to start Sherlock.

3. Click the Find File tab.

   When you display the Sherlock (or Find File) dialog box, the default parameters are set to search:
   - local disks
   - by name
   - which contains
   - text you type

4. In the white text box, type *AppleW*.

5. Click the Find button **Find**.

   The system works for a moment and then displays a list of files and folders that contain AppleW, as shown in Illustration A.

   *The Items Found window has two panes: the upper pane lists the items that match the criteria you specified; the lower pane gives the **path** to the location of any item you select.*

6. Click the first item in the list to display the folders or path of the item selected.

   In the illustration, the path of the About AppleWorks Help document is displayed.

   If no item is selected or multiple items are selected, no path is displayed.

7. Locate the AppleWorks application program entry.

8. Double-click the entry.

9. AppleWorks starts.

10. Click OK on the first screen, then press **⌘**+**Q** to quit the application.

11. Activate the Items Found window and close it.

12. Close the Sherlock dialog box.

Illustration A. Items Found Window

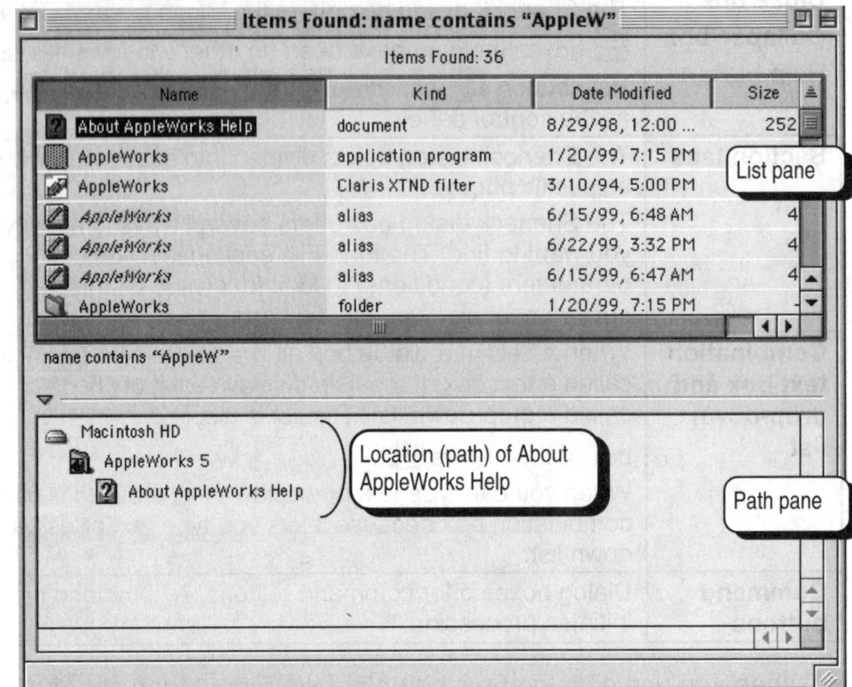

Path

The name of the disk and folder(s) that contain an item. In the illustration above, the path is Macintosh HD (disk), AppleWorks 5 (folder), About AppleWorks Help (file name).

NEXT EXERCISE

Exercise 6

Managing Your System

■ Create a Folder ■ Create an Alias ■ Save an Item to the Desktop ■ The Desktop Folder ■ Add an Item to the Apple Menu ■ Remove an Item from the Apple Menu ■ Use Trash ■ Select Multiple Items ■ Create a Folder ■ Rename an Item ■ Copy or Move Items by Dragging ■ Arrange Items on the Desktop

NOTES

Create a Folder

■ You may wish to create a folder to contain files that you create. In the following Try It! activity, you will create and name a folder.

⌨ Try It!

1. Open your hard disk window.

2. Be sure that no folder is selected. (Click on a blank area of the hard disk window if necessary.)

3. Press ⌘+N.

   OR

   Click **File** and choose **New Folder**.

   A new folder named **untitled folder** *appears in the hard disk window with its name highlighted.*

4. Type the name to *fml WP Docs*; for *fml* substitute your initials.

Create an Alias

■ An **alias** is an icon or button that opens an application, folder, or file without going through a menu. You can drag an alias from where it is created and place it on the desktop or in another folder.

■ Aliases are identified by a curving arrow that appears as part of the item's icon and the icon's name is italicized. For example, the Desktop usually contains an alias for browsing the Internet, as shown at the right.

■ Four aliases to applications appear on the desktop in the illustration that follows. The Browse the Internet alias is selected.

Alias for Internet Browser

Aliases on the Desktop

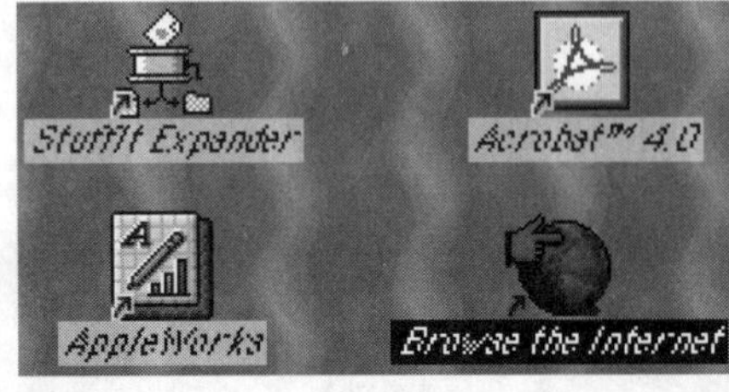

- To create an alias, select the item, such as the name of an application or file, hold **⌘**+**Option**, then click drag the item to the new location, for example, the desktop.

🖥 Try It!

1. Open the hard disk window in any view you wish (list, icons, buttons).
2. Follow the steps for your application suite below:

AppleWorks	**Microsoft Office 98**
a. Open the AppleWorks folder (usually **AppleWorks 5**).	a. Open the **Microsoft Office 98** folder.
b. Locate and select AppleWorks  or	b. Locate and select Microsoft Word or
c. Hold **⌘**+**Option**, and click and drag the item to the desktop.	c. Hold **⌘**+**Option**, and click and drag the item to the desktop.
d. Double-click the alias to start the application.	d. Double-click the alias to start the application.
e. Click **OK** to create a new word processing document.	*Word 98 opens and a new document appears.*

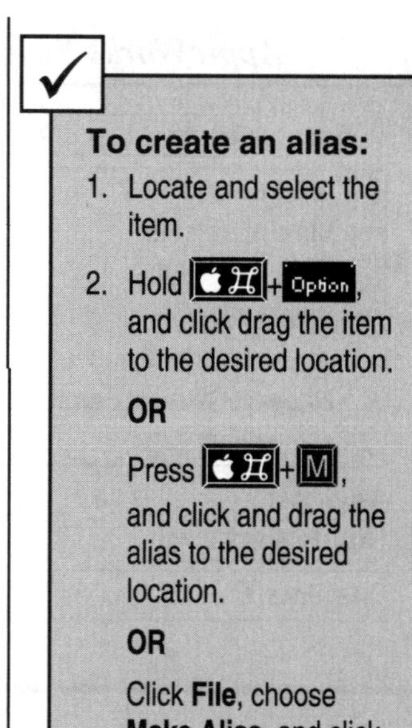

Save an Item to the Desktop

- You can copy, move, or save an item to the desktop to make it easier to open when you need it. For example, you may be working on a document in AppleWorks and need to quit work before you finish it completely. You can save the document to the desktop and double-click it the next time you want to work on it.

🖥 Try It!

1. In the document you just created, type the following two short paragraphs. Press **Return** at the end of the first line.

   Just, quiet knights often served better than zealous captains.
   No one is so suspicious of other people as the practical joker.

2. From the **File** menu, choose **Save As**.

3. Click the Desktop button **Desktop**.

4. In the text box field under Save As (AppleWorks) or Save Current Document as (Word 98), type *Maxims 1* and be sure the Document option is selected.
   The dialog box should look like the one for your application in the following illustrations.

AppleWorks Save As Dialog Box	*Word 98 Save As Dialog Box*

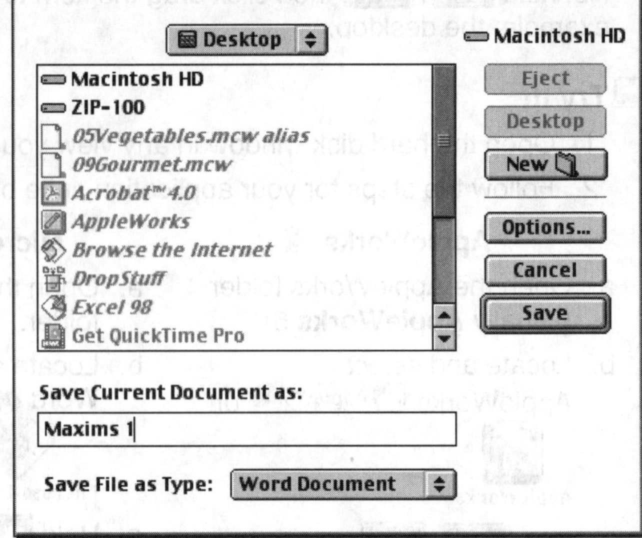

5. Click the Save button **Save**.

6. Press ⌘+Q to quit the application.

7. Double-click the Maxims 1 icon on the desktop.
   The word processing application opens and displays the document.

8. Press ⌘+Q to quit the application.

The Desktop Folder

- When you move, copy, or save an item to the desktop, it is actually stored in the Desktop folder for the drive which contains the startup system. The desktop folder for the hard disk is not visible in the list of folders, but it is there, nevertheless.

- Take care with items that you copy or move. If you copy a large item, you have two copies of it—one in its original location (the hard disk for example) and one on the desktop. If the item is large, you are doubling the amount of space used on the hard disk for the same item.

Add an Item to the Apple Menu

- If you like using the Apple menu to start programs and open folders on your computer, you can add items to the menu in several ways.

- The Apple Menu is a folder on the hard disk, so you can drag items from other folders into the Apple Menu. You can also add aliases to the Apple Menu automatically through an option on the menu itself.

Try It!

1. Click to select the AppleWorks or Word 98 alias that you placed on the desktop earlier.

2. From the **Apple** menu, choose **Automated Tasks**, **Add Alias to Apple Menu**.
   The system performs the work and then displays the message: The alias(es) have been added to the Apple Menu.

3. Click **OK**.

4. Open the **Apple** menu to verify that the alias was added.

5. Close the **Apple** menu without choosing any item (click anywhere on the desktop outside the menu).

- You can also drag an item to the Apple menu.

  - Open the Apple Menu Items folder window. (It's in the System Folder.)

  - Drag the item into (copy or move it) onto the Apple Menu Items folder window. You can create an alias of the Apple Menu Items folder, place it on the desktop, and drag items into it as well.

Remove an Item from the Apple Menu

- You can remove items you no longer wish to have on the Apple menu.

Try It!

1. Activate the hard disk window.

2. Locate the System Folder and open it to display its contents.

3. Locate the Apple Menu Items folder and open it.

4. Locate the AppleWorks or Word 98 alias you placed on the menu.

5. Drag the alias to the Trash.

   When the item touches the Trash and the icon turns dark, release the mouse button to put it in the Trash.

   OR

   Hold down the key and press the key.

   The alias is moved to the Trash (see the next section).

   OR

   Hold down the key and click the alias, and, from the context menu that appears, choose **Move to Trash**.

Use Trash

- The Trash is a folder that contains items you intend to remove from your computer. To display items that are in the Trash, double-click the Trash icon . When viewed as a list, the Trash looks like the following illustration.

Trash Viewed as List

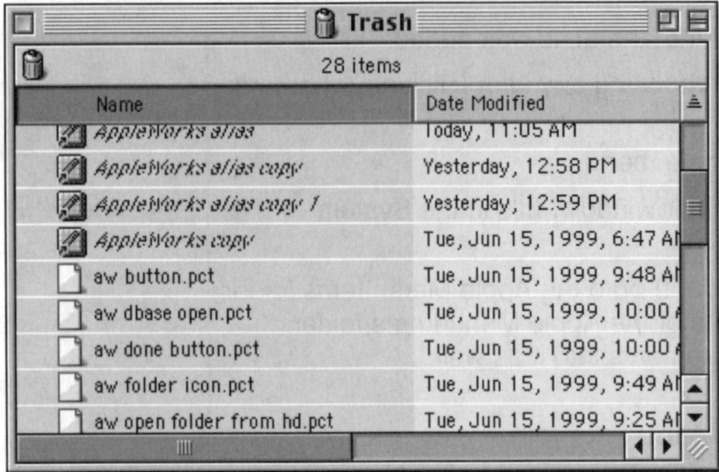

- To restore an item from the Trash to active use, do the appropriate one of the following:

  - Press ⌘+Y to restore the item to its original location (folder or desktop).

  - Drag the item to the folder to which you wish to restore it.

  - Drag it to the desktop. (You can put it in a different location later if you wish.)

Try It!

1. Double-click the Trash icon to open the Trash window.
2. Use the **View** menu to set the view to list or icons.
3. Locate the AppleWorks or Word 98 alias you just placed in the Trash.
4. Drag it back to the desktop.
   If an alias with the same name exists on the desktop, the system displays the following warning message. Sometimes the warning will tell you that a newer item of the same name exists; you must decide whether the one you want to place on the desktop should replace the existing one.

Alias Exists Message

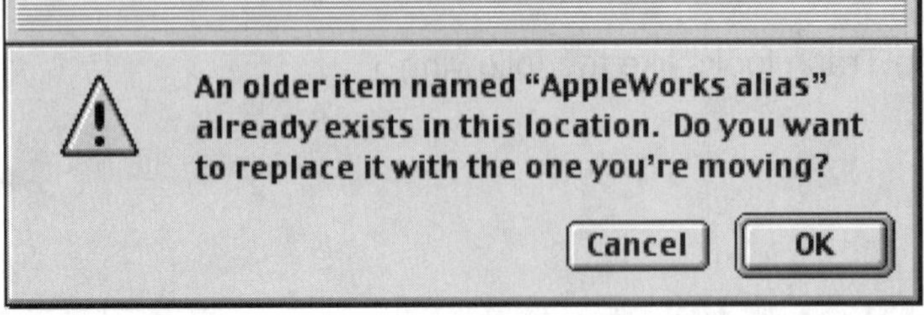

5. Click **OK**.
   The icon appears on the desktop and the previous one (if any) disappears.
6. Close the Trash window.

Empty the Trash

- You can permanently remove all items in the Trash.
  - With the Finder application active, choose **Empty Trash** from the **Special** menu.
    The system asks if you are sure you want to permanently remove the items from the computer.
  - Click [OK] to delete the items permanently.
- Once files are deleted from the trash, they cannot be recovered.
- **IMPORTANT:** Sometimes when you drag an item from a **removable disk** to the Trash, the Trash cannot store it. The system tells you that the item cannot be stored in the Trash and asks if you want to delete it immediately. You click **OK** to delete the item or **Cancel** to avoid deleting it.

Select Multiple Items

- In many windows, you can select more than one item to be processed (copied, moved, deleted, opened) at the same time.

Try It!

Select Adjacent Items

This method lets you select several items that are next to each other (adjacent).

1. Activate the hard disk window.
2. Click in a blank area of the window and drag a rectangle that surrounds several items.
   The items are selected.
3. Click in a blank area of the window to deselect the items.

Select Non-Adjacent Items

This method lets you select several items that are not next to each other.

1. Hold down the Shift key.
2. Click an item.
3. Slide down three items, and click again.
   Two non-adjacent items are selected.
4. Click in a blank area of the window to deselect the items.

Rename an Item

- You will want to rename items from time to time. For example, you may not like the word "alias" that appears on an alias icon or you need to give the new folder a name that is meaningful to you.
- The steps in the following Try It! activity work for any item that you wish to rename.

1. Create a new folder, and click the name of the folder just above the new folder.

2. Click the folder label (the words under the icon or button or the words in the list).

   The name is highlighted, as shown in the illustration below. The third item in the illustration shows a folder being renamed. Note that unwanted text remains in the name and will be deleted.

3. Change the name to *fml Documents* where *fml* is your initials, for example, *PJW Documents*.

4. Delete any unwanted text.

5. Click anywhere outside the name.

   New Folder in List and Icons Views and Folder Being Renamed

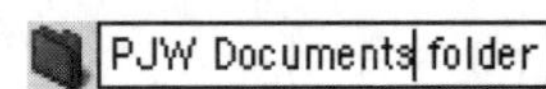

Copy or Move Items by Dragging

- You can copy or move items from one folder or one disk to another by dragging the items. To copy the item, hold down the **Option** key while dragging. If the original item is on a different disk from the disk to which you drag it, the item will be copied even if you do not hold down the **Option** key.

Move a File from the Desktop to the Hard Disk

1. Locate and open the folder you just renamed on the hard disk. (Double-click the folder name in the hard disk window.)

2. Locate the **Maxims 1** document icon on your desktop.

3. Drag the icon to the folder window.
   The Maxims 1 document is moved to the folder on your hard disk.

Copy a File from the CD-ROM

1. Place the data files CD in your CD-ROM drive.

2. Open the CD-ROM disk window.

3. Locate the folder on the CD-ROM where the Macintosh data files are stored.

4. Drag one of the files from the **Graphics** folder to the folder window.
   A copy of the data file is placed on your hard disk in the folder.

Copy a File from the Hard Disk to a Removable Disk

Note: If your system does not include a removable disk on which you can store files, you will not be able to perform the following steps.

1. Place a blank diskette in your diskette drive.

   OR

   Place a blank disk in your Iomega Zip or other removable disk drive if you have one.

2. Drag the graphics file from the folder to the removable disk.
   The file is copied to the removable disk.

Copy an Alias to the Favorites Folder

1. Close the documents folder window that you created.
2. In the hard disk window, locate and open the System folder.
3. Open the Favorites folder that is in the System folder.
4. Hold down the Option key and drag the AppleWorks or Word 98 alias from the desktop to the Favorites folder window.
   The alias is copied to the Favorites folder.
5. Click the **Apple** menu and drag down to view the Favorites item.
   A submenu opens that lists the AppleWorks or Word 98 alias. You can now start AppleWorks or Word 98 from this item.
6. Click anywhere outside the Apple menu to close it.
7. Close the Favorites window.
8. Close the hard disk window.

Arrange Items on the Desktop

■ You can align the icons or buttons on the desktop using the View menu.

Try It!

1. Click the **View** menu and point to **Arrange**.
2. From the submenu, choose **by Name**.
   The items are arranged alphabetically in columns along the right side of the desktop. Note that the Trash icon always appears in the lower right corner of the screen.
3. Drag the AppleWorks or Word 98 alias to the upper-left corner of the screen.
4. Drag the Browse the Internet alias to the middle of the screen.
5. Drag the Mail alias to the lower-left corner of the screen.
6. Use the **View** menu to rearrange the items **by Name**.

EXERCISE DIRECTIONS

Create a Folder

1. Open the hard disk window.
2. Click in any blank area of the window.
3. Press **⌘**+**N** to create a new *untitled folder*.
4. Rename the folder *My 2nd Folder*.

Create an Alias

1. With the hard disk window open, open the folder that contains the data files for this book.
2. Locate and open folder that contains word processing files for your Mac (*MS Word 98 data* or *AppleWorks WP data*).
3. Create an alias for the file **09Gourmet** and place it on the desktop.

Copy a Folder

1. In the hard disk window, select **My 2nd Folder**.
2. Hold down the **Option** key and click and drag the folder to the desktop.
   My 2nd Folder is copied to the desktop.
3. Double-click **My 2nd Folder** on the desktop.
   The folder window opens. It is empty because you have placed no files in it.
4. Close the **My 2nd Folder** window.

Rename an Object

1. Display the desktop.
2. Locate the alias for **09Gourmet**.
3. Click the name so it becomes highlighted.
4. Edit the name to read *Gourmet Letter*.
5. Click anywhere on the desktop to deselect the alias name.

Delete Objects from the Desktop

1. On the desktop, select the icon for **My 2nd Folder**.
2. Drag the folder to the Trash.
3. Drag the alias *Gourmet Letter* to the Trash.

Delete Objects from the Hard Disk

1. Return to the hard disk window.
2. Locate the folder **My 2nd Folder**.
3. Move the item to the Trash.

Restore an Object from the Trash

1. On the desktop, open the Trash window.
2. Select the alias for *Gourmet Letter*.
3. Press **⌘**+**Y** to to place it back on the desktop.
4. Delete it from the desktop again.

NEXT EXERCISE

Use Applications

■ **Launch or Start Applications** ■ **Use Launcher** ■ **Locate a Folder Using a Dialog Box**

NOTES

Launch or Start Applications

- The easy way to start an application is by double-clicking an alias for the application on the desktop. For applications that you use frequently place an alias on the desktop and use the alias to start the application. (Some programs automatically place an alias on the desktop.)

- You can start an application in all these other ways as well:

  - Add the application's alias to the **Apple Menu Items** folder and choose the application from the **Apple menu**.

  - Add the application's alias to the **Favorites** folder and choose the application from **Apple menu**, **Favorites**.

  - If you have used the application recently, choose it from **Apple menu**, **Recent Applications**.

  - Choose a document created by the application from **Apple menu**, **Recent Documents**.

  - Open the hard disk window and locate the application (alias or the application itself) and double-click. On installation, many applications place themselves in the **Applications** folder on the hard disk. You can start applications from this folder.

  - From the hard disk window or any place you store documents, double-click the name of a document created by the application. The application will start and open the document for editing.

  - Use **Launcher**.

Use Launcher

- The **Launcher** is a control panel that you can make available on the desktop when the computer starts. The **Launcher** displays buttons for application aliases placed into the **Launcher Items** folder in the System folder on the hard disk. You can also place items into Launcher by dragging them into the Launcher window itself.

🖳Try It!

To open Launcher automatically when the computer starts:

1. From the **Apple** menu, **Control Panels** submenu, choose **General Controls**.

2. Click the **Show Launcher at system startup** option.
   The next time the system starts the Launcher will appear on the desktop.

Launch or Start

Mac OS users sometimes use the term **launch** to indicate the start of an application. Launch and start can be used interchangeably.

3. Close the General Controls control panel.

To manage Launcher:

1. From the **Apple** menu, choose **Control Panels**, **Launcher**.

   Launcher opens.

2. If AppleWorks or Word 98 is not one of the buttons, copy the alias from the desktop into the Launcher window.

   ♦ Create an AppleWorks or Word 98 alias on the desktop, if necessary.

   ♦ Hold down the ⌘ key and drag the alias into the Launcher window.

3. Click the AppleWorks or Word 98 button in Launcher to start the application.

4. In AppleWorks, click the Cancel button **Cancel** on the opening screen.

5. Press ⌘+Q to quit AppleWorks or Word 98.

6. From the **Special** menu, choose **Restart** to restart the computer.

   Launcher appears at startup if you set the option Show Launcher at startup *as described in the previous Try It! activity.*

Locate a Folder Using a Dialog Box

- You may need to change to a different folder from the one that appears when you:

  - Save a file for the first time.

  - Save the file under a different name (Save as).

  - Open a file in an application.

- The dialog boxes used for these actions work in the same way. The Save As dialog box from AppleWorks is shown below.

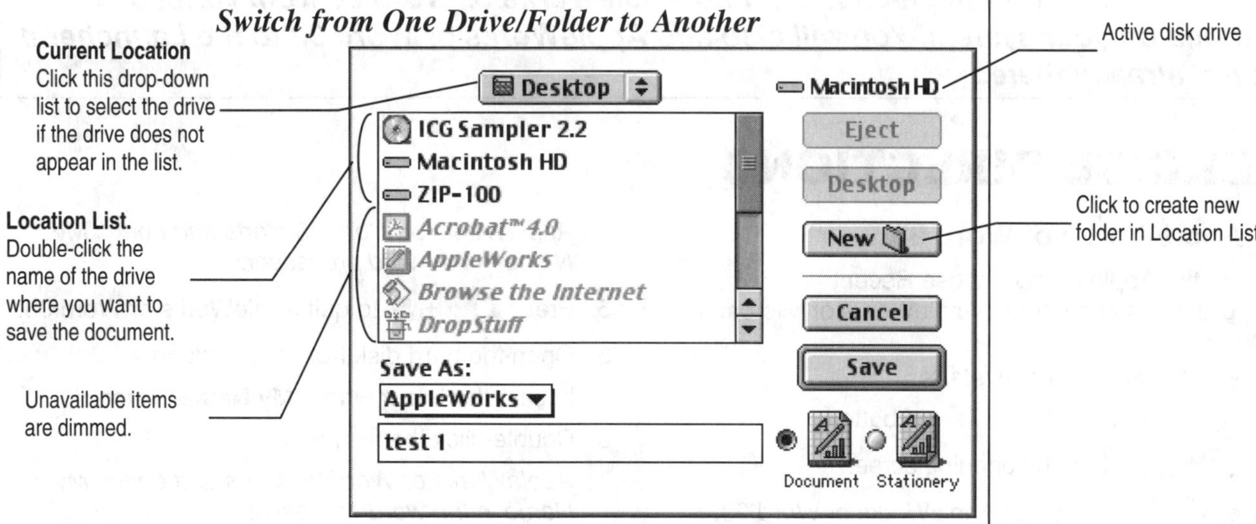

- The **current location** is a hierarchical drop-down list (the highest level appears at the top). The current location is always the desktop or a disk drive.

- The **location list** displays drives, folders, and documents. If the Desktop is the current location, your local hard disk(s), any removable disks (ZIP-100, for example), and any network connections will appear in the location list. To select a drive, double-click the drive name.

- If the current location is a drive, the location list includes folders and files. To open a folder, double-click the folder name.

- If the current location is a folder, the location list includes file names and any folders within the folder. To choose an item:

    1. Scroll to the item if necessary.

    2. Double-click the item name.

        ✓ *With some actions, such as Save As, you cannot choose a document name, you must type the name of the document in the text box.*

- If the current location does not include the document or folder you want, click the current location drop-down list and choose a different current location.

Try It!

1. Start AppleWorks or Word 98 and create a new word processing document using any of the methods outlined at the beginning of this lesson.

2. In the new document, type your name and address on three lines.

3. Choose **File**, **Save As**.

4. Switch to the folder *fml* **WP Docs** where *fml* is your initials. (You created this folder at the beginning of Exercise 6).

5. In the text box, type **My Name**.

6. Click the Save button [Save].

7. Press ⌘+Q to quit AppleWorks or Word 98.

In this exercise, you will practice starting AppleWorks or Word 98 from various locations on your system. You will also add AppleWorks or Word 98 to the Launcher if it is not already there.

EXERCISE DIRECTIONS

Start AppleWorks or Word 98

1. From the Apple menu, choose Recent Applications and choose AppleWorks or Microsoft Word.

    AppleWorks or Word 98 starts.

2. In AppleWorks, click the Cancel button [Cancel] on the opening screen.

3. Press ⌘+Q to quit AppleWorks or Word 98.

4. From the Apple menu, choose Recent Documents and double-click **My Name**.

    AppleWorks or Word 98 starts and opens My Name in the word processor.

5. Press ⌘+Q to quit AppleWorks or Word 98.

6. Open the hard disk from the desktop.

7. Locate the folder where **My Name** is stored.

8. Double-click the file name.

    AppleWorks or Word 98 starts and opens My Name in the word processor.

9. Press ⌘+Q to quit AppleWorks or Word 98.

Lesson 2B: Introduction to Windows

Exercise 1

Learn Windows Basics
■ About Microsoft Windows ■ The Desktop ■ Views
■ Modes of Operation: Web (Single-Click) and Classic Styles
■ Changing Windows 98 Views and Styles ■ Mouse for Windows ■ Select an Object
■ Open an Object ■ Windows Mouse Pointer Shapes ■ Use the Keyboard
■ Insertion Point Movement ■ Other Keys ■ Use Menus ■ Use Dialog Boxes
■ Use ScreenTips and What's This?

NOTES

About Microsoft® Windows®

- Microsoft Windows is the leading operating system software for personal computers. A dwindling number of installations still use MS- or PC-DOS® (Disk Operating System), and others run Unix, Linux, or some other operating system; most businesses, however, have adopted Windows. Apple® installations, of course, use the Mac® OS.

- Windows provides a **GUI** (Graphical User Interface). The GUI was first developed at a Xerox® think tank in California's famed Silicon Valley in the early 1970s. It was then adapted by Steve Jobs and Steve Wozniak when they created the first Apple computers.

- With a GUI, you most often use a mouse pointing device to interact with the computer through a variety of menus, icons, options, and buttons. Many of these actions can also be performed from the keyboard, but the primary interaction is visual—point and click, click and drag.

- During the 1980s, Microsoft developed its Windows GUI to compete more directly with Apple and to offer a similar appearance and consistent usage from one application to another. When you work in Windows, you can take some things for granted regardless of the software program, as you'll see as you work through the exercises in this lesson.

- To give you access to the computer and what it contains—icons, files, applications, printers, and so on—the Windows GUI uses windows. A Windows window is a rectangular area that lets you view and use a specific computer element.

The Desktop

- When you start your machine, Windows displays the desktop. A sample Windows 98 desktop is shown on the next page. The desktop you see when you start your machine may look different. The different looks of the desktop are explained in the section "Views" on page 62.

- Your desktop may include **icons** not shown in the illustration and will probably not show all those that are illustrated, and the names of your icons may be underlined. For example, you may have icons that give you access to Microsoft Office 2000 functions. This row of icons is called the

GUI

Acronym for Graphical User Interface (an acronym is a shortened form of a phrase).

Prior to GUI, users had to type commands at the keyboard to work with the computer. The GUI is convenient for many users because they point with the mouse to an icon or menu item and click. (This visual method of interaction is not so convenient for the blind and visually impaired.)

Interface

The method by which a computer system presents information to another computer or to a user.

Icon

In computer terms, a graphic symbol that represents a program, application, or other computer feature.

Office Shortcut bar and is described in a later lesson. The desktop elements are described in the table that follows the illustration.

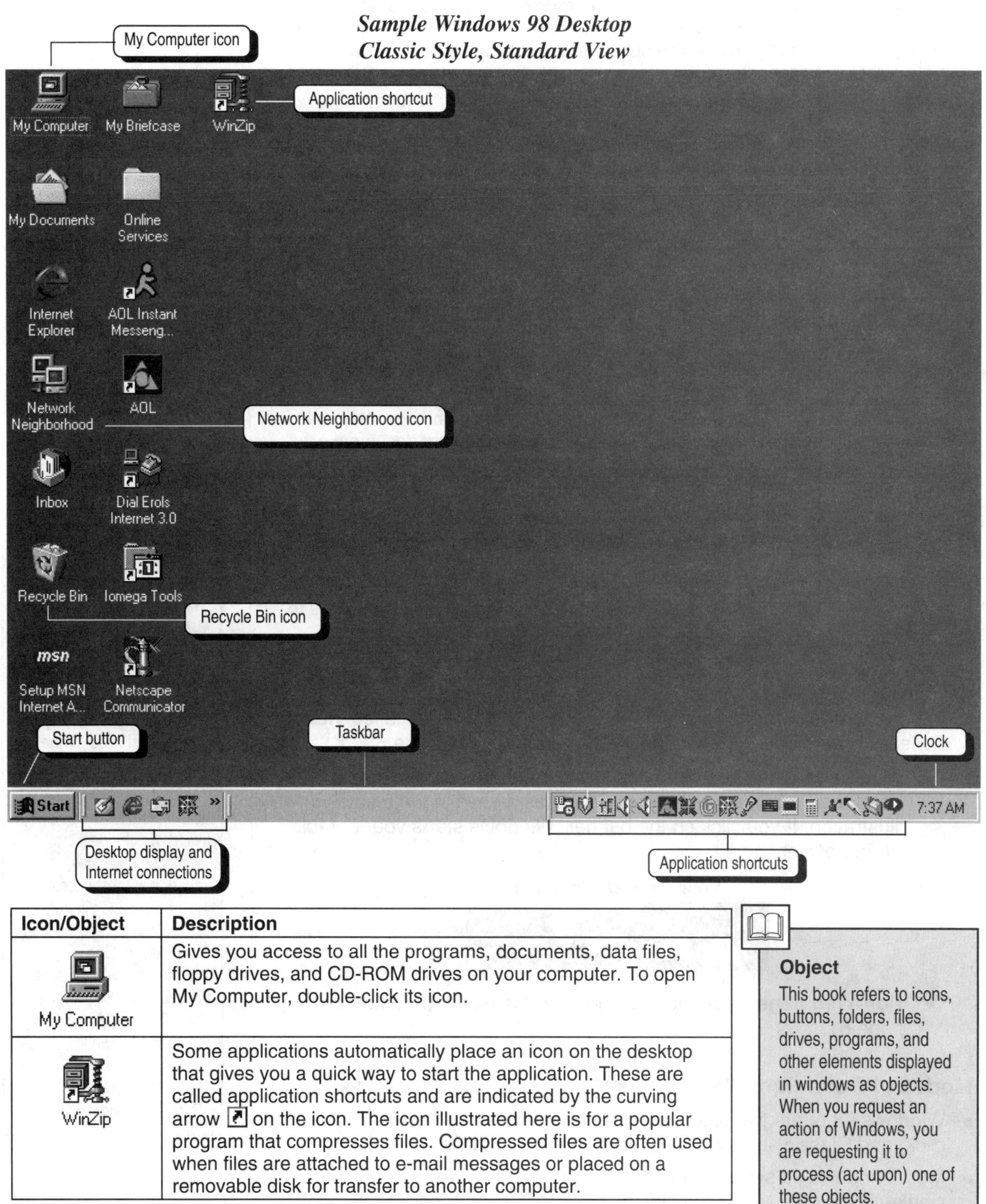

Sample Windows 98 Desktop
Classic Style, Standard View

Icon/Object	Description
My Computer	Gives you access to all the programs, documents, data files, floppy drives, and CD-ROM drives on your computer. To open My Computer, double-click its icon.
WinZip	Some applications automatically place an icon on the desktop that gives you a quick way to start the application. These are called application shortcuts and are indicated by the curving arrow on the icon. The icon illustrated here is for a popular program that compresses files. Compressed files are often used when files are attached to e-mail messages or placed on a removable disk for transfer to another computer.

Object

This book refers to icons, buttons, folders, files, drives, programs, and other elements displayed in windows as objects. When you request an action of Windows, you are requesting it to process (act upon) one of these objects.

Icon/Object	Description
 Network Neighborhood	Lets you browse through the work stations, printers, drives, and folders on your network (a group of computers that share computing resources). If you are not logged in to a network, you can open this icon but will set a message that the network cannot be found.
Recycle Bin	Stores the files you delete. Double-clicking this icon allows you to see all files deleted since you last emptied the Recycle Bin. You can retrieve any files you may have deleted by mistake (if you have not yet emptied the Recycle Bin). You can also empty the Recycle Bin to free up space on your hard drive. (Deleted files are not actually removed from your computer until you empty the Recycle Bin.)
Start	Opens the Start menu, from which you can access the programs and documents you need to begin using Windows 98.
	As part of the **taskbar**, Windows 98 displays the Show Desktop button that lets you switch to the desktop quickly. This part of the taskbar also has buttons that start Internet browsers and Outlook Express, a popular Microsoft e-mail application.
Taskbar	As you work with applications, application and document names appear on the taskbar. To switch to a different document or application, you can click its button on the taskbar.
Application shortcuts	Some applications place a button in the area at the right end of the taskbar to provide a quick way to start the application. In the illustration on the previous page, most buttons are for Corel WordPerfect suite applications, but buttons for AOL, McAfee VirusScan, Real Player, and other programs also appear.
10:55 AM	Shows the current time of day. Double-clicking it allows you to change the time, the date, or your time zone.

Views

- In Windows 98, your desktop can have two different looks called **views**. To learn how to change from one view to another, see page 63.

  - **Web page view**. The default is a dark blue background with a Windows 98 banner in the upper right, as shown in the following illustration. If you click on the banner, Windows starts your default Web browser.

View As Web Page On

  - **Non-Web page view**, the one shown in the desktop illustration on page 61.

Modes of Operation: Web (Single-Click) and Classic Styles

- Windows 98 offers two basic modes of operation—Web style (single-click) and Classic style, which is the same as Windows 95.

- Most Windows 98 systems are initially set up to work in Web style or single-click mode. Most of the instructions and illustrations in this book, however, are based on the Classic style because experience shows that

View and Modes in Other Windows

Windows that let you view computer elements, such as files and programs, appear in the view and style (Web page or classic) adopted for the desktop.

Also, if you change the view in one of the other windows, the desktop view and style also change in most cases. (You can have different views and style in different windows, but the way to do so is outside the scope of this book. See a book on Windows 98, such as Margaret Brown's *Learning Windows 98*, New York: DDC Publishing, Inc., 1998.)

newer users find it easier to work in Windows when an accidental mouse click on an icon or file does not immediately open that object.

- **Is my system in Web (single-click) or Classic style?** When **Web style** is on, the icons (pictures) on the screen are underlined or become underlined when you point to them with the mouse. This underlining means that the objects can be activated (opened) with a single click of the left mouse button.

- When **Classic style** is on, the icons are not underlined. You can look at the upper-left corner of the screen to determine which style is on, as shown in the following illustration. To change your system from the Web style to the Classic style or vice-versa, see the next section.

*Web Style
(Single-click)*

*Classic Style
and Windows 95*

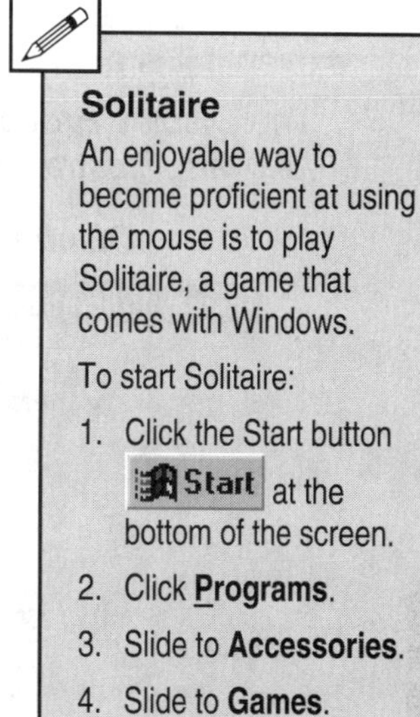

Solitaire

An enjoyable way to become proficient at using the mouse is to play Solitaire, a game that comes with Windows.

To start Solitaire:

1. Click the Start button **Start** at the bottom of the screen.
2. Click **Programs**.
3. Slide to **Accessories**.
4. Slide to **Games**.
5. Click **Solitaire**.

Changing Windows 98 Views and Styles

- Two options control the appearance of the Windows 98 desktop: **Active Desktop** and **Folder Options**.

Try It! (Windows 98 only)

To use the **Active Desktop** option to turn Web Page view on or off:

1. Right-click on a blank area of the desktop.
   A menu appears.

2. Rest the mouse pointer on **Active Desktop** or press **A** to display the submenu as shown in the following illustration.

Windows 98 Active Desktop, View As Web Page

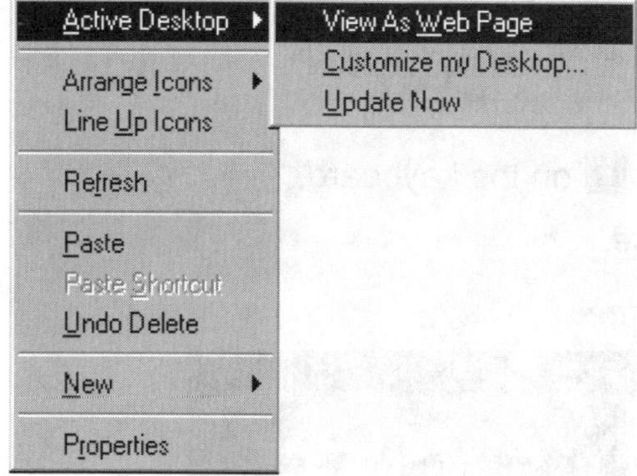

3. Click **View As Web Page** or press **W** to deselect the option.
   Note that these same actions let you turn on the option as well.
   When you turn off the View As Web Page option, the Channels bar, if any, disappears.

Try It! (Windows 98 only)

To use the **Folder Options** to change from single-click to double-click icons or vice-versa.

1. Right-click any blank area of the desktop.

2. On the menu that appears, click **Properties** or press **R**.

   The Display Properties dialog box appears.

3. Click the **Web** tab in the upper left of the dialog box. (You can click it even if it is already selected.)

   The Display Properties dialog box Web tab appears as shown in the following illustration.

Display Properties Dialog Box, Web Tab

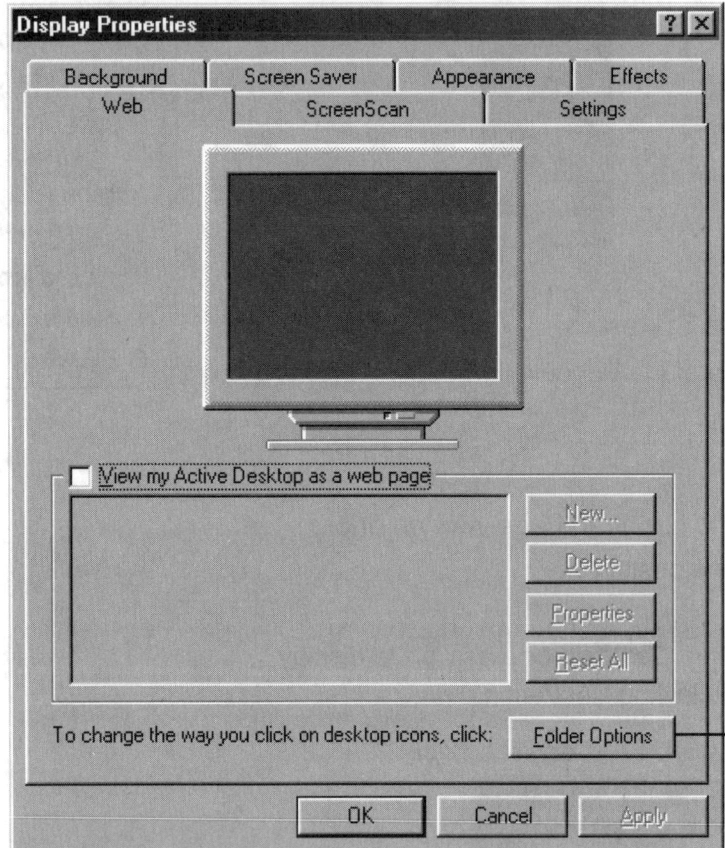

Click Folder Options button.

4. Click **Folder Options**, or press the letter **F** on the keyboard.

   Windows displays the following message.

Folder Options Message

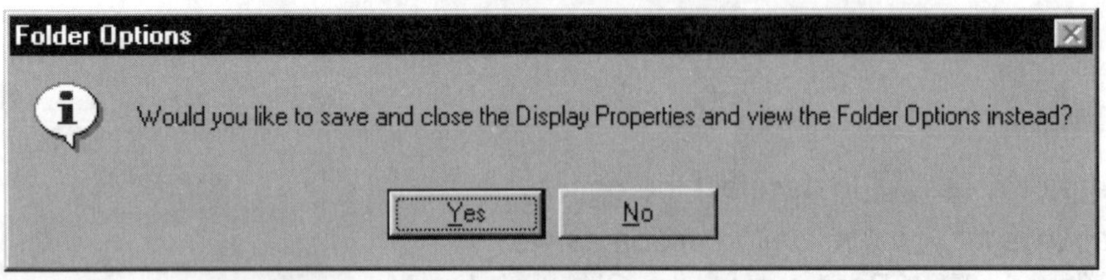

5. Click **Yes**, or press the **Enter** key.

Display Properties

The Display Properties dialog box can be opened in several different ways. You will learn others later in this lesson.

Windows displays the Folder Options dialog box shown in the next illustration.

Folder Options Dialog Box, General Tab

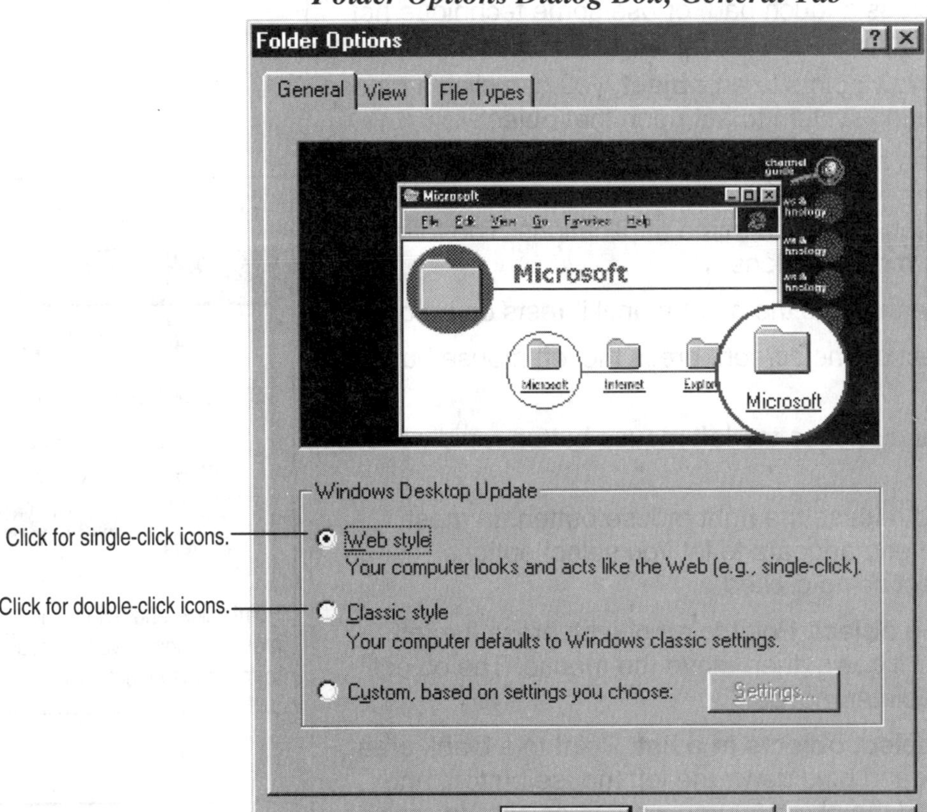

Click for single-click icons.

Click for double-click icons.

6. Click the **General** tab.

7. Click either:

   ♦ **Web style** (press the letter W)

   ♦ **Classic style** (press the letter C)

8. Click OK, or press the Enter key.

   Windows displays the desktop in the chosen style.

- You need to decide which way you want your Windows 98 environment to appear. If you are comfortable with single-click icons and the Web Page view, you can use Windows 98 with those options active.

- Be aware that in this lesson when directions say "Double-click …", you may need to translate that to "Click…" for your system.

- In addition, the illustrations of My Computer and Windows Explorer used in this lesson are taken from a Windows 98 system with Web Page view and single-click icons **turned off**. These illustrations, then, are correct for users of either Windows 95 or Windows 98.

Mouse for Windows

- The mouse is a device that lets you control a pointer on the computer monitor. When you slide the mouse across a surface, roll a ball on the mouse, drag your finger across a touch pad, or use some technique not mentioned here, the pointer moves across the screen. The pointer initially is an arrow. When the arrow points to an **object**, you can click a mouse button to request the operating system to act upon that object.

- The mouse for Windows has at least two buttons. It may have three. The IntelliMouse has two buttons with a wheel between them. The wheel can be used to change the screen display in some applications. The following terms are used to describe mouse actions.

  - **Point**. Slide the mouse to move the pointer until it rests on an object.

  - **Click**. Point at an object on the screen, press the left mouse button once, and release it.

  - **Double-click**. Press and release the left mouse button rapidly two times.

  - **Right-click**. Press and release the right mouse button. In most instances, a shortcut menu appears to let you select options appropriate to the object being clicked.

  - **Click and drag** or **drag object**. Point to an object, press the left mouse button and hold it down, then move the mouse. The object moves as the mouse pointer moves.

  - **Draw a rectangle to select objects in a list**. Point to a blank area outside an object, click and hold down the left mouse button, and draw a rectangle around the object(s) you want to select. You may begin at any corner and draw the rectangle in any direction; you release the mouse button when the rectangle includes the objects you wish to select.

  - **Drag to select text**. Point to the letter with which you want the selection to begin. Hold down the mouse button and move the mouse pointer to select the text you want, then release the mouse button. Once the text is selected, it is shaded, and you can treat the selected text as a unit for formatting, copying, cutting, or deleting.

  - **Shift+Click**. Hold down the Shift key, point to an object and click.

  - **Ctrl+Click**. Point to an object, press and hold down the Ctrl key on the keyboard, then click the left mouse button.

Select an Object

- Windows uses the term **select** to refer to marking one or more objects that you wish to work with. You can tell an object is selected when it changes color, usually from lighter to darker. Sometimes users say such an object is highlighted, which is just another way of saying that the object is **selected**.

- If more than one object is selected, you can treat the selection as if it were a single object. The table on the following page tells you how to select an object or group of objects in the two different modes of operation (styles).

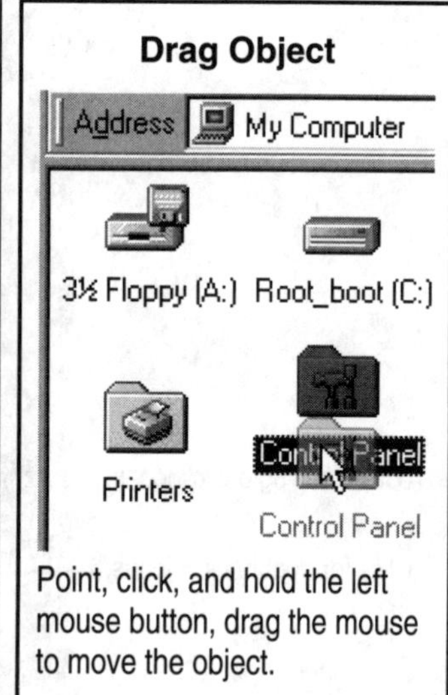

Drag Object

Point, click, and hold the left mouse button, drag the mouse to move the object.

Drag a Rectangle: Upper Left to Lower Right

Started at upper left and dragged down and to the right.

To select ...	Web style (names underlined)	Classic style (Windows 95)
One object	Point to the object.	Click the object.
Adjacent objects	Draw a rectangle around the objects to be selected. **OR** 1. Point to the first object you want to select; this action defines one corner of a rectangle. 2. Hold the `Shift` key and point to the last object to be selected; this action defines the opposite diagonal corner of the rectangle.	Draw a rectangle around the objects to be selected. **OR** 1. Click the first object you want to select; this action defines one corner of a rectangle. 2. `Shift`+Click the last object to be selected; this action defines the opposite diagonal corner of the rectangle.
Non-adjacent objects	`Ctrl`+Click on each object	`Ctrl`+Click on each object

Open an Object

- When you want to work with the feature associated with an icon or process a file, you **open** the object. The way you open an object depends on which mode of operation (Web style or Classic style) you are using.

To open ...	Web style (names underlined)	Classic style (Windows 95)
One object	Click on the object. **OR** Point to the object and press the Enter key.	Double-click the object. **OR** Select the object, and press Enter.
Multiple objects	Select the objects, and press the Enter key. *Note that on the desktop, only one of the objects will open. In most windows, all selected objects will open.*	Select the objects, and press the Enter key. *Note that on the desktop, only one of the objects will open. In most windows, all selected objects will open.*

Windows Mouse Pointer Shapes

- The mouse pointer changes shape depending on where you are in a window and what you are trying to do. Common mouse shapes are described below. Other pointer shapes will be described as you encounter them in the applications.

Pointer	Description
	Normal select. Left-slanted arrow points to objects, such as icons, menu options, or toolbar buttons.
	Busy. The system is busy processing; no other action can be performed until this pointer disappears.
	Working in background. The system is busy processing, but you can perform other actions by pointing and clicking.
	Not available. The pointer is in an area of the window where nothing can be selected or activated.
	Adjust, resize, move arrows. Two-headed arrows let you drag the boundaries of objects. When you click and drag, the object expands or shrinks in the direction you drag the boundary. **Column adjust.** Two-headed arrow on a vertical bar lets you change the width of a column. You can drag the boundary between two columns, or double-click (in most environments) to activate AutoFit, which adjusts the column to fit the longest entry.
	Horizontal resize. The horizontal version appears when the pointer rests on the middle of a left or right boundary; dragging it changes the proportions of the object.

Pointer	Description
↕	**Vertical resize.** The vertical version appears when the pointer rests on the middle of a top or bottom boundary; dragging it changes the proportions of the object.
↖ ↗	**Diagonal Resize.** The slanted versions appear when the pointer rests on a corner of the object; dragging it maintains the proportions of the object as you resize it.
✛	**Move.** In some applications, when you select a graphic or toolbar and hold the left mouse button, this four-headed arrow appears and you can drag the object.
I	**Text select.** I-beam shows where the insertion point will be positioned when you click the left mouse button. If you drag it, you select text. The insertion point (a blinking vertical bar) shows where the next key you press will take effect. For example, if you press the Backspace key, the insertion point moves left and deletes the character. The Del key deletes the character to the right of the insertion point.
🖑	**Link select.** The hand indicates that the text or icon is a link to another document or Web page.
⟋	**Line select.** Right-slanted arrow lets you click to select a line of text in word processing programs. It appears when you let the mouse pointer rest to the left of the text in an unmarked area of the screen called the **selection area**. You can drag this pointer to select multiple lines.
✛	**Cell select.** The fat cross appears as the standard pointer in spreadsheet programs. You point to a spreadsheet cell and click to select the cell.

Use the Keyboard

- The Windows keyboard shown in the illustration on the following page has the alphanumeric keys in the traditional QWERTY arrangement, with the Shift, Caps Lock, Tab, Enter, and Delete keys.

- Along the bottom row, to the right of the spacebar are the Alt, Windows, Application, and Ctrl (control) keys. To the left of the spacebar are another copy of the Alt, Windows, and Ctrl keys.

- Along the top row are the Escape (Esc) key and twelve function keys (F1 - F12), with the Print Scrn, Scroll Lock, and Pause keys. The uses of special keyboard keys, such as Ctrl, Alt, and Esc, are described as necessary throughout this book.

- Just to the right of the alphanumeric keyboard are the insertion point movement, scrolling, and Insert (Ins) and Delete (Del) keys, which are described later in this exercise.

- To the far right is the numeric keypad. When the **Num Lock** key is pressed to turn on the Num Lock indicator light above the keypad, these keys input numbers. When the Num Lock indicator light is off, these keys function as insertion point movement keys.

Windows Keyboard

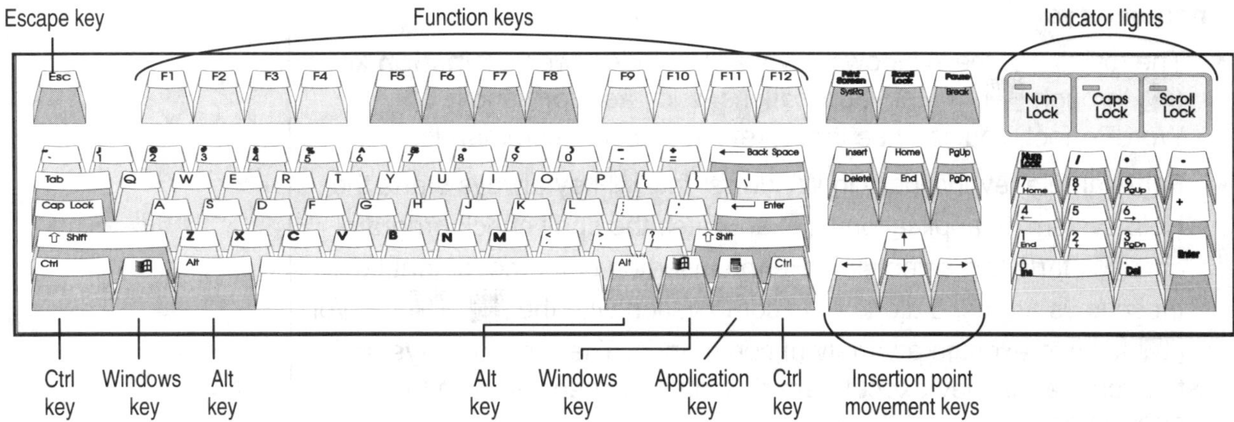

Insertion Point Movement

- You can move the insertion point (a blinking vertical line |) by pointing with the mouse and clicking to position the insertion point at the mouse pointer.

- You can also move the insertion point by using the arrow, Home, End, Page Up, and Page Down keys on the keyboard. The arrow keys are located to the right of the standard keyboard layout and are repeated on the number pad keys. To use the insertion point movement keys on the number pad, Num Lock must be off. The insertion point movement keys are illustrated below:

Insertion Point Movement Keys (Windows Keyboard)

Insert switches between Insert and Overtype modes.

Delete erases the character to the right of the insertion point or erases the selected text or object(s).

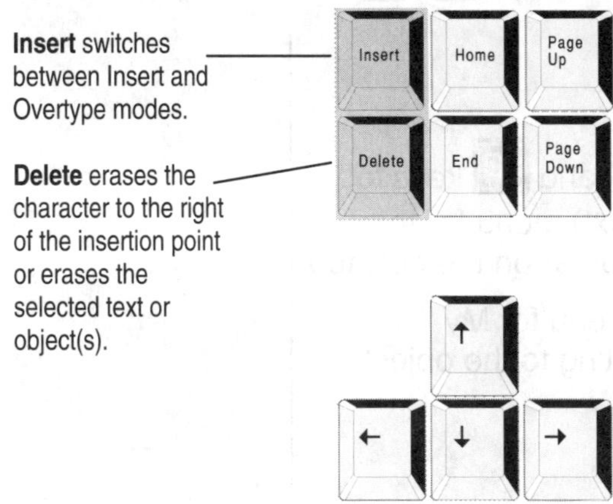

> ✓ **Alt+, Ctrl+ and Shift+**
> *Altl+F* means to hold down the Alt key and press the F key. *Ctrl+F6* means to hold down the Ctrl key and press the F6 key. *Shift+right arrow* means to hold down the Shift key and press the right arrow cursor movement key This notation is the standard way of indicating key stroke combinations.

- Each key may be pressed by itself or combined with the Ctrl key and/or Shift key.

- Ctrl + one of these keys increases insertion point movement. For example, in Word the **up arrow** () moves the insertion point up one line; Ctrl+↑ moves the insertion point up one paragraph.

- Shift + one of these keys selects text as well as moves the insertion point. For example, Shift+↑ selects up one line from the current insertion point position. Ctrl+Shift+↑ selects to the beginning of the current paragraph from the current insertion point position.

Other Keys

Function Keys

- The top row of the Windows keyboard includes twelve **function keys** (`F1` through `F12`). Within applications, such as Word and WordPerfect, you can use these keys to execute commands.

- For example, everywhere in Windows, the `F1` key always starts the Help system; in applications, `F7` activates the spell check program, and `F8` starts text selection. Like the insertion point movement keys, these keys are used alone or in combination with the `Ctrl`, `Alt`, and/or `Shift` keys to execute a variety of commands. The function keys and the commands they execute are described as necessary in the application sections of this book.

Escape Key

- The `Esc` (Escape) key is used to cancel actions. For example, if you activate a menu option that you do not want to use, pressing the `Esc` key usually closes the menu or dialog box without any command being executed.

- `Ctrl`+`Esc` is a shortcut to activate the Start menu. It is the same as clicking the Start button `Start` or pressing the Windows key.

Windows Key

- The Windows key, located between the `Ctrl` and `Alt` keys on some keyboards, opens the Start menu. It is the same as `Ctrl`+`Esc` or clicking the Start button `Start`.

Application Key

- The Application key, located between the `Ctrl` and Windows keys to the right of the spacebar, opens a shortcut (context) menu for the active object. For example, if you select My Computer on the desktop and press the Application key, the shortcut menu for My Computer opens. This action is the same as pointing to the object and right-clicking.

`Alt`+`Tab` or `Alt`+`Esc`

- `Alt`+`Tab` or `Alt`+`Esc` lets you switch from one open application to another. `Alt`+`Tab` displays a box with the icons of each application; `Alt`+`Esc` activates the application window or selects the application button on the taskbar if the application window is minimized. When the application button is selected, you can press the `Enter` key to restore the application.

Use Menus

- As illustrated by the My Computer window in the next exercise, menus appear at the top of most windows in Windows. Menus offer a list of commands from which you choose the one you want to execute. Sometimes the command is executed immediately. Sometimes the option displays a submenu. Sometimes the option displays a dialog box. A typical Windows menu (from My Computer) is illustrated below.

My Computer Menu Bar

Windows 98   **Windows 95**

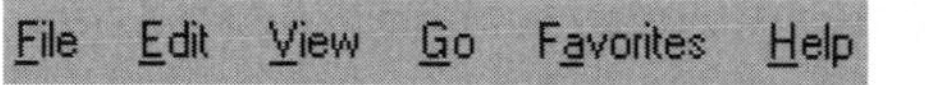

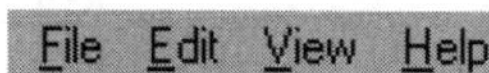

- To activate a menu, either:
  - Click the name of the menu you want to display
  - **OR**
  - Press **Alt**+the underlined letter on the menu (**Alt**+**F**, for the **File** menu, for example).

File Menu (My Computer, Windows 98)

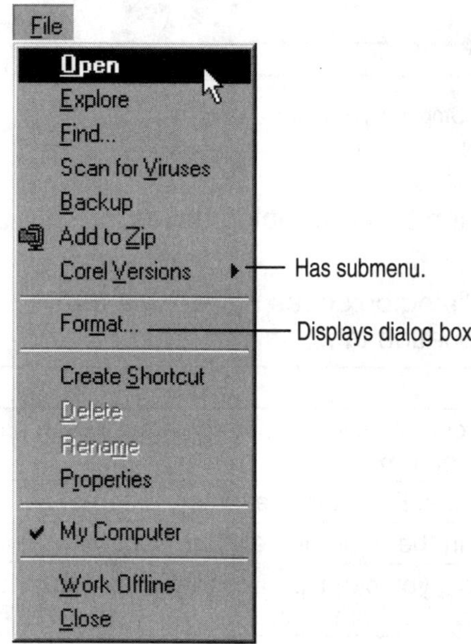

— Has submenu.

— Displays dialog box.

- Note that some commands appear in black letters while others are gray or dim. Options in black are available for selection; options in gray or dim letters are not available. Available options depend on the object (icon, folder, text, and so on) selected for processing.

- Commands followed by a small right arrow, as pointed out in the preceding illustration, offer submenus from which you choose a command. Other commands are followed by an ellipsis (...) to indicate that they activate a dialog box.

- To choose a menu option, slide the mouse to the option and click. If the option has a submenu, slide to the option, then slide to the desired command on the submenu, and then click.

Find Dialog Box

The illustrations in most of this lesson are taken from Windows 98. The differences between Windows 98 and Windows 95 objects are described as necessary throughout the lesson.

Use Dialog Boxes

- Dialog boxes are formatted windows that let you tell the system what work you want to perform. Dialog boxes are used for such things as opening files, printing documents, specifying margins for documents, setting preferences, and finding files (as shown in the following illustration).

Parameter

An entry that sets a condition or a limit for processing. For example, when you specify a word that you want a program to search for, you are setting a parameter for the search.

Find Dialog Box, Windows 98

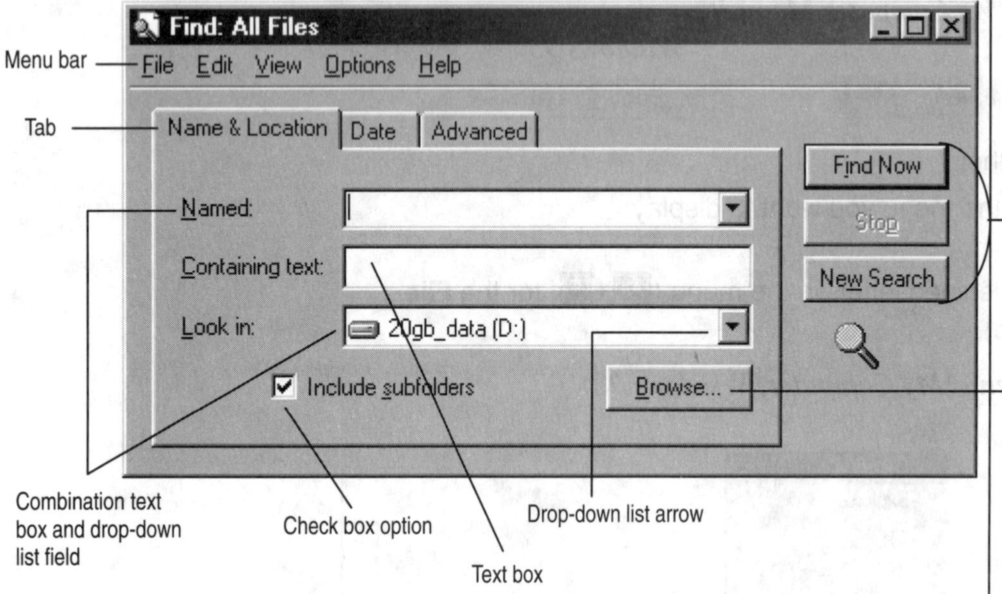

Menu bar

Tab

Combination text box and drop-down list field

Check box option

Text box

Drop-down list arrow

Command buttons

- The elements of this dialog box, common to many dialog boxes, are described in the following table.

  Windows 95: The Windows 95 Find dialog box does not include the *Containing text* field on the Name & Location tab.

Element	Description
Menu bar	Dialog boxes do not always contain menus, but some do. When a menu is available, it contains commands unique to the dialog box.
Tab	Many dialog boxes include tabs. Each tab presents a different set of options.
Text box	In a text box, you must type in the appropriate information.
Combo box	In a combo (combination) box, you can type information or click the drop-down list arrow at the right of the box to select an option from a list.
Check box	The check box lets you click to turn an option on (checked) or off (not checked). Each click either turns the option on or off. Such options are called toggles because they turn options on or off like a toggle light switch.
Command buttons	Once you've completed the body of a dialog box, you click a command button to activate the options (**parameters**) you've specified.

- To use a dialog box:
    1. Complete the fields and options to set parameters for the process.
    2. Click a command button to execute the options.

       OR

       Press the Esc key or click the Close button X to close the dialog box without executing any commands.

Use ScreenTips and What's This?

- When you rest the mouse pointer on a toolbar button, the name of the button appears. (The button shown is from Windows 98.)

- That's the simplest form of a ScreenTip. When you need more explanation, you can display a more elaborate ScreenTip using the What's This? feature.

Try It!

1. Open My Computer (double-click its icon on the desktop).
   The My Computer window opens.

   - **Windows 98 only, non-Web page view:** Point to the Control Panel folder and rest the mouse pointer there.
     A ScreenTip window opens that tells you about the Control Panel. (Windows 95 does not have an equivalent.) If you are in Web page view, the same text appears in the left side of the window.

     > Use the settings in Control Panel to personalize your computer. For example, you can specify how you want your desktop to look (Display icon), which events you want to hear sounds for (Sounds icon), the volume you prefer for audio recording (Multimedia icon), and much more.

2. Double-click the Control Panel icon (click if the name is underlined in Windows 98).
   The Control Panel window opens and displays its contents.

3. Open the Date/Time Properties dialog box (double-click the Date/Time icon or click if its name is underlined).
   The Date/Time Properties dialog box opens.

4. Click the What's This button [?] in the upper right of the dialog box.

   The mouse pointer changes to an arrow and question mark: .

5. Point to the field that displays the month and click.
   Windows 98 displays the explanation shown below. The What's This display in Windows 95 has a slightly different wording.

   > Displays your computer's current month setting.

   In some dialog boxes, you can click in a field and press Shift + F1 *to display the What's This? ScreenTip.*

6. Press the Esc key or click to cancel the ScreenTip.

7. Press the Esc key or click the Cancel button to close the Date/Time Properties dialog box without making any changes.

8. On the Control Panel window, click the Close button [X].

9. On the My Computer window, click the Close button [X].

EXERCISE DIRECTIONS

Open and Close Windows

1. Start on the desktop.

2. Select the My Computer icon .
   The My Computer icon changes color, usually to a darker color to indicate that it is selected.

3. Open the My Computer icon .
   The My Computer window opens.

4. Click the Close button ⊠ in the upper-right corner of the window.
   The My Computer window closes.

5. Open the Recycle Bin icon Recycle Bin .
   The Recycle Bin window opens.

6. Click the Close button ⊠ in the upper-right corner of the window.
   The Recycle Bin window closes.

7. Click the Start button Start

8. Move the mouse pointer to **Help** and click.
   The Windows Help window opens.

9. Click the Close button ⊠ in the upper-right corner of the window.
   The Windows Help window closes.

Minimize, Maximize, Restore, and Close

1. Open the My Computer icon My Computer to open the My Computer window.

2. Click the Minimize button ▬.
   The My Computer window becomes a button on the Windows taskbar. It looks like the following:

3. Click on the My Computer button My Computer to restore the window to its previous size and position.

4. Click the Maximize button ◻ if it is displayed.
   The My Computer window expands to fill the entire monitor screen.

   OR

   Click the Restore button ⊟ if it is displayed.
   The My Computer window shrinks to a smaller size.

5. Double-click the title bar.
   This action is the same as clicking the Maximize or Restore button, whichever is displayed.

6. Click the Close button ⊠.
   My Computer closes completely.

7. Reopen My Computer.

8. Make sure My Computer is not maximized. The Maximize button ◻ should be showing on the window. (If the Restore button ⊟ is displayed, click it to restore the window.)

9. Move your mouse pointer to the My Computer title bar.

10. Hold down the left mouse button and drag the window around on the desktop. (Be careful not to double-click.)
    The window changes its position on the desktop.

11. When the window is in a position that you like, release the left mouse button.
    Any window that is not maximized can be moved in this way. You may find it useful to move a window around to be able to see elements on the desktop that the window hides.

NEXT EXERCISE

Exercise 2

Getting Started with Windows
■ My Computer—A Typical Windows Window
■ The Edit Menu ■ The View Menu ■ The Help Menu ■ My Computer Toolbar
■ Sort Objects Using the Legend Bar ■ Shut Down Windows

NOTES

My Computer—A Typical Windows Window

■ To keep icons, files, and applications organized on your screen, Windows uses windows. A Windows window lets you:

  • View the components of your computer.

  • Review the names of folders and files on a disk or folder.

  • Look at or edit the contents of a file through an application window.

Try It!

  • To see what your computer contains, open the My Computer icon

My Computer on your desktop.

The My Computer window opens.

As shown in the illustration below, the My Computer Window displays several icons. Your icons will reflect your own computer's installed hardware and setup, and they may appear in a vertical list rather than spread across the window as illustrated. But you can recognize the window as My Computer by its title bar.

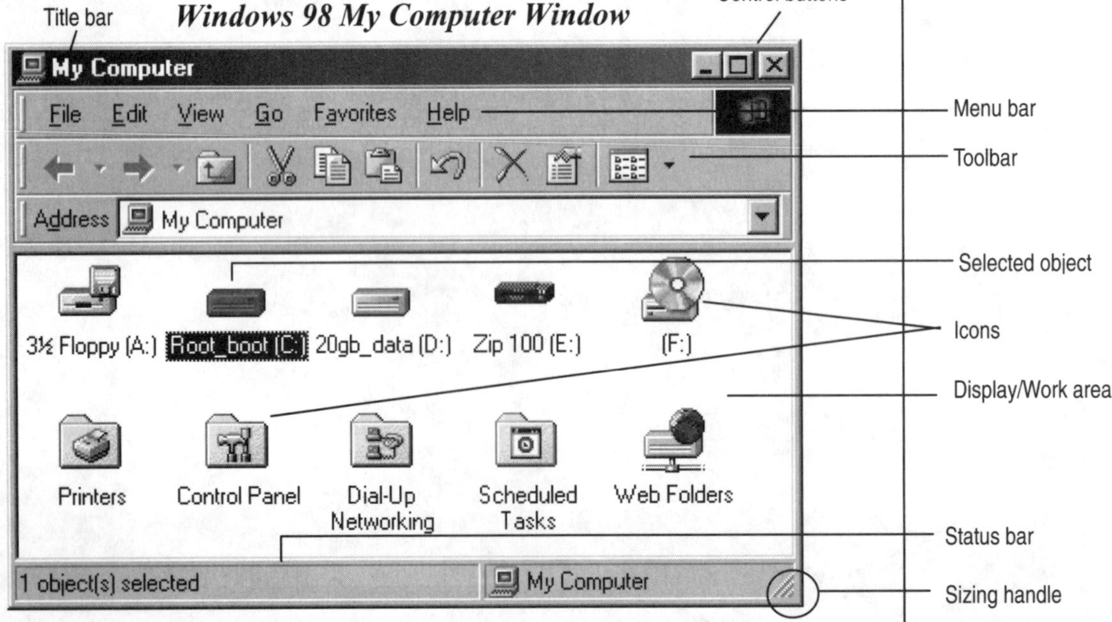

- The My Computer window has several important parts that are common to all Windows windows, as described in the table that follows.

Window Part	Description
Title bar	Identifies the application or window. When an application, such as Word, operates on a document or file, the name of the file also appears in the title bar.
Control buttons	Allow you to control the size of the window and to close it.
Minimize ▬	Turns the window into a button on the Windows taskbar. The taskbar then displays the icon for the window and its name. When a window is minimized, you can return it to its previous position by clicking its button on the taskbar.
Maximize ▢ **Restore** ▣	Different versions of the same button. When clicked, the Maximize button causes the window to take up the entire monitor screen. The Restore button appears when a window is maximized. When you click it, the window returns to the size it was before it was maximized.
Close ✕	Closes the window. If the window is an application, you exit the application.
Menu bar	Displays menu options. When you click on a menu name, a list of commands or options appears. These commands let you perform work with the objects (documents, icons) that appear in the window.
Toolbar	Contains buttons that activate a shortcut to a command. For example, a button with scissors ✂ is the standard symbol to activate the Cut function. (The button illustrated here is from Windows 95. See page 79 for more on the toolbar.) To display a toolbar if one is available, click the View menu and then click Toolbar(s) (Alt+V, T). In Windows 98, you must also choose Standard Buttons to display the Standard toolbar.
Display/Work area	Displays the results of the work you perform.
Icons	Pictorial representations of computer components or applications. You use them to move around your computer, open other windows, or start applications.
Status bar	Gives you important information about what the window contains and what work is being done. To display a status bar if it is not showing, click the View menu and then click Status Bar (Alt+V, B).
Sizing handle ◹	**Windows 98.** When you point the mouse at the sizing handle, the pointer turns into a double-headed arrow ↘. You can click and drag the sizing handle to resize the window. **Windows 95 and Windows 98.** When you point at any corner or edge of a window, the mouse pointer changes to one of several double-headed arrows. You can click and drag the corner or edge to resize the window.

Windows 98 My Computer Toolbar buttons

The Windows 98 toolbars have Web browser-like buttons. The scissors on

the Cut button Cut , for example, differ from those in Windows 95. In addition, the Windows 98 toolbars contain forward and back buttons like a browser toolbar.

The **Text Labels** for toolbar buttons can be turned on and off:

1. In the My Computer window, click **View**.

2. Choose **Toolbars**.

3. Click **Text Labels**.

If the labels are on this action turns them off. If they are off, this action turns them on.

The Edit Menu

- The <u>E</u>dit menu, available in most windows, contains such options as Cut, Copy, and Paste. You'll learn more about Edit menus in later exercises. For objects in My Computer, most <u>E</u>dit menu options are dimmed.

My Computer Edit Menu (Windows 98)

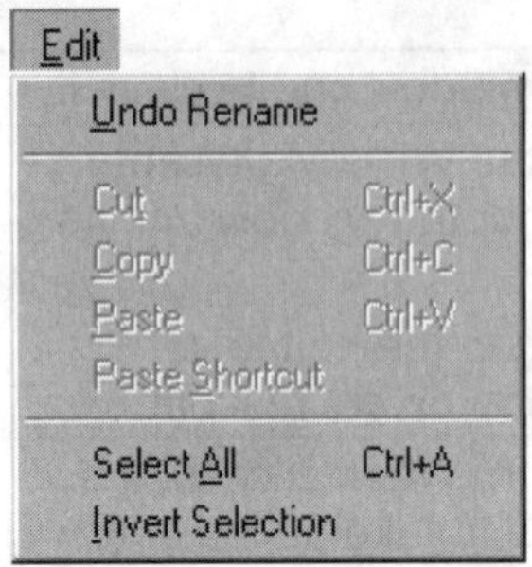

The View Menu

- The <u>V</u>iew menu, also available in most windows, lets you alter the appearance of the display area and the window itself. Click the <u>V</u>iew menu and look at the options as illustrated in the following illustration.

My Computer View Menu
Windows 98

Windows 95

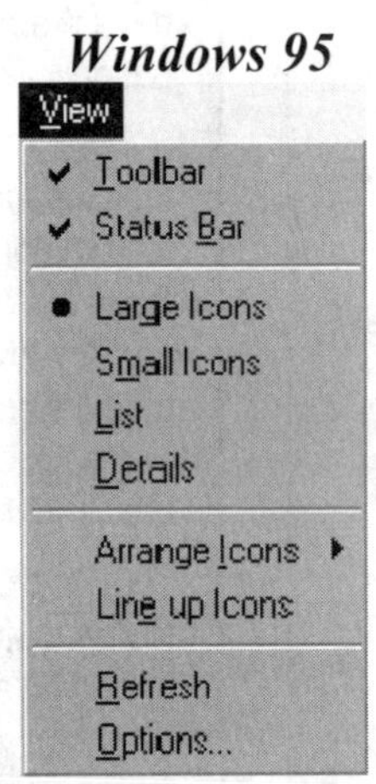

- Note the check mark beside Status <u>B</u>ar, indicating that the option is currently selected. To hide the status bar, click on the option to remove the check mark, which deselects the option.

- Four options on the menu determine how the contents of My Computer appear. In the illustration, a round dot appears next to Large Icons. Rather than a check mark, this time the selection is noted by the round black dot.

- The check mark and round dot on this menu show an important Windows distinction.

  - A check mark ✓ indicates an option that can be used at the same time as other options in the set. On the Windows 95 <u>V</u>iew menu, both the <u>T</u>oolbar and the Status <u>B</u>ar can be selected at the same time.

- A round dot ● indicates an option that cannot be used with other options in the set. (These options are said to be mutually exclusive; choosing one excludes the others.) Only one of the four choices (Large Icons, Small Icons, List, or Details) can be chosen.

The Help Menu

- Help menus are also available in most windows. You can learn about using help in Appendix B.

My Computer Toolbar

- As indicated by the button names in the following illustration, many of the toolbar buttons execute commands that are also available on one of the menus. Toolbar buttons are shortcuts to these commands. When you click on a toolbar button, the command is executed immediately.

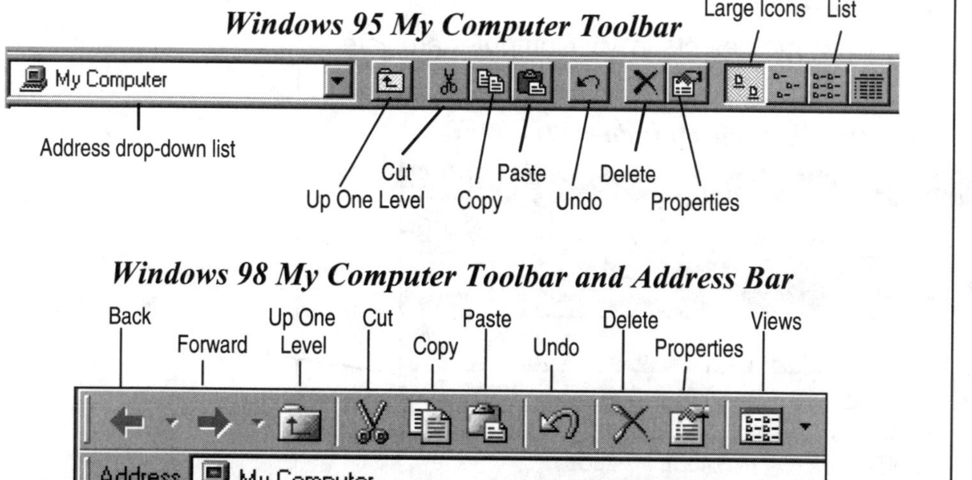

Windows 95: If the toolbar is not displayed, click the View menu and click Toolbar.

Windows 98: If the toolbar is not displayed, click the View menu, point to Toolbars, and click Standard Buttons. To display text for each standard button, click View, Toolbars, Text Labels.

- The buttons on the My Computer toolbar are typical of toolbar buttons throughout Windows. Some toolbars offer many more buttons; some offer fewer. The buttons illustrated are described in the following table.

Button	Description
Address (drop-down list or bar)	Displays a drop-down list of the objects in My Computer.
Up One Level, Cut, Copy, Paste, Undo, Delete	You'll learn more about these buttons in Exercise 7.
Properties	Displays information about the selected object. **Menu equivalent** = File, Properties (Alt+F, R)
Views	**Windows 98.** Click this button to cycle through the views listed on the following page. You can click the drop-down arrow to select from a list of these views.

Inactive buttons

When a button cannot operate on an object, nothing happens when you click it. Your computer may beep to indicate that the button cannot be used.

For most objects in My Computer, the Cut, Copy, Paste, and Delete buttons are inactive.

Button	Description
Large Icons	Changes the display to show large icons. Like the three remaining buttons, this button is available in windows that display files and folders. **Menu equivalent** = <u>V</u>iew, <u>La</u>rge Icons (**Alt**+**V**, **G**)
Small Icons	Changes the display to show small icons. **Menu equivalent** = <u>V</u>iew, S<u>m</u>all Icons (**Alt**+**V**, **M**)
List	Changes the display to a list with small icons. **Menu equivalent** = <u>V</u>iew, <u>L</u>ist (**Alt**+**V**, **L**)
Details	Changes the display to a list with small icons and information about the type and size of the objects. **Menu equivalent** = <u>V</u>iew, <u>D</u>etails (**Alt**+**V**, **D**)

Sort Objects Using the Legend Bar

- When you display the Details view, the objects in My Computer are listed as shown below.

My Computer—Details View (Windows 98)

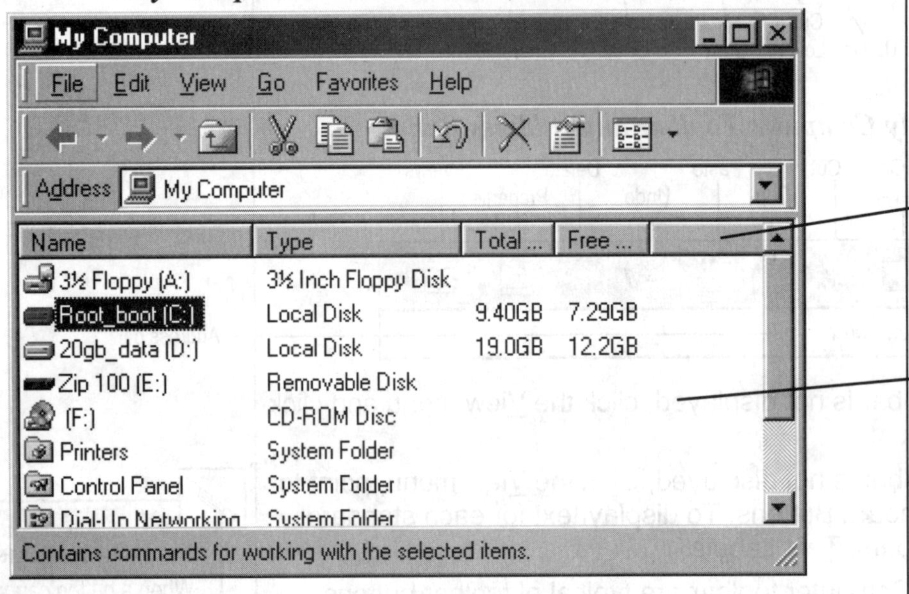

Legend bar

Details view

*Note the **legend bar** under the toolbar. This bar appears in similar windows when you select Details view.*

- You can use this bar to sort the entries in the details list.

  - Click Name to sort the entries by name.

  - Click Type to sort the entries by type of object.

  - Click Total Size to sort hard drives by their total storage space.

  - Click Free Space to sort hard drives by the amount of unused space each contains.

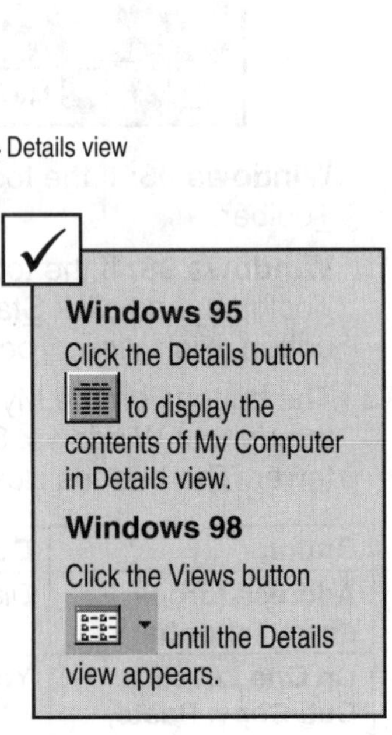

Windows 95

Click the Details button to display the contents of My Computer in Details view.

Windows 98

Click the Views button until the Details view appears.

Shut Down Windows

- To shut down Windows, click on the Start button ![Start] on the Windows taskbar and click on the Shut Down option as shown in the illustration that follows. (The options on your Start menu may be different.)

Start Menu

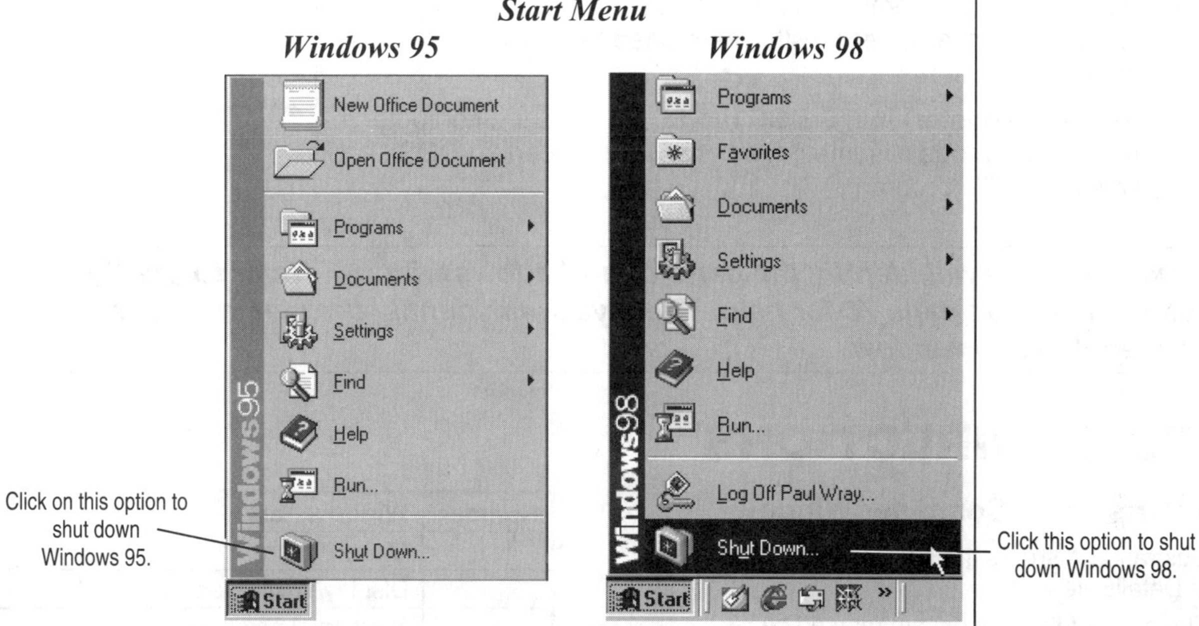

Click on this option to shut down Windows 95.

Click this option to shut down Windows 98.

- When you click **Shut Down**, the Shut Down Windows dialog box shown below appears and the desktop turns dim.

Shut Down Windows Dialog Box

(Windows 95)

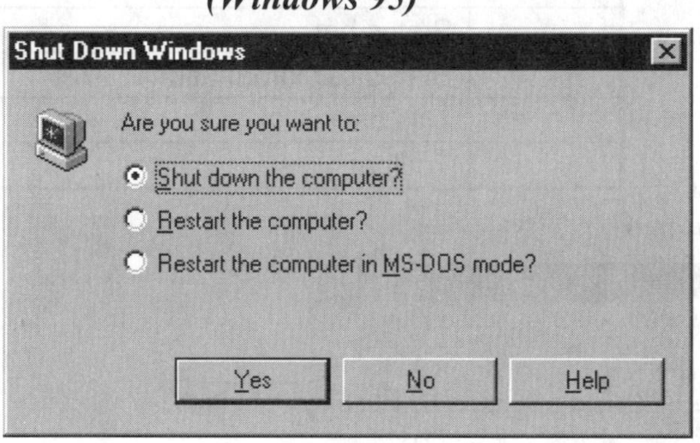

(Windows 98)

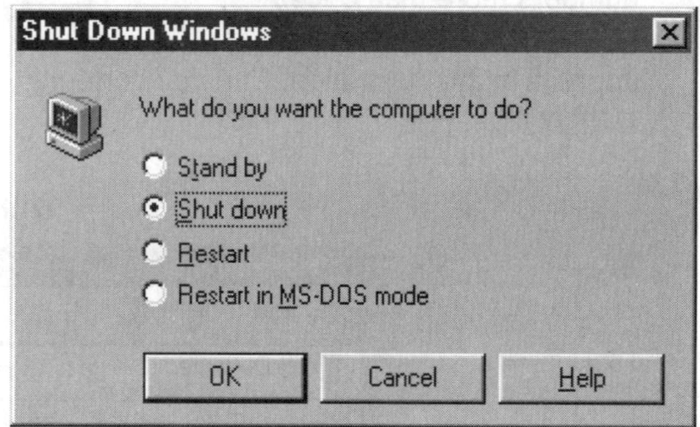

- The Shut Down Windows dialog box offers three or four options. (If you are logged on to a network, another option may appear to let you log in under another login ID.)

  - **Stand by**. This option lets you leave your computer on and available for use without restarting but using less electricity than normal. If you lose power while in stand-by mode, any unsaved work is lost. Some newer keyboards have a "sleep" button that places Windows 98 into stand-by mode. By default, Windows 98 places your computer in stand-by mode when it has been idle for 20 minutes.

  - **Shut down (the computer?)**. When you answer Yes to this option, Windows goes through its shutdown routine that may end with the message **It is now safe to turn off your computer** displayed in the middle of a dark screen. Most newer computers turn off automatically before this message appears. Watch the power light on your PC. When it goes off during shutdown, you can safely turn off other system components like the monitor, printer, and scanner.

- **Restart (the computer?)**. This option restarts your computer. If your computer has had problems, you may need to restart the computer to clean up memory and begin with a refreshed Windows environment.

- **Restart (the computer) in <u>M</u>S-DOS mode**. Restarts the computer in DOS mode. This mode is sometimes necessary for certain DOS programs and utility programs.

In this exercise, you will identify the parts of a Windows window. Refer to the My Computer window on page 76 for help. Then, you will identify the elements of a Windows application window.

EXERCISE DIRECTIONS

Identify Parts of My Computer Window

- Illustration A shows the My Computer window in Details view.

- The parts of the window are marked by numbers. Write the correct number from the illustration beside the parts of the window listed in the table at the right. You may need to use more than one number for some window parts, and you may need to use some numbers more than once.

- One windows element not yet discussed appears in the illustration. Can you correctly identify it?

Number	Window Part
	Close button
	Display/Work area
	Horizontal scroll bar
	Maximize button
	Menu bar
	Minimize button
	Drive icon
	Status bar
	Status bar information
	Title bar
	Toolbar

Illustration A

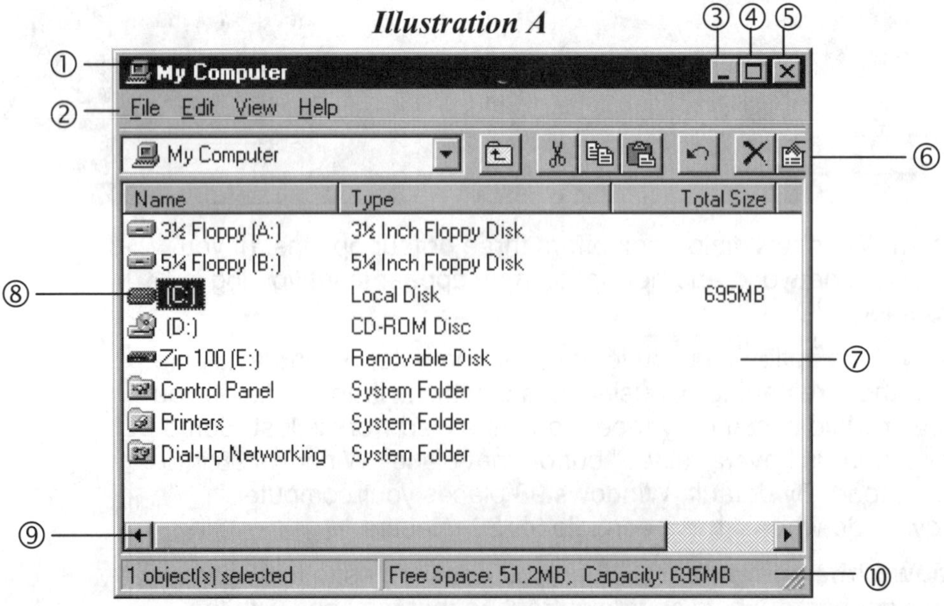

Identify Parts of Application Window

- Illustration B shows the window of the WordPad application. WordPad is a word processing program that comes with Windows.
- The parts of the window are marked by letters. Write the correct letter from the illustration beside the parts of the window listed in the table to the right. You may need to use more than one letter for some window parts, and you may need to use some letters more than once.

Letter	Window Part
	Close button
	Display/Work area
	Horizontal scroll bar
	Maximize button
	Menu bar
	Minimize button
	Ruler line
	Status bar
	Status bar information
	Title Bar
	Toolbar

Illustration B

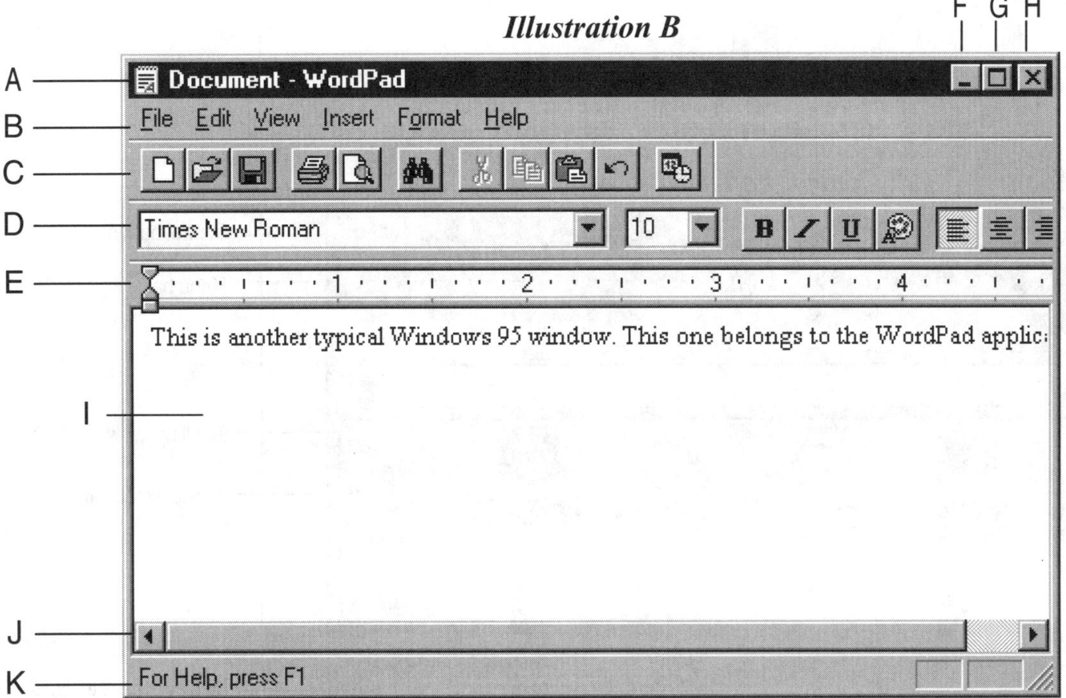

Exercise 3

Use the Control Panel
■ The Control Panel Window ■ The Active Window

NOTES

The Control Panel Window

■ The Control Panel gives you access to a number of features that let you customize your use of Windows and control the Windows environment.

Try It!

1. Open My Computer.

2. Open the Control Panel icon Control Panel .

   The Control Panel window, shown below, opens.

The Control Panel Window

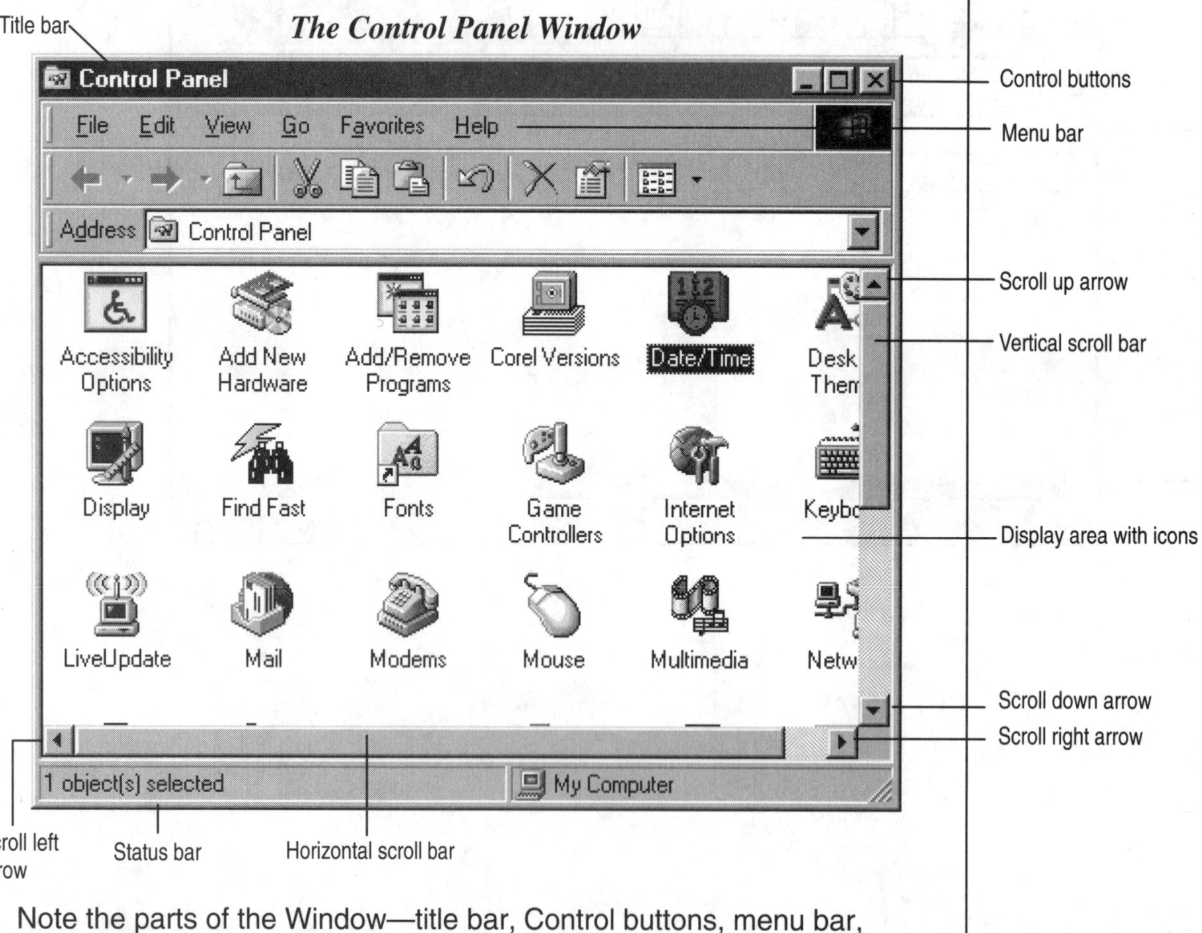

■ Note the parts of the Window—title bar, Control buttons, menu bar, display area, icons, status bar.

- The preceding illustration shows another element—a vertical scroll bar along the right side and a horizontal scroll bar along the bottom (just above the status bar). A scroll bar lets you move the display area of a window to see objects (icons or text) that lie outside the boundaries of the window. Windows uses two types of scroll bars: vertical to move up and down in a display and horizontal to move right and left. Some windows have both.

Try It!

1. Click on the gray bar and hold down the left mouse button and drag the bar in the direction you want to move. (Drag vertical scroll bars up and down, horizontal scroll bars left and right.) If your Control Panel has a scroll bar, try it.

2. You can also scroll by clicking on the arrows at either end of the scroll bar. Try using the arrows.

3. The Control Panel has a **V**iew menu. Click **View** (**Alt**+**V**) to see the options available.

   Note that the options are similar to those in My Computer. As you work with Windows, you'll find that _V_*iew menus are a chief way to control the appearance of the active window.*

4. **Windows 95:** Click **View**, **Toolbar** (**Alt**+**V**, **T**).

   Windows 98: Click **View**, **Toolbars**, **Standard Buttons** (**Alt**+**V**, **T**, **S**).

   The Control Panel toolbar appears. The Control Panel toolbar is the same as the My Computer toolbar.

The Active Window

- With Web style on (Windows 98), when you open the Control Panel from within My Computer, the My Computer window disappears. You can

  return to the My Computer window by clicking the Back button .

- With Classic style on, when you open the Control Panel from within My Computer, two windows are open. If you are using Windows 95 or Classic style, skip the three-step Try It! activity below.

Try It! (Windows 98 Web style Users Only)

Open a Second Window

1. Click the Start button.

2. Slide to **Settings** (**S**).

3. Click Control Panel.

   The Control Panel window displays. Make sure it is not maximized.

- You should now have two windows open—Control Panel and My Computer. You may be able to see both or only one. The one in which you are working is called the **active window.** You can tell which window is active because its title bar is in color (graduating from dark blue on the left to a lighter blue on the right unless your display has been changed). The inactive window has a dark gray to lighter gray title bar.

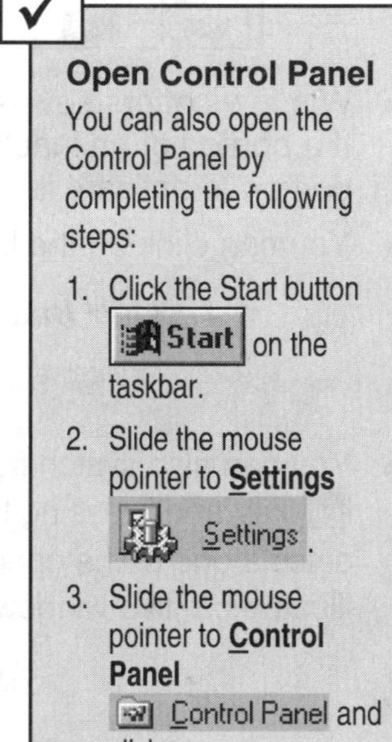

Open Control Panel

You can also open the Control Panel by completing the following steps:

1. Click the Start button [Start] on the taskbar.

2. Slide the mouse pointer to **Settings** [Settings].

3. Slide the mouse pointer to **Control Panel** [Control Panel] and click.

- In the following illustration, the Control Panel is the active window and My Computer is mostly hidden by it. A portion of the desktop forms the background.

Active and Inactive Windows

- Windows offers several ways to switch from one open window to another. If a portion of an inactive window is showing, click on the displayed portion to activate it.

- You can click on the button for the window on the taskbar.

Taskbar Buttons for My Computer and Control Panel

My Computer (inactive)  Control Panel (active)

- You can also switch from one open window to another by holding down the **Alt** key and pressing the **Tab** key. Each time you press **Alt**+**Tab**, Windows selects one of the open windows indicated by its icon. In the following illustration, five windows are open, so **Alt**+**Tab** cycles through all five.

Switch Between Open Windows

- When the icon for the window you want to activate is selected, release the **Alt** key. The window is activated.

Try It!

1. Click the hidden (inactive window) if a portion of it is showing.
2. Click the taskbar button of the inactive window to activate it.
3. Use **Alt**+**Tab** to switch to the inactive window.
4. Close the Control Panel window and the My Computer window.

> **In this exercise, you will open a couple of the objects in the Control Panel and briefly explore them.**

EXERCISE DIRECTIONS

Explore Display Properties

1. Open My Computer from the desktop.

2. Open the Control Panel.

3. Open the Display icon  Display.

   The Display Properties dialog box shown in Illustration A appears. The Windows 95 dialog box has fewer tabs than the one in the illustration.

4. Click on each tab in turn and briefly review the options.

   - Each tab lets you customize some portion of your monitor's display. If you are working on your own machine, you may wish to try some of these options.

   - If you are working on a shared machine, consider other users and do not change the settings.

5. After looking through the options, click the Cancel button [Cancel] at the bottom of the dialog box to ensure that no settings are changed.

Illustration A. Display Properties Dialog Box

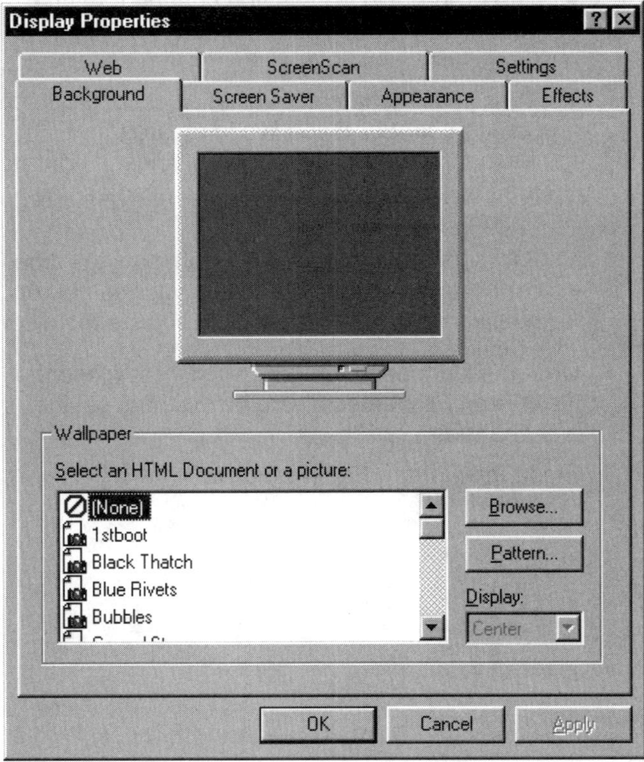

Set Date and Time

1. Open the Date/Time icon Date/Time.

   The Date/Time Properties dialog box shown in Illustration B opens.

   *In **Windows 95** and in some versions of **Windows 98**, the Date/Time Properties dialog box has two tabs Date & Time and Time Zone. In later versions of **Windows 98**, the time zone is a drop-down list at the bottom of the dialog box as shown in Illustration B.*

Illustration B. Windows 98
Date/Time Properties Dialog Box

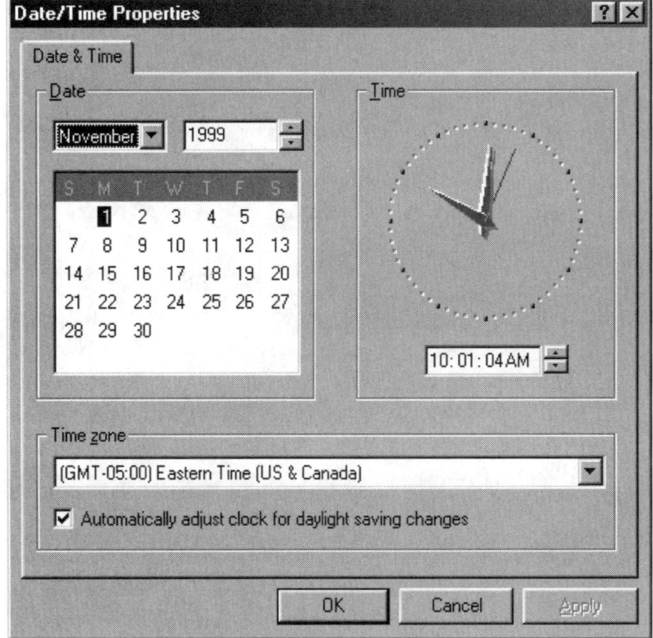

- The date and time are stored and kept current even when the power is off because a battery is used to power the date/time function.

- If you need to reset the date or time, you can use the Date/Time Properties dialog box to set the clock on your computer.

- This dialog box shows a new dialog box element, the Increase/Decrease arrows.

- When you click the up arrow, the value in the box increases. When you click the down arrow, the value decreases.

Windows 98 only

- Illustration B shows a computer set for the Eastern time zone in the United States. *GMT -(5:00)* stands for Greenwich Mean Time minus 5 hours.

- The drop-down Time zone list lets you change the time zone if you move your computer to a different time zone.

- Turn on *Automatically adjust clock for daylight saving changes* if you live in an area that always changes for daylight savings. If your area does not change, you can deselect this option (turn it off).

- If the option is on, when daylight savings time changes in the spring and fall, your computer notifies you and automatically adjusts the clock.

1. Click the Cancel button **Cancel** to close the Date/Time Properties dialog box without saving any changes.

2. Close the Control Panel window.

Windows 95 Only

1. Click the Time Zone tab.

   The Time Zone tab displays, as shown in Illustration C.

Illustration C. Windows 95 Date/Time Properties,Time Zone Tab

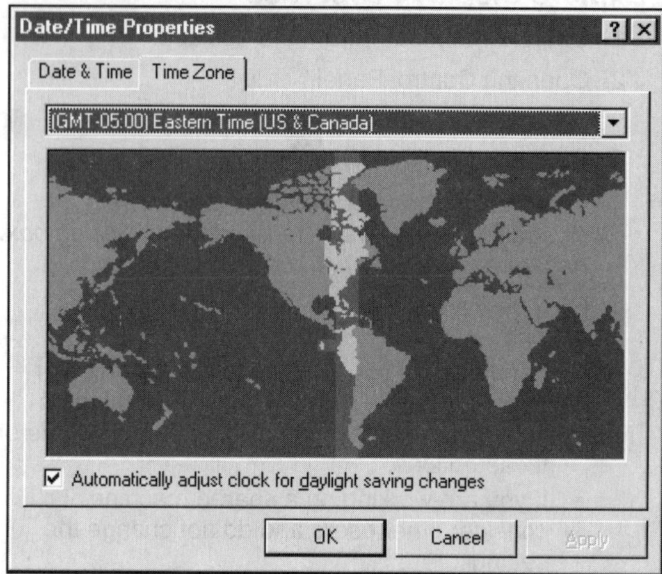

- Illustration C shows a computer set for the Eastern time zone in the United States. (Your display may not show the highlighted time zone.)

- The drop-down list lets you change the time zone if you move your computer to a different time zone.

- Turn on *Automatically adjust clock for daylight saving changes* if you live in an area that always changes for daylight savings. If your area does not change, you can deselect this option (turn it off).

- If the option is on, when daylight savings time changes in the spring and fall, your computer notifies you and automatically adjusts the clock.

2. Click the Cancel button **Cancel** to close the Date/Time Properties dialog box without saving any changes.

3. Close the Control Panel window.

NEXT EXERCISE

Find Folders and Files
■ Use the Find Dialog Box

NOTES

Use the Find Dialog Box

- A **dialog box** lets you specify criteria (input) to set **parameters** for processing. You complete the elements in the dialog box, then click a button to request processing of the options selected. In this section, you'll learn how to use the Find dialog box.

Try It!

1. Open My Computer.

2. Select drive C: in the My Computer window.

3. Click **File** (Alt+F) on the menu bar and then click **Find** (F). The Find dialog box illustrated below appears.

   *Note that your C: drive may not have a name. Drive C: in the illustration has the **drive label** Root_boot.*

   The Windows 95 dialog box does not have the Containing text field.

Windows 98 Find Dialog Box

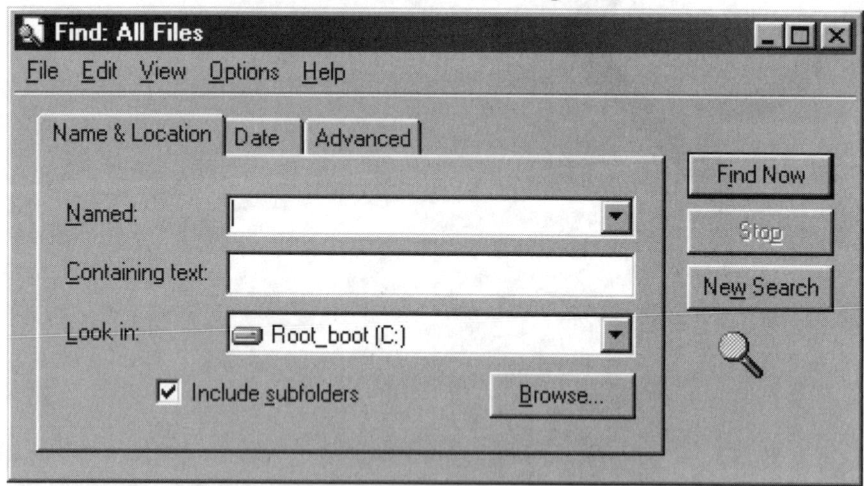

- If you open a dialog box by accident or decide at any time that you do not want to complete the action, close it before processing by:

  - Clicking the Close button  on the dialog box.

  - Clicking the Cancel button Cancel if the box has one or pressing the Esc key.

- You will learn about other elements of dialog boxes as you encounter them in this lesson and in other lessons in this book.

Parameter

An entry that sets a condition or a limit to processing. For example, when you specify a word that you want a program to search for, you are setting a parameter for the search.

Drive Label

A drive can have a name or label that helps identify its contents or use. The label can be created when the drive is created or it can be added later through the Properties dialog box.

Another way to open the Find dialog box:

1. Right-click the Start button Start.

2. Click **Find**.

> **In this exercise, you will perform a search for a file, using the Find dialog box.**

EXERCISE DIRECTIONS

Find Files

1. Open My Computer.

2. Click on the icon for drive C: ,
   to select it.

3. Click the File menu, and then click
   Find.

   *The Find: All Files dialog box opens
   (Illustration A) with the insertion
   point (blinking vertical line)
   positioned in the Named box.*

4. In the Named box, type *WIN** as
   shown in Illustration A. Do NOT
   press the Enter key.

   The asterisk is called a **wildcard***. It
   stands for any letters following
   WIN.*

5. Press the Tab key twice to move
   the insertion point to the Look in
   box. (Skip the Containing text box.)

6. In the Look in box, type
   C:\WINDOWS. Be sure to use the \
   (backslash). Do NOT press the
   Enter key.

   *These search parameters tell
   Windows to look for all files that
   begin with the letters WIN.*

7. Deselect the *Include subfolders*
   option so that Windows looks only
   in the WINDOWS folder.

8. Click the Find Now button
   Find Now .

   *Windows searches for the files and
   displays the results in a new
   section (called a* **pane***) of the Find
   dialog box, as shown in
   Illustration B.*

   *Note that the title bar of the dialog
   box now displays the entry in the
   Named box.*

9. Click the Maximize button to
   expand the Find window. You can
   now see a larger number of the
   files that meet your search criteria.

10. Close the Find dialog box.

11. Close My Computer.

Illustration A. Find Dialog Box, Name & Location Tab

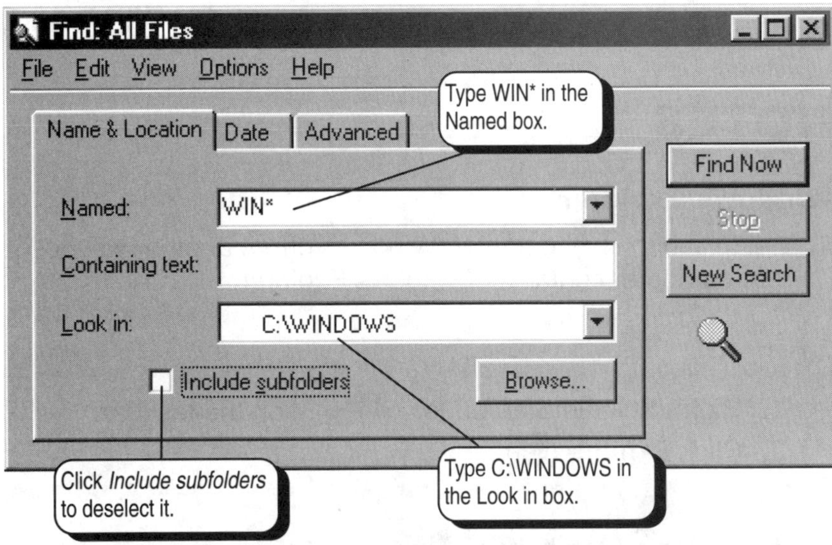

*Illustration B. Results of Find WIN**

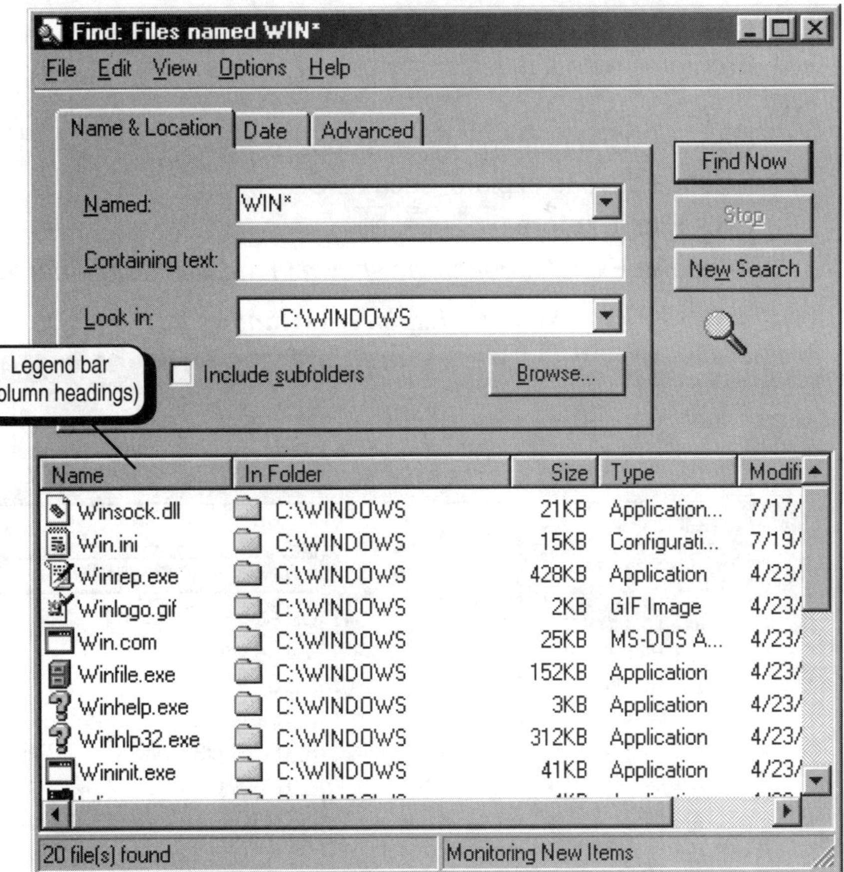

Exercise 5

Use Windows Explorer

■ Windows Explorer ■ How Windows Organizes Permanent Storage
■ Move Around in Windows Explorer

NOTES

Windows Explorer

- In addition to My Computer, Windows offers another way to look at what your computer contains—Windows Explorer.

💻 Try It!

1. Right-click the Start button **[🏁 Start]** on the taskbar.
2. Click **Explore** (**E**) .

OR

1. Click the Start button **[🏁 Start]** and slide your mouse pointer to **Programs** (**P**) .
2. Click the Windows Explorer **[🔍 Windows Explorer]** entry on the Programs menu. (It is usually one of the last entries on the menu.)

OR

1. Open My Computer on the desktop.
2. Select a drive to explore, such as C:.
3. Click **File**, **Explore** (**Alt**+**F**, **E**) .

   Windows Explorer opens, as shown in the illustration that follows.

Windows Explorer (Windows 98)

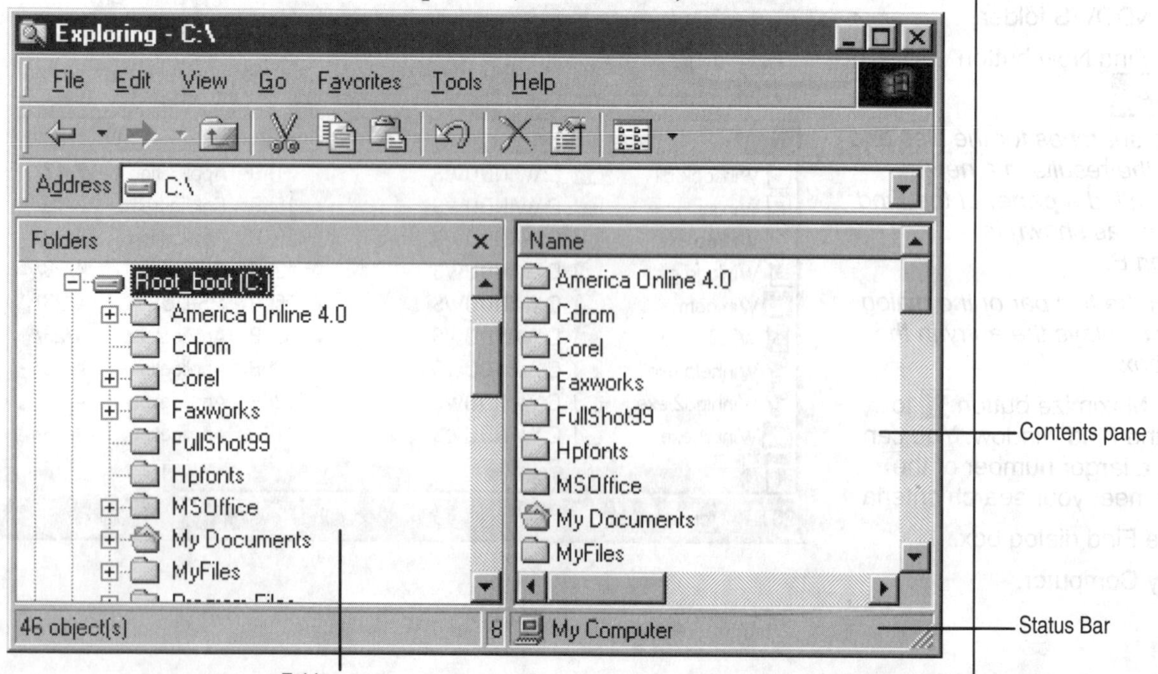

Explorers

Try not to confuse Windows Explorer with Internet Explorer, Microsoft's Web browser. Windows Explorer lets you look at what's on your computer; Internet Explorer lets you look at what's on the Internet.

- The Windows Explorer window is divided into two parts called **panes**.
  - The left pane, Folders, shows the folders in the drive currently selected. It also lists the other drives on your computer, which you can see by scrolling up and down.
  - The right pane lists the folders and files in the folder selected in the left pane.
- The following table describes the parts of the Windows Explorer window.

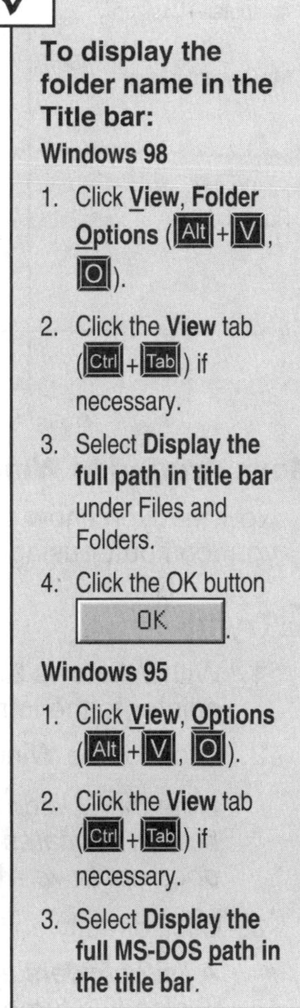

Window Part	Description
Title bar	Tells which drive and folder you are currently exploring.
Menu bar	Offers menu options. Note the addition of a **Tools** menu (Alt+T).
Toolbar and Address Bar	The Standard toolbar and Address Bar appear as on other windows. You can turn them on and off through: **Windows 98: View, Toolbars—Standard Buttons** or **Address Bar** (Alt+V, T, S or A). **Windows 95: View, Toolbar** (Alt+V, T) Windows 95 displays the address drop-down list in the left of the window.
Folders pane	Pane that lists all folders on your computer. **Windows 98 only.** Note the Close button X at the right end of the Folders bar. If you click this close button, the Folders pane closes. To reopen it, click **View, Explorer Bar, Folders** (Alt+E, O).
Right (Contents) pane	The right pane lists the objects in the folder currently selected in the Folders pane. The illustration on the previous page shows Details view. **Windows 98:** To switch views, click **View, Large Icons** (Alt+V, G), **Small Icons** (M), **List** (L), or **Details** (D) **OR** use the Views button on the toolbar. **Windows 95:** To switch views, **View, Large Icons** (Alt+V, G), **Small Icons** (M), **List** (L), or **Details** (D) **OR** use one of the four View buttons on the toolbar – Large icons; Small icons; List; Details.
Status bar	Gives information about the number and size of objects selected in the panes.

How Windows Organizes Permanent Storage

- Windows organizes permanent storage by drive letter, folder name, and file name. In your computer, the highest level of organization is the Desktop, which contains My Computer, which contains drives. Drives contain folders. Folders contain other folders and files.

- When you look at the Explorer window, you see this organization in list form. The hierarchy is reflected by dotted lines, as shown in the illustration that follows.

  Note that in the illustrations in this exercise, only the menu remains at the top of the window. The toolbar and address information have been turned off. Yours may be on.

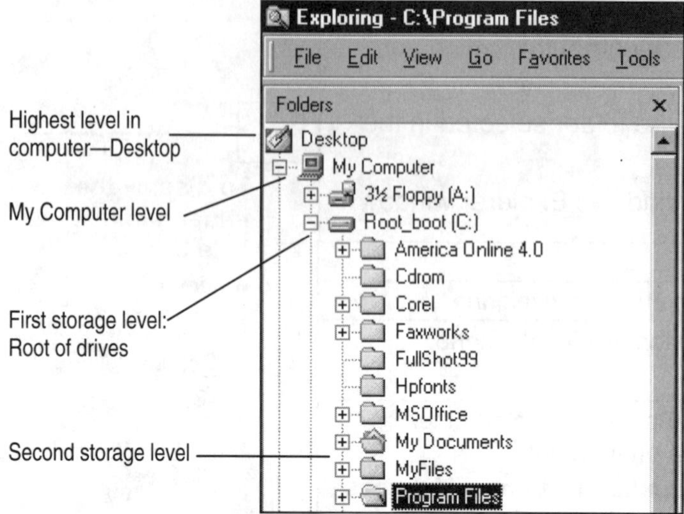

Organization Reflected in Windows Explorer

Move Around in Windows Explorer

- Now that you know something of its organization, you can look through your computer using Windows Explorer.

Try It!

1. With Windows Explorer open and maximized, move your mouse pointer to the left pane.

2. Look for the Windows folder ⊞ 🗀 Windows.

   *Note the ⊞ sign to the left of the folder. This sign, called the **Expand** button, indicates that the folder contains additional folders. If a folder does not have a ⊞, it contains only files.*

3. Click directly on the ⊞ sign.

   *A list of folders appears underneath the Windows folder, and the ⊞ sign has turned into a ⊟ sign called the **Collapse** button because it collapses the list in the left pane. Your screen should look something like the one in the following illustration. The contents of your Windows folder will be different. (So far, the right pane has not changed unless you accidentally clicked a folder.)*

Portion of Expanded Windows Folder in Explorer's Left Pane

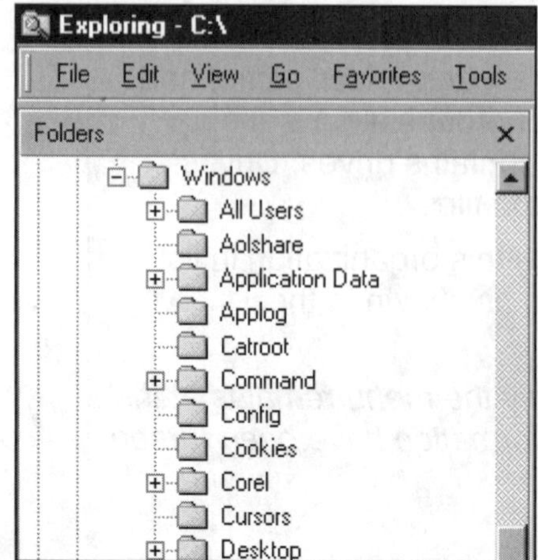

Root of Drives

The **root** folder of a drive is the highest level of organization within the drive.

Display Windows Folder

If the Windows folder does not appear in the left pane, use the scroll bar on the right side of the pane; click and drag it down until you see the Windows folder. The Windows folder is usually near the bottom of the list because folders and files are listed alphabetically.

Scroll bar
Click and hold the left mouse button and drag the scroll bar down.

4. Click the Windows folder 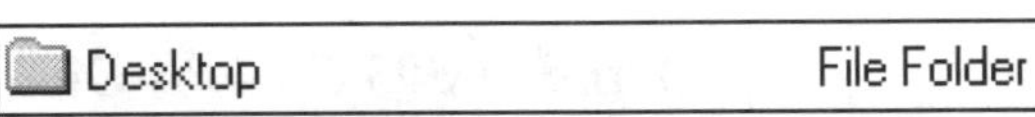 in the left pane.

The Windows folder looks open 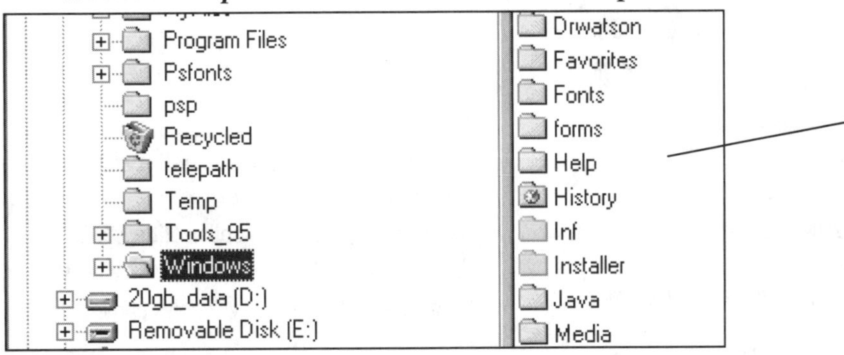 *, and its contents are displayed in the right pane, as shown in the following illustration.*

Windows Explorer with Windows Folder Open

Portion of contents of Windows folder

- In Explorer, folders are indicated by the folder icon. For example, if you have Details view on, you may see the desktop folder that looks like this:

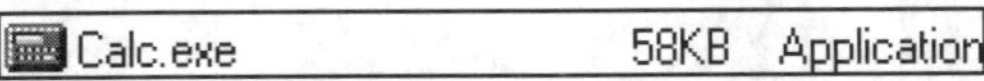

<table><tr><td>Desktop</td><td>File Folder</td></tr></table>

- Files are indicated by other icons. If the file belongs to an application, such as Word, the Word icon ▦ appears to the left of the file name in Explorer's right pane.

▦ Try It!

Locate a File

1. Make sure that the Windows folder is open.

2. Move your mouse pointer to the right pane.

3. Switch to Details view if it is not already selected. (Use the **View** (Alt+V) menu or the Views button ▦ ▾.)

4. Click on the scroll bar to the right of the pane, hold down the left mouse button, and drag down until you see the entry that looks like the following:

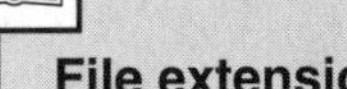

<table><tr><td>Calc.exe</td><td>58KB</td><td>Application</td></tr></table>

Note that the list is usually alphabetical by folder name, then by file name. If the names are not alphabetical, click on the Name button Name *in the legend bar at the top of the pane.*

*Your Calc (calculator) may not include the .exe **file extension** that appears above. It will, however, have the calculator icon and the word* Application*.*

5. Look at other files in the list.

Each is identified by an icon as well as the file name. In Details view, the file type and date and time modified also appear. As you work with Explorer, you'll learn to recognize the icons for different types of files.

Subfolder

Sometimes folders within other folders are called subfolders.

File extension

Three-character code that identifies the type of file. **.exe** identifies an application or program file. **.dll** identifies another type of program file. **.doc** indicates a Microsoft Word document.

Display File Extensions

<table>
<tr><th>

Windows 98

</th><th>

Windows 95

</th></tr>
<tr><td>

1. Click **V**iew ....**Alt**+**V**

2. Click **Folder O**ptions ....**O**

3. Click the **View** tab if it is not already selected.

   The Folder Options dialog box appears, as shown in the illustration that follows.

4. Deselect (uncheck) the option **Hide file extensions for known file types**.

   "Known" means that Windows can identify the application that uses the file type.

5. Click **OK** ....**Enter**

   The file extensions now appear with the file names in the right pane.

</td><td>

1. Click **V**iew ....**Alt**+**V**

2. Click **O**ptions ....**O**

3. Click the **View** tab if it is not already selected.

   The Options dialog box appears, as shown in the illustration that follows.

4. Deselect (uncheck) the option **Hide MS-DOS file extensions for file types that are registered** ....**E**

   "Registered" means that Windows can identify the application that uses the file type.

5. Click **OK** ....**Enter**

   The file extensions now appear with the file names in the right pane.

</td></tr>
</table>

Windows 98 Folder Options Dialog Box

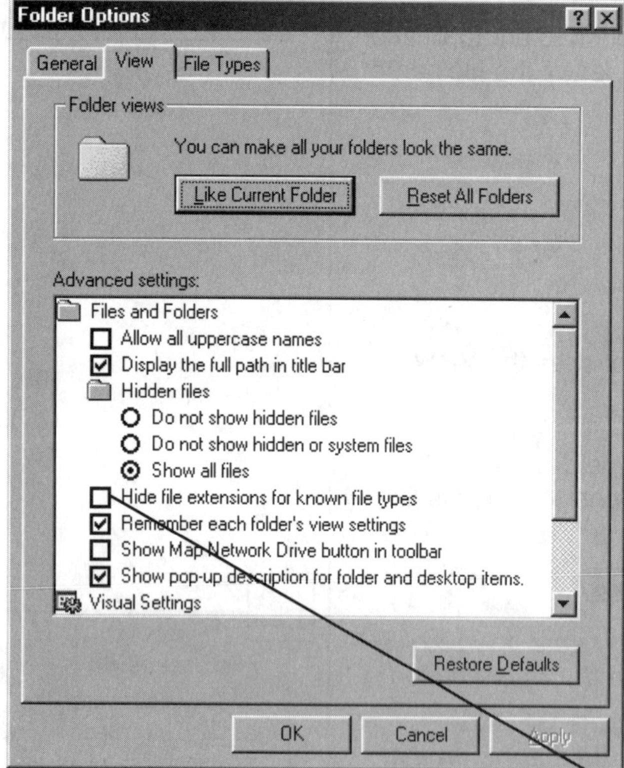

Windows 95 Options Dialog Box

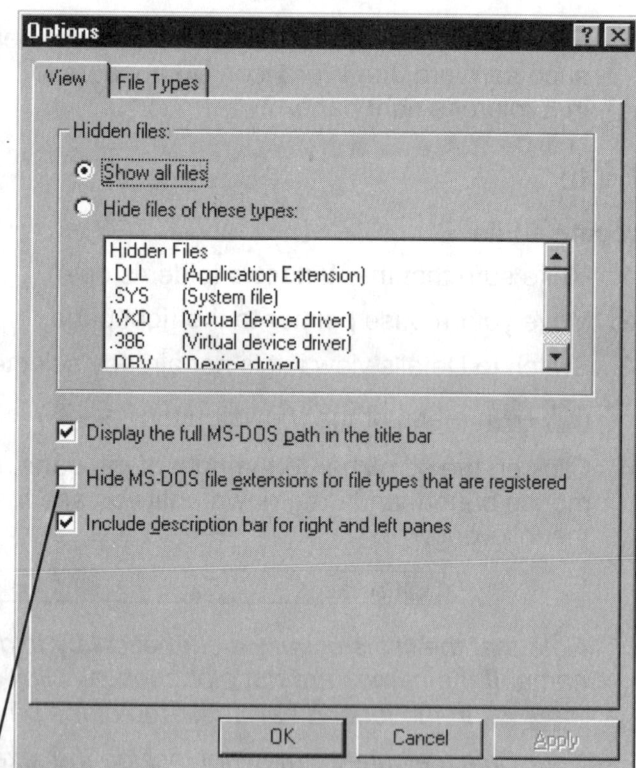

Deselect this option to show file extensions.

> *In this exercise, you will move around in Explorer to find out more about what your computer contains. You will also adjust pane and column widths in Explorer and start two programs from Explorer.*

EXERCISE DIRECTIONS

Explore Folders

1. Start Windows Explorer (if it is not already open) either from the Start menu or from My Computer.

2. Maximize the Explorer window if necessary.

3. Click View, Details to display the information in Details view.

4. Scroll down in the left pane until you find the Program Files folder.

5. Double-click the Program Files folder.

   The contents of Program Files are displayed in the right pane, as shown in Illustration A.

   This folder contains a great many other folders. Most of the folders store application programs.

Illustration A. Contents of Program Files Folder

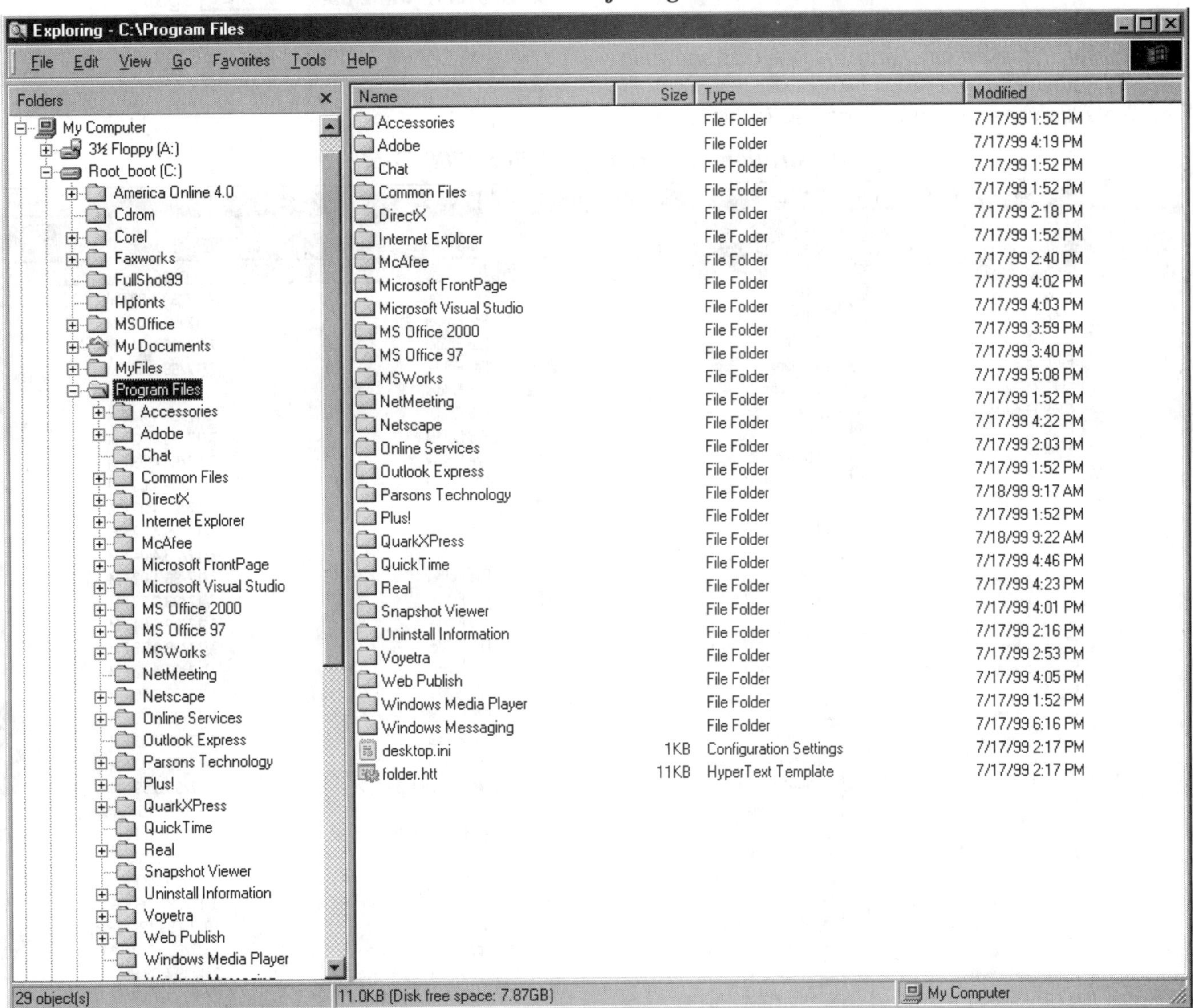

Locate Microsoft Office Folder

1. Look through the list of folders in the right pane, and double-click the **Microsoft Office** folder or the name of the folder where your version of Microsoft Office is installed.

   In the Illustration A, no Microsoft Office folder appears because the application was installed in the MS Office 2000 to prevent confusing it with other versions of Microsoft Office installed on the computer. Note the folder MS Office 97 in the illustration.

   If you are using Microsoft Office 95, your version may be installed in a folder called MSOffice on the C: drive rather than in Program Files.

   When you double-click, the Microsoft Office folder opens and its contents appear in the right pane.

2. Double-click the **Office** folder in the right pane.

   Its icon in the left pane appears open, as shown in Illustration B.

   Note the variety of folders and files in this folder.

3. Return to the left pane and locate the **Accessories** folder. Expand the Program Files folder if it is collapsed.

4. Double-click the **Accessories** folder to open it.
   The contents are displayed in the right pane.

5. Move to the right pane.

6. Click the Type button [Type] in the legend bar to sort the folders and files alphabetically by type.
   The list is rearranged alphabetically by type of object. File folders normally appear first followed by files.

7. Click the Name button [Name] in the legend bar to sort the objects by name.
   What order are the objects in now?

8. Click the Name button [Name] again.
   What order are the objects in now?

Illustration B. Microsoft Office 2000 Folder

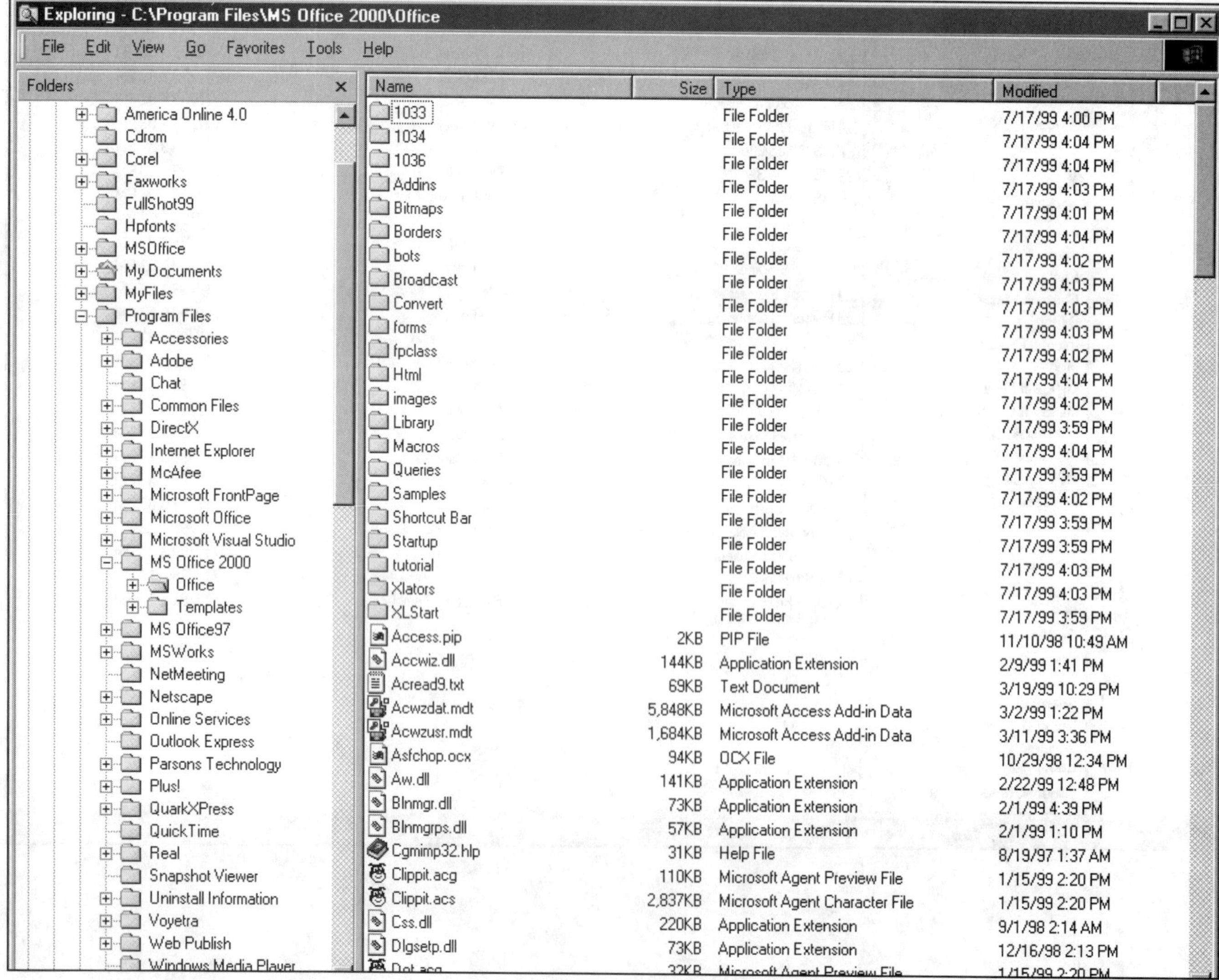

Adjust Pane and Column Widths

If information you want to see is hidden because a pane or a column is too narrow, you can adjust pane and column widths.

1. Move your mouse pointer to the thin gray bar that separates the two panes of the Explorer Window.

   The pointer becomes a two-headed arrow ↔, as shown in Illustration C.

2. With the mouse pointer in the arrow shape, click and drag the bar to the left or the right to enlarge or shrink the left pane.

3. Now move your mouse pointer to the line that divides the Name and Size buttons in the legend bar in the right pane.

A two-headed arrow with a vertical bar ✛ appears, as shown in Illustration D.

4. Click and drag the dividing line right to expand or left to shrink the width of the column.

5. Double-click the dividing line between the column names to adjust the width automatically to the longest entry in the column.

   This way you can adjust the size of the panes and columns so you can see the information that was hidden.

6. Leave Windows Explorer open.

Illustration C. Drag Pane Separator

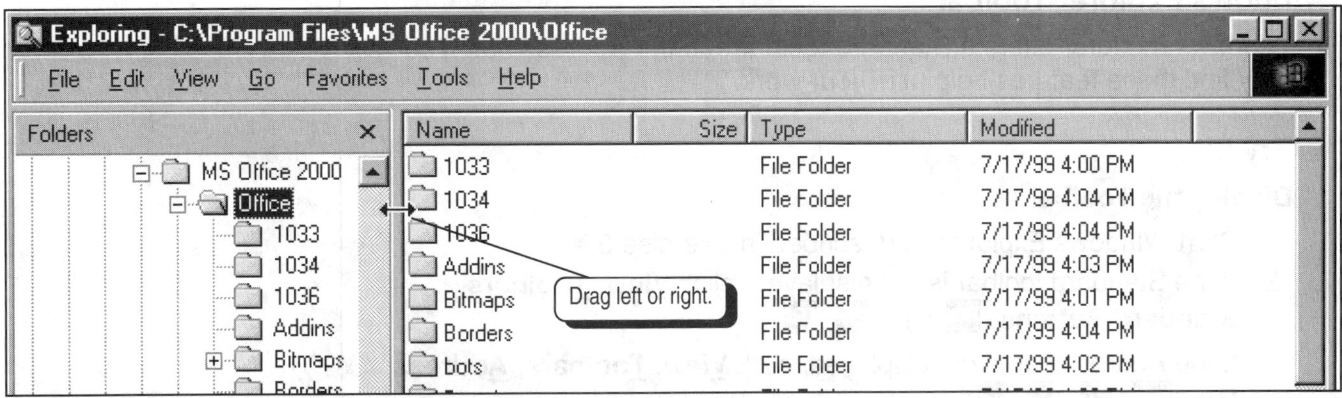

Illustration D. Adjust Details Column Widths

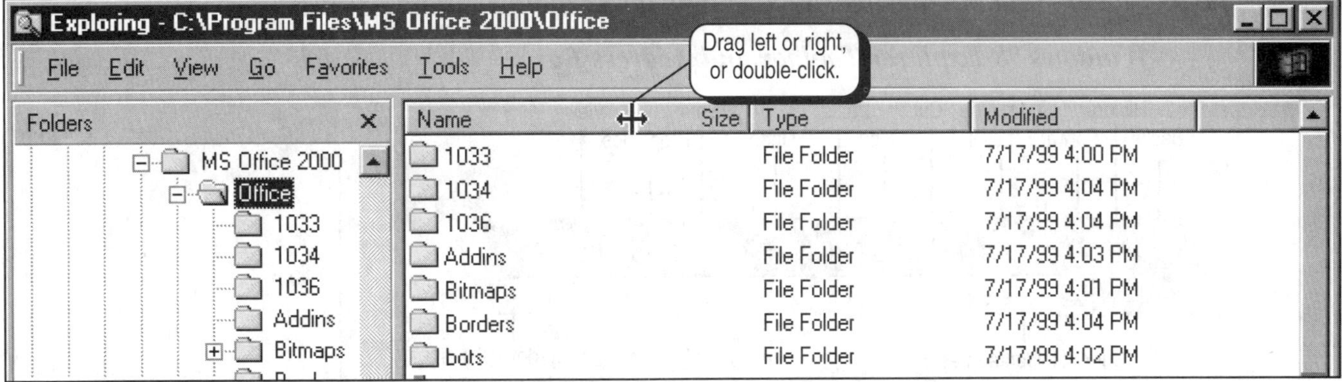

Start a Program

1. In the **Microsoft Office\Office** folder, locate the **Excel.exe** entry Excel.exe

2. Double-click the file name.

   Excel starts and displays a blank spreadsheet.

   You can start programs from Windows Explorer in this way at any time. Locate the application's .exe file and double-click it or select it and press Enter.

3. Close Excel by clicking on the Close button X on the title bar.

4. In the left pane of Windows Explorer, locate the **Accessories** folder and open it.

   Its contents appear in the right pane.

5. Locate the **Wordpad.exe** entry and double-click it to start WordPad.

   WordPad starts and displays a blank document.

6. Close WordPad by clicking on the Close button X on the title bar.

7. Close Windows Explorer.

Manage Files with Windows Explorer
■ Windows Explorer Toolbar ■ Use Windows Explorer ■ Create and Name a Folder
■ Refresh the Explorer Window ■ Create a Shortcut
■ Copy or Move Objects Using Menus or the Toolbar ■ Copy or Move Objects by Dragging
■ Rename an Object ■ Delete an Object from the Desktop
■ Delete Objects using Windows Explorer

NOTES

Windows Explorer Toolbar

■ Windows Explorer offers a Standard toolbar and the Address bar. You may find these features helpful in your work.

🖥 Try It!

Display the Toolbar

1. Start Windows Explorer as described in Exercise 5.
2. If the Standard toolbar is not displayed, click **View**, **Toolbars**, **Standard Buttons** (Alt+V, T, S).
3. If the Address bar is not displayed, click **View**, **Toolbars**, **Address Bar** (Alt+V, T, A).

   The toolbar and Address bar, illustrated below, appear underneath the menu bar. Your buttons may have names under them.

Windows 98 Explorer Toolbar and Address Bar

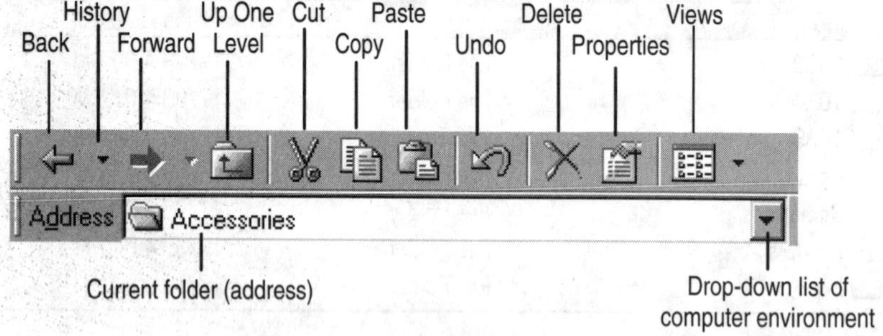

Windows 95 Explorer Toolbar

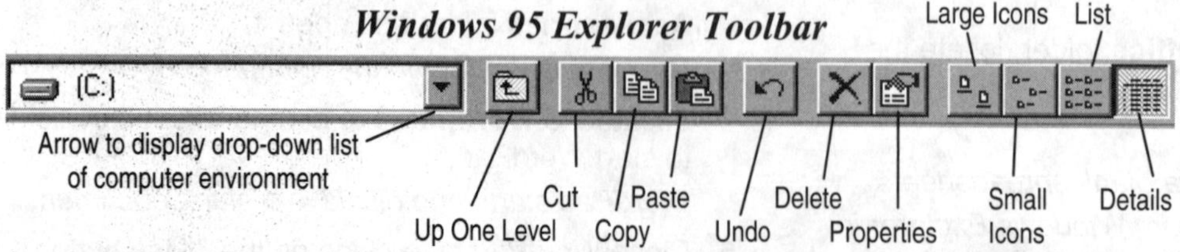

■ The elements of the toolbar and Address bar are described in the following table.

Button	Windows 98	Windows 95	Description
Back, History, Forward		(none)	Click the Back button to return to a previous location. Click the Forward button to revisit a location after you've used the Back button. Both the Back and Forward buttons have History drop-down lists to let you choose a specific location that you've already visited.
Up One Level			Available on windows that display folder contents; lets you move up one level in the folder organization.
Cut			Removes a selected object and places it on the Clipboard, a special area of Windows memory. You can then paste the object into another place. This button is used throughout Windows and its menu equivalent and keyboard shortcut are always the same. **Menu equivalent = Edit, Cut (Alt+E, T)** **Keyboard shortcut = Ctrl+X**
Copy			Places a copy of a selected object on the Clipboard. You can then paste the copy into another place. **Menu equivalent = Edit, Copy (Alt+E, C)** **Keyboard shortcut = Ctrl+C**
Paste			Pastes the contents of the Clipboard into the selected area. **Menu equivalent = Edit, Paste (Alt+E, P)** **Keyboard shortcut = Ctrl+V**
Undo			Reverses the most recent action. You can use this button to correct errors and to reverse actions that you did not want to perform. **Menu equivalent = Edit, Undo (Alt+E, U)** **Keyboard shortcut = Ctrl+Z**
Delete			Sends the object currently selected to the Recycle Bin unless the object is on a removable disk.
Properties			Displays the properties box for the selected object. **Menu equivalent = File, Properties (Alt+F, R)** **Keyboard shortcut = Right-click the object, select Properties from the shortcut menu.**
Views		**Large icons** **Small icons** **List** **Details**	The Views button works the same in My Computer. They change the appearance of objects in the right pane. **Menu equivalent = View, as Web Page (Alt+V, W)** (Windows 98 only) **Menu equivalent = View, Large Icons (Alt+V, G)** **Menu equivalent = View, Small Icons (Alt+V, M)** **Menu equivalent = View, List (Alt+V, L)** **Menu equivalent = View, Details (Alt+V, D)**
Address	**Address bar**	**Address drop-down list**	Shows the name of the object currently open. Click the drop-down list arrow at the end of the address bar to display a list of the components of your computer, just as in a My Computer list. You can use this list to change to other drives and folders in Windows Explorer.

Use Windows Explorer

■ Through Explorer, you can perform a number of file and desktop
management tasks. In this section, you will learn to:
  • Create and name a folder
  • Refresh the Explorer window
  • Create a shortcut
  • Copy or move objects using menus or the toolbar
  • Copy or move objects by dragging
  • Rename an object
  • Delete an object from the desktop
  • Delete objects using Windows Explorer

Create and Name a Folder

■ To create a folder, you select the folder into which you want to place the
new folder, then use the menu to create the folder.

🖥 Try It!

Create a New Folder at the Root Level of Drive C:

1. With Windows Explorer displayed, open drive C: by clicking on its
   icon.

2. Click **File**, **New**, **Folder** (Alt+N, F).

   The File New menu appears, as shown in the following illustration.

Explorer File New Menu

   *Windows creates the folder and places it at the bottom of the list of
   folders and files in the right pane, as shown in the illustration below.*

New Folder in Explorer

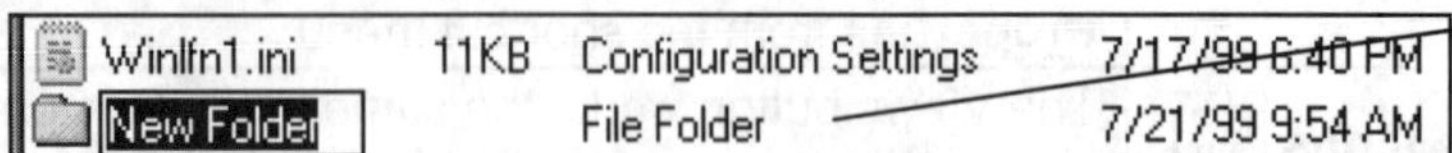

New Folder appears at the
bottom of the list.

   Note that the name is surrounded by a rectangular box New Folder *.
   This box indicates that the object name can be edited. You are now
   ready to give the New Folder a name.*

3. Type *My 1st Folder* and press the Enter key.

   *Because the text in the box was highlighted, what you type replaces
   the previous entry. You now have a new folder on drive C: called My
   1st Folder.*

Refresh the Explorer Window

■ Note that the folder is still listed in the right pane after all the file names.
You can display it alphabetically in the list of folders.

🖥 Try It!

- Click **<u>V</u>iew**, **<u>R</u>efresh** (Alt+V, R).

  My 1st Folder is now listed among the folders in the correct alphabetical position. You may need to scroll up to find it.

- Refreshing the Explorer window is necessary from time to time when you have been processing a lot of files and folders. Explorer reads the disk once when you open it, but may not retrieve information from the disk again unless the changes have been made through Explorer.

  For example, suppose you have Explorer open, then start Microsoft Excel and create a new spreadsheet. If you return to Explorer, you may not see the new spreadsheet in the right pane of the folder where you saved it until you refresh the display.

Create a Shortcut

- A shortcut is an icon that lets you open an application, folder, or file without going through the Start menu, My Computer, or Windows Explorer. You can drag a shortcut from where it is created and place it on the desktop or in another folder.

- Shortcuts are identified by a curving arrow  that appears as part of the object's icon. For example, a shortcut to PowerPoint on the desktop might look like the one at right.

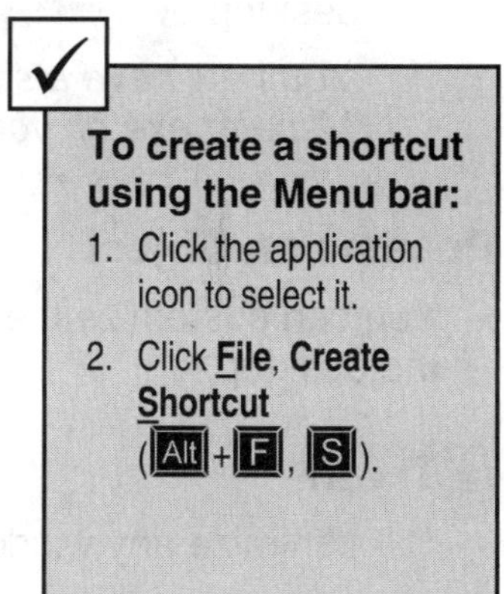

🖥 Try It!

1. Locate and open the **Accessories** folder. It is in the Program Files folder on drive C:.

2. Locate the **WordPad** application icon ▨ Wordpad.exe in the right pane.

3. Right-click on the icon to display a shortcut menu.

4. Click **Create <u>S</u>hortcut** (S) on the menu.

   Windows creates the shortcut and places it at the bottom of the list in the right pane: ▨ Shortcut to Wordpad.exe .

   You can create a shortcut to any object displayed in the Explorer window in this way.

To create a shortcut using the Menu bar:

1. Click the application icon to select it.

2. Click **<u>F</u>ile**, **Create Shortcut** (Alt+F, S).

Copy or Move Objects Using Menus or the Toolbar

- To create a shortcut in the same location as the original file is probably not very useful. You may wish, therefore, to copy or move the shortcut to a different location.

🖥 Try It!

- In the steps that follow, you will copy the WordPad shortcut to the desktop.

  1. Locate the shortcut to WordPad ▨ Shortcut to Wordpad.exe .

  2. Right-click on it to display a shortcut menu, and click **<u>C</u>opy** (C).

     OR

Click to select the shortcut, and click the Copy button 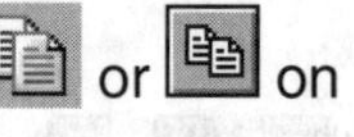 or on the toolbar.

Copy leaves the shortcut in its original location and places a copy of it on the Clipboard.

3. **Windows 98:** Click the Show Desktop button on the taskbar.

   Windows 95: Click the Minimize button to minimize Explorer.

   The desktop is displayed.

4. Press Ctrl+V to paste the shortcut on the desktop.

   The Shortcut to WordPad appears on the desktop, as shown at the right.

Shortcut to Wordpad.exe on Desktop

Copy or Move Objects by Dragging

■ You can drag the object from the Windows Explorer window to the desktop rather than use the menu options or the toolbar.

Try It!

1. Move the mouse pointer to the Windows taskbar and click on Exploring.

2. If the window is maximized, click the Restore button so that a part of the desktop appears behind the Explorer window.

3. Locate the **Mspaint.exe** file in the Accessories folder.

4. Create a shortcut to the file.

5. Use Ctrl+left mouse button and drag a copy of the shortcut to the desktop.

   You now have a shortcut to Wordpad.exe and a shortcut to Mspaint.exe on your desktop.

Rename an Object

■ You can customize the names of objects in the Explorer window and on the desktop.

Try It!

1. Minimize any windows that are displayed to reveal the desktop.

2. Locate the **Shortcut to Wordpad.exe** icon and click on it once to select it.

3. Press the F2 key.

   This action surrounds the shortcut name with a box, indicating that it is ready for editing, as shown at the right.

4. To replace the text, just begin typing.

   OR

   To edit the text, press the left or right arrow key to position the insertion point where you want to begin editing.

5. Make the entry read *WordPad*.

6. When you finish editing or typing, press the Enter key.

   The icon remains selected.

7. Click on any blank area of the screen to deselect the icon.

Delete an Object from the Desktop

■ Although it is easy to place shortcuts on the desktop, it is a good idea to copy to the desktop only those objects that you use frequently. It is unlikely that you will use WordPad regularly. You can safely remove its shortcut from the desktop.

🖳 Try It!

1. Click and drag the WordPad shortcut across the desktop to the Recycle Bin icon 🗑 Recycled .

2. When the Recycle Bin icon 🗑 Recycled is selected, release the mouse button.

   Windows displays a message like the following:

Confirm File Delete Message

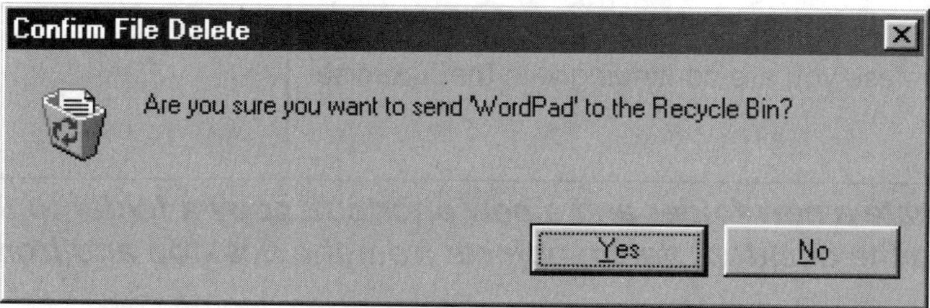

3. Click the **Yes** button [Yes] (Enter or Alt+Y) to confirm that you want to delete the shortcut.

4. Double-click the Recycle Bin icon 🗑 Recycled to open the Recycle Bin.

5. Locate the shortcut you just deleted. It will be listed as WordPad with a type of Shortcut.

6. Click the name and drag it to the desktop.
   The shortcut is restored.

7. Close the Recycle Bin.

8. Select the WordPad shortcut again.

9. Press the Del key.

   Windows displays the Confirm File Delete mesage.

10. Click the **Yes** button [Yes] (Enter or Alt+Y).

    You can use either method to remove objects from the desktop. And you can restore objects to the desktop by dragging them from the Recycle Bin list to the desktop.

Delete Objects using Windows Explorer

🖳 Try It!

1. Select the **Shortcut to Mspaint** in the Accessories folder.

2. Press the Delete button ✖ on the toolbar or press the Del key.

3. Answer **Yes** to the Confirm File Delete message.

4. Display the desktop.

   - ♦ **Windows 98:** Click the Show Desktop button [image].
   - ♦ **Windows 95:** Click the Explorer Minimize button [_].

5. Open the Recycle Bin (double-click the icon).

6. Verify that the **Shortcut to Mspaint** is in the Recycle Bin.

   Objects deleted in this way are sent to the Recycle Bin. Note that objects deleted from removable media, such as diskettes, are not sent to the Recycle Bin. Once deleted, they cannot be restored from the Recycle Bin.

7. Locate **My 1st Folder** that you created in an earlier Try It!. (It is located in the root folder of Drive C:.)

8. Click the folder name.

9. Click the [X] button or press the [Del] key.

10. Answer **Yes** to the Confirm File Delete message.

11. Close Windows Explorer unless you are continuing with the Exercise Directions.

In this exercise, you will create a new folder and a new shortcut, copy a folder to the desktop, move a shortcut to the desktop, delete objects from the desktop and from the Explorer window.

EXERCISE DIRECTIONS

Create a Folder

1. Open Windows Explorer.
2. Locate and open the Program Files folder in the left pane.
3. Locate and open the Accessories folder in the left pane.
4. Click File, New, Folder.
   The New Folder icon appears at the bottom of the list.
5. Name the folder *My 2nd Folder*.

Copy a Folder

1. Click the Restore button [image] on Windows Explorer, if necessary, to reveal a portion of the desktop.
2. Select **My 2nd Folder**.
3. Hold down the [Ctrl] key and click and drag the folder to the desktop.
   My 2nd Folder is copied to the desktop.
4. Double-click **My 2nd Folder** on the desktop.
   The folder window opens. It is empty because you have placed no files in it.
5. Close the **My 2nd Folder** window.

Rename a Folder

1. In the right pane of Windows Explorer, select **My 2nd Folder**.
2. Press the [F2] key, or right-click the name and select Rename.
   The name is displayed in edit mode.
3. Delete the word *2nd* to make the name read **My Folder**.
4. Press the Enter key.

Delete a Folder

1. Locate **My 2nd Folder** on the desktop.
2. Drag it to the Recycle Bin to delete it.
3. Answer Yes to the Confirm Folder Delete message.
4. Locate and select **My Folder** in the Accessories folder.
5. Click the Delete button [X] or press the [Del] key.
6. Answer Yes to the Confirm Folder Delete message.

Create a Shortcut

1. Restore the Explorer window, if necessary, to reveal a portion of the desktop.

2. In Explorer, open the Windows folder.

3. Click the Type button `Type` in the legend bar at the top of the right pane to sort the files by file type.

4. Locate the file **Explorer.exe**.

5. Click and drag the file name to the desktop.
   Windows creates a shortcut for Windows Explorer on the desktop.
   Note that this is another way to create a shortcut for .exe files. If you drag a document to the desktop in this way, you create a copy of the document on the desktop.

6. Minimize Windows Explorer.

7. Double-click the **Shortcut to Explorer.exe**.
   Another Windows Explorer window opens. The original window is still open and minimized.

8. Close the visible Windows Explorer window.

Rename a Shortcut

1. Switch to the desktop if you are not already there.

2. Select the **Shortcut to Explorer** if necessary.

3. Press the `F2` key and edit the name to read *Windows Explorer*.

4. Press the Enter key after typing the new name.

Move a Shortcut

1. Restore Windows Explorer from the Windows taskbar and open the Windows folder, if it is not open.

2. Locate the **Notepad.exe** file.

3. Right-click the file name.

4. Select Create Shortcut from the shortcut menu.

5. With the shortcut selected, click the Cut button on the toolbar.
   The shortcut remains displayed with its icon dimmed, but it is on the Clipboard.

6. Minimize Windows Explorer.
   Explorer becomes a button on the Windows taskbar.

7. Click on any blank area of the desktop.

8. Press Ctrl+V to paste the shortcut.
   The Shortcut to Notepad.exe joins the icons on the desktop.

Delete a Shortcut

1. On the desktop, select the **Shortcut to Notepad**.

2. Press the Delete key.

3. Answer Yes to the Confirm File Delete message.

4. On the desktop, select the Windows Explorer shortcut.

5. Press the Delete key.

6. Answer Yes to the Confirm File Delete message.

7. Close all open windows.

Exercise 7

Work with Files and Folders in Windows Explorer
■ Select Multiple Objects ■ Copy Folders/Files from One Folder to Another
■ Copy Folders/Files from One Drive to Another ■ Use the Start Menu

NOTES

Select Multiple Objects

■ In windows that display lists, including many application Open dialog
boxes, you can select more than one object to be processed (copied,
moved, deleted, opened) at the same time.

Windows 98

To select an object, point
to the object and let the
mouse pointer rest on the
object until the object is
selected.

Try It!

1. Open Windows Explorer and maximize it.
2. Open the C: drive if it is not already open.
3. In the right pane, select the first object displayed in the list.
4. Slide your mouse down about 10 objects.
5. Press the **Shift** key and select the object.

   *All the objects from the first through the last object you clicked are
   selected.*

6. Click anywhere outside the list to deselect the objects.

Try It!

1. Select the second object in the list.
2. Hold down the **Ctrl** key and select the sixth object in the list.
3. Hold down the **Ctrl** key and select the ninth and tenth objects in the
   list.
4. Click anywhere outside the list to deselect the objects.

Copy Folders/Files from One Folder to Another

■ You may want to copy or move files to improve the organization of your
permanent storage. This section explains how to copy or move folders
and files from one folder to another.

Try It!

Use the Toolbar

1. In the right pane, open the **Program Files** folder.
2. Open the **Accessories** folder.
3. Create a shortcut to Mspaint as described in Exercise 6.
4. Click on the root of Drive C:.
5. Create a new folder called **My 3rd Folder**.

6. **Windows 98:** Use the Back button ⬅ to return to the **Accessories** folder.

   Windows 95: Locate and open the **Accessories** folder.

7. Locate and select the **Shortcut to Mspaint**.

8. Click the Copy button, or right-click on the shortcut and click **Copy**.

9. **Windows 98:** Use the Forward button ➡ to return to the root of Drive C:.

   Windows 95: Locate and open the C: drive.

10. Locate **My 3rd Folder** and open it.

11. Click the Paste button, or right-click **My 3rd Folder** and click **Paste**.

    The shortcut appears in the right pane. It has been copied to My 3rd Folder.

Try It!

Drag the Object

1. Open the **Program Files** folder.

2. Open the **Accessories** folder.

3. Click on the **Shortcut to WordPad.exe**.

   If you need to create the shortcut, do so as described in Exercise 6.

4. In the left pane of Windows Explorer, display **My 3rd Folder** (the destination). Do NOT open the folder. You should not select it in any way. Just display it in the pane.

   You may need to shift between the two panes more than once to display the object to be copied in the right pane and the desired destination folder in the left pane.

5. Click on the shortcut in the right pane.

6. Hold down the **Ctrl** key and the left mouse button and drag the icon to the left pane. (If you do not hold down the **Ctrl** key, the object will be moved rather than copied.)

7. Drag the shortcut until **My 3rd Folder** is highlighted, as in the illustration that follows, and then release the mouse button.

Dragging to Copy an Object

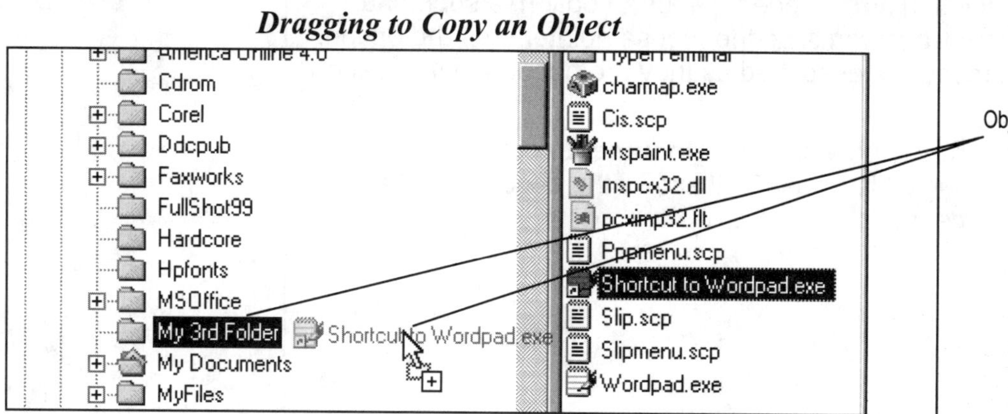

Object being dragged and destination folder highlighted

8. Open **My 3rd Folder** to see that the shortcut was copied. (Click the **My 3rd Folder** icon.)

9. Close Windows Explorer.

Copy Folders/Files from One Drive to Another

- The procedures for copying a folder or file from one drive (or disk) to another are the same as for copying from one folder to another, except that rather than a destination folder on the current drive, you select a different destination drive and folder.

- Suppose you want to copy a file from the hard drive to a diskette. You select the file in the right pane of Windows Explorer. You can then use the Copy button  or drag it to the destination drive.

- When the object you copy is a folder, the entire contents of the folder are copied. If the copy takes more than a few seconds, Windows displays a progress message box, indicating that the operation is taking place.

Copy/Move Progress Message Box

Use the Start Menu

- So far in this lesson, the focus has been on understanding and using the Windows environment through My Computer and Windows Explorer. These two tools are very important in managing your computer and files.

- Your primary use of Windows will be as a means of starting other applications. Windows, after all, is the operating system. Your real work will be done using Word, Excel, and other applications. To start applications, you begin with the Start button ![Start], which opens the Start menu. A sample Start menu is shown in the illustration on the following page.

- Note that if a right pointing arrow appears after an option, a submenu appears automatically when you slide the mouse pointer over the option. The options on the menu are described as they are needed in the rest of this book.

- When you move the mouse pointer to the **Documents** option, a list similar to the one on page 112 appears. It shows the documents that have been opened recently.

Start Menu

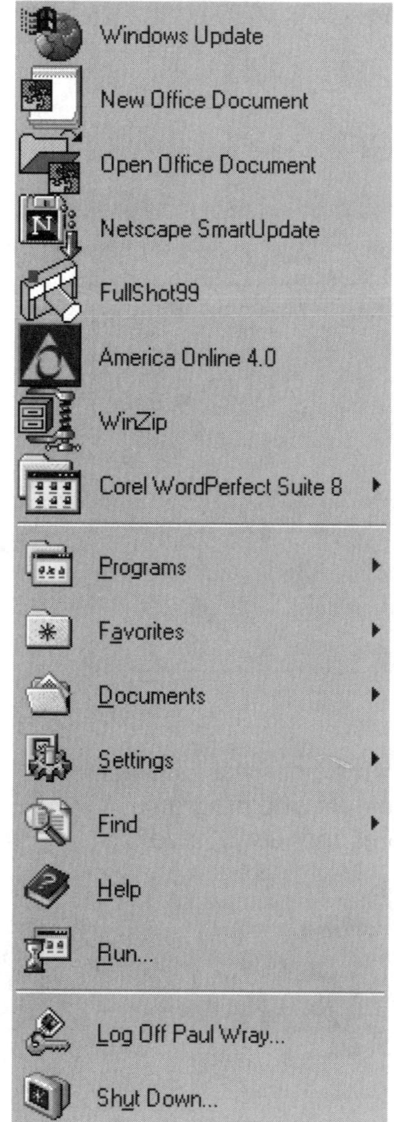

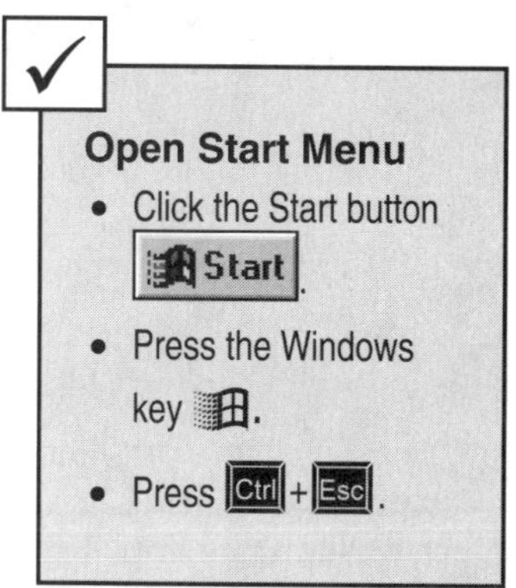

Try It!

1. Click the Start button **Start**.

2. Click **Documents** (**D**).

3. Click a file that you created. If you do not see one that you created, click a document that you recognize.
   The application for the document starts and the document opens.

4. Click on the Close button **X** of the application to exit the application.

Start Menu, Documents Option

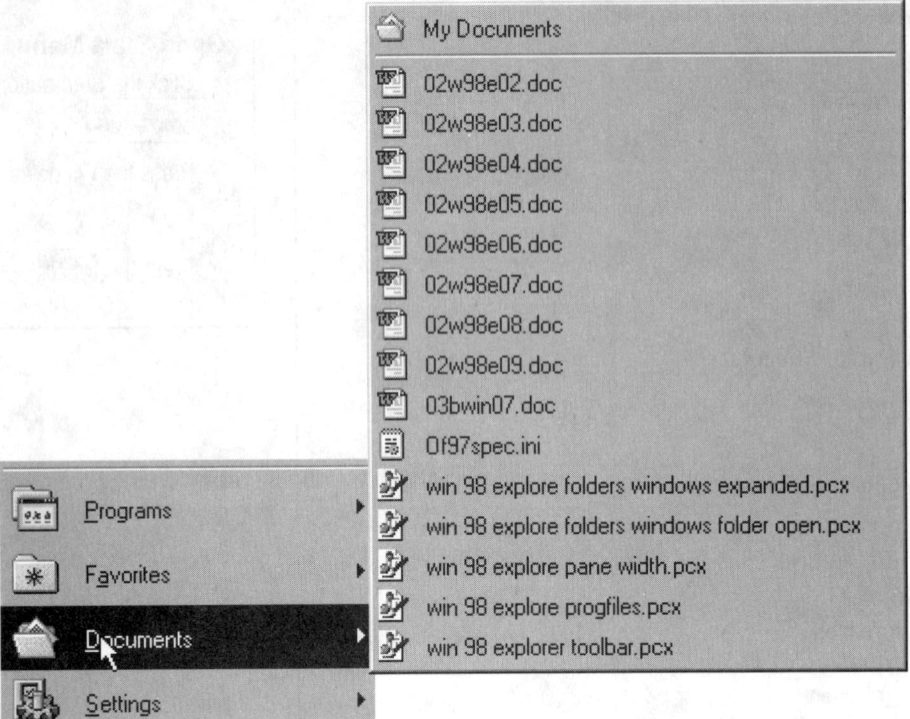

- When you move the mouse pointer to the **Programs** option, a list similar to the following appears. It shows the program folders and program names available on your computer. Your Programs menu will have different choices from those illustrated.

Start Menu, Programs Option (Portion)

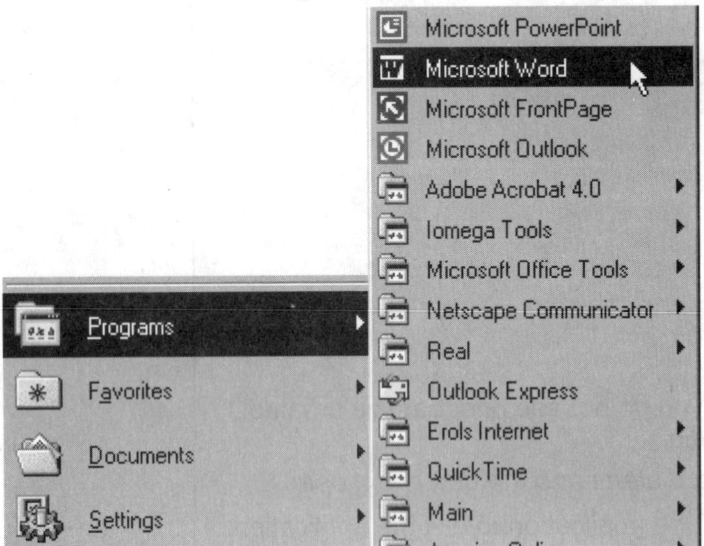

⌨ Try It!

1. Click the Start button ⊞ Start.

2. Click **Programs**.

3. Slide your mouse to your word processing program, and click to start it.

4. Click on the Close button ⊠ of the application to close the document and exit the application.

> *In this exercise, select and delete multiple objects in Windows Explorer. You will also create two shortcuts, select and copy them, and delete a folder.*

EXERCISE DIRECTIONS

Select and Delete Multiple Objects

1. Return to the left pane and select the C: drive. You may need to scroll to reveal the icon for drive C:.

   The contents of C: appear in the right pane.

2. Locate the folder **My 3rd Folder** in the right pane.

3. Open it to reveal the two shortcuts you copied into the folder in the Try It! activities.

4. Click on the first shortcut.

5. Hold down the **Ctrl** key and click on the second shortcut.

6. Delete the two shortcuts, using either the ✕ button or the **Del** key.

7. Answer Yes to the Confirm File Delete message.

Copy Objects

1. Open the **Program Files** folder.

2. Open the **Accessories** folder.

3. Create a shortcut for WordPad, if necessary

4. Create a shortcut for Mspaint, if necessary.

5. Select the two shortcuts by holding down the **Ctrl** key while clicking on them.

6. Copy the shortcuts to **My 3rd Folder** using the procedure you prefer (Copy button 📋 📋 or **Ctrl** + dragging).

Delete a Folder

1. Restore the Windows Explorer window so that a portion of the desktop is showing.

2. Move the window (click and drag on the title bar) so that the Recycle Bin icon 🗑 Recycled is visible on the desktop.

3. From Windows Explorer, select and drag **My 3rd Folder** to the Recycle Bin.

4. Answer Yes to the Confirm Folder Delete message.

5. Close Windows Explorer.

NEXT LESSON

Lesson 3: Word Processing

Exercise 1: Get Started

- Start the Word Processor and Create a New Document
- About AppleWorks
- About Microsoft Word 98 for Mac OS
- About Microsoft Works
- About Microsoft Word 97 and 2000 for Windows
- About Corel WordPerfect
- Change the Default Font Size
- What is a Paragraph?
- Proofreader's Mark for Paragraph
- Type Text
- Save an Unnamed Document

Exercise 2: Open, Save As, Edit, Save, and Print

- Open a Document
- Save As
- Insert the Date
- Edit Text
- Insert and Overtype Modes
- Undo
- Redo/Revert
- Save
- Print Preview (Word and MS Works Only)
- Print

Exercise 3: Format Paragraphs

- Toolbar and Button Bar Formatting Commands
- Align Paragraphs
- Indent First Line
- Indent Paragraphs Left and Right
- Create Hanging Indent

Exercise 4: Format Text

- Fonts and Font Names
- Change Font
- Change Font Size
- Use Bold, Italic, and Underline
- Proofreader's Marks for Bold, Italic, and Underline
- Change Text Color
- Use Symbols

Exercise 5: Change Words

- Spell Check
- Automatic Spell Checking (Word and Corel WordPerfect)
- Use the Thesaurus
- Find and Replace Text

Exercise 6: Bullets and Numbering; Cut or Copy, and Paste Text

- Introduction to Bullets and Numbering
- Create an Unordered (Bulleted) List
- Create an Ordered List
- Cut, Copy, and Paste Text

Exercise 7: Use Paragraph Spacing and Default Tab Stops

- Control Spacing within Paragraphs
- Control Spacing between Paragraphs
- Use Default Tab Stops

Exercise 8: Work with Multiple Page Documents

- Insert Page Breaks
- Set Margins
- Use Headers and Footers

Exercise 9: Challenge Exercises

Get Started

■ **Start the Word Processor and Create a New Document** ■ **About AppleWorks**
■ **About Microsoft Word 98 for Mac OS** ■ **About Microsoft Works**
■ **About Microsoft Word 97 and 2000 for Windows** ■ **About Corel WordPerfect**
■ **Change the Default Font Size** ■ **What is a Paragraph?**
■ **Proofreader's Mark for Paragraph** ■ **Type Text** ■ **Save an Unnamed Document**

NOTES

Start the Word Processor and Create a New Document

■ When a word processor starts, a new document is ready for you to begin typing. In Windows applications and Word 98, the title bar usually displays *Document1*; in AppleWorks, the title bar displays *untitled (WP)*. The names indicate that the documents have not yet been saved.

■ In each word processor you can open additional new documents. When you create new documents during the same word processor **session**, the number of the document increases; for example, MS Works displays *Unsaved Document2* for the second new document created in a session.

■ The remainder of this exercise is divided into four sections. Locate the section for your word processor and review the information. Then turn to the section *Change the Default Font Size* on page 132 to continue.

- AppleWorks, below
- Microsoft Word 98 for Mac OS, page 119
- Microsoft Works, page 122
- Microsoft Word for Windows, page 126
- Corel WordPerfect, page 129
- Change the Default Font Size, 132

About AppleWorks

**Try It!**

Start AppleWorks and Create New Document

1. Start AppleWorks from **Launcher** by clicking the AppleWorks button shown at the right.

   OR

   Start AppleWorks from the **desktop** by double-clicking the AppleWorks alias illustrated at the right.

   AppleWorks displays the New Document window.

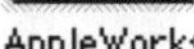

Session

A session begins when you start an application and ends when you exit the application.

AppleWorks New Document Window

New Document
AppleWorks
Word Processing
Drawing
Painting
Spreadsheet
Database
Communications
Create New Document
Use Assistant or Stationery
Create a new word processing document.
Cancel
OK

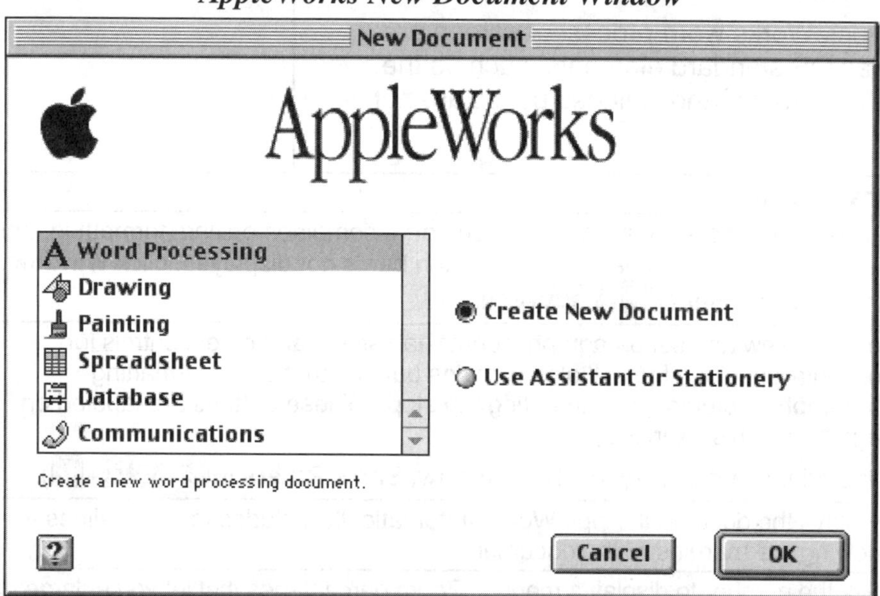

2. In the New Document window, choose **Word Processing**.
3. Select **Create New Document**.
4. Click OK (Return).

   AppleWorks creates a new word processing document. The AppleWorks screen is shown in the following illustration.

AppleWorks Window

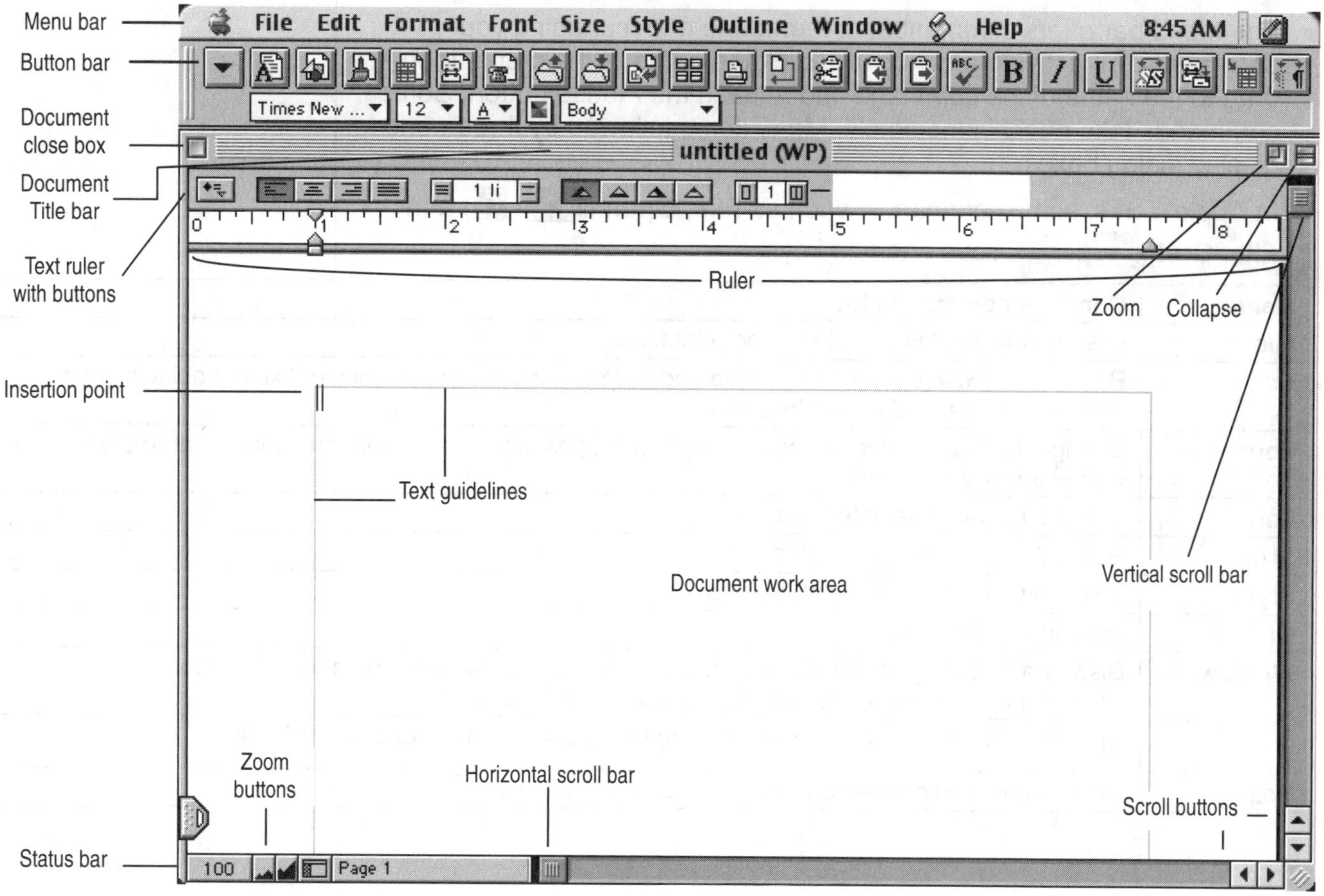
Menu bar
Button bar
Document close box
Document Title bar
Text ruler with buttons
Insertion point
File Edit Format Font Size Style Outline Window Help
8:45 AM
Times New ...
12
Body
untitled (WP)
Ruler
Zoom
Collapse
Text guidelines
Document work area
Vertical scroll bar
Zoom buttons
Horizontal scroll bar
Scroll buttons
Status bar
100
Page 1

AppleWorks Word Processor Window

- Many of the elements of the AppleWorks word processor screen are already familiar to you. The Mac OS standard elements, such as the Apple menu, menu bar, and close, zoom, and collapse boxes are not described in the following table.

Window Item	Description
Button bar	AppleWorks has an application button bar; it combines editing, formatting, and file management commands. If the button bar is not displayed, click **Window, Show Button Bar** (Shift + Command + X).
Text Ruler	Lets you view and set paragraph indents, tab stops, and other controls for horizontal spacing of text. It also contains buttons that aid in formatting paragraphs, columns, and inserting tab stops. These buttons are labeled on page 119 in this exercise. If the ruler is not displayed, click **Window, Show Rulers** (Shift + Command + U).
Document work area with Text Guidelines	Displays the document. AppleWorks automatically includes text guidelines showing the margins of the document.
Zoom buttons [100]	Click the number to display a menu of Zoom percentages that let you enlarge or shrink the size of text and graphics in the window. Click the Zoom-out control to display the window at one-half the current zoom value. Click the Zoom-in control to display the window at twice the current Zoom value.

Menu and Button Bars

AppleWorks Menu Bar

| File | Edit | Format | Font | Size | Style | Outline | Window | ◊ | Help |

- The Menu bar offers commands for formatting and managing your documents. To activate a command, click the name of the menu, then drag to the name of the command and release the mouse button. Some commands take effect immediately. Menu items followed by three periods display dialog boxes.

- In AppleWorks, some commands, such as **File, Open** (Command + O) and **File, Quit** (Command + Q), have shortcut keys.

Menu	Contains commands to:
File	Create, retrieve, lay out, store, and print files.
Edit	Rearrange document contents, undo and redo actions, find and replace text and objects, insert special features, and set preferences.
Format	Change the appearance of documents, paragraphs, and text, and insert special features and work with headers and footers.
Font	Select the font for selected text.
Size	Select the font size for selected text.
Style	Select emphasis style for selected text.
Outline	Work in Outline view.
Window	Display and arrange currently open documents. This menu also contains options for showing/hiding some tools, such as the rulers and button bar.
◊	Open the Scripts folder; AppleWorks scripts are outside the scope of this book.
Help	Get explanations of components, commands, and options.

- The button bar, shown in the following illustration, has buttons for creating, opening, saving, and printing documents. It also has buttons for checking spelling, cutting, copying, pasting, and undoing and redoing typing and commands. Buttons are described as you use them in the exercises in this lesson. Only buttons used in this text are called out in the illustration. You can turn on **Help**, **Show Balloons** and point to a button to learn the names of other buttons.

- If the symbol is gray or dimmed, the button is currently unavailable.

AppleWorks Word Processor Button Bar

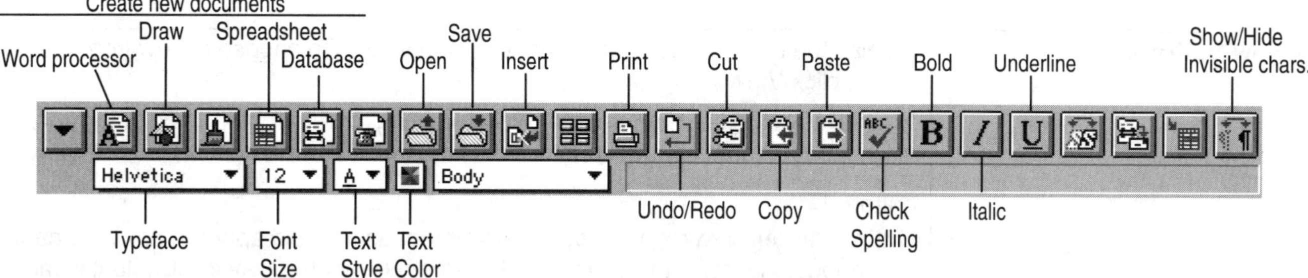

- The Text Ruler also offers buttons to help in formatting documents. If the ruler is not displayed, click **Window, Show Rulers** (Shift+⌘+U).

AppleWorks Word Processor Text Ruler Buttons

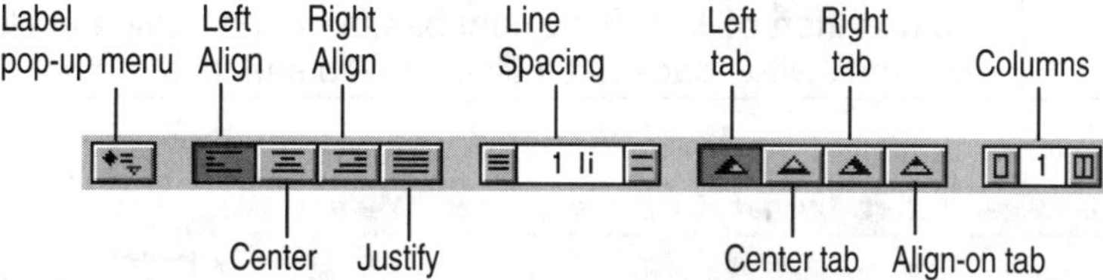

About Microsoft Word 98 for Mac OS

Try It!

Start Word 98 and Create New Document

1. Start Word 98 from **Launcher** by clicking the Word 98 button shown at the right.

   OR

   Start Word 98 from the **desktop** by double-clicking the Word 98 alias illustrated at the right.

   Word 98 creates a new word processing document when it starts. The Word 98 screen is shown in the illustration on the following page.

Launcher Button

Desktop Alias

Word 98 Window

- Many of the elements of the Word 98 window are already familiar to you. The Mac OS standard elements, such as the Apple menu, menu bar, and close, zoom, and collapse boxes are not described in the following table.

Window Item	Description
Toolbars	By default, Word 98 displays two toolbars: **Standard** and **Formatting**. Other toolbars are available if you click **View, Toolbars**.

Window Item	Description
Ruler	Lets you view and set paragraph indents, tab stops, and other controls for horizontal spacing of text. If the ruler is not displayed, click **View, Ruler**.
Selection area	Unmarked area along the left side of the document window. When you move the mouse pointer into this area, it turns into a right-pointing arrow ➤. When you click while pointing with this arrow, you select the line, paragraph, or object to the right.
Document work area window and text boundaries	Displays the document. You can display text guidelines (not shown in the illustration) in Page Layout or Online Layout view; click **Tools**, **Preferences, View tab, Text Boundaries**.
View buttons	Display the document in one of the following views. To choose a view from the menu, click **View**. **Normal View** ▤ is often best for typing, editing, and formatting text quickly. To view the document as it will print, click **File**, **Print Preview** or the Print Preview button. **Online Layout View** ▤ shows the document as it would appear on a Web page. Text appears larger and wraps to fit the window—not the way it will actually print. **Page Layout View** ▤ is used when you want to position graphics on a page, edit headers and footers, and adjust page margins. It is also used for working with page columns and drawing objects. **Outline View** ▤ lets you build an outline using Word's built-in heading styles. You can then build a document based on the outline in Normal or Page Layout view and switch back to Outline view to see its structure.

Word 98 Window

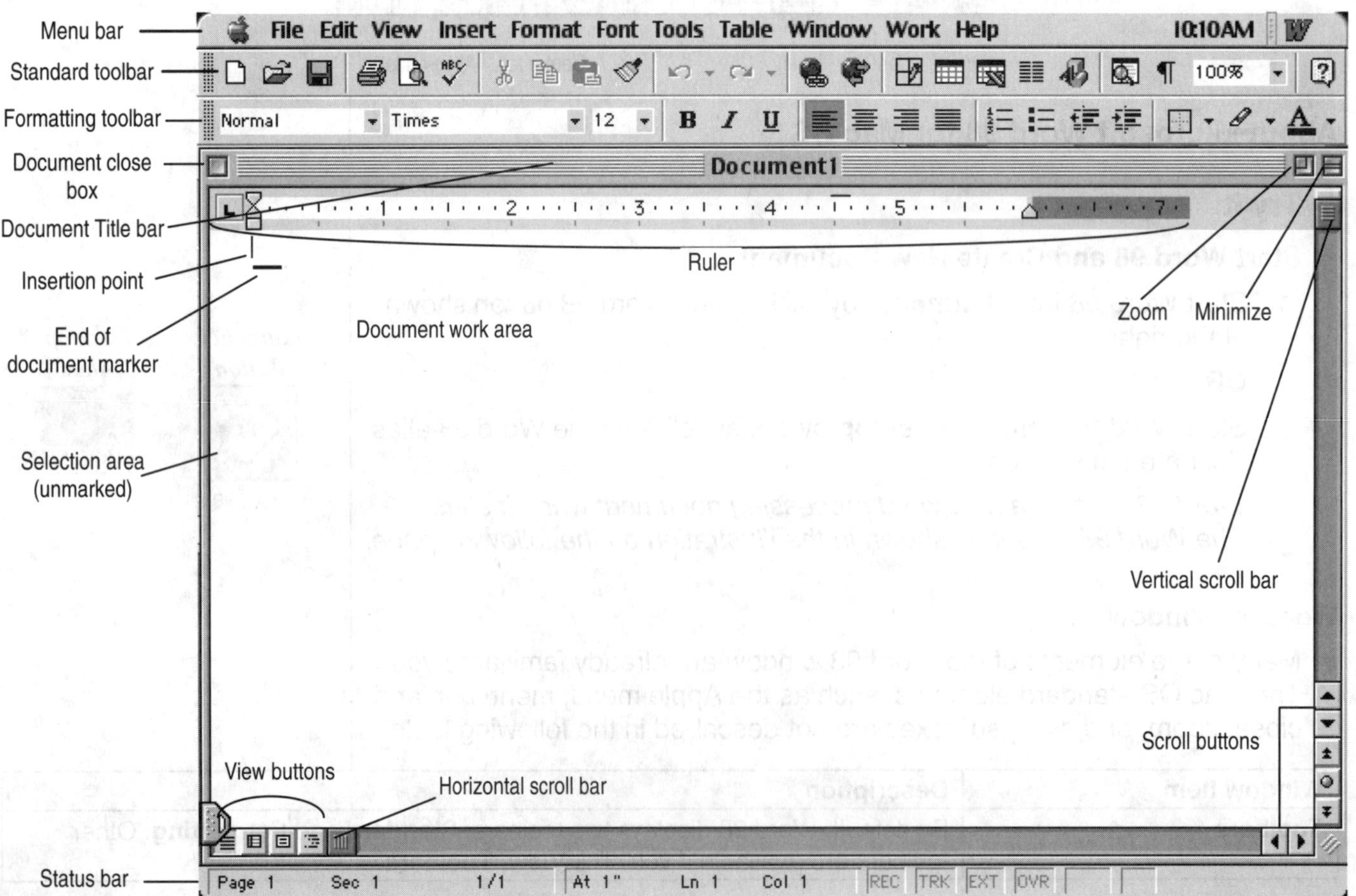

Menu and Toolbars

Word 98 Menu Bar

| 🍎 File Edit View Insert Format Font Tools Table Window Work Help | 10:08 AM W |

- The Menu bar offers commands for formatting and managing your documents. To activate a command, click the name of the menu, then drag to the name of the command and release the mouse button. Some commands take effect immediately. Menu items followed by three periods display dialog boxes.

- In Word 98, some commands, such as **File**, **Open** (⌘+O) and **File**, **Quit** (⌘+Q), have shortcut keys.

Menu	Contains commands to:
File	Create, retrieve, lay out, store, and print files.
Edit	Rearrange document contents, undo and redo actions, and find and replace text and objects.
View	Choose the way in which a document is displayed, and work with headers and footers.
Insert	Insert page breaks, date and time, and other objects, such as graphics and files.
Format	Change the appearance of documents, paragraphs, and text.
Font	Change the font for selected text.
Tools	Check spelling and grammar, perform mail merge, run macros, customize documents, and set preferences.
Table	Create and format tables and sort data.
Window	Display and arrange currently open documents.
Work	Create a list of frequently used documents.
Help	Get explanations of components, commands, and options.

Word 98 Standard and Formatting Toolbars

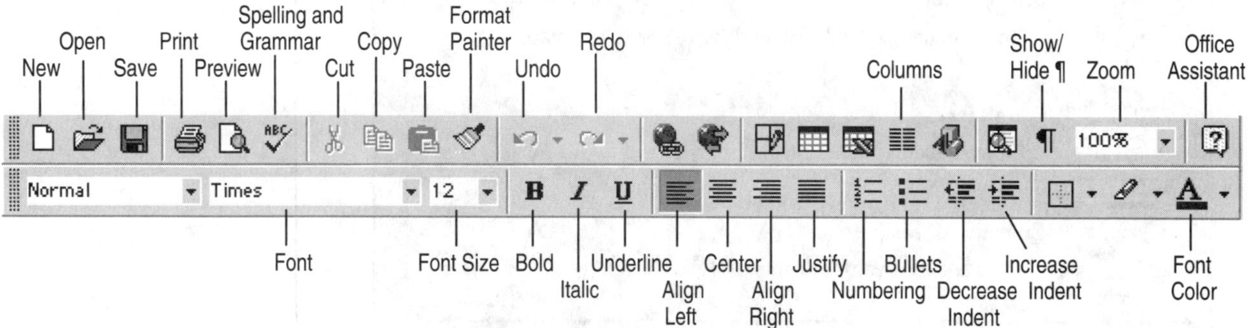

- Word 98's Standard toolbar, the upper toolbar in the previous illustration, has buttons for creating, opening, saving, and printing documents. It also has buttons for checking spelling, cutting, copying, pasting, and undoing and redoing typing and commands.

- The Formatting toolbar, the lower one in the previous illustration, has buttons for changing the font and font size, emphasizing text, aligning and indenting paragraphs, and changing the color of text.

- If the button's symbol is gray or dimmed, the button is currently unavailable.

- Toolbar buttons are described as you use them in the exercises in this lesson. Microsoft Word has several different toolbars, and the buttons may differ from those shown on the previous page. Only buttons used in this text are called out in the illustration. You can point to a button and read its ScreenTip to learn the names of other buttons.

About Microsoft Works

Try It!

Start MS Works and Create New Document

1. Click the Start button 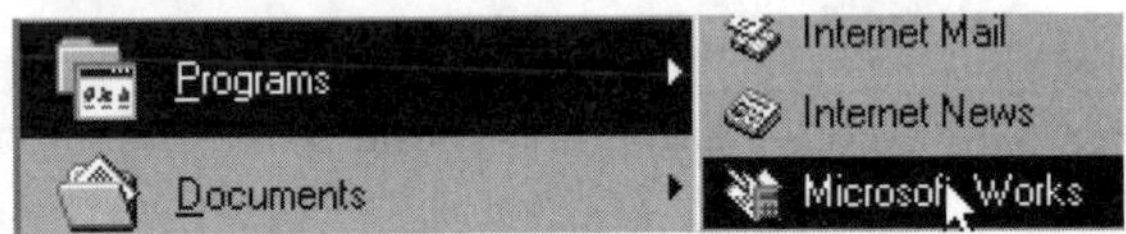, **Programs**.

2. Move to **Microsoft Works** and click, as shown below.

The Works Task Launcher appears.

Works Task Launcher

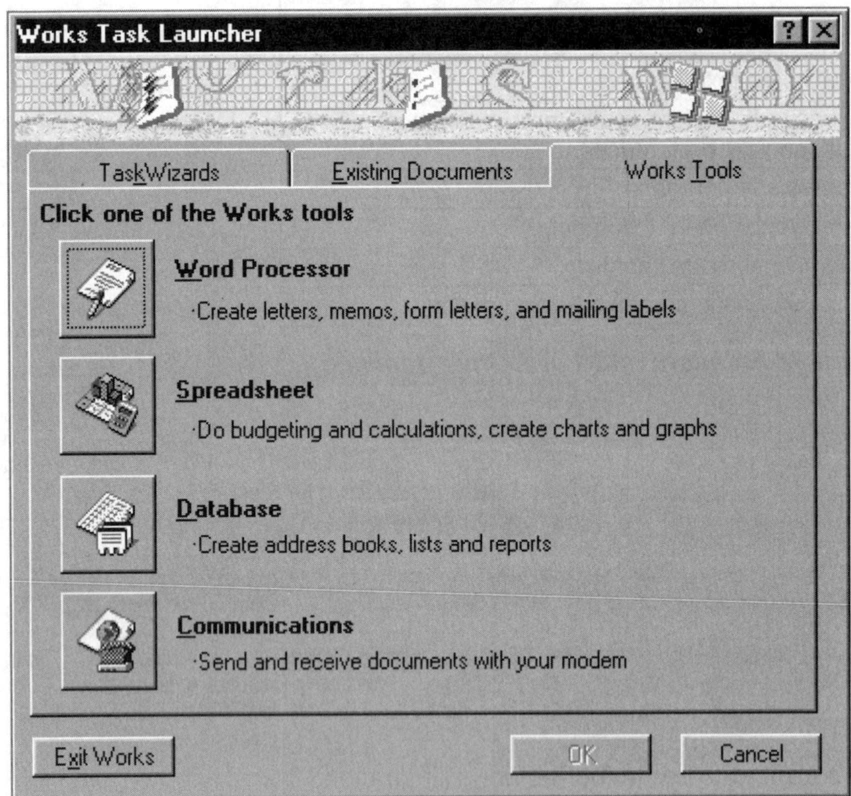

3. Click the **Works Tools** tab (**Alt**+**T**).

4. Click the **Word Processor** button (**Alt**+**W**).

   MS Works starts and creates a new word processing document. The Works window is shown in the following illustration.

MS Works Word Processor Window

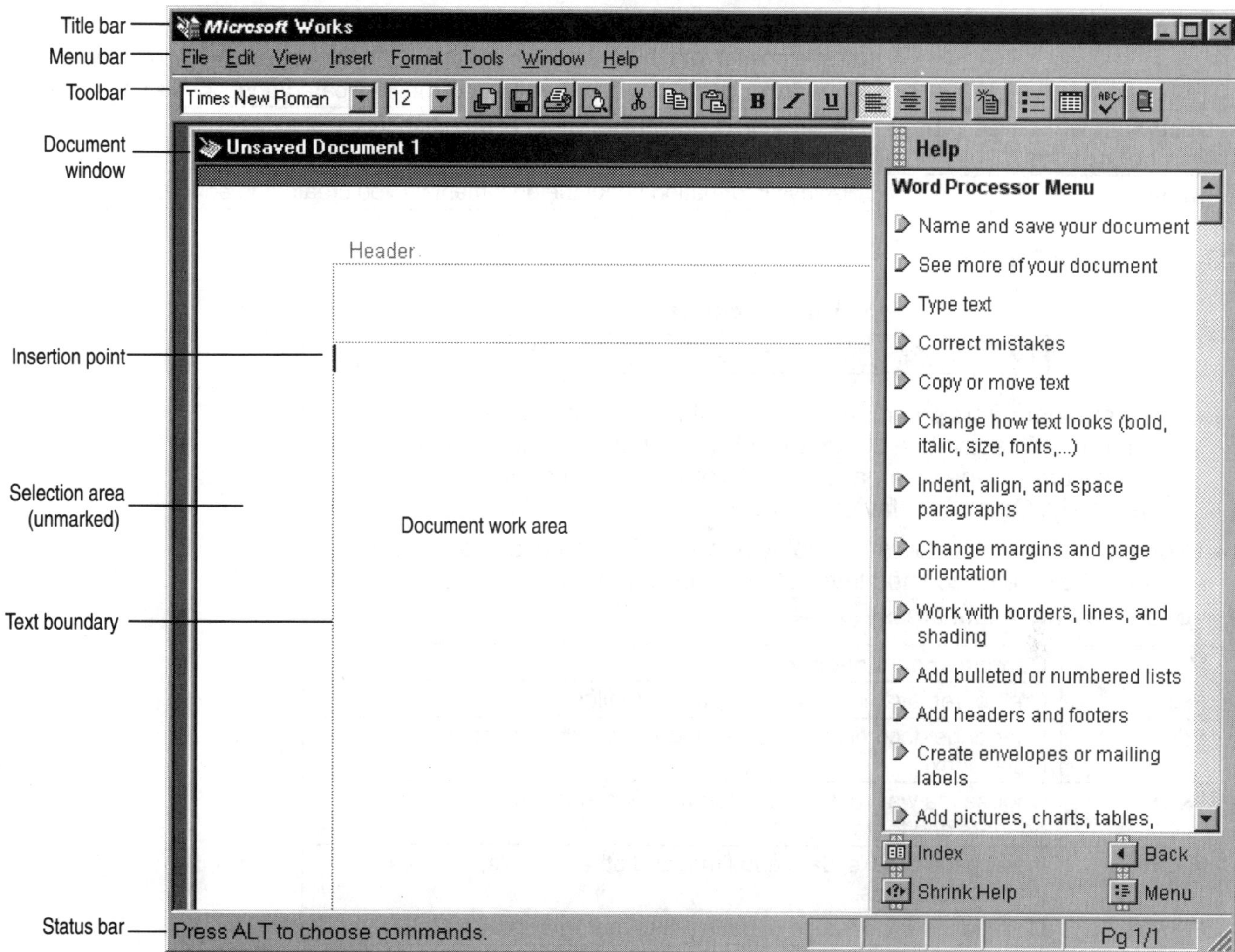

MS Works Word Processor Window

- Many of the elements of the MS Works word processor window are already familiar to you. The Windows standard elements, such as the control buttons (close and minimize, for example), are not included here.

Window Item	Description
Application Control icon	Click the **Application Control** icon at the left end of the title bar to display the Application Control menu, which has options for controlling the appearance of the application window.
Document Control icon	Click the **Document Control** icon to display the Document Control menu. When the document window is maximized, the icon appears at the left end of the menu bar. Otherwise, the icon appears at the left end of the document window's title bar. The menu has options for controlling the appearance of the document window.
Toolbar	Combines editing, formatting, and file management commands. If the toolbar is not displayed, click **View**, **Toolbar** (Alt+V, T).
Ruler	Lets you view and set paragraph indents, tab stops, and other controls for horizontal spacing of text. If the ruler is not displayed, click **View**, **Ruler** (Alt+V, R).

Window Item	Description
Selection area	Unmarked area along the left side of the document window. When you move the mouse pointer into this area, it turns into a right-pointing arrow ↗. When you click while pointing with this arrow, you select the line, paragraph, or object to the right.
Document work area with Text boundaries	Displays the document. MS Works automatically includes text guidelines that show the margins of the document and the header and footer areas.
Status bar	Displays information about the document as you create and edit it.

Menu Bar and Toolbar

MS Works Menu Bar

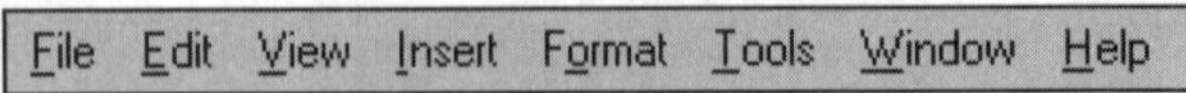

- The Menu bar offers commands for formatting and managing your documents. To activate a command, click the name of the menu then click the name of the command. Some commands take effect immediately. Others display dialog boxes.

- You can use shortcut keys to display a menu. These keystrokes are indicated by the underlined letter of the word on the menu; for example, to open the **File** menu, press **Alt**+**F**.

Menu	Contains commands to:
File	Create, retrieve, lay out, store, and print files.
Edit	Rearrange document contents, undo and redo actions, and find and replace text.
View	Choose the way in which a document is displayed, and work with headers and footers.
Insert	Insert page breaks, date and time, and other objects, such as graphics and files.
Format	Change the appearance of documents, paragraphs, and text.
Tools	Check spelling and grammar, perform mail merge, run macros, customize documents, and set options for the word processor.
Window	Display and arrange currently open documents.
Help	Get explanations of components, commands, and options.

- The MS Works word processor toolbar has buttons for creating, opening, saving, and printing documents. It also has buttons for checking spelling, cutting, copying, and pasting. Toolbar buttons are described as you use them in the exercises in this lesson.

- If the symbol is gray or dimmed, the button is currently inactive.

MS Works Word Processor Toolbar

124

About Microsoft Word 97 and 2000 for Windows

🖥 Try It!

Start Word and Create New Document

1. Click the Start button **Start**, **Programs**.
2. Move to **Microsoft Word** and click.
   Word creates a new document when it opens.

- The Word 97 window shown in the illustration on the following page is typical of Word windows. The major difference between the Word 2000 and the Word 97 windows is that in Word 2000, the Standard and Formatting toolbars are initially on the same line of the window. You can drag the Formatting toolbar to the second line to make its appearance similar to the illustration.

Word Window

- Many of the elements of the Word window are already familiar to you. The Windows standard elements, such as the control buttons (Close and Minimize, for example), are not included here.

Window Item	Description
Application and Document Control icons Word 97: Word 2000:	Click the Application Control icon at the left end of the title bar to display the Application Control menu. The menu has options for controlling the appearance of the application window.
	Click the Document Control icon to display the Document Control menu. When the document window is maximized, the icon appears at the left end of the menu bar. When the document window is not maximized, the icon appears at the left end of the document window's title bar. The menu has options for controlling the appearance of the document window.
	In **Word 2000**, only one icon appears, but it functions as a document control when two or more documents are open and as an document/application control when only one document is open.

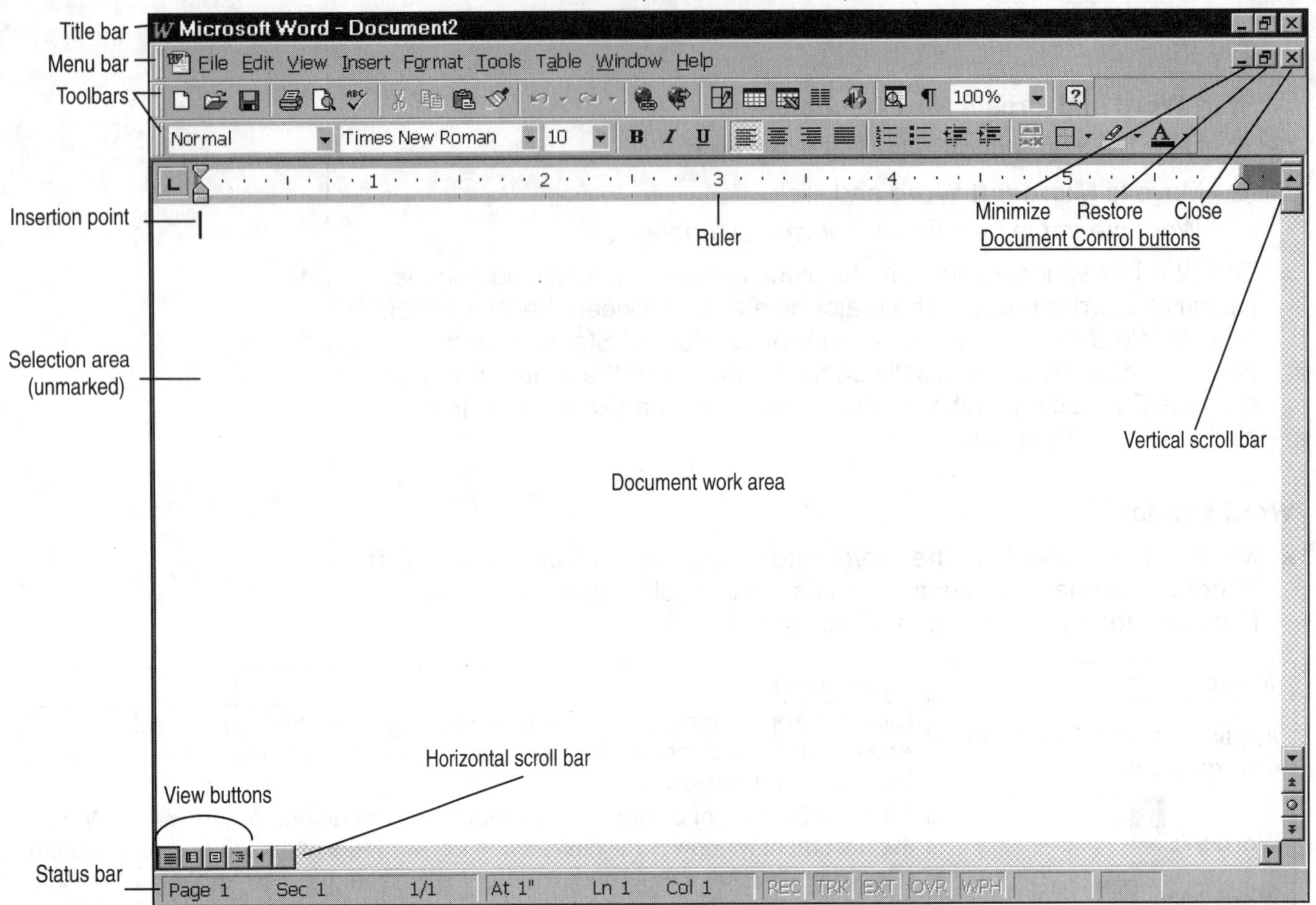

Window Item	Description
Toolbars	By default, Word display two toolbars: **Standard** and **Formatting**. Other toolbars are available if you click **View, Toolbars** (Alt+V, T). In Word 97, these two toolbars are on separate window lines, as shown in the illustration. In Word 2000, they are on the same line. In either version of Word, you can drag the toolbars to other positions on the Word window.
Ruler	Lets you view and set paragraph indents, tab stops, and other controls for horizontal spacing of text. If the ruler is not displayed, click **View, Ruler** (Alt+V, R).
Selection area	Unmarked area along the left side of the document window. When you move the mouse pointer into this area, it turns into a right-pointing arrow. When you click while pointing with this arrow, you select the line, paragraph, or object to the right.
Document work area window and text boundaries	Displays the document. You can display text guidelines in Word in Page or Print Layout view. **Tools, Options, View tab, Text Boundaries** (Alt+T, O, **View** tab, X)
View buttons	Display the document in one of the following views. **Normal** view ≡ is often best for typing, editing, and formatting text quickly. To view the document as it will print, use Print Preview. **Menu equivalent: View, Normal** (Alt+V, N) **Online Layout** (**Word 97**) or **Web Layout** (**Word 2000**) shows the document as it would appear on a Web page. Text appears larger and wraps to fit the window—not the way it will actually print.

Window Item	Description
View buttons (Cont.)	Menu equivalent: <u>V</u>iew, Onli<u>n</u>e Layout (`Alt`+`V`, `E`)
	Menu equivalent: <u>V</u>iew, <u>W</u>eb Layout (`Alt`+`V`, `W`)
	Page or Print Layout view is used when you want to position graphics on a page, edit headers and footers, and adjust page margins. It is also used for working with page columns and drawing objects. Word 2000 calls this view **Print Layout**.
	Menu equivalent: <u>V</u>iew, <u>P</u>age or <u>P</u>rint Layout (`Alt`+`V`, `P`)
	Outline view lets you build an outline using Word's built-in heading styles. You can then build a document based on the outline in Normal or Page Layout view and switch back to Outline view to see its structure.
	Menu equivalent: <u>V</u>iew, <u>O</u>utline (`Alt`+`V`, `O`)

Menu Bar and Toolbars

Word Menu Bar

<u>F</u>ile   <u>E</u>dit   <u>V</u>iew   <u>I</u>nsert   F<u>o</u>rmat   <u>T</u>ools   T<u>a</u>ble   <u>W</u>indow   <u>H</u>elp

- The Menu bar offers commands for formatting and managing your documents. To activate a command, click the name of the menu then click the name of the command. Some commands take effect immediately. Others display dialog boxes.

- In Word, shortcut keys to display a menu are indicated by the underlined letter of the menu; for example, to open the **File** menu, press `Alt`+`F`.

Menu	Contains commands to:
<u>F</u>ile	Create, retrieve, lay out, store, and print files.
<u>E</u>dit	Rearrange document contents, undo and redo actions, and find and replace text and objects.
<u>V</u>iew	Choose the way in which a document is displayed, and work with headers and footers.
<u>I</u>nsert	Insert page breaks, date and time, and other objects, such as graphics and files.
F<u>o</u>rmat	Change the appearance of documents, paragraphs, and text.
<u>T</u>ools	Check spelling and grammar, perform mail merge, run macros, customize documents, and set options for the word processor.
T<u>a</u>ble	Create and format tables and sort data.
<u>W</u>indow	Display and arrange currently open documents.
<u>H</u>elp	Get explanations of components, commands, and options.

Word Standard and Formatting Toolbars

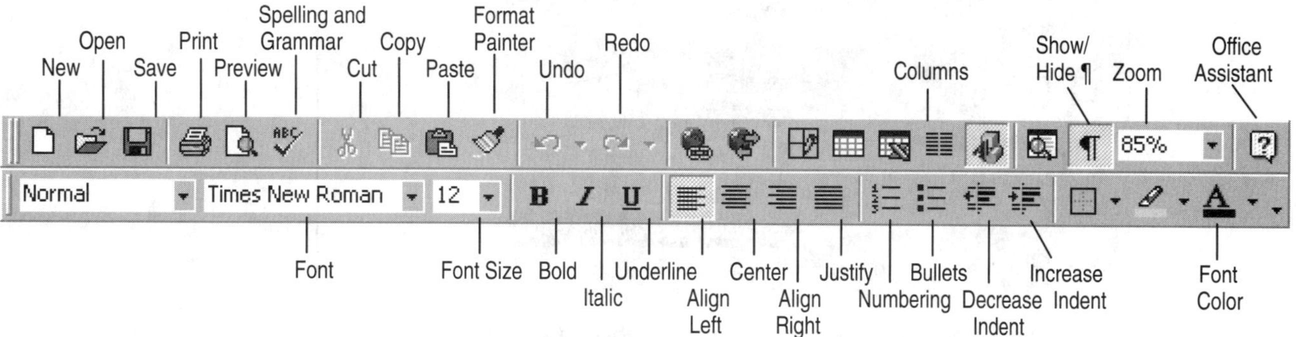

- Word's Standard toolbar, the upper toolbar in the previous illustration, has buttons for creating, opening, saving, and printing documents. It also has buttons for checking spelling, cutting, copying, pasting, and undoing and redoing typing and commands.

- Word's Formatting toolbar, the lower one in the previous illustration, has buttons for changing the font and font size, emphasizing text, aligning and indenting paragraphs, and changing the color of text.

- If the button's symbol is gray or dimmed, the button is currently inactive.

- Toolbar buttons are described as you use them in the exercises in this lesson. Microsoft Word has several different toolbars, and the buttons may differ from those shown on the previous page. Only buttons used in this text are called out in the illustration. You can point to a button and read its ScreenTip to learn the names of other buttons.

- **The More Buttons button**. If both the Standard and Formatting toolbars are on the same line on the window, you will see the More Buttons button at the end of the toolbar. Click the More Buttons button to see additional buttons, as shown in the following illustration:

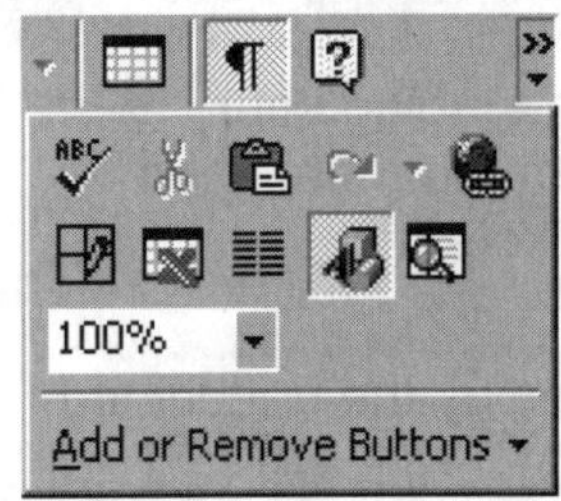

More Buttons Button Activated

About Corel WordPerfect

Try It!

Start WordPerfect and Create New Document

- Click the Corel WordPerfect icon on the right end of the task bar.

OR

1. Click the Start button.

2. Point to **Corel WordPerfect Suite**, **Corel WordPerfect**, and click.

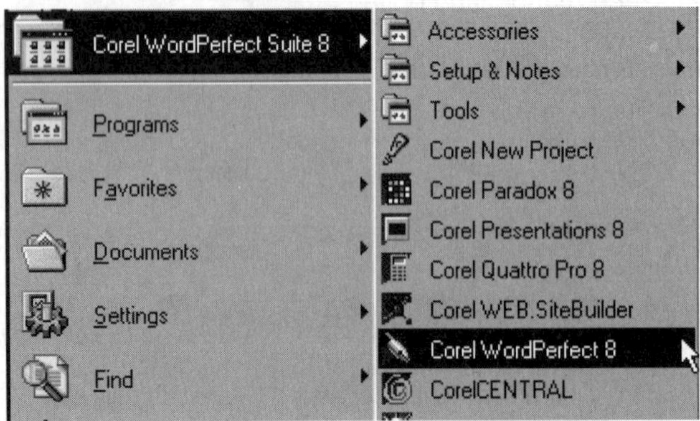

Corel WordPerfect creates a new document when it starts.

- The Corel WordPerfect 8 window is shown in the following illustration.

WordPerfect Window

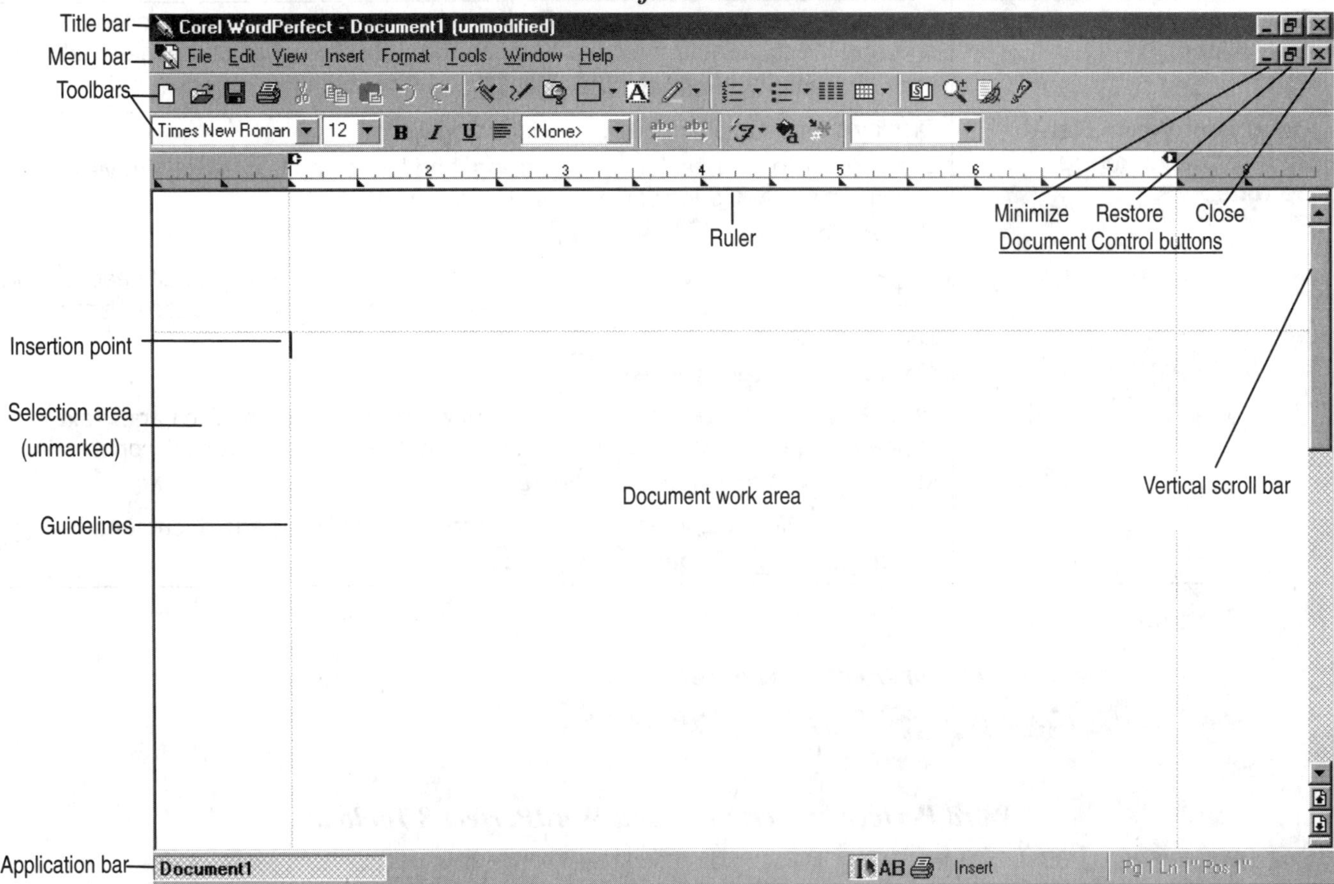

WordPerfect Window

■ Many of the elements of the WordPerfect window are already familiar to you. The Windows standard elements, such as the control buttons (Close and Minimize, for example), are not included in the following table.

Window Item	Description
Application and Document Control icons	**Application and Document Control icons:** At the left end of the menu bar, click the Application Control icon on the title bar to display the Application Control menu. The menu lets you control the application window, offering the same commands as the application control buttons at the right end of the title bar. The Document Control icon, if any, at the left end of the menu bar, lets you control the document window, offering the same commands as the document control buttons at the right end of the menu bar.
Toolbars	By default, WordPerfect displays two toolbars: **WordPerfect 8** and **Property**. Other toolbars are available if you click **View, Toolbars** (Alt+V, T).
Ruler	Lets you view and set paragraph indents, tab stops, and other controls for horizontal spacing of text. If the ruler is not displayed, click **View, Ruler** (Alt+V, R).
Selection area	Unmarked area along the left side of the document window. When you move the mouse pointer into this area, it turns into a right-pointing arrow. When you click while pointing with this arrow, you select the line, paragraph, or object to the right.

Window Item	Description
Document work area and Guidelines	By default, WordPerfect starts in Page view which includes text guidelines showing the document margins. You can turn off some or all of these guidelines through **V**iew, **G**uidelines (**Alt**+**V**, **U**).
Document Views views accessible via menu options.	Display the document in one of the following views. **Draft** view is often best for typing, editing, and formatting text quickly. To view the document as it will print, you can use Page view. Menu: **V**iew, **D**raft (**Alt**+**V**, **D**) **Page** view is used when you want to position graphics on a page, edit headers and footers, and adjust page margins. It is also used for working with page columns and drawing objects. Menu: **V**iew, **P**age (**Alt**+**V**, **P**) **Web Page** view shows the document as it would appear on a Web page. Text appears larger and wraps to fit the window—not the way it will actually print. Menu: **V**iew, We**b** Page (**Alt**+**V**, **B**) **Two Pages** view lets you view facing pages in a multiple-page document. Menu: **V**iew, T**w**o Pages (**Alt**+**V**, **W**)

Menu Bar and Toolbars

Corel WordPerfect Menu Bar

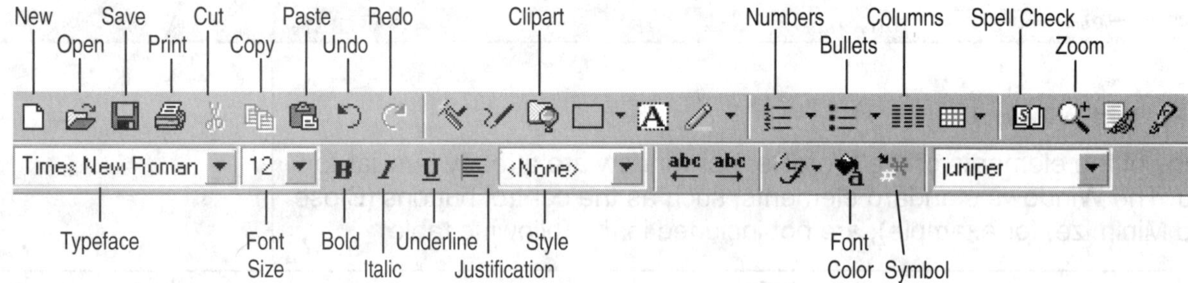

Word Perfect Property Bar and WordPerfect 8 Toolbar

- The Menu bar offers commands for formatting and managing your documents. To activate a command, click the name of the menu then click the name of the command. Some commands take effect immediately. Others display dialog boxes.

- In Corel WordPerfect, shortcut keys to display a menu are indicated by the underlined letter of the menu; for example, to open the **File** menu, press **Alt**+**F**.

Menu	Contains commands to:
File	Create, retrieve, lay out, store, and print files.
Edit	Rearrange document contents, undo and redo actions, and find and replace text and objects.
View	Choose the way in which a document is displayed, and work with headers and footers.
Insert	Insert page breaks, date and time, and other objects, such as graphics and files.
Format	Change the appearance of documents, paragraphs, and text.
Tools	Check spelling and grammar, perform mail merge, run macros, customize documents, and set options for the word processor.
Window	Display and arrange currently open documents.
Help	Get explanations of components, commands, and options.

- The toolbars, shown on the previous page, have buttons for creating, opening, saving, and printing documents. They also have buttons for checking spelling, cutting, copying, pasting, and undoing and redoing typing and commands. Toolbar buttons are described as you use them in the exercises in this lesson.

- If the symbol is gray or dimmed, the button is currently inactive.

Change the Default Font Size

- The **default** font and font size for the word processors referred to in this text are described in the following table:

Word Processor	Default Font	Default Size
AppleWorks	Geneva	12
Word 98	Times	12
Microsoft Works	Times New Roman	10
Microsoft Word 97	Times New Roman	10
Microsoft Word 2000	Times New Roman	12
Corel WordPerfect	Times New Roman	12

- To make them easy to read, most of the illustrations in this book were created using the Times New Roman 12 point as the font; therefore, most of the data files for Windows word processors also use 12-point, Times New Roman. For AppleWorks, data files were created using either Helvetica, 12 point or Times, 12 point.

- So that your solutions to exercises more closely match the illustrations, you may wish to change the default font and size if necessary.

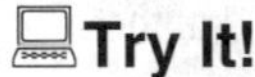

Try It!

Check Current Defaults

- You can check the default in your word processor when you start a new document.

- Look at the font information on the toolbar or button bar.

If it looks like the top illustration below, the default has been changed. If it looks like the lower illustration, the default has not been changed.

Check MS Works and Word 97 Default and Font Size

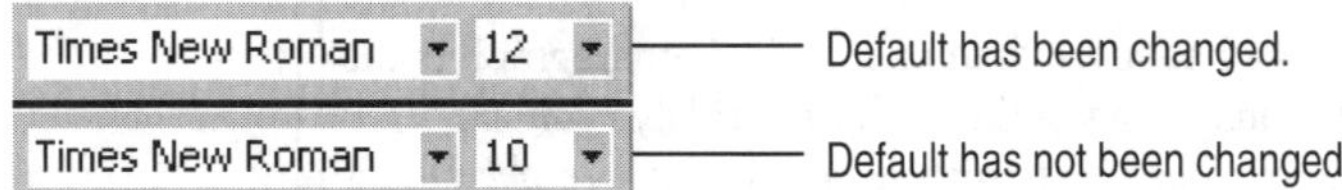

Try It!

- Change the default font size in MS Works and Word 97 to 12 points.

Default

A default value is a parameter used by the software unless you change it. Word sets default margins, font, font size, and paragraph formats so that you can begin working without worrying about those settings.

Point

Font size is measured in **points**. A font size of 12 points means that the tallest letter is about 1/6 of an inch high. A font size of 36 points means that the tallest letter is about 1/2 inch tall.

Change Default Font and Size

What is a Paragraph?

- Word processors generally do not format text line-by-line. Instead, they format each paragraph as a unit. A paragraph is the text between the place you press **Enter** or **Return** and the place you press it again. If you want a blank line, you press the **Enter** or **Return** key twice, creating a blank paragraph which also happens to be a blank line. The following illustration shows three paragraphs.

Paragraph ending symbol

AppleWorks Paragraphs

> This·is·a·paragraph·of·one·line↵
> ↵
> The·preceding·paragraph·has·no·text·while·this·one·has·more·than·one·line.··The·paragraph·
> is·the·major·unit·of·formatting·in·the·AppleWorks·word·processor.·Each·time·you·press·the·
> Return·key,·you·are·creating·a·paragraph·whether·it·contains·no·text,·one·word,·several·
> words,·or·several·lines.

Paragraph ending symbol

Word 98 Paragraphs

> This·is·a·paragraph·of·one·line.·¶
> ¶
> The·preceding·paragraph·has·no·text·while·this·one·has·more·than·one·line.·The·
> paragraph·is·the·major·unit·of·formatting·in·Word·98.·Each·time·you·press·the·Return·
> key,·you·are·creating·a·paragraph·whether·it·contains·no·text,·one·word,·several·words,·or·
> several·lines.·¶

MS Works and Word 97 and 2000 Paragraphs

Paragraph ending symbol

> This·is·a·paragraph·of·one·line.¶
> ¶
> The·preceding·paragraph·has·no·text·while·this·one·has·more·than·one·line.·The·
> paragraph·is·the·major·unit·of·formatting·in·Windows·word·processors.·Each·time·you·
> press·the·Enter·key,·you·are·creating·a·paragraph·whether·it·contains·no·text,·one·word,·
> several·words,·or·several·lines.¶

Paragraph ending symbol

WordPerfect Paragraphs

> This·is·a·paragraph·of·one·line.·¶
> ¶
> The·preceding·paragraph·has·no·text·while·this·one·has·more·than·one·line.·The·paragraph·is·the·
> major·unit·of·formatting·in·Corel·WordPerfect.·Each·time·you·press·the·Enter·key,·you·are·
> creating·a·new·paragraph·whether·it·contains·no·text,·one·line,·several·words,·or·several·lines.·¶

Proofreader's Mark for Paragraph

- The proofreader's mark for paragraph is the ¶ symbol. When you see this symbol in the Exercise Directions, end the paragraph (press the **Enter** or **Return** key).

Type Text

- To get started with the word processor, you simply begin typing in the blank screen. The insertion point (blinking vertical line) indicates where the next character will appear.

Try It!

- Type the following lines. Press the **Enter** or **Return** key at the end of each line.

  To learn word processing, you must practice.
  Without practice, you cannot improve your knowledge and skills.
  With practice, you can become good at word processing.

Save an Unnamed Document

- Although word processors display *untitled* or *Document1* on the title bar, the document does not have a name until you save it.

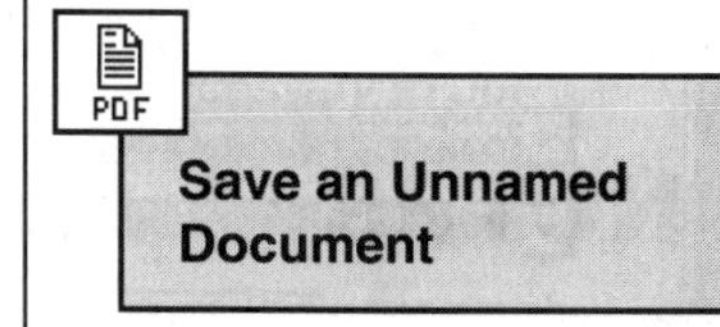

Try It!

1. Save the document you just created.
2. Name it **Mydoc**.

In this exercise, you will type a few sentences and watch how the word processor window changes. Pay special attention to the status bar at the bottom of the window. You will also correct any typing errors and save the document.

EXERCISE DIRECTIONS

Create and Save a New Document

1. Create a new word processor document.
2. Save the document as **Firstdoc**.

Simple Typing

1. Starting at the first available line in the document window, type the text shown in Illustration A.

   If you make a mistake while typing, don't worry about correcting it until you have typed the entire document.

2. Press **Enter** or **Return** twice at the end of the first paragraph to create a blank line between paragraphs.

Correct Errors

1. Read through what you typed and check for errors.

2. To correct errors, point with the mouse to the word you need to change and click once.

   This action places the insertion point (blinking vertical line) in the incorrect word.

3. Once in the word, use one or more of the following actions to correct it:

   a. Position the insertion point next to the error using the mouse pointer or the left and right arrow keys.

   b. Type the correction.

   c. Delete the incorrect letters.

4. Press **Ctrl**+**S** (Windows) or **⌘**+**S** to save the document again.

5. Close the document and exit the word processor.

Illustration A

Word processing software lets you type, format, save, and print text documents. With practice, you can combine text with clip art and illustrations from other applications.¶¶
Each time you press the Enter or Return key, you create a new paragraph. To create a blank line, press the Enter or Return key twice at the end of a paragraph. A blank line is a paragraph with no text.

Exercise 2

Open, Save As, Edit, Save, and Print
■ Open a Document ■ Save As ■ Insert the Date ■ Edit Text
■ Insert and Overtype Modes ■ Undo ■ Redo/Revert ■ Save
■ Print Preview (MS Works and Word Only) ■ Print

NOTES

Open a Document

■ To open a document so you can work with it, you click the Open button, choose a menu option, or find the document and double-click its file name. If the word processor is started, the easy way to start opening a document is to click the Open button.

Try It!

1. Start your word processor.

2. Click the Open button (AppleWorks) or (Word 98 and Windows) or use the **File**, **Open** menu command.

3. Using the dialog box, locate and open the folder that contains **Firstdoc**, which you created in Exercise 1.

   OR

   Locate the folder that contains the data files.

   Open **Firstdoc** from your folder, or open **02Firstdoc** from the data files.

■ From now on, in all exercises, the instructions will simply direct you to open the appropriate file. You will need to start the application, locate the file, and open it using any method you wish.

Save As

■ Sometimes you change a document but want to save it under a different name, leaving the original document unchanged.

Try It!

Change the Document

1. Place the insertion point at the top of the document.

2. Insert two blank paragraphs (press Enter or Return twice).

3. Move the insertion point back to the top of the document.

4. Type *Word Processors and Paragraphs*.

5. Save the document as **Firstdoc2**.

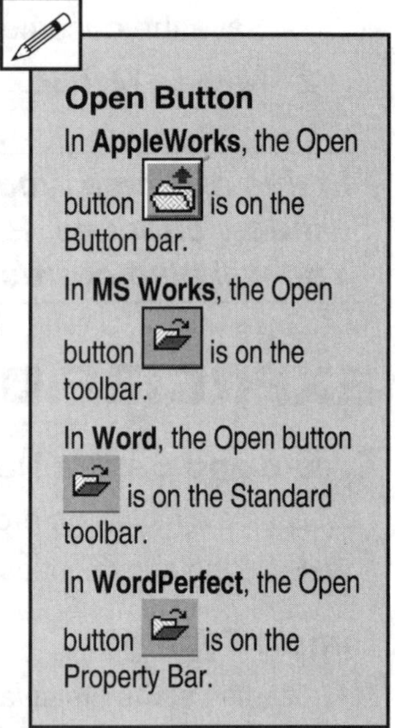

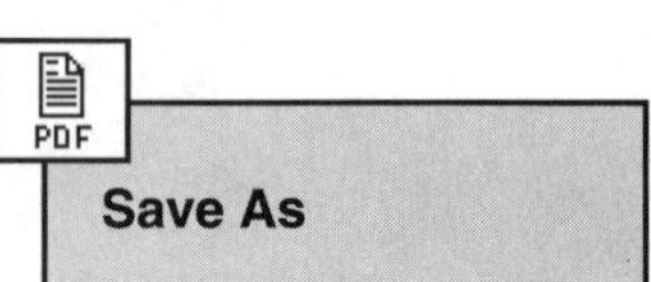

134

Insert the Date

- Word processors offer you an easy way to insert the current date into a document. The Date function is particularly useful in letters and memos.

- You can insert the date so that:

  - The **inserted date does not change** when you open or print the document on another day. In AppleWorks, such a date is called a **Fixed Date**. In Windows word processors, you deselect an option to insert a date that doesn't change.

  - The **date changes automatically** each time you open or print the document on a different day. In AppleWorks, you use the Edit, Insert Date command. In Windows, you select the option that causes the inserted date to change.

Try It!

1. Place the insertion point at the top of **Firstdoc2**.
2. Insert two blank paragraphs.
3. Move the insertion point to the top of the document.
4. Insert a fixed date.

   *When you see the phrase **Today's Date** in the exercise illustrations in this book, insert the current date as a fixed date.*

5. Leave **Firstdoc2** open.

Edit Text

- Editing text involves inserting, deleting, and replacing letters, words, phrases, sentences, and paragraphs.

  To insert text:
  1. Place the insertion point where you want the text to appear.
  2. Type the text.

  To delete a letter (Mac OS):
  1. Place the insertion point to the right of the letter.
  2. Press the Del key.

     Some Mac keyboards include a ⌦ Forward Delete key, which deletes the letter to the right of the insertion point.

  To delete a letter (Windows):
  1. Place the insertion point to the right or left of the letter.
  2. If the letter is to the right of the insertion point, press the Del key.

     OR

     If the letter is to the left of the insertion point, press the Backspace key.

  To delete a word or more:
  1. Select the text to be deleted.
  2. Press the Del key.

  To replace text:
  1. Select the text to be replaced.
  2. Type the replacement text.

Automatic Update

For most of your letters, memos, and reports, it is a good idea **not** to update the date automatically. Often, you want to retain the original date of the document as a permanent record.

Insert Fixed Date

Typing Replaces Selected Text

Some word processing applications allow you to avoid replacing selected text. In MS Works and Word, for example, the **Tools**, **Options**, **Edit(ing)** tab lets you de-select the option **Typing Replaces Selection**. When this option is off, typed text is inserted to the left of the selected text.

The equivalent option in Word 98 is **Tools**, **Preferences**, **Edit** tab, **Typing replaces selection**.

OR

Use combinations of insertion and deletion.

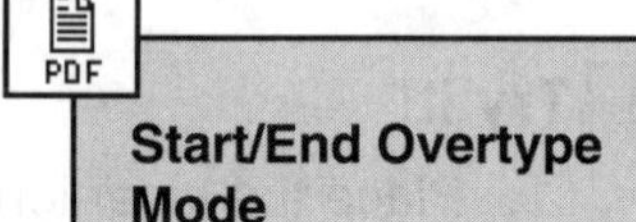Try It!

1. Select the word *text* in the first paragraph of **Firstdoc2**
2. Delete it.
3. Select the words *Enter or Return* the first time they occur in the second paragraph.
4. **Mac OS**: Type *Return*. **Windows**: Type *Enter*.
5. Select the words *Enter or Return* the second time they appear in the second paragraph.
6. Delete the phrase.
7. **Mac OS**: Type *Return*. **Windows**: Type *Enter*.
8. Leave the document open.

Insert and Overtype Modes

- In all word processors **except AppleWorks**, you can also edit text by using Insert and Overtype modes. (In WordPerfect, this is called **Typeover** mode.) By default, most word processors start in **Insert mode**. Characters you type appear at the insertion point and existing text moves to the right.

- In **Overtype mode**, the system replaces existing text one character at a time as you type. Each keystroke replaces a character until you reach the end of the paragraph. At the end of the paragraph, your new text appears as if inserted.

Undo

- Most word processors offer an **Undo** feature. Undo removes the most recent edit.

- Some word processors, such as Word, let you undo as many as 300 actions. As you type and format paragraphs and text, they store the actions in their undo **buffer** or **stack**. To undo actions in reverse order, continue to use the undo command.

Try It!

Undo One Action

1. In **Firstdoc2** select the date.
2. Delete it.
3. Undo the deletion.

   AppleWorks: ⌘+Z or Undo/Redo button

   Word 98: ⌘+Z or Undo button

   MS Works: Ctrl+Z

   Word/WordPerfect: Ctrl+Z or Undo button

4. Leave the document open.

Start/End Overtype Mode

Buffer (stack)

A buffer is an area in memory that a program uses to store data temporarily. Actions are stored in the undo buffer and can be used to reverse actions until you exit the word processor.

Undo Several Actions

In some Windows word processors, you can click the drop-down list arrow next to the Undo button to select more than one action to undo.

Redo/Revert

- After you have undone an action, you can redo it using one of the actions listed below. (In AppleWorks, this is also known as Revert.) Redo/Revert works like undo except that it reinstates the action you reversed. Word processors that let you undo more than the most recent action also allow you to redo more than the most recent undone action.

- **AppleWorks:** `⌘`+`Z` or Undo/Redo button

  Word 98: `⌘`+`Y` or Undo button

  MS Works: `Ctrl`+`Z`

  Word: `Ctrl`+`Y` or Redo button

  WordPerfect: Redo button

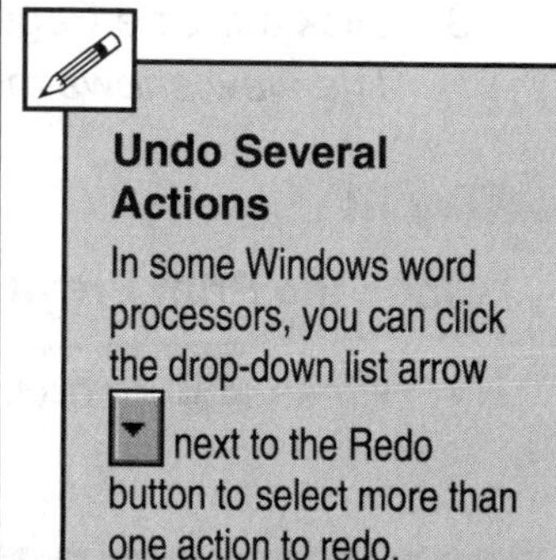

Undo Several Actions

In some Windows word processors, you can click the drop-down list arrow next to the Redo button to select more than one action to redo.

Save

- If a document has been saved once, it has a name. If you make changes to the document, you need to save it again. Save your work often. Any changes that have not been saved are lost if your computer suffers a power failure.

Try It!

- Save **Firstdoc2**.

  AppleWorks: `⌘`+`S` or Save Document button

  Word 98: `⌘`+`S` or Save button

  Windows: `Ctrl`+`S` or Save button

Print Preview (Word and MS Works Only)

- To see a document as it will appear when printed, use Print Preview. The document appears in the Print Preview window, as shown in the sample from MS Works on the next page.

Try It!

1. Click the Print Preview button.

   MS Works has buttons for use in Print Preview. Word has a separate Print Preview toolbar.

2. Move the magnifying glass pointer to the document window and click. *The preview enlarges.*

3. Click the document again. *The preview reduces to a smaller percentage.*

4. Save the document.

Try It!

Edit in Print Preview (Word Only)

1. Click the Magnifier button to turn it off.

   When you move the pointer back to the document, it changes to an I-beam, indicating that you can edit the document in Print Preview.

AppleWorks and WordPerfect

AppleWorks does not provide a separate print preview mode. You can view an entire page by clicking the Zoom-out control at the bottom of the window.

WordPerfect accomplishes print preview with **View**, **Page** or **View**, **Two Pages**.

2. Click the Magnifier button 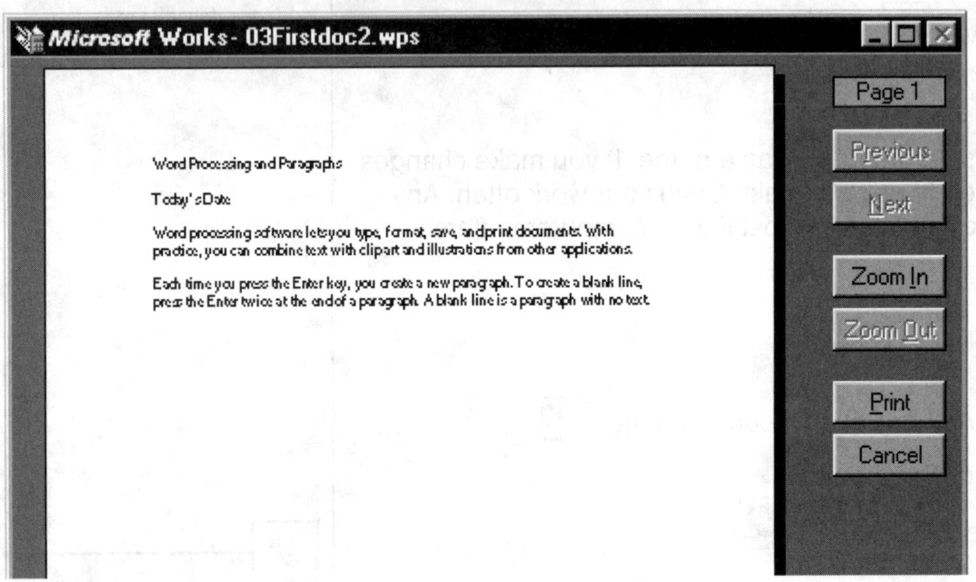 again to turn it back on and end edit mode.

3. Click the One Page button ▣.
   The view shows the entire page.

🖳 Try It!

Close the Print Preview Window

- Press Esc or click Cancel (MS Works) or click Close (Word).

MS Works Print Preview

Microsoft Works - 03Firstdoc2.wps

Word Processing and Paragraphs

Today's Date

Word processing software lets you type, format, save, and print documents. With practice, you can combine text with clipart and illustrations from other applications.

Each time you press the Enter key, you create a new paragraph. To create a blank line, press the Enter twice at the end of a paragraph. A blank line is a paragraph with no text.

Page 1 · Previous · Next · Zoom In · Zoom Out · Print · Cancel

Print

- When you are satisfied with the document's appearance, you are ready to print it. Before starting to print, be sure that your printer is turned on and ready to print.

🖳 Try It!

1. Print **Firstdoc2**.

   - **AppleWorks:**   Click the Print button 🖨.

   - **Word 98:**   Click the Print button 🖨 on the Standard toolbar, and click the Print button [**Print**] on the dialog box.

   - **Windows:**   Click the Print button 🖨. If a dialog box appears, click the Print button [Print].

   The document prints using the current printer settings.

2. Save and close the document. Exit the word processor unless you are continuing with the Exercise Directions.

In this exercise, you will create and format some notes of advice about using a word processor.

EXERCISE DIRECTIONS

Create a Document

1. Create a new document and type the text shown in Illustration A. Start at the first available line in the document window.

   The illustration uses one space after a period at the end of a sentence.

2. Insert today's date on the first line of the new document.

3. Press **Enter** (**return**) where the proofreader's mark for a new paragraph appears.

   If you make a mistake, don't worry about correcting it until you have typed the entire document.

4. Correct any errors you find.

5. Save the document as **Advice**.

6. Print Preview the document, if your word processor permits.

7. Print the document.

8. Close the document, and exit the word processor.

Illustration A

Today's date ¶¶ Learn what you need to know to finish the job at hand. As you take on more difficult assignments, you can expand your knowledge. ¶¶ For example, to use AppleWorks to create documents, you need to start the AppleWorks word processor, type the desired text, press Return to end paragraphs and create blank lines, save, and print what you've created. ¶¶ If you can handle these tasks, you can create a wide variety of documents. You can write full-block letters, single-spaced stories, acceptable memos, class notes, and e-mail messages. ¶

Exercise 3

Format Paragraphs
■ Toolbar and Button Bar Formatting Commands ■ Align Paragraphs
■ Indent Paragraphs ■ Indent First Line
■ Indent Paragraphs Left and Right ■ Create Hanging Indent

NOTES

Toolbar and Button Bar Formatting Commands

■ Using the buttons on the toolbars, you can apply the most commonly used formats to text and paragraphs. **Text** formatting controls the look of the characters—letters, numbers, and symbols—in a document. **Paragraph** formatting controls the position and spacing of the lines within a paragraph.

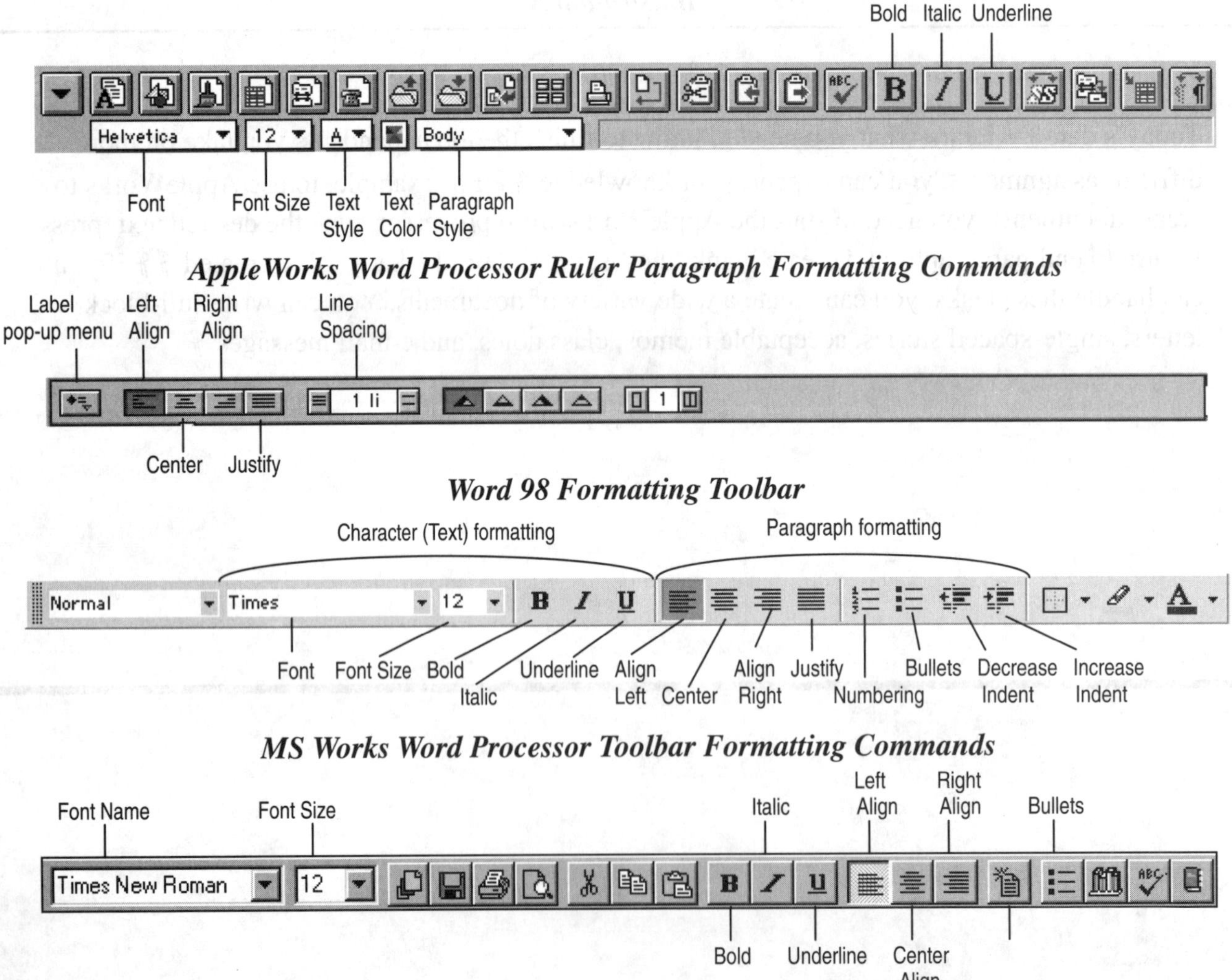

AppleWorks Word Processor Button Bar Formatting Commands

AppleWorks Word Processor Ruler Paragraph Formatting Commands

Word 98 Formatting Toolbar

MS Works Word Processor Toolbar Formatting Commands

Word 97 & 2000 Formatting Toolbar

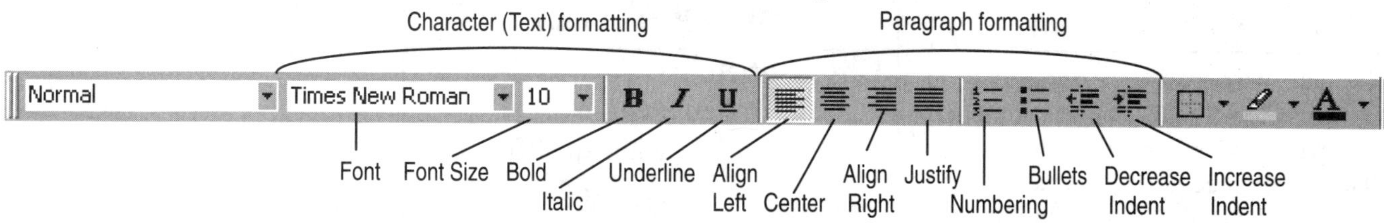

WordPerfect Property Bar and WordPerfect 8 Toolbar

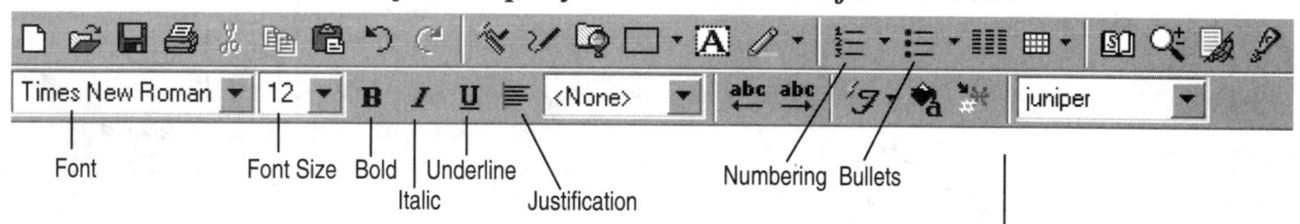

Align Paragraphs

- Paragraphs can be positioned horizontally with one of the basic **alignment** or **justification** techniques, as shown in the following table. In most word processors, you can place the insertion point anywhere in the paragraph and then apply the formatting you want.

- In **WordPerfect**, however, because you can also format lines individually, it is usually best to place the insertion point at the beginning of the paragraph.

- Also, when you want to apply the same format to several consecutive paragraphs, in **Word**, **MS Works**, and **AppleWorks**, you can select any part of the paragraphs to be formatted. You do not need to select all the text in the paragraphs.

- When you want to apply the same format to several consecutive paragraphs in **WordPerfect**, you place the insertion point at the beginning of the first paragraph to be formatted and apply the format. All following paragraphs then use the formatting applied to the first (unless a different format has previously been applied).

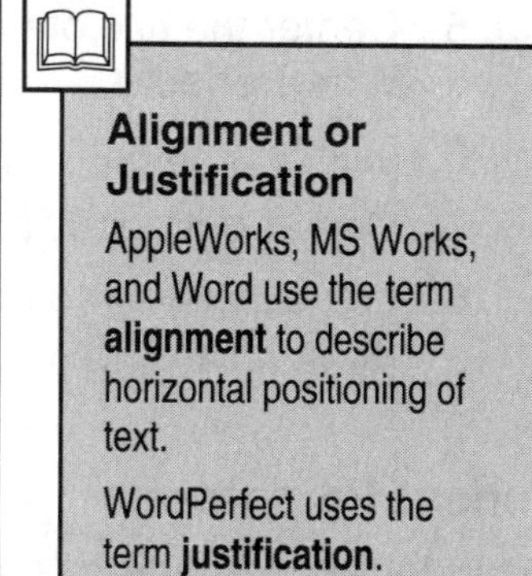

Alignment or Justification

AppleWorks, MS Works, and Word use the term **alignment** to describe horizontal positioning of text.

WordPerfect uses the term **justification**.

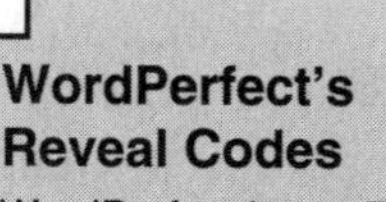

WordPerfect's Reveal Codes

WordPerfect has a Reveal Codes feature that displays the hidden codes for formatting.

Left Alignment	*Center Alignment*
A left-aligned paragraph begins at the left and wraps unevenly on the right.	A centered paragraph has lines that are evenly divided on each side of the mid-point. Shorter lines look like this.

Justify (Full in WordPerfect)	*Right Alignment*
In a justified paragraph, the text begins at the left but wraps evenly at the right margin. The word processor adds space to each line to make all lines, except the last, end at the same place.	In a right-aligned paragraph, text ends at the right margin and wraps unevenly at the left margin. It is often used for dates and other single-line paragraphs that you want aligned at the right margin.

All Justification *(WordPerfect only)*	**Line Justification** *(WordPerfect only)*
In an **All** justified paragraph in WordPerfect, the text begins at the left but wraps evenly at the right margin. The word processor adds space to each line to make all lines, including the last, end at the same place.	Left-justified line Centered line Right-justified line

💻 Try It!

1. Open 🖅 **Firstdoc2**, or open 💿 **03Firstdoc2** from the data files.
2. Save the document as **Firstdoc3**.
3. Right-align the date. (Use line justification in WordPerfect.)
4. Change the date to today's date.
5. Center the title of the document. (Use line justification in WordPerfect.)
6. Justify both body paragraphs. In WordPerfect use **Full**.
7. Center both body paragraphs.
8. Left-align the two body paragraphs.
9. Save and close the document, but leave your word processor open.

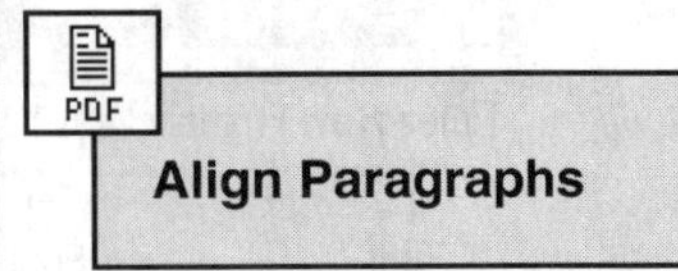

Indent Paragraphs

- Indented paragraphs are commonly used to set information apart. Note the kinds of indenting shown below.

Indented Paragraphs

> The first line of the paragraph is indented from the left while the rest of the lines begin at the left margin. This format is often used to indicated paragraphing when no extra space between paragraphs is specified. This is called a first line indent.
>
>   This paragraph is indented from the left by 1". All lines begin 1" from the left margin and wrap at the right margin.
>
>   This paragraph is indented from the left by 1" and from the right by 1". All lines begin 1" from the left margin and wrap 1" from the right margin.
>
> This paragraph is indented from the right by 1". All lines begin at the left margin and wrap 1" from the right margin.
>
> This is a hanging indented paragraph. Its first line starts at the left margin and all others are indented by 0.5". Hanging indents of this type are often used for bibliographic entries in reports and paper.

Indent First Line

Try It!

First line indents can be created by pressing the **Tab** key before the first word of the paragraph, or by use of the paragraph formatting dialog box.

1. Open ⊙ **03Marianne** in your word processor. Ignore any wavy underlines in the document

2. Place the insertion point at the beginning of the first paragraph, and press the **Tab** key.

   The first line is indented 0.5".

3. Move to the second paragraph and use the paragraph formatting dialog box to set a first line indent of 0.5".

   Note that in WordPerfect the first-line indent is applied to all remaining paragraphs.

4. Save the document as **Marianne**; leave the document open.

Indent Paragraphs Left and Right

- Left-indented paragraphs are used to call attention to information by setting it off from the rest of the body of the document. In sales letters, for example, special offers are often presented in indented paragraphs.

- With most word processors, you can set the left and right paragraph indents using the ruler, as well as through the paragraph formatting dialog box.

- Microsoft Word provides toolbar buttons for increasing (and decreasing) the left indent.

**Try It!**

1. Indent the third paragraph of **Marianne** 1" from the left.

2. Indent the fourth paragraph 1" from the left and 1" from the right.

3. Save the document; leave it open.

Create Hanging Indent

- In a **hanging indent**, the first line of the paragraph extends to the left of the remaining lines. If the text extends beyond two lines, the third and following lines align with the second line. A sample hanging indented paragraph is shown below.

Hanging Indented Paragraph

White, Bailey. *Mama Makes Up Her Mind and Other Dangers of Southern Living.* Reading, MA: Addison-Wesley Publishing Company, 1993.

- Some word processors, such as AppleWorks and MS Works, set hanging indents by using a positive left indent, and a negative first line indent (see the procedures on CD). Other word processors, such as Word, have a special hanging indent formatting option (see the procedures).

Tab and First Line

In some word processors, pressing the Tab key at the beginning of the paragraph may set a first line indent. This action is controlled through the **Tools**, **Options**, **Edit** tab, **Tabs and backspace set left indent** option.

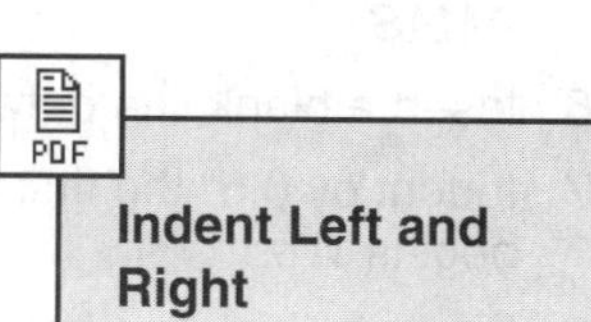

Indent Left and Right

To remove first-line indent in WordPerfect:

In WordPerfect, you may wish to remove the first line indent before applying the hanging indent.

1. Place the insertion at the beginning of the paragraph.

2. Click **Format**.

3. Click **Paragraph**.

4. Click **Format**.

5. Change **First line indent** to 0".

6. Click **OK**.

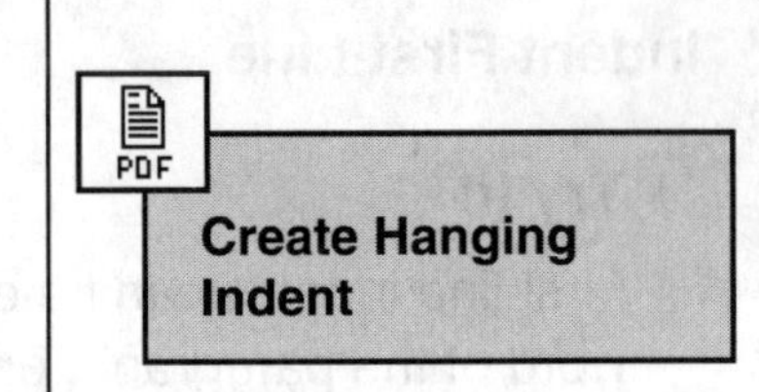

🖳 Try It!

1. Place the insertion point in the last paragraph of the document.
2. Create a hanging indent of 0.5".
3. Save the document.
4. Close the document, but leave the word processor open.

In this exercise, you will use paragraph formatting to change the appearance of a letter.

EXERCISE DIRECTIONS

1. Start your word processor.
2. Open 💿 **03Goode** from the data files.
3. Save the document as **Goode**.

Insert Blank Paragraphs

1. Insert a blank line before *Today's Date*.
2. Insert two blank lines between the date and the inside address.
3. Insert a blank line between the last line of the inside address and the salutation.
4. Insert a blank line after the salutation.
5. Insert a blank line between *representative.* and *AMAS*.
6. Insert a blank line between *Number.)* and *We*.
7. Indent by 0.5" the first line of the paragraph that begins *We*.
8. Insert a blank line between *long.* and *SPECIAL*.
9. Insert a blank line before *Sincerely*.
10. Insert three blank lines between *Sincerely,* and *Otto*.
11. Insert a blank line between *Representative* and *OM*.

12. Replace *yo* with your initials.
13. Save the document.

    Your document should now look as shown in Illustration A.

Format the Paragraphs

1. Center the first three lines.
2. Replace *Today's Date* with the current date.
3. Indent 0.5" the first line of the paragraph that begins *Thank you*.
4. Center the paragraph that begins with *AMAS*.
5. Center the paragraph that begins with *(Note:*.
6. Indent the SPECIAL OFFER paragraph 1" from both the left and the right.
7. Print Preview the document if your word processor includes that feature.
8. Compare your results to Illustration B.
9. Save the document.
10. Print the document.
11. Close the document, and exit the word processor.

Illustration A. 03Goode

After-Market Automotive Specialists
7000 Transmission Drive
Detroit, MI 48242

— *Center all three paragraphs.*

Today's Date — *Replace with the current date.*

Mr. Warren T. Goode
GOODE Auto Parts
9874 Return Place
Manufacturers, IL 62206

Dear Mr. Goode:

Indent first line 0.5".

Thank you for enrolling in AMAS Online, our new Internet-based service designed to enhance your relationship with After-Market Automotive Specialists and your sales representative.

AMAS Online pre-assigned password: WTG1001
(Note: Your User ID is your AMAS Customer Number.)

— *Center both paragraphs.*

We recommend that you change the password the first time you use our automated ordering system. Follow the simple online directions to change your password to any combination of letters and numbers from six-to-eight characters long.

Indent 1". → SPECIAL OFFER! We have just acquired a new shipment of Frammis Automatic Transmssion Syrup (FATS). If you order online, we will give you the special price of 40% off the normal wholesale price of $18 per 24-quart case or $10.80 per case. ← *Indent 1".*

Sincerely,

Otto Matic
Marketing and Sales Representative

OM/yo

After-Market Automotive Specialists
7000 Transmission Drive
Detroit, MI 48242

Today's Date

Mr. Warren T. Goode
GOODE Auto Parts
9874 Return Place
Manufacturers, IL 62206

Dear Mr. Goode:

Thank you for enrolling in AMAS Online, our new Internet-based service designed to enhance your relationship with After-Market Automotive Specialists and your sales representative.

AMAS Online pre-assigned password: WTG1001
(Note: Your User ID is your AMAS Customer Number.)

We recommend that you change the password the first time you use our automated ordering system. Follow the simple online directions to change your password to any combination of letters and numbers from six-to-eight characters long.

SPECIAL OFFER! We have just acquired a new shipment
of Frammis Automatic Transmission Syrup (FATS). If you
order online, we will give you the special price of 40% off
the normal wholesale price of $18 per 24-quart case or
$10.80 per case.

Sincerely,

Otto Matic
Marketing and Sales Representative

OM/yo

NEXT EXERCISE

Exercise 4

Format Text
■ Fonts and Font Names ■ Change Font ■ Change Font Size
■ Use Bold, Italic, and Underline ■ Proofreader's Marks for Bold, Italic, and Underline
■ Change Text Color ■ Use Symbols

NOTES

Fonts and Font Names

■ The term **font**, also called typeface, refers to the look of characters.

Serif and Sans Serif Fonts

- **Alphanumeric** fonts traditionally used for the body of documents are divided into two general groups, serif and sans serif.

Serif Face Times New Roman and Times	Sans Serif Face Arial and Helvetica
Times and Times New Roman characters have serifs—little curlicues. Studies show that printed material in sans serif typefaces are easier to read.	Helvetica and Arial characters have no serifs. Most people find that when they read material online, sans serif is easier to read.

Decorative and Script Fonts

- Two other alphanumeric font types, decorative and script, are used widely for emphasis and capturing the reader's attention.

Decorative Face Braggadocio	Script Face Brush Script MT
Braggadocio may be used for flyers and attention-getting headings.	Brush Script, in small doses, is useful for emphasis and gaining a reader's attention.

Symbol Font

- A fifth font type consists of symbols.

Symbol Font, Wingdings	Symbol Font, Dingbats
(symbol characters)	(symbol characters)

Alphanumeric
Consisting of letters, numbers, and punctuation marks.

Font Faces and Names
Serif and *sans serif* are descriptions of font faces not font names. If you are asked to use a *sans serif* font, look for a font that doesn't have serifs rather than a font named sans serif.

Change Font

- By default, most Windows word processors use Times New Roman, a serif font. AppleWorks uses Geneva, a sans serif font.

- You can change the font either before or after you type the text you want in the new font.

  - **To change the font for text you type:**
    1. Place the insertion point where you want to begin typing with the new font.
    2. Change the font.
    3. Begin typing with the new font.

  - **To change the font for existing text:**
    1. Select the text to be changed. (To select one word, double-click the word. Click and drag to select more than one word.)
    2. Change the font.

Try It!

1. Open ☉**04Goode** from the data files.
2. Select the entire document. (⌘+A in Mac OS, Ctrl+A in Windows)
3. Change the font to Times (AppleWorks), Helvetica (Word 98), or Arial (Windows).
4. Save the document as **Goode4**.
5. Leave the document open.

Change Font Size

- As with changing the font, you can select the text to be changed and change the size, or you can place the insertion point where you want to begin the new size, change the size, and then type using the new size.

Try It!

1. Select the company name in the first line of **Goode4**.
2. Change the font size to 18 points.
3. Save the document, but leave it open.

Use Bold, Italic, and Underline

- **Bold,** *italic*, and <u>underline</u> are used for emphasis. Follow a simple rule for using these embellishments: emphasize sparingly. These techniques are used for headings, for book titles, and to draw attention to an important point. When overdone, they detract from the appearance of your work.

- **Bold** increases the width, height, and darkness of characters. *Italic* slants characters to the right. <u>Underline</u> draws a single line under the characters.

- Like other font changes, to apply them to existing text, select the text then apply the emphasis style. To apply them to typed text, place the insertion point, apply the style, then type using the emphasis style. To remove the emphasis style, select the text and re-apply the style.

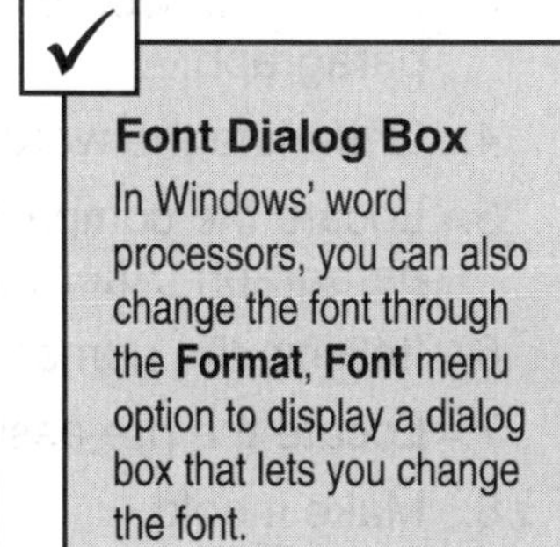

Font Dialog Box

In Windows' word processors, you can also change the font through the **Format**, **Font** menu option to display a dialog box that lets you change the font.

Change Font

Change Font Size

1. Select the second and third lines of **Goode4** (the company's address).
2. Make the two lines bold.
3. Locate the words *AMAS Online* in the first line of the first body paragraph.
4. Underline the words.
5. Locate the company name in the second line of the first body paragraph (After-Market Automotive Specialists).
6. Italicize the name.
7. Locate the pre-assigned password (WTG1001).
8. Make it bold.
9. Locate the words *SPECIAL OFFER!* at the beginning of the indented paragraph.
10. Make the phrase bold and italic.
11. Save the document, but leave it open.

Proofreader's Marks for Bold, Italic, and Underline

- The proofreader's mark for bold is a wavy underline: ﹏﹏﹏
- The proofreader's mark for italic is: ⟨After-Market⟩———— *ital*
- The proofreader's mark for underline is: ⟨AMAS Online⟩———— *underline*

Change Text Color

- Color also draws attention to text. If you do not have a color printer, colors will print in shades of gray. Cyan (Turquoise) or yellow, for example, print as light gray. Red prints as a dark gray or black.
- As with other font changes, you can select and change existing text, or place the insertion point where you want to change colors, change the color, and begin typing in the new color.

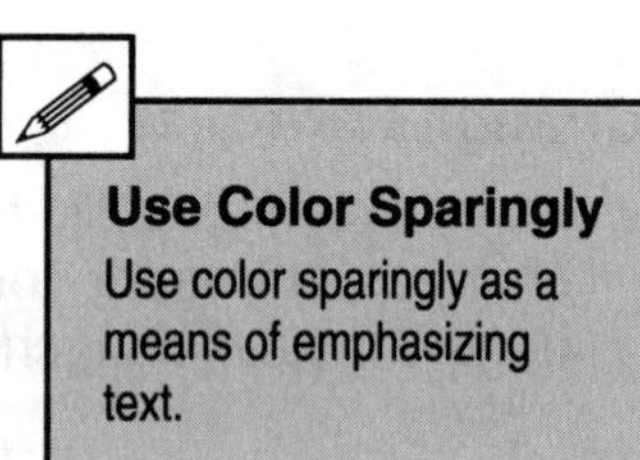

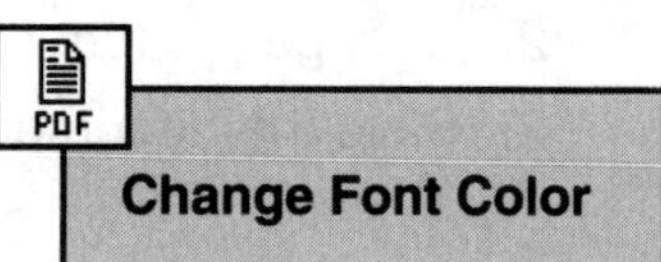

1. Select the company name at the top of the letter.
2. Change the font to a decorative font, such as Braggadocio or Britannic Bold, with a font size between 14 and 18 points. Make sure the company name fits on one line.
3. Select the first three lines (the company name and address).
4. Change the font color to blue.
5. Save the document, but leave it open.

Use Symbols

- No matter which word processor you use, you can insert symbols by typing the correct letter in the current font then changing the font of the letter to one of the symbol fonts (Symbol, Wingdings, Zapf Dingbats).

- Some word processors, such as Word, offer an **Insert**, **Symbol** command that lets you insert symbols without changing the font.

Try It!

1. Place the insertion point at the beginning of the document.
2. Insert one space before the company name.
3. Place the insertion point to the left of the space.
4. Insert the Wingdings or Zapf Dingbats symbol diamond ◆ (lowercase u).
5. Place the insertion point after the word Specialists in the company name.
6. Insert one space after the word.
7. Insert the Wingdings or Zapf Dingbats symbol diamond ◆ (lowercase u).
8. Save, print, and close the document; leave the word processor open.

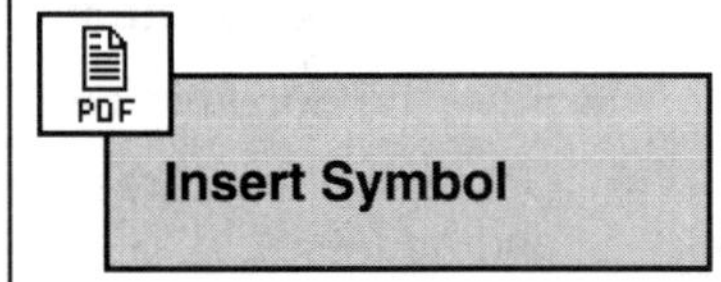

Insert Symbol

EXERCISE DIRECTIONS

Create the Letterhead

1. Open ☯ **04Coyote** from the data files.

2. Save the document as **Coyote**.

3. Center the first three lines (the company's name and address).

4. Insert one space before the word *Acme* and one space after the word *Specialties*.

5. Before the first space at the beginning of the line and after the space at the end of the line, insert the symbol described below:

   AppleWorks: Zapf Dingbats symbol ❑ (lowercase q)

   MS Works: Wingdings symbol ❑ (lowercase q)

   Word: Wingdings symbol ❑ (Use Insert, Symbol.)

   WordPerfect: Iconic Symbols symbol ❑ (Use Insert, Symbol.)

6. Select the entire first line, and change the font size to 36 points.

7. Select each of the symbols, and change the text color to red.

8. Select *Acme Specialties* and change the font color to blue.

9. Change the *Acme Specialties* font to Impact (if available), Arial Black (if available), or Arial bold.

10. Change the address, city, and state to Comic Sans MS (if available); otherwise, use Arial or Helvetica 12-point blue.

11. Save the document.

Call Attention to Text

1. In the first paragraph of the letter, italicize the words:
   Acme Jet Powered Roller Skates

2. Change the following words to blue and italic:
   your misuse of the skates

3. In the one-line paragraph above the indented paragraph, italicize the phrase:
   Acme Jet Powered Roller Skates Money-Back Warranty

4. In the indented paragraph, make the following words bold, italic, red:
   utilization of skates for any other than recreational activities

5. Save the document.

6. Change the letters *yo* after the closing to your own initials.

7. Insert one space before the PS: and one space after the question mark.

8. Before the first space of the PS: and at the end of the line, insert the symbols described below:

   AppleWorks: Zapf Dingbats symbol ★ (uppercase H).

   MS Works: Wingdings smiley face ☺ (capital J)

   Word: Wingdings smiley face ☺ (Use Insert, Symbol.)

   WordPerfect: Iconic Symobls smiley face ☺ (Use Insert, Symbol.)

9. Color the entire PS: blue, and make it bold.

10. Save the document.

Print Preview and Print

1. Print Preview the letter if your word processor includes that feature.

2. Print one copy.

3. Close the document, and exit your word processor.

Illustration A. Letter from Acme Specialties

Center all three lines.   *Insert symbol.*

Acme Specialties   *Entire name and symbols 36 pt.*
911 Mayhem Lane   *Symbols red*
Williston Park, NY 11511   *Text blue, Impact font*

Comic Sans MS 12 pt., blue

Today's Date

Mr. Wile E. Coyote
85 Roadrunner Chase
Arid Desert, AZ 85222

Dear Mr. Coyote:

We are very sorry that you believe our Acme Jet Powered Roller Skates *(ital)* are defective. We hope you have recovered from the injuries you suffered in plunging from the mesa to the valley floor. Your injuries, however, were caused by your misuse of the skates *(blue, ital)* rather than a defect in their manufacture.

Your Acme Jet Powered Roller Skates *(ital)* Money-Back Warranty states, in part:

> Manufacturer is not liable for any damage caused by product abuse, by failure to heed all safety rules as outlined by the National Skating Association, or by utilization of skates for any other than recreational activities *(bold, italic, red)*. Any violation of these limits makes this Warranty null and void.

Clearly, use of our skates on twisting mountain roads in pursuit of dinner is not a recreational activity; thus, we regret that we cannot honor your request for a new pair of skates.

Sincerely,

Allin Funn
Customer Service Manager

af/yo   *Insert symbols.*   *blue and bold*

PS: Have you tried our Acme EZ-Ride Guided Missile?

◻ Acme Specialties ◻

911 Mayhem Lane
Williston Park, NY 11511

Today's Date

Mr. Wile E. Coyote
85 Roadrunner Chase
Arid Desert, AZ 85222

Dear Mr. Coyote:

We are very sorry that you believe our *Acme Jet Powered Roller Skates* are defective. We hope you have recovered from the injuries you suffered in plunging from the mesa to the valley floor. Your injuries, however, were caused by *your misuse of the skates* rather than a defect in their manufacture.

Your *Acme Jet Powered Roller Skates* Money-Back Warranty states, in part:

> Manufacturer is not liable for any damage caused by product abuse, by failure to heed all safety rules as outlined by the National Skating Association, or by *utilization of skates for any other than recreational activities*. Any violation of these limits makes this Warranty null and void.

Clearly, use of our skates on twisting mountain roads in pursuit of dinner is not a recreational activity; thus, we regret that we cannot honor your request for a new pair of skates.

Sincerely,

Allin Funn
Customer Service Manager

af/yo

☺ **PS: Have you tried our Acme EZ-Ride Guided Missile?** ☺

NEXT EXERCISE

Exercise 5

Change Words
■ Spell Check ■ Automatic Spell Checking (Word and Corel WordPerfect)
■ Use the Thesaurus ■ Find and Replace Text

NOTES

Spell Check

- Word processors offer a spelling checker that can help you avoid many typing and spelling mistakes that you might otherwise overlook. The spell checking program scans the document and stops on words that it does not find in its dictionary. Some of these words may be spelled correctly, and you can skip them. Others are incorrect, and you can choose to:

  - Replace the error with a suggested correction.

  - Replace the error with a correction that you type.

  - Skip the error.

  - Add the word to the word processor's dictionary. For example, if your word processor marks your name as an error, you can add it to the dictionary so that the spell checking program no longer marks it as a mistake.

- In addition, most spell checking programs find repeated words and can automatically remove one of the occurrences if it is repeated unintentionally. AppleWorks does not find repeated words.

💻 Try It!

1. Open ⊙ **05Spelling** from the data files.

2. Spell check the document, correcting the errors.

   Note that the name Mertz in the third sentence is spelled correctly.

3. If you are using **AppleWorks**, proofread the fourth paragraph carefully. It contains repeated words that the AppleWorks spelling checker does not catch. Locate the repeated words and delete one of the occurrences of each repeated word.

4. Save the document as **Spelling**.

5. Close the document.

Automatic Spell Checking (Word and Corel WordPerfect)

- Some word processors, such as Microsoft Word (both Windows and Mac versions) and Corel WordPerfect, automatically check for spelling errors as you type. When they detect an error that they cannot correct automatically, they underline the word with a wavy red line, as shown in the illustration that follows.

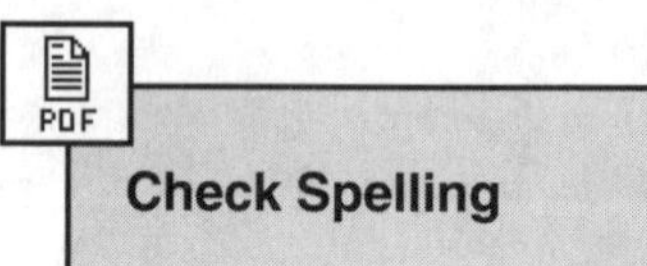

Check Spelling

Turn On/Off Automatic Spell Checking

If misspelled words are not underlined in your Word or WordPerfect document, you may need to turn on the automatic spell check feature.

Spelling Errors

> My barother was an only child.
> Sue hates broccolli.
> Fred Mertz was frightened by a water moccassin.

- The wavy underline (shown in gray) indicates that the word processor does not recognize the spelling. You need to look at each word underlined in red to determine if it is correct. *Mertz*, in the illustration above, is spelled correctly. The other underlined words need to be corrected.

Try It! (Word and Corel WordPerfect)

1. Open ☉ **05Spelling2** from the data files.

2. Save the document as **Spelling5**.

3. Place your mouse pointer on *barother*.
   The word should be underscored by a red wavy line.

4. Right-click (Windows) or `Ctrl`+click (Mac OS).
   The word processor displays a shortcut menu that gives possible corrections, as shown in the illustration that follows.

Spell Check Shortcut Menu

Word

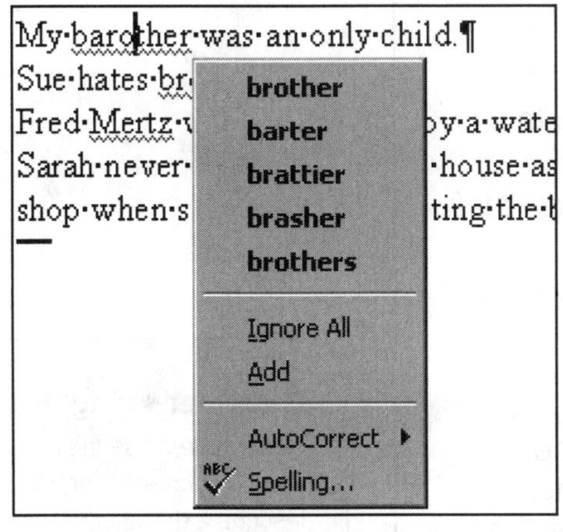

WordPerfect

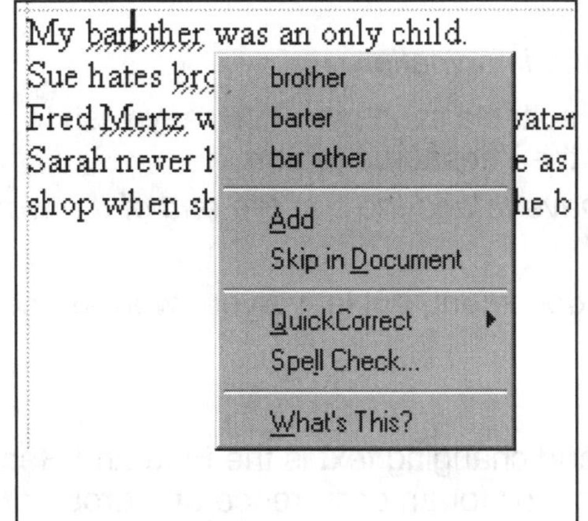

5. Click the correct word.
   If the correct word does not appear, click anywhere outside the menu and edit the word to correct the error.
   You can correct any misspelled word in this way.

6. Change the remaining errors in the document using the right-click method (steps 4-5).
   *When you right-click on a repeated word, the word processor gives you the option **Delete Repeated Word** or **Delete Duplicate**. Click the option to correct the error.*

7. Save and close the document, but leave your word processor open.

Use the Thesaurus

- Word processors offer a synonym dictionary called a **Thesaurus**. The Thesaurus can help you find the right word, and it can help you avoid repeating a word over and over in a document.

- When you choose a synonym from a Thesaurus, pay attention to the part of speech and the form of the word you are looking up. When you look up a plural noun such as *tasks*, the Thesaurus may display only the singular form. If you replace *tasks* with *job*, for example, you must add an *s* to retain the plural. Similar care must be taken with verbs to ensure that they retain their endings, such as *-ed*, *-s*, or *-ing*.

Try It!

1. Open  **05Words** from the data files.

2. Save the document as **Words**.

3. Locate the word *pretentious* in the first paragraph.

4. Use the Thesaurus to find synonyms for the word.

5. Select a suitable word, such as *pompous, arrogant*, or *ostentatious* to replace it.

6. Locate the word *evince* in the first paragraph.

7. Use the Thesaurus to replace it with *show*.

8. Go to the end of the document.

9. Insert two blank lines.

10. Type *Godzilla fires the imagination.*

11. Replace *fires* with a suitable synonym. You may wish to use the lookup command of the Thesaurus feature.

    Note that you may have to add the s *at the end of the word to retain the tense of the verb.*

12. Save and close the document, but leave your word processor open.

Find and Replace Text

- A useful tool for finding and changing text is the Find and Replace feature. You can use it to look for an occurrence of a group of letters, word, or phrase (**character string**), and you can use it to replace the letters, word, or phrase with another. The word or phrase you tell the program to look for is called the **target** or **search** string. The word or phrase to which you want to change the target string is called the **replacement** or **change** string.

Try It!

Find a Character String

1. Open  **05Godzilla** from the data files.

2. Save the document as **Godzilla**.

3. Use the Find feature to look for the word *inspire,* without any other options.

   Note that the first occurrence is in the word inspires.

4. Click Find Next to repeat the find.

Which Word?

The Thesaurus cannot tell you whether the word is one that you should use. You have to know enough about the word to use it correctly. Choosing a word from the Thesaurus without knowing its meaning and connotation can make your document sound pretentious or silly.

Use the Thesaurus

Character string

Programmers use the term **character string** to describe a group of alphanumeric and other symbols.

The **target** or **search** string is the word or phrase to be found. The **replacement** or **change** string is the word or phrase by which the target is to be replaced.

Find and Replace

Note that the next occurrence is in the word inspired.

5. Click Find Next to repeat the find.
   Note that the final occurrence is the word inspire.
6. Close the dialog box without making any changes.
7. Go to the start of the document.

Limit the Search

To prevent the program from finding words that you do not want, you can limit the search by using one or both options listed below. (Word processors, such as Word and Corel WordPerfect, offer more options than the two listed below.) These options are called **search parameters**.

Parameter
An entry that limits or controls the action of a command.

- **Match Case** or **Case sensitive** tells the program to look only for character strings that have the same capitalization as the Find argument. For example, *inspire* will not locate *Inspire* but will find *inspires. The* will not find *other* or *then* but will find *They*.

- **Find whole words only** or **Whole word** tells the program to look only for complete words that match the Find argument. For example, *inspire* will not find *inspires* or *inspired* but will find *Inspire. The* will find *the* and *The*, but not *then*, or *They*.

- If both options are selected, *inspire* will not find *Inspire* or *inspires*; it will find *inspire* only. *They* will find *They* (including occurrences in contractions such as *They're* and *They've*), but *They* will not find *they*.

Try It!

1. Use the Find feature to find the whole word *inspire*.
   Note that the program locates the word inspire in the last line of the document.
2. Close the dialog box without making any changes.
3. Go to the start of the document.

Replace Words

You can tell the Find/Replace (Find/Change) program to replace the target string with a replacement (change) string. In the Replace or Change box, type the character string to which the target character string is to be changed.

Try It!

1. Use the Find/Replace (Find/Change) feature to change the word *inspires* to *stimulates*. Select both case matching and whole words.
2. Go to the start of the document.
3. Use the Find/Replace (Find/Change) feature to change the word *inspire* to *excite*. Select both case matching and whole words.
4. Go to the start of the document.
5. In the Find box, type the word *gargantuan*.
6. In the Replace box, type the word *huge*.
7. Change all occurrences of the word.
8. Save the document.

Find and Replace Special Characters

You can tell the Find/Replace (Find/Change) program to locate and replace special characters, such as the tab and the paragraph end mark.

Try It!

1. In the Find box, specify the Tab character or Left Tab (WordPerfect).
2. In the Replace box, specify the Paragraph character or Hrt character (WordPerfect).
3. Change all occurrences.
4. Save the document.

   It should appear as shown in the following illustration.

Godzilla After Special Character Change

Godzilla stimulates the imagination. Such a huge creature strikes fear into the hearts of the unwary, scares the timid, and causes the strong to quail.

Frankenstein's monster, on the other hand, has become a tired symbol. He is no longer scary but seems more like a benevolent uncle, a symbol of scientific hubris, but not fearsome. He has inspired many imitators, but he does not excite much anxiety in the modern heart.

5. Close the document and exit the word processor unless you are continuing with the Exercise Directions.

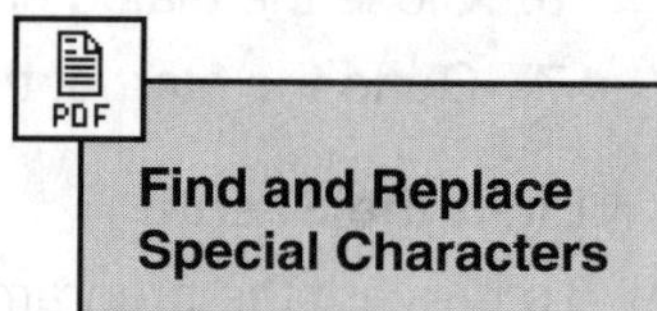

In this exercise, you will use the spelling check and Find/Replace to change words in a document.

EXERCISE DIRECTIONS

Check Spelling

1. Open **05Vegetables** from the data files.
2. Spell check the document, correcting any errors your spell check program finds.

Save, Print Preview, and Print

1. Save the document as **Vegetables**.
2. Print Preview the document if your word processor includes that feature.
3. Print one copy.

Proofread Your Printout

1. Proofread your document carefully. It contains errors that the spelling check cannot detect. See if you can find and correct them.

   Did you find the errors?

   Spell checking is no substitute for careful proofreading. It may not find wan to*; and it may not find* from *when* form *is the correct word.*
2. Correct any errors you find.
3. Print a copy of your final document.
4. Save and close the document.

Use the Thesaurus

1. Open **05Synonym** from the data files.
2. Use the Thesaurus to find a synonym for each underlined word in the file. Illustration A shows the original document.

3. Be sure to pay attention to word forms. You may have to look up related words to find a good synonym for *assured* in the last paragraph.
4. When you finish, save the document as **Synonym**.
5. Print one copy.
6. Close the document.

Illustration A. 05Synonym

A happy <u>consequence</u> of Fred's tripping over the tree root was the reaction to his <u>plight</u> of the <u>radiant</u> Myra. As he lay sprawled upon the lawn tenderly caressing the <u>bruise</u> on his shin, he looked up into her <u>benevolent</u> <u>countenance</u>. Myra <u>looked</u> at him in silent <u>interrogation</u> about his <u>pain</u>. Fred <u>assured</u> her, shyly, that he would recover. Myra licked his face, as any dog would who loved her master.

Use Find/Replace (Find/Change)

The author of the paragraph about Fred and Myra has decided to change the paragraph so that the person who trips is Horace and the dog's name is Millie.

1. Open **05Synonym**.
2. Use Find/Replace (Find/Change) to make the changes listed in the table below:

Find	Change to
Fred	Horace (change all)
Myra	Millie (change all)
licked	slurped (one occurrence)

3. Save the document as **Horace**.
4. Proofread your document on screen.
5. Print one copy.
6. Proofread again and correct any errors.
7. Print a final copy.
8. Save and close the document, and exit the word processor.

Exercise 6

Bullets and Numbering; Cut or Copy, and Paste Text
■ Introduction to Bullets and Numbering ■ Create an Unordered (Bulleted) List
■ Create an Ordered List ■ Cut, Copy, and Paste Text

NOTES

Introduction to Bullets and Numbering

■ To call readers' attention to lists of items, word processors offer bullets and numbers or letters. Use bullets to mark items in a list in which the order of the items is not important, as in a list of things you need to pack for a camping trip. Use numbers or letters when the order is important, as in the steps for pitching a tent.

■ A group of bulleted paragraphs is known as an **unordered list**; a group of numbered or lettered paragraphs is known as an **ordered list**.

Create an Unordered (Bulleted) List

■ A **bullet** is a symbol that marks the beginning of an item in an unordered list; the most common bullet is a small, filled circle (●). Other common bullets are squares (■) and diamonds (♦).

■ In **AppleWorks** bullets and automatically numbered paragraphs are part of the Label feature, which includes outlining symbols as well as bullets and automatically numbered paragraphs.

■ In **Windows** word processors, bullets, regardless of the symbol used, are associated with a Bullets feature.

Try It!

Create a Bulleted List

1. Start your word processor, and open a new document.
2. Type the following lines:

    Three important things to remember:

    Your name

    What you had for breakfast

    The date of the Norman Conquest (1066)

3. Select the last three paragraphs.
4. Make these three paragraphs a bulleted list.
5. Save the document as **Bullets**, but leave the document open.

Bullet

Symbol used to mark an item in an **unordered list** (in which the order of the items is not important).

The term **bullet** refers to the appearance of the common symbol (●), which resembles a bullet hole.

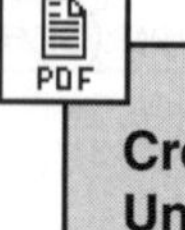

Create an Unordered (Bulleted) List

Try It!

Change the Bullet Symbol

1. In **Bullets**, select the bulleted paragraphs if they are not already selected.
2. Change the bullets to diamonds, squares, or check marks.
3. Save the document as **Diamonds**, but leave the document open.

Create an Ordered List

- Most word processors can automatically mark an ordered list with numbers or letters.

Try It!

Create a Numbered List

1. In **Diamonds**, select the bulleted paragraphs.
2. Remove the bullet symbols.
3. Number the paragraphs.
4. Save the document as **Numbers**.
5. Remove the numbers.
6. Mark the list with letters.
7. Save the document as **Letters**, but leave the document open.

Cut, Copy, and Paste Text

- You can cut and paste text to move it from one place to another. You can copy text to place a copy of it in another spot. You select the text to be moved or copied, then cut or copy it. **Cut** removes text from its current location and places it on the Clipboard. **Copy** leaves the text in its current location and places a copy of it on the Clipboard. **Paste** inserts a copy of the contents of the Clipboard at the insertion point.

- To move or copy an entire paragraph, take care to include the paragraph mark when you select the text, as shown in the following illustration. If you do not include the paragraph mark, you will copy or move just the text and not the paragraph formatting.

Selecting AppleWorks Text or Paragraph for Cut and Copy

Selecting Word 98 Text or Paragraph for Cut and Copy

Selecting Windows Text or Paragraph for Cut and Copy

MS Works 4.5 Ordered List

MS Works 4.5 does not support automatic marking of ordered lists. See the Procedures for how to create an ordered list in MS Works.

Create an Ordered (Numbered or Lettered) List

To select text:

- In all word processors, double-click to select a word.

- In **AppleWorks**, triple-click to select a line, and quadruple-click (four times) to select an entire paragraph.

- In all versions of **Word**, triple-click to select a paragraph.

- In **WordPerfect**, triple-click to select a sentence, and quadruple-click (four times) to select a paragraph.

- In all **Windows word processors** and **Word 98**, click in the selection area at the left of the window to select a line or sentence. Click and drag to select more than a line or sentence.

- To **replace text** with what you cut or copy:
  1. Select the text to be moved or copied.
  2. Cut to move the text, or copy to copy the text.
  3. Select the text to be replaced.
  4. Insert the cut or copied text.

Try It!

1. In **Letters**, if you are using Word or WordPerfect, use the Bullets feature to change the letters back to numbers so that clicking the Numbering button formats the paragraph with numbers rather than letters.
2. Remove the letters from the list.
3. Format the list (last three paragraphs) with bullets.
4. If paragraph end marks are not displayed:

AppleWorks:	Click the Show/Hide button.
MS Works:	Click **View**, **All Characters**.
Word:	Click the Show/Hide button.
WordPerfect:	Click **View**, **Show**.

5. Select the last paragraph: *The date of the Norman Conquest (1066)*. Include the paragraph mark ↵, ⌐, or ¶. Note that with most word processors you cannot select the bullet itself. It will move with the paragraph, however, if you include the paragraph mark.
6. Cut the paragraph to place the text on the Clipboard.
   The text disappears from its original location.
7. Place the insertion point just before *Your name*.
8. Click the Paste button.
   The cut text appears at the insertion point. A copy of the text remains on the Clipboard until you cut or copy something else. You can use the Clipboard contents as many times as you wish.
   Note that in WordPerfect, you may need to reapply the bullet formatting to the paragraph that begins Your name.
9. Close **Letters** without saving the changes.

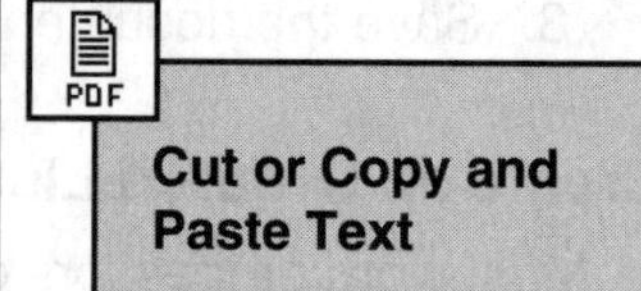

Cut or Copy and Paste Text

MS Works

If you cannot select the paragraph mark at the end of the sentence, insert a blank line after the Norman Conquest paragraph. MS Works does not allow you to select the last paragraph mark in a document.

> ***In this exercise, you will create a bulleted list and a numbered list from a list of common rules and phrases that you may have heard around your house.***

EXERCISE DIRECTIONS

Create an Unordered List

1. Open ☁ **06Rules** from the data files.
2. Choose ten rules from the list (see Illustration A).
3. Delete the rules you do not want.
4. Create a bulleted list of the ten rules. Use any order you wish.
5. Change the size of the bulleted text to 18 points.
6. Save the file as **Rules1**.

Format the Heading

1. Go to the top of the document.
2. Center the heading, and format it with a decorative font.
3. Insert a symbol of your choice before and after the heading (see Illustration B for an example). You may wish to use a different symbol in each place.
4. Format the heading with a font size of 36 points.

Save, Print Preview, and Print

1. Save the document.
2. Print Preview the document if your word processor includes that feature.
3. Print one copy.
4. Close the document, but leave the word processor open.

   A sample solution is shown in Illustration B.

Create a Numbered List

1. Open ☁ **06Rules** from the data files.
2. From the list, choose ten rules that you believe everyone in your household should follow (see Illustration A).
3. Delete the rules you do not want.
4. Create a numbered list of the ten rules.

   Hint: If the Numbering button formats the paragraphs with letters, use the Bullets feature to select the number format you want from the dialog box.

5. Put the rules in the order of their importance to you. Make the most important rule number 1; make the least important rule number 10.

   Hint: Move the rules as necessary to put them in the order you want.

6. Change the size of the text to 18 points.
7. In Word, if necessary, change the paragraph formatting to define a hanging indent of 0.5" to align the first word of each paragraph.
8. Save the file as **Rules2**.

Format the Heading

1. Go to the top of the document.
2. Insert the following three words to the left of the heading:

   My Top Ten

   The title should read:
   My Top Ten House Rules.
3. Format the heading with a decorative font.
4. Center the heading
5. Insert one or more symbols of your choice before and after the heading. You may wish to use a different symbol in each place.
6. Format the heading with a font size of 26 points.
7. If the heading with symbols does not fit on one line, decrease the point size of the text until the heading is on one line.

Save, Print Preview, and Print

1. Save the document.
2. Print Preview the document if your word processor includes that feature.
3. Print one copy.
4. Close the document, and exit the word processor.

   A sample solution is shown in Illustration C.

House Rules

Brush your hair.
Brush your teeth (using toothpaste) every day.
Clean out the garage.
Clean up this room; it's a pig sty.
Comb your hair.
Don't chew with your mouth open.
Don't forget your lunch.
Don't let dust bunnies accumulate.
Don't make me raise my voice.
Don't play with your food.
Don't talk with your mouth full.
Don't throw the ball in the house.
Drive carefully, get home early, and don't stay up too late.
Dry the dishes.
Eat your vegetables.
Get a haircut.
Get that snake out of here.
Keep it down to a dull roar.
Keep your feet off the couch.
Leave some cookies for Mom.
Leave your sister alone.
Look at me when I'm talking to you.
Make your own bed.
Mow the lawn.
No running with scissors in your hand.
Put your clean clothes away.
Put your dirty clothes in the hamper.
Quit bugging your brother.
Quit making that racket.
Rake the leaves.
Sit up straight; don't slouch.
Turn off the TV and do your homework.
Turn that music down. NOW!
Use your napkin.
Wash the dishes.
Wash your hands with soap and hot water before meals.
Wash your neck.
Wipe your feet.

Illustration B. Sample Bulleted List of House Rules

☺ House Rules ☹

- Don't make me raise my voice.
- Look at me when I'm talking to you.
- Get that snake out of here.
- Don't throw the ball in the house.
- Get a haircut.
- Keep it down to a dull roar.
- Eat your vegetables.
- Don't chew with your mouth open.
- Don't talk with your mouth full.
- Don't play with your food.

Illustration C. Sample Numbered List of House Rules

☆ ★ ☆ My Top Ten House Rules ★ ☆ ★

1. Turn that music down. NOW!
2. Turn off the TV and do your homework.
3. Don't make me raise my voice.
4. Drive carefully, get home early, and don't stay up too late.
5. Keep your feet off the couch.
6. Leave your sister alone.
7. Quit bugging your brother.
8. Look at me when I'm talking to you.
9. Don't forget your lunch.
10. Use your napkin.

Exercise 7

Use Paragraph Spacing and Default Tab Stops
■ Control Spacing within Paragraphs ■ Control Spacing between Paragraphs
■ Use Default Tab Stops

NOTES

Control Spacing within Paragraphs

■ The distance between lines within a paragraph is controlled by adjusting the **line spacing**. Most word processors set default line spacing to **auto**, **single**, or **1 line**, which adjusts the line height automatically to the accommodate the tallest character. If you increase or decrease the point size of the text, the line spacing adjusts to the new size.

Try It!

1. Start your word processor and open ☉ **07AnimalFarm** from the data files.
2. Save the document as **AnimalFarm**.
3. Select both paragraphs.
4. Change the line spacing to triple spacing (3 lines).
5. Change the line spacing to double spacing (2 lines).
6. Change the line spacing to 1.5 lines.
7. Save the document, but leave it open.

Control Spacing between Paragraphs

■ To control the distance between paragraphs, use the **Before** and **After** options in the format paragraph dialog boxes, or the **Number of lines** or **Distance in points** options.

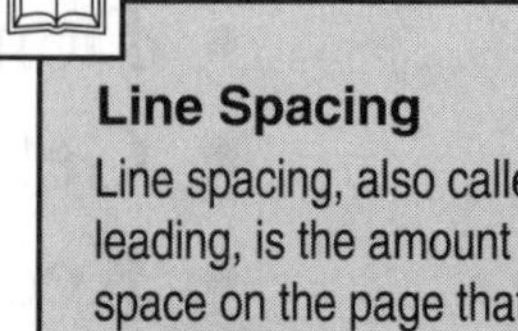

Change Line Spacing

Spacing Between Paragraphs

AppleWorks

Space Before: 12 pt ▼
Space After: 12 pt ▼

Word 98

Spacing
Before: 12 pt
After: 12 pt

MS Works

Spacing
Before: 1 li
After: 0 li

Word for Windows

Spacing
Before: 12 pt
After: 12 pt

WordPerfect

Spacing between paragraphs
● Number of lines 2
○ Distance in points 0

Sample of Spacing After

> The distance between this paragraph and the next is controlled by the After option, which has been set to 12 points.
>
> This paragraph is defined with 0 points before and 12 points after, so it is about 1 line below the preceding paragraph and one line above the next.
>
> This third paragraph is formatted the same as the second.

Spacing After = 12 pt. for these paragraphs.

- For **WordPerfect**, the <u>N</u>umber of lines field specifies the number of lines between paragraphs using the current line spacing. For example, 1 with single-spacing means that each new paragraph begins on the next available line; 2 leaves one blank line before each new paragraph, as shown in the following illustration.

WordPerfect Spacing Between Paragraphs

> The distance between this paragraph and the next one is controlled by the <u>N</u>umber of lines field in the Paragraph Format dialog box. The <u>N</u>umber of lines field has been set to 2.
>
> Note that with single-spaced paragraphs, the value of 2 in <u>N</u>umber of lines creates one blank line between successive paragraphs. A value of 1 causes each new paragraph to begin on the next line.
>
> If the line spacing is increased, the spacing between paragraphs also increases. Instead of <u>N</u>umber of lines, you may choose to specify the Spacing between lines as <u>D</u>istance in points. Although it may be confusing since 12 points equals one line, <u>N</u>umber of lines = 2 is the same as <u>D</u>istance in points = 12. <u>D</u>istance in points begins at 0 while <u>N</u>umber of lines begins at 1.

Spacing between paragraphs
<u>N</u>umber of lines = 2
<u>D</u>istance in points = 12.

Spacing with Blank Paragraphs
You may sometimes find it easier to use blank single-spaced paragraphs to provide spacing between paragraphs.

🖥️ Try It!

1. With both paragraphs in **AnimalFarm** selected, change the line spacing to **1 line**, **Auto**, or **Single**.

2. Place the insertion point at the top of the document.

3. Insert a blank paragraph.

4. In the blank paragraph, type the title: *Animal Farm.*

5. Center the title. (In **WordPerfect**, use **Fo<u>r</u>mat**, **<u>L</u>ine**, **<u>C</u>enter** [Alt+R, L, C] to avoid formatting the remaining two paragraphs.)

6. Change the title's font size to 18 point.

7. Make the title bold and italic.

8. Set the spacing between paragraphs so that 2 blank lines (24 points) appear between the title and the first body paragraph.

9. Set the spacing between the body paragraphs so that 1 blank line appears between them.

10. Double-space both body paragraphs to double spacing (2 lines).

Change Spacing Between Paragraphs

Note that in WordPerfect, you may need to readjust the Spacing between paragraphs so that only one blank line appears between the two body paragraphs.

11. Save and close the document.

Use Default Tab Stops

- By default, most word processors set a tab stop every 0.5". To indent the first line of a paragraph, you can press the Tab key once and Word indents the line ½ inch (0.5") (or you can use the first line indent in the paragraph formatting).

- Tabs are useful for indenting lines and for aligning items in lists, such as the headings of a memorandum. In this exercise, you will use the default tab stops.

- When the option to view non-printing characters is on, the tabs appear as shown in the illustrations below.

WordPerfect Tabs

By default, when you insert a Tab in the middle of a line in WordPerfect, the program formats it as a hanging indent. To insert the Tab character, press Ctrl + Tab .

Show/Hide On Non-Printing Characters Displayed

AppleWorks

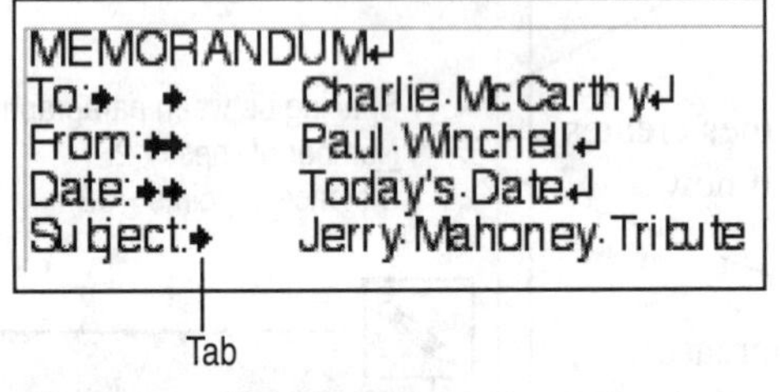

Word 98 for Mac OS

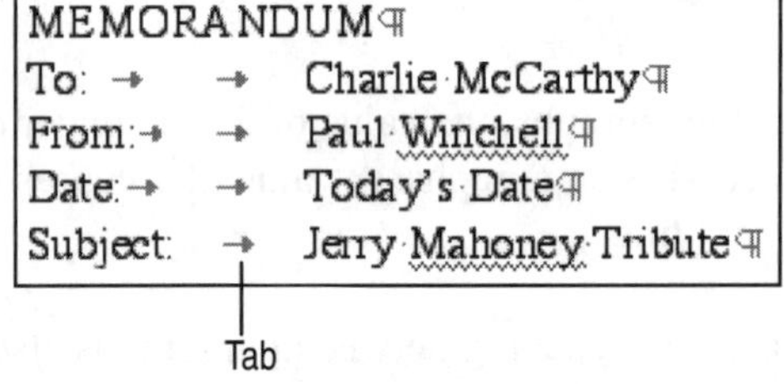

MS Works and Word for Windows

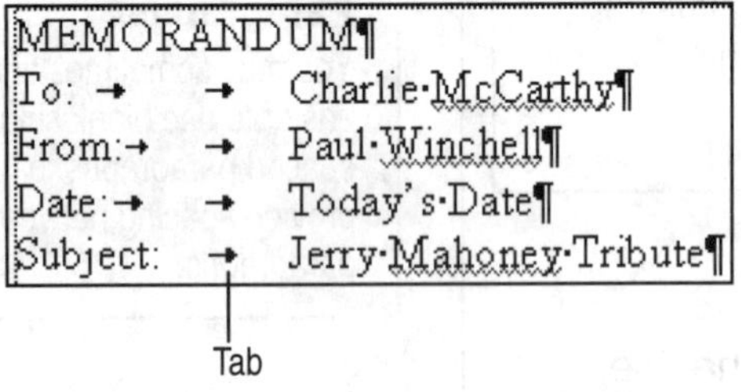

WordPerfect

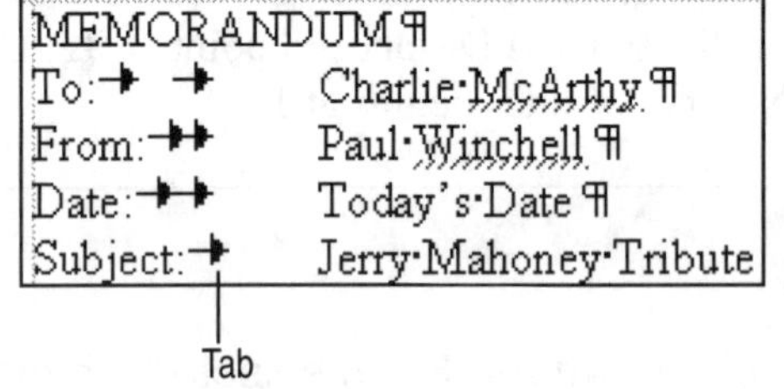

Try It!

1. Open **07Thayer** from the data files.

2. Save the document as **Thayer**.

3. Insert tabs as necessary to align the To, From, Date, and Subject entries.

4. Change *Today's Date* to the current date.

5. Save and close the document. Exit the word processor unless you are continuing with the Exercise Directions.

> **In this exercise, you will format the opening paragraphs of Charles Dickens's *A Christmas Carol*. You will also format parts of a memorandum from the president of *Guppy Aquarium Supply*.**

EXERCISE DIRECTIONS

Format the Title

1. Open 💿 **07Carol** from the data files to display the document shown in Illustration A.

2. Save the document as **Carol**.

3. Center the three title paragraphs.

4. Make the book title—*A Christmas Carol*—Helvetica or Arial, 18 point, bold.

5. Leave 2 blank lines (24 points) after the book title.

6. Make the subtitle—*Stave One*—bold.

7. Specify 1 line (12 points) after the subtitle.

8. Make third line—*Marley's Ghost*—italic.

9. Leave 2 blank lines (24 points) after the paragraph.

10. Save the document.

Format the Body Paragraphs

1. Change the spacing of the body paragraphs to double-space (2 lines).

   Note that with some word processors (MS Works, for example), when you double-space the body, an extra blank line appears above the first paragraph, giving you three blank lines between the third line of the title and the first line of the body.

2. Use the Tab key to Indent the first line of each paragraph 0.5".

3. Print Preview the document if your word processor provides that feature.

4. Save the document.

5. Print one copy.

6. Close the document, but leave the word processor open.

Illustration A: 07Carol Data File

Center all 3 lines. A Christmas Carol —— *Arial or Helvetica, 18 pt. bold, 2 lines or 24 pts. after*

Stave One ———— *Bold, 1 lines or 12 pts after*

Marley's Ghost —— *Ital, 2 lines or 24 pts after*

Marley was dead: to begin with. There is no doubt whatever about that. The register of his burial was signed by the clergyman, the clerk, the undertaker, and the chief mourner. Scrooge signed it: and Scrooge's name was good upon 'Change, for anything he chose to put his hand to. Old Marley was as dead as a door-nail.

Mind! I don't mean to say that I know, of my own knowledge, what there is particularly dead about a door-nail. I might have been inclined, myself, to regard a coffin-nail as the deadest piece of ironmongery in the trade. But the wisdom of our ancestors is in the simile; and my unhallowed hands shall not disturb it, or the Country's done for. You will therefore permit me to repeat, emphatically, that Marley was as dead as a door-nail.

Scrooge knew he was dead? Of course he did. How could it be otherwise? Scrooge and he were partners for I don't know how many years. Scrooge was his sole executor, his sole administrator, his sole assign, his sole residuary legatee, his sole friend, and sole mourner. And even Scrooge was not so dreadfully cut up by the sad event, but that he was an excellent man of business on the very day of the funeral, and solemnised it with an undoubted bargain.

The mention of Marley's funeral brings me back to the point I started from. There is no doubt that Marley was dead. This must be distinctly understood, or nothing wonderful can come of the story I am going to relate.

Indent first line of all body paragraphs 0.5".
Double-space all body paragraphs.

Format the Title

1. Open ☉ **07Memo** from the data fiiles to display the document shown in Illustration B.

2. Save the document as **Memo**.

3. Center the first two paragraphs.

4. Set the line spacing to 1 line, Auto, or Single, as appropriate to your word processor.

5. Make the company name—*Guppy Aquarium Supply*—Arial or Arial Narrow, 24 point, bold, with 1 line (12 points) after.

6. Make the second line—*Interoffice Memorandum*—Arial or Arial Narrow, 20 point, bold, with 3 lines (36 points) after.

Format the Address Information

1. Select the four address paragraphs, and set line spacing to 1.5 lines.

2. Make the following words bold:
   - To:
   - From:
   - Date:
   - Subject:

3. Press the Tab key once after To:, From:, and Date: to align the entries with the Subject: entry.

4. Make *New Products* in the subject line bold and italic.

5. Save the document.

Format the Body Paragraphs

1. Select all body paragraphs and set the spacing to 1 line, Auto, or Single, as appropriate to your word processor.

2. Place your insertion point in the first body paragraph, and specify the following:
   - 1 line before
   - 1 line after
   - First line indent of 0.3"

3. Select the next four paragraphs, and specify the following:
   - Format all four paragraphs for bullets.
   - Set the indents so that the bullet is indented from the left margin at least 0.6".

4. Select the last two body paragraphs, and specify the following:
   - 1 blank line before
   - First line indent of 0.3"

5. Save the document.

Format the Body Text

1. Make the words *NEW PRODUCTS* in the first paragraph bold.

2. Make the catalogue title—*GupAquaS*—bold and italic.

3. Make the numbers in each bullet paragraph bold.

4. Save the document.

5. Print Preview the document if your word processor provides that feature.

6. Print one copy.

7. Compare your results with Illustration C.

8. Close the document, and exit the word processor.

Illustration B. 07Memo

Guppy Aquarium Supply ———— *Center, Arial Narrow or Helvetica-Narrow, 24 point, bold with 1 line (12 pts) after.*

Interoffice Memorandum———— *Center, Arial Narrow or Helvetica-Narrow, 20 point, bold with 3 lines (36 pts) after.*

To: All staff

From: Phyte Ng Fisch, Vice-President

Date: Today's Date — *ital*

Subject: New Products

Use Tab after colon to align entries with New Products. Bold To:, From:, Date:, Subject:, Bold and italic New Products. Change line spacing to 1.5 lines

Single-space with 1 li (12 pts) before; Indent first line 0.3".

We are pleased to announce that the following NEW PRODUCTS have been added to

our product line and are included in the latest GupAquaS catalogue: ———— *One line after*

— *bold*

— *bold, ital*

18034 Micronite Filter 800

17045 Pearlite Sand and Gravel

16036 Seahorse Seafloor Panorama

15029 Balanced Aquarium #29

Single-space, bullets, bold numbers, left indent so bullet is at least 0.6" from margin.

Please refer to the catalogue and individual product fact sheets for full descriptions and

pricing of these new products. Your supervisors will be holding brief briefings on each of

these products within the near future.

Thanks to your superb efforts, we continue be the leading supplier of aquarium

necessities and accessories. Keep up the good work.

Single-space; Indent first line indent 0.3"; One line before.

Guppy Aquarium Supply

Interoffice Memorandum

To: All staff

From: Phyte Ng Fisch, Vice-President

Date: Today's Date

Subject: *New Products*

We are pleased to announce that the following **NEW PRODUCTS** have been added to our product line and are included in the latest *GupAquaS* catalogue:

- **18034** Micronite Filter 800
- **17045** Pearlite Sand and Gravel
- **16036** Seahorse Seafloor Panorama
- **15029** Balanced Aquarium #29

Please refer to the catalogue and individual product fact sheets for full descriptions and pricing of these new products. Your supervisors will be holding brief briefings on each of these products within the near future.

Thanks to your superb efforts, we continue be the leading supplier of aquarium necessities and accessories. Keep up the good work.

NEXT EXERCISE

Work with Multiple-page Documents
■ Insert Page Breaks   ■ Set Margins   ■ Use Headers and Footers

NOTES

Insert Page Breaks

■ Most word processors provide two types of page breaks: automatic and manual. Word and WordPerfect provide a third type called a forced page break that is specified as part of the paragraph formatting. Forced page breaks are not described in this lesson.

- Word processors insert an **automatic page break** when they reach the bottom margin of a page. Different word processors signal automatic page breaks in different ways.

  ♦ **AppleWorks** shows the bottom of one page and the top of the next. The guidelines indicate where the text of one page ends and the next begins.

  ♦ In Normal view, **MS Works** displays a symbol ▮▷ at the left edge of the document where the new page begins. In Page Layout view, it shows the bottom of one page and the top of the next.

  ♦ In Normal view, **Word** displays a dotted line across the window. In Page or Print Layout view, Word shows the bottom of one page and the top of the next.

  ♦ In Draft view, **WordPerfect** displays a solid line across the page. In Page view, it shows the bottom of one page and the top of the next.

- If you do not like where the automatic page break occurs, you can insert a **manual page break** to start a new page where you wish.

  ♦ **AppleWorks** shows the bottom of one page and the top of the next. The guidelines indicate where the one page ends and the next begins, and a page icon ▣ or ▤ indicates where the page break occurs.

  ♦ In Normal view, **MS Works** displays a dotted line across the window, and the symbol ▮▷ at the left edge of the document where the new page begins. In Page Layout view, it displays a dotted line where the manual page break occurs, and it shows the bottom of one page and the top of the next.

  ♦ In Normal view, **Word** displays a dotted line across the window with the words Page Break in the line. In Page or Print Layout view, Word displays the dotted line and the bottom of one page and the top of the next.

  ♦ In Draft view, **WordPerfect** displays a solid double-line across the page. In Page view, it shows the bottom of one page and the top of the next. An invisible character indicates the page break. You can view and delete the hard page break character HPg through **View**, Reveal **C**odes (Alt+V, C).

Hard Page Break
Some users and word processors refer to an inserted page break as a **hard page break**.

Try It!

1. Open ⊙ **08WebPage** from the data files.
2. Save the document as **WebPage**.
3. Scroll down, if necessary, to find the automatic page break.
4. Place your insertion point at the beginning of the heading before the paragraph in which the automatic page break occurs.
5. Insert a manual page break.
   A manual page break appears before the heading.
6. Save the document, but leave it open.

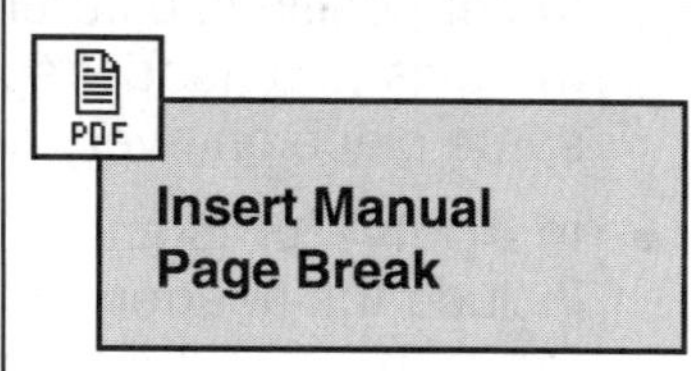

Set Margins

- For many of your documents, the word processor's default margins are appropriate. To check the default margins, create a new document and display the dialog box that lets you change margins. You can then check the default margins for new documents.

- Sometimes you may wish a page to include more (or less) text than the default margins allow. To increase the amount of text a page can hold, you make the margins smaller. (Smaller margins create longer text lines.) To decrease the amount of text a page can hold, you make the margins larger. (Larger margins create shorter text lines.)

Try It!

1. Change the margins for the entire **WebPage** document to those listed below:

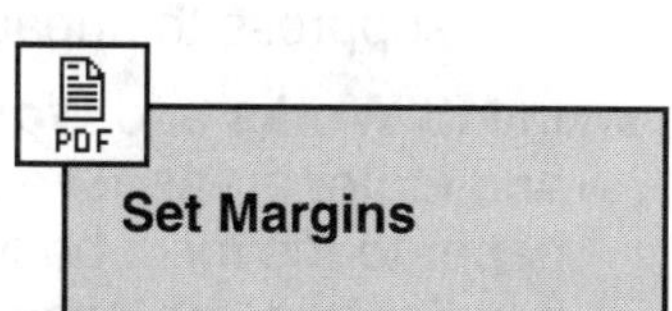

   AppleWorks & WordPerfect
   - Top   0.75"   Left   1"
   - Bottom   0.75"   Right   1"

   MS Works & Word (all versions)
   - Top   1.25"   Left   1"
   - Bottom   1.25"   Right   1"

2. Ignore any other settings in the dialog boxes.
3. Click OK to close the dialog box.
4. Remove the manual page break.
5. Insert a new manual page break so that no paragraph is separated from its heading and so that no break occurs within a paragraph.
6. Review and save the document.

Use Headers and Footers

- Headers and footers are used to insert information that appears at the top or bottom of every page. For example, in a multiple-page report, you may use headers and footers to insert your name and the page number at the top or bottom of every page.

- As a general rule, in a report like **WebPage**, the first page does not contain a header and the footer of each page displays the page number. Also, the body text of each page should start at the same distance from the top edge of the paper. Different word processors specify header and footer positions differently in relation to margins, so you have to adjust margins and header spacing to ensure that the body text starts in the same place on every page.

- In **AppleWorks** and **WordPerfect**, the top and bottom margins do not include the header and footer areas. The header area is just below the top margin, so the top margin specifies the distance from the top edge of the paper to the header (if any). The footer area is just above the bottom margin. The footer ends at the bottom margin, so the bottom margin specifies the distance from the bottom of the paper to the bottom of the footer.

  - In **AppleWorks**, you use blank lines to separate the header and footer from the body text. Thus, if you want the main text of a document to begin 1.25" from the top of the paper and the header to begin at 0.75", you need to specify a top margin of 0.75" and create a three-line header (assuming a 12-point line).

  - In **WordPerfect**, you can use blank lines or a field called *Distance between text and header* (*footer*) to separate the header or footer from the body text. Thus, if you want the body of the document to begin 1.25" from the top of the page and the header to begin at 0.75", you specify a top margin of 0.75" and a distance from text of about 0.30" for the header. These parameters keep the top line of body text aligned from page to page. WordPerfect allows you to suppress the header or footer on any page.

- In **MS Works** and **Word**, the top and bottom margins include the header and footer areas. The margins specify the distance from the edge of the paper to the main body text. Special header and footer margins specify how far from the edge of the paper the header or footer is to start. Thus, if you want the text to begin 1.25" from the top edge of the paper and the header to begin at 0.75", you need to specify a top margin of 1.25" and a header margin of 0.75", creating a header area of 0.5".

- **Note:** Because of differences in the way headers and footers are specified and appear in different word processors, the Try It! activities for headers and footers and the procedures are given for each of the word processors in the sections that follow:

  - AppleWorks, below
  - Word 98, page 181
  - MS Works, page 182
  - Word 97 & 2000, page 182
  - Corel WordPerfect, page 185

Try It! for AppleWorks

Insert a Section Break

To set the document so that no header appears on the first page but a page number appears at the bottom, you use AppleWorks, Section feature.

1. In **WebPage**, verify that the top and bottom margins are set to 0.75".

2. Place the insertion point at the end of the first page of the document after the sentence that ends *which might take several clicks to get*

back to the desired location but before the paragraph mark, as shown in the following illustration.

Place Insertion Point for Inserting Section Break

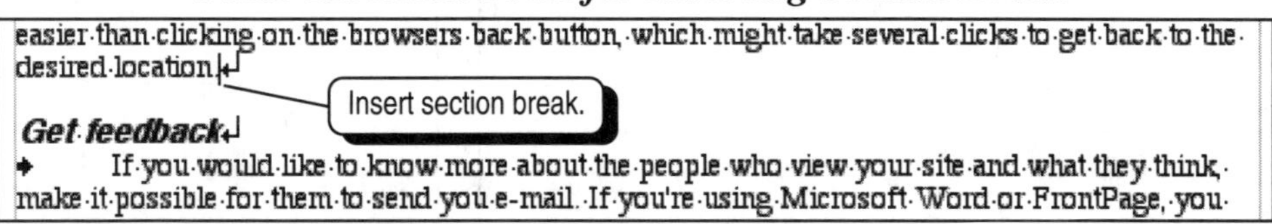

3. Press **Option** + **Enter** (not the Return key).

   OR

   Click **Format**, **Insert Section Break**.

4. Delete the paragraph mark after the section break symbol.

5. Place the insertion point anywhere in the second page.

6. Click **Format**, **Section**.

7. Complete the **Section: 2** dialog box as shown in the following illustration.

Section: 2 Dialog Box

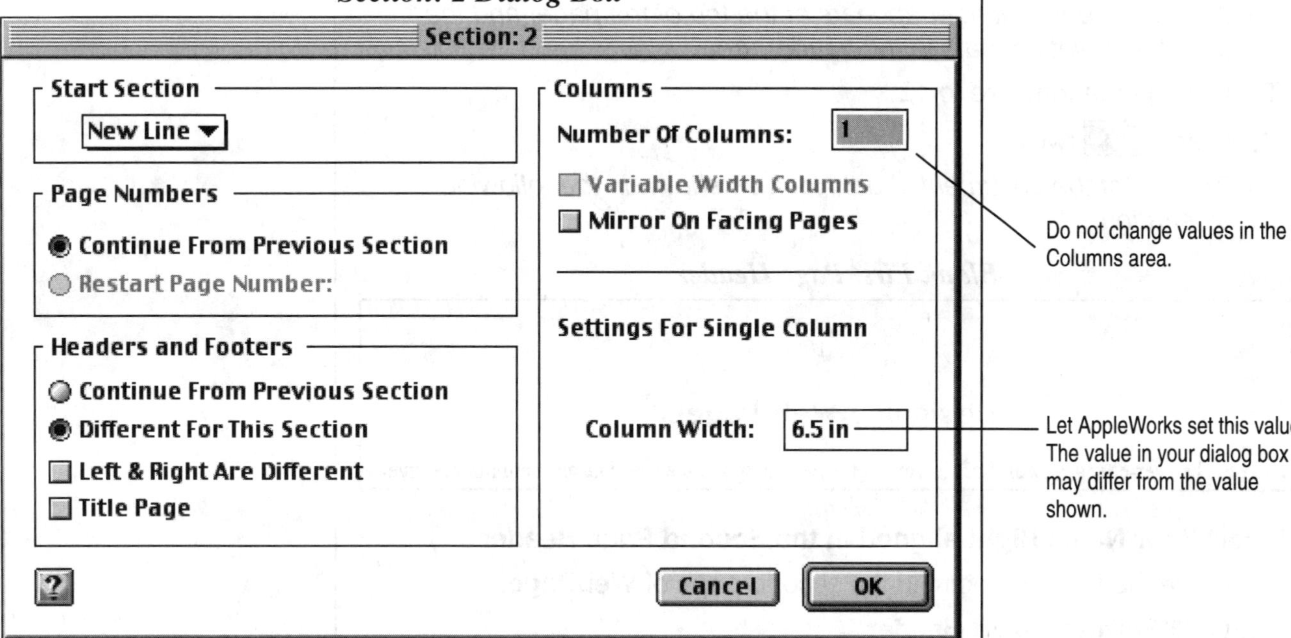

8. Insert a manual page break before the heading *Get feedback.*

   The bottom of the first page and the top of the second page should appear as shown in the following illustration. Note that a manual page break within a section has a different symbol from other manual page breaks.

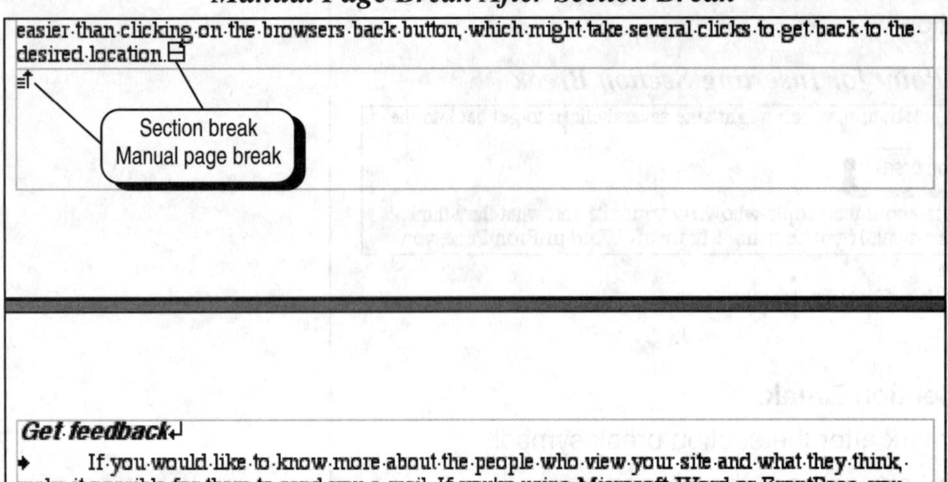

Create a Blank Header on the First Page

1. Place the insertion point in the first page of **WebPage**.

2. Click **Format**, **Insert Header**.

   A blank one-line header appears at the top of the page, and the insertion point appears in the header area.

3. Change the font size to 12

4. Press Return twice.

   The top of the document should look as shown in the following illustration.

Blank First Page Header

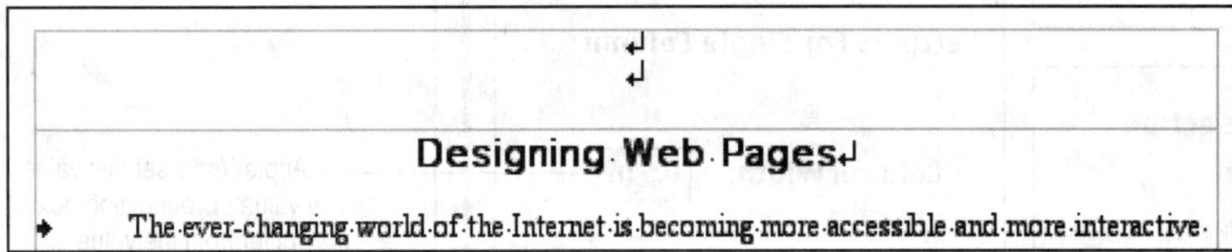

Insert Your Name Right-aligned in the Second Page Header

1. Place the insertion point in the second page of **WebPage**.

2. Click **Format**, **Insert Header**.
   A blank one-line header appears at the top of the page, and the insertion point appears in the header area.

3. In the Header area at the top of the page.

   a. Click the Right alignment button on the ruler.
   b. Type your name.
   c. Format your name as Times, 12 point, normal.
   d. Press Return twice to create two blank lines after your name.

4. Click in the body of the document.

Insert the Page Number in the Footer

1. With the insertion anywhere in the second page of **Web Page**, click **Format, Insert Footer**.

A blank one-line footer appears at the bottom of the page.

2. In the footer area:

   a. Click the Center alignment button ▤ on the ruler.
   b. Press Return once to create a blank line before the page number.
   c. Type - (hyphen) space.
   d. Click **Edit**, **Insert Page #**.
   e. Type space, - (hyphen).
   f. Format the footer as Times, 12 point, normal.

3. Click in the body of the document.

Review the Results

1. Use Zoom and scroll to review the headers and footers. The first page should have a blank header, but the footer should appear on each page.

2. Save and print the document.
   The main text on each page should be on about the same line.

3. Close the document and exit AppleWorks unless you are continuing with the Exercise directions.

Footer on Page 1
The footer on page 1 is actually in Section 2; that is why it appears when you insert a footer with the insertion point on the second page (which is in Section 2).

🖳 Try It! for Word 98

Use Page Setup to Avoid a Header on the First Page

1. Place the insertion point at the top of **WebPage**.
2. Click **File**, **Page Setup** to display the Print (Page Setup) dialog box.
3. Click the Margins button **Margins...**.
4. Click the **Margins** tab if necessary.
5. Verify that the header and footer begin 0.75" from the edges of the paper. Leave the dialog box open.
6. Click the **Layout** tab of the Page Setup dialog box.
7. Select the option **Different first page**.
8. Click **OK** (Return).
9. Click **View**, **Page Layout**. (Headers are not displayed in Normal view.)

Insert the Page Number as a Footer

1. Insert a footer that displays the page number with a hyphen on each side like this: - 1 -

2. Anywhere on the first page of the document, click **View**, **Header and Footer**.

   The Header area appears at the top of the page and the Header and Footer toolbar appears. The insertion point is in the Header area ready for you to type and insert text.

3. Click the Switch Between Header and Footer button on the Header and Footer toolbar.

4. In the footer area

   a. Click the Center button or press +.

   b. Type - (hyphen) space.

   c. On the Header and Footer toolbar, click the Insert Page Number button .

   d. Type space, - (hyphen).

   e. Ensure that the text is Times New Roman, 12 point.

   f. Select the footer text and copy it.

   g. Click the Show Next button .

   h. Paste the footer text and center the paragraph.

   This step ensures that the footer on the first page and the footer on following pages will be the same.

Insert Your Name Right-aligned in the Header on Page 2

1. Click the Switch Between Header and Footer button on the Header and Footer toolbar.

   The insertion point is positioned in the Header area of page two.

2. In the header area:

   a. Click the Align Right button or press +.

   b. Type your name.

   c. Ensure that the text is Times New Roman, 12 point.

   d. Click **Close** on the Header and Footer toolbar.

Review the Results

1. Print Preview the document to review the headers.

   The first page header should be blank and the header on page two should display your name.

2. Close Print Preview, save the document, and print it.

3. Exit Word unless you are continuing with the Exercise Directions.

Try It! for MS Works

Use Page Setup to Avoid a Header on the First Page

1. Place the insertion point at the top of **WebPage**.

2. Click **File**, **Page Setup** (+,).

3. Click the **Margins** tab (+).

4. Verify that the header and footer margins are 0.75" from the edges of the paper. Leave the dialog box open.

5. Click the **O̲ther Options** tab (Alt+O) of the Page Setup dialog box.

6. Select the option **N̲o header on first page** (Alt+N).

7. Click OK (Enter).

8. Click **V̲iew**, **P̲age Layout** (Alt+V, P).

Insert the Page Number in the Footer

1. Go to the bottom of the first page.

2. Insert a footer that displays the page number with a hyphen on each side like this: - 1 -

3. Click in the Footer area, and do the following:

   a. Click the Center Align button ≡ or press Ctrl+E.

   b. Type - (hyphen) space.

   c. Click **I̲nsert**, **P̲age Number** (Alt+I, P).

      *Works inserts the code *page* which prints as a number displays as a number in Print Preview.*

   d. Type space, - (hyphen).

   e. Ensure that the text is Times New Roman, 12 point.

Insert Your Name Right-aligned in the Header on Page 2

1. Insert a header on page two that displays your name right-aligned.

2. Click in the Header area at the top of the second page, and do the following.

   a. Click the Right Align button ≡.

   b. Type your name.

   c. Ensure that the text is Times New Roman, 12 point.

   d. Click anywhere in the body of the document.

Review the Results

1. Print Preview the document to review the headers and footer.

   The first page header should be blank and the header on page two should display your name. The footers should display the page number with a hyphen on each side.

2. Close Print Preview and save the document.

3. Print the document. Close the document and exit Works unless you are continuing with the Exercise Directions.

Try It! for Word 97 & 2000

Use Page Setup to Avoid a Header on the First Page

1. Place the insertion point at the top of **WebPage**.

2. Click **F̲ile**, **Page Set̲up** (Alt+F, U).

3. Click the **M̲argins** tab (Alt+M).

4. Verify that the header and footer begin 0.75" from the edges of the paper. Leave the dialog box open.

5. Click the **L̲ayout** tab (Alt+L) of the Page Setup dialog box.

6. Select the option **Different first page** (Alt+F).

7. Click **OK** (Enter).

8. Click **View**, **Page** or **Print Layout** (Alt+V, P). (Headers are not displayed in Normal view.)

Insert the Page Number as a Footer

1. Insert a footer that displays the page number with a hyphen on each side like this: - 1 -

2. Anywhere on the first page of the document, click **View**, **Header and Footer** (Alt+V, H).

   The Header area appears at the top of the page and the Header and Footer toolbar appears. The insertion point is in the Header area ready for you to type and insert text.

Word 97 and 2000 Header and Footer Toolbar

3. Click the Switch Between Header and Footer button on the Header and Footer toolbar.

4. In the footer area

   a. Click the Center button or press Ctrl+E.

   b. Type - (hyphen) space.

   c. On the Header and Footer toolbar, click the Insert Page Number button.

   d. Type space, - (hyphen).

   e. Ensure that the text is Times New Roman, 12 point.

   f. Copy the footer text.

   g. Click the Show Next button.

   h. Paste the footer text and center the paragraph.

   This step ensures that the footer on the first page and the footer on following pages will be the same.

Insert Your Name Right-aligned in the Header on Page 2

1. Click the Switch Between Header and Footer button.

   The insertion point is positioned in the Header area of page two.

2. In the header area:

   a. Click the Align Right button or press Ctrl+R.

   b. Type your name.

   c. Ensure that the text is Times New Roman, 12 point.

   d. Click **Close** on the Header and Footer toolbar.

Review the Results

1. Print Preview the document to review the headers.

The first page header should be blank and the header on page two should display your name.

2. Close Print Preview, save the document, and print it.

3. Exit Word unless you are continuing with the Exercise Directions.

Try It! for WordPerfect

Insert the Page Number in the Footer

1. Place the insertion point at the top of **WebPage**.

2. Click **View**, **Page** (**Alt**+**V**, **P**).

   (Headers and footers are not displayed in Draft view.)

3. Insert a footer that displays the page number with a hyphen on each side like this: - 1 -

4. Click **Insert**, **Header/Footer** (**Alt**+**I**, **H**).

5. Select **Footer A** (**F**).

6. Click **Create** (**Alt**+**C**).

   The insertion point is positioned in the footer area ready for you to type, and some new buttons appear on the Application Bar.

7. In the footer area:

   a. Click **Format**, **Line**, **Center** (**Alt**+**R**, **L**, **C**).

   b. Type - (hyphen) space.

   c. Click the Page Numbering button **#1**.

   d. Type space, - (hyphen).

   e. Ensure that the text is Times New Roman, 12 point.

   f. Click the Header/Footer Distance button.

   g. Set the value to 0.300".

   h. Click **OK** (**Enter**).

Insert Your Name Right-aligned in the Header on Page 2

1. Place the insertion point at the beginning of page two. (It should be just before the heading *Allow for Easy Navigation*.)

2. Change the top margin to 0.75".

3. Insert a header on page two that displays your name right justified.

4. Click **Insert**, **Header/Footer** (**Alt**+**I**, **H**).

5. Select **Header A** (**H**).

6. Click **Create** (**Alt**+**C**).

   The insertion point is positioned in the header area ready for you to type.

7. In the header area:

   a. Click **Format**, **Line**, **Flush Right** (**Alt**+**R**, **L**, **F**).

   b. Type your name.

   c. Ensure that the text is Times New Roman, 12 point.

   d. Click the Header/Footer Distance button ⬍ on the toolbar.

   e. Set the value to 0.300".

   f. Click [OK] ([Enter]).

   These values ensure that the body text of pages one and two begin at close to the same distance from the top of the page and that no header appears on the first page.

8. Click anywhere in the body of the first page of the document.

Review the Results

1. Click **View**, **Two Pages** ([Alt]+[V], [W]) to verify that the header appears only on page two and that the first line of body text on pages one and two align at the top.

2. Save and print the document. Close the document and exit WordPerfect unless you are continuing with the Exercise Directions.

In this exercise, you will format a book report and insert a header and footer.

EXERCISE DIRECTIONS

Open the File and Format the Document

1. Open 💿 **08Report** from the data files.

2. Save the document as **Report**.

3. Format the document as directed in Illustration A. The illustration shows the entire document on one page. Your data file may take more than one page.

   For help in paragraph and line formatting, see Exercise 3. For help with text formatting, see Exercise 4.

4. Set the left and right margins to 1.25", but leave the other margins unchanged.

5. Save the document.

Copy and Paste the Song

1. Copy the nine-line song "William Matrimatoes."

2. Paste it just before the final paragraph.

3. Be sure that there is a blank line between the last paragraph of the song and the paragraph that identifies the author and book.

4. Save the document.

General Directions

- Your objective in the remainder of this exercise is to set margins, create headers and footers, and insert manual page breaks so that:

Body Text

- Begins at 1.5" from the top edge of the paper on every page.

- No paragraph splits across pages.

Header

- Does not appear on the first page.

- Begins at 0.75" from the top edge of the paper.

- Is separated from the text by three blank lines (**AppleWorks**) or 0.6" (**WordPerfect**). (**Word's** separation from the text is automatic when you specify the header position from the edge of the page.)

- Contains your name right-aligned.
  Windows: Times New Roman, 12 point, regular (no bold, no italic)
  AppleWorks: Helvetica, 12 point, regular (no bold, no italic).

Footer

- Appears at 0.5" from the bottom edge of the paper.

- Is separated from the text by approximately 2 lines (0.3") in **AppleWorks** and **WordPerfect**.

- Appears on all pages.

- Displays - n - where n is the page number.
  Windows: Times New Roman, 12 point, regular (no bold, no italic)
  AppleWorks: Helvetica, 12 point, regular (no bold, no italic).

AppleWorks Hints

1. Set the top margin to 0.75".

2. Set the bottom margin to 0.5".

3. Insert a section break after the colon in the sentence *Ms. White concludes:*. (Be sure it is before the paragraph mark.)

4. Delete the blank paragraph after the section break.

5. Format the second section to begin on a New Line.

6. Insert a page break before the paragraph that begins *And I still miss him*.

7. On the first page, create a blank header of four lines of 12 points each.

8. On the second page, create the header with your name right-aligned.

9. Insert two blank lines above the footer text.

10. Save the document.

11. Print the document, and exit AppleWorks.

MS Works Hints

1. Set the margins as follows:
   - Top to 1.5"
   - Bottom to 1"
   - Left to 1.25"
   - Right to 1.25"
   - Header to 0.75"
   - Footer to 0.5"

2. On the Other Options tab, select No header on first page.

3. Specify the footer in the footer area on the first page.

4. On the second page, specify the header.

5. Insert a manual page break before the paragraph that begins *When spring came again*.

6. Save the document.

7. Print Preview the document.

8. Print the document, and exit Works.

Word Hints

1. Set the margins as follows to Apply to Whole document:
   - Top to 1.5"
   - Bottom to 1"
   - Left to 1.25"
   - Right to 1.25"
   - Header to 0.75"
   - Footer to 0.5"

2. On the Layout tab, select Different first page.

3. Specify the footer for the first page and copy the text to the second page, using Show Next to move from the first to the second page.

4. On the second page, specify the header, using Switch between Header and Footer to reach the header area.

5. Insert a manual page break before the paragraph that begins *When spring came again*.

6. Save the document.

7. Print Preview the document.

8. Print the document, and exit Word.

WordPerfect Hints

1. Set the top margin of the first page to 1.5".

2. Insert the footer on the first page, and set the *Distance between text and footer* to 0.30".

3. If the margins of the footer are outside the new page margins, use Format, Margins to set the footer's left and right margins to 1.25".

4. On the second page, set a top margin of 0.75".

5. Insert the header and set the *Distance between text and header* to 0.6".

6. If the margins of the header are outside the new page margins, use Format, Margins to set the header's left and right margins to 1.25".

7. Insert a manual page break before the paragraph that begins *When spring came again*.

8. Save the document.

9. Print the document, and exit WordPerfect.

Illustration A. Report (Shown on one page for ease of illustration)

Bold, 14 point all three lines

> Report on "Joe King" from
> *Mama Makes Up Her Mind*
> by Bailey White

Indent first line 0.5". — In her book, *Mama Makes Up Her Mind and Other Dangers of Southern Living*, Bailey White tells the story of Joe King, the man who allowed her to ride an old horse named Tony. The story tells of the song she and Joe King used to sing as she rode Tony, while Joe King rode a younger, more spirited Kentucky mare.

Indent all lines 1" from left margin.

> William Matrimatoes
> He's a good fisherman
> Catches hens
> Puts 'em in pens
> Wire bright
> Clock fell down
> Little mice run around
> Old dirty dishrag
> You spell out and go.

Indent first line 0.5". — She and Joe didn't understand the song. "Something wrong with that song," Joe King would say. "Sure is something wrong with that song." They couldn't figure out what was wrong, but Bailey liked it anyway, especially the "tap-tap-tapping part in the chorus."

Indent first line 0.5". — One day Tony the horse got so old that he dwindled away and died. As they dragged his carcass away,

Indent all lines 0.75" left and right.

> The mare stood up high on her feet and stared down the road where they had dragged Tony. She was trembling and shaking. Then she lifted her head and gave out a high, blowing whistle. It was almost like a cry. Joe King slapped her on the shoulder. "He's gone," Joe King said. "He ain't never coming back." The horse whistled again and Joe King gave her another comforting slap. "He's dead and gone, and you ain't never gon' see him no more."

Indent first line 0.5". — Joe King died soon after. Bailey White went to his funeral, her first. She was more surprised at Joe's being dressed in clothes she had never seen before than by the spectacle of the funeral, with his relatives and their sorrowful grief.

Indent first line 0.5". — When spring came again, Ms. White missed Joe King for the first time. He didn't come driving up in his "powdery blue pickup truck smelling like horses and saddles and axle grease and Prince Albert." Ms. White concludes:

Indent all lines 0.75" left and right.

> And I still miss him…. I think about Joe King. I remember the elegant grieving of the Kentucky mare, and the eerie, high, blowing whistle she gave. That's how I would like to mourn. But I don't have that much style. Instead, I like to take a little walk in the spring sunshine, and I say to myself:

Hanging indent of 0.50". — White, Bailey. *Mama Makes Up Her Mind and Other Dangers of Southern Living*. Reading, MA: Addison-Wesley Publishing Company, 1993.

Illustration B. Desired Result (Word 2000 shown) Page 1

Report on "Joe King" from
Mama Makes Up Her Mind
by Bailey White

In her book, *Mama Makes Up Her Mind and Other Dangers of Southern Living*, Bailey White tells the story of Joe King, the man who allowed her to ride an old horse named Tony. The story tells of the song she and Joe King used to sing as she rode Tony, while Joe King rode a younger, more spirited Kentucky mare.

> William Matrimatoes
> He's a good fisherman
> Catches hens
> Puts 'em in pens
> Wire bright
> Clock fell down
> Little mice run around
> Old dirty dishrag
> You spell out and go.

She and Joe didn't understand the song. "Something wrong with that song," Joe King would say. "Sure is something wrong with that song." They couldn't figure out what was wrong, but Bailey liked it anyway, especially the "tap-tap-tapping part in the chorus."

One day Tony the horse got so old that he dwindled away and died. As they dragged his carcass away,

> The mare stood up high on her feet and stared down the road
> where they had dragged Tony. She was trembling and shaking.
> Then she lifted her head and gave out a high, blowing whistle. It
> was almost like a cry. Joe King slapped her on the shoulder. "He's
> gone," Joe King said. "He ain't never coming back." The horse
> whistled again and Joe King gave her another comforting slap.
> "He's dead and gone, and you ain't never gon' see him no more."

Joe King died soon after. Bailey White went to his funeral, her first. She was more surprised at Joe's being dressed in clothes she had never seen before than by the spectacle of the funeral, with his relatives and their sorrowful grief.

- 1 -

Your Name

When spring came again, Ms. White missed Joe King for the first time. He didn't come driving up in his "powdery blue pickup truck smelling like horses and saddles and axle grease and Prince Albert." Ms. White concludes:

> And I still miss him…. I think about Joe King. I remember the
> elegant grieving of the Kentucky mare, and the eerie, high,
> blowing whistle she gave. That's how I would like to mourn. But I
> don't have that much style. Instead, I like to take a little walk in
> the spring sunshine, and I say to myself:

> > William Matrimatoes
> > He's a good fisherman
> > Catches hens
> > Puts 'em in pens
> > Wire bright
> > Clock fell down
> > Little mice run around
> > Old dirty dishrag
> > You spell out and go.

White, Bailey. *Mama Makes Up Her Mind and Other Dangers of Southern Living.* Reading, MA: Addison-Wesley Publishing Company, 1993.

NEXT EXERCISE

Exercise 9

■ Challenge Exercises

EXERCISE DIRECTIONS

Format a Story

1. Open ⊚ **09Fairmaiden** from the data files.

2. Save the document as **Fairmaiden**.

3. Set left and right margins of 1.25".

4. Double-space the document.

5. Change the font size for all text to 11 points.

6. Insert a title at the top of the document:

   The Fair Maiden

   Hint: In MS Works, you need to re-set the line spacing for the title to 1 line to remove the blank line above the title.

7. Center the title.

8. Make it Arial or Helvetica, 24-point bold, italic.

9. Leave 36 points (three lines) after the title paragraph.

   Hint: In some word processors you may need to remove space before the title paragraph. And, because Line spacing is already set to Double, one blank line already follows the title. You need to specify enough space after the title to bring the total to 36 points or the equivalent of three lines.

10. Save the document.

Specify a Footer

1. Set the top margin so that the body text (including the title) begins at 1.5" from the top edge of the paper on each page.

2. Set the bottom margin so that the last line of body text ends 1" from the bottom edge of the paper.

3. Center a page number in the footer 0.5" from the bottom edge of each page. Do not use hyphens.

4. Make the footer text 11 point, no bold, no italic in the font of the body text.

5. In AppleWorks and WordPerfect, separate the footer text from the body text by about 0.5".

6. Save the document.

7. Print Preview the document if your word processor includes that feature.

8. Spell check the title and save the document.

9. Print one copy.

10. Compare your first page with the first page shown in Illustration A. (Your page may end on a different line and your lines may end with different words.)

11. Close the document.

The Fair Maiden

Once upon a time, in a faraway land, a fair maiden sat musing. "I haven't been threatened for months," she sighed. "What's the world coming to when a fair maiden can go for months without even a hint of a foul play from a dragon or a pirate or an ogre? Why not even an old hag of a witch has come my way since late last summer."

At that very moment, little did the fair maiden suspect, a plot was hatching, a cauldron of wickedness was brewing, a threat to her serenity was afoot. For in the secret reaches of a dark cave (where else?) sat a sinister sister, a brooding brother, and a malodorous ogre conspiring to shatter the calm. "We'll steal her highness," hissed the sister. "We'll abduct her," vowed the brother. "We'll carry her off," growled the ogre. With many like utterances, they put their heads together, breathing in and out. With each exhalation, they spoke of new terrors. "We'll force her to eat spinach and gooseberry tarts." "We'll tie her in geometric and algebraic knots." "We'll make her do the New York Times crossword."

About the same time, a handsome youth was riding through the forest, seeking adventure. As is the way with such youths, his mind was on slaying dragons, rescuing fair maidens, and Nintendo games. "Oh," he said, "what I wouldn't give for a scaly beast to slay, an ogre to fight, an hour of Mario Brothers or Sim City!" The handsome youth rode right past the cave of the three sinister figures.

"I suppose," said the sister as she saw him ride past, "that youth thinks he can protect the fair maiden." "Perhaps," agreed the brother. "No way we'll let him," swore the ogre. So they chased the handsome youth, fell upon him, bound, gagged, and carried him trussed to their den just like the Ewoks captured Luke, Han, and Chewbacca in Star Wars.

1

Format a Letter

1. Open ⊙ **09Gourmet** from the data disk. Create the result shown in Illustration B by following the steps below.

2. Save the document as **Gourmet**.

3. Space the text as follows:

   - Two blank lines (24 points) between the city line and the date.
   - Three blank lines after the date.
   - One blank line above and below the salutation (*Dear Mr. Sturgeon:*).
   - One blank line between each paragraph of the letter.
   - One blank line above the complimentary closing (*Sincerely,*).
   - Three blank lines between the complimentary closing and the signature name.

4. Save the document.

5. Center the first three lines (the writer's name and address).

6. Format the first line with a decorative font, such as Impact, with a font size of 18 points. Use the font color red.

7. Format the writer's address lines to Arial Narrow or Arial, 12 point, bold. Make them blue.

8. Insert today's date where specified.

9. Print Preview the document if your word processor includes that feature.

10. Save the document.

11. Print one copy.

12. Close the document, and exit the word processor unless you are continuing with the Challenge Exercises.

Illustration B. Formatted Letter

Phineas Bream
814 Court Street
Scott City, KS 67871

Today's Date

Mr. Hake Sturgeon
The E-Z Gourmet
1234 Lobster Lane
Cabot Cove, ME 01333

Dear Mr. Sturgeon:

On your January TV show, seen in this area on KGLD in Garden City, KS, you demonstrated how to prepare creamy clam chowder. Fresh clams not being available here on the plains of Kansas, I substituted canned oysters. What a treat the dish turned out to be!

When I served it to my family, accompanied by a cucumber and tomato salad, the raves were long and as hearty as the chowder itself.

Thanks for such a tasty recipe.

Sincerely,

Phineas Bream

Create a Memorandum

1. Start the word processor and create a new
    document.

2. Save the document as **Latin Club**.

3. Leave the margins as set by your word processor.

4. Press Enter or Return three times.

5. Place the insertion point in the first paragraph and
    type the memorandum shown in Illustration C.

    *Note that your line endings may differ from those
    in the illustration.*

    a. For the word *MEMORANDUM*, use Times New
        Roman, 24-point bold or Geneva, 24-point
        bold.
    b. Underline the word *Memorandum*.
    c. Use the default font for all text except the
        Memorandum heading.
    d. Make To:, From:, Date:, and Subject: bold.
    e. Use default tab stops to align the address
        entries.
    f. Format the bullets and indents using the
        appropriate buttons on the Formatting toolbar.
    g. Use blank lines to separate the body
        paragraphs.
    h. Italicize the Latin words as shown.

6. Spell check the document.

7. Print Preview the document.

8. Print one copy.

9. Close the document, and exit the word processor.

Illustration C. Latin Club Memorandum

<u>MEMORANDUM</u>

To: Members of Latin Club

From: Your name

Date: Today's Date

Subject: Installation of New Officers

Ave, amici.

The year-end meeting of the Latin Club will be held on Thursday, June 4, at 3:30 in Room 225. At that time, we will officially install the following new Latin Club officers:

- Miguel Palacio, President
- Mary Jane Pastore, Vice-President
- Allison Clarke, Secretary
- Hanover Chase, Treasurer

Refreshments will be served at the end of the installation. Outgoing officers will express their appreciation to Mr. Cato, our club sponsor, and plans for travel to next year's state Junior Classical League conference will be discussed.

It has been a great year. *Gratias.*

Vale, amici.

NEXT LESSON

Lesson 4: Desktop Publishing

Exercise 1: Insert and Position a Graphic

- ♦ **About Desktop Publishing**
- ♦ **Insert a Graphic**
- ♦ **Position a Graphic**
- ♦ **Set Text Wrapping**

Exercise 2: Resize a Graphic

- ♦ **About Aspect Ratio**
- ♦ **Enlarge or Shrink a Graphic (Maintain Aspect Ratio)**
- ♦ **Stretch or Squeeze a Graphic (Distort the Aspect Ratio)**
- ♦ **Flip a Graphic**
- ♦ **Add a Border to a Page**

Exercise 3: Create a Newsletter

- ♦ **Multiple Column Formats**
- ♦ **Create a Banner Headline**
- ♦ **Insert Text from Another Document**
- ♦ **Border/Shade a Paragraph**
- ♦ **Wrap Text around a Graphic**

Insert and Position a Graphic
■ About Desktop Publishing ■ Insert a Graphic
■ Position a Graphic ■ Set Text Wrapping

NOTES

About Desktop Publishing

■ When you create documents that combine text and graphics, you are performing desktop publishing. Applications such as PageMaker, Quark XPress, and Microsoft Publisher were created specifically to make combining text and graphics easy because early word processing applications could not combine graphics and text very well. Recent versions of word processors, however, offer many of the features that used to belong solely to desktop publishing.

■ Although the word processors discussed in this text were not specifically designed to perform desktop publishing, they include many features that let you combine text and graphics to create documents that look attractive and professional.

Insert a Graphic

■ When you insert a graphic into a word processing file, it is formatted automatically in one of two ways:

- **Inline**. An inline graphic or picture is part of the paragraph into which it is inserted. It is positioned horizontally and vertically by repositioning the paragraph itself.

- **Floating**. A floating graphic can be moved anywhere on the page and causes the text to move or wrap around the image. Wrapping is controlled by text wrapping options.

■ The application suites discussed in this book offer a number of images that you can insert into documents.

- **AppleWorks** makes images available through **File**, **Library**.

- **Word 98** makes images available through **Insert**, **Picture**.

- **MS Works** makes its images available through **Insert**, **ClipArt** (**Alt**+**I**, **A**).

- **Word 97 and 2000** make images available through **Insert**, **Picture** (**Alt**+**I**, **P**).

- **Corel WordPerfect** makes its images available through **Insert**, **Graphics** (**Alt**+**I**, **G**).

■ For the Try It! activities in this exercise, you can use graphics provided by your application suite, or you can use graphics provided in the Graphics data file folder.

Clip Art Sources
Many software applications include graphics that can be incorporated into your documents. In addition, CDs with images are widely available in software outlets, bookstores, and music stores. Also, if you have access to the Internet, you can find graphic images available for downloading. Be sure that you have permission to use any images you download if you plan to distribute the document you create.

🖥️ Try It!

Type Text and Insert a Graphic

1. Start your word processor and create a new document.
2. Set the margins as follows:
   - Top margin to 0.75"
   - Bottom and footer margins so that the footer appears at 0.5" from the bottom edge of the paper
   - Left and right margins to 1.25"
3. On three separate lines, center:
   Your name
   Address
   City, State ZIP code.
4. Save the document as **My Letterhead**.
5. Make your name 16-point bold in the font and color of your choice.
6. Make your address Comic Sans MS or Arial 12 point in the color of your choice.
7. In the footer, center your telephone number and e-mail address (if you have one) on one line.
8. Separate the e-mail address from the telephone number by five spaces. (If your e-mail address turns blue and underlined to create a hyperlink, leave it as formatted.)
9. Format the footer to the same font as your address, but make its size 10 points.
10. Return to your name at the top of the document.
11. Insert a floating graphic of your choice from your application suite's clip art or library.
    You will position and size the image in later Try It! activities.
12. Save the document.

Position a Graphic

- A floating graphic can be positioned using the mouse. In most word processors, it can also be positioned by specifying the distance from the edge of the paper, margins, or text. To position an inline graphic, use paragraph formatting.

🖥️ Try It!

1. Click on the image to select it and hold the mouse button.
   Sizing handles *appear on the graphic. The sizing handles may be small white squares as shown on the following page, or they may be small black squares. Some programs, such as AppleWorks, may display sizing handles only at the corners.*

Hyperlink Format
Some word processors automatically format Web and e-mail addresses as hyperlinks. In electronic files, user can click the hyperlink address and start their Internet connections.

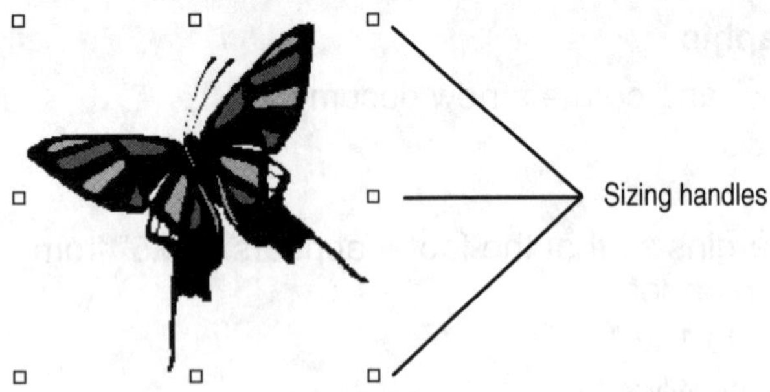

2. Click in the center of the image and drag the image toward the top-left corner of the document. If guidelines are showing, try to position its left edge at the left margin and its top edge at the top margin.

   Let the text flow around the object as necessary. You will control the position of the text in the next Try It!

3. Save the document but leave it open.

Set Text Wrapping

■ Text wrapping options tell the word processor how to flow text in relation to a floating graphic. In general, you can specify that the text wrap on all sides, one side, or only above and below the floating object. Some of these options are shown in the following illustration. Note that Word 97, Word 98, Word 2000, and WordPerfect offer more wrapping options than AppleWorks and MS Works.

Text Wrapping Options

Regular, Square, Around, Absolute

Irregular, Tight, Contour

Behind Text or None

In Front of Text

Wrap Above and Below

To wrap text only above and below an object, it is easier to use an inline graphic rather than a floating one.

⌨Try It!

1. Set the text wrap options so that the text remains centered on the page.

   - **AppleWorks** set Text Wrap to None.
   - **Word 98** set Text Wrapping to None.
   - **MS Works** set Text Wrap to Absolute. Note that this option will cause the text to move off-center. MS Works does not provide a way to prevent the text from wrapping around a floating image.
   - **Word 97** set Text Wrapping to None.
   - **Word 2000** set Text Wrapping to Behind Text.
   - **WordPerfect** set Wrapping type to Behind text.

2. Save the document.

3. Close the document and exit the word processor unless you are continuing with the Exercise Directions.

In this exercise, you will insert a graphic to embellish a memorandum and begin creating a flyer announcing an awards ceremony at Arthur Treacher Middle School.

EXERCISE DIRECTIONS

Insert Graphics in a Memorandum

1. Open ⊚**01Guppy** from the data files.

2. Save the file as **Guppy**.

3. Insert an appropriate graphic, such as a fish.

4. Make the graphic floating.

5. Set text wrapping as follows:

AppleWorks:	None
Word 98:	None
MS Works:	Absolute
Word 97:	None
Word 2000:	Behind Text
WordPerfect:	Behind Text

6. Position the graphic with its top edge at the top margin and its left edge at the left margin.

   You will resize the graphic appropriately in the next exercise.

7. Save the document.

8. Close the document but leave the word processor open.

Create a Flyer

Format the Title Text

1. Open ⊙ **01Flyer** from the data files.
2. Center all text in the document.
3. Save the document as **Flyer**.
4. Set all margins to 0.75".
5. Set the font of the title to Braggadocio, 24-point blue.

   If you do not have Braggadocio on your system, use another decorative font.

6. Insert a space before the title *Annual Awards Assembly*.
7. Before the space insert the following symbol:

AppleWorks:	❏ (Zapf Dingbats q)
MS Works :	🔔 (Wingdings %)
Word:	🔔 (Wingdings %)
WordPerfect:	{ (Iconic Symbols)

8. Insert a space and the symbol after the title.

Format the Remaining Text

1. To avoid changing the spacing between lines, format each of the following lines separately to Arial or Geneva, 24-point bold:
   date
   time
   Main Auditorium
2. Change *yyyy* of the date to the current year.
3. Format the school name to Arial or Geneva, 18-point bold.
4. Set the two address lines to Arial or Geneva, 12 point.
5. Format each of the following three lines to Arial or Geneva, 16-point bold:
   Academic Achievement
   Outstanding Citizenship
   Athletic Excellence
6. Format the *Parents...* paragraph to Times New Roman or Times, 14 point.
7. Format the final paragraph to Times New Roman or Times, 22-point bold, blue.
8. At the beginning of the last sentence, insert a symbol such as ➲ and a space. At the end of the last sentence insert a space and a symbol such as ↻.

   The flyer text should now look like that shown in Illustration A.

Insert Three Graphics

1. Insert a floating or inline graphic, such as a diploma or certificate that symbolizes academic achievement.

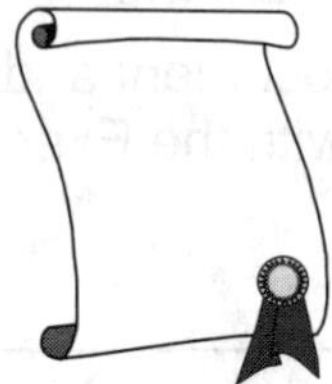

2. Set the text wrap for a floating image so that it does not displace the text.
3. Center the image above the title *Academic Achievement*.
4. Repeat steps 1-3 to insert images that symbolize *Outstanding Citizenship* and *Athletic Excellence;* for example:

5. Center them above their respective titles.

   The flyer may take up more than one page. You will size the images in the next lesson.

6. Save the document, close it, and exit the word processor.

Illustration A. Flyer Text

🔔 Annual Awards Assembly 🔔

June 10, yyyy

1:30 p.m.

Main Auditorium
Arthur Treacher Middle School
221 Fish and Chips
Whitefish Bay, WI 53211

Academic Achievement

Outstanding Citizenship

Athletic Excellence

Parents, friends, and relatives of ATMS students are cordially invited to attend.

➲ Come! Help Us Celebrate a Great Year ➲

Exercise 2

Resize a Graphic

■ About Aspect Ratio ■ Enlarge or Shrink a Graphic (Maintain Aspect Ratio)
■ Stretch or Squeeze a Graphic (Distort the Aspect Ratio) ■ Flip a Graphic
■ Add a Border to a Page

NOTES

About Aspect Ratio

■ The proportions of an image—the relationship between its height and width—are called its **aspect ratio**. When you change the size of a graphic, you can maintain its aspect ratio or distort the image's proportions, as described in the Try It! activities that follow.

Enlarge or Shrink a Graphic (Maintain Aspect Ratio)

■ To enlarge or shrink an image proportionally – to maintain its aspect ratio – you can use the mouse or a dialog box that lets you specify a scaling percentage.

Try It!

1. Create a new document in your word processor.
2. Insert a floating graphic.
3. Select the newly inserted graphic.
4. Maintaining the image's aspect ratio, drag a corner sizing handle away from the center of the image.
5. Enlarge the image to about double its original size.

   As you drag, a dotted or dashed line shows the size of the image, as shown in the following illustration from Word 97.

6. Select the graphic.
7. While maintaining the image's aspect ratio, drag a corner sizing handle toward the center of the image.
8. Shrink the image to about its original size.

   As you drag, a dotted or dashed line shows the size of the image, as shown in the following illustration from Word 97.

Stretch or Squeeze a Graphic (Distort the Aspect Ratio)

- You can stretch or squeeze an image and distort its proportions. You stretch the image to make it taller or wider; you squeeze the image to make it shorter or narrower.

Stretch a Graphic Image

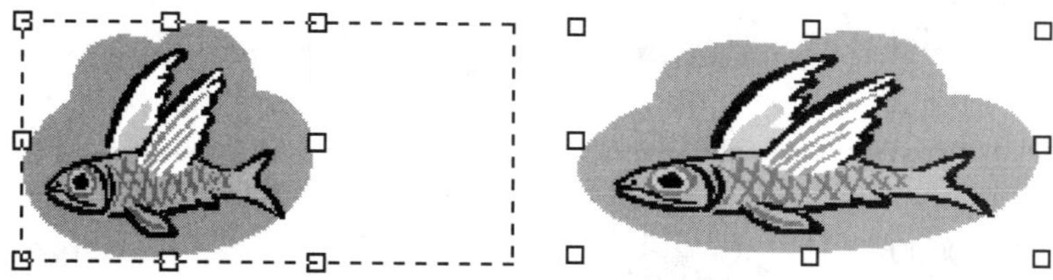

Squeeze a Graphic Image

Try It!

1. Without maintaining the aspect ratio, drag a sizing handle in a direction that will stretch the image.

   The resulting image is wider or taller, and its original aspect ratio has changed.

2. Stretch the image to about twice its original width or height.

3. Without maintaining the aspect ratio, drag a sizing handle in a direction that will squeeze the image.

   The resulting image is narrower or shorter, and its original aspect ratio has changed.

4. **MS Works:** Close the document without saving it, and exit the word processor unless you are continuing with the Exercise Directions.

   Word 98, Word 97 or **Word 2000:** Leave the document open continue with "Add a Border to a Page" on 208.

   AppleWorks or **WordPerfect:** Close the document without saving it, and continue with the next section, "Flip a Graphic."

Flip a Graphic

- **AppleWorks** and **WordPerfect** allow you to flip a graphic vertically so that it is upside down from its current orientation or horizontally so that it is reversed from its current orientation. (MS Works and Word 7 do not offer a way to flip graphics. Word 97 and 2000 offer a way, but the method involves picture editing, which is outside the scope of this book.)

- In general, graphics that have "faces" should be oriented so that they look toward the center of the page. For example, the computer image on the following page, when positioned at the left side of a document looks toward the center of the page. When it is positioned at the right edge, however, it looks toward the right edge of the page. If you insert a graphic that is not symmetrical, such as an animal or computer, you may wish to flip the image horizontally so that both images are facing the inside of the page, as shown below.

Flip a Graphic Left/Right (AppleWorks and WordPerfect)

Your Full Name
Your address
City, ST 00000

Your Full Name
Your address
City, ST 00000

Try It!

1. Create a new document.

2. Insert the following graphics as floating:
   AppleWorks: Library Animals, Bear
   WordPerfect: cdc

3. Select the graphic and drag to copy it. (AppleWorks, hold the `Option` key; WordPerfect hold the `Ctrl` key.)

4. Size and position the images side-by-side.

5. Flip one of the images horizontally so the images face each other.

6. Flip one of the images vertically.

7. Flip it vertically again.

8. If you are using **AppleWorks**, close the document without saving it and exit the word processor unless you are continuing with the Exercise Directions.

   If you are using **WordPerfect**, leave the document open and continue with the next section.

Add a Border to a Page

- **MS Works, Word 97, Word 98, Word 2000**, and **WordPerfect** provide an easy way for you to create a border around an entire page. Page borders are useful for decorating flyers and announcements.

Try It!

1. Place the insertion point at the top of the document.

2. Insert a border of your choice around the page.

3. Try at least two different borders to see how the feature works.

4. Print Preview the document, if your word processor offers this feature.

5. Close the document without saving it, and exit the word processor unless you are continuing with the Exercise Directions.

AppleWorks

To create a page border in AppleWorks requires the use of a drawing tool, which is outside the scope of this book.

💻Try It!

Complete My Letterhead

1. Open 🖮**My Letterhead**, or open ⊘**02My Letterhead**.

2. If you open **02My Letterhead**, change the text in the document to your name and address and save the document as **My Letterhead**.

3. Select the graphic.

4. Maintain the image's aspect ratio while you size the image to about 0.8" in height.

5. Move the image until its top edge is at the top margin and its right edge is about 0.5" to the left of the longest line of text.

6. Create a copy of the floating graphic.

    - In **AppleWorks** and **Word 98** hold down the `Option` key as you drag the image.

    - In all **Windows** word processors hold down the `Ctrl` key as you drag the image.

7. If you are using AppleWorks or WordPerfect and one of the images faces off the page, flip the graphic horizontally (left/right).

8. Position the copy to the right of the letterhead text so that its top edge is at the top margin and about 0.5" from the end of the longest line of your name and address.

    A sample completed letterhead is shown in the following illustration, which was created in Word 2000.

9. Save the document.

10. Close the document, and exit the word processor unless you are continuing with the Exercise Directions.

Elizabeth Bennett Darcy
10 Pemberly Place
Scott City, KS 67871

(316) 555-0404   ebdarcy@abcxyz.com

In this exercise, you will complete the memo and flyer begun in Exercise 1.

EXERCISE DIRECTIONS

Size Graphics in a Memorandum

1. Open ⌨**Guppy**, or open 💿**02Guppy** from the data files.
2. Save the file as **Guppy2**.
3. Select the graphic.

   If you have trouble selecting the graphic in WordPerfect:

   a. Point to the graphic and right-click.

   b. Choose Select Box from the shortcut menu.
4. Size the image to the height of the first two lines of the memorandum, or about 0.8".

5. Copy the graphic and position it with its top edge at the top margin and its right edge at the right margin.
6. If your software permits, flip one of the graphics as necessary so that both face the center of the page.
7. Save the document.

   The top portion of the Word 2000 result is shown in Illustration A.
8. Print Preview the document, if your word processor offers that feature.
9. Print the document.
10. Close the document but leave the word processor open.

Illustration A. Guppy2 (Word 2000)

Guppy Aquarium Supply

Interoffice Memorandum

To:　　　　　All staff

From:　　　　Phyte Ng Fisch, Vice-President

Date:　　　　Today's Date

Subject:　　*New Products*

We are pleased to announce that the following NEW PRODUCTS have been added to our product line and are included in the latest GupAquaS catalogue:

- ❑　18034 Micronite Filter 800
- ❑　17045 Pearlite Sand and Gravel
- ❑　16036 Seahorse Seafloor Panorama
- ❑　15029 Balanced Aquarium #29

Please refer to the catalogue and individual product fact sheets for full descriptions and pricing of these new products. Your supervisors will be holding brief briefings on each of these products within the near future.

Complete the Flyer

Size and Position Graphics

1. Open ⌨**Flyer**, or open 💿 **02Flyer** from the data files.

2. Save the document as **Flyer2**.

3. Change any floating graphics to inline.

4. Insert each inline graphic in the blank paragraph immediately above its title.

5. Maintain the image's aspect ratio, resize each image to about 1" tall.

    Hint: In AppleWorks, you can change images from inline to floating to size them and then change them to inline to position them.

6. Be sure all images are in centered paragraphs.

7. Adjust the line spacing so that the entire document fits on one page.

    Hint: If the image is inline, delete blank lines, if necessary, to adjust the spacing.

8. Apply a page border if you are using Word 98, MS Works, Word 97, Word 2000, or WordPerfect.

Save and Print the Document

1. Save the document.

2. Print Preview the document, if your word processor offers that feature.

3. Print one copy.

4. Compare the results with Illustration B.

    Illustration B was created in Word 2000; your graphics and symbols may differ, and you may be unable to create the page border.

5. Close the document, and exit the word processor.

Illustration B. Completed Flyer (Word 2000)

🔔 Annual Awards Assembly 🔔

June 10, yyyy

1:30 p.m.

Main Auditorium
Arthur Treacher Middle School
221 Fish and Chips
Whitefish Bay, WI 53211

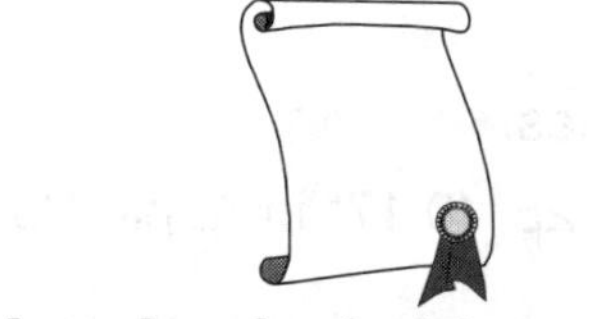

Academic Achievement

Outstanding Citizenship

Athletic Excellence

Parents, friends, and relatives of ATMS students are cordially invited to attend.

➲ Come! Help Us Celebrate a Great Year ➴

Exercise 3

Create a Newsletter
■ Multiple Column Formats ■ Create a Banner Headline
■ Insert Text from Another Document ■ Border/Shade a Paragraph
■ Wrap Text around a Graphic

NOTES

Multiple Column Formats

- Most word processors allow you to format information to be read in columns, like a newspaper or magazine. To do so, you divide the page into columns. Text begins in the one column and flows into the next column when the first column fills up. In most word processors, you can format a heading to display across all the columns, so you can format a newsletter.

🖥 Try It!

1. Open ⊙ **03Extreme** from the data files.
2. Create a three-column format with 0.25" (0.17" in AppleWorks) between columns.
3. Create no line between the columns.
4. Save the document as **Extreme**.
5. Leave the document open.

Create a Banner Headline

- A banner headline stretches across more than one column of a multi-column format.

- In **AppleWorks** and **Word**, you use a special formatting feature called **sections** to create a banner headline. Section breaks in Word and AppleWorks are shown in the following illustrations.

Word Section Break Codes, Show/Hide On

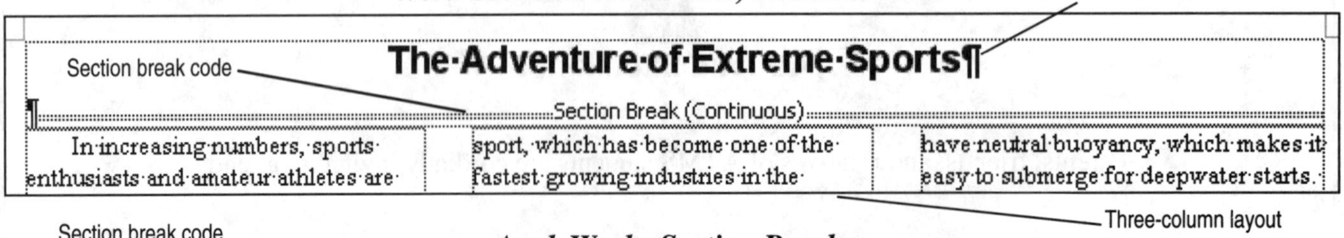

AppleWorks Section Break

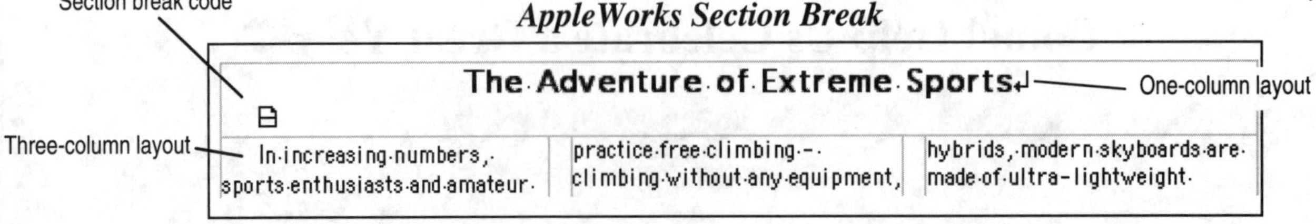

- In **MS Works**, in this exercise you will use the header to create a banner headline if the document is only one page or you do want the headline to appear on all pages. You can also use the WordArt feature, but use of that feature is outside the scope of this book.

- In **WordPerfect**, you create a banner headline by controlling where you start the multi-column format. If you followed the procedures correctly, you already have a banner headline in your WordPerfect **Extreme** document.

💻 Try It!

1. Center the title *The Adventure of Extreme Sports* as a banner headline at the top of the document.
2. Save the document, but leave it open.

Insert Text from Another Document

- When you work in desktop publishing, the text often comes from other writers. You need to bring their text into your document. Most word processors let you insert or import an entire file from another source. MS Works, however, requires that you open the other document, copy the text you want, and paste it into your document. (You can also use this method with all the other word processors.)

💻 Try It!

1. Place the insertion point at the end of the entire document.
2. Insert all the text from 💿 **03Wakeboard**.
3. Save **Extreme**, but leave the document open.

Border/Shade a Paragraph

- Most word processors let you easily put a border around or shade the paragraph. The shading may be called **fill**. In a newsletter, for example, you may wish to call attention to a paragraph by shading it. The procedures in this book and the hint boxes in the right column use shading to call attention to their content. Word 7 and AppleWorks do not include the paragraph borders and shading feature. Instead, both use drawing techniques that are outside the scope of this book.

💻 Try It!

1. Shade the paragraph under *Kayaking* with 100% turquoise or cyan. (It will print as gray on a black and white printer.)
2. Put a ½-point dark blue border around the paragraph.
3. Save the document.

Wrap Text around a Graphic

- In the previous two exercises, you inserted inline and floating graphics that were near but not within the text. This section gives you practice in inserting a floating graphic and allowing the text to flow around an image.

🖳**Try It!**

1. From your application suite's clip art, insert a floating graphic. You may wish to use a bicycle, a surfboard, or some other image that is appropriate to the subject of **Extreme**.

2. Position the graphic under one of the headings.

3. Size it using the mouse and maintaining its aspect ratio until it is about the height of four lines of the document.

4. Set the text wrapping as:

    AppleWorks: Regular or Irregular
    MS Works: Absolute
    Word 7:   Around
    Word 97 & 2000: Square or Tight
    WordPerfect: Square/Both sides or Contour/Both sides

5. Try centering the image in the column with text on both sides within the column.

6. Position the graphic at the right side of the column so text is to the left but not to the right of the image. Displace the first four lines of the paragraph without displacing the heading.

7. Position the graphic at the left side of the column so text is to the right but not to the left. Displace the first four lines of the paragraph without displacing the heading.

8. Save and close the document, and exit the word processor unless you are continuing with the Exercise Directions.

In this exercise, you will create a three-column newsletter for Arthur Treacher Middle School, using files provided. You will insert graphics and apply borders and shading to enhance the appeal of the newsletter. Note that laying out and formatting a newsletter takes time. You may not be able to complete this project in one class period.

EXERCISE DIRECTIONS

Set the Margins

1. Start the word processor and create a new document.
2. Set the top, bottom, left, and right margins to 0.75" for the entire document.
   MS Works: You are going to use the Header area for the newsletter title, so set the top margin to 1.5" and the header distance to 0.75". Set the other margins to 0.75", and the footer distance to 0.5".
3. Press the  or  .
4. Save the document as **Newsletter**.

Create the Newsletter Main Title

1. Place the insertion point in the first line of the document.
   MS Works: Place the insertion point in the Header area.
2. Type the following text:

   ATMS News and Views

3. Format the text to Arial Black, 28 points.
4. Insert a graphic.

   AppleWorks, Word 98, Word 97, Word 2000, and WordPerfect

   a. Center the title text.
   b. Insert a light bulb graphic as a floating object. (AppleWorks Education library; Word Household category)
   c. Set the wrap option as follows:
      AppleWorks: None
      Word 98:   None
      Word 97:   None
      Word 2000:   Behind Text
      WordPerfect: Behind Text
   d. Shrink the graphic to about 0.5" in height.
   e. Hold down the **Option** key (Mac OS) or **Ctrl** key (Windows), and drag a copy of the graphic to the right of the title.
   f. Position one light bulb at the left and top margins of the document and the right image at the right and top margins.
   g. Check Illustration A for how the bulbs are positioned.

MS Works

a. Place the insertion point in the title.
b. Click Format, Tabs (Alt+O, T) to display the Tabs dialog box.
c. Click Clear All (Alt+A)
d. In Tab stop position (Alt+T), type *3.5*.
e. Click Center (Alt+C).
f. Click Set (Alt+S)
g. In Tab stop position (Alt+T), type 7.
h. Click Right (Alt+R).
i. Click Set (Alt+S)
j. Click OK.
k. Position the insertion point before *ATMS*.
l. Insert a light bulb graphic as an inline object.
m. Press the Tab key between the graphic and ATMS to center the title.
n. Shrink the graphic to about 0.5" in height.
o. Select the graphic and copy it (Ctrl+C).
p. Position the insertion point at the end of the title.
q. Press the Tab key.
r. Paste the copy of the image after the tab.

5. Check Illustration A for how the bulbs are positioned.
6. Save the document.
7. If your word processor permits, place a border around the title.

   - For line style, choose a double-line border ======.

   - Choose a width of 1½ points.
     WordPerfect: Choose the double-line border at the far right of the second row of Available line styles.

   - Color the border blue.

Add the Publication Information

1. Press **return** or **Enter** once after the title to create a blank paragraph.
   Note that the new paragraph also has the border.

2. Type the following text:
   Produced by Technology Classes

3. Select the entire paragraph, including the paragraph mark.

4. Left-align the paragraph, and format the paragraph to Times New Roman, 12 point.

5. Go to the end of the paragraph.

6. Press the Tab key.

7. Type the following text. For yyyy, substitute this year.
   June 1, yyyy

8. Before the date, press the Tab key enough times (about six) to position the date at the right margin of the document.
   WordPerfect: Place the insertion point just before the letter *J.* Click Format, Line, Flush Right to position the remainder of the line at the right margin.

Save and Print Preview

1. Save the document.

2. Print Preview the document, if your word processor offers that feature.

3. Compare your document with Illustration A to see whether you have completed the title correctly.

   Note that in AppleWorks and Word 7, you will not have borders around the title.

Set the Three-Column Format

AppleWorks:

a. Place the insertion point in the last paragraph of the document.

b. Insert a section break.

c. Format the section to begin on a new line with three-column format with 0.17" between columns. (Insert the section break, then format the section.)

d. Save the document.

Word (Mac and Windows):

a. Make sure one blank paragraph with no border follows the title. (Create a blank paragraph if necessary and specify None for border.)

b. Insert a Continuous section break after the first blank paragraph.

c. Format the new section for three columns, with 0.2" between columns, no line between, and equal column width.

d. Save the document.

MS Works:

a. Make sure one blank paragraph with no border appears in the header after the publication information. (Create a blank paragraph if necessary and specify None for border.)

b. Place the insertion point in the first body paragraph of the document (outside the Header area).

c. Format the document for three columns with 0.2" between columns and no line between.

d. Save the document.

WordPerfect:

a. Make sure one blank paragraph with no border appears after the title. (Create a blank paragraph if necessary and remove the border.)

b. Place the insertion point in the paragraph that follows the borderless blank paragraph.

c. Format the document for three columns with 0.2" between columns, and no line between.

d. Save the document.

Illustration A. Newsletter Title

ATMS News and Views

Produced by Technology Classes

June 1, yyyy

Insert and Format the Awards Story

1. Place the insertion point in the first paragraph of the three-column format.

2. Insert the file ⊙ **03Announce** from the data files.

   ✓*Hint: In MS Works, open the document and copy its contents into the newsletter.*

3. Center the headline (*Principal...*). Make its text Arial, 12-point bold, with 12 points after.

4. Make sure that the first body paragraph is Times New Roman, 10 point, and format it as justified.

   The body paragraphs throughout this newsletter will be justified so that they begin at the left and right column boundaries. In WordPerfect, use Full justification.

5. Make the awards subheadings Arial, 11-point bold with one line or 12 points before.

6. Make each grade heading Times New Roman, 10-point bold.

7. Format the names as Times New Roman, 8 point.

8. Insert three floating graphics to symbolize the three awards categories.

9. Set the wrapping option to Regular (AppleWorks), Absolute (MS Works), Around (Word 7), or Square, Tight, or Contour (Word and WordPerfect).

10. Position and size them approximately as shown in Illustration B. If the names do not wrap exactly the same, that's all right. Your graphics will differ and your wrapping may differ, but make sure that no subheading is displaced.

11. Save and Print Preview the document.

Insert and Format the Retirement Story

1. Place the insertion point at the end of the document.

2. Start a new column.
   AppleWorks: Format, Insert Column Break
   MS Works: Press Enter enough times so that a blank paragraph appears at the top of the second column.
   Word: Press Ctrl+Shift+Enter
   WordPerfect: Press Ctrl+Enter

3. Insert the file ⊙ **03Retire** from the data files.

4. Format the title as Arial, 12-point bold, centered, with 3 points after the paragraph.

5. Find the paragraph that begins *School Community Wishes....*

6. Format it as Arial, 10-point bold, centered.

7. Make sure all body paragraphs are justified using Times New Roman, 10 point.

8. Insert a blank, centered line between the title and first paragraph of the retirement story.

9. Insert an inline graphic that symbolizes the principal's retirement or symbolizes the principal himself.

10. Specify 1 line or 12 points above and below the picture.

11. Size the image so that the story fits within the middle column.

12. Save and Print Preview the document.

Illustration B. Position of Images

Academic Achievement
Grade 7
Juan Guerra, Denise LeBihan, Anna Magilozzi, David Mistri, Cassandra Pierce, Walter Strate, Raisa Whittaker 
Grade 8
Carlton Doermann, Northrop Frye, John Giambalvo, Miguel Palacio, Ganga Patel, Mary Jane Pastore, Daniel Wilson
Grade 9
Larry Bommer, Maria Daniw, Sabina Romanowska, Portia Smith, William Sonoma, John Steinhart, Jane Zakrewska

Outstanding Citizenship

Grade 7
Georgia Kitch, David Mistri
Grade 8
Sandra Newcomer, Robert Plum, Mary Ellen Rhodes
Grade 9
Louise Lewis, Sonya Newcomer, Thomas Purma

Athletic Excellence
Grade 7
Maria Agnelli, Lawrence Berry, Karalea Bishop, Juan Guerra, Susan Knipp, Ronald Myrick, Harold Ohmart, Nancy VanAntwerp, Florence Wunderlich 
Grade 8
Howard Beech, Michael O'Loughlin, Miguel Palacio, Carol Ann Paul, Frieda Payne, Suzanne Rodenbeek, Winston Salem, Robert Stewart, Rosemarie Winderlin
Grade 9
Natasha Borodin, Maria Daniw, Raleigh Durham, James Holmes, Thomas Purma, William Sonoma, Paul Stookey, Barbara Timmons, Dill VanAntwerp

Insert and Format the Web Site Story

1. Place the insertion point in the blank paragraph following the story about the principal's retirement.
2. Start a new column.
3. Insert the file ◉ **03Website** from the data files.
4. Format the title to Arial, 12-point, bold, centered.
5. Justify the body paragraphs. Make sure they are Times New Roman, 10 point.
6. Place the insertion point in the first blank paragraph after the story.
7. Center the paragraph.
8. Insert an inline image of a computer in the centered paragraph.
9. Make its height about 1".
10. Below the image create a new paragraph, and type the following Web address:
    http://www.arttreach.edu
11. Format the text to Arial, 12 point, underlined, and center it.
    Your word processor may automatically format the Web address as blue, underlined.
12. Insert a blank line after the paragraph.
13. Save and Print Preview the document.

Insert and Format the Summer Story

1. Insert a blank paragraph after the Web address.
2. Place the insertion point in the blank paragraph.
3. Insert the file ◉ **03Summer** from the data files.
4. Format the title to Arial, 12-point bold, centered, with 3 points after.
5. Justify the main body paragraph, and make sure the text is Times New Roman, 10 point.
6. Select the paragraphs with the results of the survey.
7. Make the text in the survey results bold.
8. Select all the paragraphs in the story including the heading.
9. Shade the entire story in turquoise if your word processor offers the feature.
   The entire Summer story is now shaded.
10. Save and Print Preview the document.

Add Filler at the Bottom of Column 3

*When you create a newsletter, you want the three columns to have about equal amounts of information. Editors use material called **filler** to fill up the columns. In this part of the exercise, you will add filler.*

1. In a blank, centered paragraph after the survey story, insert a clip art graphic of the sun or another symbol of summer.
2. Format the paragraph with 6 points before and 6 points after.
3. If necessary, use Format, Borders to remove any shading on the paragraph.
4. In a blank paragraph after the summer graphic, type *HAVE A GREAT SUMMER!*
5. Format the new text to Arial, 12-point bold, and center the text.
6. Shrink the graphic until the last sentence fits on the page if necessary.
7. Save, Print Preview (if possible), and print one copy of the document.
8. Compare your results with Illustrations C and D. Illustration C shows a sample newsletter from Word 2000. Illustration D shows a sample newsletter from WordPerfect.
9. Close the document, and exit the word processor.

Illustration C. Sample Result for Word 2000

ATMS News and Views

Produced by Technology Classes

June 1, yyyy

Principal Happenstance Announces Annual Awards

This year's award winners in three categories were announced last week by Justby Happenstance, Principal. The awards, to be presented at the Annual Awards Assembly on June 10, "reward students who have shown outstanding academic, citizenship, and athletic abilities this year," said the principal. Award winners are listed below.

Academic Achievement

Grade 7

Juan Guerra, Denise LeBihan, Anna Magilozzi, David Mistri, Cassandra Pierce, Walter Strate, Raisa Whittaker

Grade 8

Carlton Doermann, Northrop Frye, John Giambalvo, Miguel Palacio, Ganga Patel, Mary Jane Pastore, Daniel Wilson

Grade 9

Larry Bommer, Maria Daniw, Sabina Romanowska, Portia Smith, William Sonoma, John Steinhart, Jane Zakrewska

Outstanding Citizenship

Grade 7

Georgia Kitch, David Mistri

Grade 8

Sandra Newcomer, Robert Plum, Mary Ellen Rhodes

Grade 9

Louise Lewis, Sonya Newcomer, Thomas Purma

Athletic Excellence

Grade 7

Maria Agnelli, Lawrence Berry, Karalea Bishop, Juan Guerra, Susan Knipp, Ronald Myrick, Harold Ohmart, Nancy VanAntwerp, Florence Wunderlich

Grade 8

Howard Beech, Michael O'Loughlin, Miguel Palacio, Carol Ann Paul, Frieda Payne, Suzanne Rodenbeek, Winston Salem, Robert Stewart, Rosemarie Winderlin

Grade 9

Natasha Borodin, Maria Daniw, Raleigh Durham, James Holmes, Thomas Purma, William Sonoma, Paul Stookey, Barbara Timmons, Dill VanAntwerp

Principal Happenstance Plans to Retire

After serving ATMS for more than 25 years, Principal Justby Happenstance is retiring. He began his career at ATMS 30 years ago as a mathematics teacher and 7th grade basketball coach. Twenty years ago, he was appointed as principal.

"It will be odd," Dr. Happenstance says, "not to come to Arthur Treacher after so many years of being here nearly every day. I'll miss the students, the teachers, and the staff, but I hope to keep busy in retirement. My wife and I plan to travel."

Dr. Happenstance will retain his e-mail address as jhappen@arttreach.edu and encourages current and former students, faculty, and staff to keep in touch.

School Community Wishes Dr. Happenstance Well

"It won't be the same around here without Dr. Happenstance," said Student Council President, William Sonoma. "He will be missed, but I hope he is going to have a great retirement."

"It is hard to imagine ATMS without Dr. Happenstance," said PTA president Josefina Palacio. "It seems only yesterday that he was my algebra teacher in 9th grade, and now he's old enough to retire."

Faculty Council President, Alberta Canada said that everyone will miss the support, kind words, and good leadership that Dr. Happenstance has provided.

ATMS Web Site to be Available All Summer

Technology Department Head, R. Miss Brooks announced this week that with the help of student volunteers, the ATMS World Wide Web Site will be active and updated all summer.

Students can continue to get the latest schedule update, post questions for teachers and fellow students, and perform research in ATMS's electronic library.

"We are pleased to be able to maintain the Web site rather than let it slide over the summer. The Parents for Technology Committee of the PTA found grants and gifts to support the effort. We are thankful for the support of such dedicated parents," said Ms. Brooks.

Summer Activities Include Camp, Sports, Vacation

A survey of ATMS students found that most students remain at home during the summer and participate in family activities and sports. The survey results are summarized below:

Sleepover Camp	3%
Day Camp	6%
Local Daytime Activities	30%
Summer with Relatives	2%
Vacation with Family	59%

HAVE A GREAT SUMMER!

ATMS New and Views

Produced by Technology Classes

June 1, yyyy

Principal Happenstance Announces Annual Awards

This year's award winners in three categories were announced last week by Justby Happenstance, Prin-cipal. The awards, to be presented at the Annual Awards Assembly on June 10, "reward students who have shown outstanding academic, citizenship, and athletic abilities this year," said the principal. Award winners are listed below.

Academic Achievement

Grade 7

Juan Guerra, Denise LeBihan, Anna Magilozzi, David Mistri, Cassandra Pierce, Walter Strate, Raisa Whittaker

Grade 8

Carlton Doermann, Northrop Frye, John Giambalvo, Miguel Palacio, Ganga Patel, Mary Jane Pastore, Daniel Wilson

Grade 9

Larry Bommer, Maria Daniw, Sabina Romanowska, Portia Smith, William Sonoma, John Steinhart, Jane Zakrewska

Outstanding Citizenship

Grade 7

Georgia Kitch, David Mistri

Grade 8

Sandra Newcomer, Robert Plum, Mary Ellen Rhodes

Grade 9

Louise Lewis, Sonya Newcomer, Thomas Purma

Athletic Excellence

Grade 7

Maria Agnelli, Lawrence Berry, Karalea Bishop, Juan Guerra, Susan Knipp, Ronald Myrick, Harold Ohmart, Nancy VanAntwerp, Florence Wunderlich

Grade 8

Howard Beech, Michael O'Loughlin, Miguel Palacio, Carol Ann Paul, Frieda Payne, Suzanne Rodenbeek, Winston Salem, Robert Stewart, Rosemarie Winderlin

Grade 9

Natasha Borodin, Maria Daniw, Raleigh Durham, James Holmes, Thomas Purma, William Sonoma, Paul Stookey, Barbara Timmons, Dill VanAntwerp

Principal Happenstance Plans to Retire

After serving ATMS for more than 25 years, Principal Justby Happenstance is retiring. He began his career at ATMS 30 years ago as a mathematics teacher and 7th grade basketball coach. Twenty years ago, he was appointed as principal.

"It will be odd," Dr. Happenstance says, "not to come to Arthur Treacher after so many years of being here nearly every day. I'll miss the students, the teachers, and the staff, but I hope to keep busy in retirement. My wife and I plan to travel."

Dr. Happenstance will retain his e-mail address as jhappen@arttreach.edu and encourages current and former students, faculty, and staff to keep in touch.

School Community Wishes Dr. Happenstance Well

"It won't be the same around here without Dr. Happenstance," said Student Council President, William Sonoma. "He will be missed, but I hope he is going to have a great retirement."

"It is hard to imagine ATMS without Dr. Happenstance," said PTA president Josefina Palacio. "It seems only yesterday that he was my algebra teacher in 9th grade, and now he's old enough to retire."

Faculty Council President, Alberta Canada said that everyone will miss the support, kind words, and good leadership that Dr. Happenstance has provided.

ATMS Web Site to be Available All Summer

Technology Department Head, R. Miss Brooks announced this week that with the help of student volunteers, the ATMS World Wide Web Site will be active and updated all summer.

Students can continue to get the latest schedule update, post questions for teachers and fellow students, and perform research in ATMS's electronic library.

"We are pleased to be able to maintain the Web site rather than let it slide over the summer. The Parents for Technology Committee of the PTA found grants and gifts to support the effort. We are thankful for the support of such dedicated parents," said Ms. Brooks.

http://www.arttreach.edu

Summer Activities Include Camp, Sports, Vacation

A survey of ATMS students found that most students remain at home during the summer and participate in family activities and sports. The survey results are summarized below:

Sleepover Camp	3%
Day Camp	6%
Local Daytime Activities	30%
Summer with Relatives	2%
Vacation with Family	59%

HAVE A GREAT SUMMER!

Lesson 5: Spreadsheets

Get Started with Spreadsheets

■ **What are Spreadsheets?** ■ **Spreadsheets and Word Processors**
■ **The Spreadsheet Window** ■ **Elements of a Spreadsheet Window**
■ **Select a Cell and Enter Data** ■ **Enter a Simple Addition Formula**
■ **Enter Values and Labels** ■ **Copy a Formula**
■ **Preview a Spreadsheet** ■ **Print With or Without Gridlines**

NOTES

What are Spreadsheets?

- Spreadsheets are used in business to plan and track budgets and projects and to perform financial analyses.

- Spreadsheets are tables. The box formed by the intersection of a column and row on the table is called a **cell**. To create a spreadsheet to solve a problem or provide information, you fill cells with either:

  - **Data**, which may be either text or numbers. Text data is called a **label** and cannot be used in a mathematical formula. Numeric data is called a **value** and can be used in a mathematical formula.

  - **Formulas**, which tell the spreadsheet program what data to use and how to calculate results. The cell containing the formula displays the results of the calculation. When the data in a cell changes, all the cells that rely on the data in that cell are updated. In spreadsheet terminology, these cells are said to **reference** the data cells.

- The sample spreadsheet below records statistics from a family game.

Family Game Spreadsheet

	A	B	C	D	E
1	**Date**	**Mom**	**Daughter**	**Dad**	**Winner**
2	11/3/00	87	95	153	Dad
3	11/13/00	43	90	128	Dad
4	11/15/00	95	96	102	Dad
5	12/6/00	157	116	150	Mom
6	12/8/00	122	97	67	Mom
7					
8	**Average**	100.8	98.8	120	
9	**Highest**	157	116	153	
10	**Lowest**	43	90	67	

Row identifiers · Column identifiers · Labels · Values · Results of formulas

- Modern spreadsheet applications make it easy to provide visual representations of the data and results. They do this through a **chart** feature that may guide you step-by-step through the creation of a line graph, a pie chart, or bar chart that presents the sheet's data pictorially.

Spreadsheets and Word Processors

- Once you've created a spreadsheet and its charts (if any), it is easy to combine the information with text in a word processing document. Letters, reports, and memoranda often are created in a word processor using charts or tables from the spreadsheet application to help clarify and support the message in the document.

- In the same way, you can take text from a word processor and place it into a spreadsheet. If the units of text are **delimited**—separated by tabs or commas and quotation marks or the cells of a word processing table— the spreadsheet application converts each unit of text into a cell entry.

The Spreadsheet Window

- When you start a spreadsheet application, a sheet opens and the window looks similar to other windows except that the document area is a series of rows and columns. The critical portion of the spreadsheet windows are shown below.

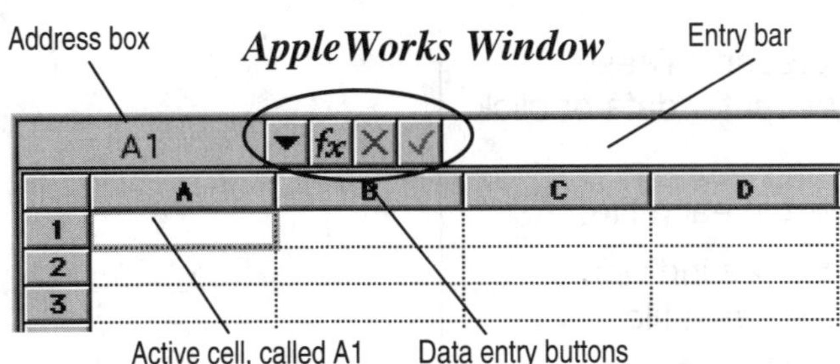

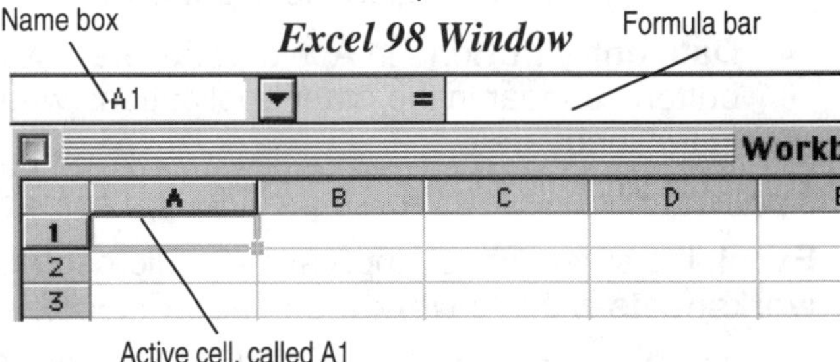

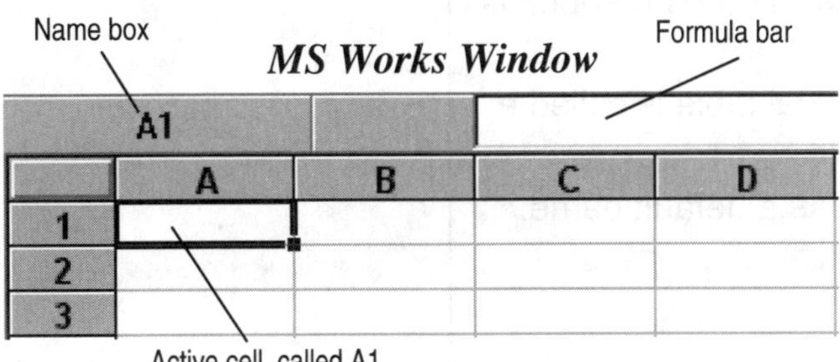

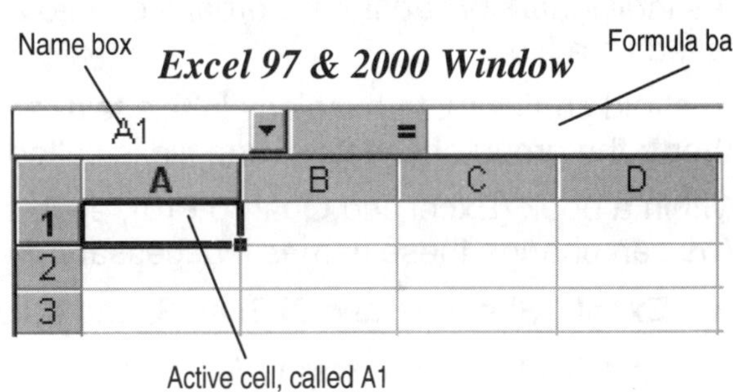

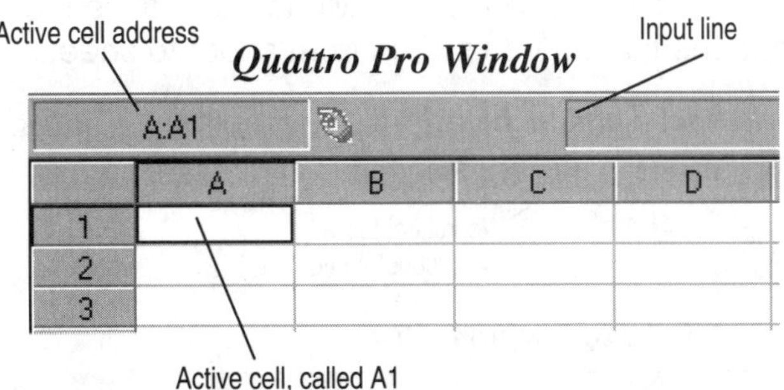

Elements of a Spreadsheet Window

- When it starts, each spreadsheet application displays a new window that contains columns and rows. Each columns is identified by a letter; each row is identified by a number.

- The intersection of a row and column forms a **cell** identified by its column and row number. In the illustrations above, cell A1, the cell at the intersection of column A, row 1, is the **active cell**. You enter data into the active cell.

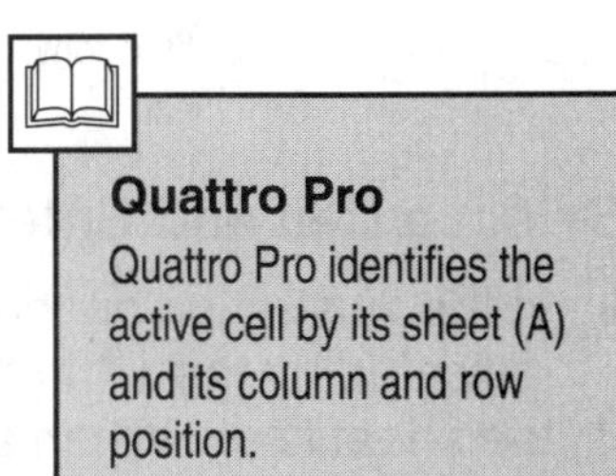

Quattro Pro

Quattro Pro identifies the active cell by its sheet (A) and its column and row position.

- In addition to the usual set of window elements—title bar, toolbars, scroll bars, and status bar—spreadsheet programs add a line just above the grid. The line contains three elements:

  - **Name box** (Excel), **Address box** (AppleWorks), **Active cell address** (Quattro Pro), which tells you which cell is selected. In this text, the term **cell address** or **cell reference** is used for all these terms. A cell is referred to by its location. For example, Cell F6 is the box at the intersection of column F and row 6. Cell B32 is column B, row 32.

  - **Formula area** (Excel), **Entry bar** (AppleWorks), **Input line** (Quattro Pro) lets you enter data into the active cell or shows you the cell's contents. If the cell contains a number, the number appears; if the cell contains the result of a formula, the formula appears. In this book, this area is called the **input area**.

  - **Data entry buttons** in AppleWorks are always present. These buttons appear in the other applications when you enter data or click in the input area.

- **AppleWorks** and **MS Works** provide one spreadsheet in each file.

- **Excel**, the spreadsheet application in Microsoft Office, has individual **worksheets** within a **workbook**; the workbook is saved as a file.

- **Quattro Pro**, the spreadsheet application in the Corel WordPerfect suite, has individual **spreadsheets** organized into a **notebook**; the notebook is saved as a file.

- To avoid confusing terminology in this text, an individual table is called a **sheet**; the group of sheets in one file is called a **book**.

- Within a book (Excel and Quattro Pro), each sheet has a default name. You can change these names if necessary.

  - **Excel:** Sheet1, Sheet2, Sheet3, and so on.

  - **Quattro Pro:** A through IV.

- In Excel and Quattro Pro, a bar at the bottom of the window identifies the sheets and contains four buttons that let you switch from sheet to sheet.

Worksheet Tabs in Excel

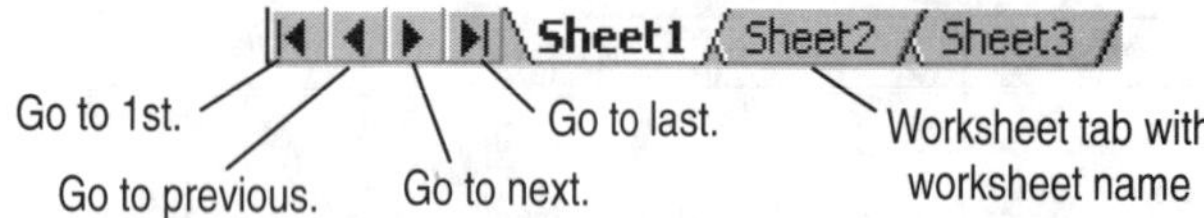

Worksheet Tabs in Quattro Pro

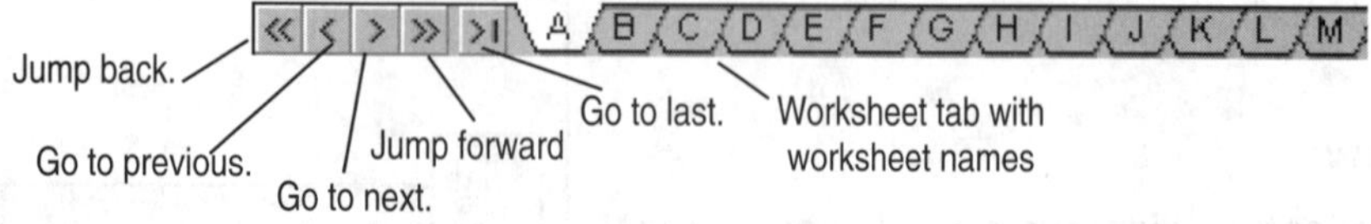

Select a Cell and Enter Data

- In the illustration on the following page, cell A1 is the **active cell** as indicated by the A1 in the cell address and the outline around the cell on the sheet itself. When a cell is **active**, you can enter data or edit the cell's contents.

Active Cell A1, Newly Opened Workbook

⌨ Try It!

1. Start your spreadsheet program.

2. Type the number *38* in cell A1.

   Note: *In AppleWorks what you enter does not appear in the cell until you press the* Return*,* Tab*, or* Enter *key. What you type appears, instead, in the Entry bar at the top of the sheet.*

3. Press the Tab key.

   The number (value) 38 appears in cell A1 and cell B1 is selected. In all the applications, pressing the Tab key enters data and selects the next cell to the right in the same row as the active cell.

Active Cell B1, Reached by Pressing Tab

4. Type the number *62*, and press the Enter or Return key.

   What happens depends on your application. As you use your spreadsheet program, you will become accustomed to what happens when you press Tab, Enter, or Return.

   In MS Works, Excel, and Quattro Pro, the arrow keys enter data and select the next cell in the direction of the arrow key you press.

5. Save the book as **Book1**.

Enter a Simple Addition Formula

⌨ Try It!

1. Use the mouse pointer to select cell B2.

   The cell is outlined and the entry in the Name box changes, as shown in the illustration that follows.

Cell B2 Active when Selected

2. Type the following formula *=a1+b1*.

   *a1 and b1 are **cell references**. The formula tells the program to add the values in A1 and B1.*

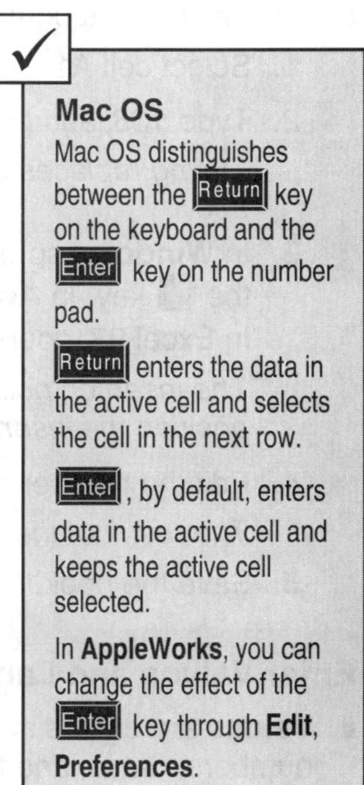

Mac OS

Mac OS distinguishes between the Return key on the keyboard and the Enter key on the number pad.

Return enters the data in the active cell and selects the cell in the next row.

Enter, by default, enters data in the active cell and keeps the active cell selected.

In **AppleWorks**, you can change the effect of the Enter key through **Edit, Preferences**.

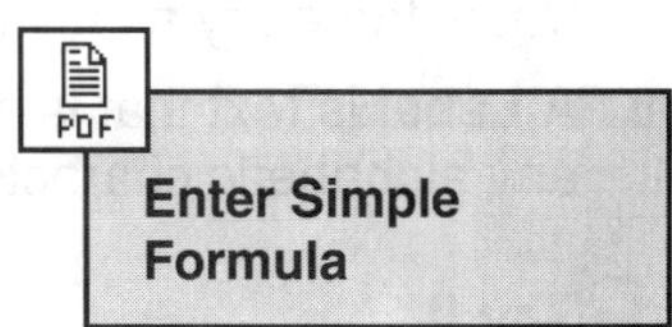

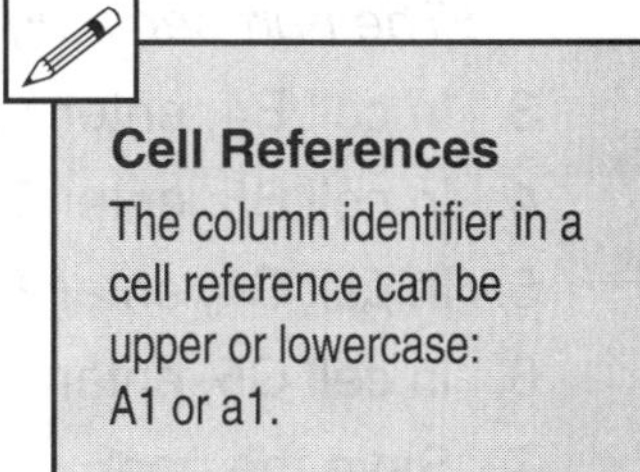

Cell References

The column identifier in a cell reference can be upper or lowercase: A1 or a1.

Note: Quattro Pro changes the = sign to a + sign. In the directions in this book, if you are using Quattro Pro, you can type a + sign rather than an = sign when you start to enter a formula.

3. Press the `Tab`, `Enter`, or `Return` key.

   The result of the formula (100) appears in cell B2.

4. Select cell B2 again (click it, or use the up arrow key).

5. Note the formula in the input area: =A1+B1 or +A1+B1 (Quattro Pro).

6. Save the book.

Try It!

- To see what happens when you change data in a referenced cell:

  1. Select cell A1.

  2. Type *138*, and press the `Tab` key.

     Typing replaces existing data, and the result in cell B2 changes to 200.

  3. In **Windows** spreadsheets, double-click cell B1 or select it and press the `F2` key. In **AppleWorks**, select the cell and click in the input area. In Excel 98, double-click cell B1.

     The insertion point appears in the data so you can edit it. You can position the insertion point using the arrow keys.

  4. Edit the number to read *162*, and press `Enter` or `Return`.

     The result of the formula (300) appears in cell B2.

  5. Save the book.

Enter Values and Labels

- **Values** are entries in a cell that can be used in formulas; values include numbers, dates, and the results of formulas. When you begin typing in a cell with one of the digits 0-9 or a period (decimal point), the program treats the entry as a value.

- A **Label** is text that is not used in a formula. When you begin typing with any alphabetic character the sheet treats the entry as a label.

Try It!

  1. In cell A4, enter *Cost*.

     The word is left-aligned, indicating that the cell contains a label. Text entries are automatically left aligned. See the Procedures for this section for how to enter a number as a label.

  2. In cell A5, enter *2588*.

     The number is right-aligned, indicating that the cell contains a value.

  3. In cell B4, enter *Price*.

  4. In cell B5, enter 3855.

  5. In cell C4, enter *Profit*.

  6. In cell C5, enter the formula *=B5-A5*

  7. Save the book.

     Your sheet should look like the one shown on the following page.

Edit Data

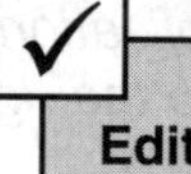

Editing Data

In all spreadsheets you can edit data by selecting the cell and clicking in the entry bar, formula bar, or input line.

Enter Numbers as Labels

228

Sheet with Labels and Values

C5	▼	= =B5-A5
	A	B	C
1	138	162	
2		300	
3			
4	Cost	Price	Profit
5	2588	3855	1267

Copy a Formula

- You can copy a formula from one cell to another. When the cell **references** are written as in the preceding example, the cell references change appropriately as you paste the formula into new cells.

Try It!

1. In cell A6, enter *1823*.
2. In cell B6, enter *2979*.
3. Select cell C5.
4. Copy the formula in cell C5.
5. Paste the formula into cell C6.
   Cell C6 displays 1156.
6. Select cell C6, and review the input area.
   The formula reads =B6-A6 or +B6-A6 (Quattro Pro). The cell references changed automatically when the formula was copied.
7. Save the book.

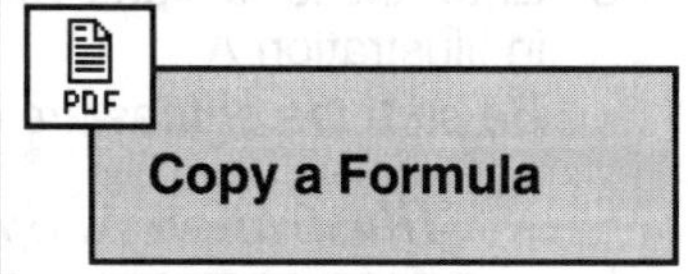

Preview a Spreadsheet

- To view your sheet as it will print, you can change the view to see how it will appear on the page.

Try It!

Print Preview your spreadsheet.

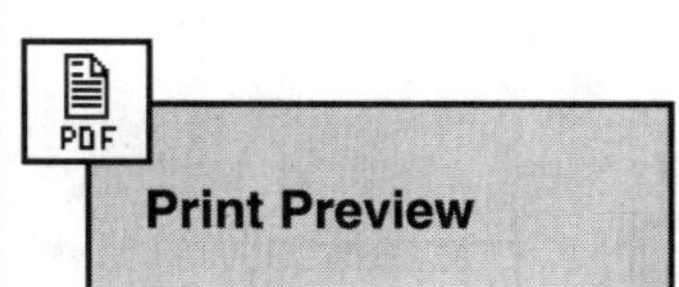

Print With or Without Gridlines

- You can print a sheet with or without column and row identifiers. You can also print with or without the lines that indicate cell boundaries (called **gridlines**). Sheet output is often easier to read if the gridlines are showing. And you may wish to see the column letters and row numbers.

Try It!

1. Set your application to print with column and row headings and gridlines.
2. Print **Book1**.
   By default, applications with multiple sheets print the current sheet.
3. Save the book.
4. Close the book and exit your spreadsheet application unless you are continuing with the Exercise Directions.

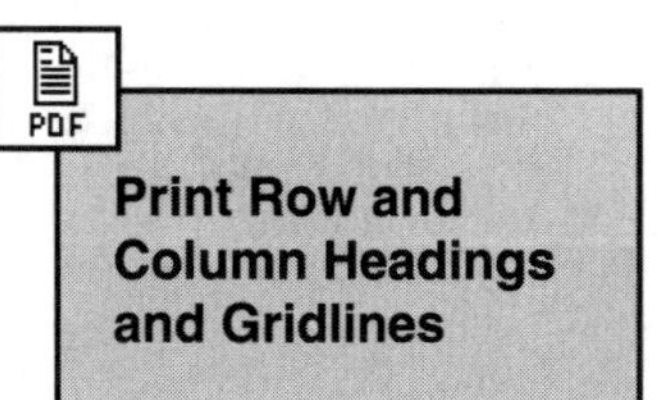

EXERCISE DIRECTIONS

Start Excel and Enter Labels and Values

1. Start your spreadsheet application to create a new spreadsheet. If the application is open, start a new book.

2. Save the book as **Shopping**.

3. Enter the labels and values in the sheet as shown in Illustration A.
   Be sure the entries are in the correct cells.

Illustration A. Spreadsheet Data

	A	B	C
1	ITEM	TRIP 1	TRIP 2
2	Chips	1.99	3.89
3	Cola	2.59	2.59
4	Popcorn	1.89	3.78

If you make a mistake, remember that you can edit a cell's contents.

Enter and Copy a Formula

1. Select cell D2.

2. Enter the following formula:

   =B2+C2

3. Select cell D2.

4. Copy its contents to D3 and D4.
   Your spreadsheet should now look like the one in Illustration B.

Illustration B. Spreadsheet with Formulas

	A	B	C	D
1	ITEM	TRIP 1	TRIP 2	
2	Chips	1.99	3.89	5.88
3	Cola	2.59	2.59	5.18
4	Popcorn	1.89	3.78	5.67

Print the Spreadsheet

1. Save the spreadsheet.

2. Turn on the options that let you print row and column headings and grdilines.

3. Preview the spreadsheet.

4. Print one copy of the spreadsheet.

5. Close the spreadsheet and exit the application.

NEXT EXERCISE

Work with Ranges, Data Formats, and the SUM Function
■ Select Columns, Fit Columns to Data, and Select Rows ■ Select a Range of Cells
■ The SUM Function ■ Use AutoSum or QuickSum ■ Format Data
■ Format Numbers ■ Align Labels

NOTES

Select Columns, Fit Columns to Data, and Select Rows

■ To operate on all entries in a column or row, you can select the entire
column or row. For example, selecting a row or column makes it easier to
insert a new one or to delete the one selected.

🖥 Try It!

Select Columns and Fit Column Widths to Data

1. Open 💿 **02Lunch** from the data files.
2. Save the book as **Lunch**.
3. Select all columns A through F, as shown below.
   Note that A1 is the active cell when you begin with column A. If you
   start with column F, F1 will be the active cell. The color of the
   selected columns depends on your application.
4. Adjust all column widths to fit the data.
5. Save the book.

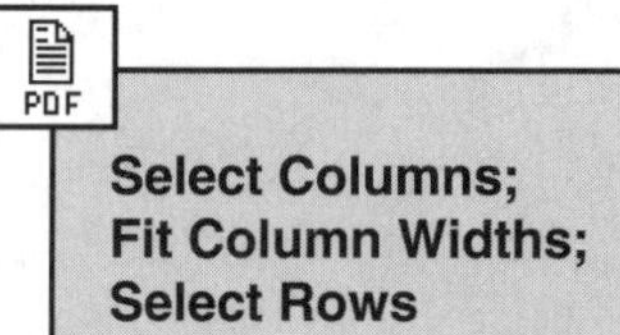

Click here and drag right.   *Columns A-F Selected*

	A	B	C	D	E	F
1	WEEK	MONDAY	TUESDAY	WEDNESDAY	THURSDAY	FRIDAY
2	3-Aug	6.48	5.22	6.48	7.59	3.6
3	10-Aug	6.48	6.48	4	6.72	4.98
4	17-Aug	6.48	10.69	3.75	6.48	2.34
5	24-Aug	6.48	6.48	7.59	4.5	3
6						

🖥 Try It!

Select Rows

1. Select rows 2 through 5 as shown on the following page.
   Note that A2 is the active cell when you begin the selection with
   row 2.
2. Click any cell to deselect the rows.

Rows 2 - 5 Selected

	A	B	C	D	E	F
1	WEEK	MONDAY	TUESDAY	WEDNESDAY	THURSDAY	FRIDAY
2	3-Aug	6.48	5.22	6.48	7.59	3.6
3	10-Aug	6.48	6.48	4	6.72	4.98
4	17-Aug	6.48	10.69	3.75	6.48	2.34
5	24-Aug	6.48	6.48	7.59	4.5	3

Select a Range of Cells

- You can select a group of cells for formatting or for inclusion in a formula. The group is called a **range**. The range is identified by the cell in its upper-left corner and the cell in its lower-right corner separated by a colon (MS Works and Excel) or two periods (AppleWorks and Quattro Pro):

  MS Works and **Excel**:   B2:B5
  AppleWorks and **Quattro Pro**: B2..B5

- In identifying ranges, this book uses a colon.

Try It!

1. Click cell B2, hold the left mouse button, and drag the pointer to cell F5.

   The cell range B2:F5 is selected, with B2 remaining the active cell.

Cell Range, B2:F5

	A	B	C	D	E	F
1	WEEK	MONDAY	TUESDAY	WEDNESDAY	THURSDAY	FRIDAY
2	3-Aug	6.48	5.22	6.48	7.59	3.6
3	10-Aug	6.48	6.48	4	6.72	4.98
4	17-Aug	6.48	10.69	3.75	6.48	2.34
5	24-Aug	6.48	6.48	7.59	4.5	3

2. Click cell F5, hold the **Shift** key, and click cell B2.

   The cell range B2:F5 is selected, with F5 as the active cell.
   It does not matter which corner you start with. The cell range name remains the same B2:F5. The active cell is the cell from which you start the selection.

   *With all the spreadsheet applications, you can use either the click and drag method or the click, hold-**Shift**, click method to select a range.*

The SUM Function

- You can create a formula for adding cells B2 through B5 by entering:

  =B2+B3+B4+B5

- If a large number of cells are to be added, it quickly becomes cumbersome to type all the cell references. Spreadsheets, therefore, provide a shorthand way of adding the values in a group of cells—the **SUM function**.

- The SUM function lets you specify a range of cells to be added up, as shown on the following page.

Click and Drag

Be careful when you click and drag to select. If you accidentally click to select, then click again and begin to drag, you will move the contents of the selected cell.

If you move the cell contents, use the Undo feature, then try selecting again.

Function

A predefined formula that performs simple or complex calculations.

=SUM(B2..B5) (**AppleWorks**)
=SUM(B2:B5) (**MS Works** and **Excel**)
@SUM(B2..B5) (**Quattro Pro**)

- The formula begins with = (equal sign) for AppleWorks, MS Works, and Excel or the @ (at) sign in Quattro Pro. Then comes the function name (SUM) and the range of cells in parentheses (B2..B5 or B2:B5). All functions follow this format called the function **syntax**.

NOTE: In all the spreadsheet applications, you can use the = sign to begin a function. Quattro Pro automatically changes = to @ when you press Enter.

In MS Works and Excel, you can enter the function using the @ sign. They automatically change @ to = when you press Enter.

Try It!

1. In **Lunch**, select cell B6.
2. Enter the SUM function for the range B2:B5.
   Reminder: AppleWorks and Quattro Pro, use two periods (B2..B5).
   The results appear in cell B6.
3. Save the book.

Use AutoSum or QuickSum

- Rather than type in the =SUM formula, you can click a button to get help in entering the SUM function for a range. In **AppleWorks**, **MS Works**, and **Excel**, this feature is called **AutoSum**. In **Quattro Pro**, it is called **QuickSum**.

Try It!

1. Use AutoSum or QuickSum to enter the SUM function for the range C2:C5.
2. Place the result in cell C6.
3. Enter the SUM function for the range B2:F2. Use AutoSum or QuickSum.
4. Copy the formula in G2 to the range G3:G5.
   a. Copy the contents of cell G2.
   b. Select the range G3:G5.
   c. Paste the copied contents.
      Note: In AppleWorks, you must paste the copy into each cell separately. AppleWorks does not paste into the entire range.
5. Copy the formula in C6 to D6:G6.
   a. Copy the contents of cell C6.
   b. Select the range D6:G6.
   c. Paste the copied contents. (In AppleWorks paste into each cell in the range.)
   Note that cell G6 contains a formula that adds the results of the formulas in cells G2:G5.
6. Save the book.

Syntax
The order in which the elements of a formula are arranged and punctuated so that the spreadsheet program can interpret and execute the elements successfully.

Function Formulas
All the functions in this book operate on ranges of contiguous values, such as B2:D5. You can combine ranges and individual cells in a function. For example:
=SUM(A1:C4,D6,E8)
=SUM(A1..C4,D6,E8)

Use AutoSum
Use QuickSum

Lunch after Try It! SUM Functions

	A	B	C	D	E	F	G	
1	WEEK	MONDAY	TUESDAY	WEDNESDAY	THURSDAY	FRIDAY		
2	3-Aug	6.48	5.22	6.48	7.59	3.6	29.37	
3	10-Aug	6.48	6.48	4	6.72	4.98	28.66	SUM of values in row
4	17-Aug	6.48	10.69	3.75	6.48	2.34	29.74	
5	24-Aug	6.48	6.48	7.59	4.5	3	28.05	
6		25.92	28.87	21.82	25.29	13.92	115.82	

SUM of values in column

Format Data

- The Formatting toolbar lets you format entries in cells by making them bold, italic, or underlined.

Format Buttons

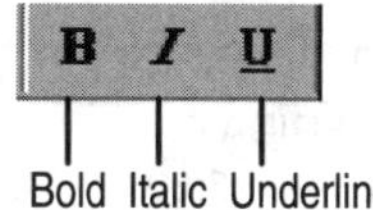

Bold Italic Underline

Try It!

1. Select the range A1:F1.

2. Click the Bold button **B**.

   You can also change the font and font size just as in your word processor. You'll use more formatting features later in this lesson.

3. Save the book.

Format Numbers

- By default, spreadsheets uses a number format called **General**. If a decimal is typed, the program retains the decimal. If a whole number is entered, the program does not automatically include a decimal. You can change the way numbers display using the formatting techniques.

- **IMPORTANT NOTE:** The value of the number may be different from its format. For example, the value 3945.6832 may be formatted to display as $3,945.68. Its value is stored in the spreadsheet as 3945.6832 and that value is used in all calculations.

Try It!

Note the values in cells D3, E5, F2, F5. The General format displays a number as it was typed. If no decimal is typed, none is shown. If one decimal place is typed, one is shown, and so on.

Number Alignment and Formats

D	E	F
WEDNESDAY	THURSDAY	FRIDAY
6.48	7.59	3.6
4	6.72	4.98
3.75	6.48	2.34
7.59	4.5	3

1. Select the range B2:F5.

2. Format the values in the range as follows:

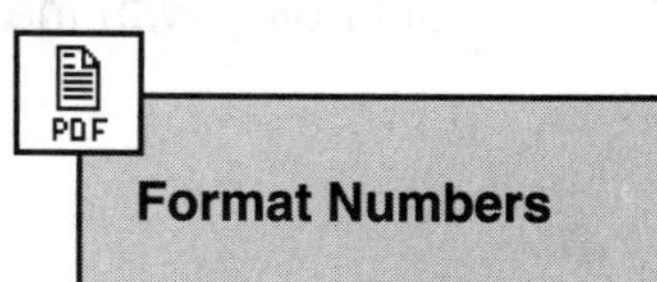

- **AppleWorks:** Fixed with 2 decimals
- **MS Works:**   Comma
- **Excel:**   Number with 2 decimals or Comma Style button
- **Quattro Pro:** Comma

3. Select the range B6:G6.
4. Format the cells for Currency.
5. Select the range G2:G5.
6. Format the cells for Currency.
7. Save the book.

Align Labels

- By default, the spreadsheet applications left-align labels and right-align values, as shown below.

Label and Value Alignment

Labels are left-aligned.

Values are right-aligned.

	A	B	C	D	E	F	G
1	WEEK	MONDAY	TUESDAY	WEDNESDAY	THURSDAY	FRIDAY	
2	3-Aug	6.48	5.22	6.48	7.59	3.60	29.37
3	10-Aug	6.48	6.48	4.00	6.72	4.98	28.66
4	17-Aug	6.48	10.69	3.75	6.48	2.34	29.74
5	24-Aug	6.48	6.48	7.59	4.50	3.00	28.05
6		$25.92	$28.87	$21.82	$25.29	$13.92	$115.82

- While you can align both labels and values in a spreadsheet, it is customary practice to leave values right-aligned so that the numbers can be lined up easily at the decimal point.

🖥 Try It!

1. Select the range A1:F1.
2. Center the labels.
3. Left-align the labels.
4. Right-align the labels.
5. Center the labels.
6. Save the book.
7. Close the book, and exit the spreadsheet application unless you are continuing with the Exercise Directions.

In this exercise, you will add additional items that Diana purchased on her shopping trips. You will use the SUM function to calculate how much she spent on each trip, and you will format the values and some of the labels.

EXERCISE DIRECTIONS

Start Excel and Enter Labels and Values

1. Open 🖅**Shopping**, or open 💿**02Shopping** from the data files.
2. Save the book as **Shopping2**.
3. Add the labels and values in the shaded areas shown in Illustration A.

Illustration A. Add Data to Shopping2

	A	B	C	D
1	ITEM	TRIP 1	TRIP 2	TOTAL
2	Chips	1.99	3.89	5.88
3	Cola	2.59	2.59	5.18
4	Popcorn	1.89	3.78	5.67
5	Bath Soap	0.99	0	
6	Shampoo	2.79	0	
7	Pens	2	0.5	
8	Paper	1.5	0	
9	TOTALS			

4. Save the workbook.

Use the SUM Function

1. Select cell B9.
2. Use the automated method to enter the SUM function for the range B2:B8.
3. Copy the formula to C9 and D9.
4. Copy the formula from D4 to the range D5:D8.
5. Save the book.

Format the Numbers

1. Select the range B2:C8.
2. Format the cells in the range with two decimal places.

   The range should appear as shown in Illustration B.

3. Select the values in the range D2:D9.
4. Format the values for Currency.
5. Select the range B9:C9.
6. Format the values for Currency.
7. Save the book.

   Your spreadsheet should now look similar to the one in Illustration B.

Illustration B. Formatted for Currency

	A	B	C	D
1	ITEM	TRIP 1	TRIP 2	TOTAL
2	Chips	1.99	3.89	$5.88
3	Cola	2.59	2.59	$5.18
4	Popcorn	1.89	3.78	$5.67
5	Bath Soap	0.99	0.00	$0.99
6	Shampoo	2.79	0.00	$2.79
7	Pens	2.00	0.50	$2.50
8	Paper	1.50	0.00	$1.50
9	TOTALS	$13.75	$10.76	$24.51

Format the Column Headings

1. Select the range A1:D1.
2. Center the headings.
3. Make the headings bold.
4. Select cell A9.
5. Make the label bold.
6. Save the book.

   Your spreadsheet should now look like the one in Illustration C.

Illustration C. Formatted Worksheet

	A	B	C	D
1	**ITEM**	**TRIP 1**	**TRIP 2**	**TOTAL**
2	Chips	1.99	3.89	$5.88
3	Cola	2.59	2.59	$5.18
4	Popcorn	1.89	3.78	$5.67
5	Bath Soap	0.99	0.00	$0.99
6	Shampoo	2.79	0.00	$2.79
7	Pens	2.00	0.50	$2.50
8	Paper	1.50	0.00	$1.50
9	**TOTALS**	$13.75	$10.76	$24.51

Save, Preview, Print

1. Save the book.
2. Preview the sheet.
3. Print one copy with gridlines and row and column headings.
4. Close the book, and exit the spreadsheet application.

Exercise 3

Use Functions
■ Use Functions ■ Paste a Function

NOTES

Use Functions

■ In Exercise 2, you used the SUM function to add up numbers in a column.
  Spreadsheets provide some other functions that you will find useful. In
  this exercise, you will work with the following:

  - **AVERAGE**, which adds all the values in the range and divides the
    total by the number of values; in other words, it calculates an
    average.

  - **MAX**, which displays the largest value in the range.

  - **MIN**, which displays the smallest value in the range.

  - **COUNT**, which displays the number of values in the range.

Paste a Function

■ Spreadsheet applications provide a way to help you avoid typing mistakes
  when you enter a formula that contains a function. AppleWorks, Excel,
  and Quattro Pro call this **Paste Function**. MS Works calls it **Easy Calc**.
  In this book, it is referred to as paste function.

🖥 Try It!

Find the Maximum Value

1. Open ⊙ **03Students** from the data files.

2. Save the workbook as **Students**.

3. Enter the following label in cell A12: *GREATEST*

4. Select cell B12.

5. Use the paste function feature to enter the following formula:

AppleWorks:	=MAX(B2..B10)
MS Works & **Excel:**	=MAX(B2:B10)
Quattro Pro:	@MAX(B2..B10)

   The result is 6.00 (or 6) for Bruce, the tallest in the group of students.

6. Save the book.

🖥 Try It!

Find the Minimum Value

1. Enter the following label in cell A13: *LEAST*

2. Select cell B13.

3. Use the paste function feature to enter the following formula:

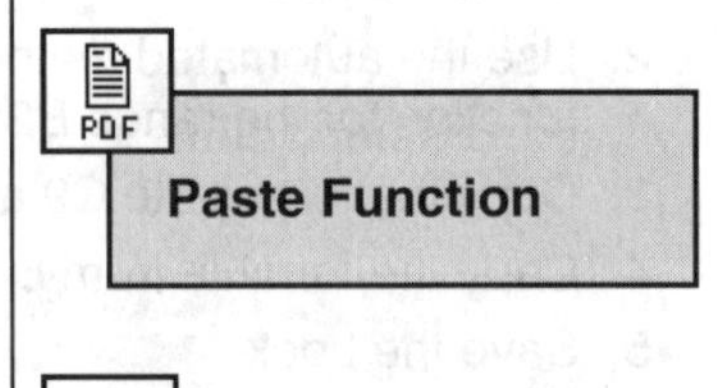

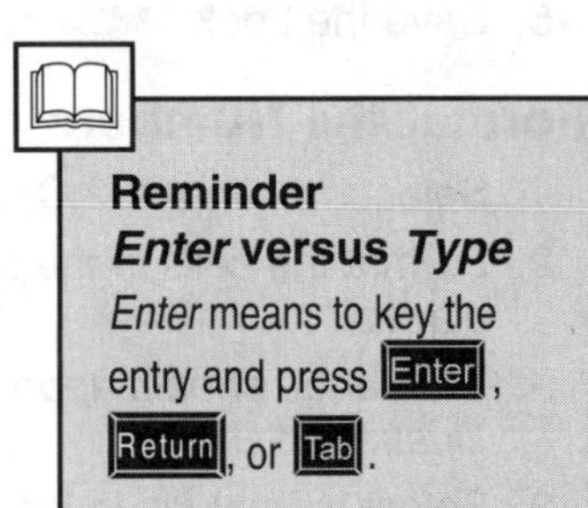

238

AppleWorks:	=MIN(B2..B10)
MS Works & **Excel:**	=MIN(B2:B10)
Quattro Pro:	@MIN(B2..B10)

The result is 5.17 for Layla, the shortest in the group of students.

4. Save the book.

Try It!

Find the Average Value

1. Enter the following label in cell A14: *AVERAGE*

2. Select cell B14.

3. Use the paste function feature to enter the following formula.

AppleWorks:	=AVERAGE(B2..B10)
MS Works:	=AVG(B2:B10)
Excel:	=AVERAGE(B2:B10)
Quattro Pro:	@AVG(B2..B10)

The result is 5.58.

4. Save the book.

Try It!

Find the Number of Values

1. Enter the following label in cell A15: *No. of Students*

2. Adjust the width of column A if necessary.

3. Select cell B15.

4. Use the paste function feature to enter the following formula required by your spreadsheet application.

AppleWorks:	=COUNT(B2..B10)
MS Works & **Excel:**	=COUNT(B2:B10)
Quattro Pro:	@COUNT(B2..B10)

The result is 9 or 9.00, the number of values in the range.

5. Save the book.

Try It!

Copy Formulas

1. Select the range B12:B14. (You don't need to repeat the COUNT function for each column.)

2. Copy the cells.

3. Paste them into the range C12:D14.

   In AppleWorks, copy all four cells, then paste into C12, then D12. The correct formulas also appear in the range C13..D14. AppleWorks does not paste in two directions at the same time.

   In all other applications, select the range C12:D14 and paste.

4. Save the book.

Format Labels and Values

1. Bold and center the labels in the range A1:D1.

2. Bold the labels in the range A12:A15.

3. Adjust the width of column A if necessary.

4. If cell B12 does not display 6.00, format the value so that it does.

5. Format the range B14:D14 (averages) with four decimal places.

6. Save and close the book. Exit the spreadsheet application unless you are continuing with the Exercise Directions.

   The sheet should look like the one in the following illustration.

Completed Students Sheet

	A	B	C	D
	STUDENT	**HEIGHT**	**WEIGHT**	**AGE**
1	**STUDENT**	**HEIGHT**	**WEIGHT**	**AGE**
2	LAMONT	5.42	143	14
3	ALLAN	5.25	103	13
4	FRANK	5.92	175	13
5	MELISSA	5.64	120	12
6	LAYLA	5.17	95	15
7	CARA	5.67	134	16
8	ZENA	5.83	160	13
9	PHILOMELA	5.33	143	13
10	BRUCE	6.00	180	15
11				
12	**GREATEST**	6.00	180.00	16.00
13	**LEAST**	5.17	95.00	12.00
14	**AVERAGE**	5.5800	139.2222	13.7778
15	**No. of Students**	9		

In this exercise, you will build a spreadsheet that contains Scrabble® scores for several people. You will paste a function to insert a formula that calculates the average score for each player. For each round, you will insert a function to determine the highest score, the lowest score, and the average score for the round.

EXERCISE DIRECTIONS

Open the Workbook and Enter Scores for Round 3

1. Open 🖸 **03Scrabble** from the data files.

2. Save the workbook as **Scrabble**.

3. Add the labels and values in the shaded areas shown in Illustration A.

4. Adjust the width of column A to fit the data.

Illustration A. Add Data to SCRABBLE

	A	B	C	D	E
1	PLAYER	ROUND 1	ROUND 2	ROUND 3	AVERAGE
2	Castillo	316	345	307	
3	Chien	295	325	320	
4	Chin, S.	295	318	301	
5	Chin, Y.	297	317	307	
6	Kardash	340	323	306	
7	Kern	283	295	298	
8	Kudja	395	370	356	
9	LeBihan	307	308	310	
10	Perro	402	299	288	
11	Rhodes	322	316	336	
12	Schwartz	275	355	304	
13	Veach	378	279	346	
14	Wang	324	339	364	
15					
16	Highest				
17	Lowest				
18	Average				
19	No. Players				

Use Paste Function to Calculate the Average for Each Player

1. Select cell E2.

2. Use the paste function feature to enter the AVERAGE (AVG) function for the first player. The player's range is B2:D2.

3. Copy the AVERAGE function in E2 to the range E3:E14, as indicated in Illustration B.

4. Save the book.

Illustration B. Copy the AVERAGE Function

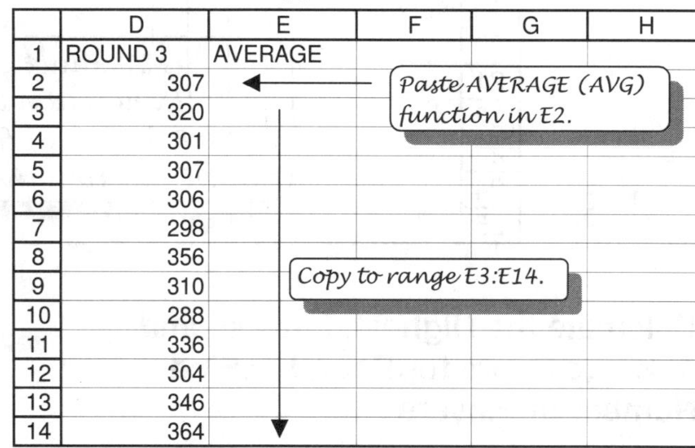

	D	E	F	G	H
1	ROUND 3	AVERAGE			
2	307				
3	320				
4	301				
5	307				
6	306				
7	298				
8	356				
9	310				
10	288				
11	336				
12	304				
13	346				
14	364				

Your worksheet should now look similar to the one in Illustration C. The number of decimals displayed on your sheet may differ.

Illustration C. Average for Each Player

	A	B	C	D	E
1	PLAYER	ROUND 1	ROUND 2	ROUND 3	AVERAGE
2	Castillo	316	345	307	322.6667
3	Chien	295	325	320	313.3333
4	Chin, S.	295	318	301	304.6667
5	Chin, Y.	297	317	307	307
6	Kardash	340	323	306	323
7	Kern	283	295	298	292
8	Kudja	395	370	356	373.6667
9	LeBihan	307	308	310	308.3333
10	Perro	402	299	288	329.6667
11	Rhodes	322	316	336	324.6667
12	Schwartz	275	355	304	311.3333
13	Veach	378	279	346	334.3333
14	Wang	324	339	364	342.3333

Illustration D. Functions to Paste and Copy

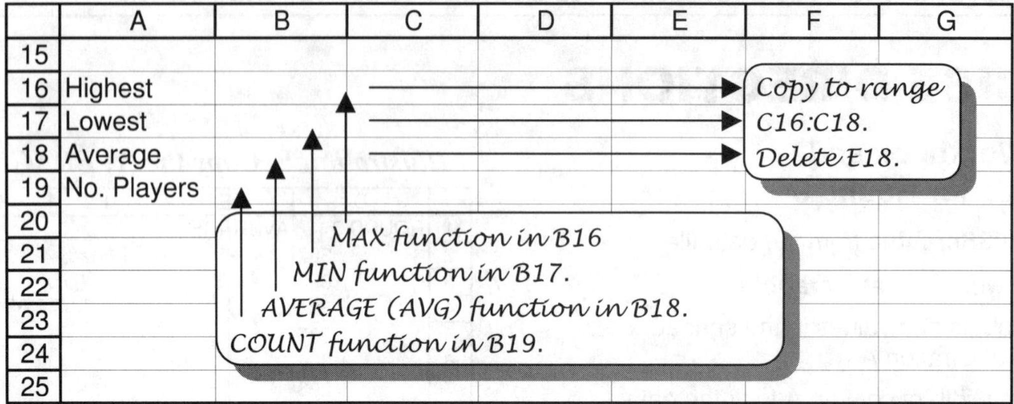

Calculate the Highest, Lowest, and Average Score for Round 1; Find the Number of Players

1. Select cell B16.
2. Use the paste function feature to enter the MAX function for the range B2:B14.
3. Select cell B17.
4. Use the paste function feature to enter the MIN function for the range B2:B14.
5. Select cell B18.
6. Use the paste function feature to enter the AVERAGE (AVG) function for the range B2:B14.
7. Select cell B19.
8. Use the paste function feature to enter the COUNT function for the range B2:B14.
9. Save the book.

   Your worksheet should now look like the one in Illustration E. Note that Excel automatically added decimals for some averages.

Illustration E. Highest, Lowest, and Average for Round 1 and Number of Players

	A	B	C	D	E
1	PLAYER	ROUND 1	ROUND 2	ROUND 3	AVERAGE
2	Castillo	316	345	307	322.6667
3	Chien	295	325	320	313.3333
4	Chin, S.	295	318	301	304.6667
5	Chin, Y.	297	317	307	307
6	Kardash	340	323	306	323
7	Kern	283	295	298	292
8	Kudja	395	370	356	373.6667
9	LeBihan	307	308	310	308.3333
10	Perro	402	299	288	329.6667
11	Rhodes	322	316	336	324.6667
12	Schwartz	275	355	304	311.3333
13	Veach	378	279	346	334.3333
14	Wang	324	339	364	342.3333
15					
16	Highest	402			
17	Lowest	275			
18	Average	325.3077			
19	No. Players	13			

Copy Highest, Lowest, and Average Formulas to the Other Rounds

1. Select range B16:B18.
2. Copy the formulas to the range C16:E18.
3. Delete the value in cell E18. (The average of the averages is not very useful information.)
4. Save the workbook.

   Your worksheet should now look like the one in Illustration F.

Illustration F. All Rounds Calculated

	A	B	C	D	E
1	PLAYER	ROUND 1	ROUND 2	ROUND 3	AVERAGE
2	Castillo	316	345	307	322.6667
3	Chien	295	325	320	313.3333
4	Chin, S.	295	318	301	304.6667
5	Chin, Y.	297	317	307	307
6	Kardash	340	323	306	323
7	Kern	283	295	298	292
8	Kudja	395	370	356	373.6667
9	LeBihan	307	308	310	308.3333
10	Perro	402	299	288	329.6667
11	Rhodes	322	316	336	324.6667
12	Schwartz	275	355	304	311.3333
13	Veach	378	279	346	334.3333
14	Wang	324	339	364	342.3333
15					
16	Highest	402	370	364	373.66667
17	Lowest	275	279	288	292
18	Average	325.3077	322.2308	318.6923	
19	No. Players	13			

Format the Averages

1. Select the range E2:E17.
2. Format the averages to display four decimal places.

   If ##### signs display because the data is too long for the column width, adjust the column width as necessary.

3. Select the range B18:D18.
4. Format the averages to display four decimal places.
5. Save the workbook.

Format the Column and Row Headings

1. Select the range A1:E1.
2. Bold and center the labels.
3. Select the range A16:A19.
4. Bold the labels.
5. Adjust all columns to fit the data.
6. Save the workbook.

   Your worksheet should now look like the one shown in Illustration G.

Save, Preview, Print

1. Preview the sheet.
2. Print one copy with gridlines but without row and column headings.
3. Close the workbook, and exit the spreadsheet application.

Illustration G. Finished Scrabble® Worksheet

	A	B	C	D	E
1	**PLAYER**	**ROUND 1**	**ROUND 2**	**ROUND 3**	**AVERAGE**
2	Castillo	316	345	307	322.6667
3	Chien	295	325	320	313.3333
4	Chin, S.	295	318	301	304.6667
5	Chin, Y.	297	317	307	307.0000
6	Kardash	340	323	306	323.0000
7	Kern	283	295	298	292.0000
8	Kudja	395	370	356	373.6667
9	LeBihan	307	308	310	308.3333
10	Perro	402	299	288	329.6667
11	Rhodes	322	316	336	324.6667
12	Schwartz	275	355	304	311.3333
13	Veach	378	279	346	334.3333
14	Wang	324	339	364	342.3333
15					
16	**Highest**	402	370	364	373.6667
17	**Lowest**	275	279	288	292.0000
18	**Average**	325.3077	322.2308	318.6923	
19	**No. Players**	13			

Exercise 4

Manage Columns and Rows and Sort Data
■ Adjust Column Widths ■ Insert Rows or Columns
■ Add a Title to a Sheet ■ Sort Data

NOTES

Adjust Column Widths

■ You have already used the feature that lets you adjust column widths to fit
the longest entry in a line. In this exercise, you will drag the column
boundary and specify a column width.

🖳 Try It!

1. Start your spreadsheet application.

2. In the new sheet, enter the names as shown below.

Text Too Long for Column B

	A	B	C
1	Suzanne	Rodenbeek	
2	Dill	Van Antwerp	

*Except in AppleWorks, parts of the labels in B1 and B2 may display
in C1 and C2.*

*It is important to understand that the longer entries are entirely within
column B. They display in column C, but the entry is only in
column B. To edit or delete Van Antwerp, for example, you must
select cell B2.*

3. Save the workbook as **Perfect**.

🖳 Try It!

Drag the Column Boundary

1. Place the mouse on the boundary between the identifiers of columns
B and C as shown in the following illustration.

*The pointer turns into a two-headed arrow. Your pointer may look
different from the one shown.*

2. Rather than double-click, click and drag the border to expand the
column so that all of Van Antwerp displays in column B. In
AppleWorks narrow the column width to fit Van Antwerp.

Drag with Mouse to Adjust Column Width

A1	▼	Width: 8.43

	A	B ┼ C
1	Suzanne	Rodenbeek
2	Dill	Van Antwerp

Numbers Too Wide

If a number is too wide to
display in a column, most
spreadsheet programs
displays ####### in the
cell to indicate that the
column is too small to
display the value.

Widen the column to
make the number appear.

3. Undo the column width adjustment to return the column to its original width by doing either of the following.

   ♦ Click the Undo button ⟲ in all except AppleWorks.

   ♦ Press Ctrl+Z or ⌘+Z.

4. Save the book.

🖥 Try It!

Specify a Column Width

The default column widths in a new sheet are listed below.

AppleWorks:	72 points (1 inch)
Excel 98:	10 digits
MS Works:	10 digits
Excel 97 & 2000:	8.43 digits
Quattro Pro:	9.00 digits

1. Select column B.

2. Except in AppleWorks, specify a column width of 12 characters. Change AppleWorks to 66 points.

3. Save the book.

   Column B is now about two characters wider than Van Antwerp.

Insert Rows or Columns

■ Sometimes you need to insert new rows or columns into your sheet. Spreadsheet applications insert new columns to the left of the column selected when you perform the insert procedure. They insert new rows above the selected row. You can also delete rows and columns.

🖥 Try It!

1. Insert a new row above row 1.

2. Insert a new column before column A.

3. Delete the new column, but leave the new row.

4. Save the book.

Add a Title to a Sheet

■ The top rows of a sheet are often used to display a title. Before adding a title, adjust the column widths for the body of the spreadsheet. In all applications except AppleWorks, you can then center the title across several columns.

🖥 Try It!

1. Select cell B1.

2. Type *Students with Perfect Attendance.*

3. Double-click the right boundary of column B.

   The column is now considerably wider than Van Antwerp, the longest name, as shown on the following page.

Specify a Column Width

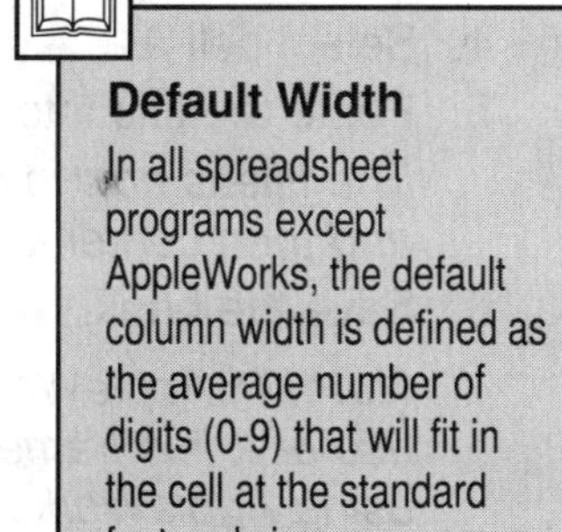

Default Width

In all spreadsheet programs except AppleWorks, the default column width is defined as the average number of digits (0-9) that will fit in the cell at the standard font and size.

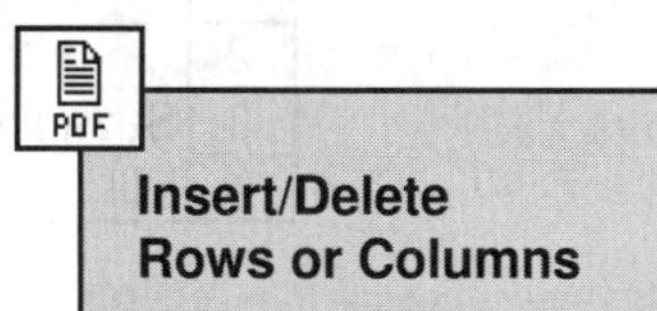

Insert/Delete Rows or Columns

Column Widths Adjusted by AutoFit with Title Entered

	A	B	C
1		Students with Perfect Attendance	
2	Suzanne	Rodenbeek	
3	Dill	Van Antwerp	

4. Undo the column width adjustment to return the column to its previous width.
5. Save the book.

Try It!

Center the Title Across Several Columns

1. Insert a new row above row 1.
2. Select cell B2.
3. Cut the title in B2.
4. Select cell A1.
5. Paste the title into cell A1.

   The title is now in cell A1. It is a good idea to insert the title in cell A1 and then center it across the columns as described below.

6. Save the book.

   Note: *In AppleWorks, to center a title across columns involves the use of a text frame, a topic outside the scope of this book. If you are using AppleWorks, continue with the next section.*

7. Center the title across the range A1:D1.
8. Save the book.

Centered Across the Range A1:D1

	A	B	C	D
1		Students with Perfect Attendance		
2				
3	Suzanne	Rodenbeek		
4	Dill	Van Antwerp		

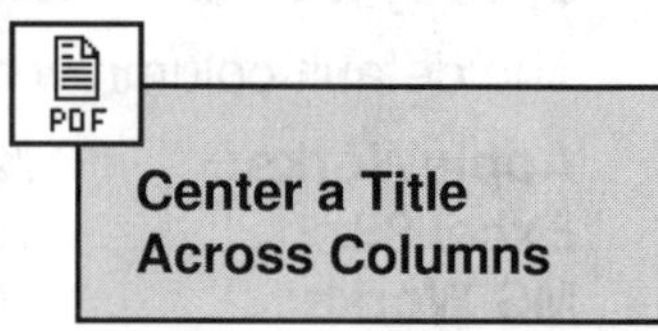
Center a Title Across Columns

Sort Data

- You may find it useful to arrange data in alphabetical or numeric order to make information easier to find.

Try It!

1. Enter the additional names and the school grades shown in the shaded portion of the illustration below.

Additional Names and School Grade

	A	B	C	D
1		Students with Perfect Attendance		
2				
3	Suzanne	Rodenbeek	7	
4	Dill	Van Antwerp	8	
5	Friedrich	Bachmann	8	
6	Marianne	Dashwood	9	
7	Alain	Delouche	6	
8	William	FitzMorris	6	

Sort Data

2. Select range A3:C8.

3. Sort the students by last name (column B or begin sorting 1st with cell B3).

4. Save the book.

5. Add the following three names to the list in the cells shown.

Three New Names and School Grade

	A	B	C
9	Wanda	FitzMorris	7
10	Walker	FitzMorris	8
11	Erin	Fitzgerald	9

6. Sort the students by last name and first name (column B, then column A, or begin sorting 1st by cell B3, and 2nd by cell A3).

7. Save the book.

8. Add the names and grades shown below in rows 12-14.

Additional Names and Grades

	A	B	C
12	Judy	Shuler	8
13	Janet	Griffith	7
14	Michael	Kimball	7

9. Insert a new row above row 3.

10. In the new row 3, enter the following headings.

Header Row (Column Titles)

	A	B	C
3	First	Last	Grade

11. Select the range A3:CI5 (A3..CI5), and sort the student list by last name, then by first name.

12. Save the book. Close the book, and exit the spreadsheet application unless you are continuing with the Exercise Directions.

Spreadsheet after Sorting by Last Name and First Name

	A	B	C	D
1	Students with Perfect Attendance			
2				
3	First	Last	Grade	
4	Friedrich	Bachmann	8	
5	Marianne	Dashwood	9	
6	Alain	Delouche	6	
7	Erin	Fitzgerald	9	
8	Walker	FitzMorris	8	
9	Wanda	FitzMorris	7	
10	William	FitzMorris	6	
11	Janet	Griffith	7	
12	Michael	Kimball	7	
13	Suzanne	Rodenbeek	7	
14	Judy	Shuler	8	
15	Dill	Van Antwerp	8	

EXERCISE DIRECTIONS

Open the Workbook and Add New Players

1. Open ⌨**Scrabble**, or open 💿**04Scrabble** from the data files.

2. Save the workbook as **Scrabble2**

3. Insert three rows above row 15.

4. Add the labels in the shaded areas shown in Illustration A.

Illustration A. Add Data to Scrabble2

	A	B	C	D	E
1	**PLAYER**	**ROUND 1**	**ROUND 2**	**ROUND 3**	**AVERAGE**
2	Castillo	316	345	307	322.6667
3	Chien	295	325	320	313.3333
4	Chin, S.	295	318	301	304.6667
5	Chin, Y.	297	317	307	307.0000
6	Kardash	340	323	306	323.0000
7	Kern	283	295	298	292.0000
8	Kudja	395	370	356	373.6667
9	LeBihan	307	308	310	308.3333
10	Perro	402	299	288	329.6667
11	Rhodes	322	316	336	324.6667
12	Schwartz	275	355	304	311.3333
13	Veach	378	279	346	334.3333
14	Wang	324	339	364	342.3333
15	VanderHoffen				
16	Reifschneider				
17	Cruz-Guerra				
18					
19	**Highest**	402	370	364	373.6667
20	**Lowest**	275	279	288	292.0000
21	**Average**	325.3077	322.2308	318.6923	
22	**No. Players**	13			

Adjust the Column Widths

1. If necessary, adjust the width of column A to fit the longest name.

2. Select all the remaining columns (B-E) and change the column width to 10.5 in all applications except AppleWorks.

   AppleWorks: Set the column width to 66 points.

Add a Title

1. Insert two rows above existing row 1.

2. Select cell A1.

3. Type the following title:

   Scrabble Scores

4. Select the range A1:E1, and center the title across the selection if your application permits.

5. Format the title text to Arial, 14-point bold.

   If some of the text is cut off at the top, you can adjust the row height. Point to the bottom boundary of the row identifier and double-click.

   Your sheet should look like the one in Illustration B. In AppleWorks, your title will be at the left, not centered across columns.

Illustration B. Scrabble Sheet with Title

	A	B	C	D	E
1			**Scrabble Scores**		
2					
3	**PLAYER**	**ROUND 1**	**ROUND 2**	**ROUND 3**	**AVERAGE**
4	Castillo	316	345	307	322.6667
5	Chien	295	325	320	313.3333
6	Chin, S.	295	318	301	304.6667
7	Chin, Y.	297	317	307	307.0000
8	Kardash	340	323	306	323.0000
9	Kern	283	295	298	292.0000
10	Kudja	395	370	356	373.6667
11	LeBihan	307	308	310	308.3333
12	Perro	402	299	288	329.6667
13	Rhodes	322	316	336	324.6667
14	Schwartz	275	355	304	311.3333
15	Veach	378	279	346	334.3333
16	Wang	324	339	364	342.3333
17	VanderHoffen				
18	Reifschneider				
19	Cruz-Guerra				
20					
21	**Highest**	402	370	364	373.6667
22	**Lowest**	275	279	288	292.0000
23	**Average**	325.3077	322.2308	318.6923	
24	**No. Players**	13			

Enter Scores for the Additional Players

1. Enter the following scores for the players just added.

	A	B	C	D
17	VanderHoffen	377	422	355
18	Reifschneider	415	332	345
19	Cruz-Guerra	303	366	325

2. If necessary, copy the formula for the player average to cells E17:E19.

   Note that Reifschneider now has the highest score in Round 1. Did the Highest value in cell B21 change automatically?

   In Excel 2000, when you insert rows or columns between a formula and its referenced cells, the program may automatically adjust the formula references.

   In other spreadsheets, when you insert rows, you must update the formulas to ensure that the new rows are included in all formulas.

3. As necessary, edit the entries in B21, B22, and B23 to correct the range to read B4:B19 (B4..B19).

4. Copy the entries in B21:B23 to C21:E23.

5. Correct the number formats as necessary and delete any value in E23.

6. Save the book.

Sort the List

1. Select the range A3:E19 or A4:E19.

2. Sort by PLAYER in Ascending order.

3. Click OK.

   Your sheet should now look like the one in Illustration C.

Illustration C. Completed Spreadsheet

	A	B	C	D	E
1	**Scrabble Scores**				
2					
3	**PLAYER**	**ROUND 1**	**ROUND 2**	**ROUND 3**	**AVERAGE**
4	Castillo	316	345	307	322.6667
5	Chien	295	325	320	313.3333
6	Chin, S.	295	318	301	304.6667
7	Chin, Y.	297	317	307	307.0000
8	Cruz-Guerra	303	366	325	331.3333
9	Kardash	340	323	306	323.0000
10	Kern	283	295	298	292.0000
11	Kudja	395	370	356	373.6667
12	LeBihan	307	308	310	308.3333
13	Perro	402	299	288	329.6667
14	Reifschneider	415	332	345	364.0000
15	Rhodes	322	316	336	324.6667
16	Schwartz	275	355	304	311.3333
17	VanderHoffen	377	422	355	384.6667
18	Veach	378	279	346	334.3333
19	Wang	324	339	364	342.3333
20					
21	**Highest**	415	422	364	384.6667
22	**Lowest**	275	279	288	292.0000
23	**Average**	332.7500	331.8125	323.0000	
24	**No. Players**	16			

Save, Preview, Print

1. Save the book.

2. Preview the sheet.

3. Print one copy with gridlines but without row and column headings.

4. Close the book, and exit the spreadsheet application.

Use Absolute References and Print Options
■ Relative and Absolute References
■ Change Print Orientation ■ Print to Fit on One Page

NOTES

Relative and Absolute References

- So far in these exercises, you have used **relative** references when building formulas. For example, when you enter a formula in cell D2 and then copy it to cells D3:D8, the cell references change automatically as the row numbers change. The reference in cell D2 is **relative**; when it is copied to a new row its references change according to its new location.

- Sometimes, however, you want to refer to the same cell in several other cells. To keep a reference from changing when a formula is copied, place a $ before the part of the reference that should not change. This is called making the reference **absolute**; the reference does not change as the location of the formula changes.

🖳 Try It!

Enter Totals and Average Stock Value

1. Open 💿 **05Stocks** from the data files.
2. Save the workbook as **Stocks**.
3. Select cell A16, and enter the label: *TOTAL*.
4. Make it bold.
5. In cell C16, enter a SUM function for the # OWNED values (range C4:C14) to find the total number of shares in the portfolio.
6. Copy the formula to cell E16 to find the total VALUE of all stocks.
7. Format cell E16 for Currency or Accounting.
8. Select cell D16, and use the paste function feature to enter the Average function to calculate the average price of the stocks.

   The last row of the worksheet should look similar to the one shown below.

Row 16 of Sample Stock Portfolio Worksheet

	A	B	C	D	E
16	**TOTAL**		7800	74.575	$ 594,107.50

🖳 Try It!

Calculate Percentages

1. Select cell F4, and enter the following formula to find what percentage AIG represents of total number of stocks.
   (Percent = # OWNED divided by TOTAL # OWNED.)
   =C4/C16

2. Copy the formula to cell F5.

   Cell F5 displays the error #DIV/0!, as shown below, or ERR.

   ### Divide by 0 Error

	F
3	**% OF STOCKS**
4	0.051282051
5	#DIV/0!

3. Edit the formula in cell F4 to read: *=C4/$C$16*

   The $ tells the program that you are making an absolute reference to cell C16.

4. Copy the formula to range F5:F14.

   The references in the first part of the formula (C4) change but the reference to cell C16 remains the same.

5. Select cell G4, and enter the formula: *=E4/$E$16*

   The formula calculates the percentage of total portfolio value represented by AIG stock.

6. Copy the formula to range G5:G14.

7. Select range F4:G14.

8. Format the values as percentages with three decimal places.

   Your sheet should look like the one in the following illustration. (In AppleWorks, the title will not be centered across columns.)

9. Save the book.

Completed Sample Stock Portfolio Worksheet

	A	B	C	D	E	F	G
1	**SAMPLE STOCK PORTFOLIO**						
2							
3	STOCK	SYMBOL	# OWNED	CURR PRICE	VALUE	% OF STOCKS	% OF PORTFOLIO
4	AMER INTL GROUP	AIG	400	110.875	44,350.00	5.128%	7.465%
5	CBS	CBS	800	52.875	42,300.00	10.256%	7.120%
6	DISNEY	DIS	700	67.500	47,250.00	8.974%	7.953%
7	GENERAL ELECTRIC	GE	1300	98.375	127,887.50	16.667%	21.526%
8	MORGAN JP & CO	JPM	600	98.625	59,175.00	7.692%	9.960%
9	COCA COLA COM	KO	600	55.125	33,075.00	7.692%	5.567%
10	LUCENT TECHNOLOGIES	LU	500	38.000	19,000.00	6.410%	3.198%
11	PFIZER, INC	PFE	1000	76.625	76,625.00	12.821%	12.897%
12	SCHLUMBERGER, LTD	SLB	600	82.325	49,395.00	7.692%	8.314%
13	AT&T CORP	T	500	56.500	28,250.00	6.410%	4.755%
14	EXXON-MOBIL CORP.	XOM	800	83.500	66,800.00	10.256%	11.244%
15							
16	TOTAL		7800	74.575	$ 594,107.50		

Change Print Orientation

■ By default, spreadsheets print in **Portrait** orientation (8½" x 11"). When a spreadsheet is wide, it prints part of the sheet on a second page. You can often cause a worksheet to print on one page by changing its print orientation to **Landscape** orientation (11" x 8½ ").

Landscape vs. Portrait

- ♦ **Landscape** orientation prints the long way on the page 11" x 8½".
- ♦ **Portrait** orientation prints the short way on an 8½" x 11" page.

Landscape

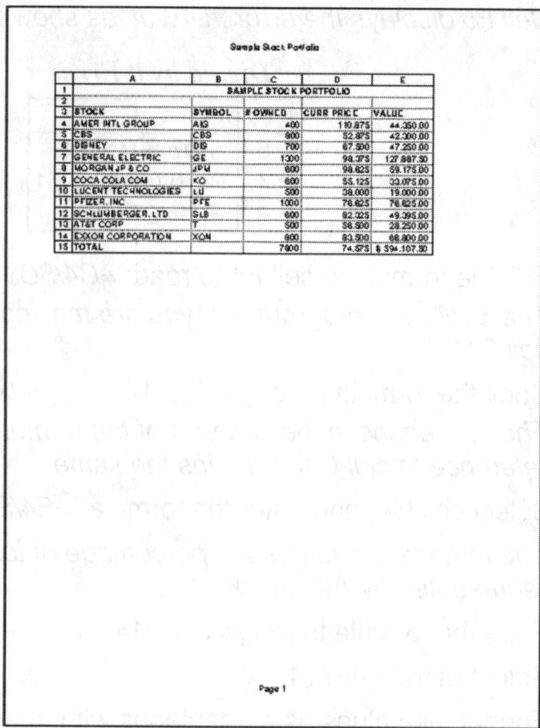

Sample Stock Portfolio

	A	B	C	D	E	F	G
1	SAMPLE STOCK PORTFOLIO						
2							
3	STOCK	SYMBOL	# OWNED	CURR PRICE	VALUE	% OF STOCKS	% OF PORTFOLIO
4	AMER INTL GROUP	AIG	400	110.875	44,350.00	5.128%	7.465%
5	CBS	CBS	800	52.875	42,300.00	10.256%	7.120%
6	DISNEY	DIS	700	67.500	47,250.00	8.974%	7.953%
7	GENERAL ELECTRIC	GE	1300	98.375	127,887.50	16.667%	21.526%
8	MORGAN JP & CO	JPM	600	98.625	59,175.00	7.692%	9.960%
9	COCA COLA COM	KO	600	55.125	33,075.00	7.692%	5.567%
10	LUCENT TECHNOLOGIES	LU	500	38.000	19,000.00	6.410%	3.199%
11	PFIZER, INC	PFE	1000	76.625	76,625.00	12.821%	12.897%
12	SCHLUMBERGER, LTD	SLB	600	82.325	49,395.00	7.692%	8.314%
13	AT&T CORP	T	500	98.500	28,250.00	6.410%	4.755%
14	EXXON CORPORATION	XON	800	83.500	66,800.00	10.256%	11.244%
15	TOTAL		7800	74.575	$ 594,107.50		

Page 1

Portrait

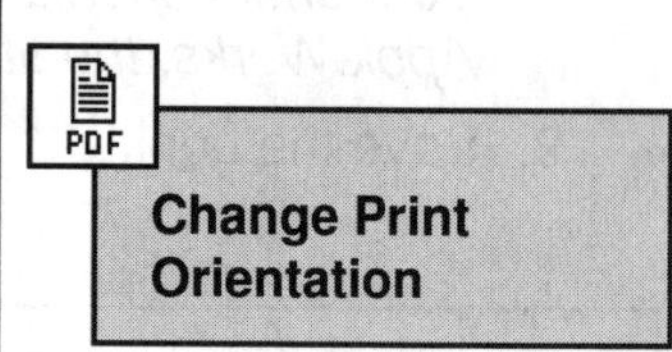

Sample Stock Portfolio

	A	B	C	D	E
1	SAMPLE STOCK PORTFOLIO				
2					
3	STOCK	SYMBOL	# OWNED	CURR PRICE	VALUE
4	AMER INTL GROUP	AIG	400	110.875	44,350.00
5	CBS	CBS	800	52.875	42,300.00
6	DISNEY	DIS	700	67.500	47,250.00
7	GENERAL ELECTRIC	GE	1300	98.375	127,887.50
8	MORGAN JP & CO	JPM	600	98.625	59,175.00
9	COCA COLA COM	KO	600	55.125	33,075.00
10	LUCENT TECHNOLOGIES	LU	500	38.000	19,000.00
11	PFIZER, INC	PFE	1000	76.625	76,625.00
12	SCHLUMBERGER, LTD	SLB	600	82.325	49,395.00
13	AT&T CORP	T	500	56.500	28,250.00
14	EXXON CORPORATION	XON	800	83.500	66,800.00
15	TOTAL		7800	74.575	$ 594,107.50

Page 1

Try It!

1. Preview the sheet.

   Note that at least one column of the worksheet appears on page 2.

2. Change the page setup to change the print orientation to Landscape.

3. Print one copy of the sheet in Landscape orientation without row or column headings and without gridlines.

4. Save the book.

   *If you are using **MS Works**, close the book and exit MS Works unless you are continuing with the Exercise Directions.*

Print to Fit on One Page

- Rather than change orientation, in many spreadsheet applications you can specify that the application fit the sheet on a single portrait page. (MS Works does not offer this automatic feature.)

Try It!

1. Change the print orientation to Portrait.

2. Leave the margins as set.

3. Set the print options so that the entire width of the sheet fits across one portrait page.

4. Preview the sheet.

5. Print one copy.

6. Save and close the book, and exit the spreadsheet application unless you are continuing with the Exercise Directions.

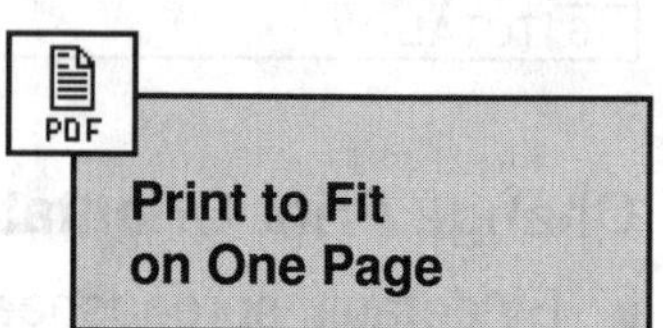

252

> **In this exercise, you will use an absolute reference to calculate what percentage of the team total each basketball player's score represents.**

EXERCISE DIRECTIONS

Open the Book and Enter New Labels

1. Open ☉ **05Basketball** from the data files.

2. Save the book as **Basketball**.

3. Add the labels and values in the shaded areas shown in Illustration A.

Illustration A. Add Scores to BASKETBALL

	A	B	C
1	Player	Score	Percent
2	Bretz	2	
3	Brokofsky	10	
4	Castillo	6	
5	Holmes	9	
6	Rhodes	15	
7	Rodriquez	7	
8	Thompson	1	
9	Veach	13	
10	Yuan	8	
11	TOTAL		

4. Select cell B11 and enter a formula to calculate the total score for the team.

5. Save the book.

Calculate the Percentage of the Total for Each Player

1. Select cell C2.

2. Enter the formula to calculate the percentage of the total score that Bretz contributed.

   *Hint: Divide Bretz's score by the total score and use an **absolute reference** to ensure that the reference does not change when the formula is copied.*

3. Copy the formula to the remaining players (range C3:C10).

4. Select the range C2:C10.

5. Format the range C2:C10 for percentages with two decimal places.

Add a Title and Format Headings

1. Insert two rows above existing row 1.

2. Type the following title in cell A1:

   BASKETBALL SCORES

3. Center the title across columns A, B, and C if your application permits.

4. Format the title as 12-point bold, italic.

5. Format *Player*, *Score*, *Percent*, and *TOTAL* to bold.

   Your worksheet should look like the one shown in Illustration B.

Illustration B. Completed Worksheet

	A	B	C
1	**BASKETBALL SCORES**		
2			
3	**Player**	**Score**	**Percent**
4	Bretz	2	2.82%
5	Brokofsky	10	14.08%
6	Castillo	6	8.45%
7	Holmes	9	12.68%
8	Rhodes	15	21.13%
9	Rodriquez	7	9.86%
10	Thompson	1	1.41%
11	Veach	13	18.31%
12	Yuan	8	11.27%
13	**TOTAL**	71	

Save, Preview, Print

1. Save the workbook.

2. Preview the document.

3. Print one copy in Portrait orientation.

4. Close the workbook, and exit the spreadsheet application.

Create a Pie Chart
■ About Pie Charts ■ Create a Pie Chart

NOTES

About Pie Charts

■ A pie chart is a circle divided into segments. Each slice of the pie represents one column or row of data. The parts of a pie chart are labeled in the illustration below.

Parts of a Pie Chart (with Legend)

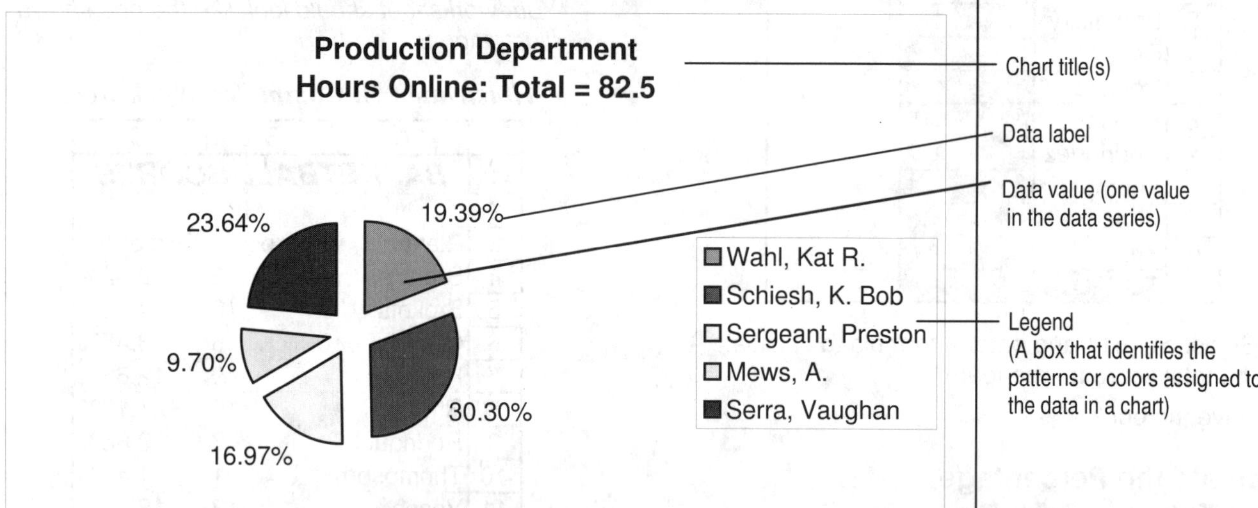

■ When you communicate the results of your work with spreadsheets, you can increase the impact of your message by including pictorial representations of your spreadsheet data. The spreadsheet applications make it easy to create charts.

Create a Pie Chart

■ Some applications provide a step-by-step guide to creating a chart; others provide dialog boxes that aid in chart creation. After creation, you can edit the chart to end up with a picture that clearly represents the data.

⌨ Try It!

Step 1: Select the Data to be Charted and the Chart Type

1. Open 💿 **06Online** from the data files.
2. Save the workbook as **Online**.
3. Select range A5:B9, as shown in the illustration on the following page.

Spreadsheet for Production Department Online Usage

	A	B	C	D
1	Online Hours -- Production Department			
2	Month of June			
3				
4	User	Hours Online	Percent of Total	
5	Wahl, Kat R.	16.0	19.39%	
6	Schiesh, K. Bob	25.0	30.30%	
7	Sergeant, Preston	14.0	16.97%	
8	Mews, A.	8.0	9.70%	
9	Serra, Vaughan	19.5	23.64%	
10	TOTALS	82.5		

Data for legend or labels

Data series (values to be charted)

4. Create a pie chart with exploded slices.

5. Use the following title:

    AppleWorks: June Online Hours -- Production Department (default font, 12-point, bold)

    MS Works: Online Hours -- Production Department (default format)

    Excel 97 & 2000: Online Hours -- Production Department (default font, 12-point, bold)

    Quattro Pro: Online Hours -- Production Department (default font, size as necessary to fit chart)

6. Use the following subtitle:

    MS Works: Month of June (default format)

    Excel 97 & 2000: Month of June (default font, 12-point regular)

    Quattro Pro: Month of June (default font, size as necessary to fit chart)

7. In **AppleWorks** and **Excel**, use a separate legend that lists each user's name with a key color for each user.

    In **MS Works** and **Quattro Pro**, show the user's name and the percentage next to the correct slice.

8. Place the chart in the application's default location. If it is on the same sheet as the data, move it below the data at the left edge of the sheet.

9. In **Excel** (all versions), format the percentages with two decimal places.

10. Save the book. Close the book, and exit the spreadsheet application unless you are continuing with the Exercise Directions.

Completed Pie Chart

AppleWorks

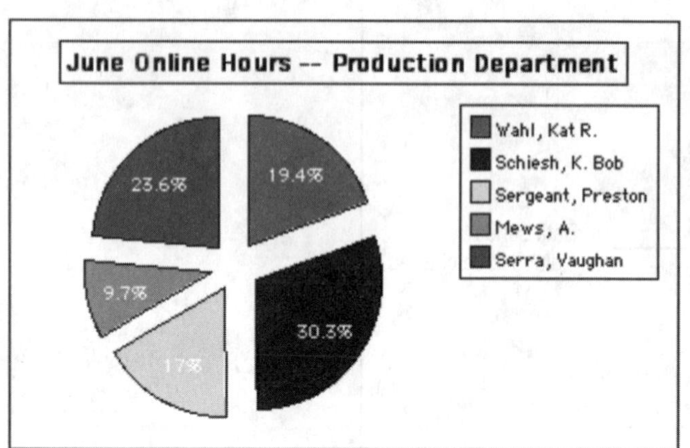

MS Works (shown greatly reduced)

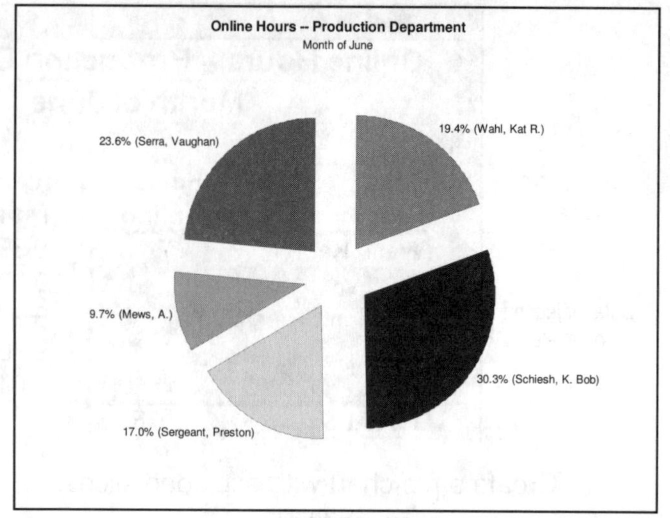

Excel

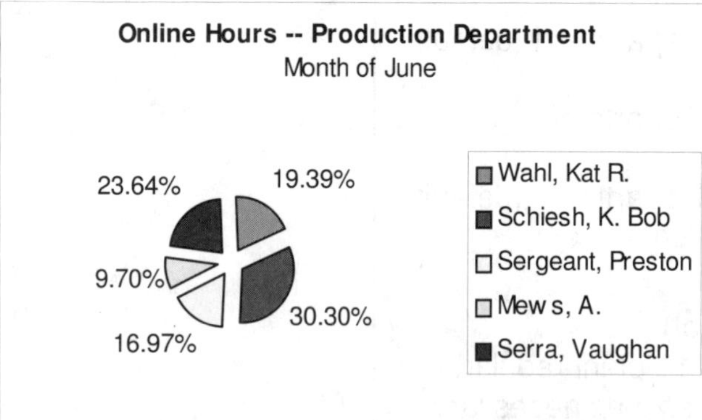

Quattro Pro

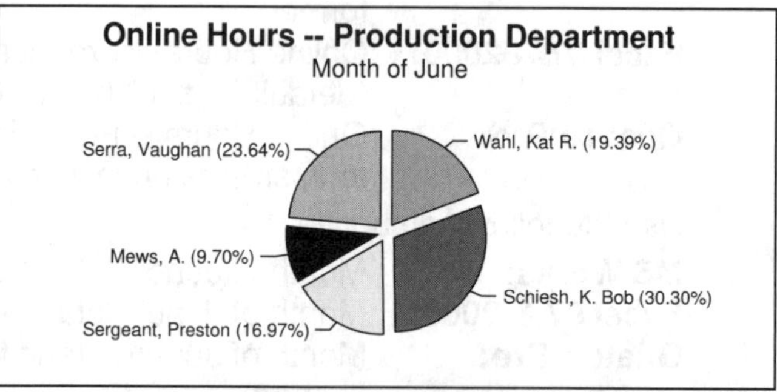

> **In this exercise, you will use the Chart Wizard to create an exploded 3-D pie chart from basketball scores.**

EXERCISE DIRECTIONS

Open the Workbook and Select the Data to Include in Chart

1. Open ⌨**Basketball**, or open 💿**06Basketball** from the data files.
2. Save the workbook as **Basketball2**.
3. Select the range A4:B12.

Create a Pie Chart

1. In all applications except AppleWorks, create a 3D exploded pie chart. In AppleWorks, create a two-dimensional exploded pie chart. Give the chart the following characteristics:

   - Legend at the right and percentages with the slices (AppleWorks and Excel).

     OR

     Names and percentages with the slices (MS Works and Quattro Pro).
   - *BASKETBALL SCORES* as the chart title.

   See the illustrations at the end of this exercise for what the charts should look like.

2. **All Excel versions**: Format the percentage labels for 2 decimal places.
3. Preview the sheet.
4. Print one copy of the sheet. In MS Works print one copy of the chart sheet.
5. Save the book.
6. Close the book and exit the spreadsheet application.

Illustration A: AppleWorks Desired Result

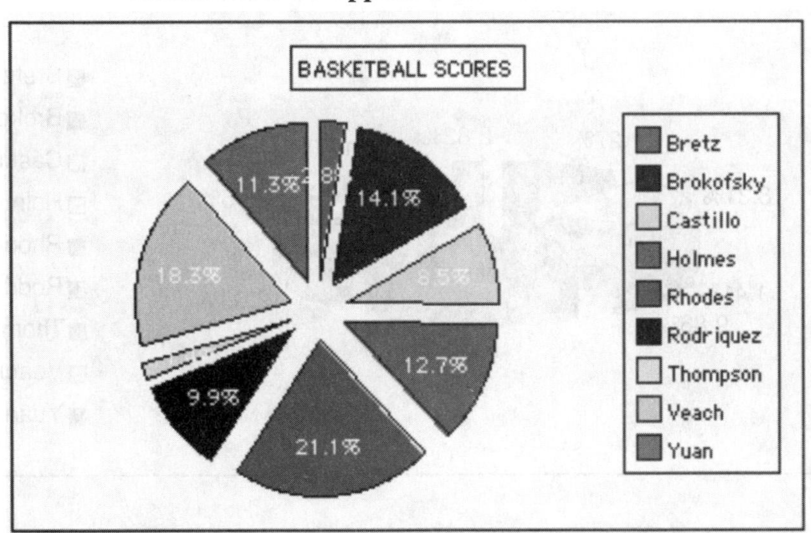

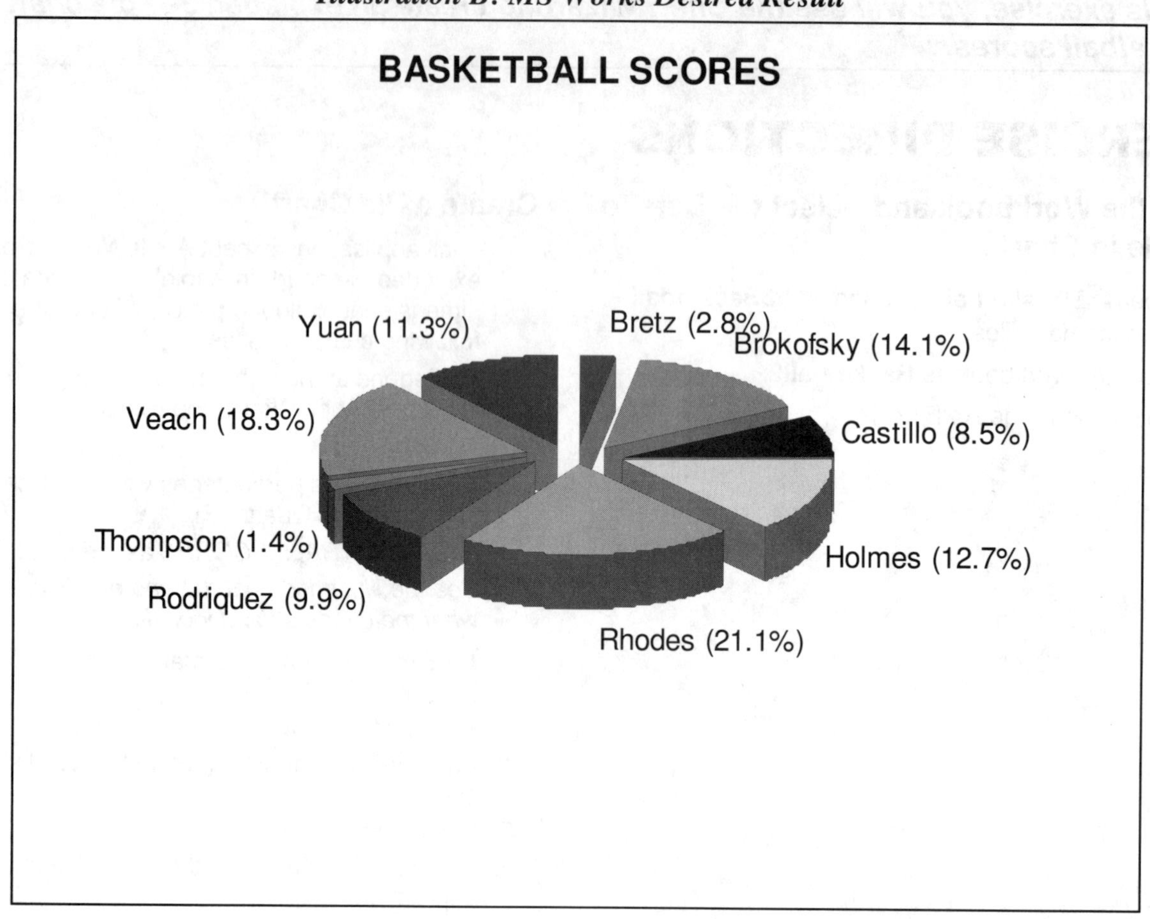

Illustration C: Excel Desired Result

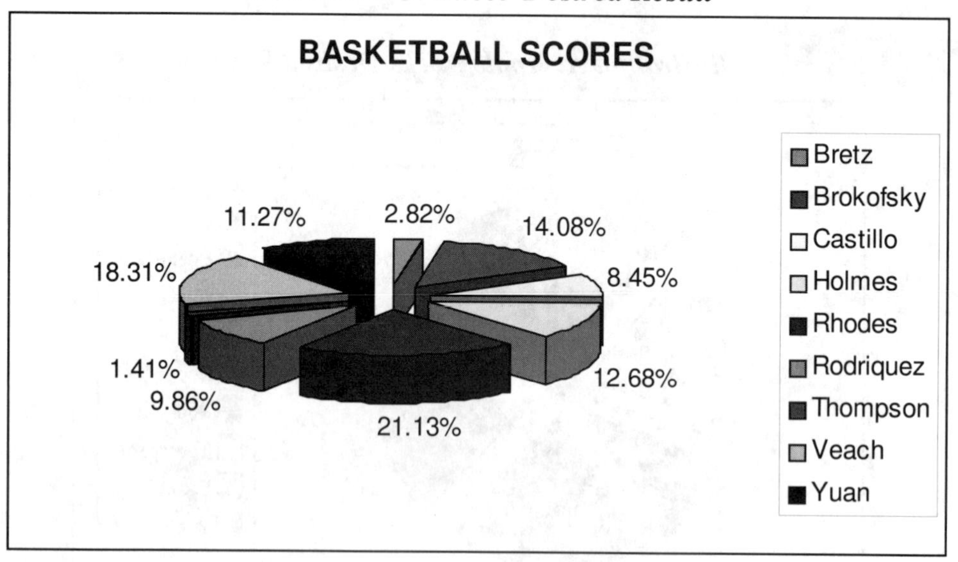

Illustration D: Quattro Pro Desired Result

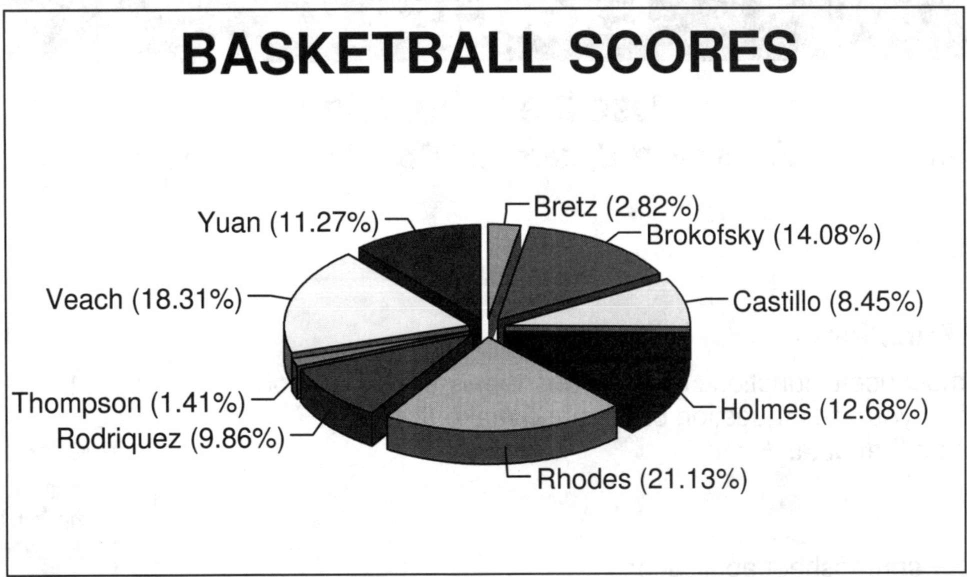

Exercise 7

Use the IF Function
■ **About the IF Function** ■ **Understand Operators** ■ **Paste the IF Function**

NOTES

About the IF Function

- One of the most useful functions in a spreadsheet is the IF function. The IF function lets you ask a question of data and make the result **conditional** on that data.

Try It!

1. Start your spreadsheet application.
2. Save the new book as **IF**.
3. In cell A1, enter *6*.
4. In cell B1, enter the following formula; be sure to type it exactly as shown below, and press Enter.

   =IF(A1=6,"YES","NO")

   The word YES appears in cell B1.

5. In cell A2, type *5*.
6. Copy the formula from B1 to B2.

   The word NO appears in cell B2.

- In this example, you entered a formula that is the equivalent of the English sentence:

   IF cell A1 is equal to 6, then display YES, otherwise display NO.

- The parts of an IF statement are labeled below.

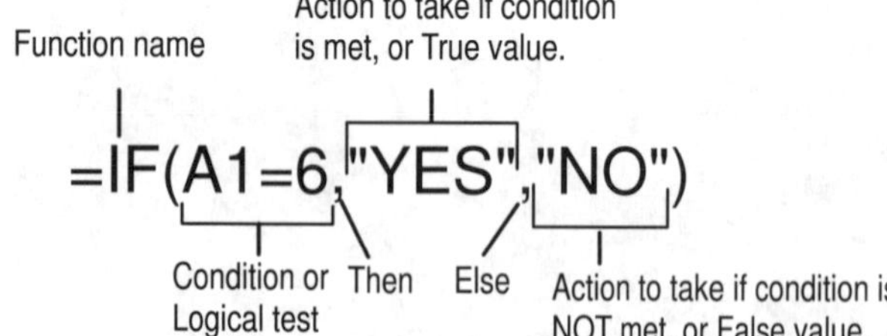

- The commas in the statement separate the phrases of the IF function. The first comma means THEN; the second means ELSE. As with other functions, the **arguments** are enclosed in parentheses.

- If you can phrase the IF statement in English, you can turn it into a formula that the application can interpret. Create the IF statement in English first, and then think about how that translates into a spreadsheet formula.

Conditional Result

A conditional result is one that can change depending on the data (or result) in another cell. An IF function sets a condition. If the condition is met, one result is used; if the condition is not met, a different result is used.

Input Area

Try typing the formula in the input area. It is easier to see the entire IF statement in that way.

Why Quotation Marks?

The quotation marks tell the spreadsheet that the word is to be treated as a word and not as the name of an object.

Argument

Element of a formula or function statement that specifies the data on which the formula is to operate.

🖥 Try It!

1. Select cell A6, and enter *3842*.

2. Select cell B6, and enter *3795*.

3. Select cell C6, and enter the following IF statement:

    =IF(A6>B6,A6-B6,A6+B6)

    The symbol > means greater than. The IF statement says, "If the value in cell A6 is greater than the value in cell B6, subtract the value in B6 from A6, else add the two values."

    The number 47 appears in cell C6.

4. Copy the number in cell B6 to cell A7 (or enter *3795* in A7).

5. Copy the number in cell A6 to cell B7 (or enter *3842* in B7).

6. Copy the formula from C6 to C7.

    The number 7637 appears in cell C7.

7. Save and close the book, but leave the application open.

Understand Operators

■ Spreadsheets use symbols to perform common arithmetic and comparison calculations. These symbols are called **operators**. The arithmetic and comparison operators are listed and described in the table that follows.

Operator	Action	Sample Use
+	Addition	=B2+C2
–	Subtraction	=B2-C2
* (asterisk)	Multiplication	=B2*C2
/ (forward slash)	Division	=B2/C2
% (percent sign)	Percent	=B2%
^ (caret)	Exponentiation	=B2^C2. For example, if B2 is 4 and C2 is 2, the result is 16 (4^2 or 4*4).
=	Equal to	=IF(A1=B1,"Equal","Unequal")
<>	Not equal to	=IF(A1<>B1,"Unequal", "Equal")
>	Greater than	=IF(A1>B1,"Greater","Less or Equal")
<	Less than	=IF(A1<B1,"Less","Greater or Equal")
>=	Greater than or equal to	=IF(A1>=B1,"Greater or Equal","Less")
<=	Less than or equal to	=IF(A1<=B1,"Less or Equal","Greater")

Paste the IF Function

- You can use the Paste Function feature to create an IF statement.

Try It!

- Build the equivalent of the following English statement:

  If the value in the Score column is 45 or more (>=45), then display the word Qualifies, else display the phrase TOO LOW!

  1. Open ⊙ **07Scores** from the data files.

  2. Save the workbook as **Scores**.

  3. Select cell C2.

  4. Use the paste function feature to enter the IF function. The completed formula should look as shown below. (Quattro Pro will display the @ symbol rather than the = sign.)

     =IF(B2>=45,"Qualifies","TOO LOW!")

     *A brief review of the paste function features of the spreadsheets is given in the procedures. For **Quattro Pro** a new procedure appears, describing the use of the Formula Composer.*

  5. Copy the IF statement in C2 to the range C3:C12.

  6. Save and close the workbook. Exit the spreadsheet program unless you are continuing with the Exercise Directions.

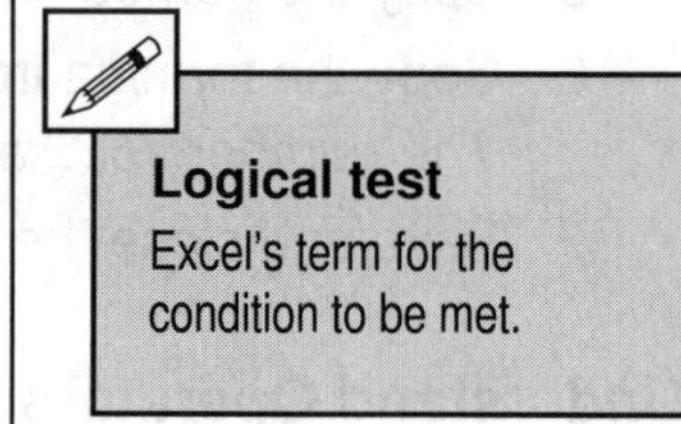

Logical test
Excel's term for the condition to be met.

In this exercise, you will use the IF function to determine whether students in a Computer Essentials class receive a PASS or FAIL grade.

EXERCISE DIRECTIONS

Open the Workbook and Enter Scores for Test 4

1. Open ⊙ **07Pass Fail** from the data files.

2. Save the workbook as **Pass Fail**.

3. Add the labels and values in the shaded areas shown in Illustration A.

4. Save the workbook.

Calculate the Average for Each Student

1. In cell G2, use the paste function feature to calculate the average test score for Howard Beech.

2. Copy the formula to the remaining students. *Your worksheet should now look like the one in Illustration B.*

3. Save the workbook.

Illustration A. Add Data to Pass Fail

	A	B	C	D	E	F	G	H
1	LAST NAME	FIRST NAME	TEST 1	TEST 2	TEST 3	TEST 4	AVERAGE	PASS/FAIL
2	Beech	Howard	78	58	79	65		
3	Doermann	Carlton	70	85	82	63		
4	Frye	Northrop	95	100	99	92		
5	Giambalvo	John	52	64	55	48		
6	Newcomer	Sandra	100	95	94	98		
7	O'Loughlin	Michael	90	88	92	91		
8	Palacio	Miguel	100	100	100	100		
9	Pastore	Mary Jane	60	65	43	55		
10	Patel	Ganga	98	97	96	93		
11	Paul	Carol Ann	87	77	83	91		
12	Payne	Frieda	67	73	84	75		
13	Plum	Robert	60	65	73	76		
14	Rhodes	Mary Ellen	88	87	86	85		
15	Rodenbeek	Suzanne	100	100	100	100		
16	Salem	Winston	63	72	78	69		
17	Stewart	Robert	54	48	62	70		
18	Wilson	Daniel	78	84	83	80		
19	Winderlin	Rosemarie	84	83	78	82		

Illustration B. Worksheet with Averages Calculated

	A	B	C	D	E	F	G	H
1	LAST NAME	FIRST NAME	TEST 1	TEST 2	TEST 3	TEST 4	AVERAGE	PASS/FAIL
2	Beech	Howard	78	58	79	65	70	
3	Doermann	Carlton	70	85	82	63	75	
4	Frye	Northrop	95	100	99	92	96.5	
5	Giambalvo	John	52	64	55	48	54.75	
6	Newcomer	Sandra	100	95	94	98	96.75	
7	O'Loughlin	Michael	90	88	92	91	90.25	
8	Palacio	Miguel	100	100	100	100	100	
9	Pastore	Mary Jane	60	65	43	55	55.75	
10	Patel	Ganga	98	97	96	93	96	
11	Paul	Carol Ann	87	77	83	91	84.5	
12	Payne	Frieda	67	73	84	75	74.75	
13	Plum	Robert	60	65	73	76	68.5	
14	Rhodes	Mary Ellen	88	87	86	85	86.5	
15	Rodenbeek	Suzanne	100	100	100	100	100	
16	Salem	Winston	63	72	78	69	70.5	
17	Stewart	Robert	54	48	62	70	58.5	
18	Wilson	Daniel	78	84	83	80	81.25	
19	Winderlin	Rosemarie	84	83	78	82	81.75	

Use Paste Function to Insert
IF Function for PASS/FAIL

The statement in English is "If the test average is 70 or more, the student passes; otherwise, the student fails."

=IF(G2>=70,"PASS","FAIL")

1. Paste the IF function into cell H2.

2. Select IF, and click OK.

3. Specify the condition: =IF(G2>=70,

4. Specify the result if the condition is true: "PASS",

5. Specify the result if the condition is false: "FAIL",

   When you complete the entry, the word PASS should appear in the cell.

If it does not, complete the following steps:

a. Select cell G2 and look at the input line.

b. Click in the input line to edit the IF statement.

c. Be sure the IF statement reads exactly as follows, with the commas, quotation marks, and parentheses as shown.

   =IF(G2>=70,"PASS","FAIL")

d. When it is correct, press Enter.

6. Copy the IF statement to cells H3 through H19.
   Your worksheet should look like the one shown in Illustration C.

7. Save the book.

Illustration C. IF Function Specified for Each Student

	A	B	C	D	E	F	G	H
1	LAST NAME	FIRST NAME	TEST 1	TEST 2	TEST 3	TEST 4	AVERAGE	PASS/FAIL
2	Beech	Howard	78	58	79	65	70	PASS
3	Doermann	Carlton	70	85	82	63	75	PASS
4	Frye	Northrop	95	100	99	92	96.5	PASS
5	Giambalvo	John	52	64	55	48	54.75	FAIL
6	Newcomer	Sandra	100	95	94	98	96.75	PASS
7	O'Loughlin	Michael	90	88	92	91	90.25	PASS
8	Palacio	Miguel	100	100	100	100	100	PASS
9	Pastore	Mary Jane	60	65	43	55	55.75	FAIL
10	Patel	Ganga	98	97	96	93	96	PASS
11	Paul	Carol Ann	87	77	83	91	84.5	PASS
12	Payne	Frieda	67	73	84	75	74.75	PASS
13	Plum	Robert	60	65	73	76	68.5	FAIL
14	Rhodes	Mary Ellen	88	87	86	85	86.5	PASS
15	Rodenbeek	Suzanne	100	100	100	100	100	PASS
16	Salem	Winston	63	72	78	69	70.5	PASS
17	Stewart	Robert	54	48	62	70	58.5	FAIL
18	Wilson	Daniel	78	84	83	80	81.25	PASS
19	Winderlin	Rosemarie	84	83	78	82	81.75	PASS

Format the Column Headings

1. Center and bold the headings over each column.

2. Center all entries in the PASS/FAIL column.

3. Format all averages with two decimals.

4. Save the workbook.

Add a Title

1. Insert two rows above existing row 1.

2. Select cell A1.

3. Type the following title:
   Computer Essentials -- 4th Period

4. Center the title across the range A1:H1 if your application permits.

5. Format the text to the default font, 14-point bold.

6. If necessary, adjust the height of the row.

   Your worksheet should look like the one in Illustration D. (In AppleWorks, the title will not be centered.

Save, Print Preview, Print

1. Save the book.

2. Preview the sheet.

3. Print one copy with gridlines only.

4. Close the workbook, and exit the spreadsheet application.

Illustration D. Desired Result

	A	B	C	D	E	F	G	H
1	**Computer Essentials -- 4th Period**							
2								
3	**LAST NAME**	**FIRST NAME**	**TEST 1**	**TEST 2**	**TEST 3**	**TEST 4**	**AVERAGE**	**PASS/FAIL**
4	Beech	Howard	78	58	79	65	70.00	PASS
5	Doermann	Carlton	70	85	82	63	75.00	PASS
6	Frye	Northrop	95	100	99	92	96.50	PASS
7	Giambalvo	John	52	64	55	48	54.75	FAIL
8	Newcomer	Sandra	100	95	94	98	96.75	PASS
9	O'Loughlin	Michael	90	88	92	91	90.25	PASS
10	Palacio	Miguel	100	100	100	100	100.00	PASS
11	Pastore	Mary Jane	60	65	43	55	55.75	FAIL
12	Patel	Ganga	98	97	96	93	96.00	PASS
13	Paul	Carol Ann	87	77	83	91	84.50	PASS
14	Payne	Frieda	67	73	84	75	74.75	PASS
15	Plum	Robert	60	65	73	76	68.50	FAIL
16	Rhodes	Mary Ellen	88	87	86	85	86.50	PASS
17	Rodenbeek	Suzanne	100	100	100	100	100.00	PASS
18	Salem	Winston	63	72	78	69	70.50	PASS
19	Stewart	Robert	54	48	62	70	58.50	FAIL
20	Wilson	Daniel	78	84	83	80	81.25	PASS
21	Winderlin	Rosemarie	84	83	78	82	81.75	PASS

Integrate Spreadsheets and Word Processing
■ Insert a Spreadsheet Chart into a Word Processing Document
■ Insert Word Processing Text into a Spreadsheet
■ Insert Spreadsheet Data into a Word Processing Document

NOTES

Insert a Spreadsheet Chart into a Word Processing Document

- As members of an application suite, word processors and spreadsheet applications are designed to work well together. You can create a spreadsheet or a chart and insert it into a word processing document, and you can create data in the word processor and import it into the spreadsheet.

💻 Try It!

1. Start the spreadsheet program and open 💿 **08Enrollment** from the data files.

2. Start the word processor and open 💿 **08Flueghel** from the data files.

3. Save the word processor document as **Flueghel1**.

4. Go to the end of the memo.

5. Switch to **08Enrollment** in the spreadsheet program.

   In AppleWorks and MS Works, use the Window menu option to switch to the spreadsheet. In the other Windows applications, click the spreadsheet's icon on the taskbar.

6. Copy the chart Flueghel College Enrollment. (It's the top chart in the spreadsheet, or Chart1 in MS Works.)

7. Switch back to the word processing document.

8. Paste the chart into the document at the insertion point (end of the document).

   The graph is inserted as an inline or floating object. Treat it as a graphic and change it to an inline object if it is floating.

9. Center the paragraph with the chart.

10. In MS Works, resize the chart to approximately 4" high. Maintain the aspect ratio.

11. Save the document.

12. Print one copy.

13. Close the file, but leave the word processor open.

14. Switch to the spreadsheet, and close **08Enrollment** without saving it.

Insert Word Processing Text into a Spreadsheet

- You can create text in the word processor and insert it into a spreadsheet.

💻 Try It!

1. Open the Word file ⊚ **08Acme** from the data files.

2. Select the entire tabbed table. Be sure to include the entirety of each row.

3. Copy the selected text.

4. Switch to the spreadsheet application and create a new document.

5. Select cell A1.

6. Paste the text into the spreadsheet.

   The spreadsheet converts the text into labels and numbers based on the kind of data after each tab. The tabs are called **delimiters**, *because they define the limits between pieces of data.*

7. In Quattro Pro, you may need to delete a blank column A, so the sheet appears as shown below.

Tabbed Text Converted to Spreadsheet

	A	B	C	D	E	F
1		Monday	Tuesday	Wednesda	Thursday	Friday
2	Week 1	58,750.75	48,763.50	44,378.65	34,832.67	59,432.18
3	Week 2	55,562.87	47,332.91	36,753.52	37,812.03	46,739.83
4	Week 3	52,374.61	50,328.40	40,293.38	40,374.72	52,983.26
5	Week 4	62,278.10	54,974.98	48,374.65	42,746.32	63,374.45

8. Adjust column widths and row heights as necessary.

9. Save the workbook as **AcmeSales**.

10. Perform the necessary formatting to make the spreadsheet appear as shown in the following illustration.

Completed Spreadsheet

	A	B	C	D	E	F	G
1				Acme Sales			
2							
3		Monday	Tuesday	Wednesday	Thursday	Friday	TOTALS
4	Week 1	58,750.75	48,763.50	44,378.65	34,832.67	59,432.18	$ 246,157.75
5	Week 2	55,562.87	47,332.91	36,753.52	37,812.03	46,739.83	$ 224,201.16
6	Week 3	52,374.61	50,328.40	40,293.38	40,374.72	52,983.26	$ 236,354.37
7	Week 4	62,278.10	54,974.98	48,374.65	42,746.32	63,374.45	$ 271,748.50
8							
9	TOTALS	$ 228,966.33	$ 201,399.79	$ 169,800.20	$ 155,765.74	$ 222,529.72	$ 978,461.78

- If necessary, select the entire spreadsheet and change the font to the default for your application and its default size. (Arial,10 point for all except AppleWorks. AppleWorks is Geneva 9 point.)

- Format the data values as numeric with commas and two decimals.

- Enter the TOTALS labels and calculate the totals with the SUM function as shown.

- Format all totals as Currency or Accounting.

- Insert two blank rows above row 1.

- Enter the title *Acme Sales* in cell A1.

- Format the title to 14-point, bold, adjust the row height if necessary, and center it across the range A1:G1 if possible.

11. Change the orientation to Landscape, and preview the spreadsheet.

12. Save the book.

13. Print one copy in Landscape orientation with row and column headings and gridlines.

14. Leave the book and the word processing document open.

Insert Spreadsheet Data into a Word Processing Document

- You can select a range of spreadsheet data and paste it into a word processing document. All applications except AppleWorks accomplish this through the **Edit**, **Paste Special** menu command.

⌨ Try It!

Prepare Letter and Insert Spreadsheet Data

1. Switch to the word processing document.

2. Delete the five rows of tabbed text.

3. Switch to the spreadsheet.

4. In Excel, turn off the options to print row and column headings (print gridlines only).

5. Select and copy the range A1:G9.

6. Switch to the word processing document.

7. Use **Edit**, **Paste Special** (for AppleWorks, see the procedures) to paste the spreadsheet into the word processing document, replacing the tabbed text.

8. Save the word processing document as **Acme**.

⌨ Try It!

Complete Formatting of the Letter

1. **AppleWorks:**

   - To create a spreadsheet frame large enough to include all columns of the sheet, set the column widths as follows:

Column A:	50 pt
Columns B..F:	66 pt
Column G:	72 pt (the default)

   - Set the display options to show gridlines only, not column or row headings.

   - Be sure only the 9 rows and columns A..G are showing.

2. If the spreadsheet object is floating, treat it as a graphic and change to an inline object.

3. Center the paragraph that contains the spreadsheet.

4. If necessary move the spreadsheet so that it follows the first paragraph of the letter.

5. Make sure there is one blank line above and one blank line below the spreadsheet.

6. Save the document, and print one copy.

7. Close the document and exit the word processor unless you are continuing with the Exercise Directions.

8. Switch to the spreadsheet, close the book (save it if prompted), and exit the spreadsheet application unless you are continuing with the Exercise Directions.

In this exercise, you will complete the memo about Flueghel College enrollment. To do so, you will copy another chart and insert it into the word processing document, and you will copy and paste spreadsheet data.

EXERCISE DIRECTIONS

Open the Documents

1. In the spreadsheet application, open ⊙**08Enrollment** from the data files.

2. Open the word processor file ⌨**Flueghel1**, or open ⊙**08Flueghel2** from the data disk.

3. Save the document as **Flueghel2**.

4. Place the insertion point at the end of the document.

5. Insert a new paragraph after the chart and left align it, and enter:
   The chart below shows the trend for total enrollment for the same five years.

6. Insert another new paragraph and left align it, and enter:
   These charts are based on the data shown below.

Insert Chart

1. Switch to the spreadsheet document (**08Enrollment**).

2. Select the line graph that shows the trend of total enrollment (the lower of the two charts).

3. Copy it.

4. Switch to the word processor.

5. Insert it as an inline object between the two final text paragraphs.

6. Center the paragraph that contains the chart.

7. In MS Works, resize the chart to approximately 4" high. Maintain the aspect ratio.

Insert Range from Spreadsheet

1. Save the document.

2. Switch to the spreadsheet document (**08Enrollment**).

3. In Excel, be sure that the gridlines are set to print.

4. **AppleWorks:**   Copy range A1..F10
   All others: Copy range A1:F8

   In AppleWorks repetition of the heading and totals rows was necessary to create the second chart.

5. Switch to the word processor.

6. Insert the copied spreadsheet data at the end of the document (see the procedures for Exercise 8).

   - **AppleWorks:** Adjust the height of row 1 to 18 pt.

   - **AppleWorks:** Size the spreadsheet frame so that the full range A1..F10 is displayed.

   - **AppleWorks:** Set the display options to show gridlines only (no row or column headings).

7. Format the inserted sheet as an inline object in a blank paragraph at the end of the document.

8. Center the paragraph with the inserted data.

9. Save the document, but leave it open.

Finish Formatting the Memo

1. Make sure there is one blank paragraph before and after each illustration.

2. Insert a manual page break before the second body paragraph.

3. Insert a footer with the page number centered.

4. Save the document.

5. Print Preview the document.

6. Print one copy.
   Your word document should now look like the one shown in Illustration B.

7. Close the document, and exit the word processor.

8. Switch to the spreadsheet, close the book, save it if prompted to do so, and exit the spreadsheet program.

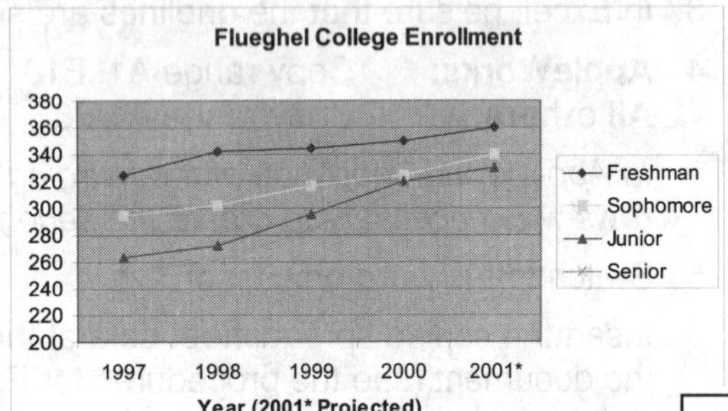

MEMORANDUM

To: Flueghel College Faculty Senate

From: O. Penn Dorr, Director of Admissions

Subject: Enrollment Trends

Date: Today's date

At the request of Professor I. M. Wise, chair of the enrollment committee, the Office of Admissions has prepared a look at recent enrollment figures here at Flueghel. The chart below shows enrollment trends by class for the past three years and projections for the years 2000 and 2001.

1

The chart below shows the trend for total enrollment for the same five years.

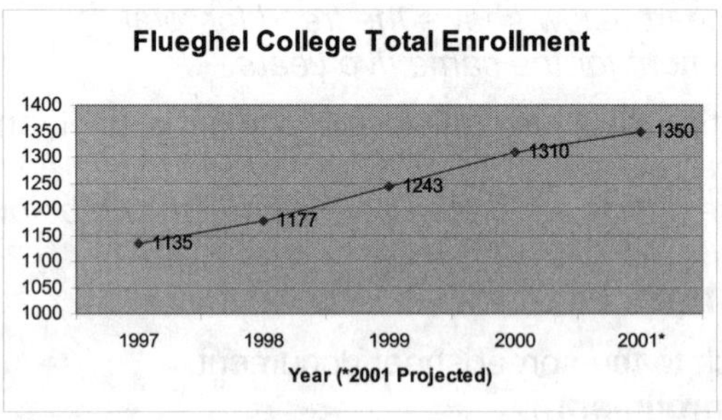

These charts are based on the data shown below.

Flueghel College Enrollment					
	1997	**1998**	**1999**	**2000**	**2001***
Freshman	325	342	345	350	360
Sophomore	295	302	317	325	340
Junior	263	272	296	320	330
Senior	252	261	285	315	320
TOTALS	1135	1177	1243	1310	1350

2

NEXT EXERCISE

Challenge Exercise
■ Structure of a Checkbook Register
■ Create a Checkbook Register

NOTES

Structure of a Checkbook Register

■ A checkbook register, like a spreadsheet, consists of rows and columns that form a grid. The checkbook register usually looks like the following:

DATE	TRANS ID	PAYEE	TYPE	AMOUNT	BALANCE
		Brought Forward			2403.46
1/3/00	2421	Mortgage	W	1,582.10	821.36

■ The columns in the grid are described below.

DATE	Date of the transaction.
TRANS ID	Identifier of the transaction. Usually this is a check number. With online banking, however, this may be an identifier assigned by the bank.
PAYEE	Name of the person or company involved in the transaction.
TYPE	Type of transaction: W = Withdrawal, D = Deposit.
AMOUNT	Amount of the transaction.
BALANCE	Amount in the account after the transaction.

■ In a checkbook register kept by hand, these columns may vary. Sometimes the manual register has two rows in the balance column to make subtraction and addition easier. In an electronic register, however, you can write an IF function to handle the calculation automatically.

■ The IF statement in the BALANCE column, in English, is:

If the transaction TYPE is W, subtract the AMOUNT from the previous BALANCE; otherwise, add the AMOUNT to the previous BALANCE.

Sample Electronic Check Register

	A	B	C	D	E	F
1			Checking -- Account # 12345678			
2	DATE	TRANS ID	PAYEE	TYPE	AMOUNT	BALANCE
3			Balance Brought Forward			2,403.46
4	1/3/00	10344	Mortgage	W	1,582.10	821.36
5	1/3/00	10345	Electric Company	W	340.89	480.47
6	1/3/00	10346	Telephone Company	W	54.97	425.50
7	1/31/00		Salary from School	D	2,674.36	3099.86
8	1/27/00		ATM Cash - Larchmont	W	300.00	2799.86

- Before starting the Exercise Directions, try to construct the IF statement for the BALANCE cell F4 in the Check Register on the previous page. Remember that text entries in the statement must be enclosed in double quotation marks. Use the questions below to help you.

Condition =IF(cell="text",

_______________________ Which cell contains the data to determine whether the amount should be added to or subtracted from the balance?

_______________________ What text indicates that the amount is to be subtracted from the balance?

Result if true(... ,balance-amount

_______________________ Which cell contains the balance from which the amount should subtracted?

_______________________ Which cell contains the amount?

Result if false(... , ... , balance+amount

_______________________ Which cell contains the balance to which the amount should added?

_______________________ Which cell contains the amount?

- The answers to these questions should help you correctly structure the IF statement for cell F4. You can then copy that formula to all the other cells.

- Write your proposed IF statement on the blank below.

____

Create a Checkbook Register

In this exercise, you will use the IF function to create a checkbook register.

Start the Spreadsheet Program and Enter the Title and Column Headings

1. Start the spreadsheet application and use the new spreadsheet created by the program.

2. Save the workbook as **Checkbook**.

3. In cell C1, enter:
   Checking -- Account # 12345678

4. In cell A2, enter *DATE*.

5. In cell B2, enter *TRANS ID*.

6. In cell C2, enter *PAYEE*.

7. In cell D2, enter *TYPE*.

8. In cell E2, enter *AMOUNT*.

9. In cell F2, enter *BALANCE*.

10. Center and bold all headings in row 2.

11. In cell C3, type:
    Balance Brought Forward.

12. Automatically adjust (AutoFit) all column widths.

    The worksheet should now look like the one in Illustration A.

13. Save the workbook.

Enter the Balance Brought Forward and Enter Some Transactions

1. In cell F3, enter the following value as the balance brought forward:

   2403.46

2. Complete the range A4:E7 with the data shown in Illustration B.

3. Format the DATE column (range A4:A18) with any date format you wish. Adjust the column width if necessary.

4. Format the TYPE range D4:D18 as centered text.

5. Select the AMOUNT and BALANCE range E3:F18, and click the Comma button to format the values.

Illustration A. Checkbook Register Headings

	A	B	C	D	E	F
1			Checking -- Account # 12345678			
2	DATE	TRANS ID	PAYEE	TYPE	AMOUNT	BALANCE
3			Balance Brought Forward			
4						
5						
6						
7						
8						
9						
10						
11						
12						
13						
14						
15						

Illustration B. Transactions for Rows 4 - 7

	A	B	C	D	E	F
1			Checking -- Account # 12345678			
2	DATE	TRANS ID	PAYEE	TYPE	AMOUNT	BALANCE
3			Balance Brought Forward			2,403.46
4	1/3/00	10344	Mortgage	W	1,582.10	
5	1/3/00	10345	Electric Company	W	340.89	
6	1/3/00	10346	Telephone Company	W	54.97	
7	1/31/00		Salary from School	D	2,674.36	

Enter the IF Statement in Cell F4

1. Select cell F4.

2. Use the paste function feature to entire the IF statement for the cell.

3. The completed statement is shown in Illustration C.

4. Check your formula (look at the input line) against the one shown below:

   =IF(D4="W",F3-E4,F3+E4)

   Did the formula you create match the one shown above?

5. Copy the formula to the range F5:F18. (If Quattro Pro displays an error box, click the Close button to ignore the error.)

   When you add entries in rows 8 - 18, the formulas in column F will be calculated automatically.

6. Add the two new transactions in the shaded area of Illustration D.

   Did the values update correctly?

7. Save and close the workbook.

   You now have a checkbook register and the knowledge to use it. You can use this register to track your own banking transactions or those of someone you know who trusts you with financial information.

Illustration C. Formula Palette for IF Function

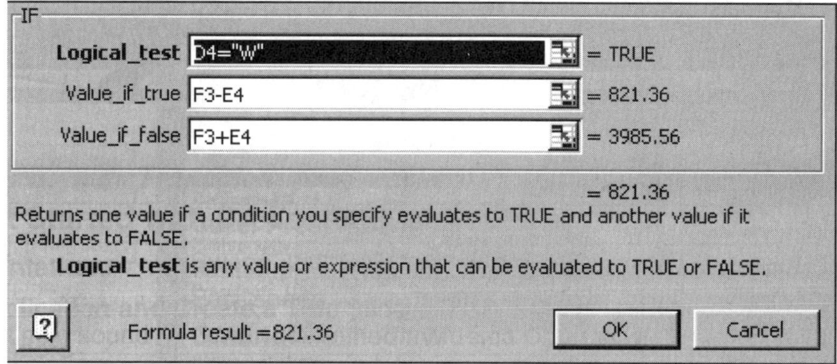

Illustration D. Completed Checkbook Register

	A	B	C	D	E	F
1			Checking -- Account # 12345678			
2	**DATE**	**TRANS ID**	**PAYEE**	**TYPE**	**AMOUNT**	**BALANCE**
3			Balance Brought Forward			2,403.46
4	1/3/00	10344	Mortgage	W	1,582.10	821.36
5	1/3/00	10345	Electric Company	W	340.89	480.47
6	1/3/00	10346	Telephone Company	W	54.97	425.50
7	1/31/00		Salary from School	D	2,674.36	3,099.86
8	1/27/00		ATM Cash - Larchmont	W	300.00	2,799.86
9	1/4/00	2419	Milburn Stone, M.D.	W	220.00	2,579.86
10						2,579.86
11						2,579.86
12						2,579.86
13						2,579.86
14						2,579.86
15						2,579.86
16						2,579.86
17						2,579.86
18						2,579.86

NEXT LESSON

Lesson 6: Databases

Exercise 1: Introduction to Databases

- What is a Database?
- What is a Database Management System?
- Types of Databases
- How Do Database Management Systems Work?
- What are Database Objects?
- How is a Table Structured?
- Field Data Types
- How are Tables Related in Access and Paradox?
- Planning a New Database

Exercise 2: Use and Modify a Database

- Open an Existing Database
- About Fields, Data Types, and Formats
- Add a Field to a Table
- Include Aids to Data Entry

Exercise 3: Create and Use a Form

- Create a Form
- Add Records in Form View
- Print Records in Form View

Exercise 4: Create a Database and Table

- Create a Database
- Enter Data in a Form

Exercise 5: Filter and Query a Database

- Filter a Database
- Filter Criteria
- Create a Query (Access or Paradox)

Exercise 6: Work with Reports

- Create a Report

Introduction to Databases

■ What is a Database? ■ What is a Database Management System?
■ Types of Databases ■ How Do Database Management Systems Work?
■ What are Database Objects? ■ How is a Table Structured? ■ Field Data Types
■ How are Tables Related in Access and Paradox? ■ Planning a New Database

NOTES

What is a Database?

■ A **database** is an organized collection of facts about a particular subject. An address book or a library's card catalog is a database. Employee or student records and inventory records are also databases. Even when these records are kept in a filing cabinet and maintained manually, they constitute a database.

Examples of Manual Database Records

Address Book Entry   *Card Catalog Entry*

Name		Call Number
Address		Author
City St Zip		Title
Telephone		Subject

■ A **computerized database** is the electronic equivalent of a manual database. It lets you organize and maintain the data using electronic tools.

What is a Database Management System?

■ An electronic database management system, such as Microsoft Access or Corel Paradox, gives you ease of data update but also provides automated ways to search, sort, ask questions of (query), and report on the data in the database. For example, suppose you wish to find all books about the U.S. Civil War in a library. To do this manually, you must read the card catalog entries and write down those with a subject of something like "U.S. History, Civil War." Such a search could be quite time-consuming. With a database management system, however, you can locate and print the records of books on the Civil War using a search function and a few simple keystrokes.

Types of Databases

■ Electronic databases are built upon tables that contain data. The database applications covered in this book are of two basic types.

- **Relational databases** (Microsoft **Access** and Corel **Paradox**) can include more than one table in a database. Each table contains a

Microsoft Office 98 for Macintosh

Office 98 for Macintosh does not offer a database application and, therefore, is not discussed in this lesson.

Uses of Databases

Businesses use their databases to answer such questions as:

Which products are performing profitably?

Which products are doing poorly?

Have we expanded our customer base within the last year?

Are we retaining customers or are they leaving us for other suppliers?

What is our cost per sale? (This question may involve analyzing database information using a spreadsheet.)

different kind of data. The idea underlying a relational database is to record each item of data only once. For example, a personal CD collection may contain many CDs by the same performer. To be efficient, a relational database for the collection stores data about the artist in one table and data about each album in another.

The tables are **related** by using an entry—called a **field**—in one table as a field in the other. In the CD collection database, for example, the table of artists can be related to the table of albums by the artist's identifier.

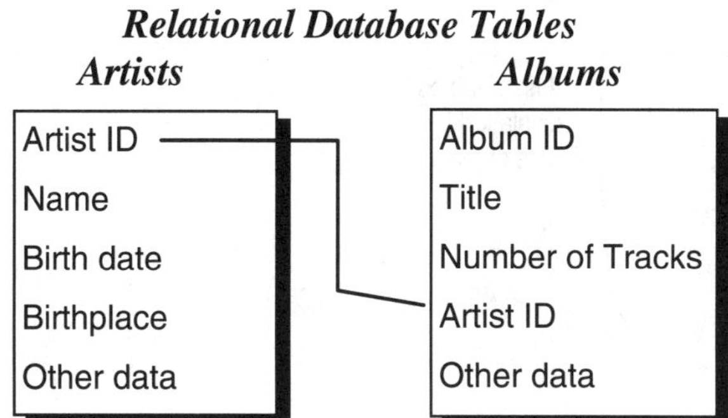

- **Flat file** databases (**AppleWorks** and **MS Works**) consist of only one table. Flat file databases can be used to maintain simple lists, but they are not as efficient as relational databases. For example, to maintain data on a CD collection, you have to enter the artist's name for each album rather than simply refer to a table of artists. And, if you want to maintain additional information on the artist (such as date of birth and other personal data), you may have to create a new database that is not directly related to the album information.

How Do Database Management Systems Work?

- **AppleWorks** and **MS Works** treat a database file just like other documents. You can display the data as a list or in a formatted view called a form. AppleWorks and MS Works include features that let you define and save the database, enter and manipulate data, and sort and report on the data.

- An **Access** database is a single file that contains **database objects**. (See page 281 for a description of database objects.) When you start Access, the **database window** appears; it contains an Objects bar with a button for each type of database object. When you click a button on the Objects bar, a list of the corresponding objects appears. In the illustration on the following page, the Tables button has been clicked.

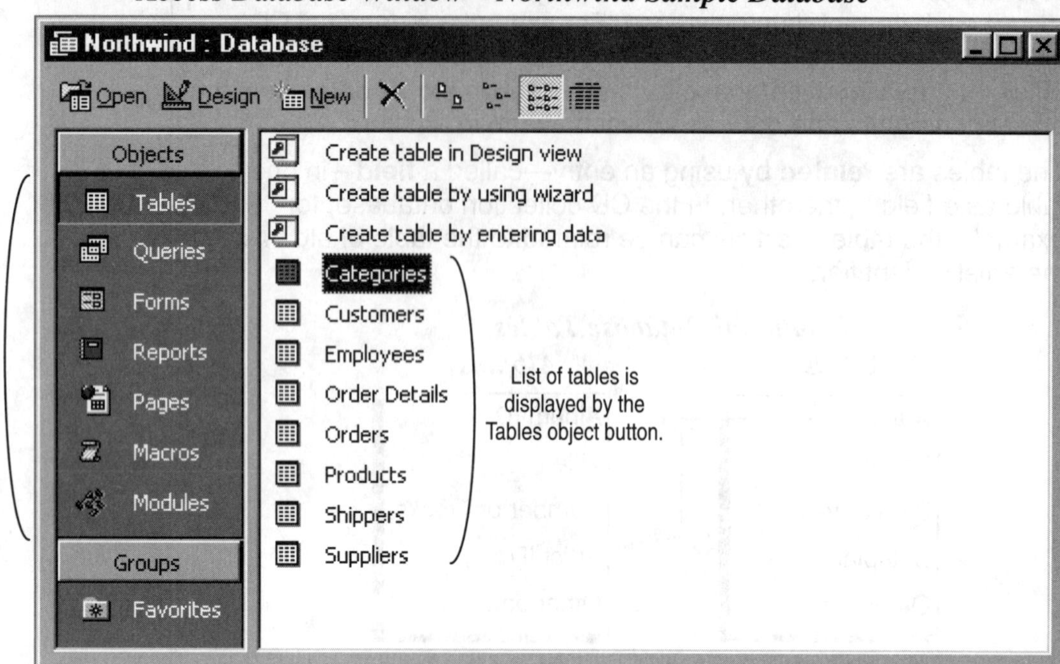

Access Database Window – Northwind Sample Database

Types of Access database objects are listed on the Objects bar.

List of tables is displayed by the Tables object button.

- A **Paradox** database consists of a variety of database objects—each in its own file—stored in the same Windows folder. (To understand fully how Paradox names a database and relates that name to the folder, see Appendix E.)

- When you start Paradox, the Project Viewer appears. You change the **Working Directory** to the correct folder, and Project Viewer displays a list of the files in the folder. The Project Viewer contains a Types pane with a button for each type of object in the database folder. You click on an option in the Types pane to display a list of the corresponding objects. In the following illustration, the Tables option has been selected.

Corel Paradox Project Viewer

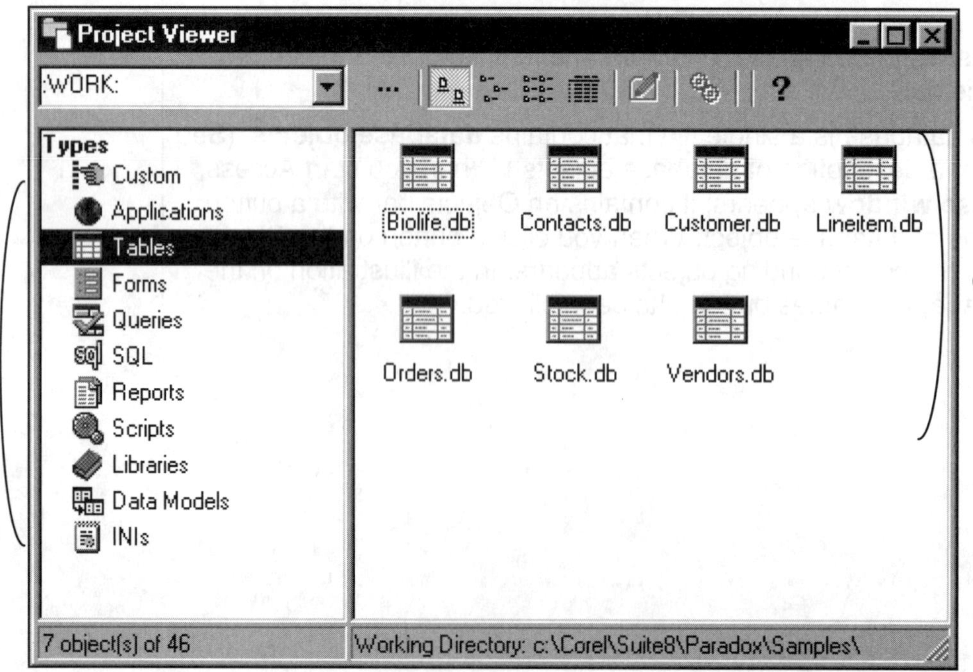

Types of Paradox database objects are listed in the Types pane.

List of tables is displayed by the Tables option.

💻 Try It!

1. Start your database program.

2. Open ⊙ **01Classic** from the data files.

3. In **AppleWorks**, look at the data in List layout, and go to step 5.
   In **MS Works**, look at the data in List view, and go to step 5.
   In **Access**, look at the database window.
   In **Paradox**, look at the Project viewer.

   - How many tables are in the database? _______________________
   - Which table might contain the release date of a disc?

   ____

   - Which table would contain the year the composer was born?

   ____

4. Open the **Musical Pieces** table.

5. Sort the data by composer's last name.

6. Answer the following questions:

   - How many musical pieces are by Johannes Brahms? __________
   - How many musical pieces are by Antonio Vivaldi? ____________
   - Who is the composer of *Concierto de Aranjuez*?

   ____

   - What is the title of the disc that contains Don Juan, op.20 by Richard Strauss?

   ____

7. In Access and Paradox, close the table without saving any changes.

8. In AppleWorks and MS Works, sort the data by **ID**.

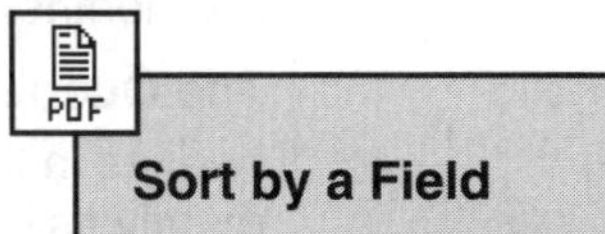

What are Database Objects?

- In the database systems covered in this lesson, you organize the data into electronic storage containers called **tables**. A table is the basic object in a database. In AppleWorks and MS Works each database contains one table.

- In Access and Paradox, each database may contain several tables, with each table storing data about one area of the subject covered by the database. For example, consider a company that sells computer hardware and software. The company database may contain one table that identifies customers, another that describes its hardware products, a third that tracks software, a fourth that maintains data about the sales force, and a fifth that tracks sales. These tables form the database.

- To help you use your database efficiently, database management systems provide **database objects**—the tools you need to maintain, search, analyze, and report on the data in your database.

Object	Description
Table	Data is displayed in rows and columns. Each column is a **field**; each row is a **record** (see the next section for a definition of these terms). AppleWorks, MS Works, Access, and Paradox all contain tables.
	In Access and Paradox, each major table includes a **primary key** field that uniquely identifies each record. The key field aids the database system in searching for records and maintaining data integrity.
	The **Tables** button ▦ Tables (▦ Tables)displays a list of all tables in the current database. It lets you open an existing table, modify its design, or create a new table.
Query	A structured way to tell Access or Paradox to retrieve data that meets certain criteria from one or more database tables. A query lets you see relationships among the data that are not apparent in the table or form views. For example, a query may request that Access or Paradox retrieve data on all printers sold within the last six months.
	The **Queries** button ▦ Queries (▦ Queries) displays a list of all queries in the current database. It lets you open an existing query, modify its design, or create a new query.
	AppleWorks and MS Works do not offer queries. AppleWorks offers a similar function called a **find** or **search**. MS Works offers a **filter** to let you specify criteria for records to be displayed.
Form	A formatted data entry window that lets you enter, display, and edit data. A form generally displays one record at a time. AppleWorks and MS Works offer Forms.
	The **Forms** button ▦ Forms (▦ Forms) displays a list of all forms in the current database. It lets you open an existing form, modify its design, or create a new form. In AppleWorks, you display the form through the Layout menu; in MS Works, you display the form through the View menu.
Report	A formatted way to display information retrieved from the database. A report formats and analyzes data you specify. Examples of reports include sales summaries, phone lists, and mailing labels.
	The **Reports** button ▦ Reports (▦ Reports) displays a list of all reports in the current database. It lets you preview the report, modify its design, or create a new report. AppleWorks and MS Works also offer ways to create reports.

- Space and time limits do not permit coverage of other objects: Access data access pages, macros, and modules, or Paradox scripts, libraries, and data models. You may see them referred to as you use the applications.

How is a Table Structured?

- A table is a grid of rows and columns. Each row contains one **record**. A record is a set of details about a specific item. For example, one record in a company's hardware inventory table could contain details on one of its NEC printers, including its product identifier, manufacturer, model number, cost, and purchase date. When database users mention the "NEC printer record," they are referring to the details in the table row that describes the printer. Similarly, a personnel record will include the employee's name, address, and so on.

Search or Filter

A search or filter is a function that extracts records from one table while a query may use more than one table.

Because AppleWorks and MS Works have only one table in each database, they use searches or filters rather than queries to extract information from a table.

- Each column in the table is a **field**, headed by a **field name**. Each row in the column contains specific data called the **field contents**. For example, the field MANUFACTURER in one of the hardware records would contain the entry NEC to identify the manufacturer of a piece of equipment. When data processing people ask, "What's in the manufacturer field?" they are asking about the field contents of the field name MANUFACTURER.

- A sample record is shown below:

Manufacturer	Type	Model	Serial No.	Pdate	Pprice	Condition
Portal MM	Computer	PMM 650 X	PMM943879	2/29/00	2000.00	Excellent

Field names — Field contents

Field Data Types

- In a database, you must define the type of data that each field (column) can contain; for example, some fields can contain text; others can contain numbers or dates. Data types are described as you use them in this lesson.

How are Tables Related in Access and Paradox?

- Database tables that share common fields are **related**. For example, in a book collection database, the Books table may use the record identifier from the Authors table to connect authors and their works. A common field that connects the tables allows you to create a **query** that lists authors and titles in the query.

Try It!

Review Data using a Form

1. Look at the **01Classic** database.
   In **AppleWorks**, look at the data in Browse layout to view the form, and go to step 5.
   In **MS Works**, look at the data in Form view, and go to step 5.
   In **Access**, click the Forms button on the Objects bar.
   In **Paradox**, click the Forms button in the Types pane.

2. Open the **Composers** form (Access and Paradox only).

   The form can be used to add a new composer to the database.

3. Scroll through some of the records, then close the Composers form.

4. Open the **Musical Pieces** form.

5. Go to the last record.

   - What is the name of the piece? _______________________
   - What is the name of the soloist? _______________________

6. Go to the 13th record.

   - What is the name of the orchestra? _______________________
   - What is the composer's name? _______________________

7. Click in the Musical Piece field.

8. Locate the first piece that includes Sonata in the title.

   - What is the soloist's name? _______________________

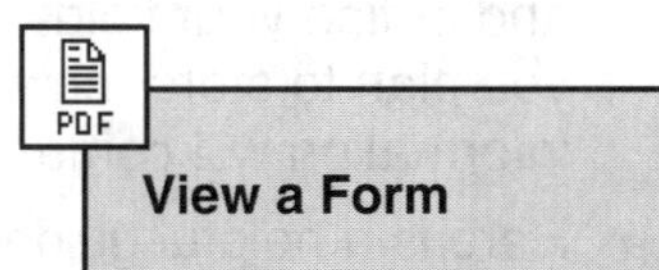

Run a Search (AppleWorks)
Apply a Filter (MS Works)
Investigate a Query (Access and Paradox)

1. In AppleWorks, display the data in List layout.
   In MS Works, display the data in List view.
   In Access and Paradox, display the queries.

2. In AppleWorks, run the search Brahms Recordings.
   In MS Works, apply the filter, Brahms Records.
   In Access and Paradox, open (run) the query Brahms Recordings.

3. Click in the Musical Piece field (column) of any record.

4. Sort the column in ascending order.

   ♦ How many recordings of Symphony No. 2 are listed in the query?
   ____

   ♦ How many recordings of the Violin Concerto in D major are listed
     in the query? _______________

5. Re-display all records in the table.

6. Close all objects and close the database.

Planning a New Database

■ Before creating tables for a new database, take time to plan your tables
  and define your fields. You should know in detail what kind of information
  you plan to store, how you want to format it, and from what source the
  information will come.

■ Here is a helpful guide:

  • Gather all your sources of information: invoice forms, employee
    records, pay stubs, order forms, product information, and so on.

  • Determine what types of information you will need to locate or report:
    names, IDs, prices, shipment dates, and so on.

  • Decide how much flexibility you need in locating and reporting the
    data. This in turn will determine how specific you must be in defining
    the fields.

  • Write down everything you want to accomplish with your database.

  • Break down information into its smallest practical units. For example,
    rather than have a field called "Name," which contains a customer's
    first, middle, and last name, it may be more useful to have three
    fields: "First Name," "Middle Initial," and "Last Name."

  • A database is only as good as the accuracy of the data it contains.
    Try to do everything possible to ensure that all data is entered
    correctly.

> **In this exercise, you will continue to explore an existing database.**

EXERCISE DIRECTIONS

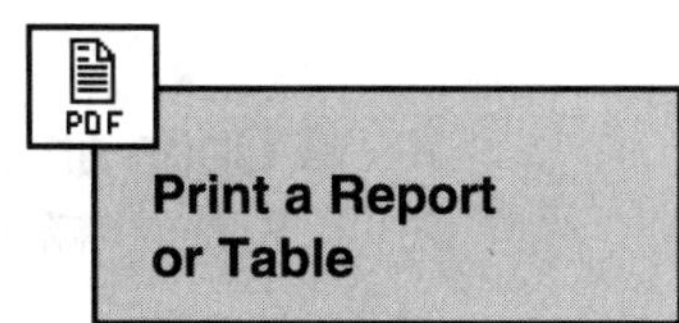

View and Print a Report

1. Start the database application if it is not already running.

2. Open 💿 **01Classic** from the data files.

3. Open the **Brahms Recordings** report.

4. View all pages of the report.

5. Print one copy of the report.

Print a Table

1. In AppleWorks, display the data in List layout.
   In MS Works, display the data in List view.
   In Access and Paradox, open the **Musical Pieces** table.

2. Print one copy of the table in Landscape orientation.

3. Close the database and exit the database application.

Exercise 2

Use and Modify a Database
■ Open an Existing Database ■ About Fields, Data Types, and Formats
■ Add a Field to a Table ■ Include Aids to Data Entry

NOTES

Open an Existing Database

■ Because database design is a profession, you may have few occasions to create a database except for your personal use. In this exercise, you will start with an existing database that already has some fields defined. You will add fields to the database to learn about elements of a database table. In the Try It! activities in this lesson, you will use a database that stores information about the library of the Rouke family.

⌨ Try It!

1. Start the database application.
2. Open ⊚ **02Library** from the data files. If your application permits, save the file as **S02Library**.
3. In AppleWorks and MS Works, display the data in List view. In Access and Paradox, open the **tblBooks** table.
4. Look at the BookID field.

Automatically Numbered Field

- The BookID field contains a number that uniquely identifies each record in the table. BookID is defined so that its value increases automatically for each new record entered. AppleWorks calls this data type **Serial Number**. MS Works refers to such a field as **Serialized**. Access calls it **AutoNumber**. Paradox calls it **Autoincrement**. In Access and Paradox, it is the **primary key field**.

- When you add a record, press the Tab key to bypass the field and let the application fill in the number. Do not type data in a field that is numbered automatically; let the software complete it. If some numbers seem to be missing, that's all right; the software always places a unique number in the field.

⌨ Try It!

- Add the following two records to the table. For ease of reading, the records are shown in two parts.

BookID	Author First	Author Last	Title
(Tab)	Sue	Grafton	"B" is for Burglar
(Tab)	John	LeCarre	Tinker, Tailor, Soldier, Spy

Publisher	Copyright	Cover	Genre	Purchase Price
Henry Holt	1985	Hard	Mystery	21.95

IMPORTANT NOTE TO ACCESS USERS
Refer to Appendix D to learn how to prepare the Access data files for use. Access does not let you perform a Save As on a database, so you must copy the data files from the CD to a hard drive and remove the read-only attribute before starting this exercise.

Make a Mistake?
If you make a mistake when entering data, you can correct it by clicking in the field and editing the data.

If you put records in a different order, don't worry. The order of records is not important.

If gaps appear in the automatically numbered fields, don't worry. The gaps do not harm the database.

Knopf	1974	Hard	Espionage	24.00

About Fields, Data Types, and Formats

- A database **field** is defined so that it stores only a certain kind of data. Some fields store text; others store numbers only; others store dates; others store Yes or No, or True or False. The kind of data a field can store is defined by its **data type**—text, number, date, and so on.

- You specify a data type for a field for at least two reasons:

  - To prevent data corruption. If you allow text to be entered in a field like Purchase Price, you cannot prevent a user from accidentally entering a letter rather than a number in the field. Yet Purchase Price should always be a number.

  - To be able to use numbers in calculations on reports and date ranges in database searches. Fields defined as text, even if they store only numbers or dates, cannot be used in calculations or to define date ranges.

- Each database application has a variety of data types for fields. Only a few data types are used in this lesson, and they are described as they are used.

- Besides the data type, some programs let you define with a **format** that specifies how the data is displayed. A number field may have a format that displays two decimals, for example. A date may be formatted to display as 10-Mar-02 or as 3/10/02.

Add a Field to a Table

- Even when you plan carefully and define your tables beforehand, you may find a need to add a field to a record. In the Rouke Library database, for example, the **tblBooks** table contains information about the original cost of the book, but the Roukes may also wish to know the current value of a book. And, since the current value depends on the how well the book has been preserved, they may wish to add a field that records each book's condition.

Try It!

1. Add a field after Purchase Price; name it *Current Value.*
2. Define its data type as number and display two decimal places.
3. Add a field after Current Value; name it *Condition.*
4. Define it as a text field.
5. After defining the fields, complete the three records as follows:

Title	Current Value	Condition
"A" is for Alibi	4.00	Excellent
"B" is for Burglar	4.00	Excellent
Tinker, Tailor, Soldier, Spy	4.00	Excellent

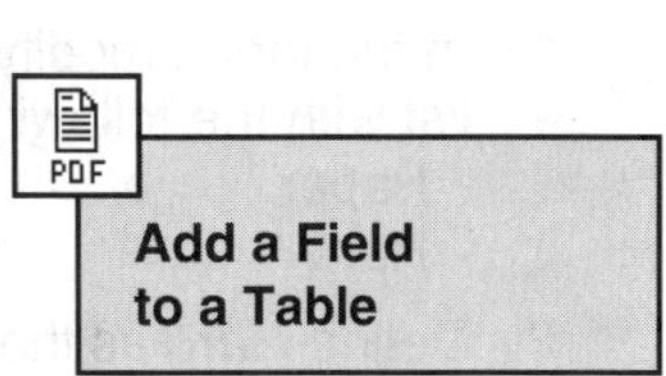

Add a Field to a Table

Include Aids to Data Entry

- One of the biggest problems facing any database creator is how to improve the accuracy of data. A misspelled entry, a missing ZIP Code in an address, or a value that is too high or too low for a field can cause problems.

- While not much can be done about a misspelled name, you can ensure that certain text entries are spelled the same every time. For example, in the Rouke's library database, only two types of book covers exist—Hard and Paper. The database designer can make the entry of the data easy in two ways:

  - Create a **default value** that is entered unless the user specifically changes it. The default value should be the one that is likely to be entered most often. In the Rouke's library, most of the books have hard covers. The default value for the field can be *Hard*.

  - Create a **lookup list** and choose the correct value rather than type it during data entry. For example, in the Rouke's library, the Condition field will always have one of four values—*Excellent, Good, Fair, Poor*. You can put these values in a list and then select the right one from the list. A value list speeds data entry, provides consistency in spelling, and, if coupled with a default value, ensures that the field always has data.

- To ensure that a field, such as a ZIP Code in an address, is always completed, you can specify the field as **Required**. During data entry, you cannot leave a record that has a required field until the field is completed.

- To be sure that a field, such as a Purchase Price, is reasonable, you can specify a range of values, a maximum value, or a minimum value as criteria that the data must meet. An easy error to make when entering dollar values with decimals, for example, is to put the decimal in the wrong place or to leave it out altogether. In the Purchase Price field for books, then, you might specify that no value can be greater than 99.99.

- Each application offers various ways to help improve the accuracy of data entry. In the next Try It! activity, you will define some of them.

Try It!

1. In the table, modify the definition of the Cover field to create a lookup list with the following values:
   Paper
   Hard

2. Define *Hard* as the default value for Cover.

   Note that the default value comes last in the list. Because the default value appears automatically, you should choose from the list only when the book does not have a hard cover.

3. For the Genre field (which indicates the kind of book), define a lookup list that reads:
   Computer
   Espionage
   Mystery
   Humor

4. Define *Humor* as the default value for Genre.

5. Define a maximum value of 99.99 for the Purchase Price field. Make Purchase Price a required field.

**Define Data
Entry Aids**

6. For the Condition field, define a lookup list that reads:
   Good
   Fair
   Poor
   Excellent

7. Define *Excellent* as the default value.

8. Add the following 5 records to the table using the data entry aids.

   The BookID field is not shown. Let your application assign the value automatically.

   Note that if you neglect to enter a Required field or specify a value outside the range for a field, the application will display a message to tell you of the error.

Author First	Author Last	Title	Publisher
Garrison	Keillor	Lake Wobegone Days	Viking
Garrison	Keillor	Leaving Home	Viking
John	LeCarre	The Secret Pilgrim	Knopf
Groucho	Marx	The Groucho Letters	Simon & Schuster
Ron	White	How Computers Work	Ziff-Davis

Copyright	Cover	Genre	Purchase Price	Current Value	Condition
1985	Hard	Humor	17.95	10.00	Excellent
1987	Hard	Humor	18.95	10.00	Excellent
1991	Hard	Espionage	20.00	8.00	Excellent
1967	Paper	Humor	6.95	0.50	Fair
1997	Paper	Computer	29.99	4.00	Good

9. Print the table.

10. Close the database and exit the database application unless you are continuing with the Exercise Directions.

Invalid Data

Invalid data is data that does not meet the restrictions set for the field. Database designers set the **validation rules** so that data that is not acceptable is rejected when entered.

EXERCISE DIRECTIONS

Open the Database Table
and Add New Data

1. Start your database application if it is not already running.

2. Open 📀**02Glasser** from the data files.

3. In Access and Paradox, open the **tblInventory** table.

4. Add the new records shown in Illustration A.

5. In AppleWorks and MS Works, save the database as **S02Glasser**.

Illustration A. Two New Records

Manufacturer	Type	Model	Serial Number	Purchase Date	Purchase Price
SLQ	Television	XS Stereo	QLS635221758	6/8/97	425.00
Portal MM	Computer	GP6 400	GP61001743	5/4/98	2000.00

Add Two New Fields and Modify Others

1. Modify the Purchase Date and Purchase Price fields as outlined in Illustration B.

2. Add the Current Value and Condition fields as outlined in Illustration B.

Illustration B. Modify the Table

Field	Data Type	Other Properties
Purchase Date	(as defined)	Cannot be earlier than 3/1/92 Required field
Purchase Price	(as defined)	Required field
Current Value	Number	Fixed display with 2 decimals. In AppleWorks, set the display values in Browse mode. Required
Condition	Text	Lookup list with: Good Fair Poor Excellent Default value = *Excellent*

Add Records 4-8

1. Update the existing records with the data shown in Illustration C. The Item column lists the manufacturer and the model.

2. Add the records shown in Illustration D using the data entry aids you specified.

3. Print the table in Landscape orientation.

4. Save and close the database and exit the database application.

Illustration C. Update Existing Records

Item	Current Value	Condition
SLQ, XL100	25.00	Poor
SLQ, XS Stereo	35.00	Good
Portal MM, GP6 400	750.00	Excellent

Illustration D. Records 4-8

Manufacturer	Type	Model	Serial Number	Purchase Date	Purchase Price	Current Value	Condition
Portal MM	Monitor	VX 1100	976389VX	5/4/99	600.00	400.00	Excellent
Mango	Computer	Power G3	XA909323FEWD	2/1/00	1800.00	1400.00	Excellent
Acton Bell	Printer	Laser Jet 4000	USMB263560	5/5/99	1499.00	900.00	Excellent
Pachelbel	Printer	BJC 5000	END 66834	12/21/99	350.00	150.00	Excellent
Portal MM	Monitor	Vivitron 15	943281V5	12/15/95	325.00	75.00	Fair

Exercise 3

Create and Use a Form
■ Create a Form ■ Add Records in Form View ■ Print Records in Form View

NOTES

Create a Form

- Rather than enter data in a table as in the previous exercise, you can enter data through a formatted layout called a **form**. With a form, you work with one record at a time. If you use a form to enter data, the data is also added it to the table on which the form is based.

- AppleWorks and MS Works create forms when a database is created. You can switch to the form at any time to review or enter data. In Access and Paradox, you must create the form after the table is defined. If you are using AppleWorks or MS Works, go to "Add Records in Form View," below. The next Try It! tells Access and Paradox users how to create a form.

⌨Try It!

Create the Form

1. Open ⊙**03Library** from the data files.

2. Create a form named **frmBooks** based on the **tblBooks** table.

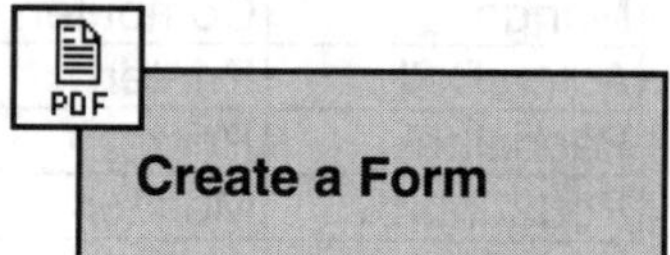

Add Records in Form View

- When you use a form to enter or edit data, the changes are automatically reflected in the table that was used as the record source for the form.

⌨Try It!

1. Switch to Browse mode in AppleWorks and Form view in the other database applications.

2. Add the new records shown on the following page. The records are shown as they appear in the Access form. If the insertion point appears in a field that is automatically numbered, press the `Tab` key to bypass and let the software complete the field.

3. In all forms, use the `Tab` key to move from field to field. All fields work the same way as in the table. For example, to display the lookup list in Paradox, press `Ctrl`+`Space`.

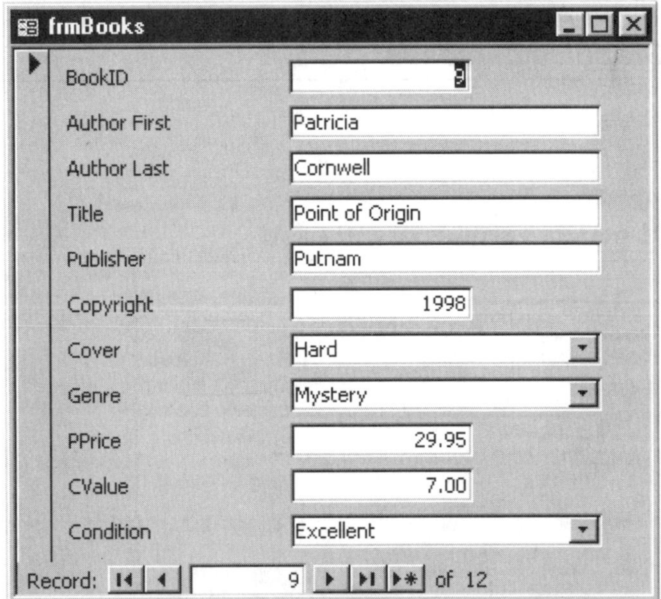
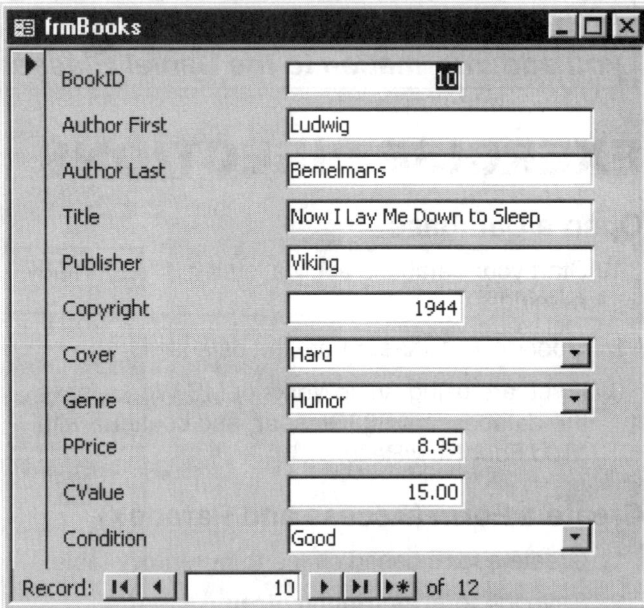
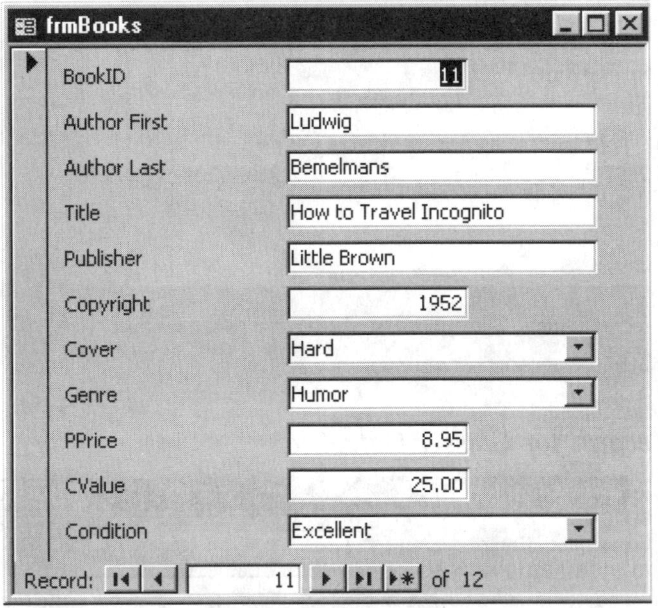
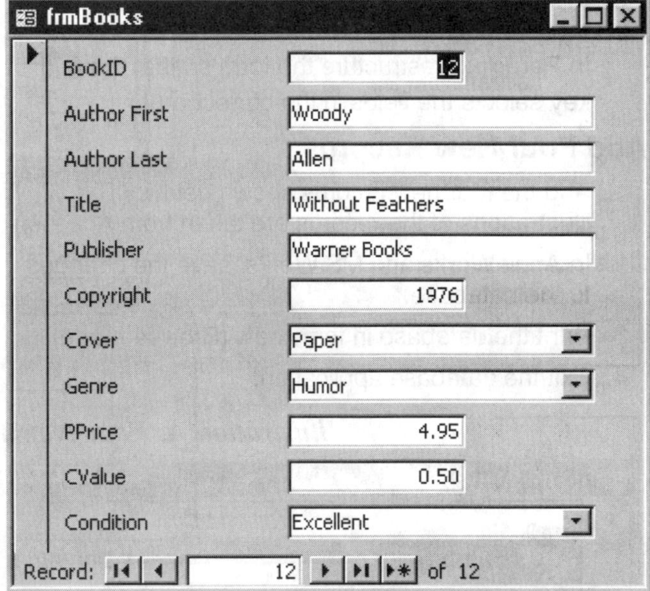

Print Records in Form View

- You can print the records in form view. Each application handles printing a little differently. See the procedures for how to print the form view.

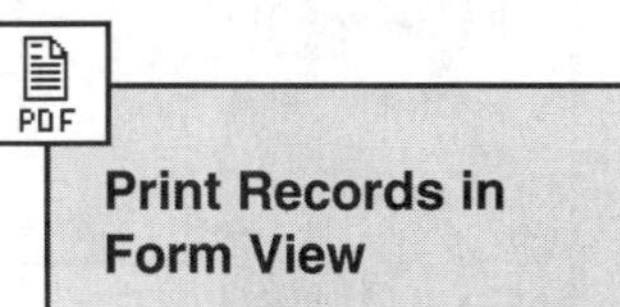

Try It!

1. Print the records in form view.

2. Close the database and exit the database application unless you are continuing with the Exercise Directions.

In this exercise, you will create a form using the AutoForm function. The form will let you add information to the Daniel Glasser Graphics database.

EXERCISE DIRECTIONS

Open a Database

1. Start your database application if it is not already running.

2. Open ⊙ **03Glasser** from the data files.

3. If you are using AppleWorks or MS Works, save the database as **S03Glasser**, and continue with "Add Four New Records."

Create a Form (Access and Paradox)

1. Create a form based on the **tblInventory** table.

2. Save the form as **frmInventory**.

3. In **Access**, change the title bar to read *frmInventory*.
   In **Paradox**, restructure the form so that the Tab key selects the fields in the correct order.

Add Four New Records

1. Add the four new records shown below. (The illustrations of the records are taken from Access.)

2. In AppleWorks and MS Works, save the changes to the database.

3. Print the database in form view (Browse mode).

4. Exit the database application.

Illustration A. Four New Records for Glasser Database

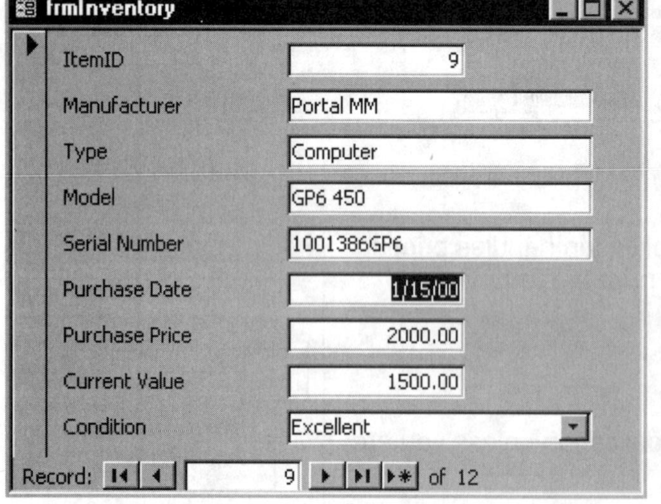

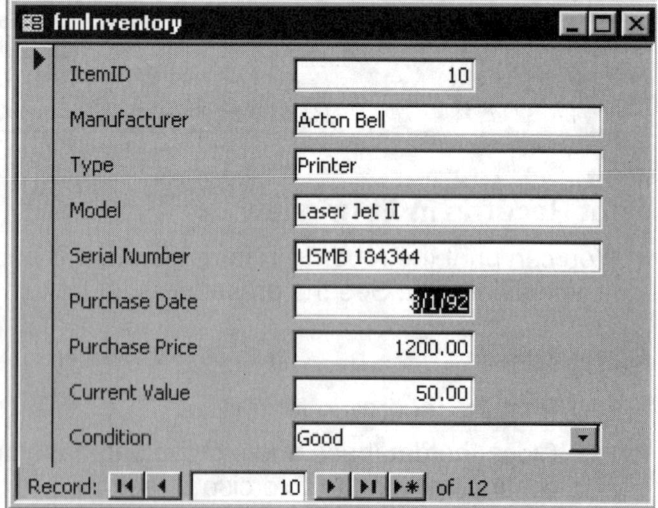

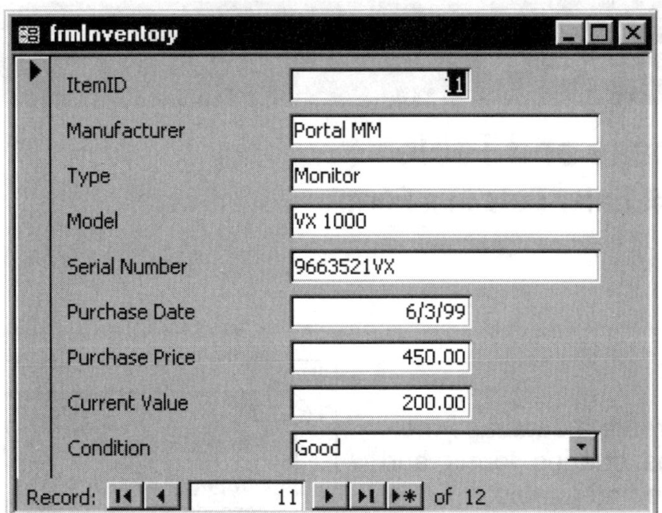

frmInventory
ItemID   11
Manufacturer   Portal MM
Type   Monitor
Model   VX 1000
Serial Number   9663521VX
Purchase Date   6/3/99
Purchase Price   450.00
Current Value   200.00
Condition   Good
Record: 11   of 12

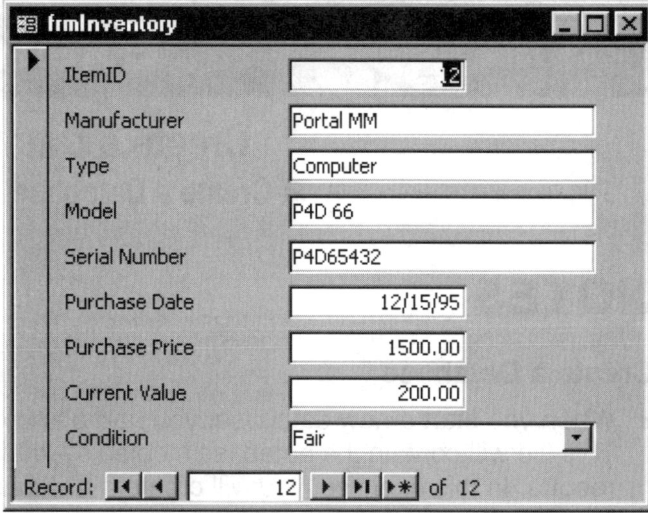

frmInventory
ItemID   12
Manufacturer   Portal MM
Type   Computer
Model   P4D 66
Serial Number   P4D65432
Purchase Date   12/15/95
Purchase Price   1500.00
Current Value   200.00
Condition   Fair
Record: 12   of 12

Exercise 4

Create a Database and Table
■ Create a Database ■ Enter Data in a Form

NOTES

Create a Database

■ When you start a new database, you name and create a database **file**. This file will contain the database's objects—tables, queries, forms, and reports. In this exercise, you will create a database and a table.

■ In the Try It! sections of this exercise, you will begin creating a database that stores data about items used by a caterer that specializes in picnics.

🖳 Try It!

1. Start your database application.

2. **AppleWorks** and **MS Works:** Create the table when you start the application; save the database as **GoodStuff**.
   Access and **Paradox:** Create a database named **GoodStuff**, then create a new table called **tblProducts**.

3. Define the fields in the table as outlined below. You will have to adjust the definitions to the features of your database application. For example, in MS Works, you can define default values, but no lookup list or other limitations.

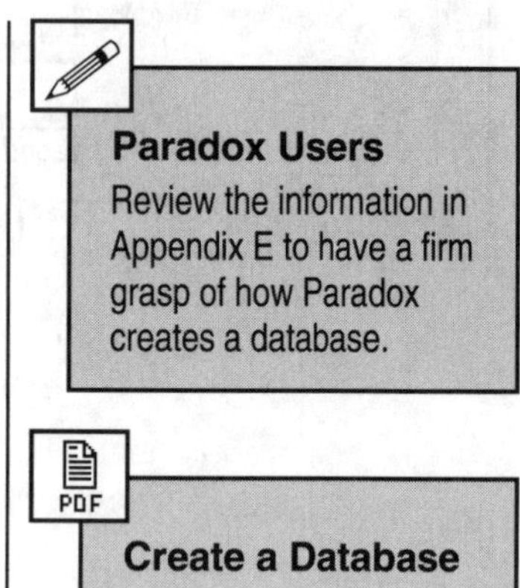

Field	Data Type	Other
Product ID	Serial Serialized AutoNumber Autoincrement	Start at 1 and increase by 1 **Access** and **Paradox**: Primary Key
Product Name	Text	Field Size = 50
Supplier	Text	Field Size = 15 Lookup List: AromaRama Meat Mart Papier, Inc. Vege-Relish
Units In Stock	Number (Integer)	Format = Integer (no decimals)
Units On Order	Number (Integer)	Format = Integer (no decimals) Default Value = 0 **Access:** Validation Rule = 0 Or 50 Or 100 Or 200 **AppleWorks & Paradox:** Minimum = 0 Maximum = 200
Unit Price	Number	Format = Fixed, 2 decimals

4. After defining the fields in AppleWorks and MS Works, save the database.

5. Add the six records shown below using the table (list view). Let the application assign the Product ID.

6. In AppleWorks and MS Works, save the database.
   In Access and Paradox, close the table.

Product Name	Supplier	Units In Stock	Units On Order	Unit Price
Bread	AromaRama	200	0	0.89
Pickles	Vege-Relish	250	0	0.95
Onions	Vege-Relish	150	0	0.69
Hot Sauce	Vege-Relish	98	200	2.98
Hamburger	Meat Mart	45	50	4.25
Ketchup	Vege-Relish	300	0	0.79

Enter Data in a Form

1. In **AppleWorks**, switch to Browse mode; in **MS Works**, switch to the form.
   In **Access** and **Paradox**, create a form based on **tblProducts**; name it **frmProducts**.

2. Use the form to enter the following six records.

3. Print the database in form view.

4. In AppleWorks and MS Works, save and close the database.
   In Access and Paradox, close the table, and close the database.

Product	Supplier	Units In Stock	Units On Order	Unit Price
Mustard	Vege-Relish	243	0	0.39
Hot Dogs	Meat Mart	75	50	2.28
Paper Plates	Papier, Inc.	90	200	0.20
Napkins	Papier, Inc.	300	0	0.59
Forks	Papier, Inc.	325	0	0.20
Spoons	Papier, Inc.	300	0	0.20

5. Exit the database application unless you are continuing with the Exercise Directions.

In this exercise, you will use the aids provided by your database application to create a personal address book.

EXERCISE DIRECTIONS

Create the Database

AppleWorks:

1. Use the Address List Assistant to create a database.

   AppleWorks displays the database in Layout Browse view ready for you to edit existing data and to add new records.

2. Save the database as **My Address Book**.

3. Edit one of the existing records to reflect your personal information.

4. Edit the other existing record to reflect the information of a friend.

5. Add at least one new record.

   If the database contains fields you do not need or do not wish to use, delete them through the Layout, Define Fields option.

6. Save the file, close the database, and exit AppleWorks.

MS Works:

1. Use the TaskWizards Address Book task to create a database.

2. Choose Personal Address book.

3. Do not add any additional or personal fields.

4. Choose to include the Alphabetized report.

5. Complete the wizard steps.

   MS Works displays the database in Form view ready for data entry.

6. Save the file as **My Address Book**.

7. Add your information as the first record.

8. Add the information of a friend as the second record.

9. Add the information of another friend as the third record.

   If the database contains fields you do not need or do not wish to use, delete them using Record, Delete Field.

10. Save the file, close the database, and exit MS Works.

Access:

1. Create a database from scratch called **My Address Book**.

2. Create a table using the wizard; select Personal, and Addresses for the table.

3. Select all sample fields.

4. Name the table **tblAddresses**.

5. Select the option to enter data directly into the table.

6. Add your information as the first record.

7. Add the information of a friend as the second record.

8. Add the information of another friend as the third record.

   If the table contains fields you do not need or do not wish to use, delete them in Design view.

9. When the table contains only the fields you want, use AutoForm to create a form for the table; name it **frmAddresses**.

10. Save and close all open objects and exit Access.

Paradox:

1. Use the Database Expert, Personal tab, Address Book option to create a database named **My Address Book**.

   Paradox displays a form with three tabs: Tables, Forms, Reports

2. Click the Forms tab.

3. Click ▢ Address (the square button).

   Paradox displays the Form.

4. Add your information as the first record.

5. Add the information of a friend as the second record.

6. Add the information of another friend as the third record.

   The My Address Book form is a navigational tool that you do not have to use. You can close the form and use the Project Viewer to open the objects in the database.

7. Save and close all open objects and exit Paradox.

NEXT EXERCISE

Filter and Query a Database
■ Filter/Search a Database ■ Filter Criteria ■ Create a Query (Access or Paradox)

NOTES

Filter a Database

■ A **filter** lets you select records in a table or form based on criteria you specify. You can use filters to reduce the number of records to be reviewed. For example, if you want to print out a list of all the computers in an inventory database, you can create a filter that displays only the computers.

🖥 Try It!

1. Start the database application.
2. Open ⊙ **05Glasser**. In AppleWorks and MS Works, save the file as **S05Glasser**.
3. Create a filter that displays all the computers in the database.
4. View the results as a table, and print the table.
5. Redisplay all records.
6. Create a filter that displays all items with a PPrice (Purchase Price) of $1200 or more and with a CValue (Current Value) of $700 or less. For comparison operators, see the next section.
7. View the results as a table, and print the table.
8. Redisplay all records.
9. Create a filter that displays all monitors that are in good condition.
10. View the results in form view and print the form.
11. Redisplay all records.
12. Close the table.
13. If you are using **AppleWorks** or **MS Works**, read about filter criteria, then continue with the Exercise Directions.

    If you are using **Access** or **Paradox**, continue with the next section.

Filter Criteria

■ **Number fields.** In all the applications except MS Works, you can use the comparison **operators** described in the table that follows to aid in your filter or query. For MS Works, all the operators are presented in English as part of the Filter dialog box.

Operator	English Meaning	Sample
=	is equal to	=100
<>	is not equal to	<>100
>	is greater than	>100
<	is less than	<100
>=	is greater than or equal to	>=100
<=	is less than or equal to	<=100

AppleWorks Find/Search

AppleWorks handles the filter as **Layout**, **Find**, or **Search**. The difference between the three is that a Search can be named and reused. A Find is not saved for reuse.

The **Find** that works as a filter is not the same as the **Find/Change** command on the Edit menu.

Recordset

Access uses the term recordset to refer to a group of records created by a query or a filter.

If the data in the recordset can be edited to change the data in the underlying table(s), the result is also called a **dynaset**. If the data cannot be edited, the results are called a **snapshot**.

Exercise 5 Procedures

- **Text fields.** The table that follows gives some sample entries for entering text criteria in filters and queries.

Desired Match	AppleWorks	Access	Paradox
Computer exactly	=Computer	Computer	=Computer
Computer anywhere in field	Computer	*Computer* (*Access changes the entry to* Like "Computer")	(not possible in filter; must use query)
begins with *Comp*	Comp (*also will find* Comp *anywhere in field*)	Comp* (*Access changes the entry to* Like "Comp*")	Comp..
begins with *Comp* or *Mon*	Comp with **Find From, All** selected then Mon with **Find From, Visible** selected	Comp* Or Mon* (*Access changes the entry to* Like "Comp*" Or Like "Mon*")	Comp.. Or Mon..
is greater than or equal to *1200* but is less than or equal to *2500*	>=1200 with **Find From, All** selected then <=2500 with **Find From, Visible** selected	>=1200 And <=2500	>=1200 And <=2500

Create a Query (Access or Paradox)

- A **query** lets you retrieve data from one or more tables and display it in a new table. In Access, queries are built on a grid similar to the one used for filtering records. In Paradox, queries are built using rows of field names from the tables from which you wish to extract data.

- A query differs from a filter in two ways. A filter shows all fields in the table; in a query you can choose to omit fields from the table. A filter works on only one table; a query can use data from more than one table. In the Try It! practices in this exercise, you will create a query that extracts data from two tables.

⌨ Try It!

1. Open ⊙ **05My Address Book** from the data files.

2. Create a new query that uses data from **tblNameAndAddress** and **tblBirthdays**.

3. In all the queries in this Try It! activity, display the following fields. (In Access, display them in the order listed.)

   - Last Name (tblNameAndAddress)
   - First Name (tblNameAndAddress)
   - Birthdate (tblBirthdays)
   - Gift (tblBirthdays)
   - Notes (tblBirthdays)
   - Address (tblNameAndAddress)
   - City (tblNameAndAddress)
   - State (tblNameAndAddress)
   - ZIP Code (tblNameAndAddress)

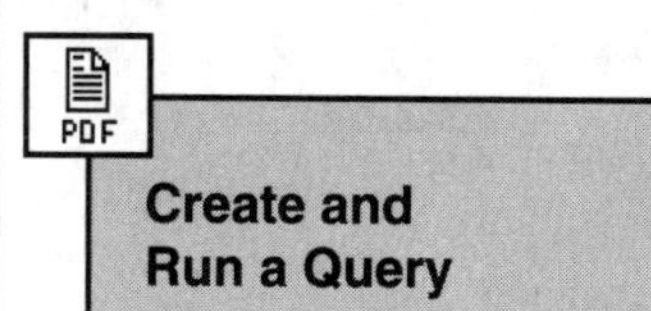
Create and Run a Query

4. In all queries, sort the resulting table by Last Name, then by First
   Name.

5. In the first query, extract the names, addresses, and birthdays of all
   those who receive gifts.

6. Name the query **qryGifts**, run the query, and print the resulting table
   in landscape orientation.

7. Copy **qryGifts**, and rename it **qryScottCity**.

8. Edit the criteria so that you display all those who live in Scott
   City, KS; run the query, and print the resulting table in Landscape
   orientation. (Be sure to remove previous criteria as part of the
   editing.)

9. Copy **qryGifts** again, and rename it **qryBirthdaysByMonth**.

10. Edit the criteria to find those with April birthdays, run the query, and
    print the resulting table in landscape orientation.

11. Change the criteria in **qryBirthdaysByMonth** to display those with
    December birthdays, and print the resulting table.

12. Find those born in March, and print the resulting table in Landscape
    orientation.

13. Close the query result and exit the database application unless you
    are continuing with the Exercise Directions.

> *In this exercise, you will filter the Rouke's library to find books in certain categories and price ranges. If you are using Access or Paradox, you will create some queries to learn about after-school activities for some students.*
>
> *Note: If you are using AppleWorks, remember that Browse mode displays a form. You can use Find or create a Search for the Filter.*

EXERCISE DIRECTIONS

Filter Records

1. Open ⊙ **05Library** from the data files.
2. In AppleWorks and MS Works, save the database as **Library5**.
3. Create a filter for the form (**frmBooks**) to list all the books in the mystery genre.
4. Print the forms for the books (except in Paradox where you can print only the first form).
5. Create a filter for the table and list all paperback books in good condition.
6. Print the table, and remove the filter.
7. Create a filter for the table (**tblBooks**) to list hard cover books with a current value (CValue) of $10.00 or more that are in excellent condition.
8. Print the table.
9. Redisplay all records.
10. In AppleWorks and MS Works, close the database and exit the database application.

Create Queries (Access and Paradox)

1. Open ⊙ **05School** from the data files.
2. Create a query that uses the **tblStudents** and the **tblActivities** tables.
3. Name the query **qryNoRelease**.

4. Include the following fields (in order listed in Access):
   - Activity
   - Last Name
   - First Name
   - Middle Name
   - Sponsor
   - Location
   - Days
   - Time
   - Release
5. Specify a criterion that lists those students whose Release field indicates No or False.
6. Run the query and print the resulting table.
7. Copy the query and rename it **qryBoysBasketball**.
8. Specify a criterion that lists the students who have signed up for Boys' Basketball.
9. Run the query and print the resulting table.
10. Copy the query and rename it **qryGirlsBasketball**.
11. Specify a criterion that lists the students who have signed up for Girls' Basketball.
12. Run the query and print the resulting table.
13. Copy the query and rename it **qryChActivities**.
14. Specify a criterion that lists the students who have signed up for Cheerleading, Chess Club, or Chorale.
15. Run the query and print the resulting table in Landscape orientation.
16. Save and close all open objects and exit the database application.

Exercise 6

Work with Reports
■ Create a Report

NOTES

Create a Report

■ **Reports** offer a way to select and format the information in a database for printing or display.

💻 **Try It!**

1. Start your database application.
2. Open ◉ **06Library** from the data files.
3. In AppleWorks and MS Works, save the database as **Library6**.
4. Create a report that displays the data in table format. (In Access, this format is called *tabular*; in AppleWorks, this format is called *columnar*).
5. Include the following fields: Genre, Author First, Author Last, Title, Copyright, PPrice, CValue, Condition.
6. Group the data by Genre; sort Genre in ascending order.
7. Within each genre, sort the books by the author's last name, author's last name, and the book's title.
8. For each type, create a summary field for PPrice and for CValue.
9. Print the page number and the current date in the footer of each page.
10. Name the report **rptValueByGenre**.
11. Title the report *Library Value by Genre*.
12. Print the report.
13. Save the database as appropriate.

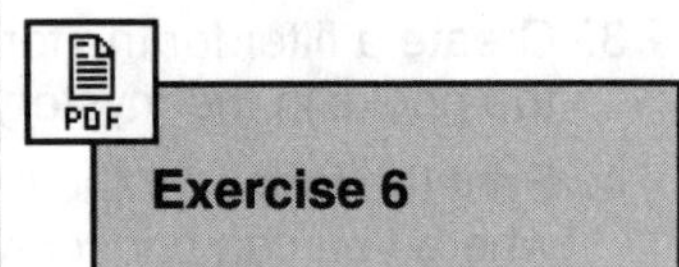

In this exercise, you will create a report for Daniel Glasser's inventory.

EXERCISE DIRECTIONS

1. Start your database application.

2. Open ☉ **06Glasser** from the data files.

3. In AppleWorks and MS Works, save the database as **Glasser6**.

4. Create a report that displays the data in table format. (In Access, this format is called *tabular*; in AppleWorks, this format is called *columnar*).

5. Include the following fields: Type, Manufacturer, Model, PDate, PPrice, CValue, Condition.

6. Group the data by Type; sort Type in ascending order.

7. Within each type, sort the items by Manufacturer and Model.

8. For each type, create a summary field for PPrice and for CValue.

9. Create a final summary for the entire report.

10. Print the page number and the current date in the footer of each page.

11. Name the report **rptValueByType**.

12. Title the report *Inventory Value by Type*.

13. Print the report.

14. Save the database as appropriate.

15. Close the report.

16. Close the database and exit the database application.

NEXT EXERCISE

Lesson 7: Presentations

Exercise 1: Get Started with Presentations

- About Presentations
- Start the Application and Create a Title Slide
- Use Placeholders
- The AppleWorks Draw Window
- The PowerPoint 98 Window
- The PowerPoint 2000 Window
- The Corel Presentations Window
- Start a New Presentation

Exercise 2: Add to an Existing Presentation

- Open a Presentation
- Add a Bulleted List Slide
- Add a Slide with a Graphic

Exercise 3: Review and Enhance a Presentation

- Review a Presentation
- Add Notes to the Presentation
- Add a Closing Slide
- Print a Presentation Using the Print Dialog Box

Exercise 4: Create a Slide Show

- About Slide Shows
- Create and Run an AppleWorks Slide Show
- Create Slide Transitions
- Add Animation Effects

Exercise 1

Get Started with Presentations
■ About Presentations ■ Start the Application and Create a Title Slide
■ Use Placeholders ■ The AppleWorks Draw Window ■ The PowerPoint 98 Window
■ The PowerPoint 2000 Window ■ The Corel Presentations Window
■ Start a New Presentation

NOTES

About Presentations

■ Presentation applications let you build documents that you can print as overhead transparencies, produce as 35mm slides (with the appropriate software), or display on a computer or computer projection system. These applications are often used to create marketing, sales, and other business presentations. Increasingly, high school and college students are using presentation software when making oral reports.

Start the Application and Create a Title Slide

■ Good presentations begin with a title slide that identifies the presentation and the general topic. Sometimes the title slide also identifies the presenter.

🖳 Try It!

1. Start your presentation application and create a new slide that includes a title and subtitle.

2. **AppleWorks:** Use the Assistant and select *Business style 1*; include a page number without a prefix, and include the following footer text: *Wright Consultants*.
   PowerPoint 98 (Mac): Use *Dads Tie* as the presentation template.
   PowerPoint 97/2000: Use *Dads Tie* as the presentation template.
   Corel Presentations: Select *Color, Dark Blue* from the Master Gallery.

3. For the title on the slide, enter *Wright Consultants*.

4. For the subtitle, enter *Technical Writing for the Computer Community*. Let the software control any word wrap.

5. Delete any other text boxes from the slide.

6. Save the presentation as **Wright1**.

7. Print one copy of the slide.

   The illustration on the following page shows the desired results.

8. Close the presentation and exit the presentation application.

MS Works
MS Works does not offer a presentations application and, therefore, is not discussed in this lesson.

Slide
A presentation page is called a slide, a common term in business for overhead transparencies as well as 35mm slides.

Create a Presentation

Complete the Title Slide

Print a Presentation

Completed Title Slides

AppleWorks

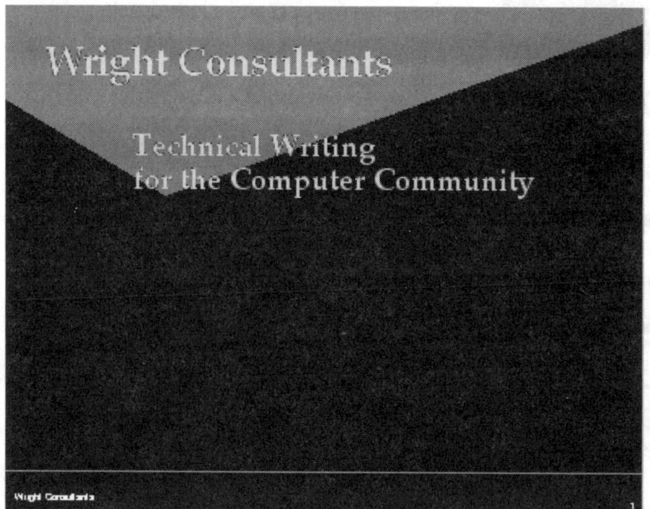

PowerPoint 98 for the Macintosh

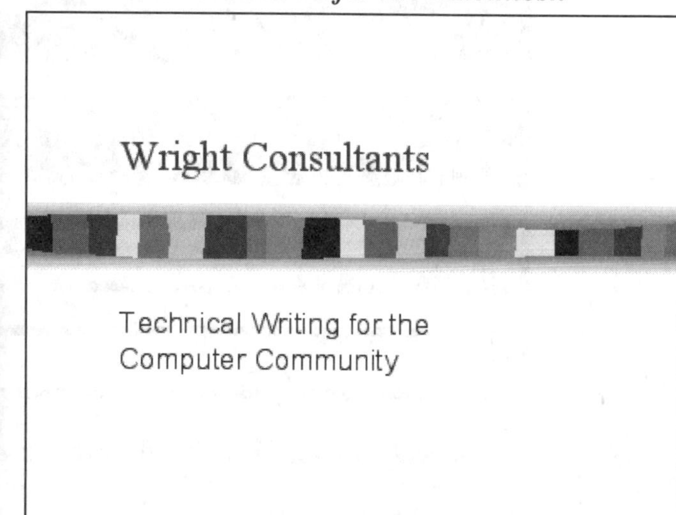

PowerPoint 97 and 2000

Corel Presentations

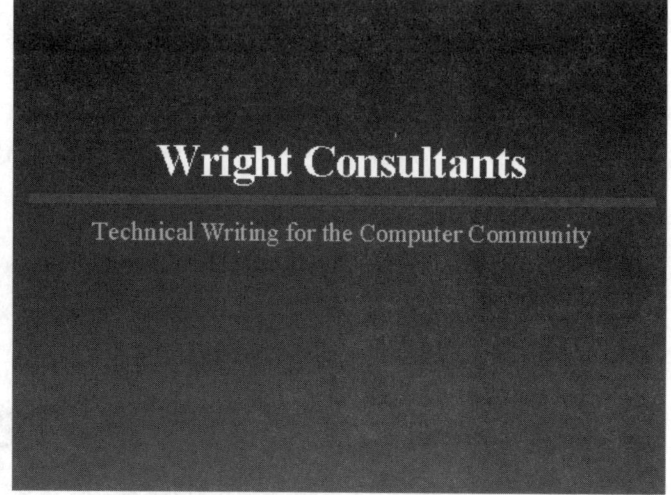

Use Placeholders

- Presentation software usually provides pre-positioned boxes called **placeholders** on each slide. Some placeholders are designed to accept text entries; others are designed for clip art or other graphic objects, such as a spreadsheet table or chart. (Graphic placeholders are described in Exercise 2.)

To use a text placeholder:

1. Click in the placeholder, or double-click the placeholder.
2. If the existing text does not disappear, delete the text.
3. Type the text you wish to insert.
4. Click outside the placeholder when finished.

   NOTE: Do not press Return or Enter inside a placeholder unless you are going to type an additional paragraph. If you press Return or Enter after a one-paragraph entry, you may end up with a blank space where you do not want it.

AppleWorks Text Placeholders

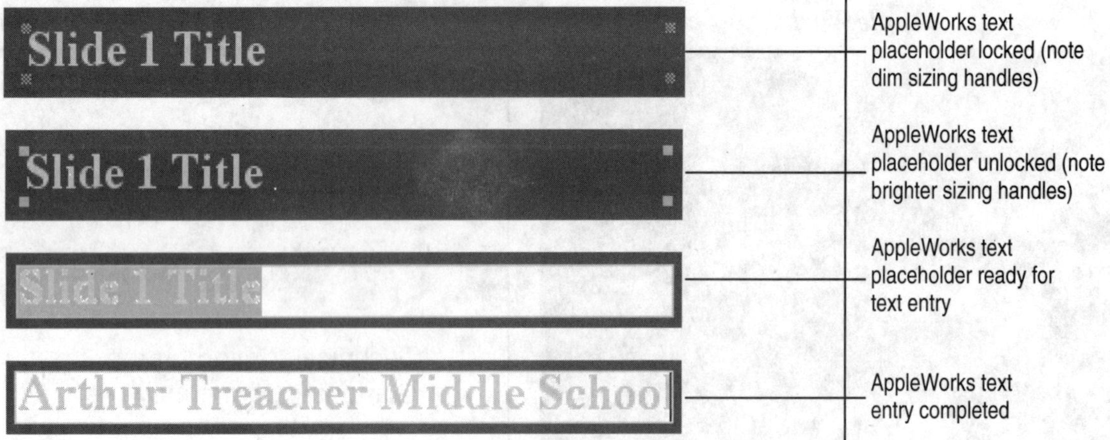

PowerPoint 98, 97, & 2000 Text Placeholders

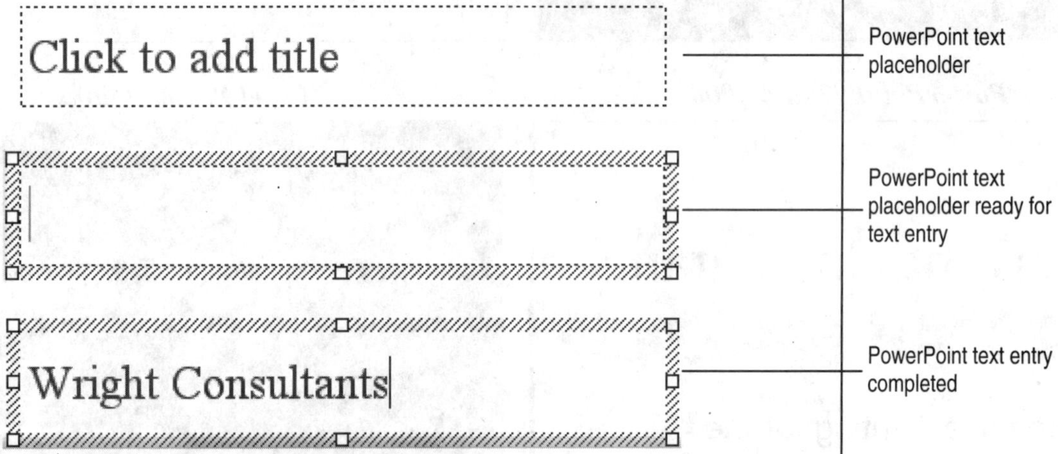

Corel Presentations Text Placeholder

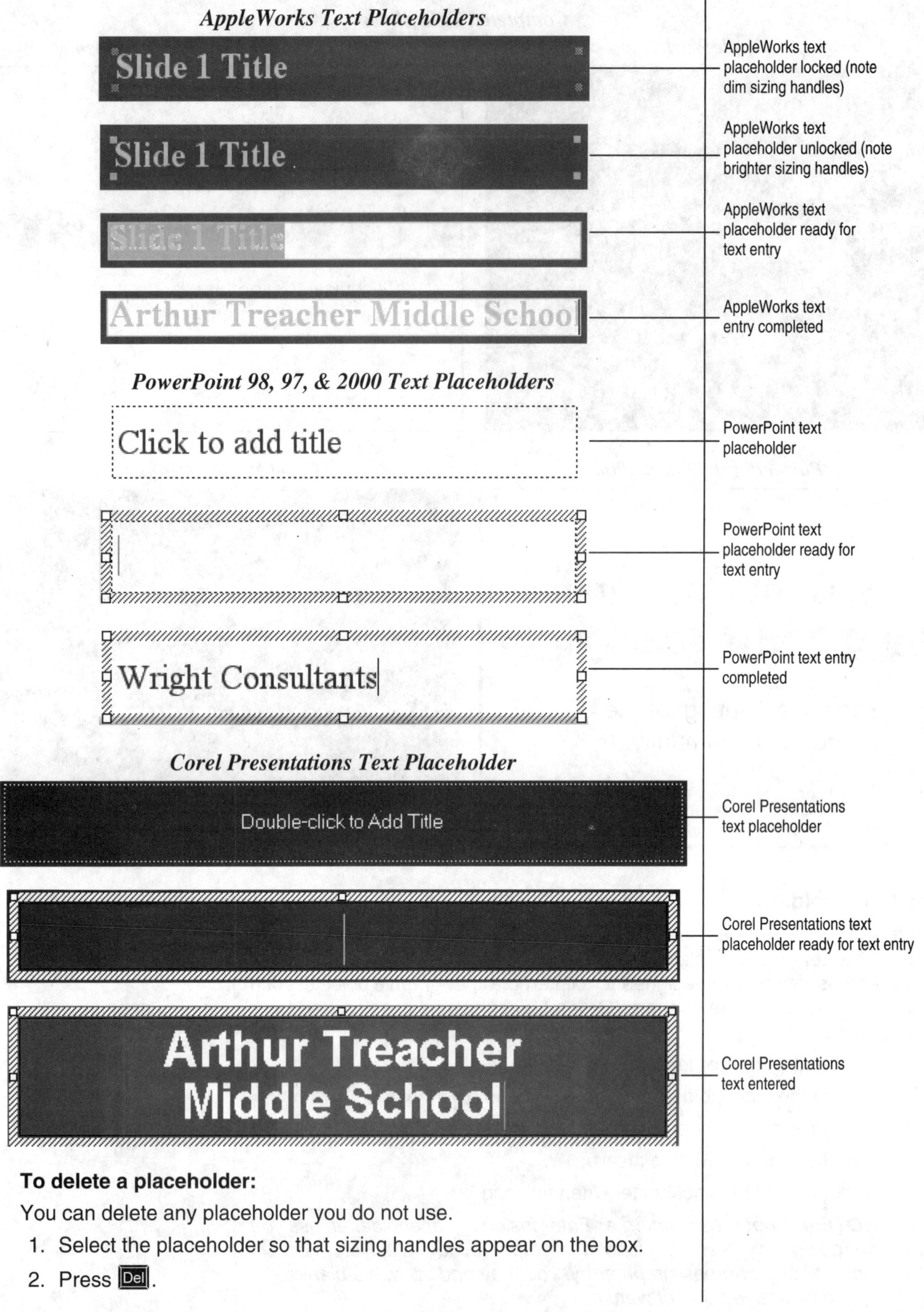

To delete a placeholder:

You can delete any placeholder you do not use.

1. Select the placeholder so that sizing handles appear on the box.
2. Press Del.

In AppleWorks, if the box is not erased, select the box and press
[Shift]+[⌘]+[H] to unlock the object, and then press [Del].

The AppleWorks Draw Window

- When you use the Assistant for presentations, AppleWorks creates a
  Draw document. The graphics tools appear at the left edge of the window.
  Buttons and tools are introduced as needed in this lesson.

AppleWorks Window for Creating Slides

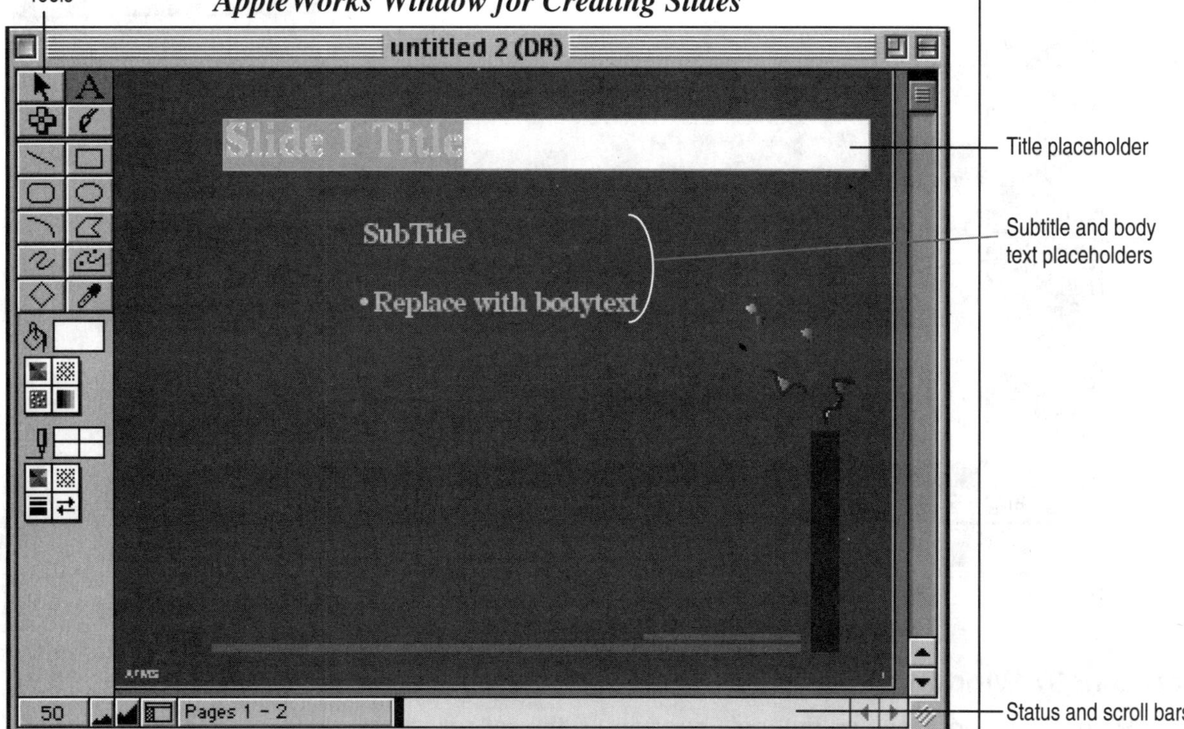

The PowerPoint 98 Window

- The PowerPoint 98 window, shown in the illustration on the following
  page, includes elements common to all Microsoft Office 98 windows—title
  bar, menu bar, toolbars, and status bar.

- In addition to the common elements, PowerPoint 98 adds a floating
  Common Tasks toolbar and some View buttons at the bottom of the
  window. The Common Tasks and View buttons will be described as
  necessary during these exercises.

- The illustration also shows the Drawing toolbar, which can be used to add
  line drawings and other graphical elements to a slide. Use of the Drawing
  toolbar is outside the scope of this book.

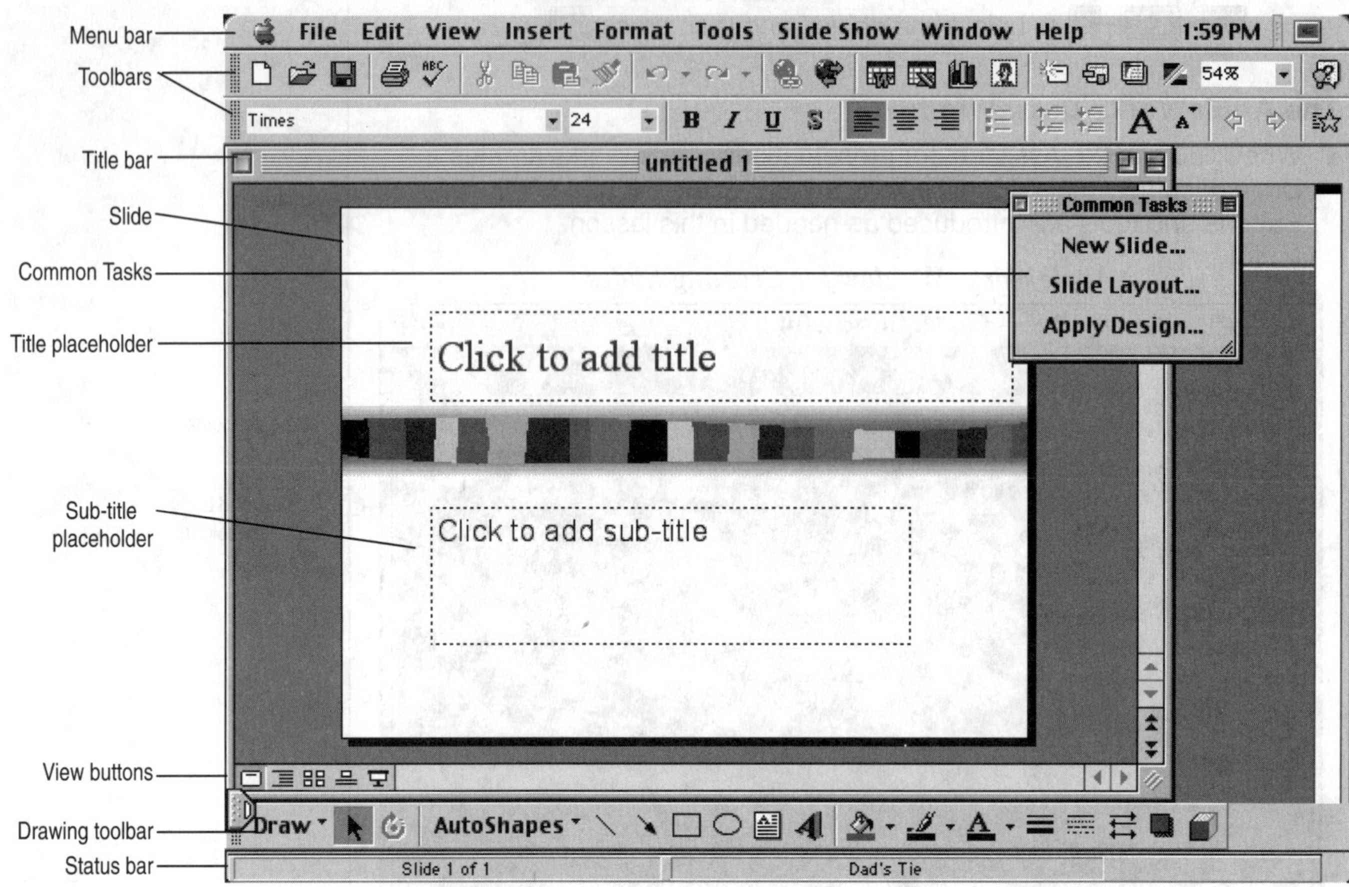

The PowerPoint 97 Window

- The PowerPoint 97 window, shown in the illustration on the following page, includes elements common to all Microsoft Office 97 windows—title bar, menu bar, toolbars, and status bar.

- In addition to the common elements, PowerPoint 97 adds a floating Common Tasks toolbar and some View buttons at the bottom of the window. The Common Tasks and View buttons will be described as necessary during these exercises.

- The illustration also shows the Drawing toolbar, which can be used to add line drawings and other graphical elements to a slide. Use of the Drawing toolbar is outside the scope of this book.

PowerPoint 97 Window

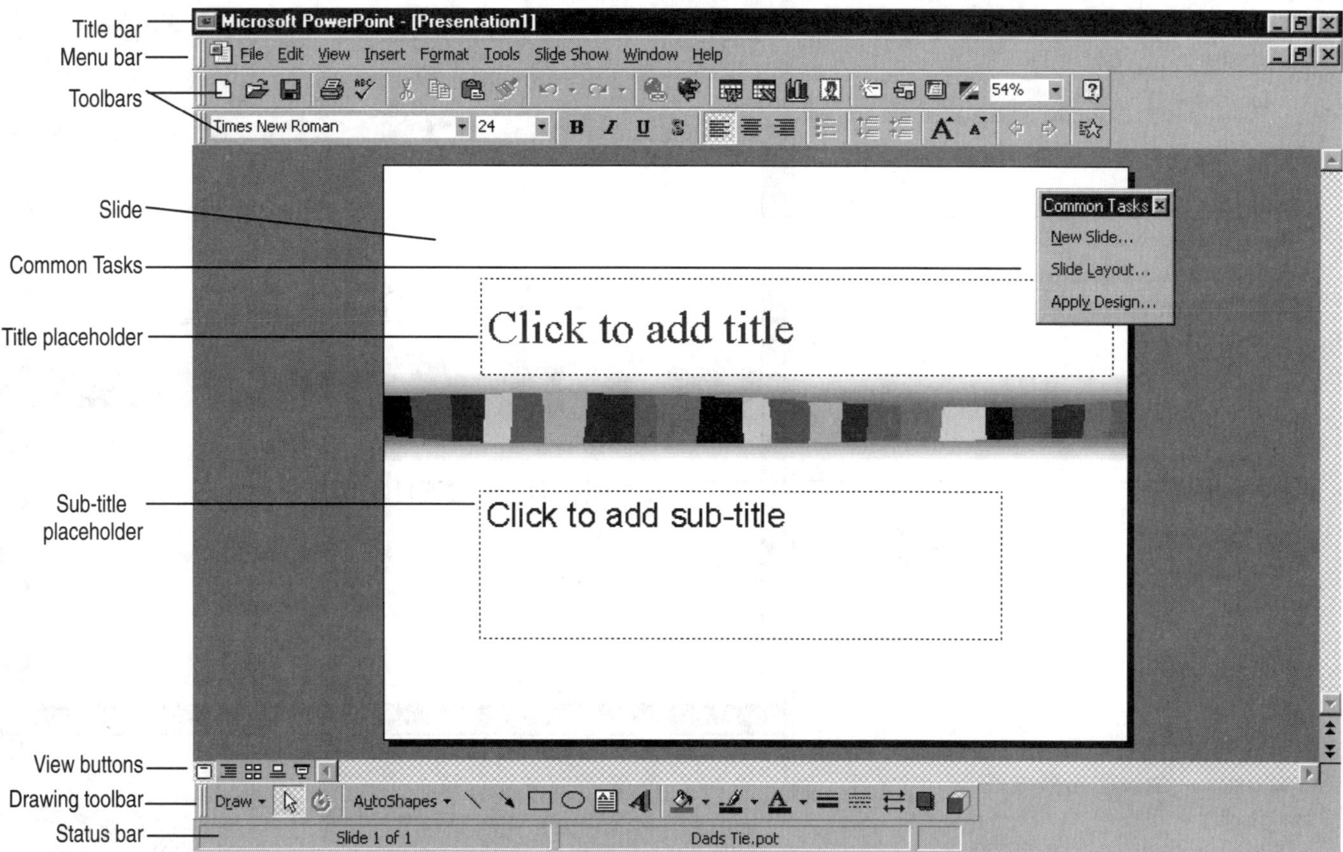

The PowerPoint 2000 Window

- The PowerPoint window, shown in the illustration on the following page, includes elements common to all Microsoft Office windows—title bar, menu bar, toolbars, and status bar. As with other Office applications, you can drag the toolbars to new positions on the screen to make more of their buttons visible.

- In addition to the common elements, PowerPoint 2000 adds a Common Tasks option on the Formatting toolbar and View buttons at the bottom of the window. The Common Tasks and View buttons will be described as necessary during these exercises.

- The illustration also shows the Drawing toolbar, which can be used to add line drawings and other graphical elements to a slide. Use of the Drawing toolbar is outside the scope of this book.

- The PowerPoint 2000 window has three panes: Outline, Slide, and Notes. As you create a presentation by adding text to slides, the **Outline pane** shows the text in outline form so you can review the organization and content of the presentation.

- The **Slide pane** shows the slide as it will appear when displayed or printed. The **Notes pane** lets you add notes that you can use as reminders of important points you want to make when giving the presentation.

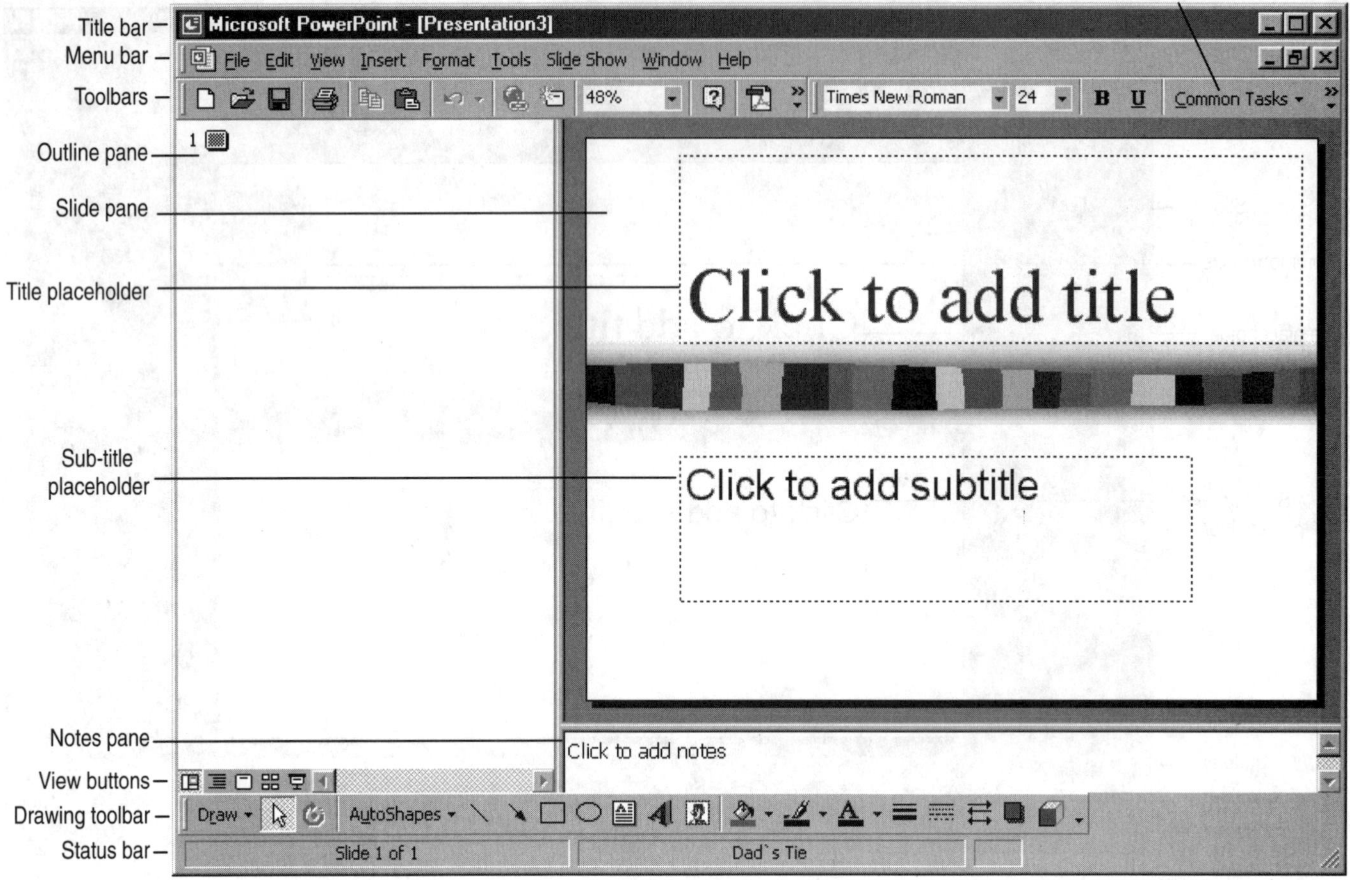

The Corel Presentations Window

■ As shown in the illustration on the following page, the Corel Presentations window includes a variety of buttons on the Toolbar and Property Bar that aid in the creation and editing of slides. At the right side of the window are four buttons that let you display the slides in different views. The toolbar buttons and view buttons will be described as they are used in this lesson.

314

Corel Presentations Window

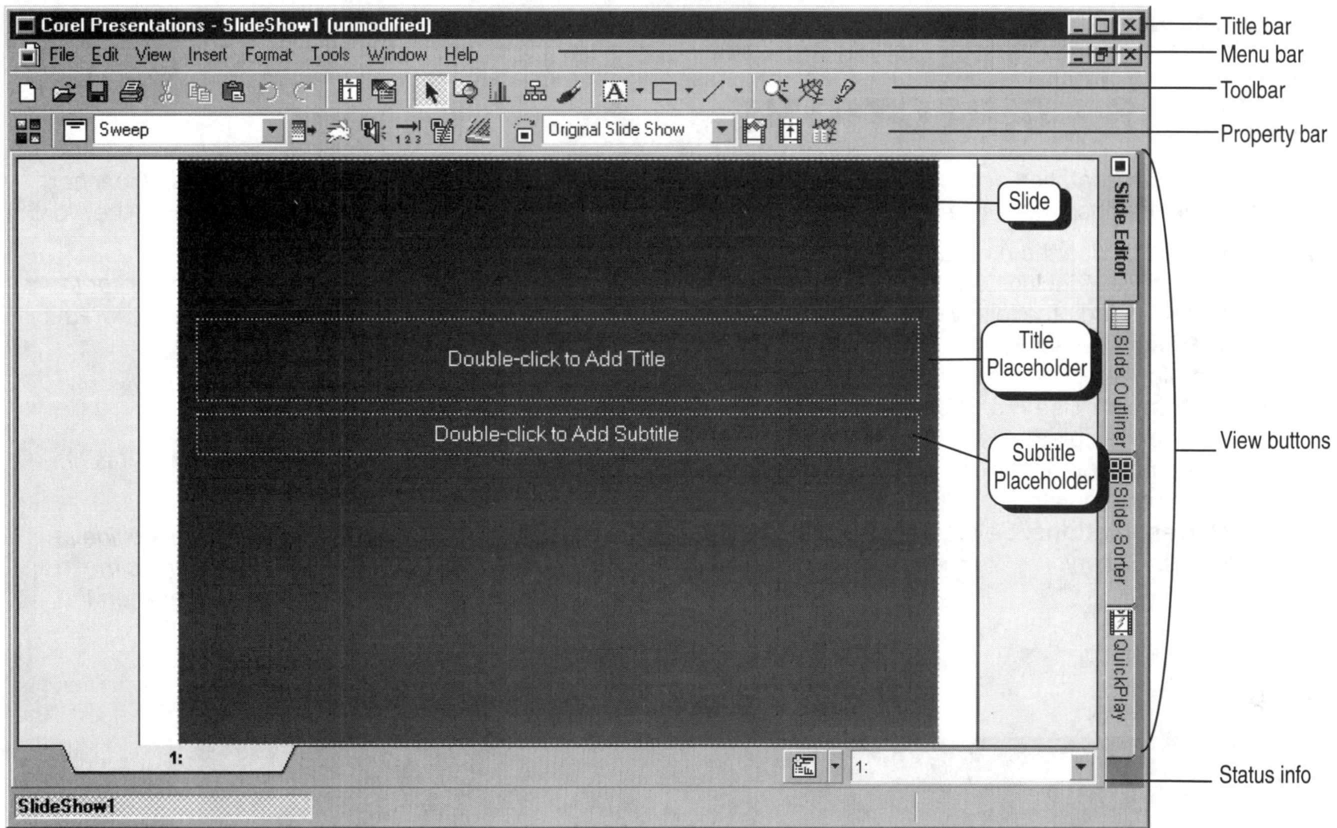

Start a New Presentation

■ When the presentation application is already running, you can create a
new presentation by using the **File**, **New** command. Each application then
lets you create a new presentation in the same way as when you start the
application.

EXERCISE DIRECTIONS

1. Start your presentation application and create a new slide that includes a title and subtitle.

2. **AppleWorks:** Use the Assistant and select *Business style 2*; include a page number without a prefix, and include the following footer text: *ATMS*.
   PowerPoint 98: Use *High Voltage* as the presentation template.
   PowerPoint 97: Use *High Voltage* as the presentation template.
   PowerPoint 2000: Use *High Voltage* as the presentation template.
   Corel Presentations: Select *Color*, *Default* from the Master Gallery.

3. For the title on the slide, enter *Arthur Treacher Middle School*. Let the software control the word wrap if any.

4. For the subtitle, enter *Learning together for the future*. Let the software control the word wrap if any.

5. Delete any other placeholders, and adjust text positions as necessary.

6. Save the presentation as **Treacher1**.

7. Print one copy of the slide.

Illustration A shows the completed title slide in PowerPoint 2000. The dot at the right is the electron that travels across the slide when the slide is displayed in a slide show.

Illustration A. Completed Title Slide

NEXT EXERCISE

Add to an Existing Presentation
■ Open a Presentation ■ Add a Bulleted List Slide ■ Add a Slide with a Graphic

NOTES

Open a Presentation

■ When you want to open an existing presentation, the specific steps depend on whether or not the application is already running. In this exercise, you will add to existing presentations.

Try It!

1. Start your presentation application.
2. Open **Wright1**, or open ☉ **02Wright1** from the data files.
3. Save the presentation as **Wright2**.

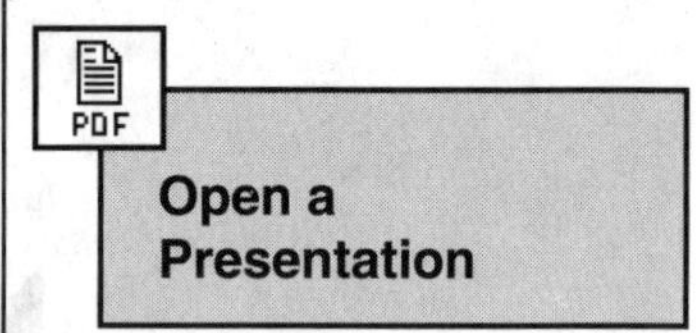

Add a Bulleted List Slide

■ To create additional information for the presentation, you add a new slide. Body text in presentations is usually formatted as bulleted list points, so many applications provide bulleted list layouts.

Try It!

1. Add a new slide to **Wright2**.
2. **AppleWorks:** Scroll to slide 2.
   PowerPoint 98: From the New Slide dialog box, select the Bulleted List layout.
   PowerPoint 97/2000: From the New Slide dialog box, select the Bulleted List layout.
   Corel Presentations: From the New Slide dialog box, select the Bulleted List layout.
3. In the title placeholder, type *Our Experience*.
4. Delete any subtitle placeholder.
5. Create a bulleted list that has the same content and structure as the following (see the illustrations that follow):
   - *Twenty years producing end-user materials*
   - *Software documentation*
     - *Applications for IBM 370 and others*
     - *Emulation software for DEC VT terminals*
     - *Variety of PC applications*
   - *Computer-based training materials*
6. Use the application's default formatting and word wrap.
7. Press `Return` or `Enter` after typing each of the first five paragraphs. Do not press `Return` or `Enter` after the last paragraph.

8. In **AppleWorks**, format the sub-bullets using the **Format**, **Paragraph** command as described in the procedures.

   In **PowerPoint 98**, **PowerPoint 2000**, and **Corel Presentations**, format the sub-bullets by clicking the Demote button ➡ or ➡ on the toolbar or by pressing the Tab key before typing any text in the paragraph. Use the default bullets provided by the application.

9. Save the presentation.

   The following illustration shows the desired results.

Completed Bulleted List Slides

AppleWorks

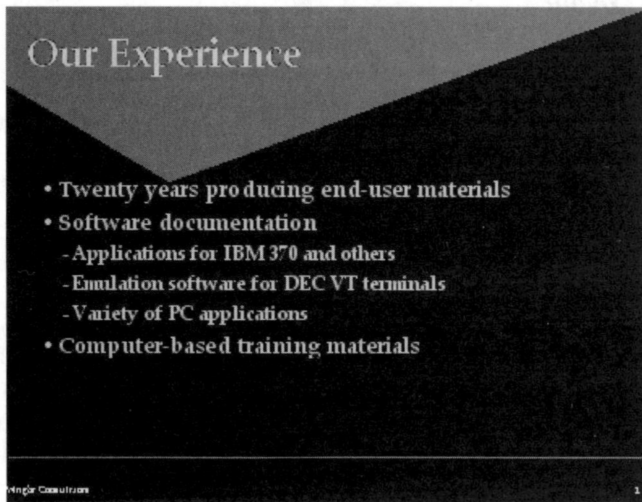

PowerPoint 98 for the Macintosh

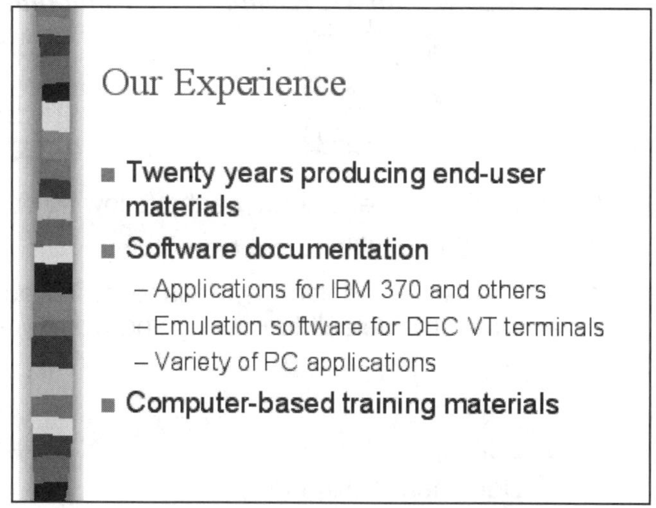

PowerPoint 97 & 2000

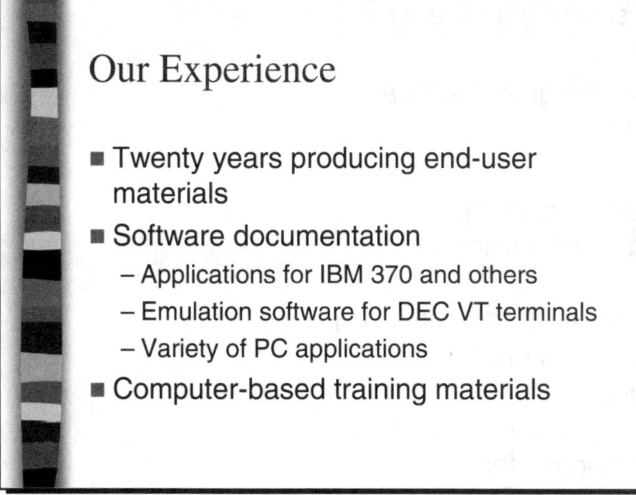

Corel Presentations

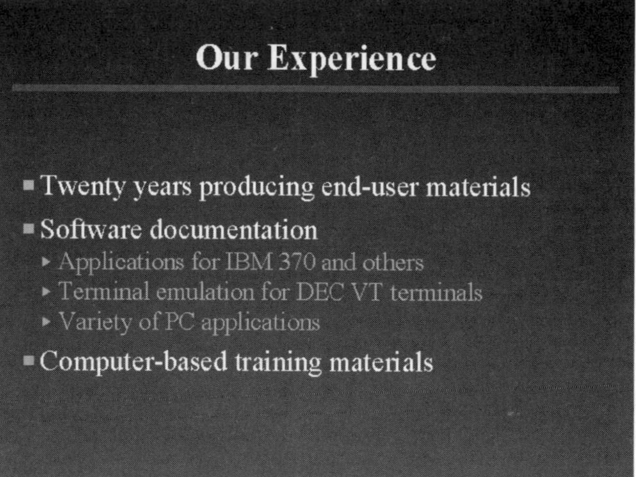

Add a Slide with a Graphic

- You can add visual interest to your presentation by including an appropriate graphic.

- AppleWorks does not provide a special slide layout for including a graphic. You must adapt the existing layout to the purposes.

- Both PowerPoint versions provide a slide layout designed to combine a bulleted list with a clip art image.

■ Corel Presentations offers a layout to place text beside a graphic, but the graphic is intended to be a chart rather than clip art; you can adapt this slide layout to create the slide with a graphic.

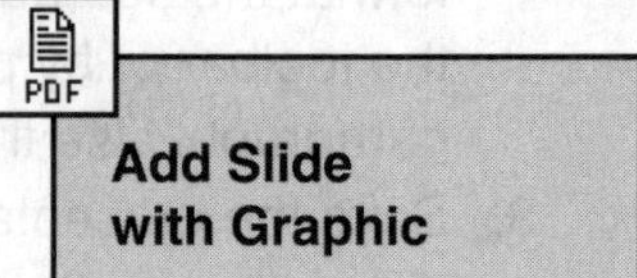

Try It!

1. **AppleWorks:** Scroll to slide 3.

   PowerPoint 98 and **PowerPoint 2000:** Insert a new slide with the Text & Clip Art layout, as shown in the following illustration.

   Corel Presentations: Insert a new slide with the Combination layout.

PowerPoint   *Corel Presentations*
Text & Clip Art Layout   *Combination Layout*

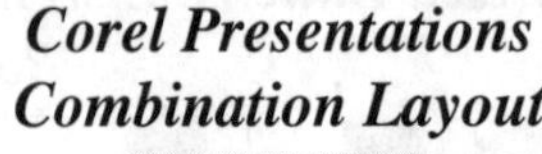 

2. In the title placeholder, type the following title: *We Offer*

3. Delete the subtitle placeholder if any.

4. In the text placeholder, type the following bullet list using the application's default formatting and word wrap.

   ♦ Planning
   ♦ Writing
   ♦ Editing
   ♦ Document design
   ♦ Layout
   ♦ Production coordination

5. In AppleWorks, move the bulleted list to the left side of the slide (see the illustration that follows this Try It! activity).

6. Insert an appropriate graphic from clip art or from the graphics data files. The desired results show the graphics listed below:

   ♦ **AppleWorks: Pens** from data files
   ♦ **PowerPoint 98:** Image from the Academic category of the Microsoft Clip Gallery. If the image illustrated is not available, choose a different appropriate graphic.
   ♦ **PowerPoint 2000: Writetools.pcx** from the graphics data files.
   ♦ **Corel Presentations: Computer\cpu\screen** from the Corel CD Clipart tab. The graphic was flipped left to right.

7. Position and size the graphic to the size shown in the illustration of the completed slide for your application. The techniques for positioning and sizing are the same as those used in the Desktop Publishing lesson.

8. Save the presentation.

9. Print the three slides in Landscape orientation.

10. Close the presentation and exit the presentation application unless you are continuing with the Exercise Directions.

Completed Text & Clip Art Slides

AppleWorks

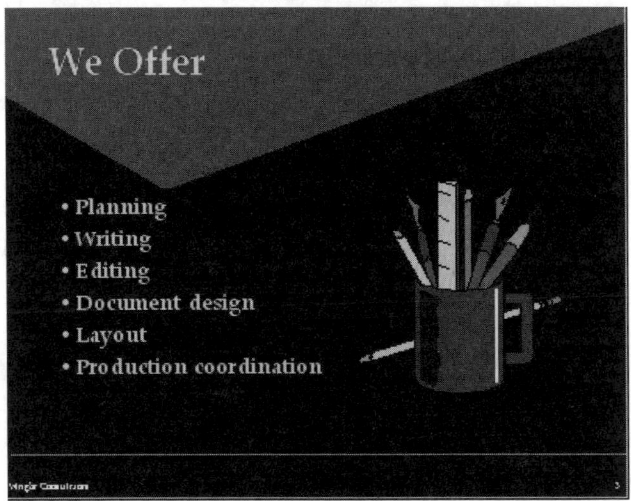

PowerPoint 98 for the Macintosh

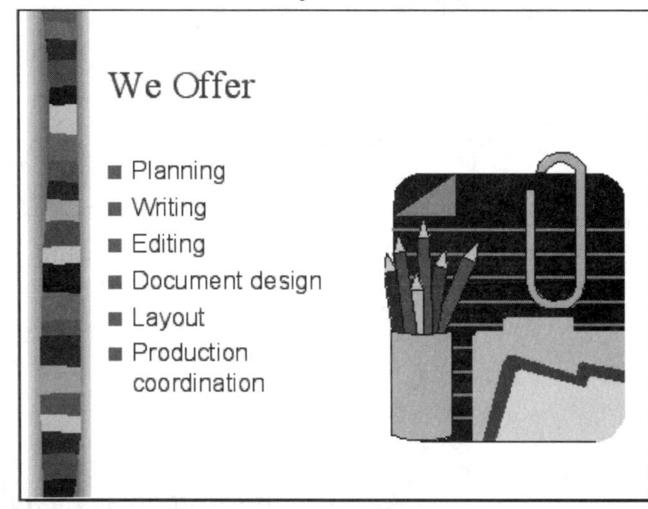

PowerPoint 97 & 2000

Corel Presentations

In this exercise, you will add two slides to the Arthur Treacher Middle School presentation.

EXERCISE DIRECTIONS

Open the Presentation

1. Open **Treacher1**, or open **02Treacher1** from the data files.
2. Save the presentation as **Treacher2**.

Add a Bulleted List Slide

1. Add a new slide to **Treacher2**.
2. **AppleWorks:** Scroll to slide 2.
   PowerPoint 98: From the New Slide dialog box, select the Bulleted List layout.
   PowerPoint 97/2000: From the New Slide dialog box, select the Bulleted List layout.
   Corel Presentations: From the New Slide dialog box, select the Bulleted List layout.
3. In the title placeholder, type *Academic Excellence*.
4. Delete any subtitle placeholder.

5. Create a bulleted list that has the same content and structure as the following:

- Best middle school library in state
- Excellent science laboratories
- Superior writing and literature programs
- State-of-the-art computer lab
    ◆ PCs with Windows 98 and MS Office 2000
    ◆ Apple Macintosh and iMac
- Modern language lab

6. Use the application's default formatting and word wrap.

7. Press **Return** or **Enter** after typing each of the first six paragraphs. Do not press **Return** or **Enter** after the last paragraph.

8. In **AppleWorks**, format the sub-bullets using the Format, Paragraph command as described in the procedures.

9. In **Powerpoint 98**, **PowerPoint 2000**, and **Corel Presentations**, format the sub-bullets by clicking the Demote button ⬇ or ➡ on the toolbar. Use the default bullets provided by the application.

10. Save the presentation.

11. Illustration A shows the desired results in PowerPoint 2000.

Illustration A. Completed Bulleted List Slide

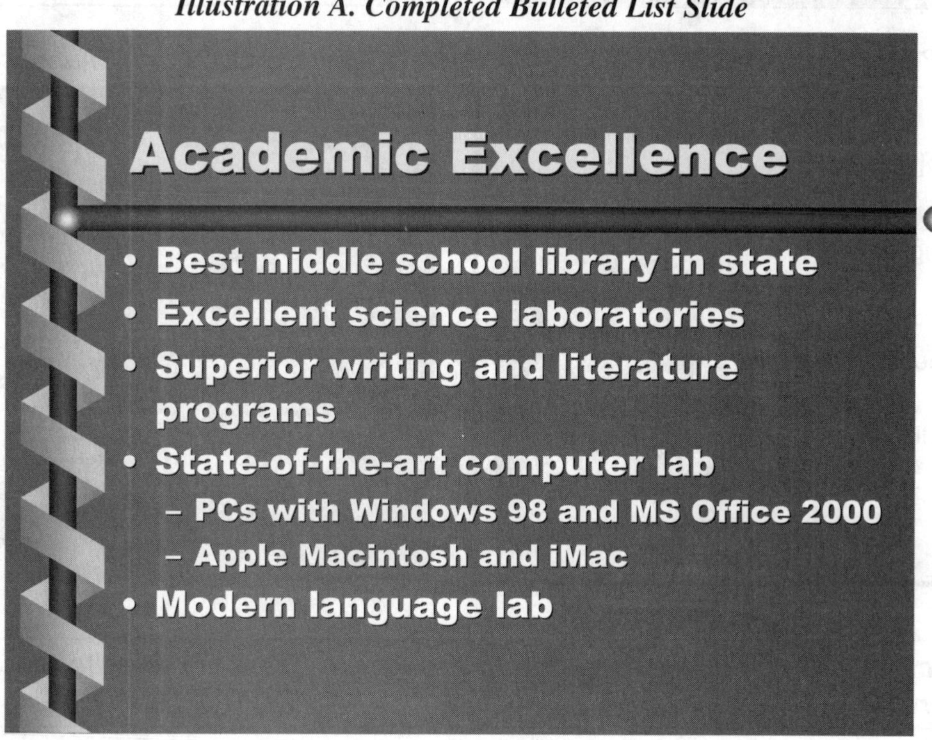

Add a Text & Clip Art Slide

1. **AppleWorks:** Scroll to slide 3.
   PowerPoint 98 and **PowerPoint 2000:** Insert a new slide with the Text & Clip Art layout.
   Corel Presentations: Insert a new slide with the Combination layout.

2. In the title placeholder, type the following title:
   Activities Galore

3. Delete the subtitle placeholder if any.

4. In the text placeholder, type the following bullet list using the application's default formatting and word wrap.

- Intramural sports
- Academic clubs
- Interscholastic sports
- Mock United Nations
- Cultural field trips
- Dramas and musicals
- Band, orchestra, and choral groups

5. In AppleWorks, move the bulleted list to the left side of the slide (see Illustration B).

6. Insert an appropriate graphic from clip art or from the graphics data files. The desired results in Illustration B show the graphics listed below:

   - **AppleWorks:** Combines three graphics data files: **Basketball**, **Color Notes**, and **Drama Mask**.
   - **PowerPoint 98:** Image from the Academic category of the Microsoft Clip Gallery. Use the Find feature of the Clip Gallery and look for *Friend* or use a different appropriate graphic.
   - **PowerPoint 97/2000:** Image from Metaphors category. Search for *stars* or *opportunity*.
   - **Corel Presentations: People\Humorous\kids0031** from the Corel CD Clipart tab.

7. Position and size the graphic(s) as shown in the illustrations of the completed slides. The techniques for positioning and sizing are the same as you used in Lesson 4, Desktop Publishing.

8. Save the presentation.

9. Print the three slides in Landscape orientation.

10. Close the presentation and exit the presentation application.

Illustration B. Completed Text & Clip Art Slide

AppleWorks

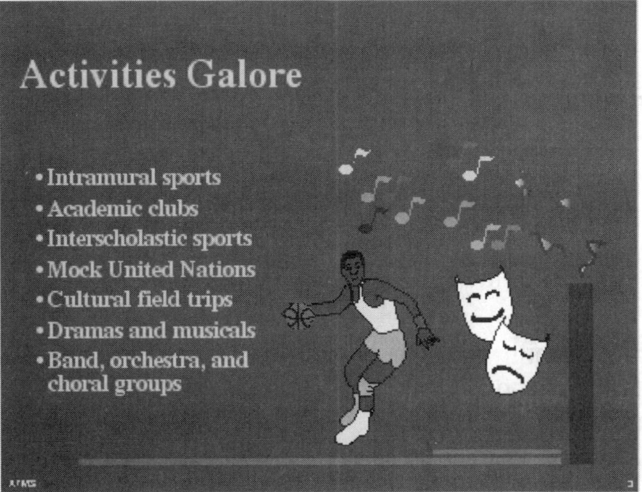

PowerPoint 98 for the Macintosh

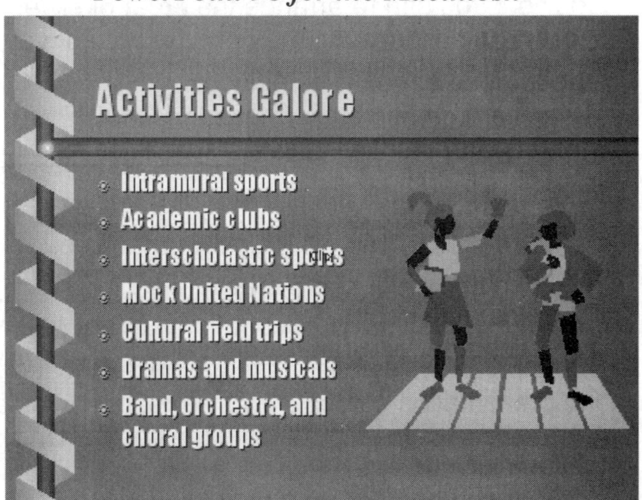

PowerPoint 97/2000

Corel Presentations

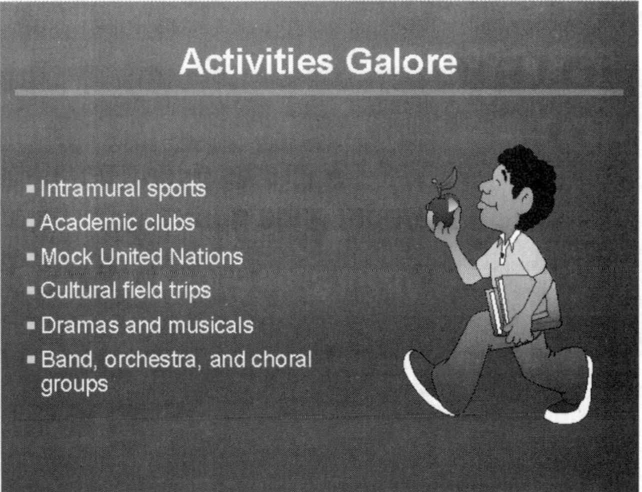

Review and Enhance a Presentation
■ Review a Presentation ■ Add Notes to the Presentation
■ Add a Closing Slide ■ Print a Presentation Using the Print Dialog Box

NOTES

Review a Presentation

- **AppleWorks.** Although AppleWorks does not offer the views discussed in this section, you should review the presentation by scrolling through it. In addition, you can re-arrange the order of slides using the Slide Show feature as described in the next exercise. If you are using AppleWorks, go to "Add Notes to the Presentation" on page 327.

- As you are creating a presentation, you should review it to be sure that:

  - You are covering the subject in sufficient detail for the audience while remaining within the time limits.

  - The presentation is logically organized.

  - You have corrected typographical and factual errors and have formatted text and illustrations appropriately.

- To help you review the presentation, applications offer various views of the presentation content. Two views, in particular—Outline and Slide Sorter—can help you evaluate the content and organization of your presentation.

- You can select a view using the View buttons on the application window. In PowerPoint, the view buttons are located at the lower left of the window; in Corel Presentations, they are located along the right side of the window oriented vertically, as illustrated in Exercise 1.

View Buttons

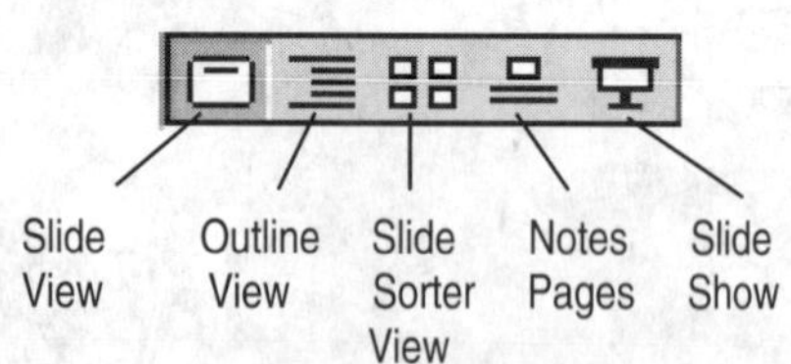

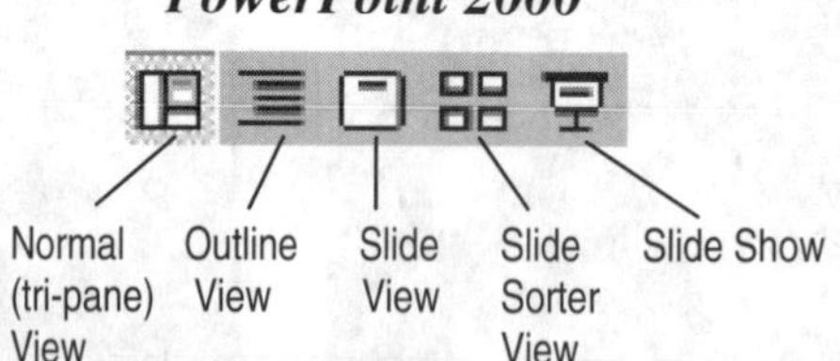

Corel Presentations (rotated to horizontal)

View Name	Application	
Normal (tri-pane) view	PowerPoint 2000	Displays the outline, slide, and notes panes. PowerPoint 2000 offers this view so that you do not have to switch among views to review organization, speaker notes, and individual slides
Slide view Slide Editor	PowerPoint (all) Corel Presentations	Displays an individual slide for editing.
Outline view Slide Outliner	PowerPoint (all) Corel Presentations	Displays the presentation in outline form.
Slide Sorter view Slide Sorter	PowerPoint (all) Corel Presentations	Displays all the slides in the presentation in miniature. In this view, you can rearrange slide order or select a slide for viewing in normal or Slide view.
Slide Show QuickPlay	PowerPoint (all) Corel Presentations	Displays the presentation as a slide show.

Try It!

Review Slide Order in Slide Sorter View

1. Open **Wright2**, or open **03Wright2** from the data files.

2. Save the presentation as **Wright3**.

3. Display the presentation in Slide Sorter view.

   The application displays all three slides in miniature, as shown in the illustration that follows.

PowerPoint 98 Slide Sorter View

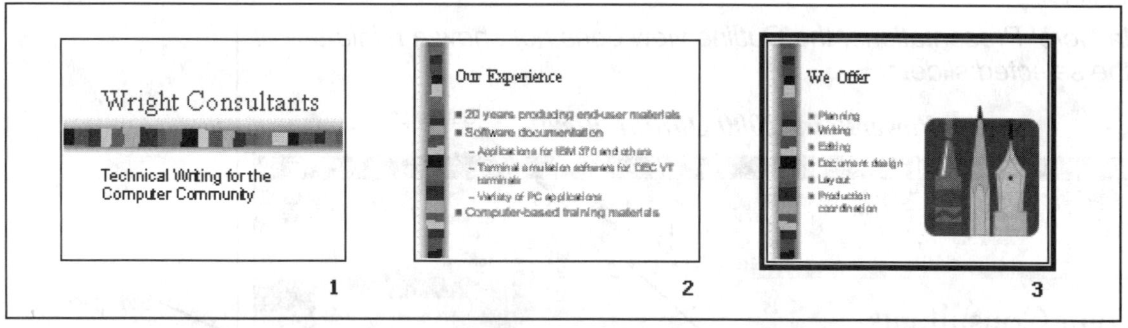

Corel Presentations Slide Sorter View

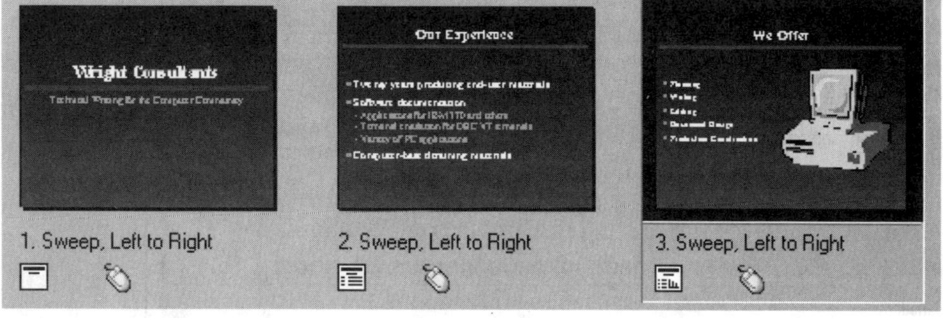

In PowerPoint, the bold border around slide 3 indicates that the slide is selected. In Corel Presentations, the selected slide looks sunken below the surface level, and the information under each slide indicates specifications for the slide show. Slide shows are described in Exercise 4.

4. Click and drag slide three to the left until a vertical line appears to the left of slide 2, and release the mouse button.

   Former slide 3 is now slide 2.

5. Click and drag current slide 3 (former slide 2) to its previous position.

6. Double-click slide 3.

   In PowerPoint 98, the slide appears in Slide view; in PowerPoint 2000, the slide appears in Normal view; in Corel Presentations, the slide appears in the Slide Editor.

7. Switch back to Slide Sorter view.

🖳 Try It!

Review Content and Organization in Outline View

- Display the presentation in Outline view.

   The text of the slides appears in outline form, as shown in the following illustration from PowerPoint 2000. You can determine whether the content is complete and organized the way you want.

   You can edit the content of the presentation in Outline view. Changes are reflected in the text displayed on the slide.

   Note that slide 3 is displayed in the upper right of the window, and the slide's icon is gray to indicate that it is selected. PowerPoint 98 works in a similar way, displaying a miniature of the selected slide in the upper right of the window.

   You can switch from slide to slide by clicking on the slide icons in the outline.

   In Corel Presentations, the Outline view does not show a miniature of the selected slide.

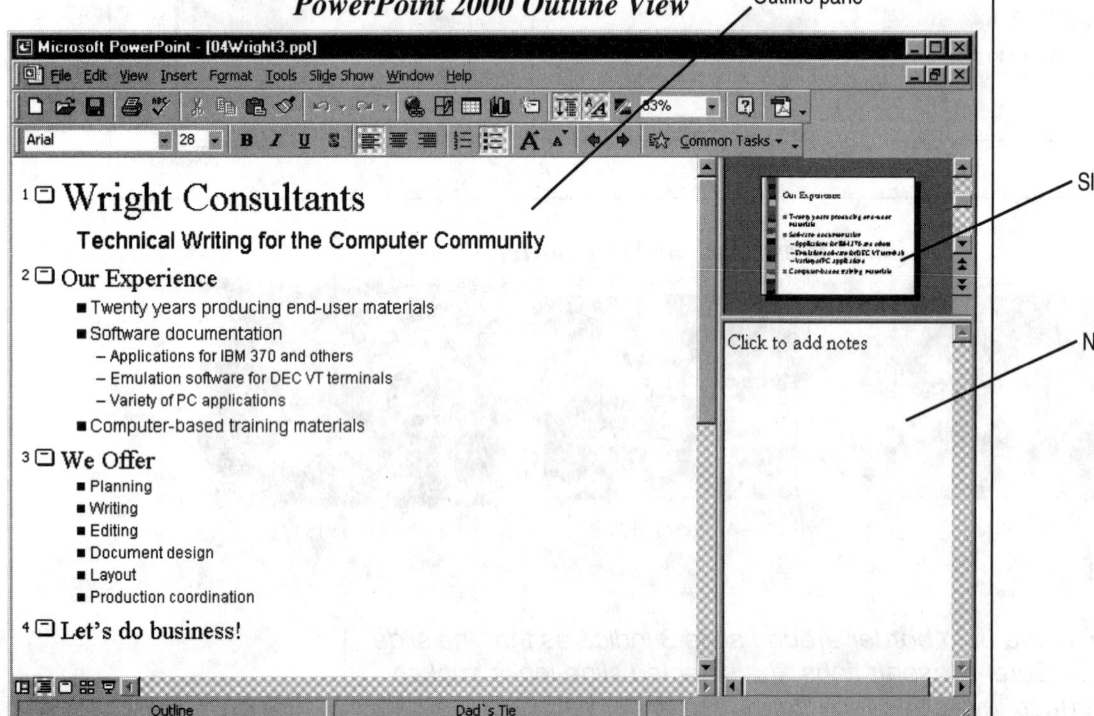

Add Notes to the Presentation

- When you make a presentation, you can often profit from notes that remind you of certain points to emphasize. These reminders—called speaker notes—can be stored with the slide to which they refer.

- **AppleWorks.** To create notes to an AppleWorks presentation, create a new word processing document and enter speaker notes for each slide. If you are using AppleWorks, go to "Add a Closing Slide," below.

🖥 Try It!

1. Display slide 3 (*We Offer*).

2. Add the following speaker note: *Carefully describe what production coordination includes.*

3. Save the presentation.

4. Display slide 1.

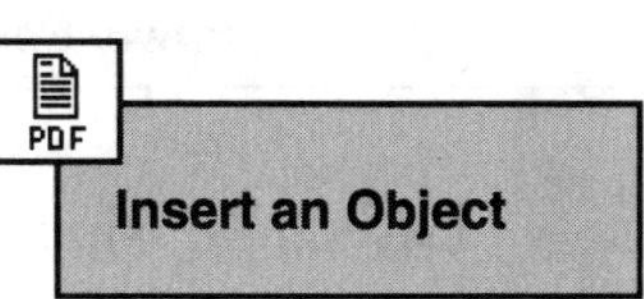

PowerPoint 2000 Note Added in Notes Pane

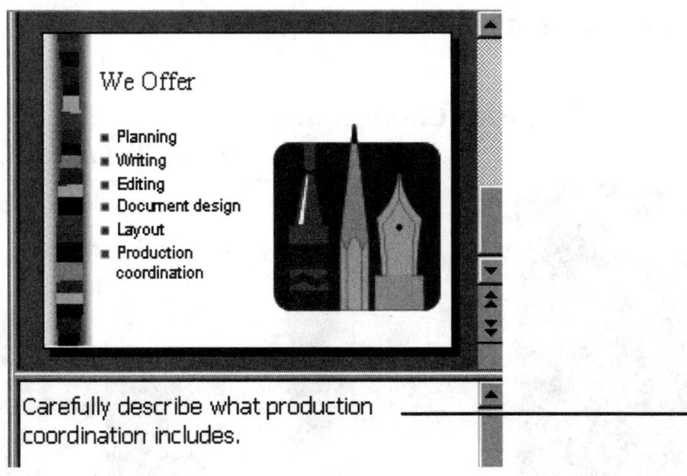

— Notes pane

Add a Closing Slide

- A presentation needs a concluding slide that encourages the audience to act or summarizes the presentation's content.

🖥 Try It!

1. **AppleWorks:** Scroll to slide 4, and go to step 5.
   PowerPoint and **Corel Presentations:** Display the presentation in Slide Sorter view.

2. Select slide 3.

3. Insert a new slide. **PowerPoint:** Use the Object layout. (You must scroll to locate it.)
   Corel Presentations: Use the Title layout.

PowerPoint
Text & Clip Art Layout

Corel Presentations
Combination Layout

The slide appears as slide 4 in Slide Sorter view.

4. Double-click slide 4.

   The view switches to Slide, Normal, or Slide Editor view.

5. In the title placeholder, type *Let's do business!*

6. Delete any subtitle placeholder.

7. **AppleWorks:** Insert a graphic from the data files. The illustration shows **Business Handshake**.

   PowerPoint 98: Insert an object from the Microsoft Clip Gallery (see the Procedures). The graphic in the illustration is from the Business category.

   PowerPoint 97/2000: Insert an object from the Microsoft Clip Gallery (see the Procedures). The graphic in the illustration can be found using *Agreement* as the search word.

   Corel Presentations: Insert a graphic from the Scrapbook or the graphics data files. The illustration shows group001 from the Scrapbook Clipart tab.

   The desired results are shown in the following illustration.

8. Save the presentation.

Completed Closing Slides

AppleWorks

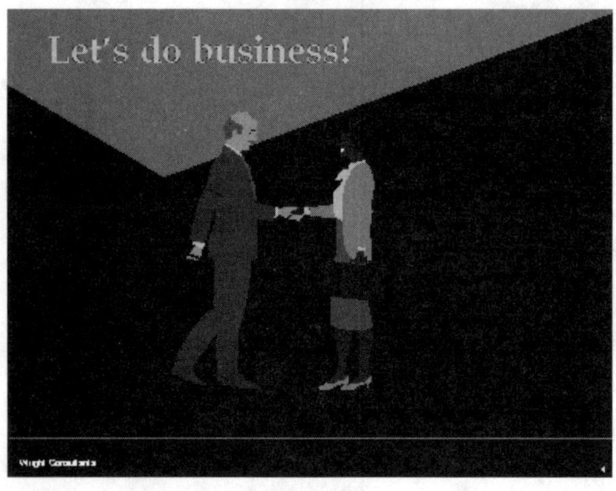

PowerPoint 98 for the Macintosh

PowerPoint 97/2000

Corel Presentations

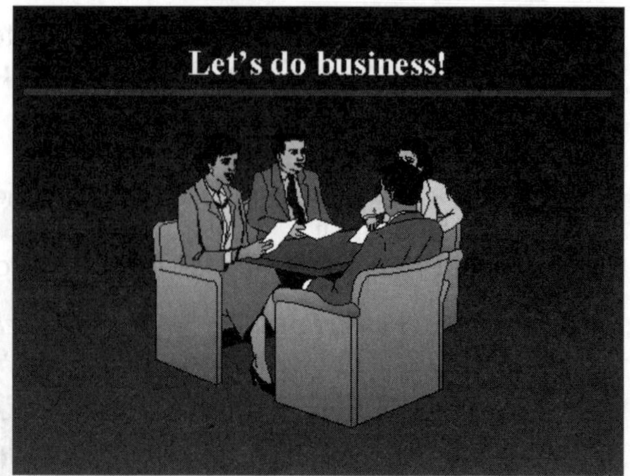

Print a Presentation Using the Print Dialog Box

- Most presentation applications let you print:
  - Slides.
  - Handouts or Audience Notes, which puts two or more slides on each page to be distributed to the audience so the audience can take notes.
  - Speaker notes, which include an image of each slide and any notes you have written for it.
- **AppleWorks** does not offer printing choices.

Try It!

1. Print the slides.
2. Print handouts or audience notes, 4 per page.

   Note that Corel Presentations distinguishes between handouts and audience notes. On audience notes pages, Corel Presentations provides lines on which audience members can write.

3. Print speaker notes. In Corel Presentations, print 4 per page.
4. Close the presentation and exit the presentation application unless you are continuing with the Exercise Directions.

Wright Consultants
Technical Writing for the
Computer Community

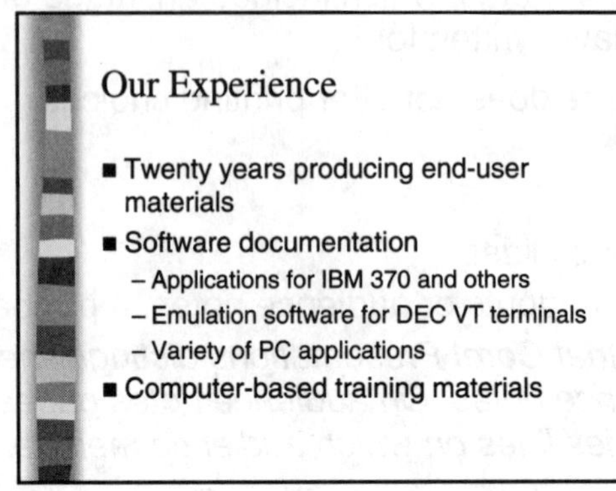
Our Experience
Twenty years producing end-user materials
Software documentation
– Applications for IBM 370 and others
– Emulation software for DEC VT terminals
– Variety of PC applications
Computer-based training materials

We Offer
Planning
Writing
Editing
Document design
Layout
Production coordination

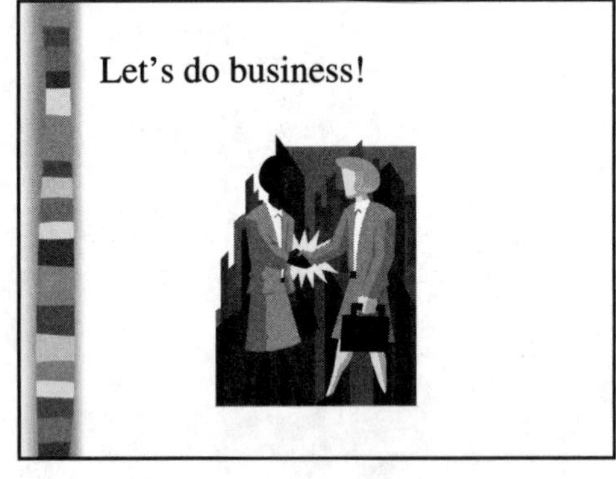
Let's do business!

1

Corel Presentations Audience Notes (4 slides per page)

In this exercise, you will review the Arthur Treacher Middle School presentation and add a closing slide.

EXERCISE DIRECTIONS

Open the Presentation

1. Open 📼**Treacher2**, or open 💿**03Treacher2** from the data files.
2. Save the presentation as **Treacher3**.

Review the Presentation

1. Review the appearance of the presentation title slide.

   Note that in AppleWorks, you scroll from slide to slide.

2. Display the presentation in Normal or Slide view.
3. Display slide 2.
4. Review its appearance.
5. Display slide 3.
6. Display the slides in Slide Sorter view.
7. Select slide 3, and add the following speaker notes.

   ATMS was league champion in interscholastic baseball last season.

   Mention last year's production of OLIVER under dramas and musicals.

Add a Closing Slide

1. **AppleWorks:** Scroll to slide 4, and go to step 5.
   PowerPoint and **Corel Presentations:** Display the presentation in Slide Sorter view.
2. Select slide 3.
3. Insert a new slide. **PowerPoint:** Use the Object layout. (You must scroll to locate it.)
   Corel Presentations: Use the Title layout.

The slide appears as slide 4 in Slide Sorter view.

4. Double-click slide 4.

   The view switches to Slide, Normal, or Slide Editor view.

5. Click the title placeholder and type *Go for a great year!*
6. Delete any subtitle placeholder.
7. **AppleWorks:** Insert **Stoplight** from the data files.
   PowerPoint 98: Delete the object placeholder and insert **Stoplight** from the data files.
   PowerPoint 2000: Delete the object placeholder and insert **Stoplight.wmf** from the data files.
   Corel Presentations: Insert **Stoplight.wmf** from the data files.
8. Resize and position the graphic as necessary.

   The desired results are shown in Illustration A.

9. Save the presentation.

Print Handouts or Audience Notes

1. **AppleWorks:** Print the presentation.
   PowerPoint: Print the handouts with 6 slides per page.
   Corel Presentations: Print audience notes with 4 slides per page.
2. **PowerPoint:** Print the notes page for slide 3.
   Corel Presentations: Print the notes page for slide 3, specifying 4 slides per page.
3. Close the presentation and exit the presentation application.

Illustration A. Completed Closing Slides

AppleWorks

PowerPoint 98 for the Macintosh

PowerPoint 2000

Corel Presentations

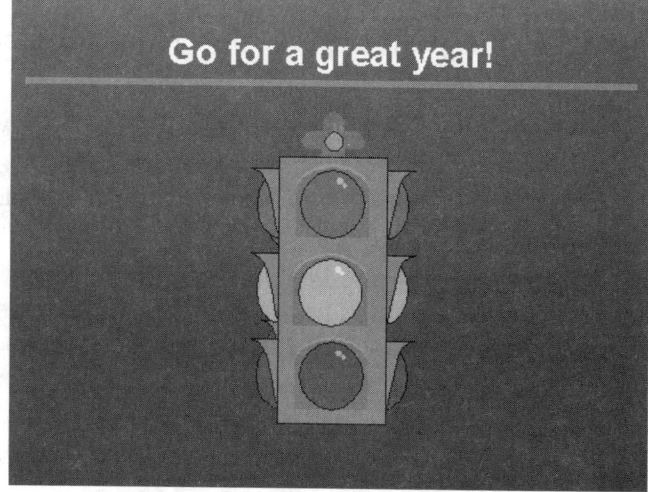

Create a Slide Show

**■ About Slide Shows ■ Create and Run an AppleWorks Slide Show
■ Create Slide Transitions ■ Add Animation Effects**

NOTES

About Slide Shows

- Presentation applications allow you to build a slide show that you can run on your computer or on a projection system. Except for AppleWorks, the options include:

  - **Transitions** from slide to slide to vary the way a slide is displayed when you run the slide show.

  - A number of **animation effects** for controlling when and how slide elements appear.

  - **Sound** to call attention to slides or slide elements.

- **AppleWorks** lets you display the slides in a show, but you have few choices about how the slide show runs.

- **PowerPoint** lets you animate slide titles, subtitles, bulleted lists, and graphics. You can add sound to play with the slide transition or with the appearance of any slide object.

- **Corel Presentations** lets you animate bulleted lists and graphic objects. You cannot animate titles or subtitles. In addition, you can specify sounds only for slide transitions, not for the appearance of a bulleted list or graphic.

- This exercise deals with AppleWorks options first. If you are using PowerPoint or Corel Presentations, go to "Create Slide Transitions" on page 335.

Create and Run an AppleWorks Slide Show

- AppleWorks lets you control the way the entire slide appears when you run a slide show.

💻 Try It!

Specify and Store Slide Show Options

1. Open ⌨️**Wright3**, or open 💿**04Wright3** from the data files.

2. Save the presentation as **Wright4**.

3. Click **Window**.

4. Choose **Slide Show**.

   AppleWorks displays the Slide Show dialog box.

5. For the slide shows in this exercise, set the options as shown in the illustration on the following page. For explanations of the other options, see the procedures.

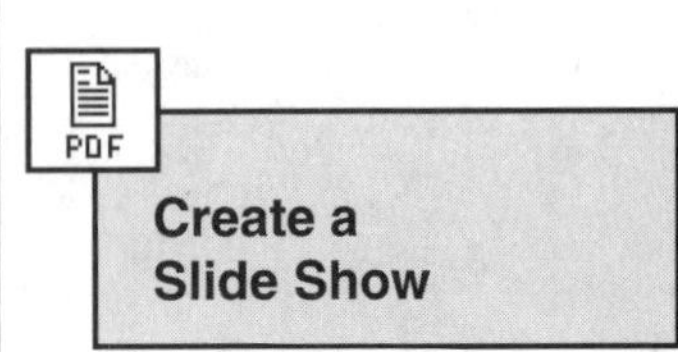

6. For **Background**, leave the defaults.

7. For **Border**, click the left button, and select a light blue to complement the slide background.

8. Click **Done** to close the dialog box and save the specifications.

9. Save the presentation.

AppleWorks Slide Show Dialog Box

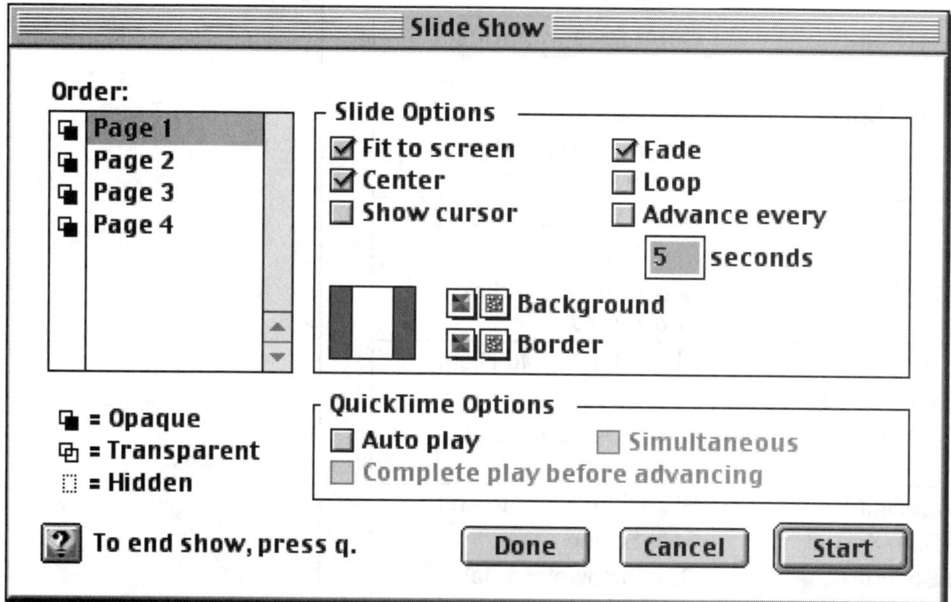

Try It!

Run the Slide Show

1. Review the slide show to be sure that no text is selected. If text is selected, it appears selected during the show.

2. Click **Window**.

3. Choose **Slide Show**.

   AppleWorks displays the Slide Show dialog box.

4. Click **Start** to start the show.

5. To move from slide to slide, click the mouse button, press **Tab**, or press **Return**.

6. Press **Q** to stop the show.

7. Close the presentation and exit AppleWorks unless you are continuing with the Exercise Directions.

Create Slide Transitions

- Slide transitions let you determine the way in which a slide first appears when you run a slide show. You can make a slide seem to grow or shrink to fit the screen, be revealed as if from behind blinds, be uncovered one direction or another, or in a variety of other ways.

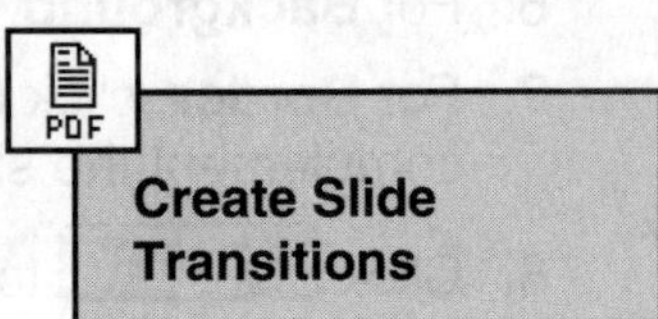

Try It!

1. Open **Wright3**, or open **04Wright3** from the data files.
2. Save the presentation as **Wright4**.
3. Display the presentation in Slide Sorter view.
4. Specify the transitions listed in the following table for the slides.
5. Save the presentation.

Slide	PowerPoint	Corel Presentations
1 (title)	Cover Down Medium Speed No Sound	Slide Out, Top to Bottom Fast Speed **C:\windows\media\chimes.wav**
2 (Our Experience)	Cover Up Medium Speed No Sound	Slide Out, Bottom to Top Fast Speed **C:\windows\media\chord.wav**
3 (We Offer)	Cover Left Medium Speed No Sound	Slide Out, Left to Right Fast Speed **C:\windows\media\ding.wav**
4 (closing)	Cover Right Medium Speed No Sound	Slide Out, Right to Left Fast Speed **C:\windows\media\notify.wav**

Add Animation Effects

- Animation effects control how individual elements on a slide appear during a slide show. You can add sound effects to draw attention to the element when it appears. If your computer is not equipped for sound, you will not be able to hear the sound effects.

- To specify animation effects involves two major procedures:

  - Select the slide objects to be animated, the order in which they will appear, and what action will cause them to appear.

  - Specify the visual and sound effects for the appearance of each object.

Try It!

1. In the tables on the following pages, locate the specifications for your application.
2. Add the animation and sound effects outlined in the table, specifying that all animation effects start on a mouse click.

   The elements are listed in the order they should appear on the slide.

3. Save the presentation after animating a slide.
4. Run the slide show to review the slide transitions and animation effects.
5. Change any transition or animation effect that is incorrect.

6. Save and close the presentation, and exit the presentation application unless you are continuing with the Exercise Directions.

PowerPoint 98

Slide	Element	Animation	Sound
1	1) Title 1	Fly From Top	Chimes
	2) Text 2	Fly From Bottom	Chimes
2	1) Title 1	Fly From Left	Camera
	2) Text 2	Fly From Left Grouped by 2nd Level Paragraphs After Animation, second color button from right	(No Sound)
3	1) Object 3	Peek From Top	Laser
	2) Title 1	Fly From Right	Cash Register
	3) Text 2	Fly From Bottom-Left Grouped by 1st Level Paragraphs After Animation, second color button from right	(No Sound)
4	1) Title 1	Fly From Bottom	Applause
	2) Picture frame 2	Dissolve	(No Sound)

PowerPoint 97 & 2000

Slide	Element	Animation	Sound
1	1) Title 1	Fly From Left	Slide Projector
	2) Text 2	Fly From Right	Chime
2	1) Title 1	Fly From Top-Right	Camera
	2) Text 2	Fly From Left Grouped by 2nd Level Paragraphs After Animation, second color button from right	(No Sound)
3	1) Object 3	Stretch From Bottom	Laser
	2) Title 1	Spiral	Cash Register
	3) Text 2	Peek From Top Grouped by 1st Level Paragraphs After Animation, second color button from right	(No Sound)
4	1) Title 1	Random Bars Horizontal	Clapping
	2) Picture frame 2	Blinds Horizontal	(No Sound)

Corel Presentations

Slide	Element	Animation
2	Bulleted List	Slide In, Left to Right One item at a time Highlight current bullet
3	Graphic	Fly In Top to Bottom Change Display Sequence to show animated objects before bulleted list
	Bulleted List	Fly In Bottom to Top One item at a time Highlight current bullet
4	Graphic	Curve In Right and Down

In this exercise, you will add transition, entry, and sound effects to the Arthur Treacher Middle School presentation. You will choose the effects and sounds you want.

EXERCISE DIRECTIONS

Open the Presentation

1. Open **Treacher3**, or open **04Treacher3** from the data files.
2. Save the presentation as **Treacher4**.
3. For PowerPoint and Corel Presentations, go to "Specify Slide Transitions" on the next page.

Set Up AppleWorks Slide Show

1. Set up the slide show to run as specified in Illustration A.
2. For the Border color, choose a light green that complements the slide background.
3. Run the slide show.

Illustration A. AppleWorks Slide Show Options

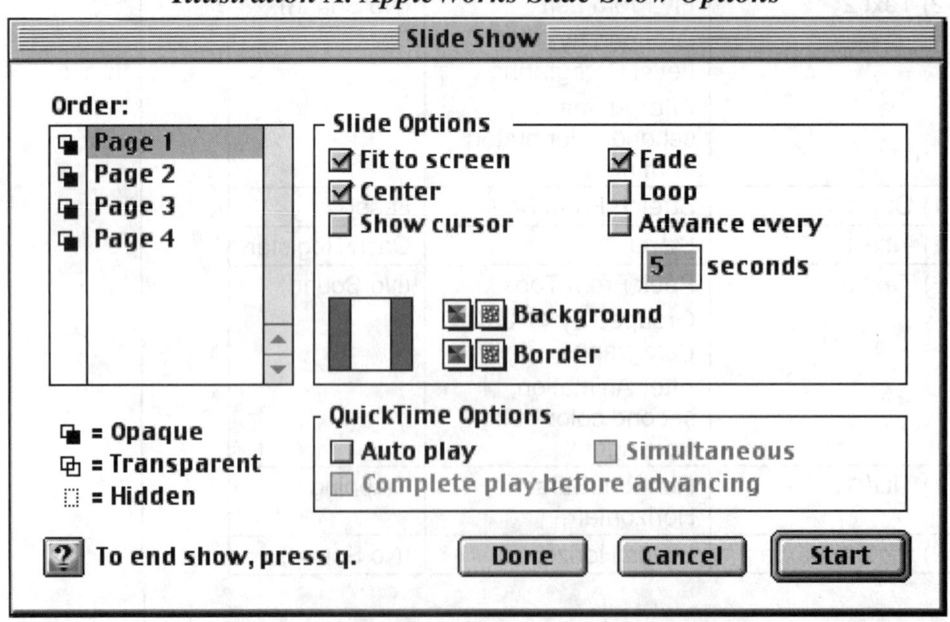

Specify Slide Transitions

1. Specify transitions for the slides as outlined in Illustration B.
2. Preview the slide transitions as often as necessary.

3. Save the presentation each time you finish specifying a transition.

Illustration B. Slide Transitions for Treacher4

Slide	PowerPoint	Corel Presentations*
1 (title)	Split Horizontal In Medium Speed Chimes, loop until next sound	Sweep, Left to Right Fast Speed **C:\windows\media\Musica Open.wav**
2 (Academic Excellence)	Split Horizontal Out77 Medium Speed Chimes, loop until next sound	Sweep, Right to Left Fast Speed **C:\windows\media\notify.wav**
3 (Activities Galore)	Split Vertical In Medium Speed Chimes, loop until next sound	Sweep, Bottom to Top Fast Speed **C:\windows\media\TADA.wav**
4 (closing)	Split Vertical Out Medium Speed Chimes, loop until next sound	Sweep, Top to Bottom Fast Speed **C:\windows\media\Utopia Asterisk.wav**

***If any suggested sound is unavailable, choose an appropriate sound.**

Specify Animation Effects

1. Specify the animation effects as outlined for your application in Illustration C.
2. Preview the animation effects as often as necessary.

3. Save the presentation each time you finish specifying an effect.
4. After specifying the effects, run the slide show.
5. Close the presentation and exit the presentation application.

Illustration C. Animation Effects Treacher4

PowerPoint 98, Treacher4

Slide	Element	Animation	Sound
1	1) Title 1	Fly From Top	Camera
	2) Text 2	Fly From Bottom	Camera
2	1) Title 1	Fly From Left	Cash Register
	2) Text 2	Fly From Right Grouped by 2nd Level Paragraphs After Animation, second color button from right	(No Sound)
3	1) Object 3	Stretch From Top	Slide Projector
	2) Title 1	Peek From Bottom	Whoosh
	3) Text 2	Stretch From Left Grouped by 1st Level Paragraphs After Animation, second color button from right	(No Sound)
4	1) Picture frame 2	Spiral	Clapping
	2) Title 1	Fly From Top-Right	(No Sound)

PowerPoint 97 & 2000, Treacher4

Slide	Element	Animation	Sound
1	1) Title 1	Fly From Top	Cash Register
	2) Text 2	Fly From Bottom	Whoosh
2	1) Title 1	Peek From Bottom	Camera
	2) Text 2	Peek From Top Grouped by 2nd Level Paragraphs After Animation, second color button from right	(No Sound)
3	1) Object 3	Stretch From Top	Laser
	2) Title 1	Dissolve	Cash Register
	3) Text 2	Peek From Left Grouped by 1st Level Paragraphs After Animation, second color button from right	(No Sound)
4	1) Picture frame 2	Spiral	Applause
	2) Title 1	Split Horizontal In	(No Sound)

Corel Presentations, Treacher4

Slide	Element	Animation
2	Bulleted List	Fly In, Right to Left Medium speed One item at a time Highlight current bullet
3	Graphic	Fly In From Corner, Left and Up Medium speed Display Sequence: Show animated objects before bulleted list
	Bulleted List	Fly In From Corner, Right and Down Medium speed One item at a time Highlight current bullet
4	Graphic	Curve In, Left and Up Medium speed

Lesson 8: Computer Communications

Exercise 1: Learn about File Server Local Area Networks

- Introduction to Computer Communications
- File Server Local Area Networks (LANs)
- File Server Network Components
- Network Use
- Structure of a File Server Network
- Explore a File Server Network

Exercise 2: Learn about Peer-to-Peer Networks

- Introduction to Peer-to-Peer Networks
- Explore a Peer-to-Peer Network on Windows
- Explore a Peer-to-Peer Network on Mac OS

Exercise 3: Learn about the Internet

- The Internet
- Internet Addresses—URLs (Uniform Resource Locators)
- Internet Use
- Introduction to Internet Explorer for Windows
- Introduction to Internet Explorer for Mac OS
- The World Wide Web
- Online Services
- Electronic Mail (E-mail)
- File Transfer Protocol (FTP)

Exercise 4: Learn about Other Communications Methods

- Wide Area Networks (WANs)
- Intranets
- Telecommuting
- PC-to-Mainframe Communications

Learn about File Server Local Area Networks

■ Introduction to Computer Communications ■ File Server Local Area Networks (LANs)
■ File Server Network Components ■ Network Use
■ Structure of a File Server Network ■ Explore a File Server Network

NOTES

Introduction to Computer Communications

■ All computers communicate. The CPU talks to the hard drive controller; the video card communicates with the monitor and the CPU. The printer and the CPU talk to each other. Each element uses a **communications protocol**—a set of send and receive signals following rules that have been agreed upon by computer manufacturers or established by governmental or professional organizations.

■ For example, when you print a document, the program in the computer that handles printing sends a signal to the printer that asks whether it is ready to receive data. The printer normally signals that it is ready. When its print **buffer** is full, the printer signals the computer that it cannot receive more data. The computer waits, periodically asking if the printer is ready for more, until the printer signals its readiness.

■ But when people talk of computer communications, they usually mean the ability of one computer to talk with other computers. When personal computers became common in businesses, users began to look for ways to make it possible for personal computers to share data and programs with one another.

■ The first solution was **sneaker net**. Users copied files from one computer and carried them to another. That method, however useful, had limits. If the receiving computer was across town, it took a while for the communication to be completed. In addition, businesses have large amounts of data residing under the control of their mainframe computers, but the personal computers on desktops at first couldn't make use of that data. Communication was a problem that needed to be solved.

■ Today, PC users can share data and programs over networks; they can use the facilities of the company's mainframe computers using terminal emulation software and hardware. They can communicate with colleagues in remote locations through networks, electronic mail, and the Internet and World Wide Web.

■ If you use a personal computer in a reasonably large organization— school, university, or company—you probably work on a Local Area Network or LAN. Your computer can work **locally**, using the programs and drives that are installed on it. Your computer, however, is also a **workstation**, a machine that can use the drives, folders, files, and programs on the network. LANs generally operate in one of two configurations:

Buffer
A temporary storage area that holds data until it is used.

Sneaker net
Because so many computer users dress casually, wearing sneakers rather than dress shoes, the method of walking with diskettes from one computer to another became known as sneaker net.

- **File server**, in which a central computer or group of computers controls access to the network's facilities. File server networks are described in this exercise.

- **Peer-to-peer**, in which users share the resources of their local machines with one another. Peer-to-peer networks are described in the next exercise.

File Server Local Area Networks (LANs)

- On **file server** networks, one or more computers act as the central filing system for the **clients** on the network. Data and programs that are to be shared reside on the disk drives controlled by the network programs.

- File server LANs usually involve users in the same building or group of neighboring buildings that can be connected directly by cables.

File Server Network Components

- File server networks include the following elements:

    - The **server** provides files or services to other computers. The server has hard drives and programs that let it communicate with other computers and provide services to them.

    - **Client workstations** are computers that request files or services from servers. Most modern networks can mix computers of different types and capabilities, including Apple machines running Mac OS, PCs running Windows or DOS, and computers running the Unix or Linux operating systems. In a peer-to-peer network, each computer operates as a client when it requests services from other computers and as a server when it provides services to other computers. (See Exercise 2.)

    - **Printers** may be shared across the network. Each shared printer is identified by a name. When users want to print, they choose a printer through the application they are using. Other peripherals, such as scanners or plotters, are managed in the same way as printers.

    - **Network cards** convert binary data from the computer into signals that can be transmitted over cables to and from other computers. Each workstation requires a network card in one of its bus slots. Network cards are specific to the type of network to which the workstation is connected.

    - **Cables** connect computers to one another and to the server.

        - **Coaxial** cable is similar to the cable used for most cable television systems. It consists of two conductors—a central wire and an outer woven wire—wrapped in outer insulation and separated by an inner layer of insulation. For some years, coaxial cable was the most common type of network cabling. Coaxial cables connect to computers and network outlets in the same way that a television connects to a VCR. The end of the cable has a cap that screws on to the outlet and secures the conductor in the center of the outlet.

        - **Twin twisted pair**, similar to telephone wires, consists of pairs of wires twisted together. The twisting improves resistance to interference. In the past few years, this method of cabling has overtaken coaxial cable as the most common for new network

Client
A client is a workstation that is actively using the network's facilities.

installations. Connections are made with snap-in connectors that are usually slightly larger than normal telephone connections to prevent confusing the two.

  ♦ **Fiber optic cable**, which uses light to communicate, consists of a glass filament encased in a plastic coating. The light travels along the filament and reflects off the coating.

- When network wiring stretches over long distances, a series of **hubs** may be used to strengthen signals transmitted along the cables. The distance from one hub to another depends on the cable type; fiber optic cables allow the longest runs without a hub to boost the signal.

Network Use

- When you turn on a computer attached to a network, the computer boots up, but before you can start using it, you are requested for a **login name** or **username** and **password**. The login name (also called **user ID**) identifies you to the network and the password ensures that only an authorized person can use the name. If you do not have a valid login name or you don't remember your password, you are not allowed to use the network.

- If you cancel the login process, you can use the machine as a stand-alone computer, but some drives, programs, data files, and printers may be unavailable.

  ✓ *All the illustrations in this section are drawn from DDC's Novell file server network. The objects on your network will have different names.*

Windows Login Screen for Novell Network

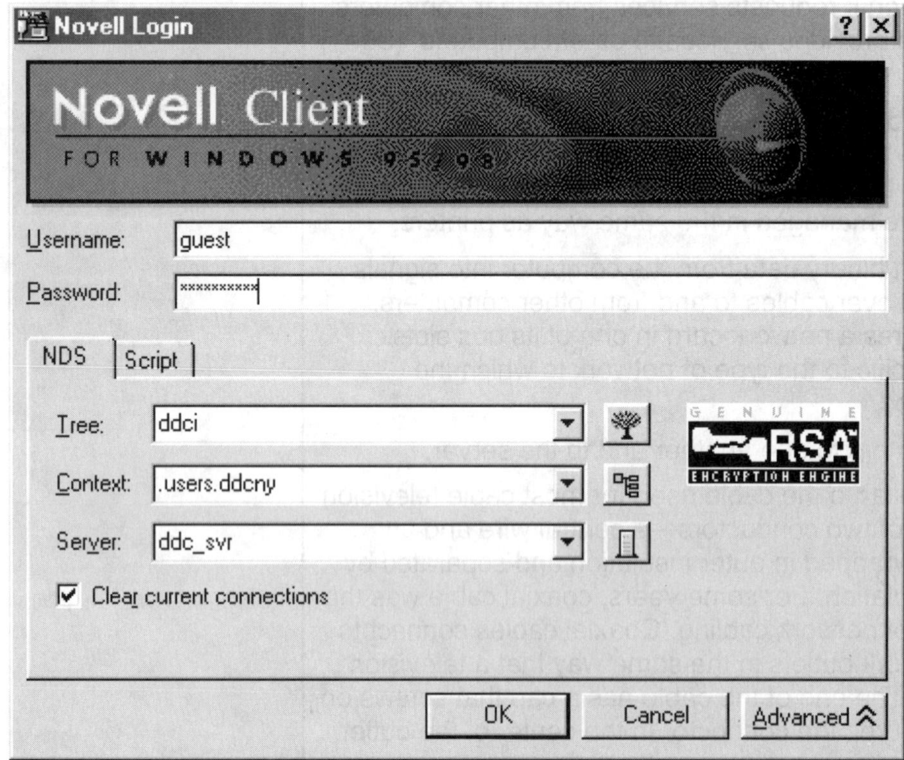

MacOS Login Screen for Novell Network

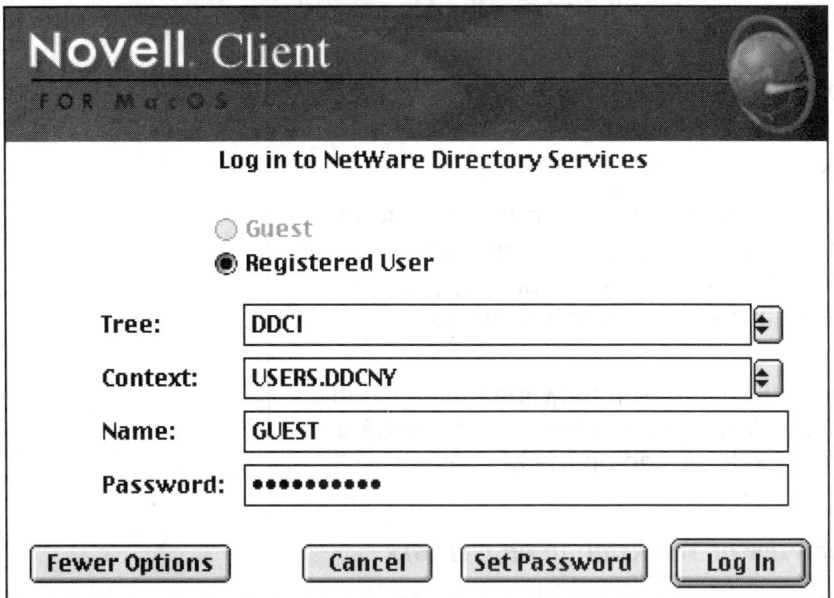

Log in, sign on, or log on?
Some networks call the process of connecting and identifying users as a **login procedure;** you log in to the network. Others use the term **sign on** to mean the same thing; still others use **log on** and you have a **logon name** or **ID**. All these terms mean the same thing: identify yourself and provide the password to determine what drives, folders, files, and programs you can use.

- The **login name** is a string of characters assigned by network administration that identifies you as a network user. The rights to use network folders and files are associated with the login name.

- On LANs your access is usually restricted to certain drives, folders, and files. On a file server network, maintaining access rights is the job of the **network administrator**. The network administrator assigns login IDs, defines and maintains access rights, ensures that backups are performed regularly, and works to keep the network operating smoothly.

Structure of a File Server Network

- A Novell file server network has a hierarchical structure:

Sample Tree in Windows

Tree in Mac OS
The tree shown in the illustration is also reflected on the Mac. The Windows view is shown because it shows the hierarchical structure.

- **Tree.** A network may have several trees. In the preceding illustration, Ddci is the tree.

- **Organization.** A tree may have several organizations. In the sample tree illustration, DDCNY is the organization.

- **Organization unit.** An organization may have several organization units. In the sample tree illustration, USERS is the organization unit.

- **Server.** An organization unit may have several servers. Server names usually represent disk drives under the server's control.

- **Volume.** A volume is a name given to a disk drive or a portion of a disk drive. In Windows, drive identifiers (letters) are **mapped** (assigned) to a volume or portion of a volume. These drive letters appear in Windows Explorer just like local drives. On the Macintosh, a volume to which you have access appears on the desktop.

- **Folder.** A container for files on a volume.

Explore a File Server Network

- Once the LAN accepts your user ID and password (the technical term is **authenticates**), the login program runs a script that defines your access to network facilities in detail. When the script has completed, you can begin using the drives and other network components that you are authorized to use.

- In Windows, you can use Windows Explorer to review the drives to which your workstation has access. The following illustration shows the LAN drives as they appear in Windows Explorer and on the Macintosh desktop.

Sample Windows Explorer View of Workstation on Network

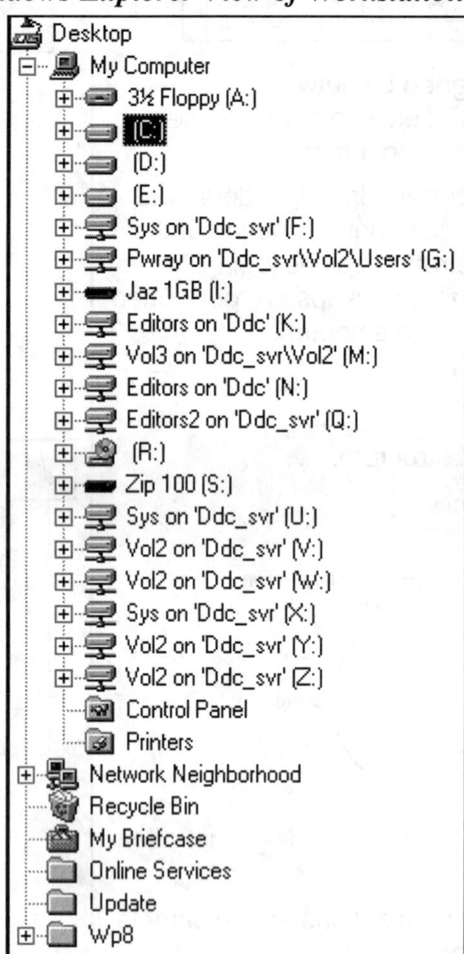

- In the preceding illustration, drives F:, G:, K:, M:, N:, and Q:, and U: through Z: are network drives. The drive identifier includes the name of the volume to which the drive is mapped (assigned). Thus, drives K: and N: are mapped to the same volume—Editors. Similarly, drives V:, W:, Y:, and Z: are mapped to volume Vol2.

- In Mac OS, the features—such as drives and printers—appear as icons or windows on the desktop. The Mac OS illustration that follows shows the volumes (drives) and network printers to which the user has access.

Sample Mac OS Desktop of Workstation on Network

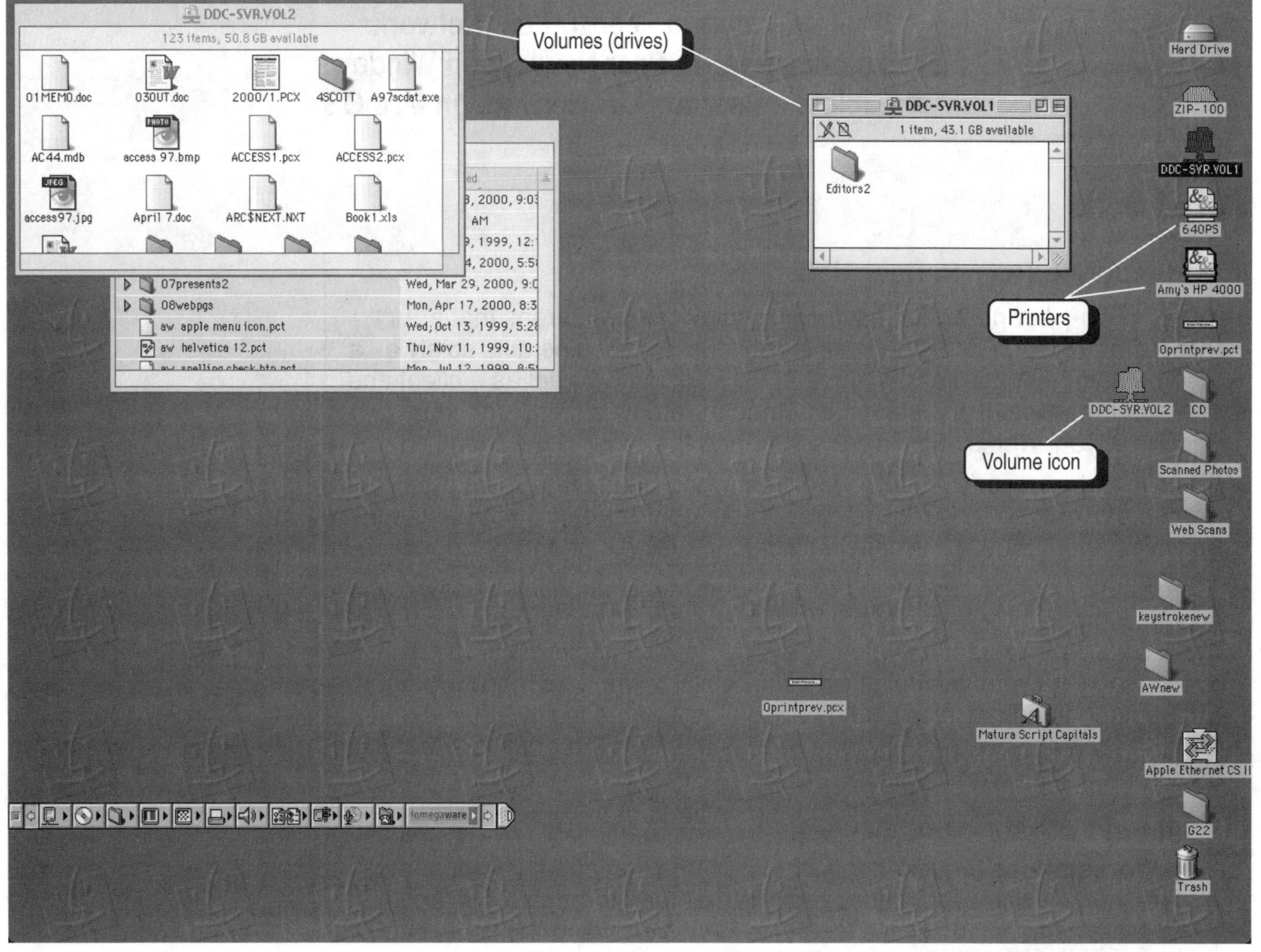

Exercise 2

Learn about Peer-to-Peer Networks
■ Introduction to Peer-to-Peer Networks
■ Explore a Peer-to-Peer Network on Windows
■ Explore a Peer-to-Peer Network on Mac OS

NOTES

Introduction to Peer-to-Peer Networks

■ On **peer-to-peer** networks, each workstation has disk areas that are accessible to other users. In such a network, no machine acts solely as a server. If you want a file from another workstation, you act as a client and the other machine is the server; if someone retrieves files from your machine, your workstation is the server and the other is the client.

■ Peer-to-peer networks usually work best when only a few users are involved. Because they require direct cable connection from workstation to workstation, they are usually restricted to a single geographic location.

■ Combinations of file server and peer-to-peer networks often exist within a single company. Several users who are working on the same project may work on a peer-to-peer network. They may need, for example, to retain close working-group control of specific files. But when members of the group need to communicate with or use files that belong to the organization as a whole, they may access the file server network that everyone in the company uses.

Peer-to-Peer Network Components

• **Workstations** are independent computers that can share data and resources with each other directly rather than through a server. Users can control access to the resources on their machines, even if, in practice, much of the administration of the network is handled by one user.

• **Printers** are shared across the network. Each printer is identified by a name. When users want to print, they choose a printer through the application they are using. Other peripherals are managed in the same way as printers.

• **Network cards** are specific to the type of peer-to-peer network being used. They convert binary data from the computer into signals that can be transmitted over cables to and from other computers.

• **Cables** connect computers to one another.

■ The remainder of this exercise is divided into two parts. The first part, which begins on the next page, discusses a Windows peer-to-peer network. The second, which begins on page 353, deals with a Mac OS peer-to-peer network.

Explore a Peer-to-Peer Network on Windows

- You can explore a peer-to-peer network on Windows through Windows Explorer. The illustration that follows shows a five-workstation, peer-to-peer network displayed in Windows Explorer.

Five-Workstation, Peer-to-Peer Network on Windows

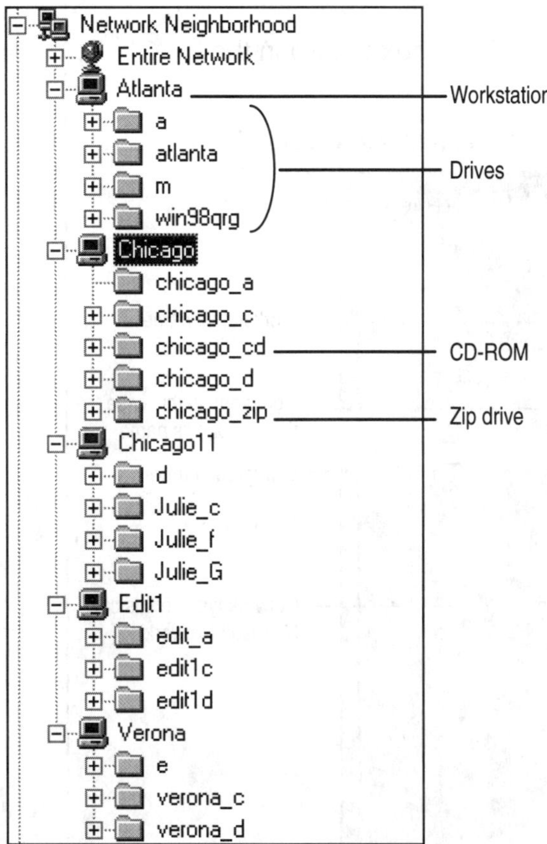

- Any drive on a machine can be shared. Note, for example, the Chicago workstation can give other users access to its CD-ROM and a Zip drive that provides additional storage on 100 Mbyte, removable disks.

- When you right-click on one of the workstations or drives, a shortcut menu appears, as shown in the illustration that follows. (For the **Sharing** option, see later in this exercise on page 351.)

Windows Peer-to-Peer Workstation Shortcut Menu

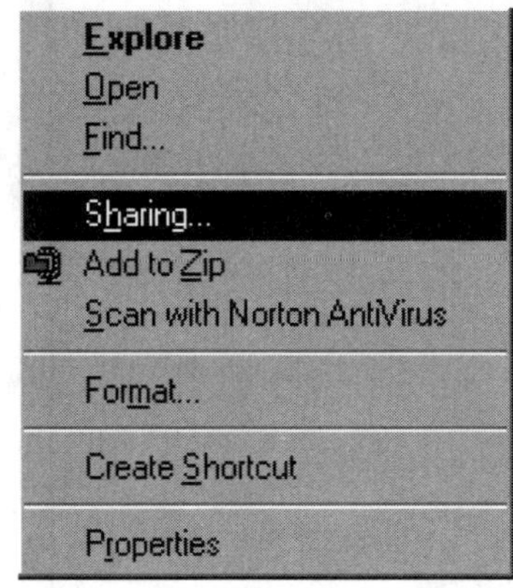

🖥 Try It!

View Workstation's Properties

1. Open the Network Neighborhood window.
2. Right-click the icon of a workstation.
3. Click **P**roperties (⬛).
4. Click the General tab to display the dialog box shown in the illustration that follows.

Windows Peer-to-Peer Workstation Properties, General Tab

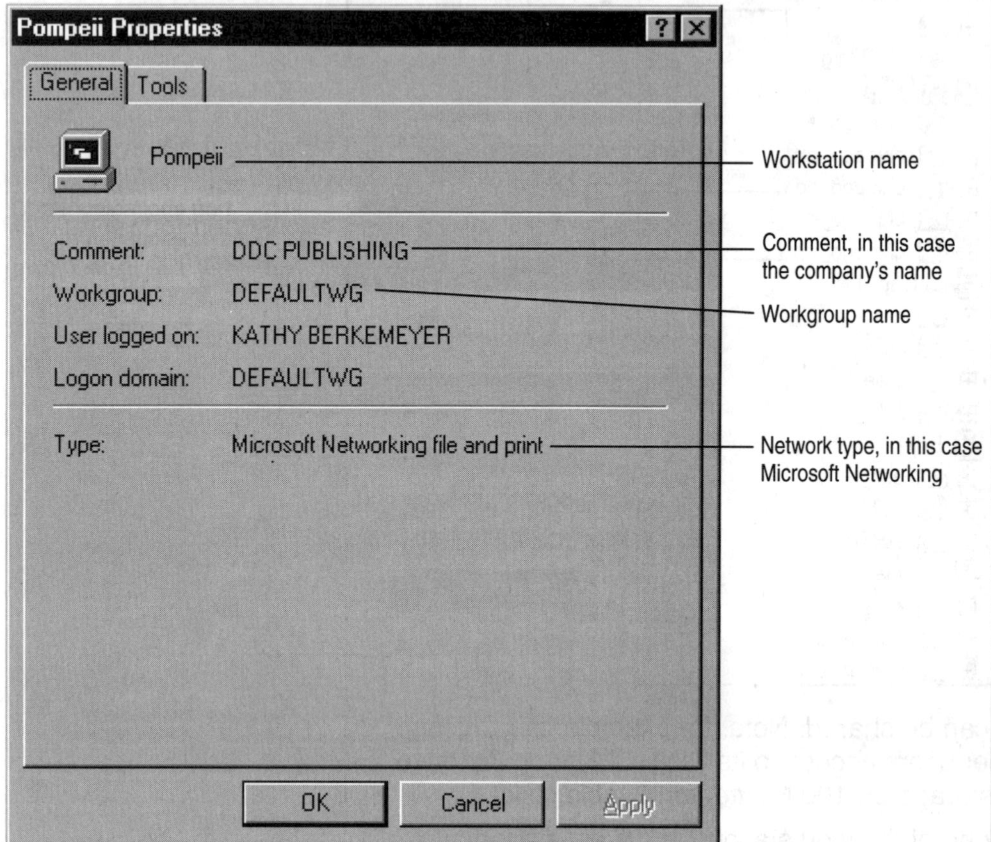

- The Tools tab of the workstation Properties dialog box offers options that let the workstation user control access to it, as shown in the illustration on the following page.

Windows Peer-to-Peer Workstation Properties, Tools Tab

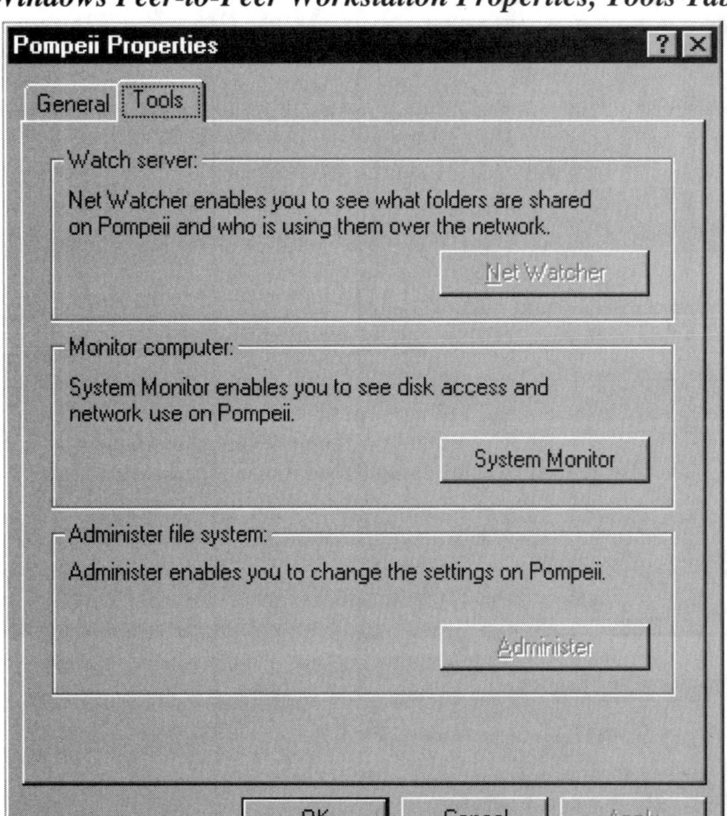

Sharing Windows Workstation Resources

Workstation **resources** include drives, folders, files, printers, scanners, and other peripherals. Access to these resources is managed through the **Sharing** option on the shortcut menu or the **Administer** button on the Tools tab of the Properties dialog box.

When you click the **Sharing** option or the **Administer** button, the Properties dialog box Sharing tab appears, as shown in the illustration on the next page.

✓ *Note that the Sharing tab appears on the Properties dialog box only when you activate the Sharing option or Administer button. It does not appear when you select Properties from the shortcut menu.*

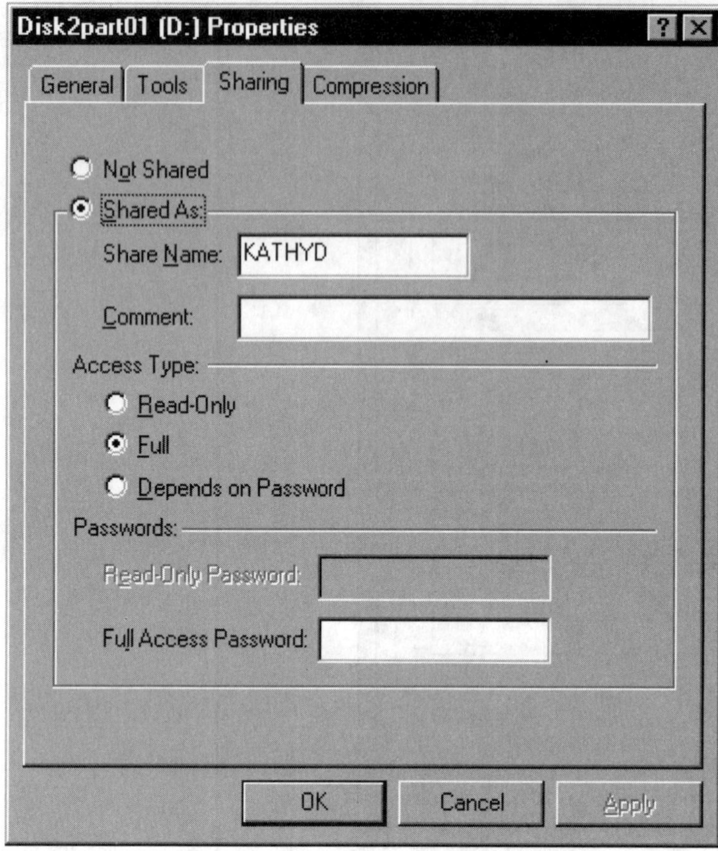

- You can set the workstation to **N<u>o</u>t Shared** (Alt+O) or **<u>S</u>hared As** (Alt+S). If it is shared, you enter a name to identify the drive and a comment to further identify the resource.

- In the Access Type section, you can authorize:

  - **<u>R</u>ead-Only** (Alt+R) access, which allows other users to retrieve files but not to save to the workstation or drive.

  - **<u>F</u>ull** (Alt+F) access, which allows other users to retrieve files, save files, and manage folders.

  - **<u>D</u>epends on Password** (Alt+D), which gives other users read-only or full access depending on the password they enter.

- In the Passwords section, you can specify a password for **R<u>e</u>ad-Only** (Alt+E) or **Fu<u>l</u>l Access** (Alt+L).

Explore a Peer-to-Peer Network on Mac OS

- Macintosh computers have a built-in capability to create and operate in a peer-to-peer network. The software is already installed in the machines; no further software is necessary for a small network, and you can control who is allowed to share the resources of your machine. Setting up a Mac OS peer-to-peer network involves:

  - Cabling the machines. (This section does not cover how to connect machines.)

  - Starting File Sharing.

  - Defining users and groups.

  - Specifying which resources are shared.

  - Choosing the resources to be used.

Start/Stop File Sharing

1. Click the **Apple** menu.

2. Choose **Control Panels**.

3. Choose **File Sharing**.

   The system displays the File Sharing dialog box, as shown in the following illustration.

Mac OS File Sharing Dialog Box, Start/Stop Tab

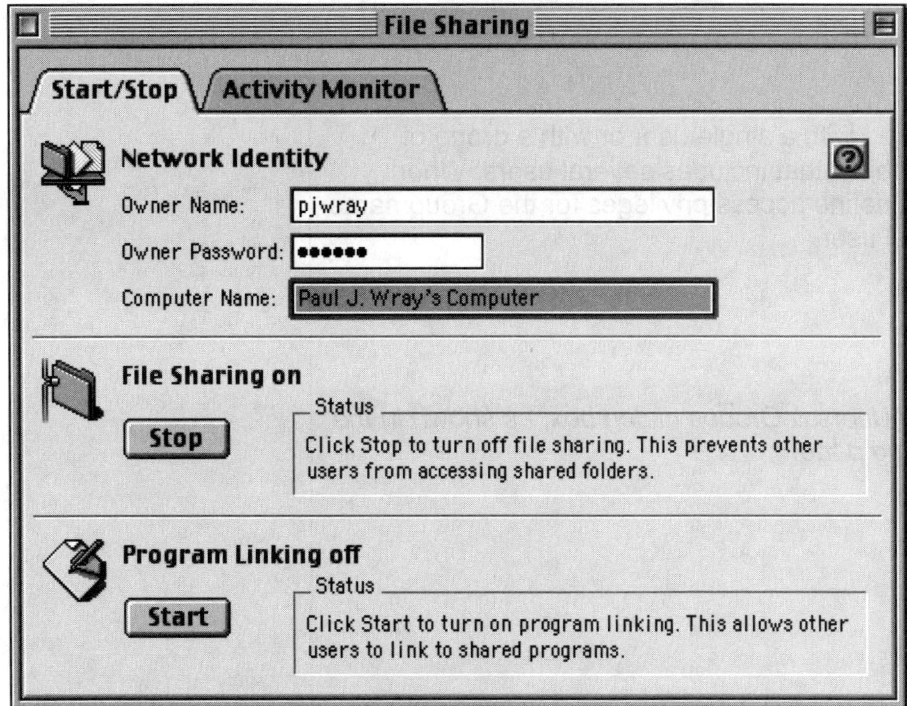

4. If File Sharing is off, click **Start**.

   After a short time, the Stop button appears, and file sharing is ready to use.

   Note that this dialog box includes an option for Program Linking. Sharing programs between computers slows down the network so program linking is generally inadvisable. In addition, any linked program must be designed and licensed for network use.

AppleTalk and LocalTalk

AppleTalk and its replacement, LocalTalk, support either a File server or peer-to-peer network. Because the file sharing protocol is part of Mac OS and is easy to install, anyone with more than one Macintosh machine can easily set up a peer-to-peer network.

For a full description of how to create such a network, see Sharon Zardetto Aker, *The Macintosh Bible*, 7th Edition, Berkeley, CA: Peachpit Press, 1998, pp. 909-926.

Reminder
To close a dialog box, click the close box.

View Network Activity

- Click the Activity Monitor tab of the File Sharing dialog box.

Mac OS File Sharing Dialog Box, Activity Monitor Tab

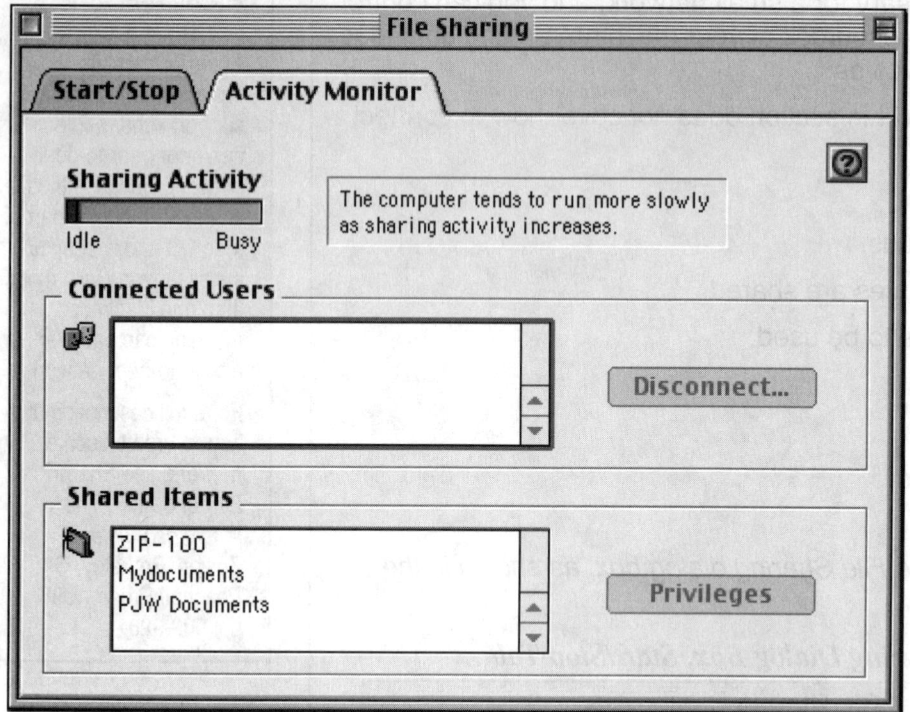

View Users & Groups

Folders and files can be shared with a single user or with a group of users. A **Group** is a named object that includes several users. When defining file sharing, you can define access privileges for the Group name rather than for each individual user.

1. Click the **Apple** menu.
2. Choose **Control Panels**.
3. Choose **Users & Groups**.

   The system displays the Users & Groups dialog box, as shown in the illustration on the following page.

Mac OS File Users & Groups

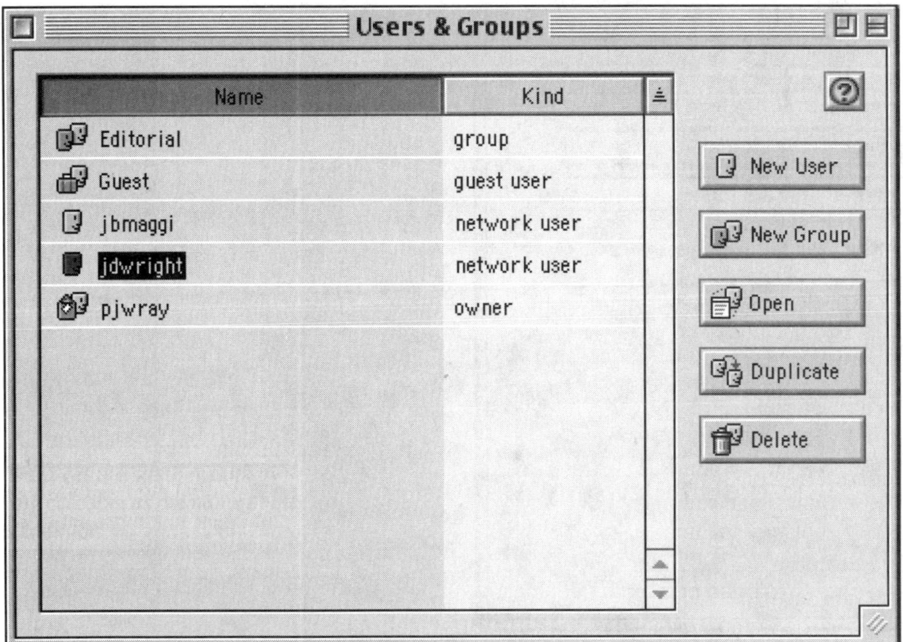

4. To view the members of a group, double-click the group name.

    To add a new group, click New Group.

Mac OS Group Definition Dialog Box

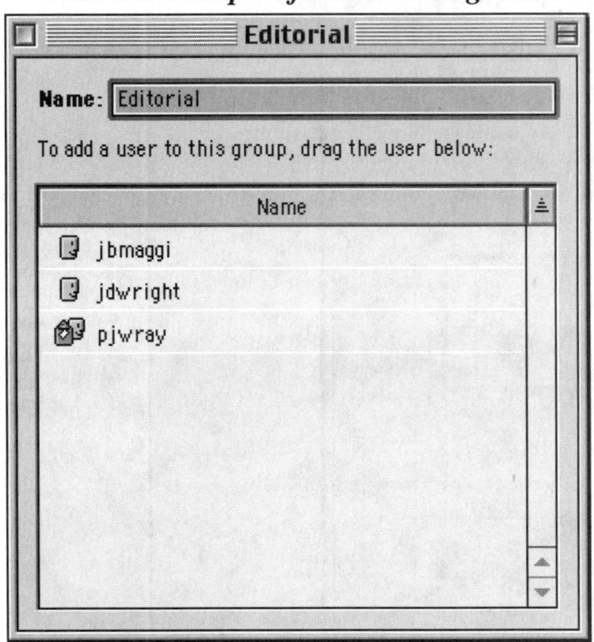

5. To view information about a user, double-click the user's name.

    To add a new user, click New User.

    The system displays a dialog box like the one on the following page. You can edit the user's information.

Mac OS User Identity Dialog Box

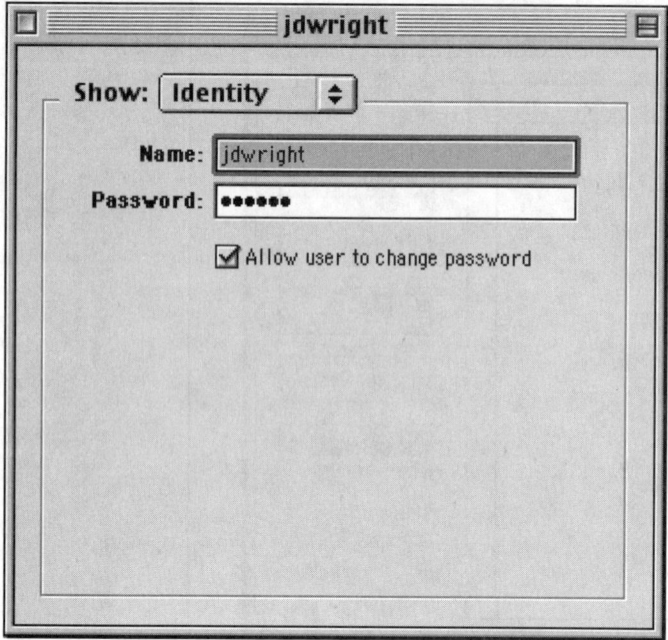

6. To view the sharing information for the user or group, click the arrows next to Identity and choose Sharing.

Mac OS User Sharing Dialog Box

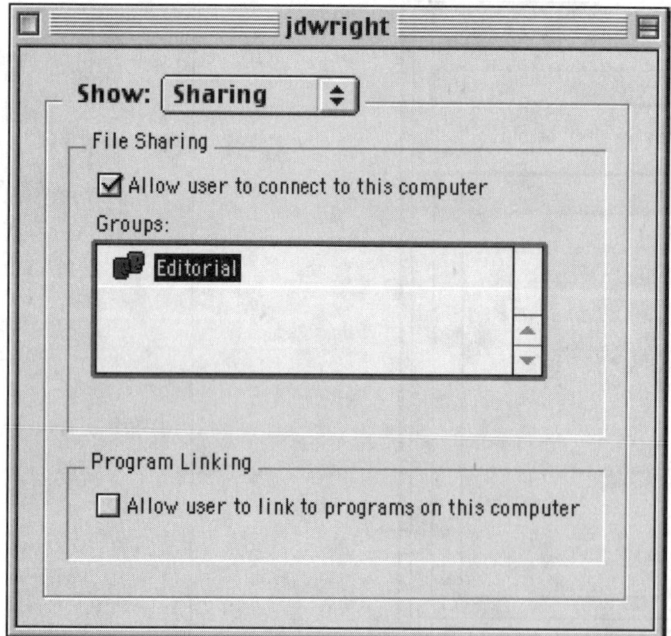

Share Mac OS Workstation Resources

Workstation **resources** include drives, folders, files, printers, scanners, and other peripherals. Access to these resources is managed through the Finder menu. Once File Sharing has started and some users have been defined, you can define the objects on your computer that are to be shared.

1. Open the drive or folder to be shared.

2. Click **File** on the Finder menu.

3. Choose **Get Info**.

4. Choose **Sharing**.

   The system displays a dialog box similar to the one in the following illustration, which indicates who can share the object.

Mac OS File Sharing Dialog Box

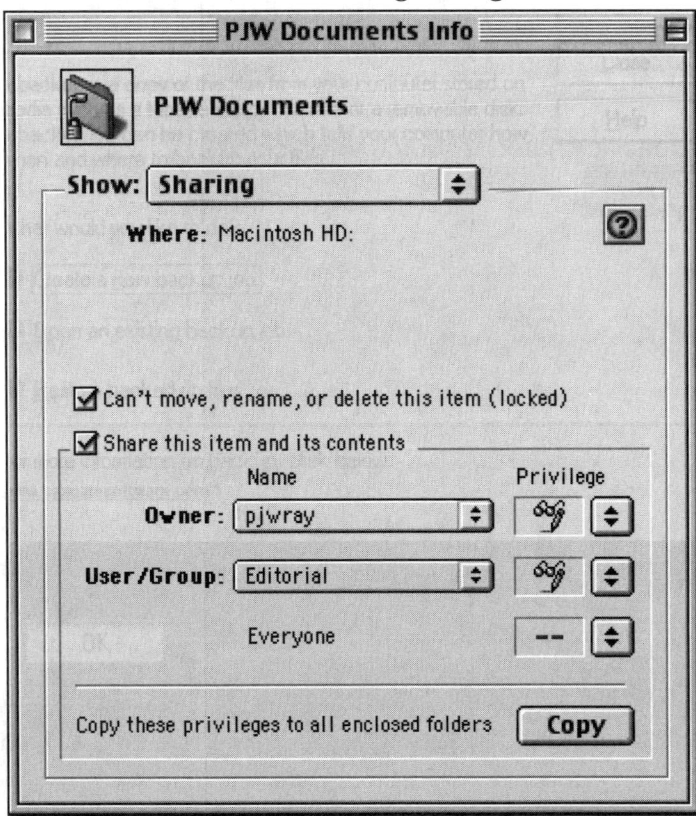

The options on the dialog box are described below.

Option	Effect
Can't move, rename, or delete this item (locked).	Prevents users from moving, renaming, or deleting the resource.
Share this item and its contents.	Permits resource to be shared.
Owner	Defines who controls the resource.
User/Group	To permit use by a single user.
Privilege	**Read & Write**. Permits user to retrieve and save files to this resource (normal use). **Read only**. Permits user to retrieve but not save files to this resource. **Write only (Drop box)**. Users can save files to the resource but cannot retrieve them from it. **None**. User cannot use the resource.
Everyone	This option can be used to define rights for any user on the network. You may wish, for example, for all network users to have Read only privileges for the resource.

Gain Access to Other Shared Resources

1. Click the **Apple** menu.
2. Select **Chooser**.
3. Click the **AppleShare** icon in the left pane.
4. In the right pane, click the computer to which you want to connect.
5. Click [OK].
6. In the next dialog box, enter your user name and password, and click [OK].
7. In the next dialog box, select the specific shared resource to which you want to connect, and click [OK].

NEXT EXERCISE

Exercise 3

Learn about the Internet

■ **The Internet** ■ **Internet Addresses—URLs (Uniform Resource Locators)** ■ **Internet Use**
■ **Introduction to Internet Explorer** ■ **The World Wide Web** ■ **Online Services**
■ **Electronic Mail (E-mail)** ■ **File Transfer Protocol (FTP)**

NOTES

The Internet

■ The Internet is a network of computers. It combines client-server and peer-to-peer networking to make it possible for computer users all over the globe to share the network's facilities and to communicate with other users.

■ The Internet resulted from the desire to have computers talk to one another so that users could share information, data, and ideas. It originated as a way for researchers, especially in defense industries and universities, to share information. With the introduction of the World Wide Web in 1989, businesses, schools, governments, and non-profit organizations realized that it would be a valuable tool to communicate with customers and clients and to provide information and services.

■ Now nearly every television and radio commercial and newspaper and magazine ad gives an address where the company or organization can be contacted on the Internet.

■ The Internet is a large number of computers linked by a variety of connections—cables, telephone lines, satellites. They pass information back and forth using the communications protocol called **TCP/IP** (Transmission Control Protocol/Internet Protocol). TCP/IP is actually a suite of protocols that work together to make the Internet work. TCP/IP performs the following communications functions:

- Permits login from remote computers.
- Routes data between Internet servers.
- Makes sure that data packets are error-free and assembled in the right sequence.
- Converts text-based domain names into numerical IP (Internet Protocol) addresses.

■ The computers that form the Internet can be divided into the following groups:

- **Clients** are computers that connect to the Internet to do research and send e-mail. Most personal computers that access the Internet are in this category. Client computers access the Internet in one of three ways:
  - Online service, such as America Online (AOL) or Prodigy.
  - Internet Service Provider.
  - Direct access through a dedicated communications line (telephone or cable television) that is continuously connected to the Internet.

- **Online services** provide a variety of shopping, research, and e-mail services and also provide access to the Internet. America Online (AOL), Prodigy, and CompuServe are the most well-known of these services. Such services are not actually part of the Internet, but most users do not distinguish between AOL and the Internet.

- **Internet Service Providers (ISPs)** are computers that provide other computers with access to the Internet. Networks such as Earthlink, NetCom, and AT&T Worldnet are ISPs.

- **Internet servers** (sometimes called hosts) are computers that provide access to information. When an Internet user contacts an Internet site, the computer that contains the site is a server. Internet servers may also act as clients when they request a link to another site. Some servers offer specialized services, such as e-mail and file transfer.

  - **Search engines or sites** are Internet computers dedicated to providing information about other Internet sites. Yahoo!, excite, and Lycos started life as search engines but now have expanded to offer a wide range of services in addition to search capabilities.
  - **E-mail servers** are computers that provide electronic mail boxes and service.
  - **File transfer protocol (FTP) servers** are computers dedicated to allowing the transfer of files from one computer to another.

Internet Addresses—URLs (Uniform Resource Locators)

- Because the Internet is not a single network but a collection of networks, a naming system called the **domain** name system is used to identify the exact location of Internet servers and their primary Internet activity. It is something like the telephone numbering system that includes country codes, area codes, and individual phone numbers.

- An Internet address (IP address) is made up of a four-part series of numbers. The domain name system translates the numbers into a user-friendly system of text-based names. So instead of typing in 128.337.392.449 to order a pizza over the Internet, you can type in "www.pizzahut.com." Text is easier to remember.

- To locate an Internet site, you enter an address, called a **URL (uniform resource locator)**. Usually this address is a group of characters that looks like the following:

      http://www.ddcpub.com

  - **http** stands for HyperText Transfer Protocol, the communications protocol used by sites on the World Wide Web.

  - **www** stands for World Wide Web, the largest part of the Internet.

  - **ddcpub** is the name used to identify the organization who is responsible for the content of the site. It is usually some form of the name of the company or organization, for example, ddcpub is the identifier for DDC Publishing, Inc.

  - **com** is the **domain** identifier. Different types of organizations have different domain names.

- Common Internet domains include the following:

Domain:	Used By:
.com	commercial/business
.gov	government
.edu	educational
.org	various organizations, usually non-profit
.mil	military
.net	network resources

- In addition, many domain names include an abbreviation of the country where the site is located; for example, *uk* in a URL indicates a site in the United Kingdom (Great Britain and Northern Ireland).

- The Internet includes:
  - The World Wide Web
  - E-mail servers
  - File Transfer Protocol sites

- The Internet also includes Gopher, Usenet, and Telnet, which are defined at the right but not otherwise described in this book.

Internet Use

- To use the Internet you need:
  - **Internet browser**, such as Microsoft Internet Explorer or Netscape Navigator. A browser is an application that:
    - Lets you connect to the Internet either directly or through a modem and a telephone line using an ISP or online service.
    - Lets you enter URLs.
    - Displays information provided by an Internet site.
    - Lets you save or print displayed information so it can be reviewed later.
    - Recognizes and lets you activate connections (called **hyperlinks)** to other addresses.
    - Lets you save addresses that you'd like to visit again using **favorites** (Internet Explorer) or **bookmarks** (Netscape Navigator).
  - **Modem and telephone line** or a direct connection that lets your computer communicate with others. Modem speed is given in **bits per second (BPS)**. A modem that operates at 28,800 BPS sends that many bits every second. The faster the modem, the quicker communications with other computers take place.
  - **ISP** or **online service** (or direct Internet connection) that gives you access to the Internet.

Introduction to Internet Explorer for Windows

- This book does not go into detail about how to use Internet Explorer, one of the most popular Internet browser applications available. This section provides a brief look at the Internet Explorer window and what it contains.

Gopher

A browsing system for Internet resources that predates the World Wide Web. Gopher works much like a directory, listing Internet sites in a menu.

Usenet

A global system of discussion groups called newsgroups. Many Internet browsers include a newsreader program to access the newsgroups.

Telnet

A program that lets one computer log on to a remote computer. Telnet is often used to search libraries and databases.

Windows Internet Explorer Window

The numbered callouts (❶ ❷ ❸ ❹) point to parts of the Internet Explorer window showing the Smithsonian Institution page (http://www.si.edu).

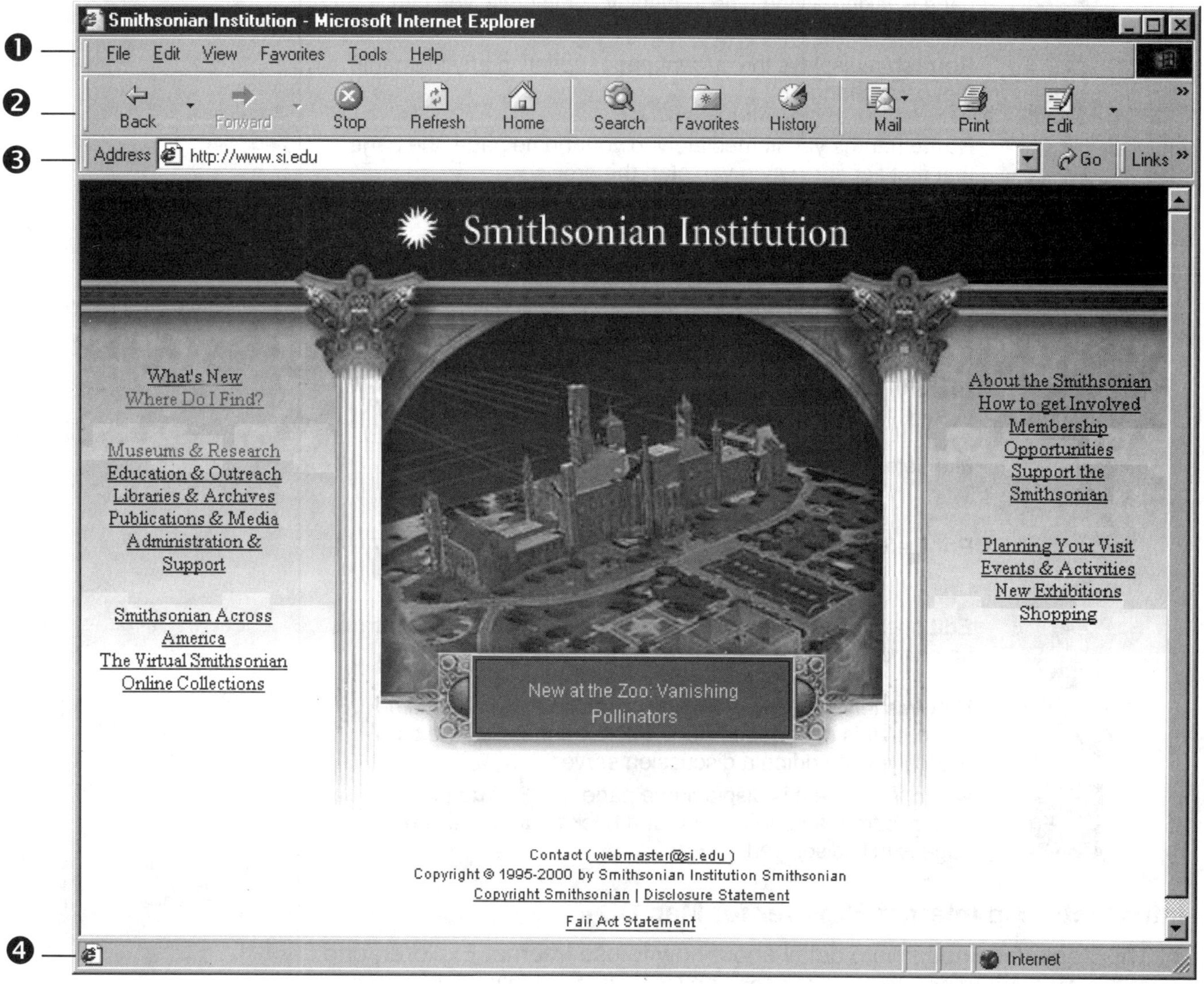

❶ The **menu bar** gives access to functions that let you open HTML documents saved on your machine, save and print Web pages, perform some edits (copy and paste, for example), change your view of Internet displays, move from one Internet site to another, save favorite sites so you can revisit them, and get help.

❷ **Toolbar buttons** are described below.

❸ In the Address box, you enter the URL of the site you want to visit.

❹ The **status bar** provides information about your use of Internet Explorer.

HTML (HyperText MarkUp Language)
HTML is the most common of the programming languages used in building Web pages.

■ Internet Explorer's toolbar has several buttons that help you find your way around the Internet.

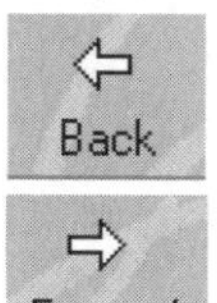

Back lets you return to the previous page.

Forward lets you move to a page you previously viewed. This button is active only if you have previously used the Back button.

Stop interrupts the attempt to display the current page. If a page is taking a long time to display completely, you can click this button to stop the display.

Refresh redisplays the current page, updating any elements that have changed.

Home returns you immediately to your home page, the page that first appears when you start the browser.

Search lets you search the Internet for information.

Favorites lets you save site addresses so you can revisit them later.

History lets you review and return to sites that you have visited.

Mail lets you send e-mail.

Print lets you print the currently displayed page.

Edit opens the current Web page in Microsoft Word so it can be edited.

Discuss lets you link to a discussion server. The first time you click this button, Internet Explorer starts a wizard that guides you in adding a discussion server.

When the system is displaying a page, the **Status icon** changes from an *e* to a globe and back to an *e* until the page is fully displayed.

Introduction to Internet Explorer for Mac OS

- This book does not go into detail about how to use Internet Explorer, one of the most popular Internet browser applications available. This section provides a brief look at the Internet Explorer window and what it contains.

❶ The **menu bar** gives access to functions that let you open HTML documents saved on your machine, save and print Web pages, perform some edits (copy and paste, for example), change your view of Internet displays, move from one Internet site to another, save favorite sites so you can revisit them, and get help.

❷ **Button bar buttons** are described below.

❸ In the **Address box**, you enter the URL of the site you want to visit.

❹ These buttons provide links to various sites; the defaults are for Apple and Microsoft Web sites.

❺ The **status bar** provides information about your use of Internet Explorer.

HTML (HyperText MarkUp Language)

HTML is the most common of the programming languages used in building Web pages.

364

Mac OS Internet Explorer Window

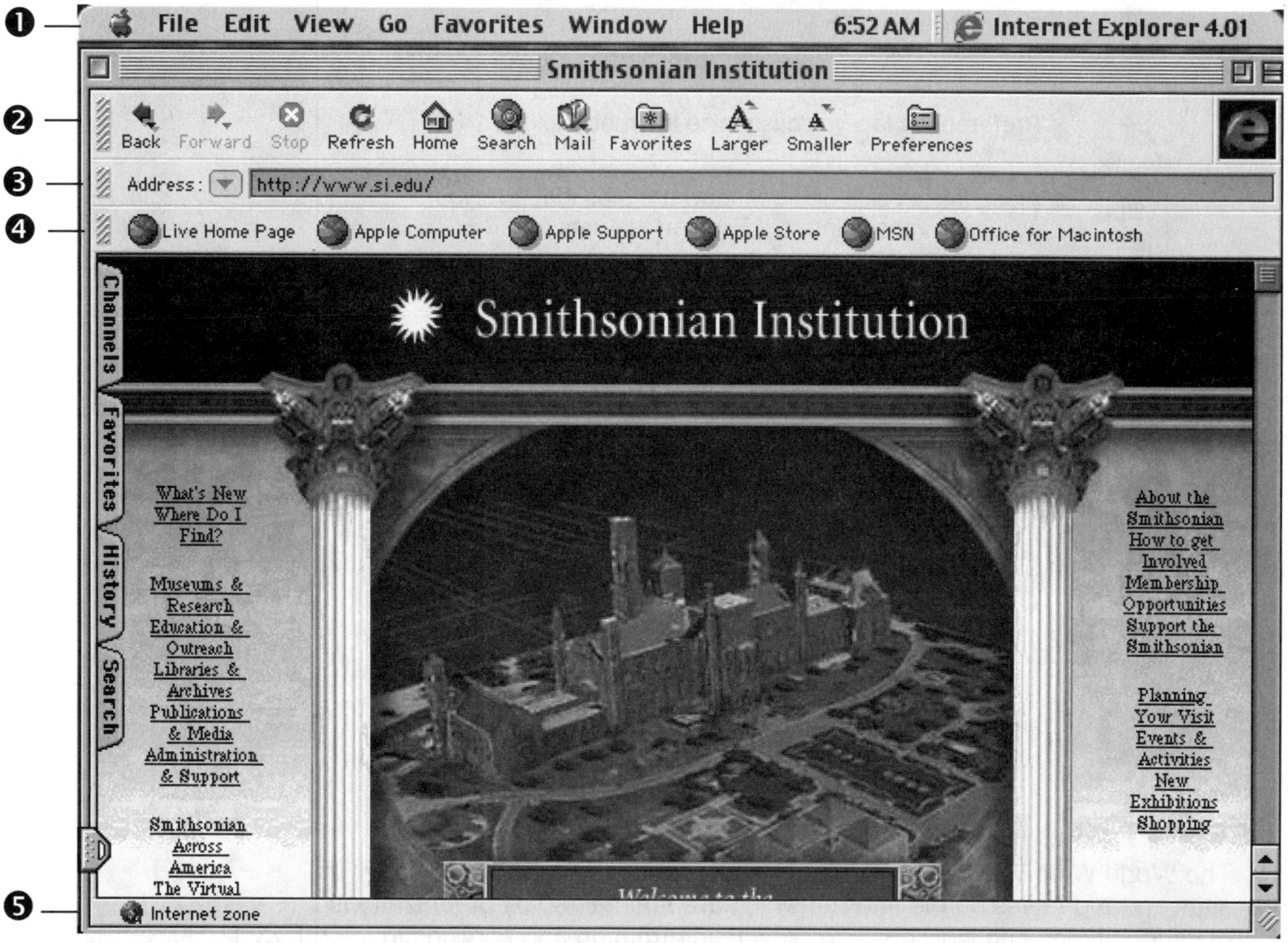

❶ File   Edit   View   Go   Favorites   Window   Help   6:52 AM   Internet Explorer 4.01

Smithsonian Institution

❷ Back Forward Stop Refresh Home Search Mail Favorites Larger Smaller Preferences

❸ Address: http://www.si.edu/

❹ Live Home Page   Apple Computer   Apple Support   Apple Store   MSN   Office for Macintosh

Channels / Favorites / History / Search

Smithsonian Institution

What's New
Where Do I
Find?

Museums &
Research
Education &
Outreach
Libraries &
Archives
Publications
& Media
Administration
& Support

Smithsonian
Across
America
The Virtual

About the
Smithsonian
How to get
Involved
Membership
Opportunities
Support the
Smithsonian

Planning
Your Visit
Events &
Activities
New
Exhibitions
Shopping

Welcome to the

❺ Internet zone

- Internet Explorer's button bar has several buttons that help you find your way around the Internet.

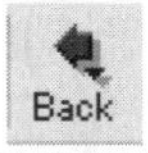

Back lets you return to the previous page.

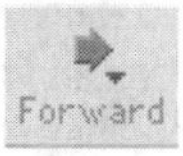

Forward lets you move to a page you previously viewed. This button is active only if you have previously used the Back button.

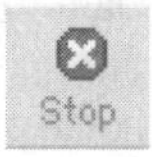

Stop interrupts the attempt to display the current page. If a page is taking a long time to display completely, you can click this button to stop the display.

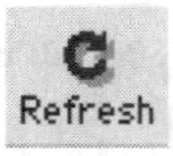

Refresh redisplays the current page, updating any elements that have changed.

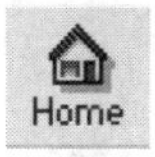

Home returns you immediately to your home page, the page that first appears when you start the browser.

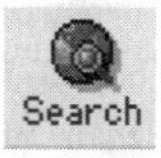

Search lets you search the Internet for information.

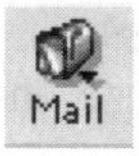

Mail lets you send e-mail.

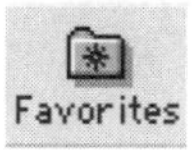

Favorites lets you save site addresses so you can revisit them later.

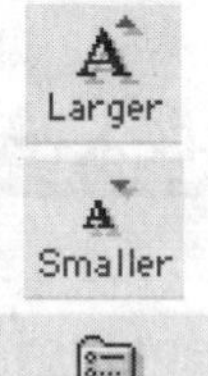
Larger enlarges the font size of the text displayed on the screen.

Smaller reduces the font size of the text displayed on the screen.

Preferences lets you customize Internet Explorer.

Along the left side of the window are tabs that give you access to various Internet Explorer features.

A **Channel** is a Web site designed to deliver content from the Internet to your computer.

Favorites lets you activate the URL of a site you have saved.

History lets you review and return to sites that you have visited.

Search lets you search the Internet for information.

When the system is displaying a page, the **Status icon** changes from an *e* to a globe and back to an *e* until the page is fully displayed.

The World Wide Web

- The World Wide Web portion of the Internet contains **Web sites**. Web sites are addresses on the Internet which are maintained by organizations of various types and individuals to provide information and services to Internet users.

- A Web site is built from **Web pages**, which are specially designed and formatted to display text and graphics. Most Web pages are built using the programming language called HTML (**H**yper**T**ext **M**ark**U**p **L**anguage). Many Web pages also include objects that are presented using Java, another programming language.

- When you enter the URL of a Web site, you are taken to the site's **home page**, the page from which the Web site expects you to start to explore the information or services it offers. (If you know or have saved the URL of a different page within the site, you can go directly to that page by entering its full address.) The home page of the Smithsonian Institution (**www.si.edu***)* is shown in the illustrations of the Internet Explorer windows earlier in this exercise.

- When a Web page is displayed, you can point your mouse to graphics or underlined text. When the mouse pointer turns to a hand , you can click to activate a link to another page or another Web site.

Smithsonian Home Page

Web sites change constantly. As companies and organizations stress new services and new information, they change their Web sites. The current Smithsonian Institution home page may have a different appearance from the one illustrated in this book and on the accompanying CD-ROM.

The illustrations and the simulated site on the CD were created in August of 2000; the site may have changed since then.

Online Services

- America Online (AOL), Microsoft Network, Prodigy, and CompuServe (which is now owned by AOL) are online services that provide more than just a connection to the Internet. They offer a large number of services that may connect you to Web sites, but just as often keep you within the services hosted by the service itself. For example, when you sign on to AOL, the two opening windows offer a variety of options, only two of which take you immediately to the Internet. The other services, including Channels, Mail Center, and People Connection, are all part of the services offered by AOL. The Welcome Window is shown in the illustration below.

AOL Welcome Window

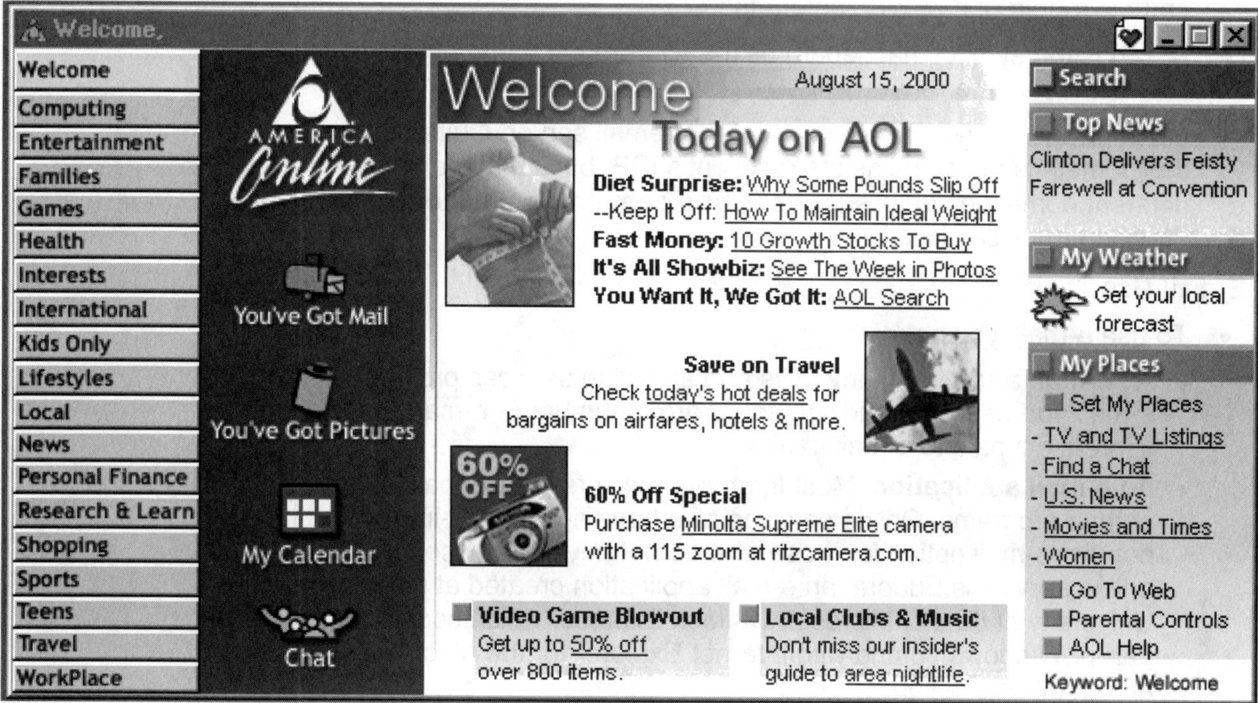

- The AOL Channels bar at the left of the Welcome screen provides links to many services besides the Internet.

Electronic Mail (E-mail)

- Very early on, networks provided a way to pass messages from one user to another. Novell networks, for example, offer a way to broadcast messages to one or more users. These messages are sent and then disappear. They are not saved on the network and cannot be reviewed after they are first viewed.

- Software companies developed electronic mail (e-mail) applications to provide a way to save messages, make sure that messages were received by the addressee, and provide more privacy in their transmission.

- At first, these e-mail systems were internal. Internal e-mail systems have been in use for some time in most companies. If you need to send an agenda for a meeting to several co-workers, you can address an e-mail message to them.

- With the explosion in growth of the Internet, companies recognized the value of e-mail from one organization to another. Thus, they began to provide e-mail capabilities that used the Internet to send messages anywhere.

- E-mail finds its destination because it has been properly addressed. The e-mail address has three components, as shown in the example that follows:

    username@earthlink.net

  - **username** is the **e-mail ID**. It is an identifier that tells who is sending or receiving the message. Most often, this part of the address identifies a specific person, but sometimes you can send a message to a company or organization without a specific person's name. An entry is required, however, before the @.

  - **@ (at)** is the symbol that separates the ID from the name of the e-mail domain name.

  - **earthlink.net** is the domain name of the e-mail server. Quite often, this domain is the same as the recipient's ISP, but it may be a different domain entirely, such as **yahoo.com** or **hotmail.com**, which provide e-mail services.

E-mail Use

- To use e-mail, you need:

  - An **e-mail address**. Many ISPs and all online services provide e-mail addresses. In addition, there are a number of e-mail servers devoted to e-mail traffic.

  - An **e-mail application**. Most Internet browsers offer e-mail as one of their programs. Online services also have e-mail built-in. A popular e-mail option for those who do not have a browser or online service is Eudora, an e-mail application created at the University of Illinois. Microsoft Outlook Express, which comes as part of Windows 98 and with Internet Explorer for the Mac, is also an e-mail application.

- Once you have an e-mail account established, you can test whether it works properly, by sending a message to **learn@ddcpub.com**. *Learn* will reply to acknowledge receipt of the message. (Don't address questions to *learn*; the reply is automated and used for testing only.)

File Attachments

- Besides sending messages to co-workers and friends, e-mail users often attach files to their messages.

- For example, if you want to share a story you have written with a friend, you can attach the story to an e-mail message and send it along. When the friend receives the message, the e-mail application notifies him or her that a file is attached, and the friend can download the file to the local computer.

- Many files are transferred this way every day, but there is a faster alternative called FTP that is often used for large files (see following page).

File Transfer Protocol (FTP)

- **File Transfer Protocol (FTP)** is another area of the Internet. FTP sites let users **download** (retrieve files from a server) and **upload** (send files to a server). The Internet includes a number of FTP sites and users take advantage of FTP capabilities, especially when they have large files that they need to download or upload.

- FTP sites are specially designed to shorten the time it takes to transfer files. Most sites require a password and authorized access to their files and folders. Most also maintain an **anonymous logon**, which gives access to limited areas of the site.

In this exercise, you will explore some of the World Wide Web. If you have access to the Internet, you will look at the Smithsonian Institution site. If you do not have access to the Internet, you will use Internet Explorer to simulate access to the Web site by opening a file from the data disk.

EXERCISE DIRECTIONS

Mac without Internet Access

1. Start Internet Explorer.

2. If any window appears other than the Internet Explorer windows, close it.

   Internet Explorer may display a message saying it cannot locate the home page.

3. When Internet Explorer opens, click File.

4. Choose Offline Browsing.

5. Click File.

6. Click Open File to display the open dialog box.

7. Locate and open ☺ **www-si-edu.htm** from the data files.

8. Continue with "Activate Some Links" on page 370.

Mac with Internet Access

1. Double-click the Browse the Internet icon

    on the desktop.

2. Connect to the Internet.

3. Enter the following URL: *http://www.si.edu.*

   Internet Explorer opens the Smithsonian Institution's home page.

4. Continue with "Activate Some Links" on page 370.

Windows without Internet Access

1. Start Internet Explorer using Start, Programs.

2. If any window except the Internet Explorer window appears, close it.

   Internet Explorer displays a message indicating that the Web page is unavailable offline.

3. Click File, Work Offline.

4. Click File, Open.

   Internet Explore displays the Open dialog box with a blank Open field.

5. Click the Browse button [Browse...].

6. In the dialog box that appears, locate and open the file ☺ **www-si-edu.htm** in the data files.

   - Select the file name and click the Open button [Open]

     OR

   - Double-click the file name

   The Open dialog box appears as shown below with the file name in the Open field.

Open Dialog Box

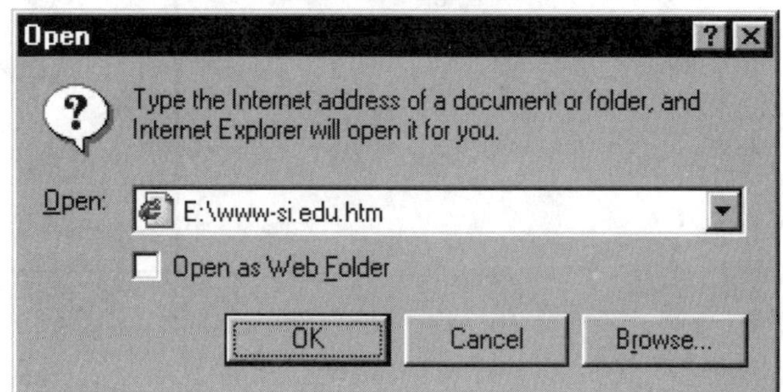

7. Click **OK**.

The remaining steps in this exercise are the same as for those who have Internet access.

8. Continue with "Activate Some Links," below.

Windows with Internet Access

1. Start your browser and connect to the Internet.

2. Open the page that has the following URL:
   http://www.ddcpub.com

   The remaining steps in this exercise are the same as for those who do not have Internet access.

3. Continue with *Activate Some Links*, below.

Activate Some Links

The Smithsonian Institution Web home page appears. (It may differ from the one illustrated which was captured in August 2000. Only a portion of the page is shown.)

1. Click the link: <u>Where Do I Find?</u>

   You know the text is a link because it is underlined and when you point to it, the mouse pointer turns into a hand.

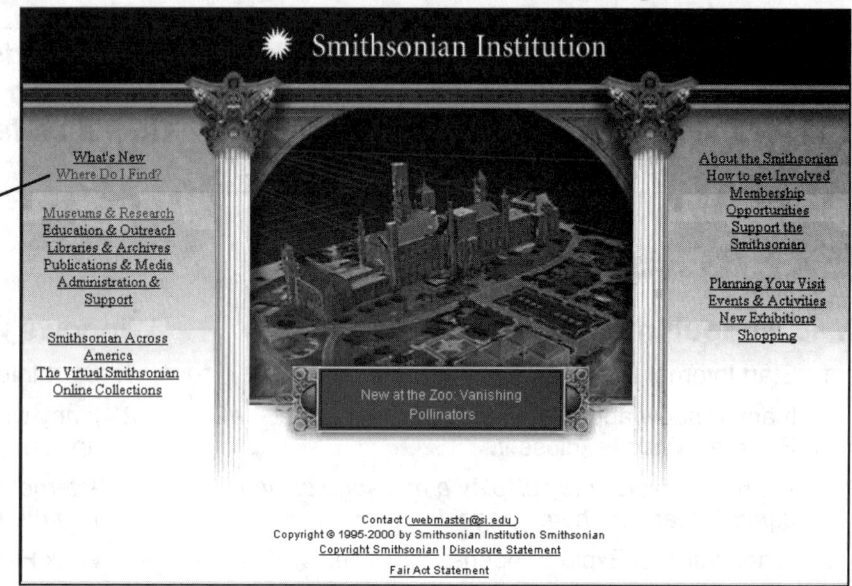

Smithsonian Institution Home Page

The Encyclopedia Smithsonian page opens.

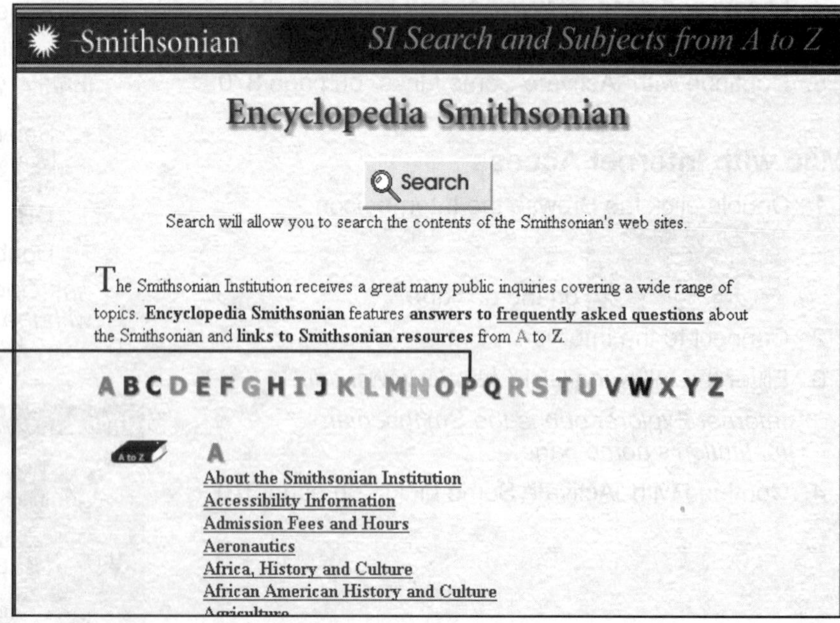

Encyclopedia Smithsonian

2. Click the letter **P**.
   Like many Web page elements, this is a graphic that also serves as a link.

The Encyclopedia Page displays links that begin with the letter P.

3. Click the link: <u>Pandas</u>.

Encyclopedia Smithsonian, Letter P

✹ Smithsonian   *SI Search and Subjects from A to Z*

P
Pandas
Paleoanthropology
Paleobiology
Pendulum, Foucault
Performing Arts
Pianos
Photography
Physical Sciences
Presidents, U.S.
Primates
Printing Technology
Political History
Postal History
Publications

Q
Quilts

R
Railroads
Reptiles
Research Centers
Revolutionary War, American

The links to information about pandas appear.

4. Click on the following link:
<u>Giant Panda Reading List</u>

Links to Information about Pandas

- Pandas:
  - Giant Panda Reading List
  - Red Panda Web Site
  - FONZ Panda Page
  - Smithsonian scientists team up with colleagues in China to save pandas
- Primates:
  - Golden Lion Tamarin Conservation Program
  - Great Ape House at the National Zoo
  - Orangutan Language Project
- Reptiles and Amphibians:
  - Division of Reptiles and Amphibians at the National Museum of Natural History
  - Photo Exhibit: *Green Sea Turtles and Costa Rica's Tropical Rainforest*
  - Reptiles and Amphibians, Reading Lists
  - Reptile Discovery Center at the National Zoo
  - Reptile and Amphibian Hall at the National Museum of Natural History
  - Sounds of North American Frogs , Smithsonian Folkways Recording
  - Declining Amphibian Populations Task Force
- Small Mammals
  - Bat Facts
  - Bats, Selected Publications
  - Small Mammal House at the National Zoo
- Wildlife Pictures, Sources for

DEPARTMENT OF **VERTEBRATE ZOOLOGY**

The Giant Panda Reading List page opens. The top portion is shown at the right.

Links to Information about Pandas

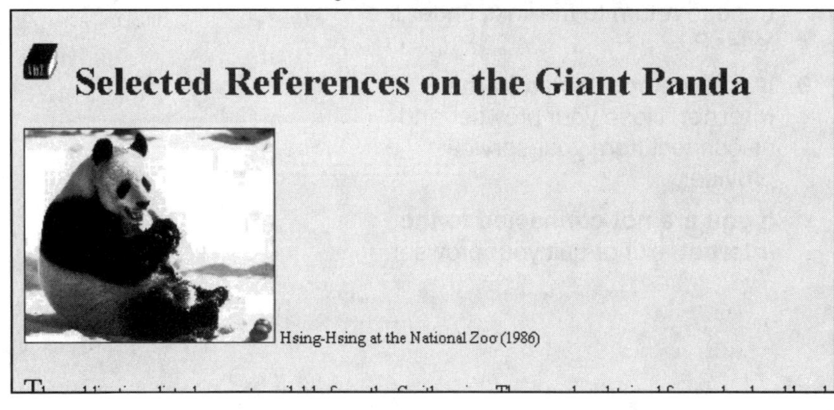

Selected References on the Giant Panda

Hsing-Hsing at the National Zoo (1986)

5. Scroll down to review some of the references.

6. Click the Back button on your browser.

7. Click the link: FONZ Panda Page.

   The Friends of the National Zoo Panda Page appears.

8. Scroll down to review the page.

9. Click the Back button on your browser.

10. Click the Back button on your browser again.

11. Click the link: Pendulum, Foucault.

Review Foucault Pendulum Page and Use Navigation Buttons

1. Review the page.

2. Scroll down to read material that is not visible at first.

3. Click the Back button to return to the list of links under the letter P.

4. Click the Back button until you reach the Smithsonian Institution home page.

5. Click the Forward button twice to return to the links under the letter P.

6. **If you are connected to the Internet**, close your browser and disconnect from your service provider.

   If you are not connected to the Internet, exit or quit your browser.

FONZ Panda Page

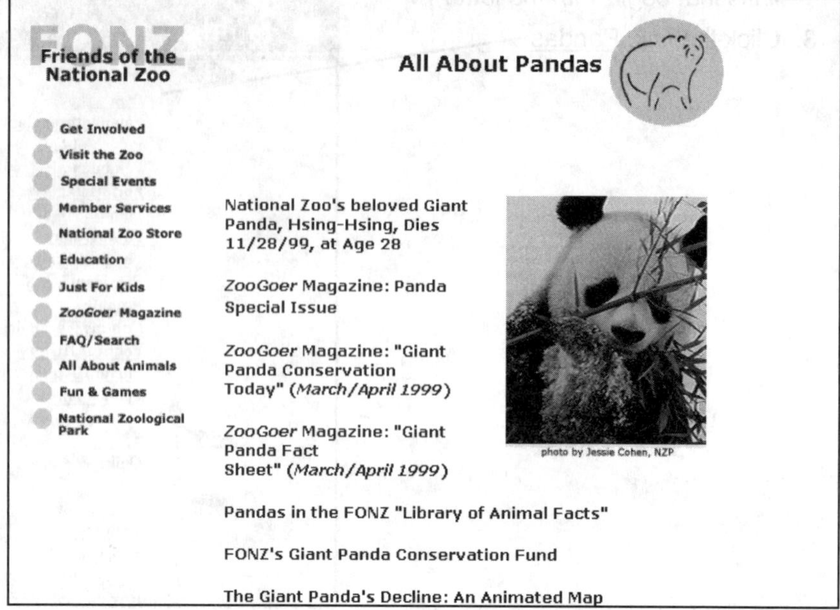

Foucault Pendulum Page

Foucault Pendulum

Information or research assistance regarding pendulums is frequently requested from the Smithsonian Institution. The following information has been prepared by the National Museum of American History's Division of Physical Sciences in cooperation with the Visitor Information and Associates' Reception Center's Public Inquiry Mail and Telephone Information Service Unit to assist those interested in this topic.

The Foucault Pendulum is named for the French physicist Jean Foucault (pronounced "Foo-koh), who first used it in 1851 to demonstrate the rotation of the earth. It was the first satisfactory demonstration of the earth's rotation using laboratory apparatus rather than astronomical observations.

If you start a Foucault Pendulum swinging in one direction, after a few hours you will notice that it is swinging in a quite different direction. How does this happen?

Imagine you are in a museum located at the north pole and that the museum has a Foucault Pendulum suspended from the ceiling at a point exactly over the pole. When you set the pendulum swinging it will continue to swing in the same direction unless it is pushed or pulled in some other direction. (This is due to a basic law of nature called Newton's First Law.) The earth, on the other hand, will rotate once every 24 hours underneath the pendulum. Thus if you stood watching the pendulum, after a quarter of an hour or so, you would be likely to notice that the line of the pendulum's swing has changed to a different direction. This would be especially clear if one marked the position of the line of swing in the morning and had the pendulum

NEXT EXERCISE

Exercise 4

Learn about Other Communications Methods
■ Wide Area Networks (WANs) ■ Intranets
■ Telecommuting ■ PC-to-Mainframe Communications

NOTES

Wide Area Networks (WANs)

- Another kind of network is called a **Wide Area Network** (**WAN**). In some companies, a WAN is used to connect workers in different geographic locations. In the central location, the network operates like a LAN. Workers outside the central location communicate with the network via modem, satellite, or leased telephone lines through hardware and software facilities called *gateways*. The gateways give distant users access to the services of the central location.

- Some people reserve the term WAN for networks that serve only members of the same company or organization. Others consider AOL, Prodigy, CompuServe, World Wide Web, and even the Internet as WANs.

Intranets

- Many users within an organization may have access to the Internet, using their Internet browsers to find information, send e-mail, and exchange files with co-workers. But when they leave the Internet, many of them have to use other applications to review information and exchange files.

- Increasingly, therefore, companies are creating internal Webs to allow employees to access company information using the same application they use to access the Internet. These internal Webs are known as **intranets**.

- Intranets are created and managed within an organization. Users outside the organization generally cannot gain access to them. This means that information that is inappropriate for an Internet site, such as personnel policies or intra-company news, can be provided on an intranet. Using their Internet browsers, workers can use the intranet in the same way they use the Internet.

- Some companies also provide access to their intranets to authorized outside users. For example, a company may wish a supplier to be able to review specifications for a purchase that is about to be made. The supplier then uses an Internet browser, contacts the intranet (often through the Internet), and gains access to the intranet through an ID and password. The companies that provide such access call this an **extranet**.

- An intranet may have connections to the Internet, but these connections are constructed to prevent unauthorized access. The term **firewall** is used to describe protecting a network or computer from unauthorized access.

Telecommuting

- More and more workers are working away from the office. Some of them simply use their PCs as local machines and communicate with the office only when they have files they want to send or receive. Such users may use the Internet or e-mail service as their way to communicate with the office and never actually log in to the office's computers.

- Other workers, however, connect via telephone lines and work directly on the office network. Telecommuting of this type requires hardware and software on both the workstation and the server. Usually the telecommuter starts the communications software on the workstation, dials up the office computer, and logs in as a network user. The full facilities of the company's network are then available to the workstation.

PC-to-Mainframe Communications

- To use a company's mainframe computing capacity, workers require a **terminal**. Terminals are pieces of hardware that have no software of their own. They are connected to the mainframe computer via cables and their communication is managed by a **controller**, another piece of hardware that provides the link between terminals (one controller could handle many terminals) and the mainframe. Terminals are single-use devices; they cannot function apart from the mainframe. If they get disconnected from the computer or the mainframe stops working, their users are no longer computing.

- In the first days of the personal computer, users thought it would be good to use them just like terminals. But terminals operate differently from PCs. PCs do not require controllers and ordinarily do not speak the same language as controllers. Often workers who needed both a personal computer and access to the company's mainframe had both a PC and a terminal on their desks. Soon after the introduction of IBM's PC in the early 1980s, however, both hardware and software solutions were created.

- **Terminal emulation software**, programs that mimicked mainframe terminals, was created as early as 1981 for computers built by Digital Equipment Corporation. DEC mainframes used ASCII (American Standard Code for Information Interchange) for encoding characters. Since PCs also used ASCII, it was possible to create software that let a PC work with a DEC mainframe.

- IBM mainframes, however, were a different matter. Rather than use ASCII codes, they use a coding system called EBCDIC (sometimes pronounced EB-sid-ick, short for Extended Binary Coded Decimal Interchange Code). Differences between the ASCII and EBCDIC coding systems made it necessary to create **terminal emulation hardware** so the PC and the IBM mainframe could communicate.

- In most installations where PCs and mainframes communicate today, a combination of hardware and software does the job. In many companies, users are connected to a local area network and log on (or sign on) to the organization's mainframe without disconnecting from the network. The personal computer then operates not only as an independent machine but also as a network workstation and as a mainframe terminal.

NEXT LESSON

Lesson 9: Computer Care

Exercise 1: Manage Your Disks

- ♦ **Check a Disk for Problems**
- ♦ **Create a Startup Disk**
- ♦ **Defragment the Hard Drive**
- ♦ **Format a Diskette**

Exercise 2: Use Backup

- ♦ **Back Up Files**
- ♦ **Restore Backed Up Files**

Exercise 3: Learn about Virus Protection

- ♦ **Protect against Viruses**
- ♦ **Run a Virus Scan**

Exercise 4: Add Software to Your Computer

- ♦ **Install Software**
- ♦ **Windows Installation**
- ♦ **Mac OS Installation**
- ♦ **Install a Printer in Windows**
- ♦ **Install a Printer in Mac OS**

Exercise 5: Keep Your Computer System Clean

- ♦ **General Care Instructions**
- ♦ **Clean the Monitor**
- ♦ **Save Energy and Preserve Screens**
- ♦ **Clean the Keyboard**
- ♦ **Clean the Mouse**
- ♦ **Clean the Cases**
- ♦ **Maintain Computers and Peripherals**

Manage Your Disks
■ Check a Disk for Problems ■ Create a Startup Disk
■ Defragment the Hard Drive ■ Format a Diskette

NOTES

Check a Disk for Problems

■ If you have ever turned off your computer before its shutdown was complete or had to reboot because the system failed, you may have seen the operating system run a check of your hard drive when you next started your computer.

■ Windows runs ScanDisk, a program that determines if a disk is damaged or contains data that seems not to be part of a file. Mac OS runs a similar program, Disk First Aid, to verify that the disk is not damaged. You can run such checking programs at any time.

Try It!

Check a Windows Hard Drive for Problems

1. Open the My Computer window.

2. Select the drive containing the disk you want to check.

3. Click **File** (Alt+F)

4. Click **Properties** (R) to display the Properties dialog box.

5. Click the Tools tab (Ctrl+Tab) to display the Tools options; the Error-checking status portion of the tab is shown in the illustration that follows.

Drive C: Properties Dialog Box, Tools Tab

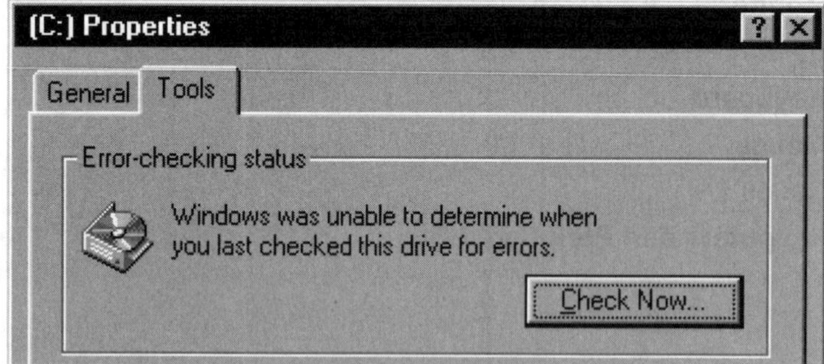

6. Click Check Now button [Check Now...] to display the ScanDisk dialog box, as shown in the illustration on the following page.

   If you have a program such as Norton Utilities installed on your machine, some of the options described in this section may be unavailable.

ScanDisk Dialog Box

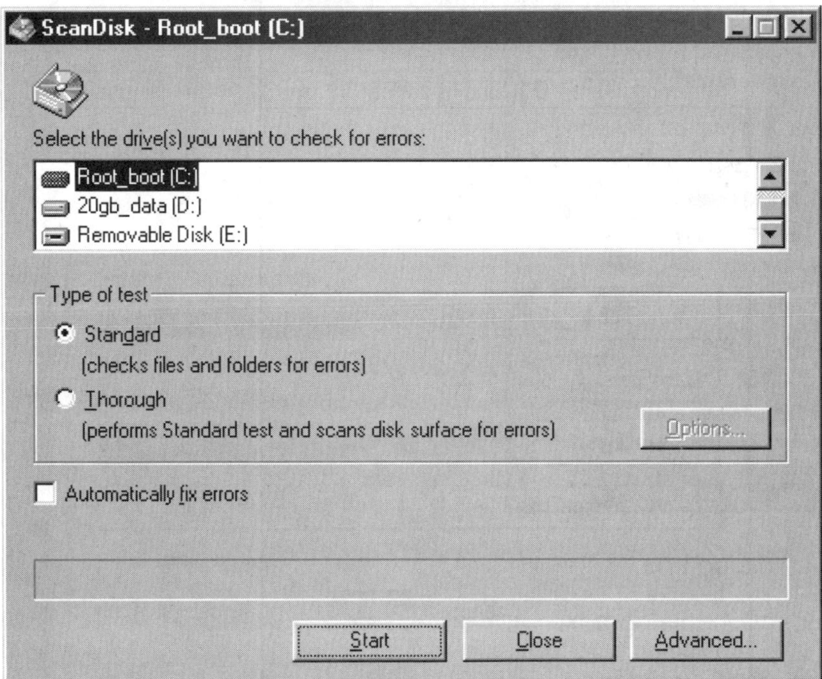

7. Select the drive(s) you want to check.

8. Select **Standard** (**Alt**+**D**) for a check of files and folders.

   OR

   Select **Thorough** (**Alt**+**T**) to also check the disk surface for errors. Usually the Standard check is sufficient.

   If you believe your disk or diskette may be damaged, run the Thorough check.

   IMPORTANT: *Select **Thorough** if you are scanning a diskette. If Windows detects surface errors, copy data you want to save to another disk. Then try reformatting the diskette. If the reformat results show errors, discard the diskette. Damaged diskettes can cause you to lose data.*

   *Unless you believe something has damaged your hard drive, it is not generally necessary to select **Thorough** when checking a hard drive. Any bad spots on hard drives have been removed from the system's knowledge by the manufacturer or computer vendor. While almost all hard disks contain some bad sectors, the system knows about them and does not use them when saving.*

   *When saving to diskettes, however, the system will attempt to write to bad sectors because it has no way of knowing about them. Thus, use **Thorough** when scanning diskettes.*

9. Select **Automatically fix errors** (**Alt**+**F**) if you want windows to fix any file errors it encounters.

10. Click **Start** (**Alt**+**S**).

    Windows scans the disk and then displays the ScanDisk Results message box, as shown in the illustration on the following page.

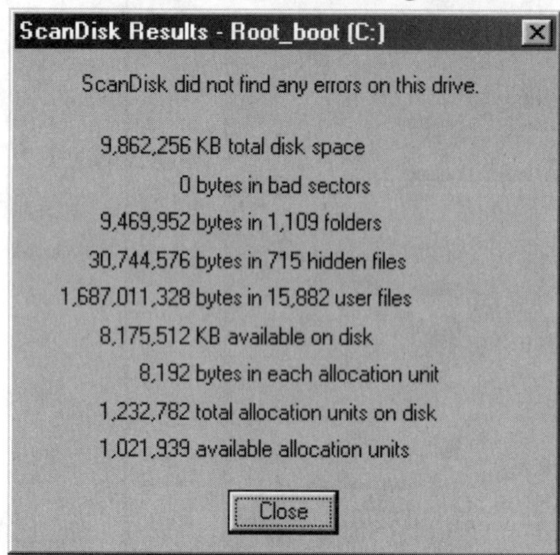

ScanDisk Results Message Box

11. Click **Close** on the Results dialog box.

12. Click **Close** on the ScanDisk dialog box.

13. Click **OK** on the Properties dialog box.

Try It!

Check a Mac OS Hard Drive for Problems

1. Open the hard drive.

2. Locate and open the **Utilities** folder.

3. Double-click **Disk First Aid**.

   Mac OS displays the Disk First Aid dialog box, as shown in the following illustration.

Disk First Aid Dialog Box

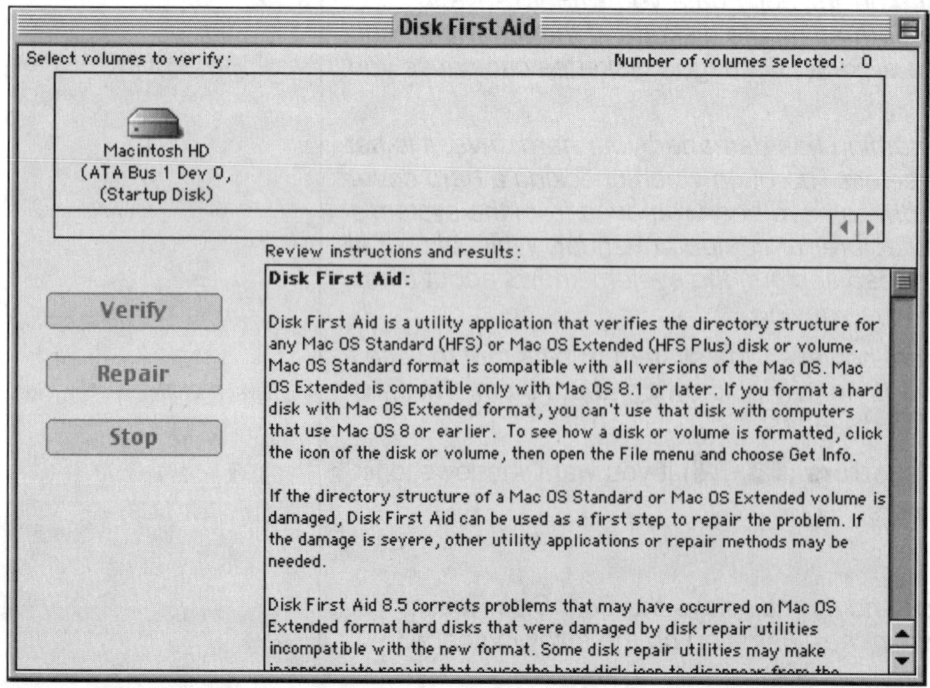

The right side of the dialog box explains what Disk First Aid does.

4. In the upper part of the dialog box, select the disk to be checked.

   If more than one disk is shown, you can select multiple disks by holding down the **Shift** *key while clicking. The explanation disappears from the right half of the window, and a list of actions appears.*

5. Click the Verify button **Verify**.

   Mac OS runs the program. If it encounters problems, it displays a report.

6. If Disk First Aid reports problems with the disk, select the same drive and click the Repair button **Repair** to allow Disk First Aid to fix the problem if it can.

7. Close the Disk First Aid dialog box (use **File**, **Quit** or press **⌘**+**Q**).Disk First Aid Results

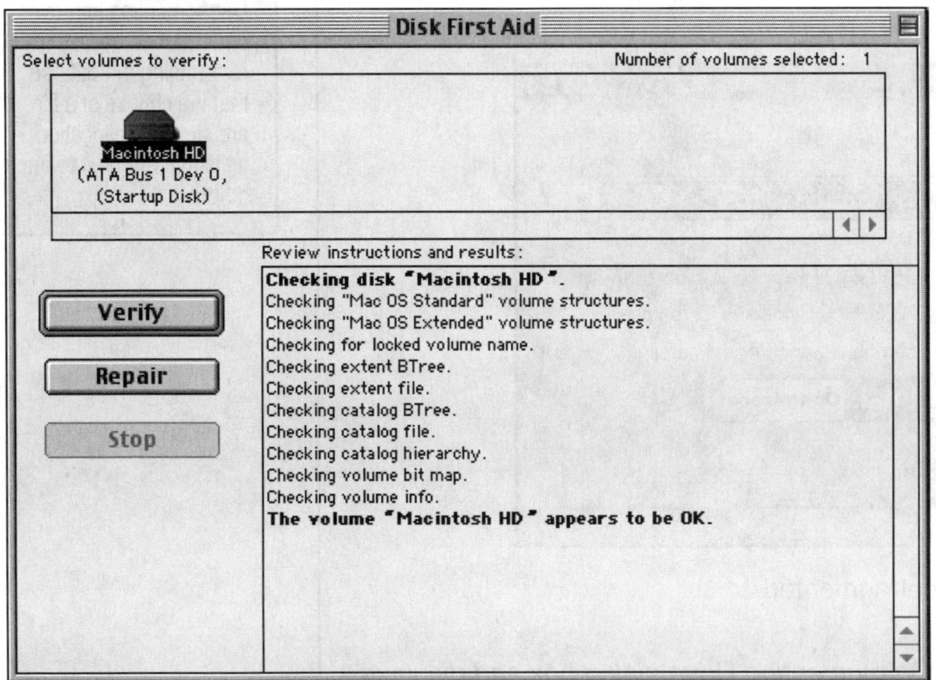

Create a Startup Disk

- If you do not already have one, you should create a startup disk for your computer. If you have problems starting up, you can use the startup disk to boot your computer, copy critical files as backup, run diagnostic programs, and fix any problems.

- Mac OS does not offer a specific program for creating a startup disk. If your Mac includes an Iomega Zip™ or Jaz™ drive, you can use the Iomega utilities to create a startup disk. The procedures describe creating a startup (emergency rescue) disk with Iomega.

- Windows 95 and 98 offer an easy way to create a startup disk, as described in the procedures.

Create a Startup Disk

Mac OS Startup

The Mac OS installation CD (or CD of System Software) can also be used to start the Mac.

Defragment the Hard Drive

- Occasionally, you may need to let Windows **defragment** the hard drive. Depending on how much you use your computer, you should run the defragmenting procedure about once a month.

- To defragment the hard drive on a Mac OS computer, you need a third party program such as AltSoft's DiskExpress, La Cie's Silverlining, or Symantec's Norton Utilities. Mac OS does not include a defragmentation program.

Try It! (Windows only)

1. Click the Start button ![Start].

2. Slide to <u>P</u>rograms, Accessories, System Tools, and click Disk Defragmenter ![Disk Defragmenter].
   The dialog box shown below appears.

Select Drive Dialog Box

3. Select the drive to be defragmented.

4. Click OK.
   Windows displays the Defragmenting Drive dialog box and displays the progress of the procedure, as shown in the following illustration.

Defragmenting Drive C Dialog Box

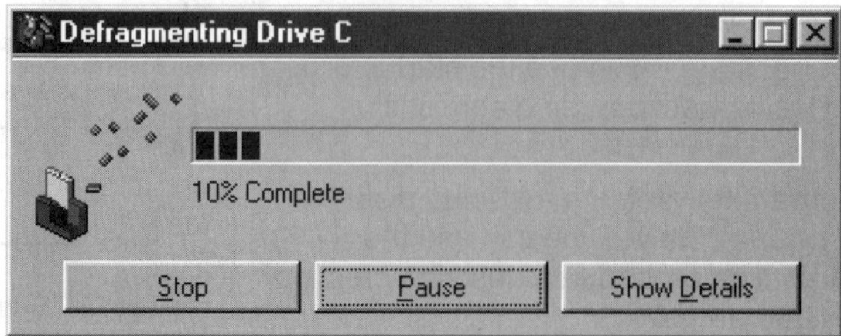

When defragmentation is complete, the dialog box on the following page appears.

Disk Defragmenter Dialog Box

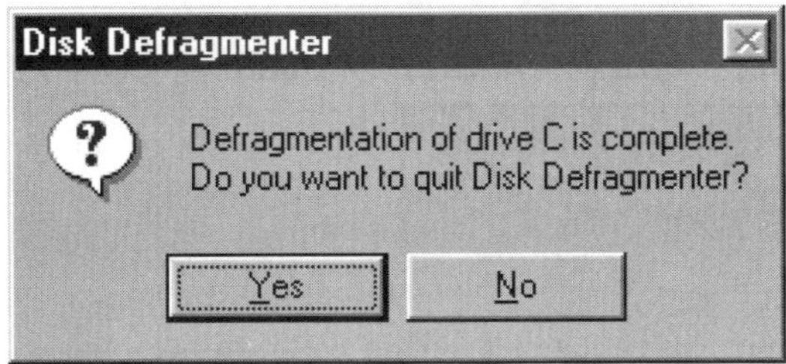

5. Click the Yes button [Yes   ].

Defragmentation Settings

The defragmentation function provides settings that you can specify. After running the defragmentation procedure once, you can adjust the settings for defragmenting your disk. To do so:

1. Complete steps 1 and 2 as described on the previous page.

2. Click the Settings button [Settings...].

    The Disk Defragmenter Settings dialog box appears, as shown in the following illustration.

    The default options, shown in the illustration, fully defragment the drive to provide the most efficient performance. Change them only if you have reason to do so.

Disk Defragmenter Settings

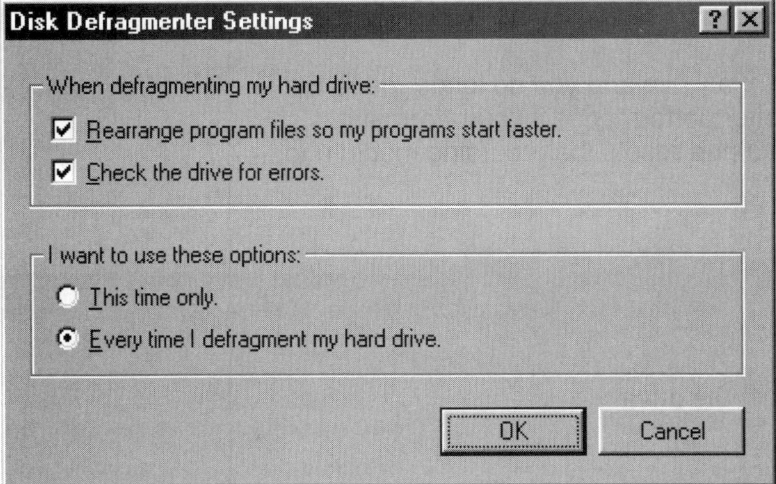

Use My Computer to Start Defragmentation

You can also start the defragmentation procedure through My Computer, as described below.

1. Open My Computer, and select the drive to be defragmented.

2. Click File, Properties to display the Properties dialog box.

3. Click Tools to display the Tools tab, and look at the Defragmentation status, as shown in the illustration on the following page.

Note that Windows indicates either that it cannot determine when the drive was last defragmented or the date of the most recent defragmentation.

Drive C: Properties Dialog Box, Tools Tab, Defragmentation Status

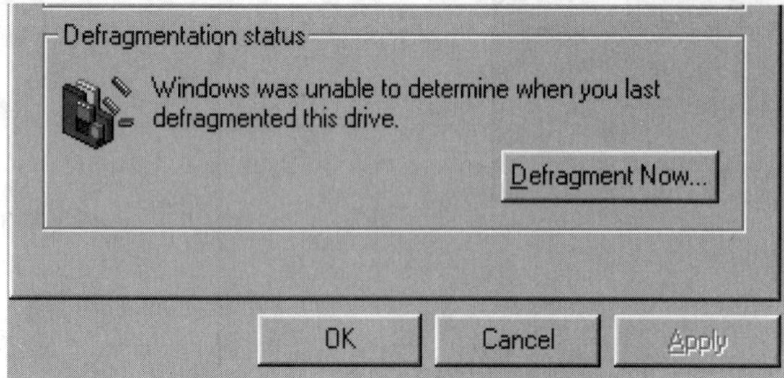

4. Click the <u>D</u>efragment Now button Defragment Now....

   Windows displays the Defragmenting Drive progress box shown on page 383.

Format a Diskette

- Most diskettes come preformatted to be compatible with your computer. When you buy them, be sure to get diskettes that are formatted for use with your machine:

  - Windows formats are sometimes still called MS-DOS or PC-DOS or even IBM PC compatible.

  - Mac OS compatible disks are variously called Apple or Mac formatted.

- When you have used a diskette for a while and you no longer need the data stored on it, you may get better performance if you reformat it. Formatting erases all existing data and resets the recording medium to receive new data.

Try It!

Format a Windows Disk

1. Place the disk in the drive.
2. Open My Computer and select the drive.
3. Click **File** (Alt+F).
4. Click **For<u>m</u>at** (M) to display the Format dialog box, as shown in the illustration on the following page.

Format Dialog Box

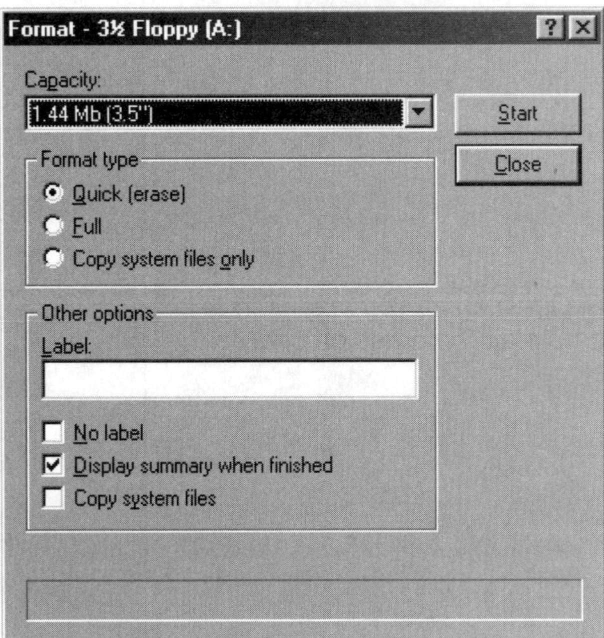

5. Choose the options you want for the format.

    ♦ **Quick** (Alt+Q) simply erases the files.

    ♦ **Full** (Alt+F) erases the files and restructures the recording medium into allocation units.

    ♦ **Copy system files only** (Alt+O) places the files needed to start your computer on the disk without erasing any existing files on the diskette.

    ♦ **Label** (Alt+L) lets you specify a label for the diskette. Labels can be helpful in identifying the owner or content of a diskette.

    ♦ **No label** (Alt+N) indicates that you do not want a label on the diskette.

    ♦ **Display summary when finished** (Alt+D) tells Windows to display information about the disk after the formatting is complete.

    ♦ **Copy system files** (Alt+Y) tells Windows to format the diskette and copy the system files to it.

6. To format, click the Start button Start (Alt+S).

7. To exit the format program, click the Close button Close (Alt+C).

    Copy System Files. *When you copy the system files to a diskette in this way, you can boot your machine in MS-DOS mode by placing the diskette in the drive and turning on the machine. The system opens to the prompt for the A: drive. Although you can start your computer with a diskette to which these system files have been copied, the diskette does not contain all the information of a startup diskette and should not be considered a substitute for it.*

Format a Mac OS Disk

1. Insert a disk in the drive.

2. Select the drive on the desktop.

3. Click **Special**.

4. Click **Erase**.

5. Click the Erase button `Erase`.

   If you are formatting a Zip, Jaz, or SyQuest drive, you may wish to use the tools provided by the vendor to start the erase procedure.

NEXT EXERCISE

Use Backup
■ Back Up Files ■ Restore Backed Up Files

NOTES

Back Up Files

- Backup makes sure that you can return to a known starting point on any of your files rather than have to create them all over again.

- **Backup** is the process of copying files from your hard drive to a medium that can be stored elsewhere and retrieved when you need to restore the data because the hard drive is damaged, the file becomes corrupted, or the file is accidentally erased.

- If you work on a computer that is not connected to a network, you need to be certain that you back up your files frequently.

- If you work on a network, your system administration probably handles backup for your network files. You still need to back up any local files that you do not want to lose.

- **Frequency of backup** depends on the data you have and how much you use your machine. At least once a week you should ensure that all new and changed files are backed up. You should run backup every day if you use your hard drive to create files that you do not want to lose.

- Windows provides a backup program that you can use to perform periodic backups. In addition, a number of vendors offer backup utilities. This exercise covers the backup program that comes with Windows 98.

- Mac OS does not provide a backup program. You must copy the files you wish to back up to a removable medium. You may wish to use a compression program, such as StuffIt from Aladdin Systems, to compress the files as you copy them. In addition, many vendors, such as Retrospect, Dantz, and Leader Technologies, offer programs specifically designed to back up your system. This exercise does not describe backup for the Mac.

Moving Files

Moving files from the hard disk to a diskette when you no longer need them is a good idea, but it is not a backup. Moving does not ensure the integrity of the files that remain on the hard drive; backup does.

Removable Media

Many companies provide special drives with removable media that can be used for backup. These include tape drives, which usually come with their own backup software, and other removable disks, such as Iomega Zip and Jazz and SyQuest.

Try It! (Windows Only)

Prepare for Backup

1. Collect enough clean, formatted diskettes to contain the data you intend to back up. Windows compresses data as it performs the backup, so you need fewer diskettes than the total number of bytes to be backed up, but you are likely to need several depending on the amount of data you intend to include.

2. Open the My Computer window, and select a drive.

3. Click File, Properties, and click the Tools tab. (This dialog box is illustrated in Exercise 1 in this lesson.)

4. Click the <u>B</u>ackup Now button [Backup Now...] to start the backup process with the Microsoft Backup dialog box, as shown in the following illustration.

Microsoft Backup Dialog Box

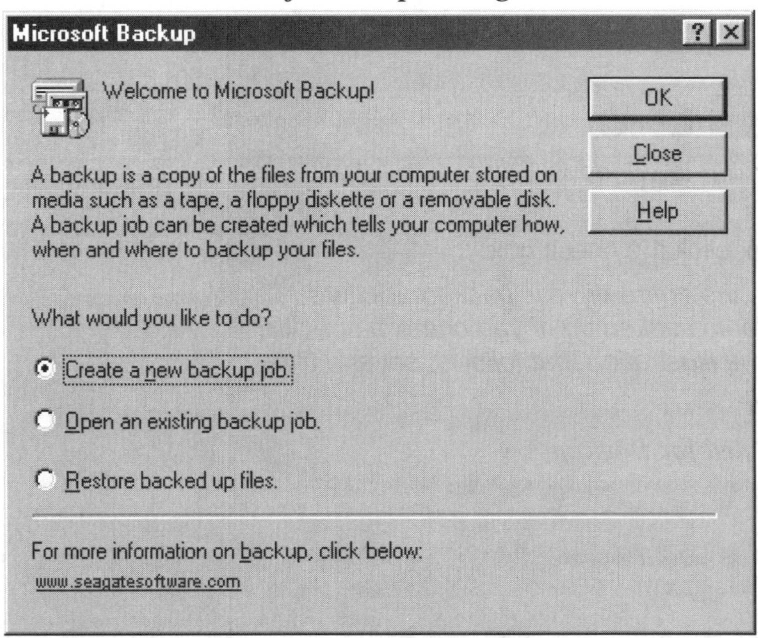

5. Select **Create a <u>n</u>ew backup job** ([Alt]+[N]).

6. Click [OK].

   The Backup Wizard begins, as shown in the following illustration.

7. For this Try It!, select **Back up s<u>e</u>lected files, folders, and drives** ([Alt]+[E]).

Backup Wizard Dialog Box, Choose What to Back Up

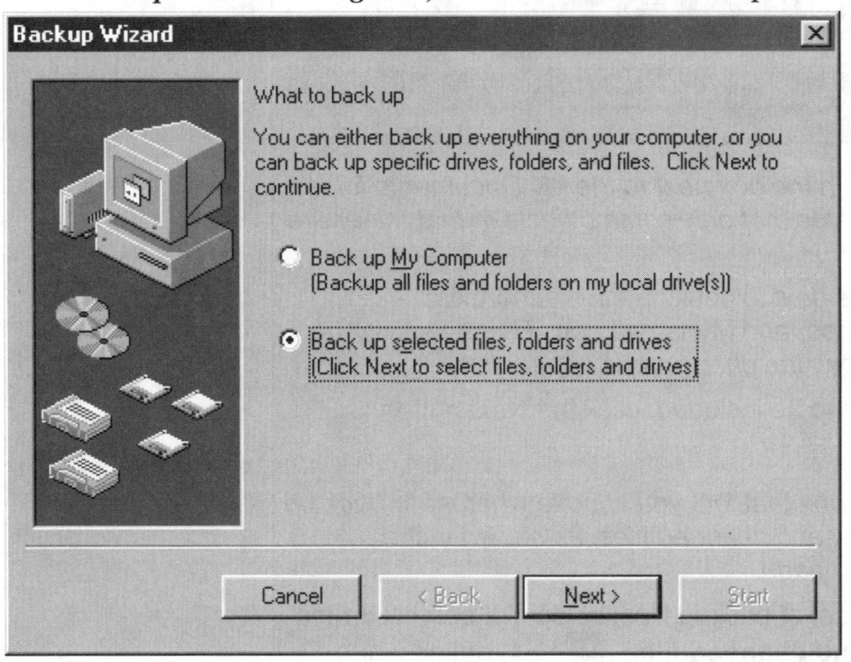

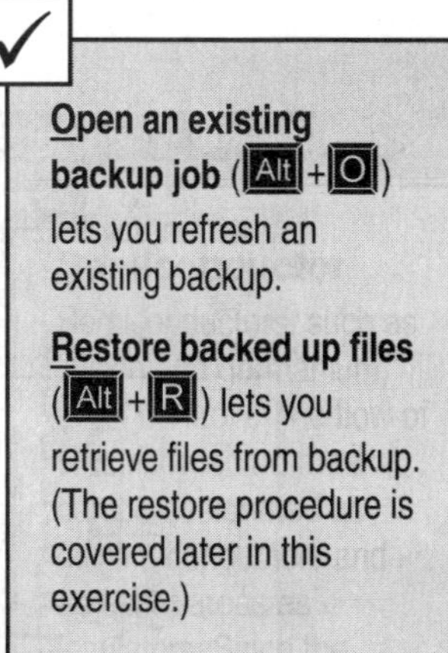

<u>O</u>pen an existing backup job ([Alt]+[O]) lets you refresh an existing backup.

Restore backed up files ([Alt]+[R]) lets you retrieve files from backup. (The restore procedure is covered later in this exercise.)

Back up <u>M</u>y Computer

This option backs up everything on your computer.

Use this option once each time you add software or hardware to your computer.

Restore from the complete system backup only in case of disaster.

Select Objects for Backup

The Backup Wizard lets you choose to back up entire drives, specific folders, or specific files. You display objects in the window in the same way that you do in Windows Explorer except that each object is preceded by a check box.

Try It!

1. Click the <u>N</u>ext button [<u>N</u>ext >] (⌐Alt⌐+⌐N⌐).

   Backup displays a window similar to Windows Explorer to let you choose which files to back up.

2. To select an object for backup, click the check box.

   Note that if you check a drive, the entire drive is backed up. If you check a folder, the entire folder is backed up. If you check a specific file, that file is backed up. In the illustration that follows, several files have been selected for backup.

Objects Selected for Backup

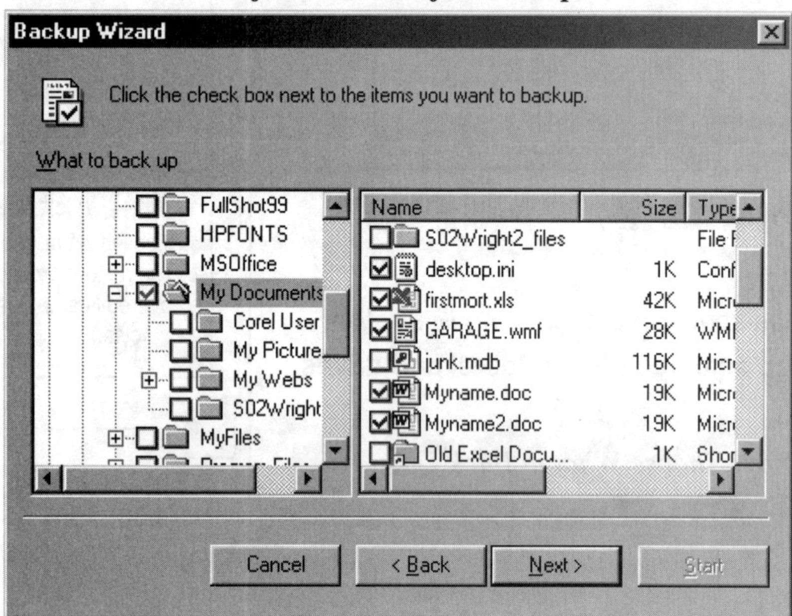

   Note the gray checkmark in the box next to the My Documents folder. The gray check box indicates that only some objects in that folder are included in the backup.

   Note the dark checkmarks next to desktop.ini, firstmort.xls, GARAGE.wmf, Myname.doc, *and* Myname2.doc. *These files will be backed up. (In your window, the checkmarks appear in blue.)*

3. After selecting the objects to be included, click the <u>N</u>ext button
   [<u>N</u>ext >] (⌐Alt⌐+⌐N⌐).

   Backup displays a dialog box that lets you choose whether to back up all the files or only the new and changed files, as shown in the illustration on the following page.

4. If you are creating a new set of backup files, select **All selected files** (⌐Alt⌐+⌐A⌐). Use the **N<u>e</u>w and changed files** (⌐Alt⌐+⌐N⌐) option when you are refreshing an existing backup set.

Backup Wizard, Back Up All Selected Files

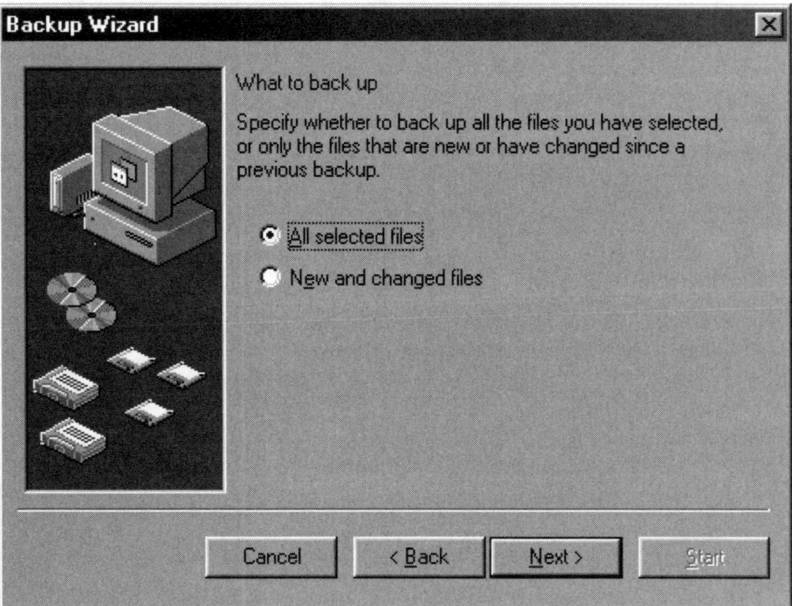

⌨ Try It!

Select Backup Destination

1. Click the <u>N</u>ext button **Next >** (**Alt**+**N**).

   Backup displays a dialog box that lets you choose where to back up, as shown in the following illustration.

2. In the second field, choose the location of your backup disk and give the file a name that you will remember. In the illustration, the file is named by drive letter and the date.

   The extension .qic is added by the Backup Wizard.

Backup Wizard, Choose a Destination for the Backup

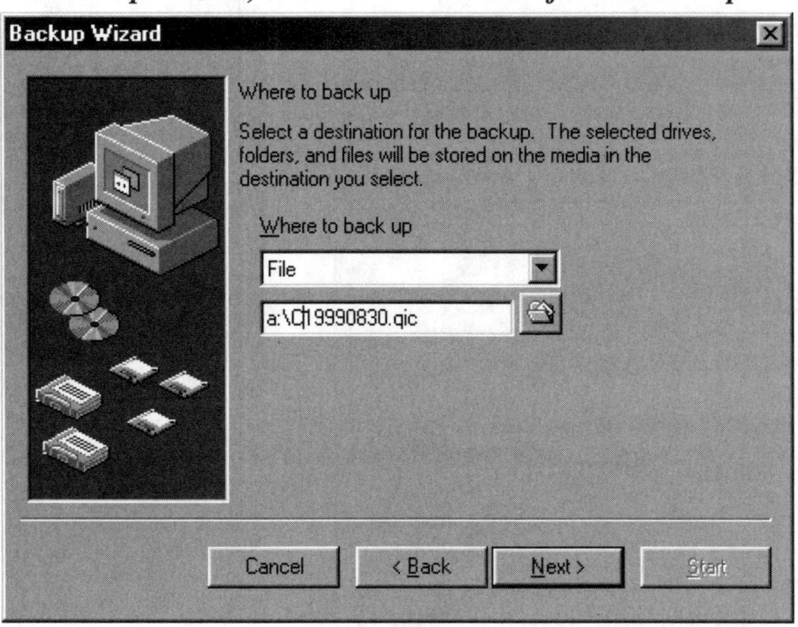

3. Click the <u>N</u>ext button _Next >_ (**Alt**+**N**).

    The wizard displays a dialog box that lets you choose how backup will operate.

Backup Wizard, How to Back Up

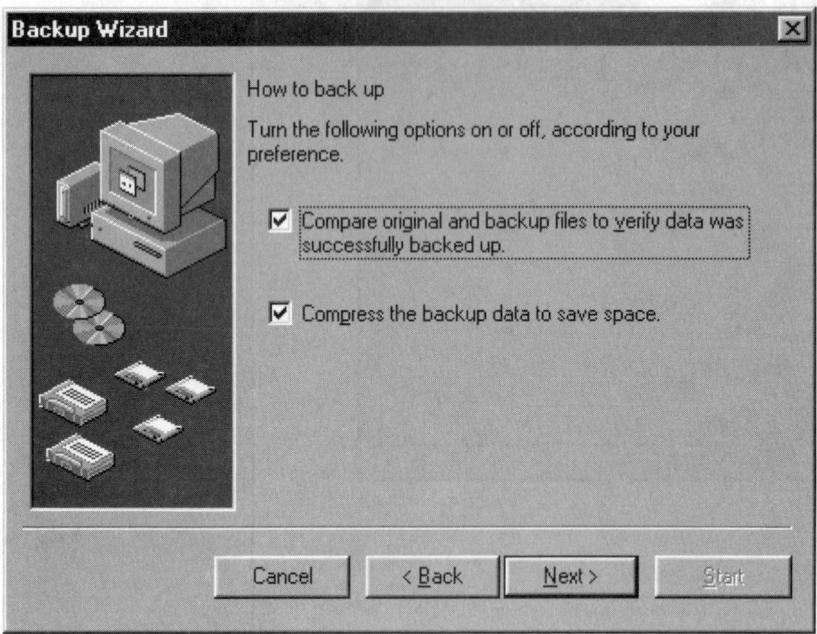

4. Select both options.

    The comparison ensures proper backup and compression saves valuable disk space.

5. Click the <u>N</u>ext button _Next >_ (**Alt**+**N**).

    The wizard displays a dialog box that lets you name the backup job, as shown in the following illustration.

6. Give the job a name that will tell you its purpose.

Backup Wizard, Name the Backup Job

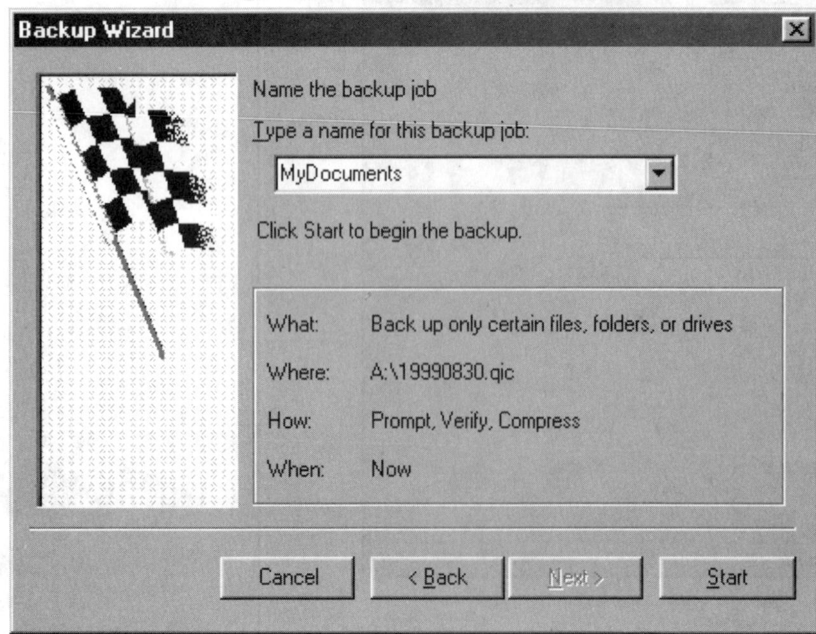

🖥 Try It!

Start Backup

1. After naming the job, click the <u>S</u>tart button [<u>S</u>tart] (Alt+S).

   Backup starts and displays a dialog box that marks the progress of the operation.

   When the job is completed, Backup displays the following message.

Operation Completed Message

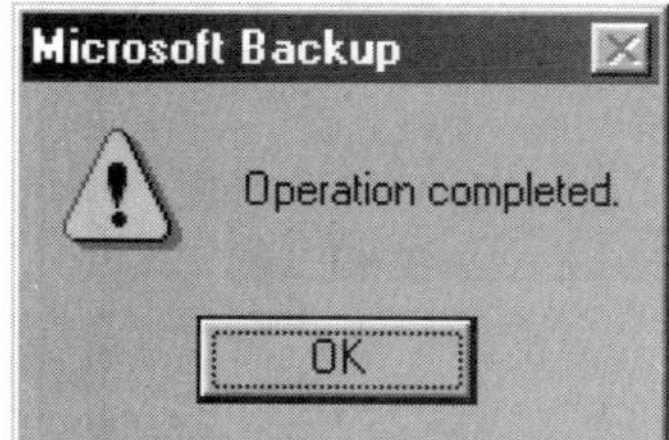

2. Click [OK].

   The progress dialog box indicates whether the operation was successful, as shown in the following illustration.

Backup Progress, After Completion

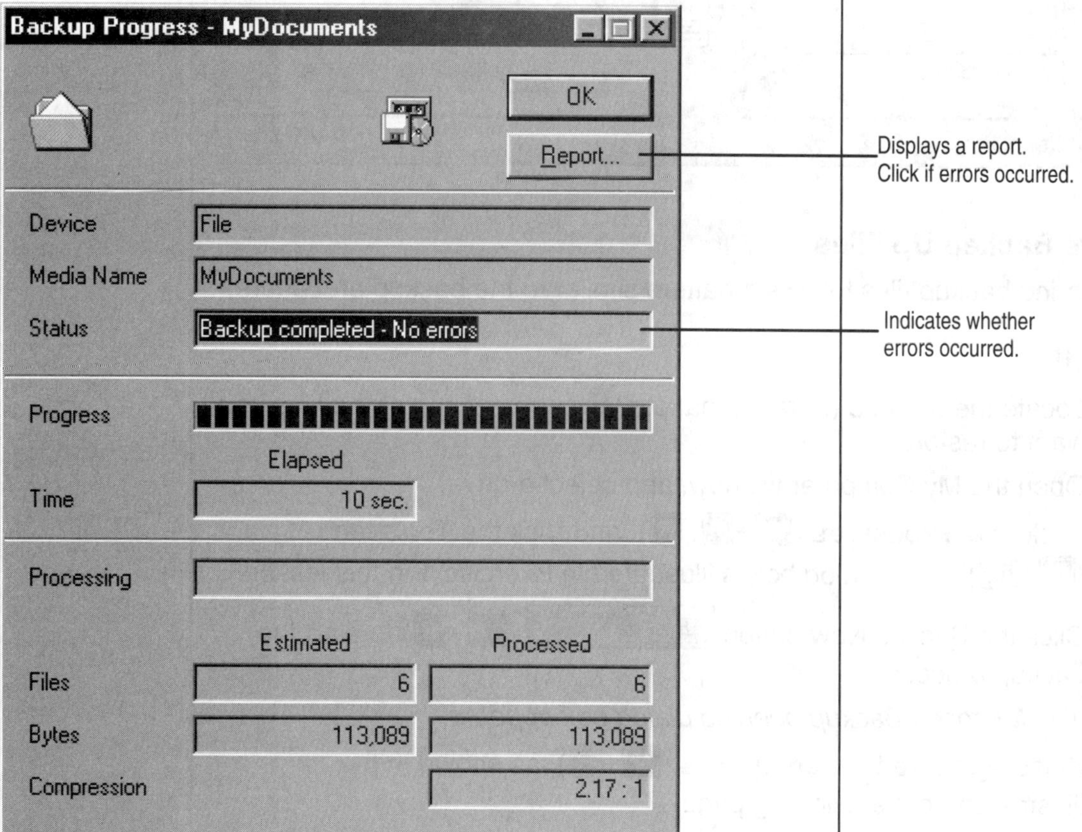

Displays a report. Click if errors occurred.

Indicates whether errors occurred.

3. Click [OK] to close the dialog box.

   Backup displays the Microsoft Backup dialog box for the backup job just completed, as shown in the illustration on the following page.

4. Click the Close button ⊠ on the dialog box to close it.

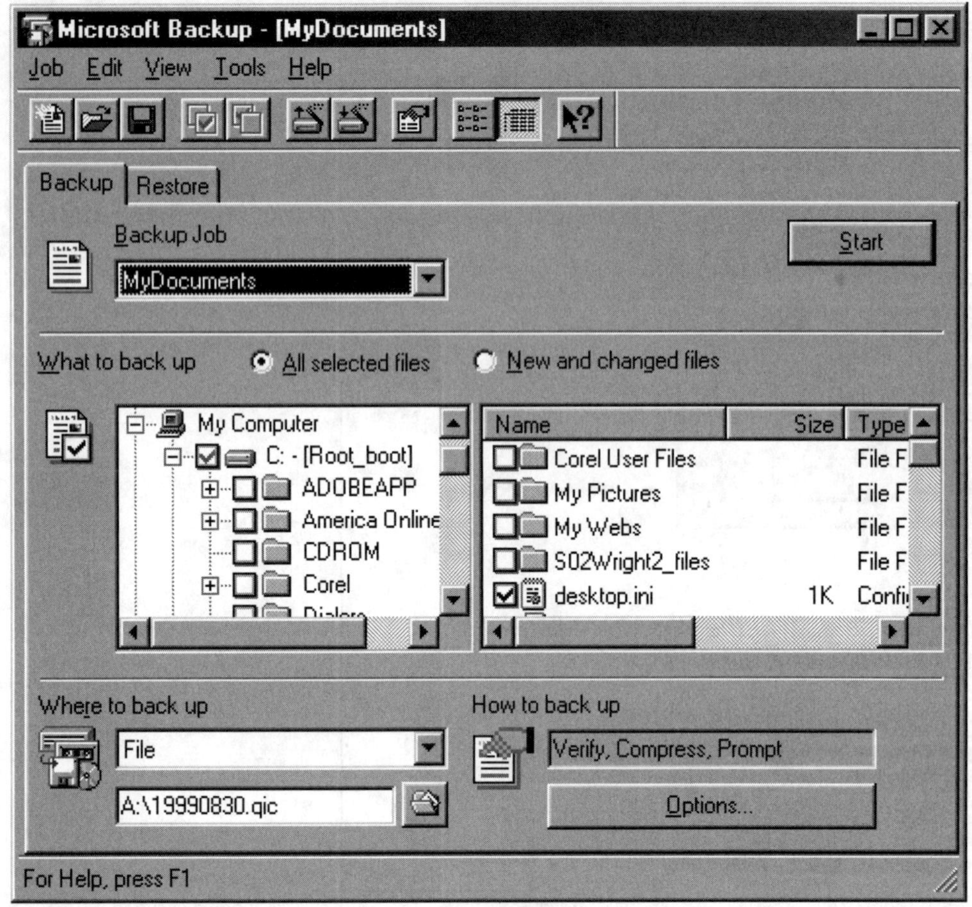

Restore Backed Up Files

- Restoring backup files follows a pattern similar to the backup procedure.

💻 Try It!

1. Locate the diskette (or tape) that contains the backup of the files you want to restore.

2. Open the My Computer window, and select a drive.

3. Click **File**, **Properties** (Alt + F, R), and click the Tools tab (Ctrl + Tab). (This dialog box is illustrated in Exercise 1 in this lesson.)

4. Click the **Backup Now** button Backup Now... (Alt + B) to start the backup process.

   The Microsoft Backup opening dialog box appears.

5. Select **Restore backed up files** (Alt + R), as shown in the illustration on the following page.

Select Restore

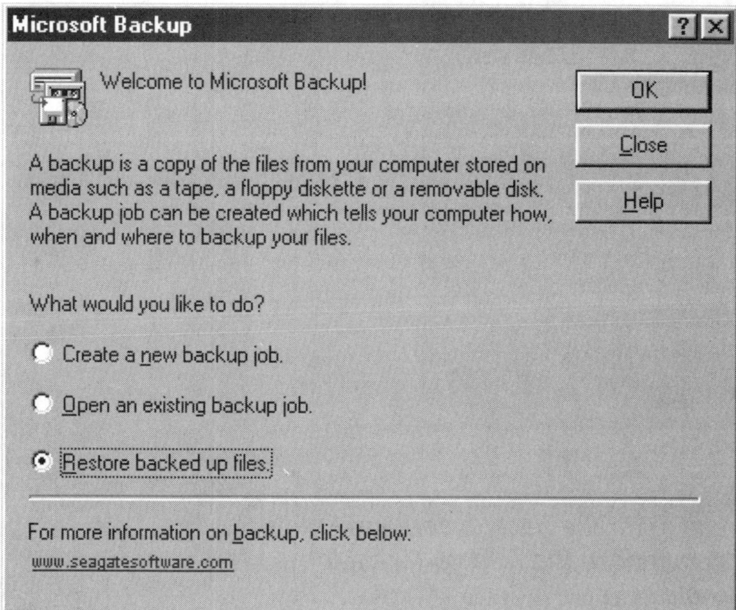

Try It!

Select Where, What, and How to Restore

1. Click [OK].

   The Restore Wizard starts and asks you to choose the backup file from which you want to restore.

Restore Wizard, Choose Location and File From which to Restore

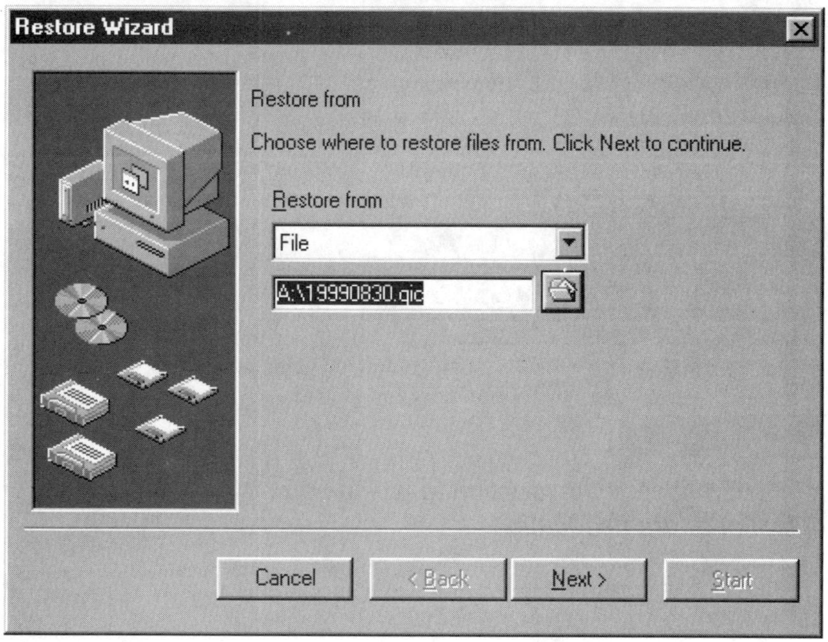

2. Select the drive and file that contains the backup file.

3. Click the Next button [Next >] (Alt+N).

   A box appears that lets you choose the backup set from which you want to restore the files.

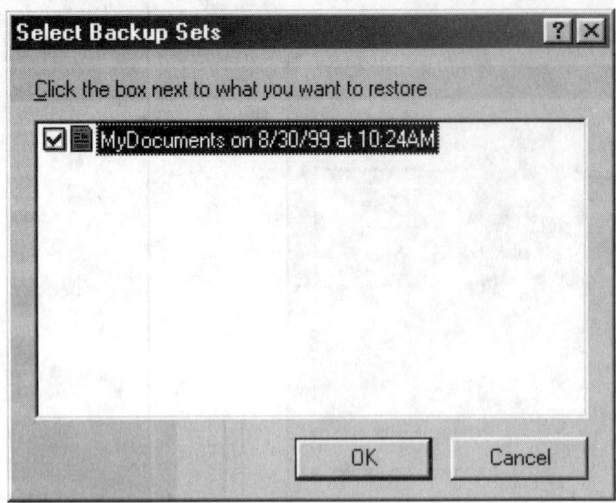

4. Click [OK].

Backup creates a temporary catalog for the backup set, and then displays a dialog box that lets you choose the files you want to restore, as shown in the following illustration.

Restore Wizard, Choose Objects to Restore

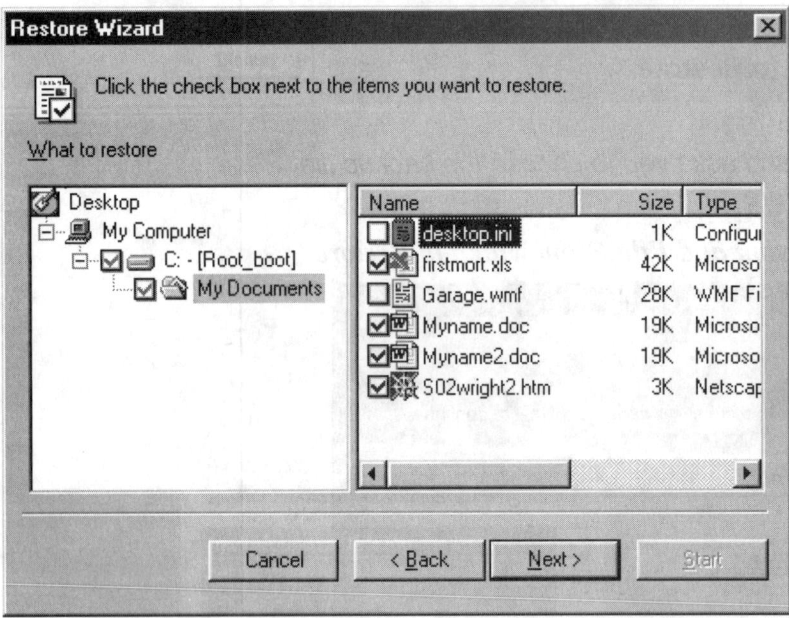

5. Select the files to be restored.

6. Click the Next button [Next >] (Alt+N).

The next wizard dialog box lets you specify the location to which you want the files restored—original or alternate location.

Restore Wizard, Choose Where to Restore

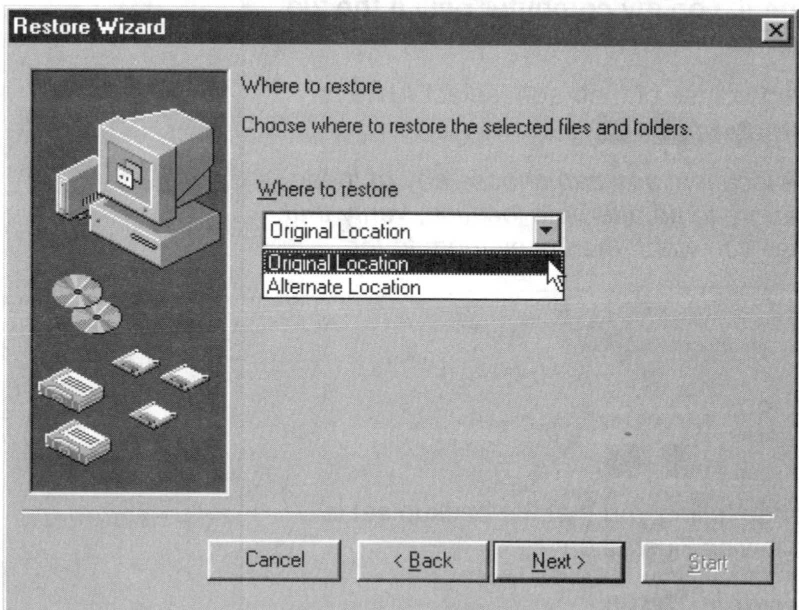

7. Choose Original Location if you want the files to be placed on their original drives in their original folders.

   Choose Alternate Location if you want to place the files elsewhere. The wizard will ask you for the alternate location.

8. Click the <u>N</u>ext button Next > (Alt+N).

   The next wizard dialog box lets you specify how the files are to be restored.

Restore Wizard, How to Restore Files

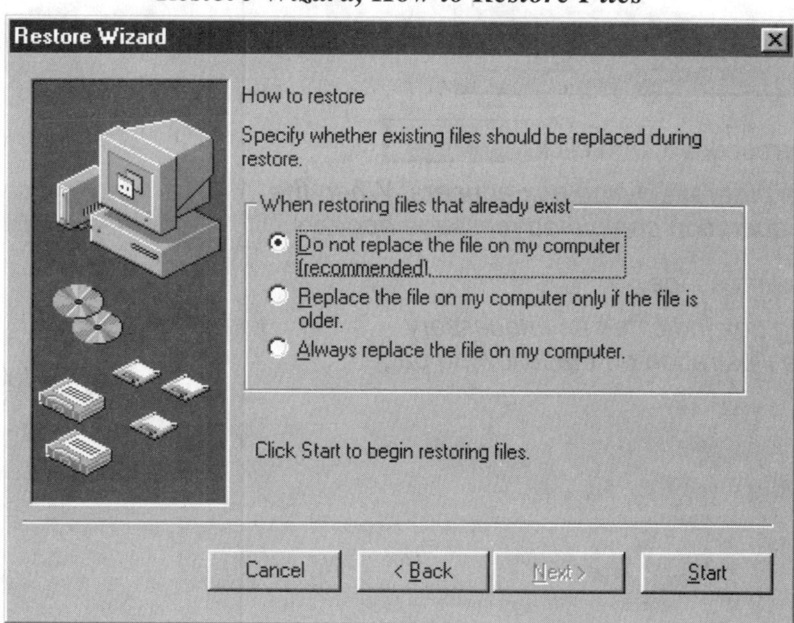

9. Choose the option that suits the kind of restoration you are performing.

   If the files have been deleted, select **<u>D</u>o not replace the file on my computer** (Alt+D).

If your backup files may contain newer versions than those on your computer, select **Replace the file on my computer only if the file is older** (Alt+R).

If you want to replace files regardless of their age, select **Always replace the file on my computer** (Alt+A).

If you restore to an alternate location, you can choose any of these options. You may wish to restore to an alternate location, verify that the restored files are the ones you want, then copy them to the original location.

Try It!

Start and Complete the Operation

1. Click the Start button [Start] (Alt+S).

2. The wizard displays a message telling you that the backup set is required, as shown in the following illustration.

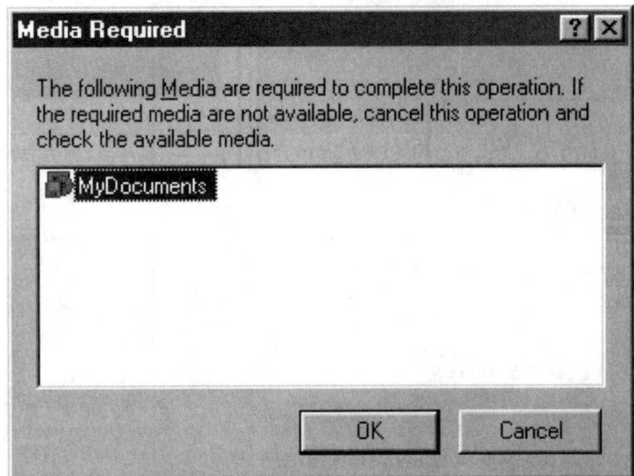

Media Required Message

3. Be sure the disk is in the correct drive, and click [OK].

   The procedure begins and a progress dialog box appears. When the restoration is complete, the operation completed message appears.

4. Click [OK] to close the message.

   The Restore Progress dialog box indicates any necessary information, as shown in the illustration on the following page.

Restore Progress, Skipped Files Reported

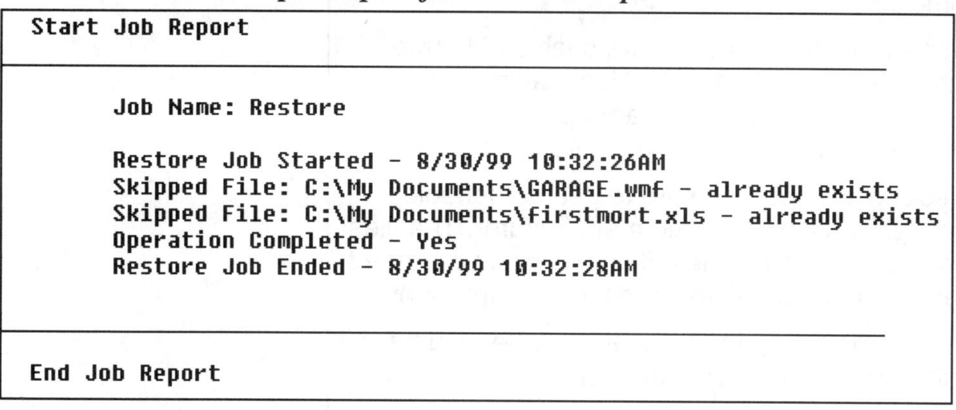

5. Click the <u>R</u>eport button [<u>R</u>eport...] (**Alt**+**R**) to view the report if you are not sure why files were skipped or not restored.

   The report is displayed in Notepad. A sample report is shown in the following illustration.

Sample Report from Restore Operation

```
Start Job Report
________________________________________________


    Job Name: Restore

    Restore Job Started - 8/30/99 10:32:26AM
    Skipped File: C:\My Documents\GARAGE.wmf - already exists
    Skipped File: C:\My Documents\firstmort.xls - already exists
    Operation Completed - Yes
    Restore Job Ended - 8/30/99 10:32:28AM

________________________________________________

End Job Report
```

6. After viewing the report, exit Notepad.

7. Click [OK] on the Restore Progress dialog box.

8. Click the <u>C</u>lose button [<u>C</u>lose] (**Alt**+**C**) on the Microsoft Backup (Restore) dialog box.

Learn about Virus Protection
■ Protect against Viruses   ■ Run a Virus Scan

NOTES

Protect against Viruses

■ Computer viruses range from trivially irritating to horrifyingly devastating. Some are nearly harmless; the Have a Nice Day virus, for example, simply turns every Microsoft Word document (.DOC) into a template (.DOT) file when it is saved. Once the virus is eliminated, the data in the .DOT file can be copied back into a .DOC. Many users may not know that such a virus has infected their files.

■ Other viruses can cripple your machine or make it completely unusable. Some of these viruses attack the integrity of the hard drive and destroy the system's ability to save and retrieve files. Others reformat the hard drive, or infect the boot information on the disk so that you cannot start your machine.

■ Viruses are the products of malice. Those who create them and those who knowingly pass them on to others are the worst kind of vandal who deserve the strongest condemnation; they do not deserve even grudging admiration, no matter how skillful their programming.

■ You can help protect your computer against viruses by being watchful and cautious and taking simple steps.

- Install and regularly use virus-checking software, such as McAfee VirusScan, Norton AntiVirus, or Dr. Solomon's Virex (also from McAfee). These programs check files as they are opened on your computer to ensure that no known virus can infect your machine.

- If you have a virus-checking program, be sure to get the periodic updates to the virus recognition files from the manufacturer. The files are available via downloads from Web sites. It is especially important to keep your virus scanner up to date if you use the Web frequently.

- Run the virus scan on your disks regularly, especially after you have transferred files from the Web or another computer.

- Download files from Web sites with caution. Be sure you can trust the source of the files you are taking from the Web to your local machine. When in doubt, don't download.

- Do not open e-mail from any source you do not recognize. E-mail is a frequent carrier of viruses, and some virus creators piggy-back disk-destroying viruses on **spam** (junk e-mail), luring unsuspecting users into infecting their local computers.

- Borrow diskettes only from people you trust. Scan the disk for viruses as the first step in transferring files from it to your machine.

- Pay attention to messages from Microsoft applications. For example, if you save a file from the Web as HTML, you can open the file in

Internet Explorer from the folder where you saved it. When you start to open it, Internet Explorer displays the message shown in the illustration that follows. (The illustration is from Windows, but the Mac OS version contains the same information.)

Internet Explorer, Caution about Viruses

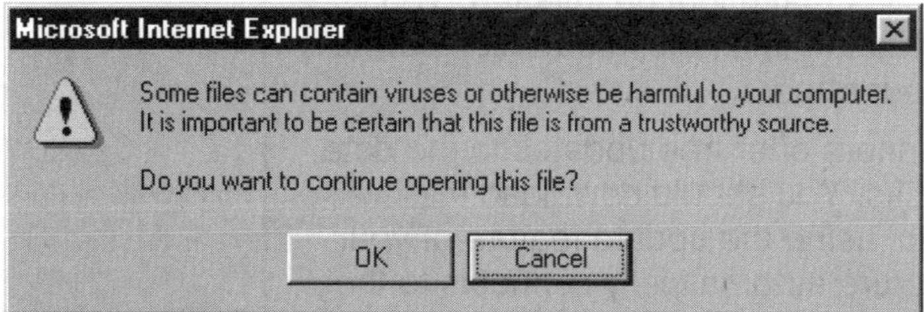

- Similarly, Microsoft Office applications warn you if they encounter a macro in a file. For example, if the Word template (.DOT) file has a macro that runs automatically, Word displays the message shown in the illustration that follows when you open the template. (The illustration is from Windows, but the Mac OS version contains the same information.)

Microsoft Office Macro Warning

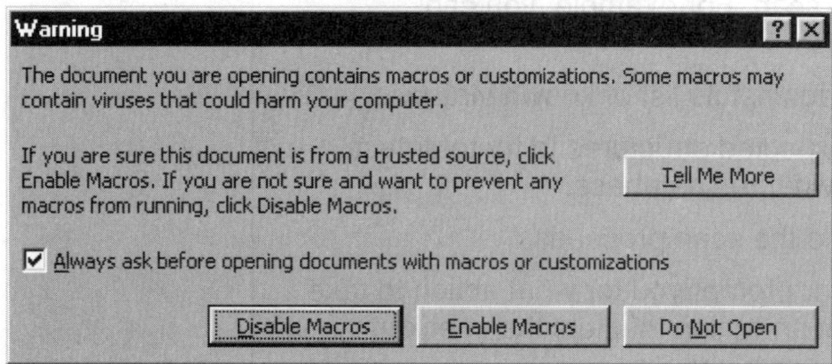

- **Heed these warnings.** Do not open the file if you have any doubts about the file. Click Cancel or Do Not Open until you are sure it is safe to do so.

Run a Virus Scan

- When you install virus protection software, it automatically places itself as a watchdog over the activity on your system. When files are opened or downloaded or when you look at the contents of diskettes, the virus scanner checks each action to be sure that no file or disk houses a recognizable virus.

- To check whether the virus protection is active in windows, point to the icon for the automatic virus scanner that appears in your Windows taskbar. The illustration that follows shows the McAfee Vshield icon and the ScreenTip that tells you the application is enabled.

Check Automatic Virus Protection in Windows

- In Mac OS, the virus scan icon appears on the Control Strip, as shown at the right. Click the black arrow to display a pop-up menu. If the pop-up menu shows **On** selected, automatic virus protection is enabled.

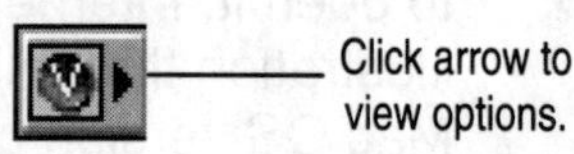

- Besides this automatic protection, virus scanners let you scan your system or a disk for viruses at any time. Virus scanners offer a variety of options for diagnosing and repairing files that might be infected. You should read your program's documentation and help information carefully to learn the options that best meet your needs.

- **Update Virus Protection.** Virus scanners offer free updates to the data that they use when scanning your disks. You should download the latest virus protection at least once a month, using the update feature of your virus scanner. In most cases, this feature automatically connects to the correct Web site and downloads the latest virus protection data files.

- For example, the automatic update feature of Virex on Mac OS can be started from within the Virex program by clicking the eUpdate button.

- **Run a Scan.** Even with automatic protection on, you may wish to check your disks for viruses periodically. In general, virus checkers do the following during a scan:

  - Let you specify which drives are checked.

  - Let you specify options for the scan. For example, you can include/exclude certain file types.

  - Check each file on the drives against its list of known viruses.

  - Check files for unusual or unexpected structures to try to detect viruses that are not in the known-virus database.

  - Display status information while the scan proceeds.

  - If a virus is found, take action or prompt you for what action to take. Most virus checkers let you set an option that lets the checker automatically repair files with known viruses.

  - Create a report that list any viruses found and the action taken. The report also lists files that may be infected and should be monitored.

- **Sample Windows Scan.** The illustration on the following page shows the McAfee VirusScan opening dialog box for scanning Windows drives. The dialog box has three tabs.

  - The Where & What tab lets you specify which drives, files, and folders are to be included in the scan.

  - The Actions tab of the VirusScan dialog box, lets you specify what action the scanner is to take if it encounters an infected file.

  - The Reports tab of the VirusScan dialog box lets you specify how VirusScan is to report its results.

VirusScan Dialog Box

Where & What Tab

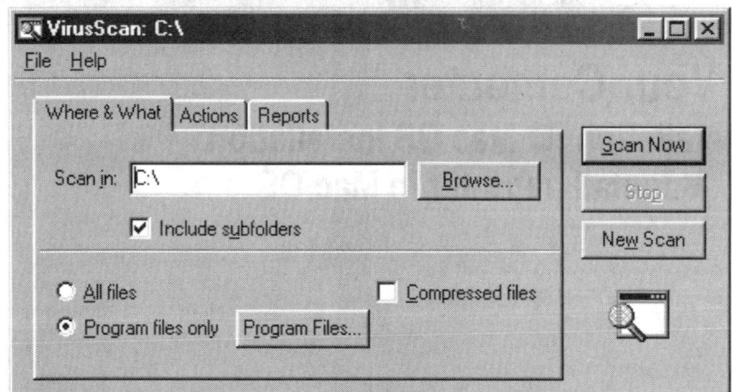

Actions Tab

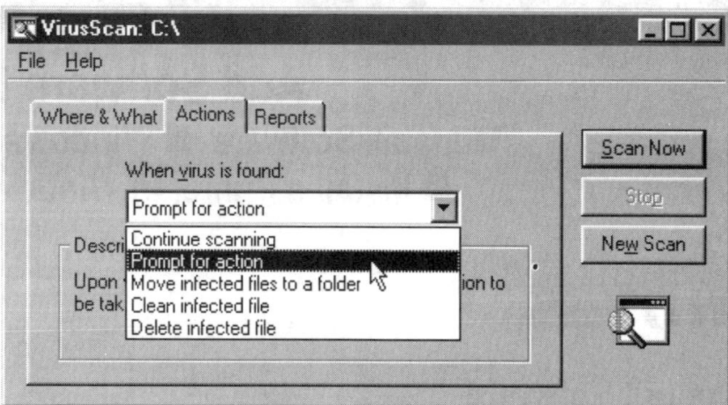

Reports Tab

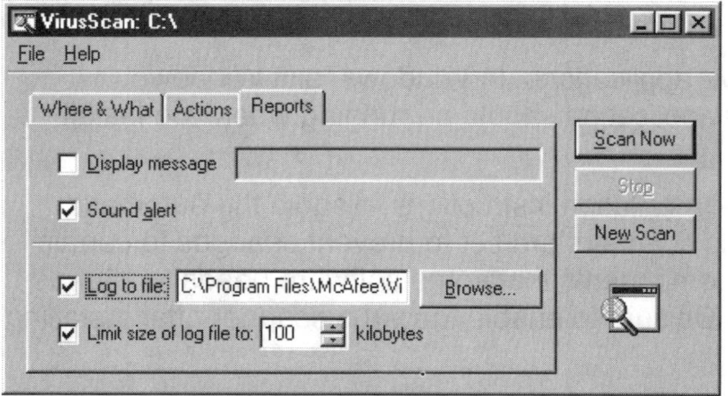

- **Sample Mac OS Scan**. The following illustration shows the Virex dialog box for scanning drives on the Mac OS.

Mac OS Virex Dialog Box

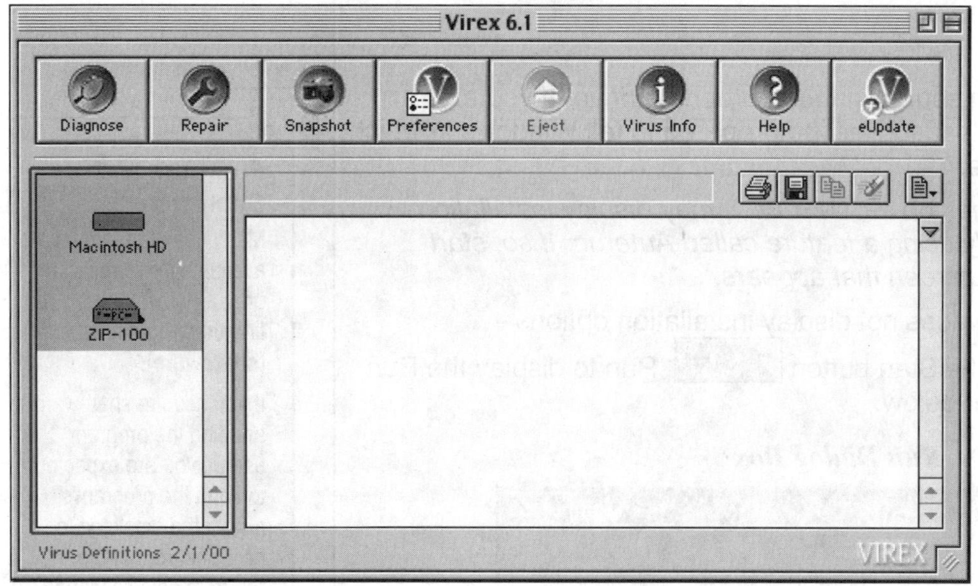

- The Diagnose, Repair, and Snapshot buttons start scan procedures. The Preferences button lets you set options for Virex. The Virus Info button gives you information about known viruses.

Add Software to Your Computer
■ Install Software ■ Windows Installation ■ Mac OS Installation
■ Install a Printer in Windows ■ Install a Printer in Mac OS

NOTES

Install Software

■ When you purchase a new software package or need to re-install an application, read through the installation instructions before attempting to add it to your system. Generally, the following advice is helpful.

- Shut down all active applications. In Windows, exit Windows Explorer. No other application should be running when you install software.

- If requested by the installation instructions, disable the automatic virus scanner. Virus scanners are set to prevent changes to certain operating system components that some software needs to alter as part of installation. Be sure to enable the virus scanner after installing the new software.

- Most software nowadays comes on a CD-ROM. In Windows, you will find it helpful to know the drive letter of your CD-ROM drive.

- Learn whether your software uses Install or Setup as the command to start installation.

Windows Installation

1. Place the installation source in the appropriate drive. If you are installing from downloaded files, be prepared to tell Windows in which folder the files reside.

   If your software comes on a CD-ROM, it may display installation options automatically using a feature called Autorun. If so, start installation from the screen that appears.

2. If your new software does not display installation options automatically, click the Start button , Run to display the Run dialog box, as shown below.

Run Dialog Box

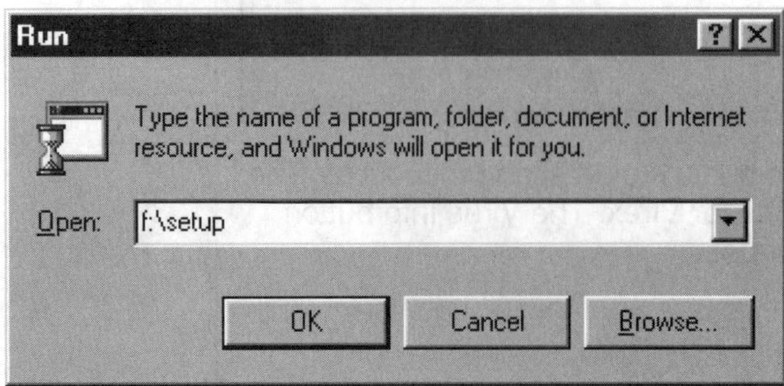

Scan First

If you download software from the Web or acquire free software from any source, scan the installation files for viruses before starting installation.

Freeware and Shareware

Many useful programs are available free (**freeware**) or at a nominal cost if you find the program useful (**shareware**).

If you acquire shareware and find the program useful, you are expected to send the program's author the small fee to help ensure that the program gets continued support.

3. In the <u>O</u>pen text box, type the path of the installation program, or use the <u>B</u>rowse button [Browse...] to locate the installation program.

4. Click [OK].

    The installation program starts.

5. Carefully follow the instructions that appear on the screen and in the documentation that accompanies the software.

Mac OS Installation

- The following is a general guide to installing software from a CD-ROM.

    1. Insert the CD-ROM in your CD-ROM or DVD drive.

    2. Double-click the icon for the CD on the desktop.

    3. In the CD window, double-click the install icon or follow the instructions that may appear in the window.

        The installation program starts. The illustrations below show the AppleWorks 5 CD with the Install AppleWorks icon selected, and the window for installing Microsoft Office 98.

    4. Carefully follow the instructions that appear on the screen and in any documentation that accompanies the software.

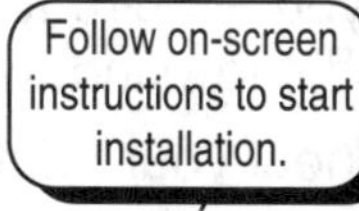

Sample Mac OS Installation Startups

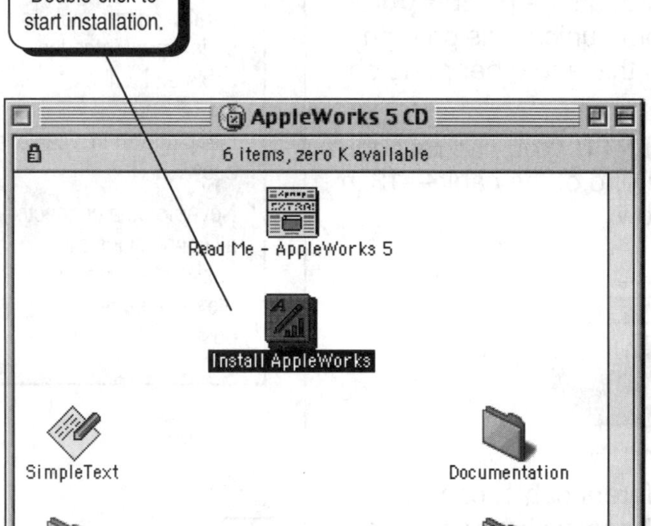

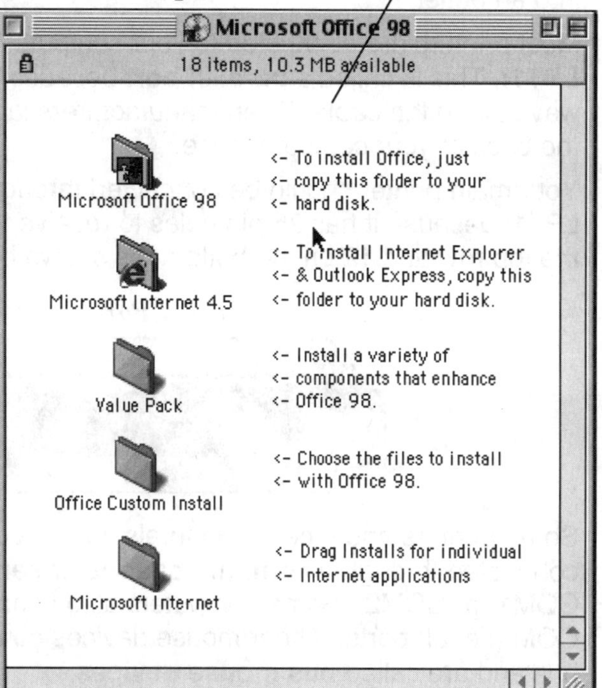

If you double-click an option such as Value Pack in the Microsoft Office 98 window, another window opens, as shown in the illustration on the following page.

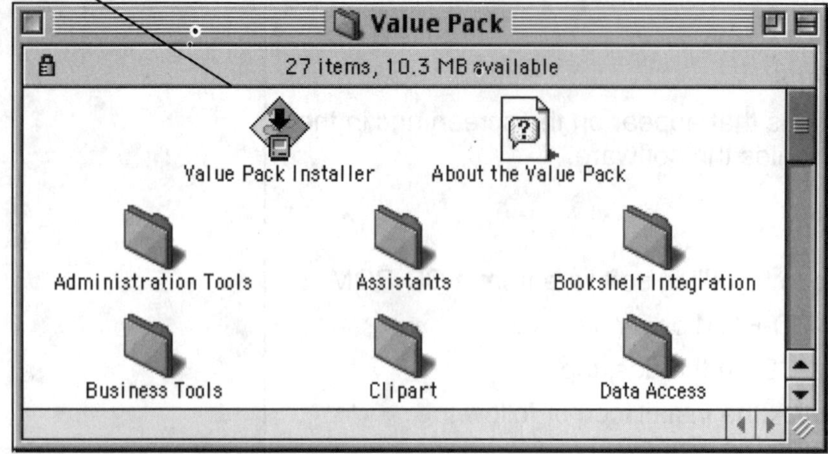

Install a Printer in Windows

- When you acquire a printer, you must connect its cable to the computer and add it to Windows' list of printers before you can use it.

- To connect your printer, shut down your computer and connect the printer cable to the correct computer **port** (see below) and plug the electric cord into an outlet.

- Most printers are connected to your computer through the **printer port LPT1:**. This is called a **parallel port** because communications go both ways along the cable. Often manufacturers label this and other ports on the back of your computer case.

- Your main printer should be connected through LPT1:. You can recognize LPT1: because it has 25 pin holes to receive the end of the cable—13 in the top row and 12 on the bottom, as shown below.

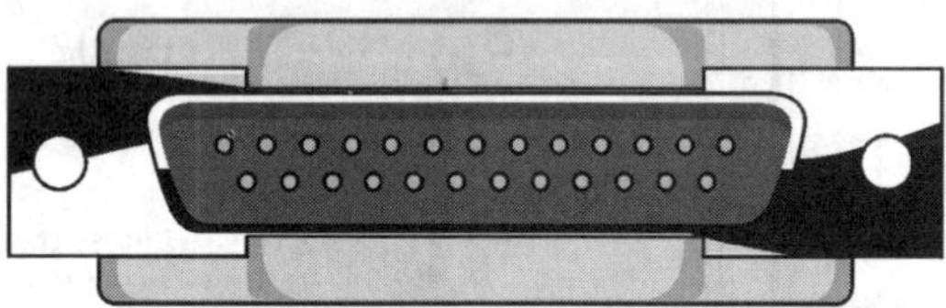

- Some printers and other peripherals, using a different cable, can be connected through a **communications** or **serial port** with a name like COM1: or COM2:. Some computers also connect the mouse to one of the COM (serial) ports. (Other mouse devices connect directly through the bus and are called **bus mouse devices**.)

- Once you have connected your printer and plugged it in, you are ready to add your **printer driver** (software that lets the printer work) to Windows. To do so, complete the procedure outlined in the steps that follow.

Try It!

1. Have your Windows installation CD-ROM or disks handy. You may need them to install the printer.

2. Turn on your computer and get Windows started.

3. Turn on your printer.

Connecting Cables

Computer cables and connectors are built so that you cannot connect a parallel printer cable to a serial port. Match the cable end to the correct socket and you will find that plugging in a cable is easy.

Never force a connector; all connections slide easily into place when they are properly positioned.

Automatic Recognition

Windows may recognize the new device automatically and display a dialog box that gives you the option to install the device.

4. Open the My Computer window, and double-click the Printers

    icon Printers to open the Printers folder, shown in the following illustration.

Printers Folder Opened

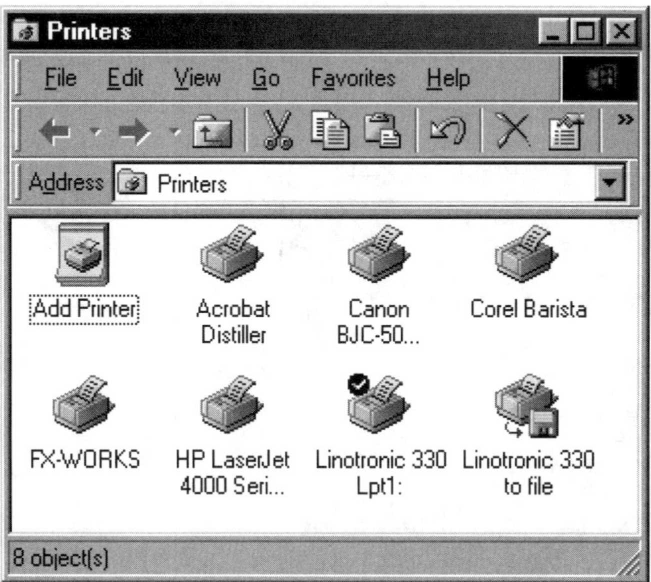

Try It!

Start the Procedure and Select a Printer

1. Double-click the Add Printer icon Add Printer to start the Add Printer Wizard.

    The Add Printer Wizard starts and displays a dialog box to get you started.

2. Click the Next button Next > to display the dialog box shown below.

Add Printer Wizard, Step 1, Choose Local or Network

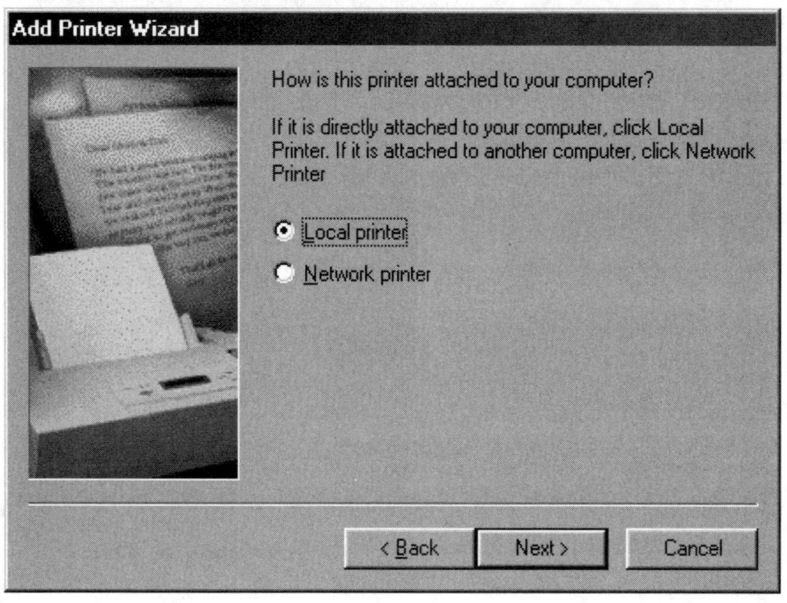

3. Select Local printer to install the printer driver on your computer.

    If you are on a network and know the network address of the printer, you can choose Network printer.

4. Click the Next button [Next >] to display the next dialog box as shown below.

Add Printer Wizard, Step 2, Select a Printer

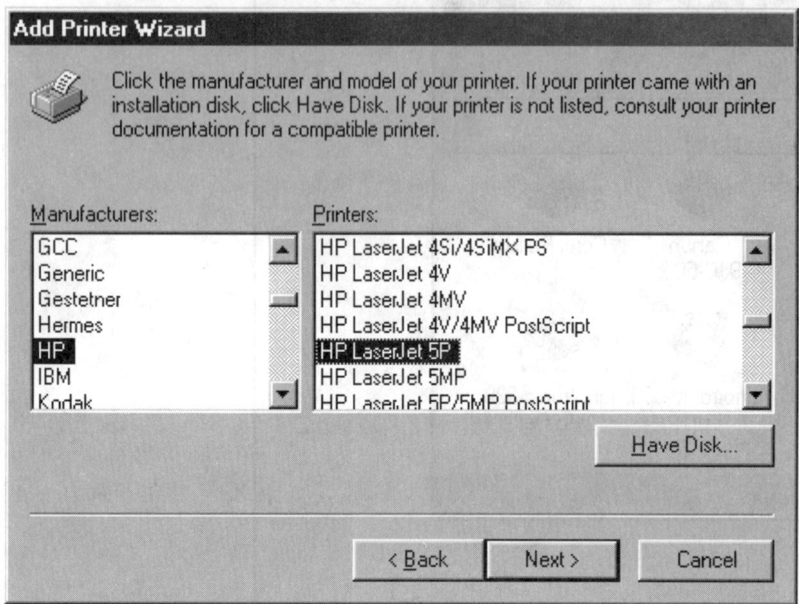

5. In the left pane, Manufacturers, select the manufacturer of your printer. (If the manufacturer is not listed, you may need to follow installation instructions provided by the printer maker rather than the procedure outlined here.)

6. In the right pane, select the specific printer you are installing.

    If your manufacturer provides a driver file on disk, place the disk in the appropriate drive and click the Have Disk button [Have Disk...].

    The Add Printer Wizard displays a dialog box that allows you to specify the location of the printer driver file. (The box offers a Browse button to help you locate the file.)

    If you are uncertain about whether to click the Have Disk button, do not use it. Windows contains drivers for all the printers listed in the second Add Printer Wizard dialog box.

7. When you have selected the manufacturer and the printer, click the Next button [Next >] to display the third wizard dialog box, shown on the next page.

🖳 Try It!

Select a Port, Name the Printer, and Print a Test Page

Add Printer Wizard, Step 3, Select a Port

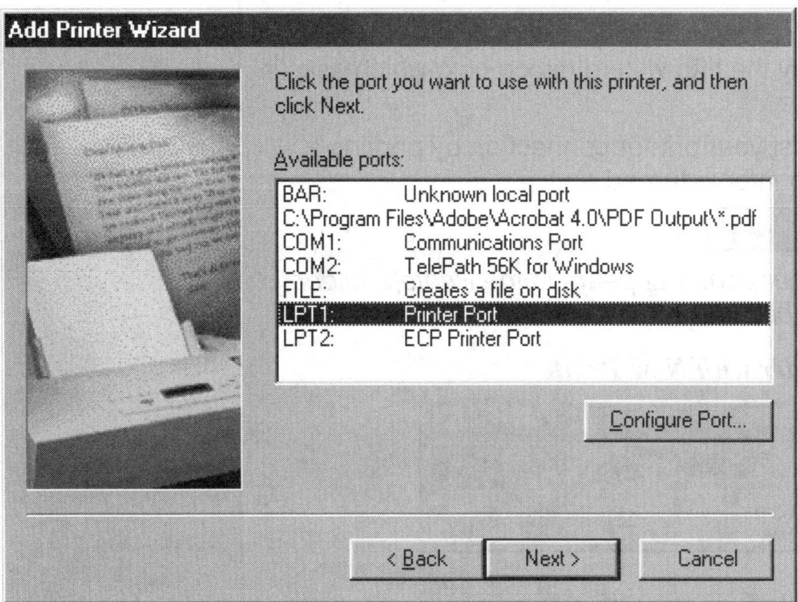

1. Select the port where the printer is connected. Normally this is LPT1: as shown in the illustration.

   Unless you know you need to change port settings, do not click the Configure Port button. The default configuration is correct for most printers.

2. After selecting the port, click the Next button [Next >] to display the fourth wizard dialog box, shown in the following illustration.

Add Printer Wizard, Step 4, Name the Printer

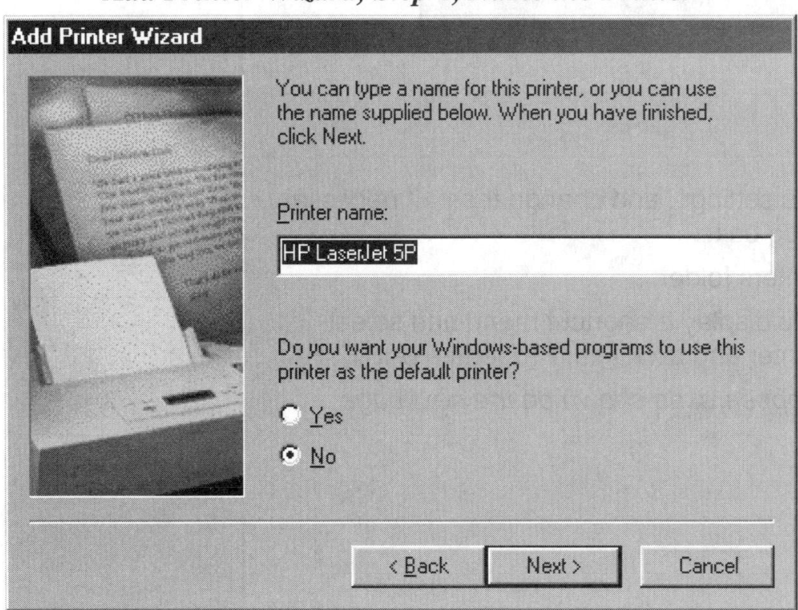

3. Accept the <u>P</u>rinter name displayed or type a new name.

4. If this printer is the one you plan to use most of the time, select <u>Y</u>es to the question *Do you want your Windows-based programs to use this printer as the default printer?*.

5. After naming the printer and setting its default status, click the Next button $\boxed{\text{Next >}}$ to display the fifth wizard dialog box, which asks if you want to print a test page.

6. Click <u>Y</u>es to let Windows test your printer connection by printing a test page. (Make sure the printer is turned on.)

7. Click the Finish button $\boxed{\text{Finish}}$.

   The test page prints and your printer appears in the Printers folder, as shown in the illustration below.

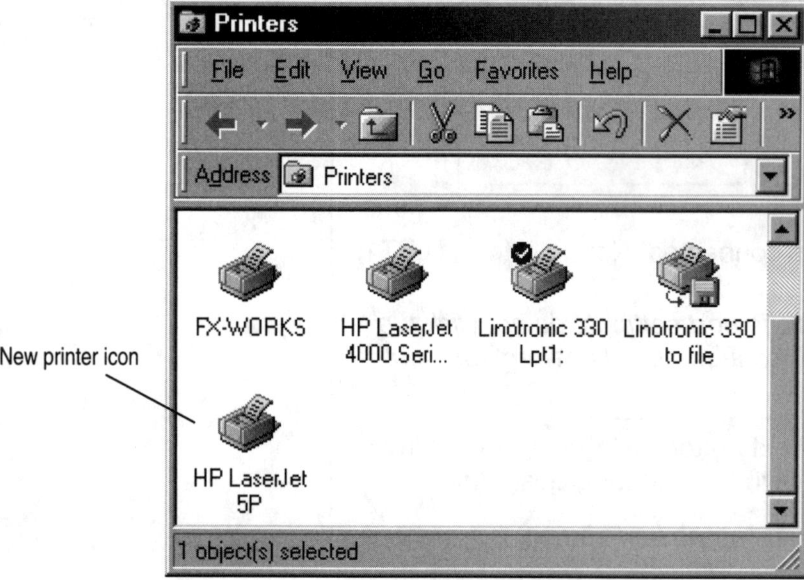

Printers Folder with New Printer

New printer icon

⌨ Try It!

Check the Printer Properties

- You can review the printer's settings, and change them, if necessary, through the Properties dialog box.

1. Select the printer in the Printers folder.

2. Right-click the printer icon to display a shortcut menu and select P<u>r</u>operties, or select the printer and click <u>F</u>ile, P<u>r</u>operties (Alt+F, R).

   The Properties dialog box appears, as shown on the next page.

Printer Properties Dialog Box, Details Tab

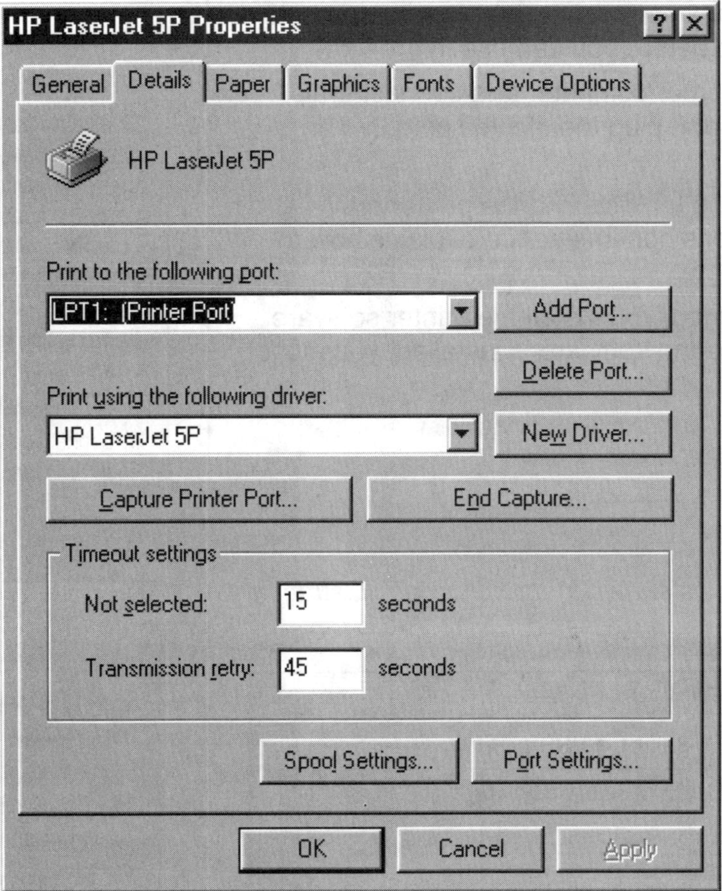

- Do not change the default settings unless recommended by the manufacturer.

- If you acquire an updated printer driver, click the New Driver button [New Driver...] on the Details tab in the dialog box. The Add Printer Wizard guides you through adding the driver.

Printing

- You can check printing as it is running by double-clicking the printer icon in the Printers folder or double-clicking the printer icon that appears at the far right of the task bar. A dialog box appears that lets you monitor printing progress. All files sent to the printer are listed in the dialog box.

Install a Printer in Mac OS

- When you acquire a printer, you must connect its cable to the computer and install the appropriate software before you can use it.

- To connect your printer, shut down your computer and connect the printer cable to the correct computer **port** and plug the electric cord into an outlet.

- In Mac OS, you need the instructions for installing the printer provided by the manufacturer. The manufacturer's documentation explains how to connect the printer to your Macintosh.

- Once the printer is correctly connected, you install the printer software provided by the manufacturer. Once the software is installed, you must use Chooser to select the printer.

Try It!

1. Click the Apple menu.

2. Select **Chooser**.

   The Chooser window appears, as shown in the following illustration.

Chooser

3. In the left pane, select the printer you want to use.

   Note that some printer connections require that AppleTalk be active. If it should be active and is not, a message tells you to make it active when you try to close Chooser.

4. Click the Close box ▣ to close Chooser.

   You may receive a message telling you that your printer choice has changed and that you need to change it in the applications when you want to print.

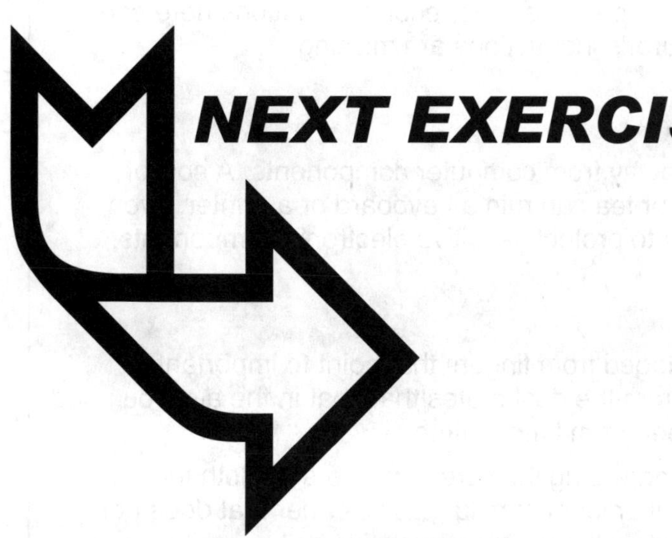
NEXT EXERCISE

Exercise 5

Keep Your Computer System Clean

■ General Care Instructions ■ Clean the Monitor ■ Save Energy and Preserve Screens
■ Clean the Keyboard ■ Clean the Mouse ■ Clean the Cases
■ Maintain Computers and Peripherals

NOTES

IMPORTANT NOTE

- **Before cleaning any computer component, shut the computer down and disconnect from electricity sources.**

- The recommendations in this exercise are based on the instructions from several computer manufacturers. Read the manufacturer's instructions and rely on them whenever possible. The recommendations here can help when the manufacturer's instructions are missing.

General Care Instructions

- Keep food and drink far away from computer components. A spill of coffee, water, soda pop, or tea can ruin a keyboard or a printer, even though manufacturers try to protect sensitive electronic components.

Clean the Monitor

- Monitor screens get smudged from fingers that point to important displays. They get dirty from the dust motes that float in the air. You need to clean the monitor screen from time to time.

- Manufacturers recommend wiping the screen with a soft cloth that has been sprayed with a small amount of mild glass cleaner that does not contain alcohol. Do not spray the monitor screen directly.

- Gently wipe the screen with the cloth and let it dry before restarting your computer. Specially prepared and individually packaged screen cleaning cloths are available from computer stores.

Save Energy and Preserve Screens

- Both Windows and Mac OS let you establish settings that can help you conserve energy when your machine's components are not active. These energy conservation settings supersede the need for screen saver programs, even though Windows offers a number of built-in screen savers.

- Screen savers, however artful and attractive, are not really necessary. They were invented to prevent displays from leaving ghostly patterns on the monitor screen because of a process called "burn-in." Since your computer can automatically turn the monitor dark when no processing has taken place for a while, screen savers can be eliminated.

Advice on Mac Care

The Mac OS Help system has good advice about caring for your Macintosh computer.

With Finder displayed:

1. Click **Help**.
2. Choose **Help Center**.
3. Click **About Your Macintosh**.
4. Click **Health, safety, and maintenance**.
5. Click the desired topic in the right pane of the Help window:

   - **Health-related informaton about computer use**
   - **Safety instructions**
   - **Handling your computer equipment**
   - **Cleaning your computer equipment**

- Screen saver programs also take up valuable room in memory and on the hard disk, and they sometimes interfere with other applications. Use the energy saving settings of your operating system and avoid screen savers.

**Try It!**

Control System Energy Use in Windows

1. Open the Control Panel.

2. Double-click the Display icon Display.

3. Click the Screen Saver tab (Ctrl+Tab).

   The Display Properties dialog box appears, as shown below.

   Display Properties Dialog Box, Screen Saver Tab

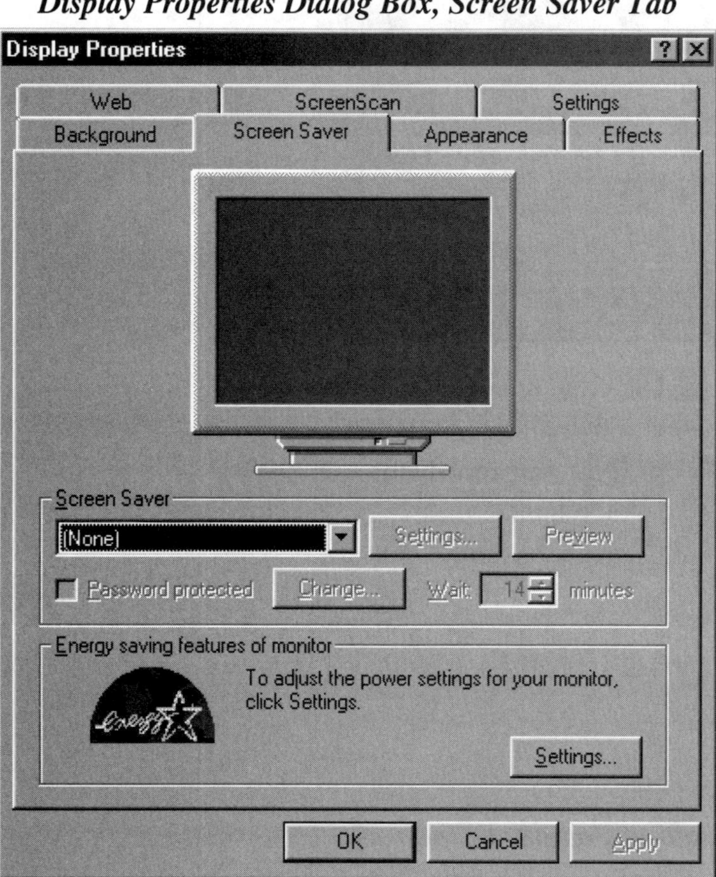

4. Click the **S**ettings button Settings... (Alt+S) in the **Energy saving features of monitor** section.

   Windows 98 displays the Power Management Properties dialog box shown in the illustration on the following page.

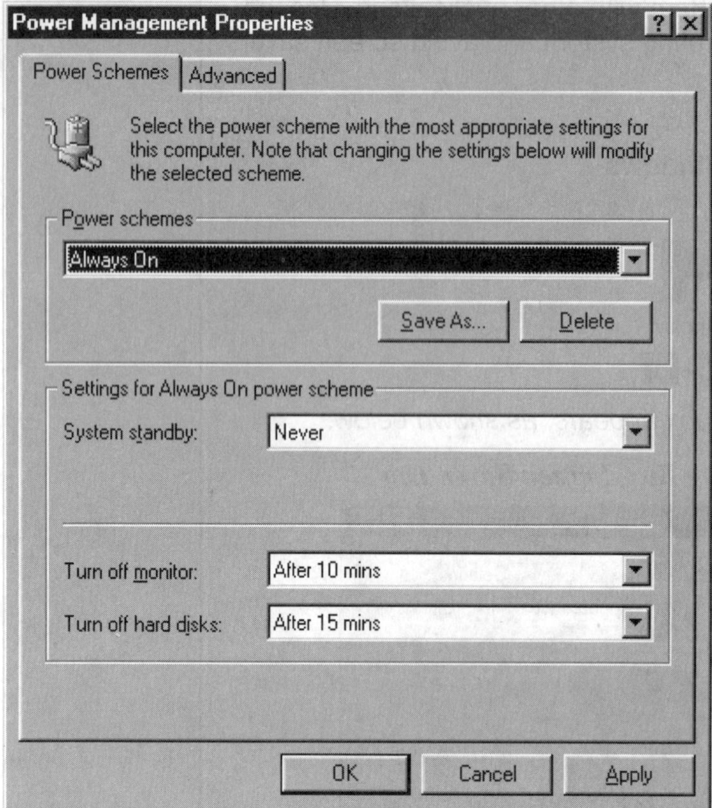

5. Select **Turn off monitor** (Alt+M,) and specify the number of minutes or hours before the monitor automatically turns dark.

6. Select **Turn off hard disks** (Alt+I,) and specify the number of minutes or hours before the hard disk turns off.

7. Generally, you should leave the other settings as the defaults.

8. Click **OK** .

9. Click **OK** again to close the Display Properties dialog box.

Try It!

Control System Energy Use in Mac OS

1. From the Apple menu, select **Control Panels**.

2. Click **Energy Saver**.

   The Energy Saver dialog box appears, as shown in the following illustration.

3. If **Hide Details** is not displayed, click **Show Details** .

4. Select the timings for your system by sliding the indicator to the left or right.

   The timings shown in the illustration on the following page are the system defaults.

5. When finished, click the Close box .

Energy Save Dialog Box with Details

Clean the Keyboard

- Use a can of compressed air that has a long, small-diameter straw inserted in the nozzle. Spray between the keys to remove any dust and other particles.

- If you do spill liquid on your keyboard, immediately turn your keyboard upside down to drain out the liquid and shut down your system. After letting the keyboard drain, hold the keyboard upside down and use the compressed air can to remove the remaining moisture. You may be able to salvage the keyboard by quick action.

- To clean the keyboard case and keys, spray a soft, lint-free cloth with a small amount of non-alcohol cleaner and gently wipe the keys and the case. Do not spray the keyboard directly. After wiping with the cloth, use compressed air to remove any cloth particles that may remain between the keys.

Clean the Mouse

- The mouse consists of a case with two or more buttons and perhaps a wheel (the IntelliMouse). The mouse works because, as you slide it across the surface, a rolling ball activates electrical contacts that cause the mouse pointer to move.

- If you turn your mouse over, you will see that the ball is held in place by a circular holder that can be turned to allow removal of the ball from the inside of the mouse.

Try It!

1. Turn the mouse upside down and remove the circular cover.

2. Cup your hand over the ball and turn the mouse right side up to allow the ball to drop into your cupped hand.

3. Once the ball is free, use the sticky side of adhesive tape to remove any lint or other particles that cling to the ball.

4. Use rubbing alcohol on a cotton swab to remove any debris from the inside of the mouse.

5. Allow the mouse to dry completely after cleaning.

6. Replace the mouse ball and cover after the mouse is dry.

- To clean the outside of the mouse, use a soft cloth that has been sprayed with a small amount of cleaner and gently wipe the outside of the mouse. Let the mouse dry completely after cleaning.

Clean the Cases

- To clean the cases of your monitor, computer, printer, speakers, and other peripherals, spray a soft, lint-free cloth with a small amount of non-alcohol cleaner. Gently wipe away any smudges and dust.

- Allow the surfaces to dry completely before using your computer again.

Maintain Computers and Peripherals

- Keep all manufacturer's instructions on the maintenance and care of your computer, printer, and other peripherals. Follow the manufacturer's instructions carefully when performing any maintenance.

- Pay attention to announcements of new printer drivers and other maintenance software. Acquire new maintenance software as soon as possible to keep your system up to date.

- When changing ink or toner cartridges in printers, read the installation instructions completely through before starting the procedure. Be careful to follow manufacturer's instructions for cleaning the printer when you change the ink or toner cartridge.

- Make sure that the paper and ink or toner you use meet manufacturer's standards.

Appendixes

A Brief History of Computers
■ **History of Computers** ■ **Early Computing Machines** ■ **Vacuum Tube Computers**
■ **Semiconductors and Portable Programs** ■ **The Personal Computer**

NOTES

History of Computers

■ The electronic digital computer, the kind you are using with this book, is an invention of the 20th century. Computer-like functions, however, have been around for years. Some people date the invention of the computer to the invention of the **abacus**, a device on which beads are manipulated to perform calculations. The abacus is still used in many Asian nations.

■ Other computer historians point to Frenchman Joseph Marie Jacquard. Jacquard automated a loom that operated by dropping needles through holes punched in cards. Every time a needle passed through a hole, it lifted a weaving thread. Needles that did not drop through caused their weaving threads to lower. The weaving shuttle then passed through the threads and a pattern developed. Because the needles were either up or down (on or off, like binary numbers), the Jacquard loom is considered a true digital computer.
(http://www.bess.net/whats_new/June2/science_and_nature/)

Early Computing Machines

■ Two computing machines were the forefathers of modern electronic computers. In the mid-1800s, Charles Babbage constructed a mechanical device that he called the Difference Engine. It could perform complicated calculations by working with the differences in positions of various levers and gears.

■ Because it was mechanical and used metal, as the arrangement of gears and levers became increasingly complex, the performance of the Difference Engine was hurt by the expansion and contraction of its metal components. Changes in temperature and humidity seriously impaired its efficiency. Imprecision in the manufacture of its components and the quality of the materials also caused problems. The metal-working technology of the day wasn't up to the demands of Babbage's design.
(http://www.gmcc.ab.ca/~supy/lec02.htm)

■ In 1890, the US Census was projected to take more than 10 years. But Herman Hollerith built a punched card machine to process census data and sped things up considerably. Later, he founded Hollerith Tabulating Company, which eventually became IBM.

Computer History

For a more detailed look at the history of computers, see the Web sites listed in the text and the following site, maintained by the IEEE Computing organization.

http://www.computer.org/50/history/

A good pictorial history with significant dates in the history of computing can be found at the following URL.

http://www.computer.org/computer/timeline

Vacuum Tube Computers

- In the 1940s, at the University of Pennsylvania, a group of electronics experts developed the computer ENIAC, which is often credited as the first modern computer. ENIAC bears little resemblance to today's computers. It could be programmed only by rewiring. Its vacuum tubes heated its environment so much that tubes were constantly burning out. Since ENIAC was being used to help the military calculate weapons' trajectories for World War II, a team of people worked inside the computer to replace vacuum tubes as they burned out.

- Other computers were also being developed in the 1940s. An interesting term for resolving computer problems came into use at that time. Grace Hopper was a programmer hired to work on the computers Mark I and Mark II at Harvard University. In 1945, she found a moth dead in the jaws of a mechanical relay, causing the machine to malfunction. She glued the bug into the operator's logbook; after that, resolving programming and other computer problems was known as **debugging**.

Semiconductors and Portable Programs

- The spread of the electronic computer was made possible by the invention of the transistor by John Bardeen, William Shockley, and Walter Brattain at Bell Laboratories in the late 1940s. The transistor (TRANsfer reSISTOR) replaced vacuum tubes in radios and televisions and created a new industry—semiconductors. Semiconductors, naturally occurring substances such as silicon and germanium, make it possible to place the functions of a computer on a thin wafer, the microchip.

- In the 1950s, transistors began replacing vacuum tubes in computers. Tens of transistors could be placed in the same amount of space as one vacuum tube, so computers became smaller. In addition, transistors didn't burn out or overheat like vacuum tubes, so computers became more reliable.

- One other development hastened the spread of computers. The 1940s and 1950s saw a critical change in the way computers are programmed. To program ENIAC, a host of wires had to be moved and reconnected. The programming was tedious, time-consuming, and couldn't be transferred from one computer to another.

- The invention of programming languages and the ability of computers to accept instructions through holes punched in cards allowed computers to work on a variety of scientific, mathematical, and business problems. These uses of the computer came to be called **applications** because they *applied* the computer to solving problems. The term application is still used today to refer to the use of computer programs to perform specific tasks.

- By the 1970s, IBM, Sperry-Rand (now UniSys), Digital Equipment Corporation (DEC), Data General and other computer manufacturers had their machines in most companies and universities. But the early 1980s saw the computer change from a large tool used by experts and specially trained personnel into a consumer electronics product.

Debug

While the first "debugging" involved a real insect, the term today is used for investigating and solving any hardware or software problem.

Semiconductor

Semiconductors, such as silicon and germanium, allow control of the flow of electricity; some areas can be designated as current conductors and adjacent areas as insulators. Since the areas of conductivity can be defined selectively, these substances are called **semiconductors**.

Metals, such as copper, are **conductors**. They conduct electricity non-selectively; areas of copper cannot be designated for conduction and insulation. All parts of copper conduct current.

The Personal Computer

- Apple Corporation was founded in the mid-1970s. Initially, the founders, Steve Jobs and Steve Wozniak, thought the Apple® computer would be a machine for electronics hobbyists to compete with the popular Commodore and Atari computers.

- One application, the VisiCalc spreadsheet, changed that. Graduates with Masters in Business Administration (MBAs) learned that VisiCalc could run on Apple machines. These MBAs, in a wide variety of companies, began buying and using Apples to perform business analyses. The personal computer revolution was on.

- Microsoft's Bill Gates and others purchased, developed, and marketed DOS, the <u>D</u>isk <u>O</u>perating <u>S</u>ystem. When it was adopted as the operating system for IBM's PC in 1981, DOS became the operating system with which all others had to compete.

- The IBM PC took over the personal computer revolution begun by Apple. Because so many businesses relied on IBM for their large computers (called mainframes, see Lesson 1), they purchased large numbers of PCs, primarily to take advantage of spreadsheet and word processing programs.

- Students who graduated from high school or college before 1985 seldom had access to personal computers. By the end of the 1980s, many schools boasted computer laboratories where PCs were available.

- The table below illustrates how far computing has come since the 1940s. It compares ENIAC with the 450 mHz Pentium processor, a CPU microchip from the Intel Corporation.

ENIAC Versus 450 mHz Pentium

Even if you are not using a computer with a 450 mHz Pentium III, your personal computer has more capacity and is far faster than ENIAC.

Measurement	ENIAC	450mHz Pentium
Speed	5,000 additions per second	900,000,000 additions/second
Memory	200 digits	16,000,000 digits
Elements	18,000 vacuum tubes	
	6,000 switches .	
	70,000 resistors	4,000,000+ transistors (CPU)
	10,000 capacitors	
	1,500 relays	
Size	10 feet tall x 1,800 square feet	9" x 12" x 3"
Weight	30 tons	6 pounds

(http://www.gmcc.ab.ca/~supy/lec02.htm, and http://mbhs.bergtraum.k12.ny.us/cybereng/nyt/databox.htm)

Personal computer revolution

A lively and opinionated review of the beginnings of the PC revolution is provided by:

Cringely, Robert X. *Accidental Empires: How the Boys of Silicon Valley Make Their Millions, Battle Foreign Competition, and Still Can't Get a Date.* Reading, MA: Addison Wesley, 1992.

NEXT APPENDIX

Appendix B

Use Windows 98 Help

■ Start Help ■ The Help Window ■ Use Help Contents ■ Use the Help Index
■ Use Search ■ Click Here and Related Topics ■ Print a Topic

NOTES

Start Help

💻 Try It!

■ To get Help in Windows 98 at any time:

1. Click the Start button **🏁 Start** on the Windows taskbar, press the
   Windows key **⊞**, or press **Ctrl**+**Esc**.

   The Start menu appears.

2. Click <u>H</u>elp.

   *The Windows Help window appears, as shown below. The tab
   selected in the window is the one last used.*

Windows Help: Contents Tab

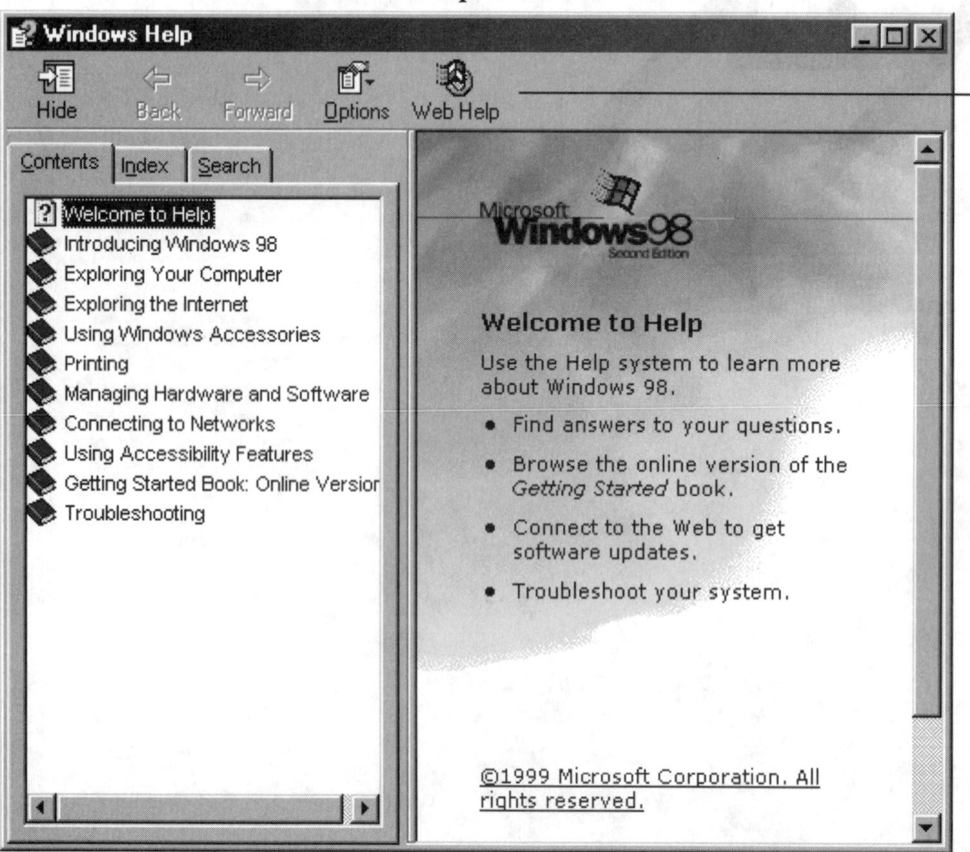

> **Whose Help?**
>
> When you open Help from
> the Start menu (as well as
> from My Computer or
> Windows Explorer), the
> help you get is for
> Windows 98. When you
> use the Help menu in a
> program, such as Word,
> PowerPoint, or Excel, the
> help is only for that
> program.

The Help Window

- The Help window has two panes. The left pane lets you select a topic to explore; the right pane displays the details of the topic. As you use the Help window, you may need to enlarge and shrink the panes. The border between the two panes can be dragged right or left, and the outside borders of the window can be dragged as necessary to see the contents of each pane.

- The Help toolbar has a Hide button **Hide** that lets you hide the left pane of the window. When the left pane is hidden, the Show button **Show** appears. Click the Show button to redisplay the left pane.

- The Back button **Back** becomes active after you view the details of a topic; clicking it takes you back to the previous topic. The Forward button **Forward** becomes active after you have used the Back button; clicking it returns you to the topic from which you clicked the Back button.

- The Options button **Options** displays a menu that lets you choose from Hide/Show Tabs, Back, Forward, Home, Stop, Refresh, Internet Options, 2 Web Help, Print, Search Highlight On/Off. For ordinary use of Windows Help, these options are not needed.

- The Web Help button **Web Help** lets you connect to the Microsoft Windows help Web page if you can connect to the Internet.

Use Help Contents

- The tabs below the toolbar in the Help window let you obtain help in several ways. The Contents tab, shown selected in the illustration on the previous page, presents help topics in a table of contents format showing only the major headings. When you point to a topic, it displays as underlined text, like a hyperlink on a Web page.

Try It!

Help for Changing the Background of the Desktop

1. Click the Contents tab **Contents**, if it is not already selected.

2. Click **Exploring Your Computer**.

   The book icon at the left of the heading opens, and the subheadings appear in a list as shown in the illustration on the following page.

Exploring Your Computer Options

3. Click ◆ Customize Windows 98 .

    The subheading opens with a list of additional subheadings, as shown below.

Customize Windows 98 Topics

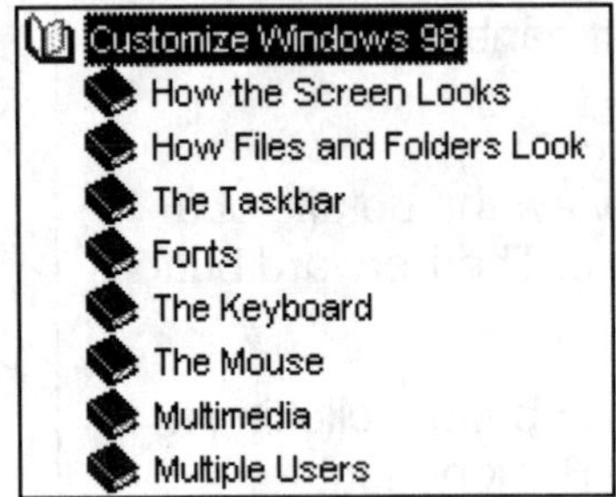

4. Click ◆ How the Screen Looks .

    The subheading opens and displays a list of Help topics, as shown in the following illustration. The question mark icons indicate topics for which information will appear in the right pane.

How the Screen Looks Topics

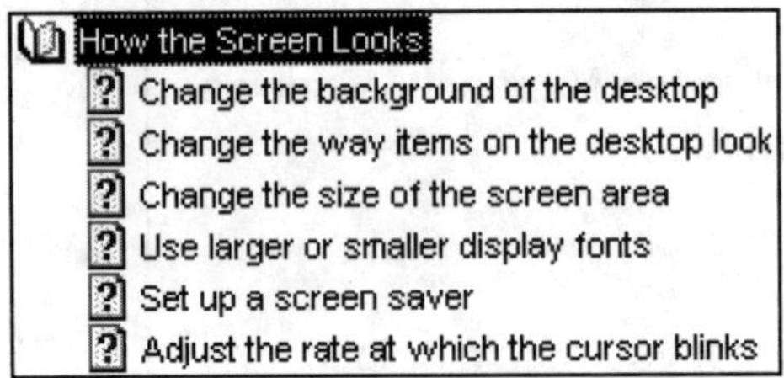

5. Click ? Change the background of the desktop .

    The right Help pane displays step-by-step instructions for changing the Desktop background, as shown in the illustration on the following page.

Windows Help Step-by-Step Instructions

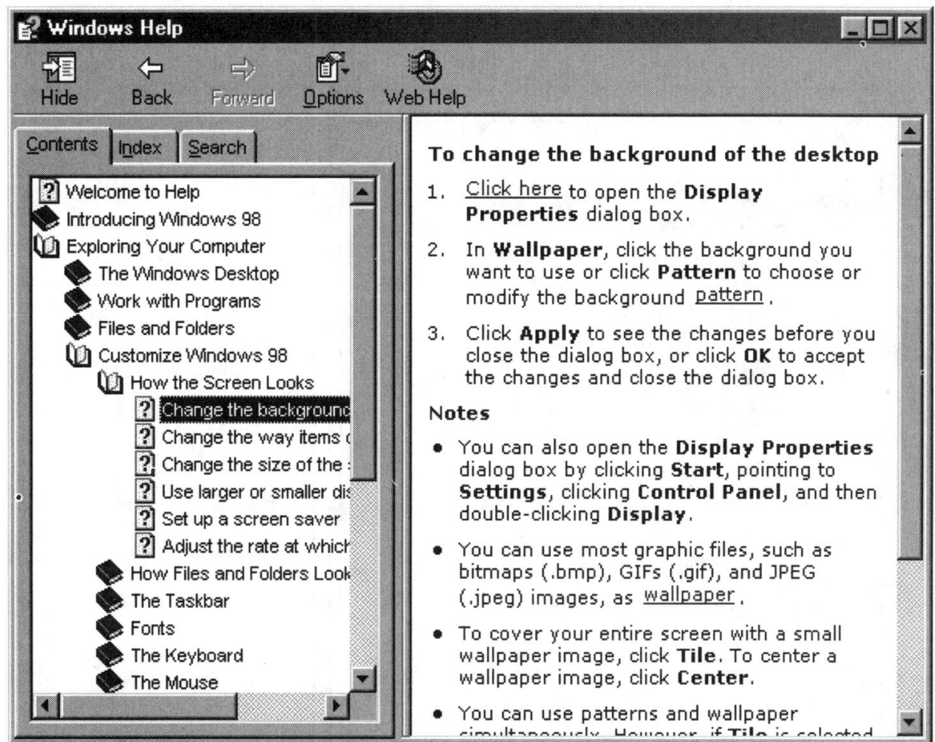

6. Review the instructions, then click [?] Welcome to Help to redisplay the Welcome message.

   This step in using Help is unnecessary, but for the purposes of this exercise, you should start again with the Welcome message.

7. Leave the Help Window open with both panes displayed.

Use the Help Index

Try It!

1. Click the Index tab.

   The Windows Help window dialog box displays all topics alphabetically, as shown in the illustration on the following page.

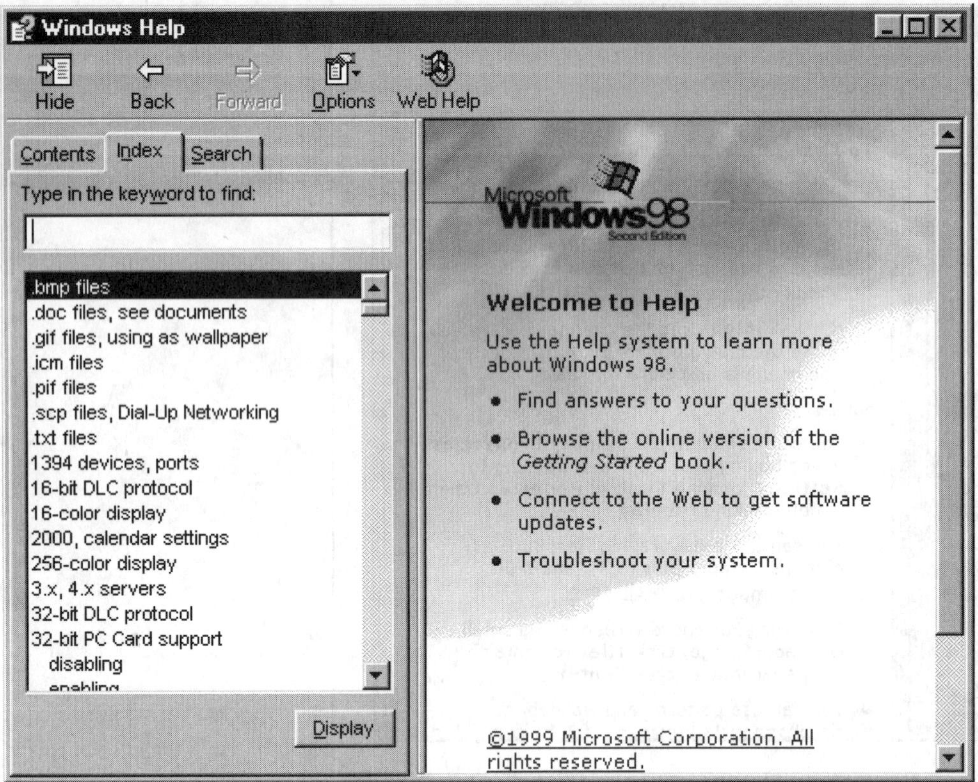

2. Select and delete any text in the *Type in the keyword to find* box.
3. Start to type *background of desktop.*

   Before you finish the words, the list jumps to a topic that starts with the letters you type. Thus, to find help using the Index tab, type the first few letters of the subject about which you want help.

Help Index Tab: Background

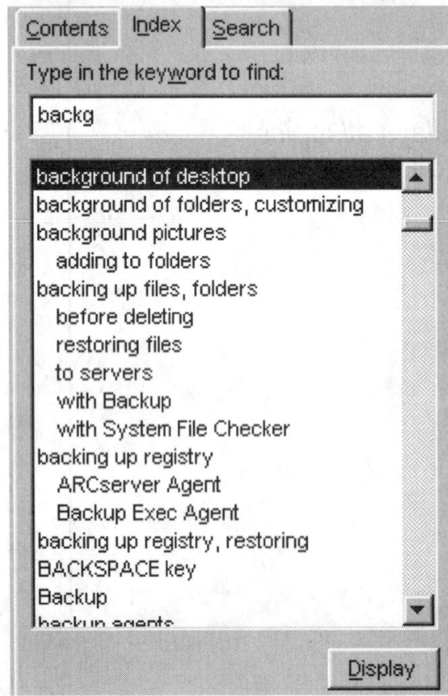

4. Double-click the desired topic (*background of desktop*), or click the topic and click the <u>D</u>isplay button | Display | (Alt+D).

   The Topics Found dialog box appears with a list of topics from which you can choose, as shown in the following illustration.

Topics Found Dialog Box

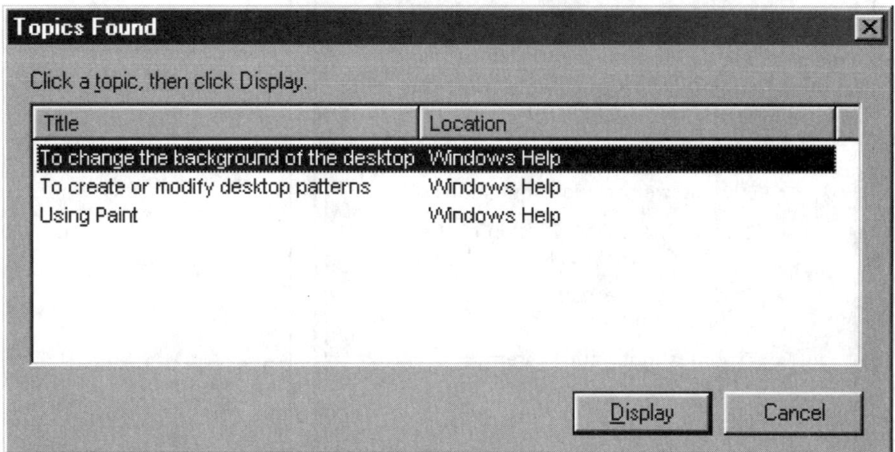

5. Double-click *To change the background of the desktop*, or click it and click the <u>D</u>isplay button | Display |.

   The step-by-step instructions illustrated on page 427 appear in the right pane. You used a different path to the topic, but the result was the same.

6. Click the Back button | Back | to redisplay the Welcome message.
   This step in using Help is unnecessary, but for the purposes of this exercise, you should start again with the Welcome message.

7. Leave the Help Window open with both panes displayed.

Use Search

Try It!

1. Click the <u>S</u>earch tab | Search |.
   The Help window appears as shown on the following page.

Windows Help: Search Tab

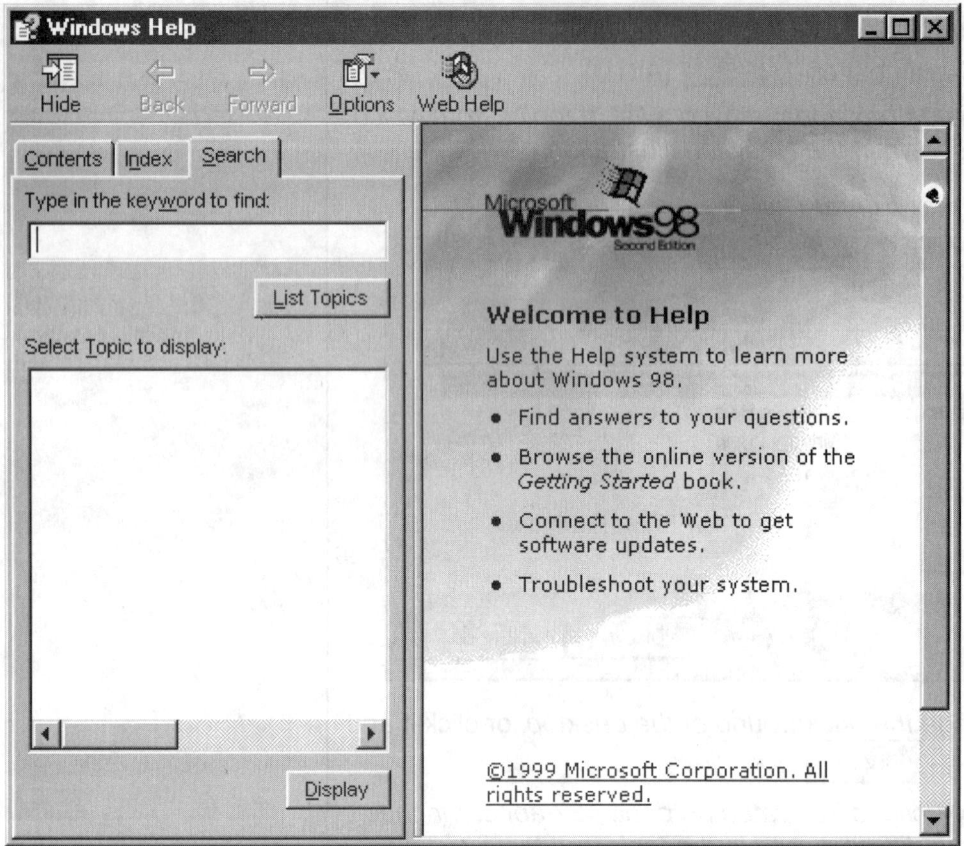

2. In the *Type in the keyword to find* text box, type the words *desktop background.*

3. Click the List Topics button ⌈ List Topics ⌋.

   Windows searches for topics. If the search takes a long time, you can cancel it. The results display in the Select Topic to display list box, as shown below.

Results of Help Topic Search

4. Double-click *To change the background of the desktop,* or click it and click the Display button ⌈ Display ⌋.

   The step-by-step instructions illustrated on the following page and on page 427 appear in the right pane. Note that the search words are highlighted.

You used a different path to the topic, but the result was the same. You can turn off the highlighting using the Options button Search Highlight Off option.

Results of Search

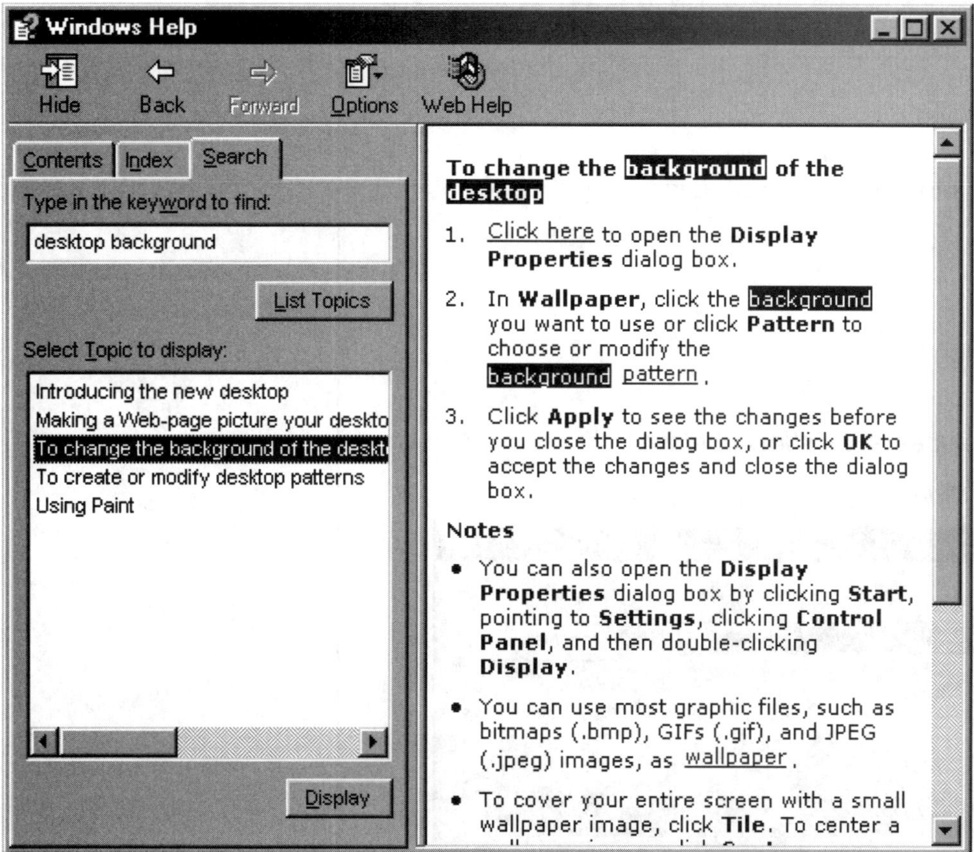

Click Here and Related Topics

- Many Help topics have underlined entries in blue. *Click here* options usually display a Windows dialog box. When Help displays a dialog box, you can use it as if you had displayed it yourself.

- Single words, such as *wallpaper* in the previous illustration, display a definition of the term in a pop-up box. When Help displays a definition, click again to dismiss the definition pop-up box.

- The blue phrase Related Topics often appears at the bottom of a topic. You may wish to review the related topics.

Try It!

1. Scroll down to the bottom of the topic to see the item Related Topics.

2. Click Related Topics.

   A pop-up list of related topics appears.

3. Click the option you'd like to review.

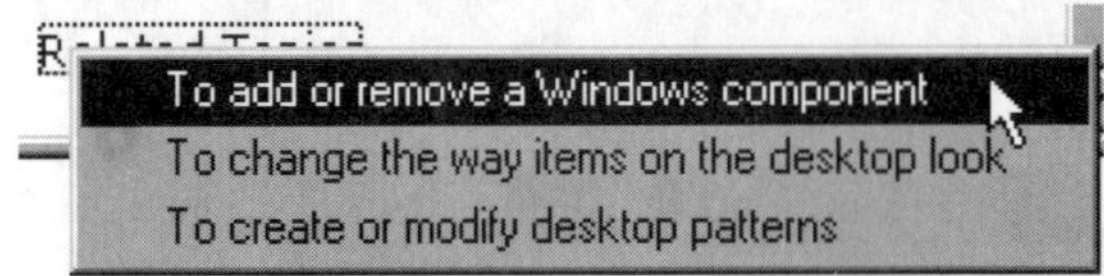
Related Topics Pop-up List

Print a Topic

■ You may wish to print the information displayed in the right pane.

🖥️ Try It!

1. Click the Options button **Options**.
2. Click the Print option.

   The Print dialog box appears, as shown below.

Print Dialog Box for Help Topics

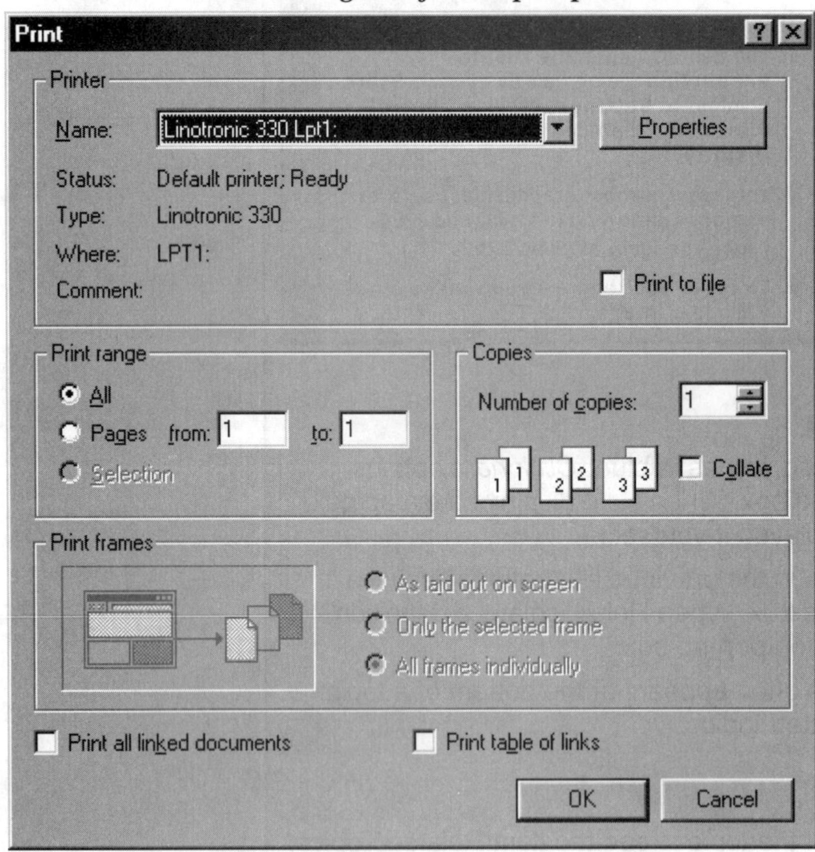

3. If desired, choose one of the link options.

   If you click Print all linked documents, *any documents linked to the topic also print.* Print table of links *also prints a table that lists any links in the topic.*

4. Click **OK**.
5. Click the Close button ☒ on the Help window to close it.

432

NEXT APPENDIX

Appendix C

Use Mac OS Help

■ Start Help ■ The Help Window ■ Use Contents ■ Use the Search Feature

NOTES

Start Help

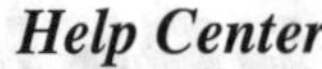 **Try It!**

- To display the Help Center window:

    1. Click **Help** on the menu bar.

    2. Choose **Help Center**.

        The Help Center window appears, as shown in the following illustration. You may find options on this window helpful in learning about your computer and using the DVD or CD player.

Help Center

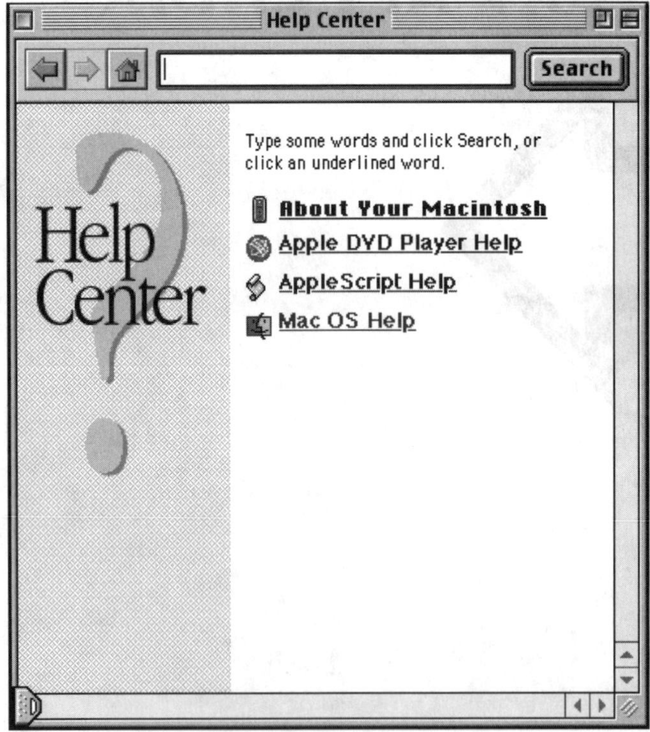

Whose Help?

When you open Help from the Finder menu, the help you get is for Mac OS. When you use the Help menu in a program, such as AppleWorks, Word, PowerPoint, or Excel, the help is only for that program.

Try It!

- To display the Mac OS Help window:

    1. Choose **Mac OS Help** from the Help menu.

        OR

        Click **Mac OS Help** on the Help Center window.

    OR

1. Click on a blank area of the desktop.
2. Press the **Help** button on the keyboard.

   The Mac OS Help window appears, as shown in the following illustration.

Mac OS Help Window

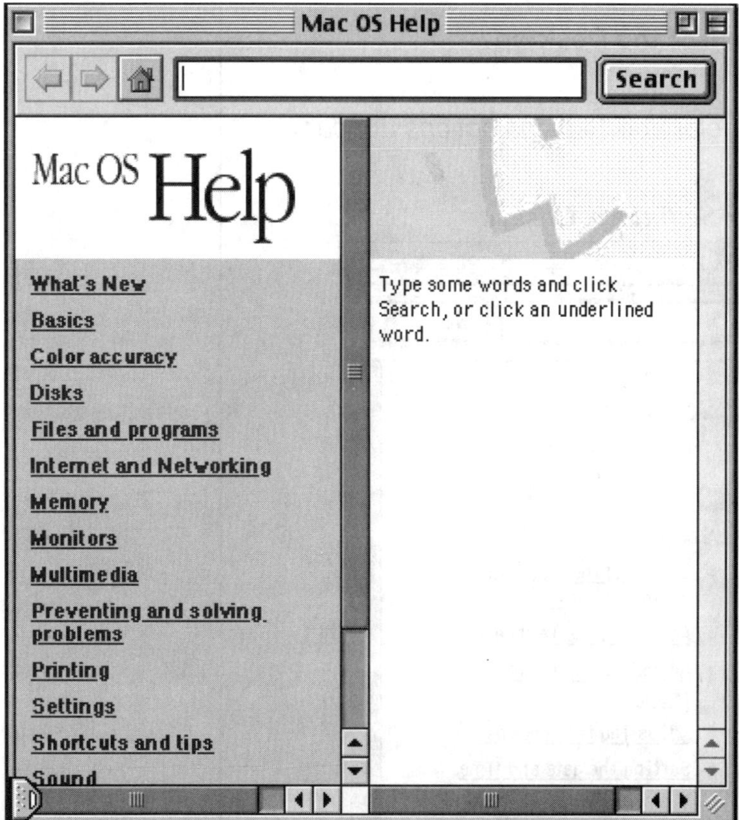

The Help Window

- The Help window has two panes. The left pane lets you select a topic to explore; the right pane displays additional options.

- The Help button bar has three buttons than can help you navigate within help.

- The Back button becomes active after you have left the initial window; clicking it takes you back to the previous window.

- The Forward button becomes active after you have used the Back button; clicking it returns you to the window from which you clicked the Back button.

- The Help Center button takes you to the Help Center window shown on the previous page.

Use Contents

- The left pane of the Help window (shown on the previous page) displays a series of topics which you may explore. You may need to guess at the appropriate topic for finding the information you need.

Try It!

Help for Changing the Appearance of the Desktop

1. Click **Settings**.

   The option turns to a different color and Settings options appear in the right pane.

Help Window after Settings is Clicked

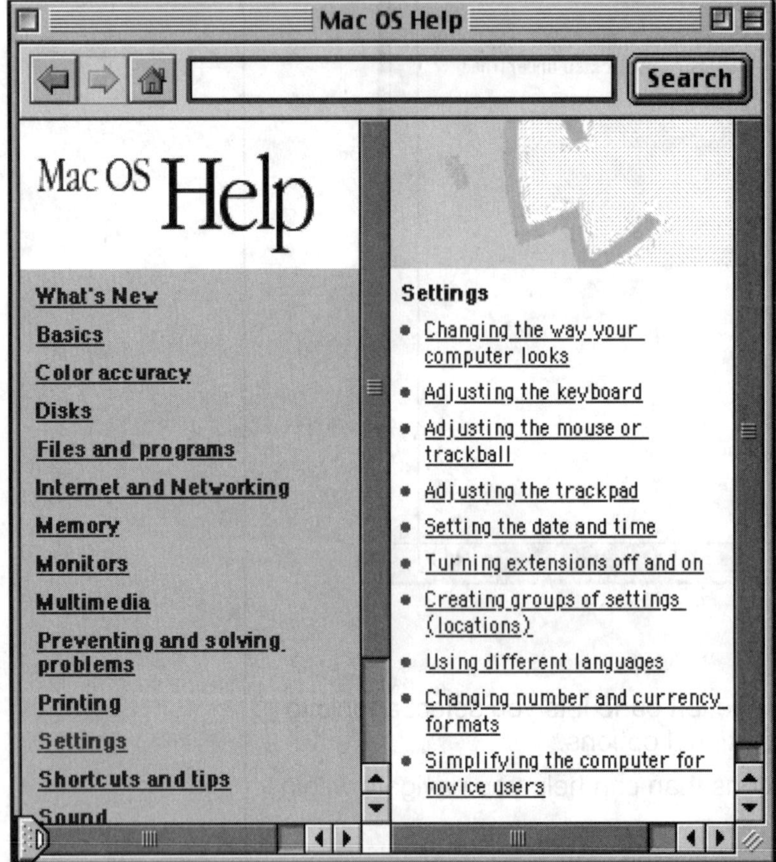

2. Under Settings, click **Changing the way your computer looks**.

   The system displays the help screen shown in the following illustration.

3. After viewing the help, close the help window.

Help Topic Details Window

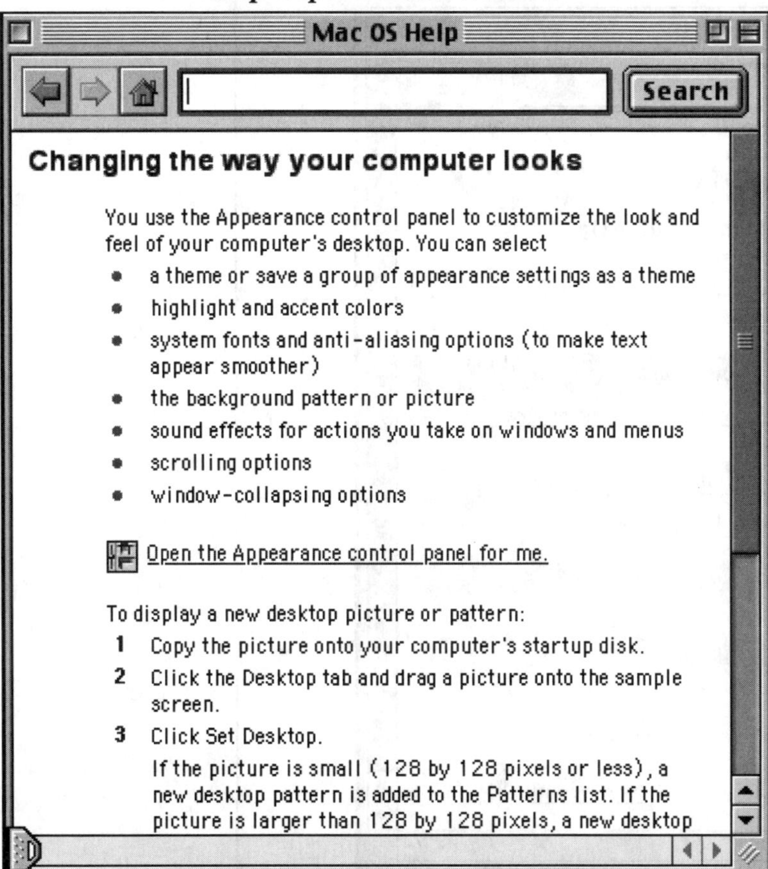

Use the Search Feature

Try It!

1. Start **Mac OS Help**.
2. In the search box, type *desktop*, as shown in the following illustration.

Search Feature

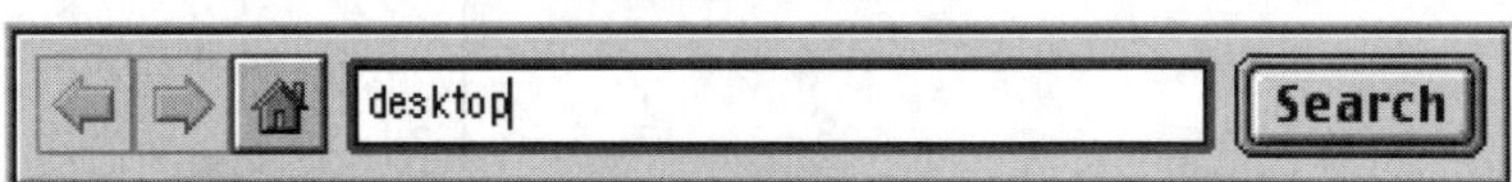

3. Click the Search button.

   The system displays the first page of the Search Results as shown in the illustration on the following page.

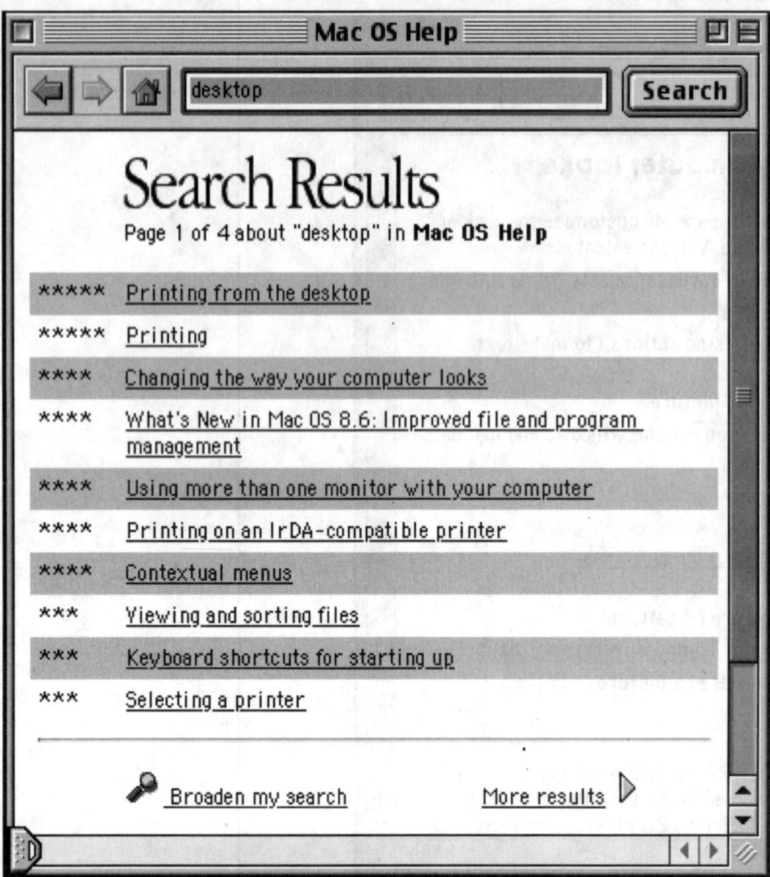

4. Locate and click the option you want—**Changing the way your computer looks**.

   The system displays the same Help topic details you viewed in the previous Try It! activity (page 437), except that the word desktop *still appears in the Search textbox.*

5. Close the help window.

NEXT APPENDIX

Prepare Access Data Files
■ Copy the Data Files and Deselect the Read-only Attribute

NOTES

Copy the Data Files and Deselect the Read-only Attribute

- Access does not let you perform a Save As on a database. This feature means that you must complete the following steps to make the Access data files usable:

  1. Copy the Access data files to a hard drive.

  2. Open Windows Explorer, and locate the drive and folder where you stored the copies.

  3. Select all the Access data files.

  4. Right-click on the selected files.

  5. Select **Properties** (**R**) from the shortcut menu.

  6. Deselect **Read-only** (**Alt**+**R**) in the Attributes section as shown in the illustration below:

  7. Click **OK**.

Deselect Read-only Attribute

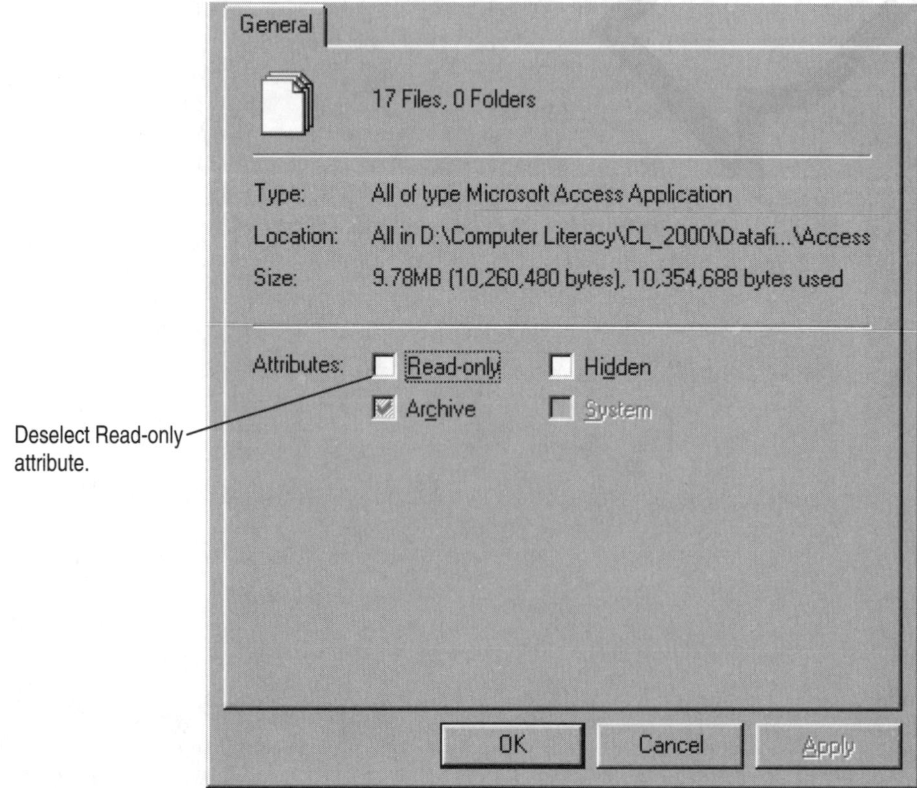

Deselect Read-only attribute.

NEXT APPENDIX

Appendix E

Understand Paradox Database Structure
■ Copy the Data Files and Deselect the Read-only Attribute
■ Change the Working Directory ■ Paradox Aliases

NOTES

Copy the Data Files and Deselect the Read-only Attribute

■ Paradox does not let you perform a Save As on a database. This feature means that you must complete the following steps to make the Paradox data files usable:

1. Copy the Paradox data file folders to a hard drive.
2. Open Windows Explorer, and locate the drive and folder where you stored the copied folders.
3. Open a data file folder such as **01Classic**.
4. Select all the files within the folder.
5. Right-click on the selected files.
6. Select **Properties** (**R**) from the shortcut menu.
7. Deselect **Read-only** (**Alt**+**R**) in the Attributes section as shown in the illustration below:
8. Repeat steps 3-7 for each data file folder.
9. Click **OK**.

Deselect Read-only Attribute

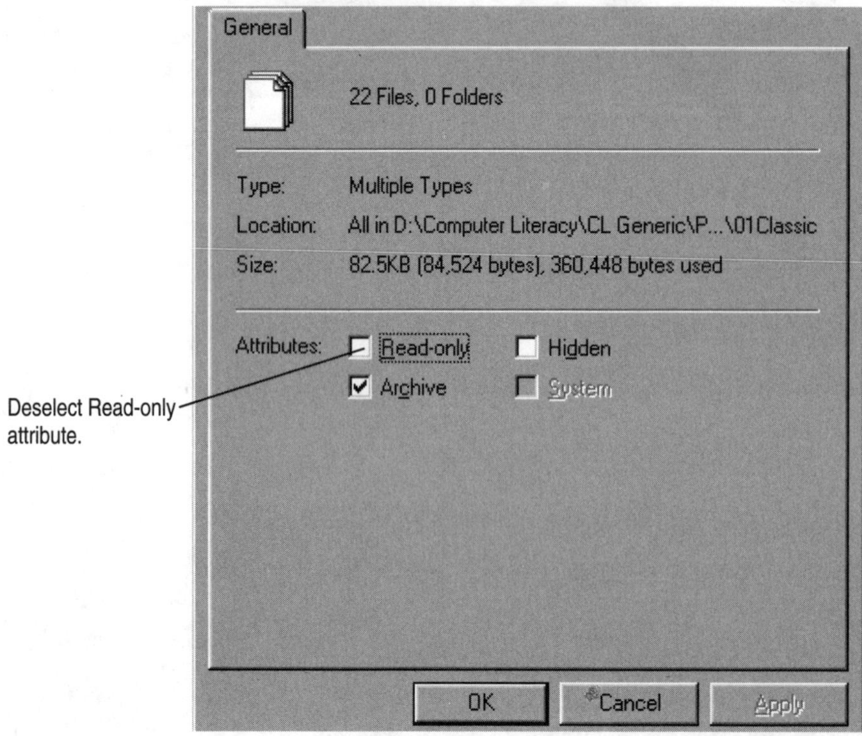

Change the Working Directory

- Paradox generally stores objects from one database in a single folder. The data files for this book are stored in folders that have the same name as the database mentioned in the text. When you want to open a database (in this case a folder with the object files), complete the steps below.

  1. Start Paradox.
  2. Click **File** (Alt+F).
  3. Click **Working Directory** (W).
  4. Click the Browse button Browse... (Alt+B).

     Paradox displays the Directory Browser.

Directory Browser

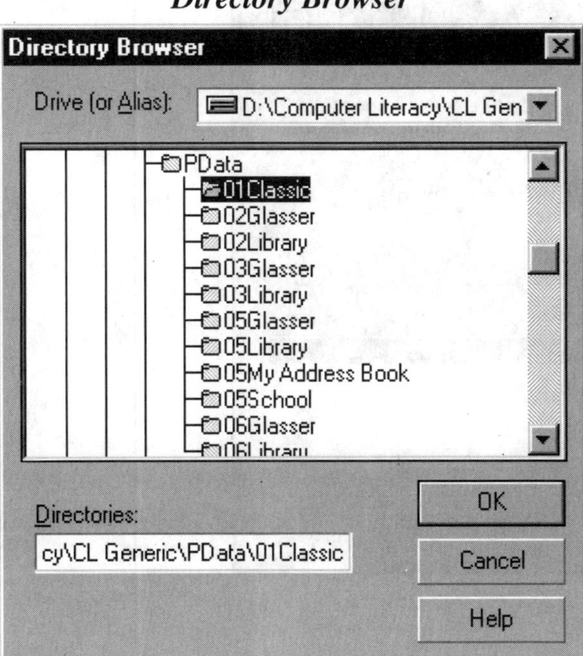

  5. Click the Paradox data folder.
  6. Select the desired folder (database) name.
  7. Click OK.

     The Project Viewer will then display the objects in the folder.

Paradox Aliases

- Paradox can name databases by the use of aliases that are defined with the **Tools**, **Alias Manager** command. Aliases have the following characteristics:

  - They need not have the same name as the folder which contains the database object files.

  - They function like shortcuts by providing a quick way to change the Working Directory to the correct folder for a database.

  - Like shortcuts, if the database object files are moved, the alias no longer points to the correct folder.

- The aliases themselves are not copied when database object files are copied from one folder to another.

- The Paradox data files on the CD-ROM, therefore, do not have aliases. The chief consequence of this fact is that the **Startup Expert**, which displays aliases in its lower pane, will not list the data file names. After Exercise 4 (Lesson 6), however, when you have created a database using the Database Expert, the database name will appear in the Startup Expert window because Paradox creates the appropriate alias.

- The Open a database option on the Startup Expert will not open a data file for you. When the Startup Expert appears, click the Cancel button Cancel (Alt+C) and use the File, Working Directory command to open the database.

Startup Expert

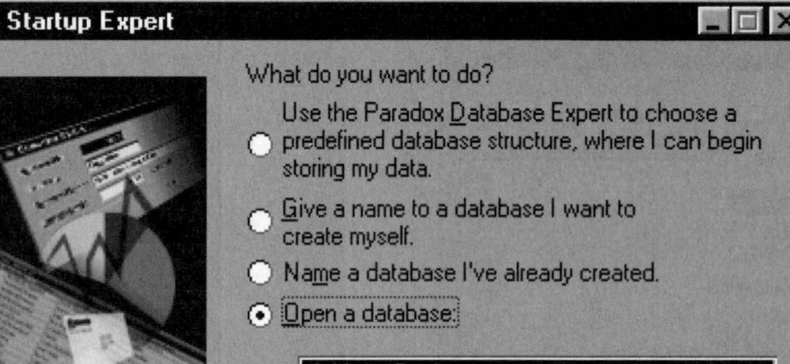

Fast-teach Learning Books

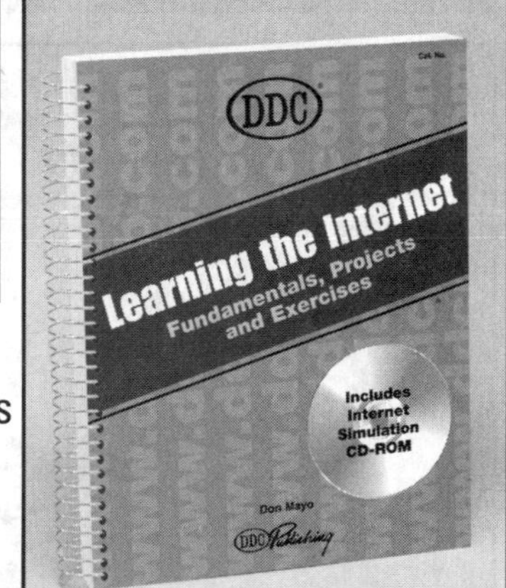

How we designed each book

Each self-paced hands-on text gives you the software concept and each exercise's objective in simple language. Next to the exercise we provide the keystrokes and the illustrated layout; step by simple step—graded and cumulative learning.

Did we make one for you?

$27 each

Title	Cat. No.
Creating a Web Page w/ Office 97	Z23
Corel® Office 7	Z12
Corel® WordPerfect® 7	Z16
Corel® WordPerfect® 8	Z31
DOS + Windows	Z7
English Skills through Word Processing	Z34
Excel 97	Z21
Excel 5 for Windows®	E9
Excel 7 for Windows® 95	Z11
Internet	Z57
Internet for Business	Z27
Internet for Kids	Z25
Keyboarding/Word Processing with Word 97	Z24
Keyboarding/Word Processing for Kids	Z33
Lotus 1-2-3 Rel. 2.2–4.0 for DOS	L9
Lotus 1-2-3 Rel. 4 & 5 for Windows	B9
Microsoft Office 97	Z19
Microsoft Office for Windows 95	Z6
PowerPoint 97	Z22
Windows® 3.1 – A Quick Study	WQS1
Windows® 95	Z3
Windows® 98	Z26
Word 97	Z20
Word 6 for Windows®	1WDW6
Word 7 for Windows® 95	Z10
WordPerfect 6 for Windows®	Z9
WordPerfect 6.1 for Windows®	H9
Works 4 for Windows® 95	Z8

Microsoft® OFFICE 2000

$29 each

Title	Cat. No.
Accounting Applications with Excel 2000	Z41
Access 2000	Z38
Create a Web Page with Office 2000	Z43
Computer Literacy with Office 2000	Z54
Excel 2000	Z39
FrontPage 2000	Z49
Keyboarding & Word Processing with Word 2000	Z55
Office 2000	Z35
Office 2000 Deluxe Edition $34	Z35D

* Includes advanced exercises and illustrated solutions for most exercises

Title	Cat. No.
Office 2000 Advanced Skills: An Integrated Approach	Z51
PowerPoint 2000	Z40
Publisher 2000	Z47
Windows 2000	Z44
Word 2000	Z37

Includes CD-ROM

to order call
800-528-3897
or fax 800-528-3862
Preview our books online at:
http://www.ddcpub.com

Learning Programming

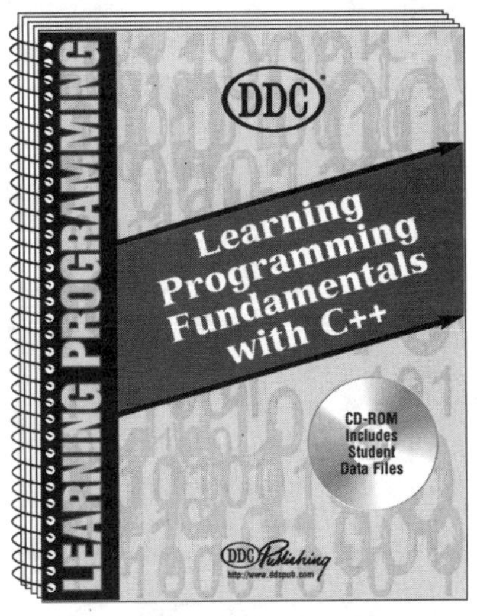

- **Suitable for HS, post-secondary, or continuing-ed introductory courses**
- **Hands-on exercises designed to teach programming concepts**
- **Labs at each Chapter's end covering intro through advanced subjects and a range of difficulty**
- **Chapter Notes provide conceptual info in easy to understand sentences and bullet lists**

$35 ea. **60+ HOURS OF INSTRUCTION**

Learning Programming Fundamentals with C++
$35 Cat. No. Z68 • ISBN 1-58577-022-1

Learning Java
$35 Cat. No. Z66 • ISBN 1-58577-020-5

Learning HTML
$35 Cat. No. Z59 • ISBN 1-58577-961-8

Learning C++
$35 Cat. No. Z69 • ISBN 1-58577-023-X

Learning C
$35 Cat. No. Z70 • ISBN 1-56243-974-X

$15 Solutions on CD-ROM
for Z66, Z68, Z69, Z70 • Cat. No. Z68SL

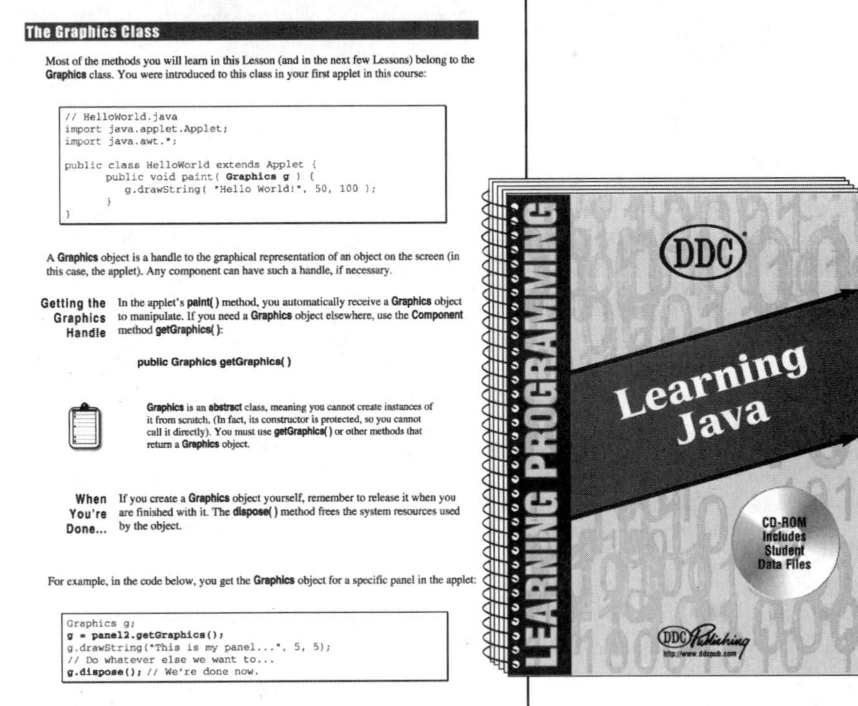

Inheritance in Java

extends How do you create a subclass in Java? By using an extends clause in your class declaration. For example:

```
public class Client extends Person {
    int status;
    public void setStatus( int status ) {
        // Body of method...
    }
    public int getStatus( ) {
        // Body of method...
    }
    // etc...
}
```

The Object Class Where does Java's inheritance hierarchy begin? With a class called Object. If you declare a class without the extends clause, the class extends Object.

Multiple Inheritance C++ supports multiple inheritance, the ability to create a subclass from more than one ancestor. For example:

Figure 6-3: An example of multiple inheritance

Multiple inheritance offers some benefits. But it can cause problems, too. If, in this example, **Actor.speak( )** and **Criminal.speak( )** behave differently, which one is called by **Politician**?

Java escapes this problem by avoiding multiple inheritance. But it reclaims some of the benefits through *interfaces* (discussed later).

The Graphics Class

Most of the methods you will learn in this Lesson (and in the next few Lessons) belong to the **Graphics** class. You were introduced to this class in your first applet in this course:

```
// HelloWorld.java
import java.applet.Applet;
import java.awt.*;

public class HelloWorld extends Applet {
    public void paint( Graphics g ) {
        g.drawString( "Hello World!", 50, 100 );
    }
}
```

A **Graphics** object is a handle to the graphical representation of an object on the screen (in this case, the applet). Any component can have such a handle, if necessary.

Getting the Graphics Handle In the applet's **paint( )** method, you automatically receive a **Graphics** object to manipulate. If you need a **Graphics** object elsewhere, use the **Component** method getGraphics( ):

```
public Graphics getGraphics( )
```

Graphics is an **abstract** class, meaning you cannot create instances of it from scratch. (In fact, its constructor is protected, so you cannot call it directly). You must use getGraphics( ) or other methods that return a **Graphics** object.

When You're Done... If you create a **Graphics** object yourself, remember to release it when you are finished with it. The **dispose( )** method frees the system resources used by the object.

For example, in the code below, you get the **Graphics** object for a specific panel in the applet:

```
Graphics g;
g = panel2.getGraphics();
g.drawString("This is my panel...", 5, 5);
// Do whatever else we want to...
g.dispose(); // We're done now.
```


Preview our books online at: http://www.ddcpub.com

Microsoft® Office 2000 Advanced Skills: *An Integrated Approach*

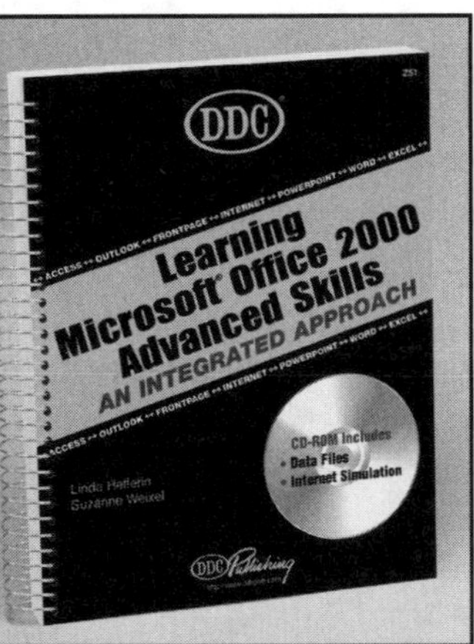

For use following Learning Office 2000, when students have mastered basic skills in each application. Each exercise incorporates more than one application. For example:

- Embed charts and graphs in reports (Word & Excel)
- Link tables to presentations (Word & PowerPoint)
- Create a mail merge using a query (Access & Word)
- Perform a merge with calculations (Excel & Access)

This book teaches students five different kinds of integration:

- Survival Skill Integration ■ Productivity Integration ■ Power Integration
- Web Page Integration ■ Internet Integration

These integration skills reflect the way power users work with Office in a real-world business setting using several different applications in combination to finish a complex task.

$29 *60 Exercises*
Cat. No. Z51
ISBN 1-56243-774-7
Includes CD-ROM

SUPPORT MATERIALS

Cat. No. Z51TE	Annotated Teacher Edition with Solution Files	$50
Cat. No. BTZ51	Tests in a three-ring binder	$100
Cat. No. SLZ5	Solutions on CD-ROM	$15
Cat. No. SLZ5SL	Solutions on CD-ROM Site License	$65
Cat. No. VA51	Visual Aids on Diskette (25 PowerPoint Slides)	$50
Cat. No. SLB51	Printouts of solutions in a three-ring binder	$50
Cat. No. DLZ51	Distance Learning Template CD-ROM	$150

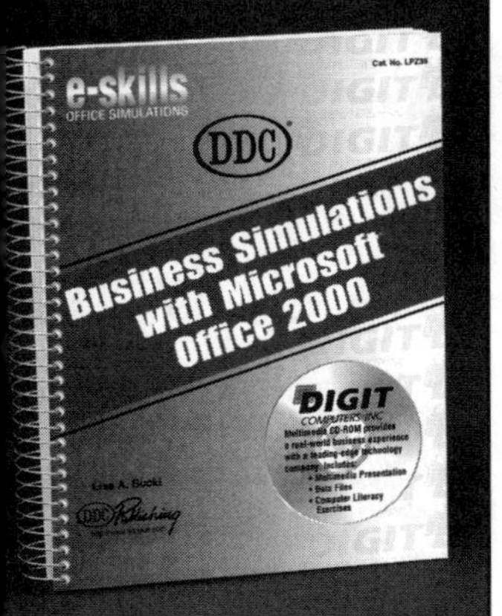

Business Simulations with Microsoft® Office 2000

Know the pressures and rewards of being a regional sales manager in

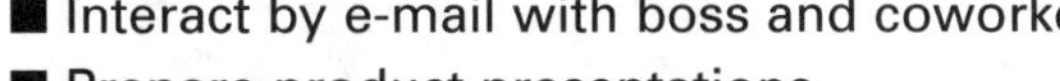

In 25 realistic business simulation projects, students use critical thinking, communications, and cross-curriculum study skills. They hone computer skills as they:

- Interact by e-mail with boss and coworkers
- Prepare product presentations
- Budget finances with spreadsheets and databases
- Make key business decisions

$29 Spiral
Cat. No. LPZ35
ISBN 1-56243-861-1
Includes CD-ROM

$15 Solutions CD-ROM with Instructor Support Material.
Get hints, tips, and sample solutions. Cat. No. SLLP

Preview our books online at: http://www.ddcpub.com

275 Madison Avenue, New York, NY 10016
phone 800-528-3897 • fax 800-528-3862

#8-2KZ51&LPZ35

FREE CATALOG
AND
UPDATED LISTING

We don't just have books that find your answers faster; we also have books that teach you how to use your computer without the fairy tales and the gobbledygook.

We also have books to improve your typing, spelling and punctuation.

Return this card for a free catalog and mailing list update.

275 Madison Avenue,
New York, NY 10016

☐ Please send me your catalog and put me on your mailing list.

Name

Firm (if any)

Address

City, State, Zip

Phone (800) 528-3897   Fax (800) 528-3862

SEE OUR COMPLETE CATALOG ON THE INTERNET @: http://www.ddcpub.com

---

FREE CATALOG
AND
UPDATED LISTING

We don't just have books that find your answers faster; we also have books that teach you how to use your computer without the fairy tales and the gobbledygook.

We also have books to improve your typing, spelling and punctuation.

Return this card for a free catalog and mailing list update.

275 Madison Avenue,
New York, NY 10016

☐ Please send me your catalog and put me on your mailing list.

Name

Firm (if any)

Address

City, State, Zip

Phone (800) 528-3897   Fax (800) 528-3862

SEE OUR COMPLETE CATALOG ON THE INTERNET @: http://www.ddcpub.com

---

FREE CATALOG
AND
UPDATED LISTING

We don't just have books that find your answers faster; we also have books that teach you how to use your computer without the fairy tales and the gobbledygook.

We also have books to improve your typing, spelling and punctuation.

Return this card for a free catalog and mailing list update.

DDC Publishing

275 Madison Avenue,
New York, NY 10016

☐ Please send me your catalog and put me on your mailing list.

Name

Firm (if any)

Address

City, State, Zip

Phone (800) 528-3897   Fax (800) 528-3862

SEE OUR COMPLETE CATALOG ON THE INTERNET @: http://www.ddcpub.com

BUSINESS REPLY MAIL
FIRST-CLASS MAIL   PERMIT NO. 7321   NEW YORK, N.Y.

POSTAGE WILL BE PAID BY ADDRESSEE

275 Madison Avenue
New York, NY 10157-0410

BUSINESS REPLY MAIL
FIRST-CLASS MAIL   PERMIT NO. 7321   NEW YORK, N.Y.

POSTAGE WILL BE PAID BY ADDRESSEE

275 Madison Avenue
New York, NY 10157-0410

BUSINESS REPLY MAIL
FIRST-CLASS MAIL   PERMIT NO. 7321   NEW YORK, N.Y.

POSTAGE WILL BE PAID BY ADDRESSEE

275 Madison Avenue
New York, NY 10157-0410

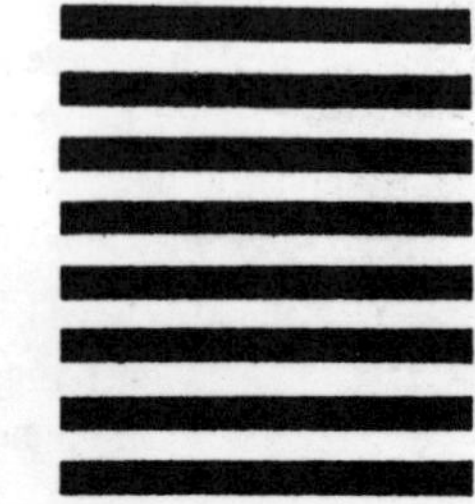